The Palgrave Handbook of Auto/Biography

Julie M. Parsons · Anne Chappell
Editors

The Palgrave Handbook of Auto/Biography

Editors
Julie M. Parsons
University of Plymouth
Plymouth, UK

Anne Chappell
Brunel University London
London, UK

ISBN 978-3-030-31973-1   ISBN 978-3-030-31974-8   (eBook)
https://doi.org/10.1007/978-3-030-31974-8

Cover image: © 'Gala Parc' by David Chappell, April 2019

This Palgrave Macmillan imprint is published by the registered company Springer Nature Switzerland AG
The registered company address is: Gewerbestrasse 11, 6330 Cham, Switzerland

For Chris
—Julie M. Parsons

For David, Sam and Jack.
—Anne Chappell

Foreword

The Palgrave Handbook of Auto/Biography is a welcome addition to the scholarly work on Auto/Biography. The authors of most of the articles and the editors themselves have a long affiliation to The British Sociological Association (BSA) Study Group on Auto/Biography (A/B). As such, it is worth noting the importance of that organisation for the development of Auto/Biographical Studies and therefore the work before us.

The BSA Auto/Biography group was formed from a New Year initiating conference held on the 1st and 2nd of January 1992 and organised by David Morgan and Liz Stanley (then of the University of Manchester) and consequent, in part, upon the researches that led to Stanley's *The Auto/Biographical I*—a volume that became a founding text for the sociology of auto/biography. There soon followed in 1993 a special issue of the *BSA's Primary Journal, Sociology*, entitled 'Auto/Biography in Sociology' (edited by David Morgan and Liz Stanley) that consolidated Auto/Biography as an area of study and was a fillip to the nascent Study Group. The Editorial Introduction to the issue provided the best conspectus of the sociology of auto/biography to date. Some of the attendees at the 1992 Auto/Biography conference are represented in the volume herewith and others from the group have presented at various of the scores of conferences that have successfully followed the founding event. An enduring practice of the Auto/Biography Study Group has been that, whilst promoting publication, conference presentation and intellectual exchange, it has been done within a republic of scholarly affection. This ethos and the commitment it generated has had consequences: Study Group members, as their careers developed, were increasingly responsible for inaugurating programmes of Auto/Biographical

Studies and related areas (particularly at Masters and Doctoral levels) at numerous institutions within the UK system of Higher Education. For a Study Group, this is not a small nor an unimportant achievement.

There is a long, detailed and useful dissertation to be written on why the area of sociology represented by the Study Group should have arisen when it did. Certainly, it was not the first time such matters had been of interest to social scientists. The distinguished work of the Chicago School of sociology alone was evidence of that. However, there was a marked losing sight of this sociological tradition by the 1970s and 1980s both in the UK and the USA. A renaissance was needed and the Study Group became part of one. Its first publication—a modest, pre-internet, few-page bulletin—set the tone for how it was to go about its work, describing Auto/Biography as follows:

> as the activity of attempting to render a succession of narrative moments relating to a life in such a way as to make them comprehensible to others, who in turn may complement or alter them and so become part of the Auto/ Biographical project… Additionally, the term Auto/Biography demonstrates an alacrity to recognise that all biography has some impression of the biographer upon it and that no autobiography can be produced by an individual entirely ungoverned by the social. (Erben et al. 1992: 1)

Also, from the beginning, ordinary lives were explicitly given more attention than those publicly regarded as exceptional. The epigraph of the Auto/ Biography journal is Dr. Johnson's maxim that 'there has rarely passed a life of which a judicious and faithful narrative would not be useful… no species of writing seems more worthy of cultivation than biography' (Johnson 1750: 1). Further, it was not just the lives themselves that were of importance to the Study Group's endeavours but the study of those telling those lives and the meaning of the notions of biography and autobiography per se. From this first 1992 bulletin, the Study Group has not been without a continuous publication and for the last twenty-one years, under the exemplary, untiring and exceptional editorship of Andrew Sparkes, it has produced a regular academic journal containing high quality, original articles. Within its journal and through its monographs, the Study Group has accomplished the analysis and understanding of lives, identity and selfhood in numerous ways and via numerous methods: through action research, through archival research, through participant observation, through prosopography, through in-depth interview, through auto-ethnography, through case-study, through auto-fiction, through psychoanalysis, through literature and history, through art, cinema and virtual worlds and so on.

Of course, it was not only in the formative BSA Auto/Biography Study Group that interest in the study of lives in novel ways was of interest. There were additional, co-extensive developments during this time. To a degree, this 'biographical turn' was brought about by a feeling that *some* of the High Theory of the 1970s and 1980s was proving repetitive, too self-involved, too remote from persons and too inaccessible. By the 1980s, it was felt increasingly within parts of the social sciences and humanities that it was time to bring human actors back on the stage. As a result, there is now a large body of work within an encompassing human sciences concerned with lives and the nature of selfhood. The growing interest in autobiographical and biographical forms in terms of individuals, themes and disciplines is illustrated by the popularity of the comprehensive two-volume *Encyclopedia of Life Writing* of 2001 edited by Margaretta Jolly, to which a number of Auto/Biography Study Group members made contributions.

A consciousness of the notion of narrative (of ways the ineluctable nature of time plays itself out in lives) and the exploration of that complex filigree of places and spaces represented by the interplay of structure and agency have been central to the Study Group's research mission. As such, the intricacies of lives in social context remain as fascinating now as they have always been and are well represented in what follows in this volume.

Michael Erben
Southampton Education School
Southampton, UK

References

Johnson, S. (1750). The Dignity and Usefulness of Biography. *The Rambler*, p. 60.
Erben, M., Morgan, D. H. J., & Stanley, L. (1992). *Editorial, Auto/Biography, 1*(1), 1–9.

Acknowledgements

The significance of auto/biography has evolved over the last three decades. This is exemplified in the work of the British Sociological Associations' Auto/Biography (BSA A/B) Study Group. In part, this book is a tribute to all scholars, past, present and future, who have been or are yet to become acquainted with auto/biography and/or the Auto/Biography Study Group.

The initial convenors and editors of the Auto/Biography Study Group from 1992 consisted of Michael Erben, David Morgan and Liz Stanley. Subsequent convenors and conference organisers are Jenny Byrne, Anne Chappell, Gill Clarke, Andrew Sparkes and Carly Stewart, with Michael maintaining a lead role throughout. Of course, there are also a host of other committed regular contributors to the group, journal and the field of auto/biographical. Not least for Julie on a personal note, her former doctoral supervisor and research mentor Gayle Letherby, a passionate and committed champion of auto/biography, who introduced her to auto/biography and the Study Group in 2010. Anne's experience is that the group conferences and journals, and the colleagues who contribute, have created productive spaces to talk and think in auto/biographical ways. The academic support and encouragement provided by these colleagues are profound in their influence on both research and confidence-building. The Auto/Biography Study Group is a unique and rich academic environment that has made a significant contribution to the development of auto/biography, and we feel very privileged to be part of it. We are very grateful to all involved.

This Palgrave Macmillan Handbook of Auto/Biography has only been made possible with the commitment of all nine part editors and twenty-eight chapter authors, to whom we are very grateful. Similarly, the support from Sharla Plant and Poppy Hull at Palgrave Macmillan.

A note from Julie: Anne and I have worked together on this handbook over the last four years, meeting regularly through Skype and spending time together in the British Library, as well as at Wolfson College, Oxford, Friends House, London and Dartington Hall, Devon, before and during various BSA Auto/Biography conferences. Throughout this time, Anne has been unwavering in her commitment to both the book and the Auto/Biography Study Group. It has been an enormously enjoyable experience and we have had some laughs along the way for which I am truly thankful.

A note from Anne: It has been an absolute pleasure to work on this with Julie over the last four years. We have had great fun as well as fascinating auto/biographical conversations. It has been a wonderfully collaborative academic adventure with both Julie and all the contributors. I would like to thank David, Neil, Heather and Alfie for entertaining conversations about both auto/biography and the book cover.

Introduction

We are delighted to welcome you to the *Palgrave Macmillan Handbook of Auto/Biography*. In this collection, we demonstrate that auto/biography offers endless possibilities for providing insights into the lives of others and the self. It is through first-hand accounts that lives and circumstances become known, providing opportunities for understanding the meanings that people make of their experience(s), as well as the impact of this meaning-making on their lives and the lives of others: 'if men [sic] define situations as real, they are real in their consequences' (Thomas and Thomas 1928: 572). Indeed, we agree with Letherby (2015: 130):

> …that all writing is in some ways auto/biography in that all texts bear traces of the author and are to some extent personal statements (Denzin and Lincoln 1994) within which the writer works from the self to the other and back again. Research writings, then, include intersections of the public/ private domains of the researcher and the researched. (Stanley 1993a)

One of the most exciting things about auto/biography is its interdisciplinary nature and relevance to a range of substantive concerns. *The Palgrave Macmillan Handbook of Auto/Biography* draws on work from fields such as the arts, cultural difference; dis/ability, education, families; health, history; human geography, philosophy; sociology and social justice. Moreover, many of the part editors and contributors have long-standing and active connections with the British Sociological Association's Auto/ Biography Study Group (established in 1992). The group draws from a varied and wide-ranging field of scholars interested in the intersections of autobiography and biography in past and present lives, and the implications of this for our understanding of the social world.

The rationale for *The Palgrave Macmillan Handbook of Auto/Biography* emerged from a conversation between us at the British Sociological Association (BSA) Auto/Biography Study Group Silver Jubilee Summer Conference, at Wolfson College, Oxford in July 2016. Julie had given a paper on fieldwork she was conducting on commensality (eating together around a table) as part of a Sociology of Health and Illness Mildred Blaxter Postdoctoral fellowship.

The focus of the paper was on the benefits for participants sharing a lunch time meal at a prisoner resettlement scheme (RS) with men released on temporary licence from the local prison and others referred from probation, collectively referred to as 'trainees' (Parsons 2017). During the paper, Julie explained how she had published a book from her recently completed doctoral study entitled *Gender, Class and Food, Families, Bodies and Health* (2015). The book highlighted how our everyday foodways, or ways of doing food, can be divisive, enabling individuals to make distinctions between and across social groups. This was used to contrast to the commensality research which demonstrated how food could also be a useful means of bringing people together. Anne was curious about the book and Julie explained that, whilst it had been based on her doctoral research *An Auto/Biographical study of relationships with food*, the reviewers had requested that Julie should 'limit any auto/biographical reflections and to use these only if strictly necessary to make a point'. This resulted in a book of rich, thick descriptions (Geertz 1973) from research respondents, with little if any auto/biographical data (Parsons 2015). This is not the first instance of a misunderstanding in relation to the use of auto/biography. In Julie's doctoral thesis, she explains that:

> … after a brief presentation of the rationale for my work, one of the key note speakers at a University event (a senior academic involved in applied empirical sociology) took me to one side and said; 'you're not serious about the auto/biographical focus of your research are you?' (2014: 78)

However, Julie goes on to add that this was not a typical response. Usually after a presentation of some of the data from her food research, audience members would share their own food stories, highlighting how food memories, like other lived experiences of the everyday are simultaneously both individual and collective.

Anne's experiences during her Ph.D. were similar in that people who she discussed her research with were both cautious and sceptical about her chosen methodological approach that was underpinned by auto/biography. Anne noted that the focus for the project:

> …arose from my range of personal and professional experiences, and the associated observations of those of others… this project did not begin as a process of seeking to know and understand myself, however the consideration of others' understandings of themselves has inevitably prompted reflections on the self. (Chappell: 2014: 61)

As Anne came to understand more about auto/biography, it became clear that these reflections on the self, in researching with others, were inevitable and important given Stanley's observation that:

> The notion of auto/biography involves the insistence that accounts of other lives influence how we see and understand our own and that our understandings of our own lives will impact upon how we interpret other lives. (Stanley 1994: i)

It was these individual experiences of research, along with our observations of different academic collectives that prompted the discussion at the conference which lead to the idea for the book. It was the appeal of auto/biography as a means to make explicit the links or otherwise between the individual and the social, the public and the private that we were keen to curate into an academic artefact as a resource for those seeking to work in this area. It was also important to illustrate the ways in which auto/biography ensures an engagement with a cannon of previous work, as Brennan and Letherby (2017: 160) explain:

> Auto/Biography is academically rigorous, highlighting the social location of the writer and making clear the author's role in the process of constructing rather than discovering the story/the knowledge (Mykhalovskiy 1996; Stanley 1993a; Letherby 2003). Furthermore, auto/biographical study—either focusing on one, several or many lives—demonstrates how individuals are social selves, fashioned from interwoven biographies (Elias 2001; Goodwin 2012; Cotterill and Letherby 1993), and how a focus on the individual can contribute to an understanding of the general. (Mills 1959; Stanley 1992; Ellis and Bochner 2000)

It is no accident, therefore, that scholars working in the field of auto/biography make reference to the work of Mills' (1959) *Sociological Imagination* and the search for common vocabularies within and beyond the individual.

Book Outline

The book is in nine parts, each containing three chapters with introductions from part editors who are established researchers, most of whom are members of the BSA Auto/Biography Study Group. These parts provide the reader with current, previously unpublished research from authors at different stages in their careers: doctoral students, early career researchers, established professors and practitioners. The content will appeal to those with interests in a wide range of areas including, but not limited to, auto/biography, auto-ethnography, epistolary traditions, narrative analysis, life writing, the arts, cultural studies, education, geography, history, philosophy, politics, sociology, reflexivity, geography, research in practice and the sociology of everyday life.

The part titles are indicative of the general theme which has framed the writing of the chapters within it. The parts have been organised alphabetically. What follows is the summary of the parts through abstracts written by the part editors. We wanted to ensure that the part editors' voices are central in presenting their ideas so that these are shared directly with the reader rather than through the filter of us as editors.

Creativity and Collaboration

Gayle Letherby

The chapters in this part highlight how auto/biographical working across disciplines and genres enriches the telling of individual and group stories. With a focus on marginalised and excluded groups (Douglas and Carless); grief and memorialisation (Davidson) and the hidden emotional labour and subsequent burnout of a medical practitioner (Compton), the authors reflect on their use and analysis of creative and artistic approaches including music, poetry, art, dance and tattooing. As such, these pieces engage with the 'personal as political' through a consideration of (often) hidden/untellable stories, embodiment and emotion. Individually and as a collection they challenge and extent social scientific understandings of method, methodology and epistemology both in terms of the tools used and in terms of working practices.

Families and Relationships: Auto/Biography and Family—A Natural Affinity?

David Morgan

There is a particularly intimate relationship between family practices and auto/biographical practices. The stories told help to construct families in space (homes, households) and, through intergenerational relationships, over time. Further, generational family practices over time provide major links between autobiography and history.

Epistolary Lives: Fragments, Sensibility, Assemblages in Auto/Biographical Research

Maria Tamboukou

As a genre of communication, letter-writing is almost universal—a phenomenon with diverse geographies and histories. Letters carry the immediacy of the moment they are written in and are thus considered to be 'nearer' to experience and life. Letters are also particularly 'private documents': their intimate character allows for thoughts, inner feelings and emotions to be expressed. Rather than imposing an overarching meaning derived from a central organising narrative authority or character, epistolary narratives offer multiple perspectives and thus reveal complex layers of meaning. Of course working with letters as documents of life raises a quite complex spectrum of questions around representation, context, truth, power, desire, identity, subjectivity, memory and ethics, questions that are now well identified and richly explored in the field of auto/biographical research. However, epistolary narratives have their own take on these questions and indeed demand ways of analysis that are particularly oriented to the specificities of their ontological and epistemological nature. The main argument of this part is that letters have opened up rich fields of inquiries in auto/biographical research, whilst the chapters comprising it point to new and emerging ways of reading, analysing and 'rewriting' letters.

Geography Matters: Spatiality and Auto/Biography

John Barker and Emma Wainwright

Whilst geographers have long explored the significance of space and place, more recently a diverse range of geographers (see Roche 2011) have begun to consider the role of space, narrative and auto/biography, for example, in exploring issues around health (Milligan et al. 2011), mobility (Sattlegger and Rau 2016) and urban studies (Valentine and Sadgrove 2014). In attempting to explore how narratives of lifepaths draw upon and can be navigated in geographical ways, this part brings together academics from Youth Studies, Education and Human Geography to consider interdisciplinary approaches to geography and biography. In doing so, the part considers a range of auto/biographical experiences from a range of social groups and locations. Chapter 11 (Cullen, Barker and Alldred) explore the spatial and temporal rhythms of young women with caring responsibilities. Chapter 13 (Hayes) considers the role of space, place and nature in biographical accounts. Chapter 13 maps autobiographical narratives of social housing tenants and the everyday challenges faced in moving off welfare. Together, the part illustrates some of the diverse ways in which auto/biography and spatiality are interwoven.

Madness, *Dys*-order and Autist/Biography: Auto/Biographical Challenges to Psychiatric Dominance

Kay Inckle

Psychiatric medicine remains a dominant force in contemporary society, orchestrating who and what is normal, and what practices should be used to achieve normalcy. Psychiatry is based on binary structures which separate the bad, the mad and the irrational from the normal, sane and reasonable. Positioned as irrational, insane and disordered, the mad can never narrate credible self-knowledge and are therefore always written about, objectified and diagnosed. What happens, then, when those who are mad/disordered/atypical narrate their critical and creative auto/biographical accounts? To answer this question, this part presents three auto/biographical accounts which explore neurodiversity, eating dys-order and madness to reveal how auto/biographical approaches are essential for revealing and challenging the power underpinning the medical hegemony and proffering alternative and more productive ways of knowing and being mad, disordered and diverse.

Prison Lives

Dennis Smith

This part will consider the importance of past lives for the theory and practice of auto/biographical study. It will present three chapters of original historical research. The object of this part is to deploy a historical perspective in order to locate the high-profile lives of specific writers and political activists in the context of life and death struggles underway over generations in divided societies where the rights and obligations of powerful establishments and those over whom they exercise their power are in dispute. These conflicts are vividly and sometimes dramatically on display in the case of insurgents and rebels who stand up for exploited and neglected groups in confrontations that test the strength not only of personal character but also of competing ideologies, interests and sociopolitical alliances. In such cases, the heavy hand of imperialist oppression and the answering demand for individual freedom are set directly against each other, most evidently in the case of critics and insurgents that are incarcerated by regimes that wish to punish and silence them. The three chapters in this part draw together three such instances. They explore, in turn, the intellectual and methodological challenges and opportunities involved in narrating and analysing the following cases: first, Antonio Gramsci (1891–1937); second, Bobby Sands (1954–1981), and, finally, Nelson Mandela (1918–2013).

Professional Lives

Jenny Byrne

The three chapters in this part offer original research focusing on the lived experiences of individuals within their different professional contexts and how they view their working lives, their professional identity and sense of self. The auto/biographies are set against a landscape of neoliberal agendas, marketisation of services, performativity, accountability and the rise of managerialism that has disrupted traditional concepts of being a professional. Using auto/biographical accounts of academics in Higher Education (Selway, Byrne and Chappell), early career teachers (Stone) and millennials working in the private sector (Byrne) a reappraisal of professional life in the twenty-first century, that is subject to 'liquid modernity', is presented (Bauman 2000). The chapters provide an enriched and up-to-date understanding of what it means to be a professional, and thus add to the theory and practice of auto/biography in this field of study.

'Race' and Cultural Difference

Geraldine Brown

Auto/Biography provides a means of capturing the multiplicity of ways in which our lives, intersects with power, the subject under investigation, the theoretical approach utilised the stories told by participants in our research and how we make sense and reproduce these stories. As highlighted in the opening introduction, in the UK, there is an array of literature that explores narratives and their relevance in our lives (Parsons and Chappell 2020). However, it is possible to suggest that less attention has been paid to how auto/biography offers individuals a valuable tool to capture the multifaceted ways factors such as 'race', racism and a process of racialisation shape and are implicated in how certain sections of British society live and experience their social world. The contributors in this part are three Black men who use auto/biography as a tool to interrogate such power relations. Sharing snapshots of his life, Paul Grant explores the relationship of autobiography to the practice of black socialism in the twenty-first-century UK. Gurnam Singh reflects on 35 years in Higher Education as a student and faculty member drawing on his journey from childhood to adulthood and through the education system as someone from a working-class Sikh family who migrated to a northern town and entered the academy. And, Carver Anderson's work highlights contradictions associated with notions of community and his story shows his multiple connections to the choices he has made in key areas of his life.

Social Justice and Disability: Voices from the Inside

Chrissie Rogers

The chapters in this part engage with stories of disability and social justice. The narratives are gained through carrying out qualitative research from a particular position: that of the 'insider'. All three chapters take an auto/biographical sociological position, whereby the researchers are explicit about their positionality and reflexive in their analysis. From gaining and main-taining access with hard to reach groups, to broad assumptions based on the researcher's personal background and public others' perceptions, stories of social and embodied injustices are told. Stigmatised identities and the social gaze occur as persistent themes when drilling down into the life story and auto/biographical accounts. The first chapter begins this part and explains the very beginnings of a challenging research process with adults who have been through the criminal justice system and family members. What is dis-covered in Chrissie's chapter, is the emotive life story research, from the very inception, is unpredictable, chaotic and often hidden from the post-project sanitised formal write-up. The second chapter questions whether experiences of dwarfism could ever be separated from the exploitative historical and cultural portrayals which have plagued and blighted the fight for social jus-tice both inside and outside of a community. Kelly-Mae's auto/biographical reflections as a mother with a son with Dwarfism are woven throughout, in pursuit of social justice. The final chapter in this part utilises reflexive writ-ing as Amy, an autistic woman, examines disability within higher education as she reflects upon her experiences of 'passing' as 'normal' at an academic conference. Critically, she considers the decision-making process behind her reasons to present as a hybrid of an autistic and non-autistic researcher. All three chapters highlight the importance, benefits and challenges of doing auto/biographical disability research.

Concluding Thoughts

The chapters provide invaluable insights into the lives of others and/or selves, through the use of documents, diaries, letters, photographs and/or reflections on personal experience, past, present and future. The format of the chap-ters is mostly as might be expected in academic work, whilst some authors play with how the text is structured, organised and presented on the page. Authors also use a range of creative methods for delineating the voices of those represented in the text. It is these voices that make auto/biographical work so illuminating. They provide invaluable accounts across a number of different fields that explore aspects of the social world and the experiences of those within it. Authors utilise a range of academic perspectives and philosophical orientations, and their accounts cover the famous and/or infa-mous through to the everyday. It has been, and continues to be, a privilege to bear witness to the testimonies of the experiences of those represented here. This handbook is therefore an invaluable resource to understand how auto/biography has been used over time for those with an interest in it and/or considering the use of auto/biography in their work or research.

In 1993, Stanley wrote that there were 'a number of signs that the intellectual wind in Britain is now blowing fairly briskly in an auto/biographical direction' (Stanley 1993b: 1). Our commitment in collaborating with colleagues on this book has been to draw some of that scholarship over the last three decades together in this collection.

Julie M. Parsons
Anne Chappell

References

Bauman, Z. (2000). *Liquid Modernity*. Cambridge: Polity Press.

Brennan, M., & Letherby, G. (2017). Auto/Biographical Approaches to Researching Death and Dying: Connections, Continuums, Contrasts. *Mortality, 22*(2), 155–169.

Chappell, A. (2014). *Professional Learning: Teachers' Narratives of Experience*. Unpublished Ph.D. London: Brunel University London. http://bura.brunel.ac.uk/handle/2438/10933.

Cotterill, P., & Letherby, G. (1993). Weaving Stories: Personal Auto/Biographies in Feminist Research. *Sociology, 27*, 67–79.

Denzin, N., & Lincoln, Y., (1994). *Handbook of Qualitative Research*. London: Sage.

Elias, N. (2001). *The Society of Individuals*. New York: Continuum.

Ellis, C., & Bochner, A. P. (2000). Autoethnography, Personal Narrative, Reflexivity: Researcher as Subject. In N. Denzin & Y. Lincoln (Eds.), *Handbook of Qualitative Research* (2nd ed., pp. 733–768). Thousand Oaks: Sage.

Geertz, C. (1973). *The Interpretation of Cultures*. New York: Perseus Books.

Goodwin, J. (2012). Editor's Introduction: Biographical Research—Researching "Lives" at the Intersection of History and Biography. In J. Goodwin, (Ed.), *Sage Biographical Research* (Vols. 1–4, pp. xix–xxxvi). London: Sage.

Letherby, G. (2003). *Feminist Research in Theory and Practice*. Buckingham: Open University.

Letherby, G. (2015). Bathwater, Babies and Other Losses: A Personal and Academic Story. *Mortality, 20*(2), 128–144.

Milligan, C., Roberts, C., & Mort, M. (2011). Telecare and Older People: Who Cares Where? *Social Science & Medicine Journal, 72*(3), 347–354.

Mills, C. W. (1959). *The Sociological Imagination*. London: Penguin.

Mykhalovskiy, E. (1996). Reconsidering Table Talk: Critical Thoughts on the Relationship Between Sociology, Autobiography and Self-indulgence. *Qualitative Sociology, 19*, 131–151.

Parsons, J. (2014). *'Ourfoodstories@email.com', an Auto/Biographical Study of Relationships with Food*, Ph.D. thesis. http://hdl.handle.net/10026.1/2920.

Parsons, J. M. (2015). *Gender, Class and Food: Families, Bodies and Health.* Basingstoke: Palgrave Macmillan.

Parsons, J. M. (2017). Cooking with Offenders to Improve Health and Wellbeing. *Special Issue of the British Food Journal on Cooking, Health and Evidence, 119* (5), 1079–1090.

Parsons, J., & A. Chappell (eds.) (2020). *The Palgrave Macmillan Handbook of Auto/Biography.* Basingstoke: Palgrave Macmillan.

Roche, M. (2011). Special Issue: New Zealand Geography, Biography and Autobiography. *New Zealand Geographer, 67*(2), 73–142.

Sattlegger, L., & Rau, H. (2016). Carlessness in a Car-Centric World: A Reconstructive Approach to Qualitative Mobility Biographies Research. *Journal of Transport Geography, 53*(C), 22–31. Elsevier.

Stanley, L. (1992). *The Auto/Biographical I: Theory and Practice of Feminist Auto/Biography*. Manchester: Manchester University Press.

Stanley, L. (1993a). On Auto/Biography in Sociology. *Sociology, 27*, 41–52.

Stanley, L. (1993b). Editorial. *Auto/biography, 2*(1), 1–5.

Stanley, L. (1994). Introduction: Lives and Works and Auto/Biographical Occasions. *Auto/biography, 3*(1 and 2), i–ii.

Thomas, W. I., & Thomas, D. S. (1928). *The Child in America: Behavior Problems and Programs*. New York: Knopf.

Valentine, G., & Sadgrove, J. (2014). Biographical Narratives of Encounter: The Significance of Mobility and Emplacement in Shaping Attitudes Towards Difference. *Urban Studies, 51*(9), 1979–1994.

Contents

Notes on Contributors

Pam Alldred is Professor of Social Work at Nottingham Trent University, UK. She researches sexualities, parenting and sex education and has led two large international EU-funded projects on gender-related violence and sexual violence. The first (GAP Work) produced free training resources to help youth practitioners to challenge gender-related violence (https://sites.brunel.ac.uk/gap) and the second (USV React) piloted sexual violence first-responder training for staff in universities in six countries, and shares training resources (www.USVReact/eu). Recent publications include Sociology and the New Materialism (2016) and the Handbook of Youth Work Practice (2018). She is an editor for the journals *Sex Education, and Gender and Education.*

Rev. Carver Anderson is a practical theologian and social scientist with over 35 years' experience as a qualified social worker, working with families and communities plagued by multiple and complex needs and challenges. He is one of the Executive Directors and cofounder of the Bringing Hope Charity in Birmingham. He is an Honorary Fellow at the University of Birmingham's Edward Cadbury Centre for Public Understanding of Religion and a Visiting Academic at Birmingham City University, School of Social Science. His interests lie principally in practical theology and social ethics. He has written in the areas associated with developing community-led and community-involved perspectives relating to violence, practical theology and desistance, interfaith relationships and family support. Carver is currently working on a Black Public Practical theology towards engage black young men.

Karin Bacon lectures in Primary Science and Social Studies education at the Marino Institute of Education, an associate college of education at Trinity College, Dublin. She works with undergraduate and Professional Masters' students and coordinates a module on Inquiry-Based Learning on a Masters programme in Early Childhood Education. She completed her doctoral degree in children's inquiry at the School of Education, Trinity College and holds a Masters in Science Education. She spent seven years at the Munich International School before returning to Ireland in 1999 to work in the area of professional development and in-service training for teachers of the Irish primary curriculum. In 2007, she founded and was the first head of the International School of Dublin. Her research interests include Inquiry-Based Learning, comparative education with an emphasis on International Schools and Early Childhood Curriculum—particularly within the areas of SESE and Continuing Professional Development with an emphasis on reflective narrative practice.

John Barker is Senior Lecturer in the Department of Education at Middlesex University, London, UK. John is a Geographer and, over the past 25 years, has undertaken numerous research projects funded by UK Government, local authorities and local charities, exploring different aspects of the lives of children and young people, particularly around care, play and mobility. Widely published in a range of internationally renowned journals, John has particular interests in post-structural and post-human approaches to research, as well as a keen interest in children-centred methods and methodological and ethical issues in research.

Julia Brannen is Professor of the sociology of the family at the Thomas Coram Research Unit, UCL, Institute of Education London and a Fellow of the Academy of Social Science. Her research covers the family lives of parents, children and young people, work-family issues in Britain and Europe, intergenerational relationships and food in families. She has a particular interest in methodology, including mixed methods, biographical approaches and comparative research.

Geraldine Brown background is in the disciplines of Sociology and Social Policy and a key goal is to make a difference. She is an experienced researcher and has been involved in developing and delivering research-informed training to practitioners, community workers and policy makers. Geraldine adopts an 'action research' approach to her work and has undertaken research with communities identified in policy as 'marginalised' 'excluded' or 'hard to reach'. 'She has carried out research with; pregnant teenagers and young mothers', Black and Minority Ethnic communities' 'criminalised men and women,' older people with a mental health need and young carers. This research employs methods that aim to reduce the nexus between the researcher and the researched and, in so doing, produce knowledge that is grounded in the lived reality of the participants she engages in her work. Her doctoral research adopted an auto/biographical approach to exploring how activist working in African Caribbean communities understood and responded to 'urban gun crime'.

Jenny Byrne has taught in all phases of education. She is an Associate Professor at The University of Southampton where she lectures in Biographical Studies and Education. She is a convenor of the Auto/ Biography Study Group. She has published several articles in the Auto/ Biography Yearbook and a BSA Auto/Biography Monograph, We just gelled—the story of 5/67: a biographical and Durkheimian analysis of a school reunion (2012). Her research interests include the cultural and social factors that affect well-being and personhood, the lives of women writers; currently, she is developing her work on Enid Blyton, as well as The Ashington Art Group.

David Carless is a Visiting Research Professor at Queen's University Belfast. His professional background spans the performing arts, health and physical education. In his research, he uses stories—in various forms—to understand critical aspects of human experience and to share the understandings that ensue with others. His arts-based and performative research has informed more than sixty journal articles and book chapters; eight audio CDs; six films (available on YouTube); numerous live performances; commissioned research and evaluation projects; and invited lectures, workshops, seminars and keynotes. Together with Kitrina Douglas, he is co-presenter of the *Qualitative Conversations* series (available on YouTube) and co-author of *Sport and Physical Activity for Mental Health* and *Life Story Research in Sport: Understanding the Experiences of Elite and Professional Athletes Through Narrative*.

Anne Chappell is Senior Lecturer and Divisional Lead in the Department of Education at Brunel University London. Her background is in education and sociology, with particular research interests in policy, professionals, auto/ biography, narrative methodologies and the ethical exploration and representation of experiences. She has undertaken a number of research projects and published in areas such as teachers' professional lives, the experiences of university students, education for university staff and the development of tuition centres. Anne is co-convener of the British Sociological Association (BSA) BSA Auto/Biography Study Group.

Theresa Compton is a lecturer in biomedical science at the Peninsula Medical School, University of Plymouth. Her previous experience of a career as a medically qualified doctor informs her work in the medical school supporting students' personal development and well-being and she is often asked to provide advice to other academic tutors and externally to healthcare professionals on well-being issues. As a result of this work, Theresa was recently awarded a 'Personal Tutoring and Academic Advising' joint CRA (Centre for Recording Achievement) and SEDA (Staff and Educational Development) award. Research interests include student support, student engagement and small group teaching.

Fin Cullen is Senior Lecturer at St Mary's University Twickenham, UK. She worked in the field of youth work for over a decade. She is the co-editor of 'Research and Research methods for Youth Practitioners' (2011) and the 2018 SAGE 'Handbook of Youth Work Practice'. Fin has researched in the areas of youth homelessness, youth friendship cultures, professional identities, sex-gender equalities in education, gender-related violence and young carer experiences. Fin's main research interests explore sex-gender equalities, feminist pedagogy, young people's cultures and (inter)professional identities in education and youth services.

Deborah Davidson is Associate Professor at York University in Toronto. She is a feminist sociologist and a qualitative researcher with research and writing interests in the areas of health and well-being, loss and bereavement, disability, family and mothering, and pedagogy. Her current research includes commemorative tattoos and digital archiving. Methodologically, she has expertise in qualitative and creative methodologies and is particularly experienced in collaborative research, participatory methods, auto/biographical approaches, and researching sensitive topics with marginalised populations. She is a lover of all creatures, great and small, especially her canine and feline family members.

Kitrina Douglas is a Professor at the University of West London. Previously, she worked as the Director of the Boomerang-Project.org.uk an arts-based network for public engagement and performance of social science research, and Co-director/producer with David Carless of the YouTube qualitative research series 'Qualitative Conversations'. Together they have written two academic books, produced three music, poetry and story CDs, toured five ethno-dramas in the UK, USA and/or New Zealand, and their documentary/

films have been watched in 52 countries and are available on YouTube: https://www.youtube.com/channel/UCkWCTy8bNOY6JlvX_yg-Uig. As an independent scholar, Kitrina has conducted research for a variety of organisations including the Department of Health (UK), UK sport, Women's Sport and Fitness Foundation, the Addiction Recovery Agency and NHS Trusts. Since 2012, she has had a fractional contract at Leeds Beckett University where she was named Researcher of the Year in 2014.

Paul Grant is a recovering academic who teaches yoga and tai chi in the West Midlands. He is currently working on a Fanonian analysis of the HBO series 'The Wire', death, injustice, contradiction, impatience, humour and hope.

Erla Hulda Halldórsdóttir is a lecturer/assistant professor in women's and gender history, University of Iceland. Her research field is women's history, biography, correspondence and historical literacy (writing). Among her published work in Icelandic is the monograph Nútímans konur (2011) [*Women of Modernity. Women's Education and the Construction of Gender in Iceland 1850-1903*]. Among recent works in English is: 'A biography of her own. The historical narrative and Sigríður Pálsdóttir (1809–1871)', in *Biography, Gender and History: Nordic Perspectives*. Eds. Erla Hulda Halldórsdóttir, Tiina Kinnunen, Maarit Leskelä-Kärki and Birgitte Possing (Turku: k&h, 2016); "'Do Not Let Anyone See This Ugly Scrawling': Literacy Practices and the Women's Household at Hallfreðarstaðir 1817–1829", *Life Writing* (2015). Halldórsdóttir is currently working on the biography of Sigríður Pálsdóttir and a project on women, suffrage and agency in twentieth-century Iceland.

Tracy Ann Hayes is Lecturer in Health, Psychology and Social Studies at the University of Cumbria, UK. In 2018, she was awarded Ph.D. in Transdisciplinary research in Outdoor Studies by Lancaster University, for her research into the relationship that young people have with the natural environment. Having previously achieved B.Sc. in Natural Sciences and M.A. in Youth Work and Community Development, she embraces transdisciplinary methodologies which utilise creative and narrative approaches to research nature; human-nonhuman/more-than-human relationships; outdoor learning and play; geographies of children, youth and families; youth work and informal learning.

Alyssa Hillary is an Autistic Ph.D. student in the Interdisciplinary Neuroscience Programme at the University of Rhode Island (USA). Officially, they work on augmentative and alternative communication, both in the form of brain–computer interfaces and as used by autistic adults. Unofficially but more prolifically, they write about issues related to neurodiversity and representation in fiction, media, scientific research and now life writing. Their work has appeared in *Criptiques*, on Disability in Kidlit, in International Perspectives on Teaching with Disability, and in several Autonomous Press anthologies.

Kay Inckle is a lecturer in sociology at the University of Liverpool (UK). Her work (and life) are based on user-led and critical approaches to self-injury and 'mental health', disability, gender and sexuality and creative research methods. She has a number of publications including her recent book *Safe with Self-Injury: A Practical Guide to Understanding, Responding and Harm-Reduction* (with PCCS Books) and a (very critical) commentary in Disability & Society, *Unreasonable Adjustments: The Additional Unpaid Labor of Disabled Academics* (2018). She is also a vegan, hand-cyclist, swimmer, dancer and a qualified Pilates instructor.

Gayle Letherby is Honorary Professor of Sociology at Plymouth University and Visiting Professor at the University of Greenwich. Alongside substantive interests in reproductive and non/parental identities; gender, health and well-being; loss and bereavement; travel and transport mobility and working and gender and identity within institutions (including universities and prisons) she has an international reputation in research methodology. Expertise in this area includes feminist and qualitative approaches and in auto/biography and creative reflexivity (with reference to data collection and presentation). Gayle is currently co-editor of the *Sage journal Methodological Innovations* and is in the process of editing the *Handbook of Feminist Research* for Routledge. For examples of non-academic writing and pieces written for general readership, see http://arwenackcerebrals.blogspot.co.uk/ and https://www.abctales.com/user/gletherby.

Elodie Marandet is a qualitative researcher based in the UK with interests in the restructuring of the welfare state, including family and welfare-to-work policies; post-compulsory education; gender; and neoliberalism and global governance, with a focus on aid relations. She has a Ph.D. from Brunel University. Her work has been published in the *British Educational Research Journal* and *Space and Polity* and she recently contributed to a volume of a Springer Major Reference Work on the *Geographies of Children and Young People*. Elodie is a member of the consultancy network *Keep Your Shoes Dirty* and has worked as a tutor at the Institute of Development Studies, London, UK.

Ellen McHugh is a researcher and lecturer in the Department of Education, Brunel University London, UK. She has a Ph.D. in Geography from the University of Reading. Her research interests lie in transnation-alism, belonging, identity, welfare and well-being, education and young people. She recently completed a project on 'successful students' from a widening participation background and a research project for a housing association looking at tenants' financial capability and well-being. Ellen is currently undertaking research looking at the growth and role of tuition centres for children of primary school age (4–11) in the UK.

David Morgan is an Emeritus Professor in Sociology at the University of Manchester where he taught for over 35 years. Main interests have included family studies, men and masculinities, everyday life and auto/biography. He is a founding member of the BSA Auto/Biography Study Group. Recent books are *Acquaintances: The Space Between Intimates and Strangers* (OU Press, 2009), *Rethinking family practices* (Palgrave Macmillan, 2011) and *Snobbery* (Policy Press, 2019).

Jenifer Nicholson started her professional life as a linguist, first in teaching, both in schools and adult education. When she moved into the management of Adult Education, focusing on its quality and purpose, she became interested in the life and work of Antonio Gramsci. She studied his life, ideas and political practice for an M.A. and subsequently a Ph.D. at Southampton University. She is now an independent researcher and has published articles in La Gramsciana and several in Auto/Biography Yearbooks. She is currently working on a book about Gramsci and the influential, but neglected, women in his life. The book will incorporate little known material from the archives in Rome and Moscow. She is also interested in new approaches to presenting a life.

Bríd O'Farrell received her doctorate from the school of sociology in Trinity College Dublin in 2008. She is currently working as a teacher of the Feldenkrais Method and is training to become a humanistic Psychotherapist. She maintains a keen interest in creative social research methods which attempt to represent the complexity of embodied experience, particularly marginalised and stigmatised lived experience.

Denis O'Hearn is an academic and activist who has worked in Ireland, Turkey and the USA. His books include a biography of the Irish hunger striker Bobby Sands (Nothing But an Unfinished Song) and a study of mutual aid among Cossacks, Zapatistas, and prisoners in solitary confinement (Living at the Edges of Capitalism: Adventures in Exile and Mutual Aid). After living many years in Belfast, Northern Ireland, he is now Dean of Liberal Arts and Professor of Sociology at the University of Texas at El Paso (UTEP).

Julie M. Parsons is Associate Professor in Sociology. She recently completed an Independent Social Research Foundation (ISRF) mid-career fellowship (2016–2017), working on a Photographic electronic Narrative (PeN) project with men released on temporary licence from the local prison and others serving community sentences on placement at a local resettlement scheme (RS), which is ongoing. This followed a Sociology of Health and Illness (SHI) Foundation Mildred Blaxter fellowship (2015–2016), exploring commensality (eating together) as a tool for health, well-being, social inclusion and community resilience at the same RS. Her book *Gender, Class and Food, Families, Bodies and Health* (Palgrave Macmillan 2015), was shortlisted for the Foundation of Health and Illness (FHI) book prize in 2016. She was programme lead for the M.Sc. in Social Research from 2010–2014 and is currently programme lead for the B.Sc. (Hons) in Sociology. She is convener of the British Sociological Association (BSA) Food Study Group, a member of the BSA Auto/Biography Study Group, the BSA Medical Sociology Study Group and the British Society of Criminology.

Elizaveta Polukhina is Associate Professor in the Faculty of Social Sciences at the National Research University Higher School of Economics (HSE), Moscow, Russia. Her projects and research interests are related to the issues of everyday life in post-soviet Russia, housing studies, social mobility and sociological research methods. She is the author of numerous methodological articles focusing on the ethnographic case-study application, online observation, the potential of integrating qualitative and quantitative strategies with data. Elizaveta contributes to the courses 'Research designs: How to Combine Different Methods in One Research', 'Methodology and Methods of Sociological Research' and the Research Seminar (HSE, Moscow). She is a member of the Editorial Board of the international journal *The Qualitative Report* (USA). Personal page: http://www.hse.ru/en/staff/polukhina.

Chrissie Rogers is Professor of Sociology at the University of Kent, Canterbury, UK. Her recent research funded by the Leverhulme Trust called *Care-less Spaces: Prisoners with learning difficulties and their families* (RF-2016-613\8) involved life story interviews with adults who have offended and have learning difficulties (LD) and/or social, emotional, mental health problems (SEMH), mothers of offenders and professionals who work with these groups of people. Chrissie has begun to publish from this research in *Methodological Innovations*, and the *Oxford Research Encyclopedia*. Chrissie has previously written on mothering/parenting, intellectual/learning disability, ethics of care, intimacy and education. Her most recent book *Intellectual*

Disability and Being Human develops a care ethics model of disability. Chrissie graduated from the University of Essex (2005) with a Ph.D. in Sociology (ESRC) and was awarded an ESRC postdoctoral fellowship at the University of Cambridge (2004/2005). Her Ph.D. was qualitative research with mothers and fathers who have children identified with 'special educational needs', which she published as *Parenting and Inclusive Education* in 2007.

Kelly-Mae Saville is a research associate and seminar tutor in the School of Languages and Social Sciences at Aston University, Birmingham. Currently undertaking a Ph.D., her thesis explores the experiences of mothering children with dwarfism in a biotechnical advanced medical age, where disabled identities and perspectives on 'health' are at times contested. As an averaged statured member of the dwarfism community, she uses auto/biography to highlight and critique the blurred boundary nature of this type of 'insider' research.

Aiden Seery is Senior Tutor in Trinity College, Dublin and has just completed a three-year term as Director of the Trinity Research Centre for Cultures, Academic Values and Education (CAVE) in the School of Education. The Centre conducts research into higher education and is the largest such centre in Ireland. Educated at University college, Dublin, the Hochschule fur Philosophie and the Ludwig Maximilian University, Munich and Trinity College (Ph.D. 1995), his research interests include: higher education and self-formation, *Bildungstheorie*, narrative philosophy and biography, and the philosophical foundations of educational research. He lectures and writes on educational theory and philosophy, higher education, educational research methods with a special interest in auto/biography.

Irene Selway has been a teacher across a range of education sectors for most of her adult working life. She was a community adult educator in further education before studying for a degree and subsequently taught primary school children before moving to teaching adults in further education. From there, she moved to teach in universities. She completed her Ph.D. with a focus on auto/biography at the University of Southampton. She has been an active member of the BSA Auto/Biography Study Group and has published several articles in Auto/Biography and the Auto/Biography Yearbook. She is now an independent scholar.

Amy Simmons is a Ph.D. student, studying sociology (disability studies branch) at the University of Bradford. Her research interests include autism and transition in further and higher education. She is an Autistic self-advocate and uses auto/biography and in-depth interviewing to explore the stigma of autism, the downplaying of difference, and the value of support in the life of an autistic person, drawing upon the work of Goffman and Foucault to inform her analysis. She has a degree from Aston University and a master's degree from the University of Birmingham. She began her Ph.D. at Aston University, before continuing her studies at the University of Bradford, giving her plenty of experience to draw on for her research on autism and transition in further and higher education.

Gurnam Singh is an Associate Professor of Social Work and Post Graduate Research Degrees Lead for the Faculty of Health and Life Sciences at Coventry University. He is also Visiting Professor of Social Work at the University of Chester and Visiting Fellow in Race and Education at the University of Arts, London. Before entering academia, he worked as a professional Social Worker. Dr. Singh completed his Ph.D. from the University of Warwick in 2004 and in 2009 he was awarded a National Teaching Fellowship by the HEA for his work on Critical Pedagogy an Inclusion in Higher Education. More recently became a Fellow of the Royal Society of Arts (RSA). His main area of research is anti-racist theory and practice and critical pedagogy as it relates both to social work and higher education. He is seen as one of the leading thinkers on the issue of disparities in attainment in Higher Education and he has published over 50 peer review articles, book chapters and research reports and has presented over 150 papers conference papers across the world. Dr. Singh also has an extensive media and public profile and regularly offers commentary on policy developments.

Dennis Smith studied Modern History at Christ's College, Cambridge and Sociology at the London School of Economics. As a historical sociologist, his work has ranged from Victorian cities such as Birmingham and Sheffield (the focus of his doctorate since published as *Conflict and Compromise. Class Formation in English Society 1830–1914*, Routledge, 2016, 2nd ed.) through to post-war ex-colonies of the British Empire, especially apartheid-ridden South Africa and Burma under military dictatorship. His most recent book entitled *Civilized Rebels*. An Inside Story of the West's Retreat from Global Power, Routledge, 2018, focused on four prisoners: Oscar Wilde, Jean Améry, Nelson Mandela and Aung San Suu Kyi. He is currently writing about Brexit, the European Union and the West. He is Emeritus Professor of Sociology at Loughborough University, UK. The research on which this chapter is based drew on public available materials and was entirely financed by the author. For further details, see https://www.lboro.ac.uk/departments/socialsciences/staff/honorary/dennis-smith/ and http://lboro.academia.edu/DennisSmith.

Phil Smith is former Professor of Special Education at Eastern Michigan University (USA), and Mad as hell. He's published in many journals, book chapters, and some books, including *Whatever Happened to Inclusion? The Place of Students with Intellectual Disabilities in Education* (2010), *Both Sides of the Table: Autoethnographies of Educators Learning and Teaching With/In [Dis]ability* (2013), *Disability and Diversity: An Introduction* (2014) and *Writhing Writing: Moving Towards a Mad Poetics* (2018). A published poet, playwright, novelist, and visual artist, he's worked as an activist, and served on the boards of directors of a number of national and state organisations. He is past President of the Society for Disability Studies.

Liz Stanley holds the established Chair of Sociology at the University of Edinburgh and has just completed a period as an ESRC Professorial Research Fellow. A feminist sociologist who works on cultural and historical topics, she uses these investigations to explore questions concerning epistemology and ontology as well as methodology. Her 1992 book *The Auto/Biographical I*, and a special issue of the journal *Sociology* she edited with David Morgan, were the first publications to develop the analytical idea of auto/biography. Please see her university website for more detail on research projects and publications: http://www.sociology.ed.ac.uk/people/staff/stanley_liz.

Glenn Stone has worked as a primary school teacher and is currently a Principal Lecturer in Education at the University of Chichester where he coordinates the undergraduate Initial Teacher Education programme. Glenn has a special interest in the training of teachers and their perspectives on school accountability, performativity and the standards agenda. His doctorate study focused on conceptions of professionalism held by student teachers. He continues to research the role of Initial Teacher Education in shaping the professionalism of teachers.

Maria Tamboukou is Professor of Feminist Studies at the University of East London, UK and Leverhulme Research Fellow in 2018–2019. She has held visiting research positions in a number of institutions and is currently Affiliated Professor in Gender Studies at Linnaeus University Sweden, Adjunct Professor at the Institute for Educational Research at Griffith University, Australia and member of the Scientific Board of the 'Hannah Arendt' Centre for Political Studies at the University of Verona, Italy. Maria's research activity develops in the areas of philosophies and epistemologies in the social sciences, feminist theories, narrative analytics and archival research. She is the author of 7 monographs, 2 co-authored books, 3 co-edited volumes on research methods and more than 80 articles and book chapters. Writing histories of the present is the central focus of her work, currently configured as an assemblage of feminist genealogies. Recent publications include the monographs *Sewing, Writing and Fighting, Gendering the Memory of Work, Women Workers' Education*, as well as the co-authored book *The Archive Project*. Please see the author's website for more details on research projects and publications: https://sites.google.com/site/mariatamboukoupersonalblog/home.

Dimitra Vassiliadou holds a Ph.D. in modern history from the University of Crete (2015). Currently, she is a postdoctoral researcher at the University of Athens and teaches at the Hellenic Open University. She is a co-editor of two collective volumes, on *Gender History and Masculinities*, respectively. In her monograph *The Tropic of Writing: Family Ties and Emotions in Modern Greece, 1850–1930* (Gutenberg, Athens 2018), which is based on correspondences, she traces the emotional cultures of middle-class families. She is the recipient of many fellowships; most recently, she received a two-year fellowship from the Greek State Scholarships Foundation, for her new project, which focuses on autobiographical discourses of melancholy and explores the historical transformation of a disorderly emotion into a disease.

Emma Wainwright is a reader and a Geographer in the Department of Education and the Institute of Environment, Health and Societies, Brunel University London, UK. She has expertise in the geographies and sociologies of education, training and welfare-to-work; housing; family, parenting and care; embodiment, bodywork and emotional labour, and has published extensively in *Sociology, Education and Geography* journals. Emma has led research projects funded by the ESRC, the British Academy, Barclays, the Learning and Skills Council, and the Money Advice Service. Emma is currently editor of the *British Educational Research Journal*.

List of Figures

List of Tables

1

A Case for Auto/Biography

Julie M. Parsons and Anne Chappell

Introduction

In this chapter, we make a case for auto/biography, as it lies at the heart of the sociological imagination, emphasising as it does the links between biography and history, the public and the private (Mills 1959). We consider both auto/biography as an epistemological orientation and a methodological approach. This involves reflection on the field of auto/biography, as well as specific reflections on auto/biographical research in practice. To begin, we provide a very brief history of auto/biography as we understand it in the social sciences.

Following Durkheim's work in 1897, in the early 1900s there was a range of academic work that started to focus on the lives of people and the different means by which those lives could be explored (Thomas and Znaniecki 1918; Thomas and Thomas 1928; Mills 1959). Erben noted this work as key within the Chicago School (1998a) in providing an important basis for the development of auto/biography as a field of study. What followed later were key works such as 'Documents of Life' (Plummer 1983), 'Time and Narrative' (Ricoeur 1984), 'Destiny Obscure' (Burnett 1984) and 'A History of Private Lives' (Prost and

J. M. Parsons (✉)
University of Plymouth, Plymouth, UK
e-mail: jmparsons@plymouth.ac.uk

A. Chappell
Brunel University London, London, UK
e-mail: anne.chappell@brunel.ac.uk

© The Author(s) 2020
J. M. Parsons and A. Chappell (eds.), *The Palgrave Handbook of Auto/Biography*,
https://doi.org/10.1007/978-3-030-31974-8_1

Vincent 1991) which explored the underpinnings of the auto/biographical in relation to different lives, the ways in which those lives were recorded, and theories for how they could be understood and subsequently represented. This work laid the foundation for Michael Erben, David Morgan and Liz Stanley to convene the British Sociological Association's Auto/Biography Study Group in 1992. The group was committed to understanding lives because, as Stanley (1993a: 2) notes:

> Lives are an interesting place to be, partly because there are so few areas of work in the social sciences and humanities which do not involve auto/biography in one form or another, but perhaps mainly because the auto/biographical forms a radical departure – truly a reconceptualisation – in the way we think and work as well as in the subject matter we deal with.

At the time, Stanley suggested that auto/biography was essential for the social sciences as:

> …maximally it mounts a principled and concerted attack on conventional views that 'works' are separate from lives, that there can be an epistemology which is not ontologically based. That science can be objective. Auto/biography intends an epistemological revolution within the social sciences. (Stanley 1993a: i)

In order to initiate this 'revolution', the group convenors began publishing a bulletin in 1992 and held a conference that led to a special issue of the journal Sociology in 1993. The bulletin became a self-published journal in 1994 and was then picked up by a publisher in 1998. In 2007, the publication changed to the Auto/Biography Yearbook and, in 2019, Auto/Biography Review. The work of the group sat alongside, but discrete from, the developing fields of narrative, biography, and life history, amongst others.

The material in the journals has consistently been rich, interdisciplinary and challenging in nature, edited from 1998 to the present day by Andrew Sparkes whilst Jenny Byrne, Gill Clarke and Michael Erben, and latterly Anne Chappell, led on maintaining the pattern of two conferences a year. Alongside this there have been a range of significant books, including monographs published by the Study Group, that have contributed directly and significantly to the field of auto/biography (Stanley 1992; Morgan 1996; Evans 1999; Plummer 2001; Sparkes 2002; Clarke 2008; Abbott 2009; Tamboukou 2010c; Byrne 2012; Stanley 2013; Letherby 2014; Dickinson and Erben 2016). In addition, there have been an array of journal articles and conference presentations related to auto/biography beyond those of the

Study Group, which David Morgan recently noted in an interview conducted in preparation for this book. The legacy of the Study Group is key to the work presented here. This book demonstrates how auto/biographical work continues to offer a significant provocation in social science research.

It seems fitting that in order to introduce the Palgrave Handbook of Auto/Biography that Anne and I say something about ourselves in relation to auto/biography. Yet, there can be problems with beginnings, with where to start. Every time we consider a beginning, we have to contemplate the ending and what purpose this particular beginning serves. What stories do we want to tell and how do we represent ourselves within them? What are our multiple subject positions, the academic self, social researcher, sociologist, feminist, lecturer, teacher, student and/or mother, wife, daughter? What needs to be known about us, as researchers in order to evaluate our research, this book and how can this be known? Or as Elliott (2011: 1) asks 'how, as researchers, do we notice ourselves in ways which make the interpretative selves visible?' It is through the writing of the self and the narratives that we construct about these selves that our identities are 'forged, rehearsed and remade' (Lee and Boud 2003: 188). It is, therefore, in the act of 'doing' auto/biography that connections and reconnections are made. Hence, the 'auto', or personal experience, and 'biography', or life story, are significant in re-authorising subjectivity and experience (Mintz 2016). These generative texts provide a storied reworking of the self, situated and contextualised, yet simultaneously blurring perceived boundaries between self/other and the public/private (Sheridan 1993).

In this context, auto/biography is both a method and a text; it is a noun and a verb. Moreover, the forward slash in auto/biography is deliberate and distinguishes it from autobiography. Indeed, as Liz Stanley, one of the founding members of the study group, explains:

> auto-slash-biography… disputes the conventional genre distinction between biography and autobiography as well as the divisions between self/other, public/private, and immediacy/memory… (Stanley 1993b: 42)

Auto/Biography is not simply a shorthand representation of autobiography and/or biography but is a recognition of the interdependence of the two enterprises, as David Morgan (another founding member of the BSA Auto/Biography study group) notes:

> In writing another's life we also write or rewrite our own lives; in writing about ourselves we also consider ourselves as somebody different from the person

who routinely and unproblematically inhabits and moves through social space and time… (Morgan 1998: 655)

Following the work of Mills (1959), an auto/biographical approach concerns the development of a 'sociological imagination' that enables individuals to look at the familiar in social life and see it afresh, to emphasise how 'the social scientist is not some autonomous being standing outside of society' (Mills 1959: 204), but is shaped by biography, history and social structure. It is therefore particularly prescient in a neoliberal era of heightened individualism that auto/biography enables analysis of 'the self' within its wider context. It draws on narrative analysis and epistolary traditions. It encourages reflexivity and reflection. However, whilst auto/biography might consider 'the self' a source of analysis, it is not self-indulgent. Instead, as Gayle Letherby argues the 'self' is a 'resource for helping to make sense of the lives of others [because] it is always present and inseparable from the work we produce' (Letherby 2003: 96). Mills (1959) argues that scholars should learn:

> … to use your life experience in your intellectual work: continually to examine it and interpret it. In this sense craftsmanship [sic] is the centre of yourself and you are personally involved in every intellectual product upon which you […] work. (Mills 1959: 216)

Some of the key themes within auto/biography as practised within the social sciences relate to issues of epistemology, methodology, reflexivity, position and power. For example, in Letherby's extensive cannon of auto/biographical work (Letherby 1993, 2002, 2010, 2015 amongst others) the personal is political (Andrews 2007; Hanisch 2009) and there is an overt epistemological concern with a positioning of the self, and a commitment to a form of theorised subjectivity (Letherby 2003, 2013). Indeed, in an interview conducted with Liz Stanley in preparation for this book, she outlined her rationale for the development of the BSA Auto/Biography Study Group in the 1990s. She explains how the group developed due to some of the issues she was grappling with at the time, notably:

> …on the one hand reflexivity in an auto/biographical form, and on the other being interested in what I would now call everyday documents of life like diaries, autobiographies, biographies, testimonies and letters… There was nothing like it in sociology at that time. I knew about a/b, but it was not widely available in Britain, was largely arts and humanities, and I felt strongly there was a need for a social science perspective on such matters. Also, the sociological term auto/biography expresses the epistemological matters and issues, whereas the US journal used it descriptively just to include biographies and autobiographies, which I thought unsatisfactory.

There are links here between auto/biography and autoethnography, which is:

> an autobiographical genre of writing and research that displays multiple layers of consciousness, connecting the personal to the cultural… autoethnographers vary in their emphasis on the research process (graphy), on culture (ethnos) and on self (auto). (Ellis and Bochner 2000: 739–740)

Indeed, Brennan and Letherby (2017) argue for a continuum within auto/biography, suggesting that:

> When academics write about themselves, but acknowledge the significance of others, their work could be labelled auto/biography (what some might call autoethnography, see for example Ellis and Bochner 2000; Jackson and Mazzei 2008). When writing about others but recognising the subjectivity of the biographer, auto/biography is more appropriate. Our use of 'continuum' acknowledges that concentration on the self OR on the other is not clear cut and that, whether conscious or unconsciously 'slippage' often occurs. (Brennan and Letherby 2017: 159)

Moreover, it is these epistemological matters or how epistemology matters that link the sections in this book. Auto/Biography provides a richness that crosses, as well as tests, interdisciplinary and multidisciplinary boundaries. It asks whether it is possible to separate the self from our research encounters and, if not, how much of the 'self' do we include? Do we write ourselves in or out? Where are the boundaries of self and other and how might these be constructed, maintained or dissolved? These are important considerations in the light of Frosh's suggestion that there is 'no knowledge of the other without the engagement of the self' (Frosh 2001: 630). Hence auto/biographical work is often ethnographic or autobiographical but not always. It does however retain an epistemological challenge to what it means to be. For example, in Tamboukou's work (2010a, b) on epistolary traditions there are glimpses of her embodied, corporeal senses, which are interwoven or folded into the narratives of the other. It is the revealing of her embodied self in the research process that enlivens these biographical accounts. This does not detract from the rigour of her work but adds richness, texture and authenticity. In her work, she is looking for:

> …rich heterogeneities, narrative forms of becoming [and] a musical repetition that draws circles within the chaos of correspondence [that] is soothing for both the researcher and the reader. (Tamboukou 2010a: 8)

There are therefore many benefits in adopting an auto/biographical approach, not least in that it exposes the interconnectedness and interdependence of biography with autobiography, the self with other. This book is particularly and specifically concerned with auto/biography which sits within the field of narrative, complementing biographical and life history research. As Burnett suggests 'the outstanding merit of [auto/biography] lies in the fact that it is the direct, personal record of the individual' (1984: xi). In providing this record, the individual will choose to note, sometimes reflexively, through an account of an experience that which is significant or important to them. Frank (2013) suggests that auto/biography is both personal and social, and we recognise here the uniqueness of the account given by an individual in relation to both themselves and the audience. This may result in an account of events that is 'partial' but nonetheless valid in representing that which is constituted as valuable to the individual. Stanley talks of the ways in which auto/biography can provide the reader with 'exemplary lives' (1992: 12). Here we are interested in auto/biographies that may or may not be exemplary but tell us things about the lives that people understand that they live and the implications of this for our understanding of the human condition (Arendt 1998; Evans 1999).

Generally speaking, auto/biography is concerned with 'the myriad of everyday and frequently fleeting social practices concerned with the articulation of (often competing, sometimes discontinuous) notions of "selves" and "lives"' Stanley (1992: 40). An auto/biographical approach therefore often has an explicit:

> epistemologically oriented concern with the political ramifications of the shifting boundaries between self and other, past and present in writing and reading, fact and fiction (with) the researcher and author very much alive as agents actively at work in the textual production process. (Stanley 1992: 41)

Yet, as Richardson (1997: 2) reminds us, we are often 'restrained and limited by the kinds of cultural stories available to us'. In academic writing, we are encouraged to 'adhere to the canons of writing practices' from the nineteenth century that we should not be present in our texts and that the 'I' should be suppressed (1997: 2–3). In taking an auto/biographical approach on the other hand 'I' state that 'I' am present. Instead, we therefore ask, 'how do we write ourselves into our texts with intellectual and spiritual integrity?' (Richardson 1997: 2).

Indeed, one of the appeals of an auto/biographical approach lies in its overt positioning of the researcher, the 'self' within the research process. It explores the intricacies of the relationship between this 'self' and 'other'. It is a search for 'meaning', an attempt at understanding the motivations and to interpret the intentions that lie behind the construction of a 'life-history'. Thus, an auto/biographical approach highlights the interdependence of the two enterprises of autobiography and biography. Moreover, life history narratives 'give a means to understand identity in its sociality, since narrative identity places us within a complex web of relationships and, ultimately confounds the notion of the atomized individual' (Lawler 2008: 13). Individuals draw on wider cultural narratives and symbols in the telling of their stories, and it is these interconnections that an auto/biographical approach helps to explore. Indeed, as Letherby notes:

> … self conscious auto/biographical writing acknowledges the social location of the writer thus making clear the author's role in constructing rather than discovering the story/the knowledge. (Mykhalovskiy 1996; Stanley 1993b; Letherby 2002)

An auto/biographical approach also acknowledges that 'the self is always present and inseparable from the work we produce' (Letherby 2003: 83). Hence, researchers adopting an auto/biographical approach tend to acknowledge the role of reflexivity in their work, one that is 'respectful [of] respondents and acknowledges the subjective involvement of the researcher' (Letherby 2003: 83). Thus, for some, when doing auto/biography, the researcher takes on the position of a 'key informer' in the context of the research project, acknowledging the role of their own auto/biography throughout. This may or may not be the research focus, but it is used to 'bridge the gap between the lived experience and academic knowledge production' (Inckle 2007: 32). There are risks inherent in this approach, as the process of becoming a 'research subject as well as author, risks exposure and vulnerability' for the researcher (Inckle 2007: 31; Liamputtong 2007). Some of the emotional risks of 'exposure and vulnerability' are well documented amongst academics engaged in auto/biographical approaches (Cotterill and Letherby 1993; Inckle 2005, 2010; Letherby 2003, 2013; Sparkes 2004, 2007; Chappell et al. 2014). Yet, as Letherby claims the power balance in the respondent/researcher relationship is not static; it is fluid and dynamic (Cotterill and Letherby 1993; Letherby 2003, 2013; Ludhra and Chappell 2011). Moreover, an auto/biographical approach is also about accountability, and as researchers we have a responsibility:

...whether the stories we use are our own, or those of our informants... we need to produce 'accountable knowledge' and that we owe them (our readers and the larger community) an honesty about ourselves; who we are as characters in our own stories and as actors in our own research... (Katz-Rothman 2007: 1)

Anne: An Auto/Biographical Approach

In my doctoral research, I explored teachers' lives and their professional formation as I was concerned about the ways in which policy initiatives had resulted in them being positioned as 'missing persons' (Evans 1999: i). I knew from the outset that I wanted to share stories about the teachers that are 'rarely told' (Maguire et al. 2011) and I presented my early reflections on this in the thesis, noting that 'this research started because I was interested in the experiences of teachers like those I had worked with in school, as well as myself' (Chappell 2014: 195). Without realising it, or having the relevant knowledge to notice it at the time, my interest in the project was auto/biographical; however, it was several years into the research before I could name it as such. As I became more knowledgeable about auto/biographical approaches in research, I recognised that the challenge was to:

> work towards a position that recognises both the personhood of the researcher and the complexity of the researcher/respondent relationship and yet allows for useful things to be said. (Letherby et al. 2013: 87)

This repositioning of my thinking resulted in an understanding of my research as 'principled practice' (Drew 2006: 41) where I sought to behave:

> ... responsibly with a clear commitment to avoid taking a tick box or audit approach to the ethical considerations (MacLure, 2005)...to adopt an approach that supported ethics-in-practice to ensure that I was alert to any issues that arose (Laimputtong, 2007), particularly in relation to researcher power. Aside from the bureaucratic aspect of research ethics, I recognised that my own professional experience as a teacher in a school prior to joining the University, played a major part in the significant sense of responsibility I felt about working with the teachers and re-presenting their data. (Chappell 2014: 187–188)

As this extract illustrates, the role of my experience in designing the research and, like Andrews (2007), the sense of responsibility I had to the participants became key. In this respect, I also struggled to reconcile some of the terminology that was available in the literature:

> …such as subjectivity and objectivity; insider and outsider; identity and subjectivity; structure and agency; resistance and compliance; and actor and subject. It was difficult to work with these since using any one term resulted in the exclusion of the ideas of another: it created a dualism. This was particularly problematic in relation to actor/subject as neither term adequately captured the complexity demonstrated in the data. (Chappell 2014: 187)

I wanted to centre the teachers in the research but, in addition to the ethical considerations and concepts detailed above, was concerned about how to deal with some of the responses I received from others when I shared my ideas about my methodological approach:

> …there was a need to balance the critiques levelled at narrative work as being reductionist in its 'inspection of personal, even private, experience in the search for an interior biographical life' (Atkinson, 2009: 1.2) with my own concerns about taking an approach that took such a broad look at the social that it omitted the individual experience (Craib 1998). (Chappell 2014: 190)

In seeking to respond to these critiques and disrupt some of the 'associated assumptions about shared understandings' (Chappell 2014: 186) by finding ways to work with the terminology, I explored different ways to analyse the accounts and present the teachers' stories. This took a significant amount of time given that:

> …an enormous volume of valuable data was generated, which took me by surprise and also presented me with a challenge in how best to work with the data within the scale of the project. There were several ways that I could have presented and explored the findings, indeed I tried different approaches, and this stage in the process was much more complex than anticipated. I wanted to do justice to the teachers' stories, particularly in light of the time they had given to the project. (Chappell 2014: 190)

The challenge came in finding a way to present an academically rigorous analysis that would be defensible in the viva whilst taking account of:

> …firstly, the complexity of each individual case and the implications of this complexity for the individual teacher and; secondly, the way in which narrative data such as this can offer us a way of thinking differently about the lives

and work of teachers, with obvious interweaving of the personal and professional. (Chappell 2014: 191)

I wanted to use the teachers' particular individual experiences to illustrate the more general concerns (Evans 1999). I presented the findings in different ways drawing on Mills' ideas about using private troubles to illustrate public issue (Mills 1959).

The auto/biographical insights into the lives of teachers provided material for publication but had significant implication for other aspects of my own practice:

> As well as providing material for taught sessions, it has also made me reflect on the way in which we work with student teachers and qualified teachers who are at various stages of their teaching career. (Chappell 2014: 195)

By the end of the process, I had come to understand and recognise the critical role played by auto/biography, as both noun and verb and the associated reflexivity, in my development as a researcher as well as the development of the research:

> I have been critically reflexive at every stage of the process and attempted to make that explicit throughout the thesis. This reflexivity was necessary, in part because this level of study requires it but, most significantly to fulfil my methodological commitment to this particular research, its focus and design. (Chappell 2014: 203)

The auto/biographical approach that I took in the research and as a researcher resulted in knowledge about the lives of teachers that could not have been elicited in any other way, as well as having profound implications for my work. It is my experience of coming to think and work auto/biographically that resulted in my part in editing this collection.

Julie: Auto/Biography and Reflexivity

In my doctoral study in order to justify my auto/biographical approach and in the light of the second wave feminist slogan, the 'personal is political' (Andrews 2007; Hanisch 2009) I positioned myself as a reflexive feminist researcher and wrote:

that there are tensions within 'feminism' as a political movement and that it may be possible to follow feminist research principles without accepting the political underpinnings of feminism, I have a commitment to the Fawcett Society's mission statement 'a vision of society in which women and men enjoy equality at work, at home and in public life'. For me, being, doing or becoming a feminist is a political act. It signifies an alignment with egalitarian values. (Parsons 2014: 26)

I also reflected on previous work I had published regarding feminism, as I stated in the opening paragraph from my article in the *BSA Auto/Biography Yearbook 2010*:

The origins of my own interest in feminism can be traced back to a bookshop in Liverpool at the age of 18, where I saw a copy of Susie Orbach's book 'Fat is a Feminist Issue'. However, it lay dormant and unarticulated until the 1990s, when in another book shop, a women's bookshop in Bristol (long since closed) I bought a series of post cards with Rebecca West's (1892 – 1983) assertion that she did not know what feminism was, only that she was called a feminist when she expressed sentiments that differentiated her 'from a doormat or a prostitute'. (Parsons 2011: 53)

In adopting an auto/biographical approach for my doctoral study, I argued that I took:

… great comfort from those who have forged an auto/biographical path before me, such as Erben (1998b), Inckle (2007, 2010), Letherby (1993, 1994), Morgan (1998), Sikes (2006), Sparkes (2002, 2007), Stanley (1992), to name a few that I have met in text and in person along the way. However, it is still difficult to do, for as Pelias (2004: 1) argues, 'the desire to write from the heart' means that the researcher:
    …instead of hiding behind the illusion of objectivity, brings himself [sic] forward in the belief that an emotionally vulnerable, linguistically evocative and sensually poetic voice can place us closer to the subjects we wish to study. (Pelias 2004: i, cited in Parsons 2014: 13)

In the final writing up of the thesis, I claimed that 'it was about finding a voice, a way of presenting and positioning the self that pleases the reflexive feminist and ethical researcher in me' (Parsons 2014: 13). Indeed, the final title of my Ph.D. thesis made explicit the methodological and epistemological orientation of my work; *An 'Auto/Biographical approach to exploring relationships with food'* acknowledging the interconnectedness of biography and autobiography, the other and the self (Parsons 2014, 2015). This enabled an exploration of the individual and the social or the private troubles and public issues concerning food and foodways (Mills 1959). My relationship with food during my adolescence, for example, was influenced by a desire to conform to normative scripts of femininity, as I engaged in talk about food and bodies as a means of 'doing gender' (West and Zimmerman 1987, 2009).

In setting out the aims and objectives of my research, I was looking to examine the sameness and difference across 'our food stories'. How these 'stories' may have changed over the life course, whether they were influenced by gender or health discourses or weight management practices. Indeed, there were two interrelated purposes of my study, firstly to explore the food memories of others, and secondly to critically examine the social and cultural milieu in which these were articulated. In keeping with Mills' (1959) argument in favour of the 'sociological imagination', personal troubles and public issues are interconnected. In the former, memory is considered a creative process with emotions as markers of the construction of the self and agency (Crawford et al. 1992: 126). In the latter, as Lupton claims 'memories are sociocultural, individual and collective and contain the conditions for self-development, [so that] people grow into their emotions' (1998: 168). To reiterate, emotion 'makes a unique contribution to action and agency, without it persons are lost in time with the past a remote and future inaccessible' (Turner and Stets 2005: 417). And, as Barbalet (2001: 8) demonstrates an interest in emotion is due to increased individualism, hence an:

> autopoietic aggrandisement or development of the self without regards for other selves (a result of market and political individuation isolating self in contained universe) [means the] self [has become] a centre of emotional feeling.

In the light of this, I explained my position in auto/biographical extracts from the preface written for my Ph.D. transfer process in the summer of 2012:

> I trained as a sociologist in the early 1990s, within a 'post-modern', academic climate that appeared to reject notions of objectivity and value-freedom in social science research as potentially unrealistic, if not impossible goals… I found myself working within a scientific paradigm that valued reflexivity and interpretative approaches to research… sociologists, such as Giddens (1992) and Beck (1992) challenged the idea of a fixed and stable identity. They emphasised notions of reflexivity and the negotiation of the 'self' within

a context of shifting boundaries in which the 'meta-narratives' of modernity and the founding fathers of sociology; Mark, Weber and Durkheim were being dissolved…

…All of these notions fed into a general milieu of relativity; there were no fixed, dogmatic rules of engagement in (or with) the social world. The self was merely a free-floating product of consumption and the ontological insecurity that was bound up with this, seemed fine to me. It was against this background that I began my doctoral study, therefore there will be, a representation of the self as researcher in relation to the respondents, interplay between biography and autobiography, an exploration of the lives of the researched and the researcher and an inter-textual analysis of the whole process. For me the research process has and should always be a reflexive endeavour… (Parsons 2014: 42)

Indeed, I continue to be committed to research as a reflexive endeavour. Latterly this has entailed less in terms of auto/biographical reflection and more in terms of a commitment to giving voice to those with whom I am working (Parsons 2017b, 2018a, b, 2019; Parsons and Hocking 2018; Parsons and Pettinger 2017). In an attempt to prioritise the voice of research respondents, I have made use of 'i-poems' (Parsons 2017b), photographs (Parsons 2018b, 2019; Parsons and Pettinger 2017) and food (Parsons 2017a, 2018a).

In terms of the use of food and food memories in my doctoral study, Morgan (1996: 166) explains how 'food represents a particularly strong form of anchorage in the past [as it] serves as one of the links between historical time, individual time and household time'. Thus, foodways are, also as Scott (2009: 106) claims, 'so embedded in the domestic cultures of everyday life that they come to be regarded as natural'. There is moreover a persistent tension between 'knowing' oneself and the creation of memory. For Deleuze and Guattari (1998), memory is the membrane that allows for the correspondence between the 'sheets of the past and the layers of reality', it is a block of becoming, as Clough (2007: 29) claims:

> we write not with childhood memories but through blocs of childhood that are [always part of] becoming the child of the present. We move backwards and forwards to locate a 'self', one that is an autobiographical-techno-ontological writing block. (Clough 2007: 15)

However, my doctoral study was not just an exploration of the epistemological orientation of my approach, it also made reference to auto/biography as a research practice. When writing up my research, I noted that:

I explicitly position myself in terms of a 'theorised subjectivity' (Letherby 2013: 80) and engage in a 'constant, critical interrogation of [my] personhood – both intellectual and personal – within the knowledge production process'. I apply a critical lens to all aspects of the research process from its design to data collection, analysis and dissemination. (Parsons 2014: 77)

Moreover, in this regard I argued that:

> It is important for me that research should be guided by feminist principles of 'collaboration, reciprocity and disclosure' (Kralik et al., 2000: 909). This is because these principles are essential elements in an auto/biographical approach to research, as the researcher is inseparable from the data. This is not to assume that there is only one feminist perspective… a feminist approach to research is 'respectful of respondents' whilst acknowledging the subjective involvement of the researcher (Letherby, 2003: 5). It is usual to consider the power relationships implicit in the research process and attempt to redress this power imbalance. It is about being sensitive to the needs of those being researched. As Letherby (2003: 6) argues, 'we need to be sensitive to respondents and the relevance of our own presence in their lives and the research process'. (Parsons 2014: 94)

Hence, 'objectivity' is replaced by 'reflexive subjectivity and the politics of position' (Grbich 2004: 28–29) or theorised subjectivity (Letherby 2013). These concerns therefore became central to my doctoral study and analysis of the data. Indeed, according to Liamputtong (2007: 17):

> …self-reflexivity requires an awareness of the self in the process of creating knowledge and requires researchers to clarify how they construct their beliefs (a process of self revelation) and how these beliefs influence their data collection… the emotions and personal transformation resulting from self-reflexivity are essential components of her feminist research project.

For me, reflexivity is an important aspect of adopting an auto/biographical approach. I am committed to auto/biography and the myriad ways in which it is applied.

Auto/Biography and Arts-Based Practices

It is no accident that scholars committed to auto/biography often adopt participatory and/or arts-based practices in their work. The BSA Auto/ Biography Study Group has long been a useful forum for music, song, poetry and performance in the interests of pursuing and promoting the voices of others and selves. Moreover, there has been a recent resurgence in interest in approaches that value the participant's voice, particularly in health research, which is party motivated by an explicit requirement by funding bodies (in the UK at least) for public and patient involvement (PPI) (Cook 2012). Moreover, many of the issues faced by those committed to arts-based approaches are also applicable to auto/biography.

Indeed, auto/biography as a field as previously noted incorporates issues to do with reflexivity and ethics. These are also issues which may be addressed through participatory styles of research and creative/arts-based methods, which are adopted in order to give research respondents a voice to address, challenge and rebalance power relationships (Clarke et al. 2005; Coad 2007; Parsons and Pettinger 2017; Poudrier and Mac-Lean 2009). The use of creative/art-based methods is 'an emerging qualitative research approach [that] refers to the use of any art form (or combinations thereof) at any point in the research process (Cole and Knowles 2001; Knowles and Cole 2008) in generating, interpreting, and/or communicating knowledge' (cited in Boydell et al. 2012). It is argued that incorporating creative/art-based resources within the research process promotes dialogue and storytelling (Jones 2006). Further that knowledge conceptualised in this way is more accessible to diverse stakeholders (Colantonio et al. 2008). Moreover, Boydell et al. (2012: 30) carried out a scoping review of literature on the topic and conclude that creative/arts-based methods provide:

1. an opportunity for enhanced engagement for participants and audiences alike (e.g. Levin et al. 2007);
2. a way to enrich communication and make research accessible beyond academia (e.g. Colantonio et al. 2008); and,
3. a method for facilitating conversation and reflection during individual interviews, generating data beyond what was considered the normal scope of most interview-based methods alone (e.g. Dyches et al. 2004; Oliffe and Bottorff 2007).

Conclusion

In auto/biography, when adopting participatory and/or creative/arts-based approaches the emphasis is on research 'with' rather than doing research 'on' people (Reason and Bradbury 2001). Moreover, as previously stated, auto/biography emphasises the importance of democracy, equality, flexibility and reflexivity in the research process, which changes the nature of the traditional research relationship, and can make the researcher more of 'an outsider in the academic community' (Bergold and Thomas 2012). Indeed, this insider/outsider dilemma is a common theme within auto/biography and is explored within some of the chapters of this handbook. Overall, this handbook demonstrates some of the ways in which researchers, academics and laypeople use auto/biography to present and position themselves, to make and remake their own and others' lives and identities.

References

Abbott, J. (2009). *The Angel in the Office: The Life and Work of the Office Secretary in Victorian and Edwardian Times*. Nottingham: Russell Press.

Andrews, M. (2007). *Shaping History: Narratives of Political Change*. Cambridge: Cambridge University Press.

Arendt, H. (1998). *The Human Condition* (2nd ed.). Chicago: University of Chicago Press.

Atkinson, P. (2009). Illness Narratives Revisited: The Failure of Narrative Reductionism. *Sociological Research Online, 14*(5), 325–344.

Barbalet, J. M. (2001). *Emotion, Social Theory and Social Structure, a Macrosociological Approach*. Cambridge: Cambridge University Press.

Bergold, J., & Thomas, S. (2012). Participatory Research Methods: A Methodological Approach in Motion. *Forum Qualitative Social Research*, Special Issue on "Participatory Qualitative Research", *13*(1), Art. 30. http://www.qualitative-research.net/index.php/fqs/article/view/1801/3334.

Boydell, K. M., Gladstone, B. M., Volpe, T., Allemang, B., & Stasiulis, E. (2012). The Production and Dissemination of Knowledge: A Scoping Review of Arts-Based Health Research [40 Paragraphs]. *Forum Qualitative Sozialforschung/ Forum: Qualitative Social Research, 13*(1), Art. 32. http://nbn-resolving.de/urn:nbn:de:0114-fqs1201327.

Brennan, M., & Letherby, G. (2017). Auto/Biographical Approaches to Researching Death and Bereavement: Connections, Continuums, Contrasts. *Mortality, 22*(2), 155–169. https://doi.org/10.1080/13576275.2017.1291604.

Burnett, J. (1984). *Destiny Obscure: Autobiographies of Childhood, Education and Family from the 1820s to the 1920s*. London: Penguin.

Byrne, J. (2012). *'We Just Gelled': The Story of 5/67*. Nottingham: Russell Press.

Chappell, A. (2014). *Professional Learning: Teachers' Narratives of Experience*. Unpublished Ph.D. Brunel University London. http://bura.brunel.ac.uk/handle/2438/10933.

Chappell, A., Ernest, P., Ludhra, G., & Mendick, H. (2014). Explorations in Knowing: Thinking Psychosocially About Legitimacy. *Pedagogy, Culture and Society, 22*(1), 137–156.

Clarke, G. (2008). *The Women's Land Army: A Portrait*. Bristol: Sansom and Company.

Clarke, J., Febbraro, A., Hatzipantelis, M., & Nelson, G. (2005). Poetry and Prose: Telling the Stories of Formerly Homeless Mentally Ill People. *Qualitative Inquiry, 11*(6), 913–932.

Clough, P. T. (Ed.). (2007). *The Affective Turn: Theorizing the Social*. Durham, NC: Duke University Press.

Coad, J. (2007). Using Art-Based Techniques in Engaging Children and Young People in Health Care Consultations and/or Research. *Journal of Research in Nursing and Health, 12*(5), 487–497.

Colantonio, A., Kontos, P. C., Gilbert, J. E., Rossiter, K., Gray, J., & Keightly, M. L. (2008). After the Crash: Research-Based Theater for Knowledge Transfer. *Journal of Continuing Education in the Health Professions, 28*(3), 180–185.

Cole, A., & Knowles, G. (2001). *Lives in Context: The Art of Life History Research*. Walnut Creek, CA: Altamira.

Cook, T. (2012). Where Participatory Approaches Meet Pragmatism in Funded (Health) Research: The Challenge of Finding Meaningful Spaces. *Forum Qualitative Sozialforschung/Forum: Qualitative Social Research, 13*(1), Art. 18. http://nbn-resolving.de/urn:nbn:de:0114-fqs1201187.

Cotterill, P., & Letherby, G. (1993). Weaving Stories: Personal Auto/Biographies in Feminist Research. *Sociology, 27*, 67–79.

Craib, I. (1998). *Experiencing Identity*. London: Sage.

Crawford, J., Kippax, S., Onyx, J., Gault, U., & Benton, P. (1992). *Emotion and Gender, Constructing Meaning from Memory*. London: Sage.

Deleuze, G., & Guattari, F. (1998). *A Thousand Plateaus*. London: Athlone Press.

Dickinson, H., & Erben, M. (2016). *Nostalgia and Auto/Biography: Considering the Past in the Present*. Nottingham: Russell Press.

Drew, N. (2006). The Seagull Imperative. *Australian Community Psychologist, 18*(1), 40–41.

Durkheim, E. (1951/1897). *Suicide: A Study in Sociology*. Glencoe, Illinois: The Free Press.

Durkheim, E. (2002/1897). *Suicide: A Study in Sociology*. London: Routledge.

Dyches, T. T., Cichella, E., Olsen, S. F., & Mandleco, B. (2004). Snapshots of Life: Perspectives of School-Aged Individuals with Developmental Disabilities. *Research and Practice for Persons with Severe Disabilities, 29*(3), 172–182.

Elliott, H. (2011). Interviewing Mothers: Reflections on Closeness and Reflexivity in Research Encounters. *Studies in the Maternal, 3*(1). www.mamsie.bbk.ac.uk.

Ellis, C., & Bochner, A. P. (2000). Autoethnography, Personal Narrative, Reflexivity: Researcher as Subject. In N. Denzin & Y. Lincoln (Eds.), *Handbook of Qualitative Research* (2nd ed., pp. 733–768). Thousand Oaks: Sage.

Erben, M. (1998a). Introduction. In M. Erben (Ed.), *Biography and Education: A Reader*. London: Falmer.

Erben, M. (1998b). Biography and Research Method. In M. Erben (Ed.), *Biography and Education: A Reader*. London: Falmer.

Evans, M. (1999). *Missing Persons: The Impossibility of Auto/Biography*. London: Routledge.

Frank, A. W. (2013). *The Wounded Storyteller: Body, Illness and Ethics* (2nd ed.). Chicago: University of Chicago Press.

Frosh, S. (2001). On Reason, Discourse and Fantasy. *American Imago, 58,* 627–647.

Grbich, C. (2004). *New Approaches in Social Research*. London: Sage.

Hanisch, C. (2009). *The Personal Is Political, the Women's Liberation Movement Classic with a New Explanatory Introduction*. http://www.carolhanisch.org/CHwritings/PIP.html. Accessed 17 May 2019.

Inckle, K. (2005). Who's Hurting Who? The Ethics of Engaging the Marked Body. *Auto/Biography, 13*(3), 227–248.

Inckle, K. (2007). *Writing on the Body? Thinking Through Gendered Embodiment of the Marked Flesh*. Newcastle: Cambridge Scholars Publishing.

Inckle, K. (2010). Telling Tales? Using Ethnographic Fictions to Speak Embodied 'Truth'. *Qualitative Research Journal, 10*(1), 27–47.

Jackson, A. Y., & Mazzei, L. A. (2008). Experience and "I" in Autoethnography. *International Review of Qualitative Research, 1,* 299–318.

Jones, K. (2006). A Biographic Researcher in Pursuit of an Aesthetic: The Use of Arts-Based (Re)presentations in "Performative" Dissemination of Life Stories. *Qualitative Sociology Review, 2*(1), 66–85.

Katz-Rothman, B. (2007). Writing Ourselves in Sociology. *Methodological Innovations Online, 2*(1) (unpaginated).

Knowles, G., & Cole, A. (Eds.). (2008). *Handbook of the Arts in Social Science Research: Methods, issues and perspectives*. Thousand Oaks, CA: Sage.

Kralik, D., Koch, T., & Brady, B. (2000). Pen Pals: Correspondence as a Method for Data Generation in Qualitative Research. *Journal of Advanced Nursing, 31*(4), 909–917.

Lawler, S. (2008). *Identity, Sociological Perspectives*. Cambridge: Polity Press.

Lee, A., & Boud, D. (2003). Writing Groups, Change and Academic Identity: Research Development as Local Practice. *Studies in Higher Education, 28*(2), 187–200.

Letherby, G. (1993). The Meanings of Miscarriage. *Women's Studies International Forum, 16*(2), 165–180.

Letherby, G. (1994). Mother or Not, Mother or What? Problems of Definition and Identity. *Women's Studies International Forum, 17*(5), 525–532.

Letherby, G. (2002). Claims and Disclaimers: Knowledge, Reflexivity and Representation in Feminist Research. *Sociological Research Online, 6*(4). Retrieved from http://www.socresonline.org.uk/6/4/letherby.html.

Letherby, G. (2003). *Feminist Research in Theory and Practice*. Buckingham: Open University Press.

Letherby, G. (2010). Reflecting on Loss as a M/other and a Feminist Sociologist. *Journal of the Motherhood Initiative, 1,* 258–269.

Letherby, G. (2013). Theorised Subjectivity. In G. Letherby, J. Scott, & M. Williams (Eds.), *Objectivity and Subjectivity in Social Research* (pp. 59–78). London: Sage.

Letherby, G. (2014). *He, Himself and I: Reflections on Inter/Connected Lives*. Nottingham: Russell Press.

Letherby, G. (2015). Bathwater, Babies and Other Losses: A Personal and Academic Story. *Mortality: Promoting the Interdisciplinary Study of Death and Dying*. https://doi.org/10.1080/13576275.2014.989494.

Letherby, G., Scott, J., & Williams, M. (2013). *Objectivity and Subjectivity in Social Research*. London: Sage.

Levin, T., Scott, B. M., Borders, B., Hart, K., Lee, J., & Decanini, A. (2007). Aphasia Talks: Photography as a Means of Communication, Self-Expression, and Empowerment in Persons with Aphasia. *Topics in Stroke Rehabilitation, 14*(1), 72–84.

Liamputtong, P. (2007). *Researching the Vulnerable: A Guide to Sensitive Research Methods*. London: Sage.

Ludhra, G., & Chappell, A. (2011). 'You Were Quiet. I Did All the Marching': Research Processes Involved in Hearing the Voices of South Asian Girls. *International Journal of Adolescence and Youth, 16*(2), 101–118.

Lupton, D. (1998). *The Emotional Self*. London: Sage.

MacLure, M. (2005). 'Clarity Bordering on Stupidity': Where's the Quality in Systematic Review? *Journal of Education Policy, 20*(4), 393–416.

Maguire, M., Perryman, J., Ball, S., & Braun, A. (2011). The Ordinary School—What Is It? *British Journal of Sociology of Education, 32*(1), 1–16. *Methods, Issues and Perspectives.* Thousand Oaks, CA: Sage.

Mills, C. W. (1959). *The Sociological Imagination*. New York: Oxford University Press.

Mintz, S. (2016). Transforming the Tale: The Auto/body/ographies of Nancy Mairs. In R. Chansky & E. Hipchen (Eds.), *The Routledge Auto/Biography Studies Reader* (pp. 130–138). London: Routledge.

Morgan, D. H. J. (1996). *Family Connections*. Cambridge: Polity Press.

Morgan, D. H. J. (1998). Sociological Imaginations and Imagining Sociologies: Bodies, Auto/Biographies and Other Mysteries. *Sociology, 32*(4), 647–663.

Mykhalovskiy, E. (1996). Reconsidering Table Talk: Critical Thoughts on the Relationship Between Sociology, Autobiography and Self-Indulgence. *Qualitative Sociology, 19*(1), 131–151.

Oliffe, J. L., & Bottorff, J. L. (2007). Further Than the Eye Can See? Photo Elicitation and Research with Men. *Qualitative Health Research, 17*(6), 850–858.

Parsons, J. (2011). What Constitutes 'Doing' Feminism? Reflecting Upon the Unpublished Auto/Biographical Work of Peggy Barclay. In C. Sparkes (Ed.), *BSA Auto/Biography Yearbook 2010*. Nottingham: Russell Press.

Parsons, J. (2014). *'Ourfoodstories@email.com', an Auto/Biographical Study of Relationships with Food*. Ph.D. thesis. http://hdl.handle.net/10026.1/2920.

Parsons, J. M. (2015). *Gender, Class and Food, Families, Bodies and Health*. Basingstoke: Palgrave Macmillan.

Parsons, J. M. (2017a). Cooking with Offenders to Improve Health and Wellbeing. Special issue of the *British Food Journal* on Cooking, Health and Evidence, *119*(5), 1079–1090.

Parsons, J. M. (2017b). "I Much Prefer to Feed Other People Than to Feed Myself." The 'i-poem' as a Tool for Highlighting Ambivalence and Dissonance Within Auto/Biographical Accounts of Everyday Foodways, in a Special Issue of *The Journal of Psycho-Social Studies*, Offering Food ↔ Receiving Food, *10*(2) (unpaginated). http://www.psychosocial-studies-association.org/volume-10-issue-2-october-2017/.

Parsons, J. M. (2018a). Commensality as a Theatre for Witnessing Change for Criminalised Individuals Working at a Resettlement Scheme. *European Journal of Probation, 10*(3), 182–198. https://journals.sagepub.com/doi/10.1177/2066220318819239.

Parsons, J. M. (2018b). Virtual Social Media Spaces, a Relational Arena for 'Bearing Witness' to Desistance. *Papers from the British Criminological Conference 2018, 18*. http://www.britsoccrim.org/papers-from-the-british-criminology-conference-2018/.

Parsons, J. M. (2019). Narrative Re-scripting: Reconciling Past and Present Lives. *Auto/Biography Review 2018*, A. C. Sparkes (Ed.). British Sociological Association Auto/Biography Study Group, Russell Press, Nottingham, 111–128.

Parsons, J. M., & Hocking, S. (2018). The Lived Experience of Carrots and Risks, Voices from Within the Criminal Justice System. *ISRF Bulletin, XV1*, 32–38. https://issuu.com/isrf/docs/isrf_bulletin_issue_xvi.

Parsons, J. M., & Pettinger, C. (2017). 'Liminal Identities' and Power Struggles, Reflections on the Regulation of Everyday Foodways at a Homeless Centre and the Use of Creative Participatory Research as a Tool of Empowerment and Resistance. In A. Bleakley, L. Lynch, & G. Whelan (Eds.), *Risk and Regulation at the Interface of Medicine and the Arts* (pp. 171–189). Newcastle: Cambridge Scholars Publishing.

Pelias, R. J. (2004). *A Methodology of the Heart, Evoking Academic and Daily Life*. Walnut Creek: Alta Mira Press.

Plummer, K. (1983). *Documents of Life*. Hemel Hempstead: George Allen and Unwin Ltd.

Plummer, K. (2001). *Documents of Life 2*. London: Sage.

Poudrier, J., & Mac-Lean, R. T. (2009). "We've Fallen into the Cracks": Aboriginal Women's Experiences with Breast Cancer Through Photovoice. *Nursing Inquiry, 16*(4), 306–317.

Prost, A., & Vincent, G. (1991). *A History of Private Life V*. London: The Belknap Press.

Reason, P., & Bradbury, H. (Eds.). (2001). *Handbook of Action Research: Participative Inquiry and Practice* (pp. 91–102). London: Sage.

Richardson, L. (1997). *Fields of Play, Constructing an Academic Life*. New Brunswick, NJ: Rutgers University Press.

Ricoeur, P. (1984). *Time and Narrative* (Vol. 1). London: The University of Chicago Press.

Scott, S. (2009). *Making Sense of Everyday Life*. Cambridge: Polity Press.

Sheridan, D. (1993). Writing to the Archive: Mass Observation as Autobiography. *Sociology, 27*(1), 27–40.

Sikes, P. (2006). On Dodgy Ground? Problematics and Ethics in Educational Research. *International Journal of Research and Method in Education, 29*(1), 105–117.

Sparkes, A. (2002). *Telling Tales in Sport and Physical Activity: A Qualitative Journey*. Leeds: Human Kinetics.

Sparkes, A. (2004). Bodies, Narratives, Selves and Autobiography: The Example of Lance Armstrong. *Journal of Sport and Social Issues, 28*(4), 397–428.

Sparkes, A. (2007). Embodiment, Academics and the Audit Culture: A Story Seeking Consideration. *Qualitative Research, 7*(4), 521–550.

Stanley, L. (1992). *The Auto/Biographical I: The Theory and Practice of Feminist Auto/Biography*. Manchester: Manchester University Press.

Stanley, L. (1993a). Editorial. *Auto/biography, 2*(1). i–ix.

Stanley, L. (1993b). On Auto/Biography in Sociology. *Sociology, 37*, 41–52.

Stanley, L. (Ed.). (2013). *Documents of Life Revisited*. Farnham: Ashgate.

Tamboukou, M. (2010a). *In the Fold Between Power and Desire: Women Artists' Narratives*. Newcastle Upon Tyne: Cambridge Scholars Publishing.

Tamboukou, M. (2010b). *Nomadic Narratives, Visual Forces, Gwen John's Letters and Paintings*. New York: Peter Lang Publishing.

Tamboukou, M. (2010c). *Visual Lives: Carrington's Letters, Drawings and Paintings*. Nottingham: Russell Press.

Thomas, W. I., & Thomas, D. S. (1928). *The Child in America: Behavior Problems and Programs*. New York: Knopf.

Thomas, W. I., & Znaniecki, Z. F. (1918). *The Polish Peasant in Europe and America, Volumes I and II*. Boston: The Gorham Press.

Turner, J. H., & Stets, J. E. (2005). *The Sociology of Emotions*. New York: Cambridge University Press.

West, C., & Zimmerman, D. H. (1987). Doing Gender. *Gender and Society, 1*(2): 125–151.

West, C., & Zimmerman, D. H. (2009). Accounting for Doing Gender. *Gender and Society, 23*(1), 112–122.

Part I

Creativity and Collaboration

Gayle Letherby

The chapter authors in this part highlight how creative and collaborative auto/biographical working across disciplines and genres enriches the telling of individual and group stories. Individually and as a collection the chapters here challenge and extend social scientific understandings of method, methodology and epistemology both in terms of the tools used and in terms of working practices. Through a focus on exposing the hidden the emotional labour within medical practice (Theresa Compton, Chapter 2) researching marginalised and excluded groups (Kitrina Douglas and David Carless, Chapter 3) and exploring new ways of telling research (and other) stories (Deborah Davidson and Gayle Letherby, Chapter 4), the authors reflect on their use and analysis of creative and arts-based approaches including poetry, body tattoos, drawing and the writing of fiction. Additionally, in each of these accounts there is reflection on positive (and negative) relationships, including collaboration as colleagues, as researchers, as friends. As such, these pieces engage with the 'personal as political' through a consideration of known and hidden stories and in doing so highlight the intersections of the public/private domains of the researcher and the researched, including research on and of the self. Here, as elsewhere in this volume, and research writing in general:

> The notion of auto/biography is linked to that of the 'auto/biographical I'…. The use of 'I' explicitly recognises that … knowledge is contextual, situational, and specific, and that it will differ systematically according to the social location (as a gendered, raced, classed, sexualised person) of the particular knowledge-producer. (Stanley 1993: 49)

Research and the outputs that result are always in some ways auto/
biography in that all texts bear traces of the author and are to some extent
personal statements (Denzin and Lincoln 1994) within which the writer
works from the self to the other and back again. To paraphrase, and extend
Richardson's (1994: 515) suggestion that '[b]y writing in different ways, we
discover new aspects of our topic and our relationship to it' (see Davidson
and Letherby Chapter 4 for more detail) creative auto/biographical work
(beyond and including the written word) enable the creator to explore and
to play in ways that traditional approaches do not encourage, do not allow.

Carole Gray and Julian Malins writing in 1993 argued that there was no
one universally accepted methodological approach to research within the
arts. They suggested that creative and reflexive approaches enabled methods
and processes to be tailored to respond to practice and practice to research.
It is perhaps a truism that creativity is central to arts research but since Gray
and Malins' (1993) comments the social sciences have embraced creative,
arts-based practices including art, drama, creative writing and so on. These
approaches are used in a range of ways: as tools (method) to gather data;
as a way of engaging with and reflecting on relationships with participants
(methodology) and as a way of sharing findings and influencing policy, practice and theory as the research leads to new ways of knowing (epistemology).
Thus, 'creative methodologies' can and have been applied to both the process
and the product of research.

In a newspaper article on 'creative industries', Khai Meng (2016) reflects
on the term. He wonders if there are any uncreative industries, and if so how
do they survive. For Khai Meng, everyone is born creative but:

> … it is educated out of us at school, where we are taught literacy and numer-
> acy. Sure, there are classes called writing and art, but what's really being taught
> is conformity.
>   Young children fizz with ideas. But the moment they go to school, they
> begin to lose the freedom to explore, take risks and experiment.
>   We spend our childhoods being taught the artificial skill of passing exams.
> We learn to give teachers what they expect. By the time we get into indus-
> try, we have been conditioned to conform. We spend our days in meet-
> ings and talk about "thinking outside the box". But rarely do we step
> outside   it.   https://www.theguardian.com/media-network/2016/may/18/
> born-creative-educated-out-of-us-school-business

The same could be said of traditional social scientific teachings in method,
methodology and epistemology where being 'objective' and 'value free' were

literally the be-all and end-all. Times have changed though and not only is there a greater acceptance, insistence even, that all research is subjective (Letherby 2002, 2014) there is an increasing, and exciting, energy for looking beyond in-depth interviews and questionnaires, reports and Powerpoint presentations. In addition to utilising visual, online and other less than traditional 'tools' to discover what is going on in the social world, researchers who favour this approach, as suggested above, argue that creative methodologies encourage an emotional, embodied, involving, evolving and reflexive practice for all concerned. In the physical sciences, the use of arts-based ways of working is less established but as Compton's (Chapter 2) experience highlights when such methods are used, both for self-reflection and as teaching aids, the impact is powerful. Compton's story of leaving medicine following a long period of stress and distress is taboo. Such stories are largely absent both from academia and more generally. Similarly, Douglas and Carless (Chapter 3) report on working with others whose stories are similarly hidden, in this case because of extreme social marginalisation. They use creative approaches, here poetry, but in other work (Douglas and Carless 2013) also song to present and thus highlight the significance of lives that are generally hidden, ignored and denied. Davidson and Letherby (Chapter 24) reflecting on personal and public life experiences demonstrate how creative practices, from commemorative tattoos to writing fiction and memoir, can be beneficial to emotional well-being (for all involved). Similarly, Compton (Chapter 2) points out, with specific reference to auto/biographical reflective drawings (although the point is generalisable) such endeavours can help the creator to access unspoken hidden thoughts and emotions, including those related to loss and to grief.

Referring specifically to auto/biographical narratives, Lawler (2008: 13) argues that a written (again we can extend this to other types of creative expression) autobiography does not reflect a 'pre-given' 'identity' but rather 'identities are *produced* through the autobiographical work in which all of us engage every day'. Such auto/biographical work, as the chapters in this part show, can include telling one's story to another (colleague, friend, researcher), writing a 'fictionalised' version of one's own or another's story, and/or visual displays of self, such as drawings and bodily tattoos.

All of the chapters in this part include some **auto**/biographical reflection:

> When academics write about themselves, but acknowledge the significance of others in the story their work could be labelled **auto**/biography (what some might call autoethnography … When writing about others but recognising the subjectivity of the biographer auto/**biography** is more appropriate.

> Writing and working auto/biographically recognises the entanglement and slippage (Elliott 1999) between self and other: the fact that any autobiography involves others (especially others whose lives impact on the life of the writer) and that any biography inevitably involves traces of the autobiographical self of the biographer… (Brennan and Letherby 2017: 53).

In 1994, Liz Kelly and colleagues pointed out that although there was much discussion focusing on researcher/respondent relationships there was little on relationships between members of the research community. Kelly et al.'s (1994) concern was with those who may be experiencing oppression at work. Arguably, there is still little discussion of such issues, within academia (and elsewhere). Compton's (Chapter 2) reflections are particularly poignant here in terms of her reflections on which spaces (including work ones) where she received support and where she did not. There is some work on collaborative writing/editing [e.g. Cotterill et al. (2007), Malina and Maslin-Prothero (1998)] and the difference between this and joint publishing (another academic practice often considered to be oppressive and exploitative). As Cotterill et al. (2007) note, collaboration takes effort and compromise but the rewards can be personally, politically and theoretically relevant. Douglas and Carless (Chapter 3) and Davidson and Letherby (Chapter 4) all specifically reflect on the emotional as well as intellectual support they get from their co-authors/collaborators.

Writing about working relationship in a less 'tidy' way is useful. Just as it is now widely acknowledged that the doing of research is not neat, not 'hygienic' in the way it was once argued to be (e.g. Stanley and Wise 1993; Letherby 2003) working relationships, including research collaborations, are not neat or hygienic either, and as such relevant to both the research process and product. When collaborations work well, they provide a space:

> …where people continually expand their capacity to create the results they truly desire, where new and expansive patterns of thinking are nurtured, where collective aspiration is set free, and where people are continually learning together. (Keep and Rainbird 2002: 65)

With respect to the presentation and sharing of data, creative, arts-based approaches engage academic audiences in different ways and can also have an impact outside of the academy (e.g. Douglas and Carless 2013; Pettinger et al. 2018). Auto/Biographical work has clear epistemological (and political) implications, not least in terms of the challenge to mainstream assumptions about 'tidy research' and its attempt to counter (as well as challenge) the imbalance between researcher and researched (e.g. Letherby 2014).

Auto/Biographical research in this way serves both as a corrective to much traditional research (by which researchers 'write themselves out' of the knowledge they produce). What the chapters in this part show is how creative and arts-based approaches also are also political.

In an article focusing on the relationship between creativity and activism, Blum (2017) insists that artistic projects can be inspirational, carry strong messages and resonate with large audiences no matter what the medium. She writes:

> Whatever our chosen palette, the practice of understanding the importance of our own creative engagement is a source of potential change on its own, and a space where valuable insight can be found through reflection and sharing.   http://www.huffingtonpost.com/annette-blum/art-and-politicsthe-power_b_9511384.html

Working creatively and collaboratively for social and political change is not new. During the movement for abolition, sewing circles served as a place for women to exchange ideas and talk about political work. As Segal (2017) writes:

> Sewing Circles are among the best means for agitating and keeping alive the question of anti-slavery…. A friend in a neigboring town recently said to us, "Our Sewing Circle is doing finely, and contributes very much to keep up the agitation of the subject. Some one of the members generally reads an anti-slavery book or paper to the others during the meeting, and thus some who don't get a great deal of anti-slavery at home have an opportunity of hearing it at the circle". http://www.pbs.org/newshour/art/stitch-stitch-history-knitting-activism/

And during World War I:

> A grandmother in Belgium knitted at her window, watching the passing trains. As one train chugged by, she made a bumpy stitch in the fabric with her two needles. Another passed, and she dropped a stitch from the fabric, making an intentional hole. Later, she would risk her life by handing the fabric to a soldier—a fellow spy in the Belgian resistance, working to defeat the occupying German force.
>
> …every knitted garment is made of different combinations of just two stitches: a knit stitch, which is smooth and looks like a "v", and a purl stitch, which looks like a horizontal line or a little bump. By making a specific combination of knits and purls in a predetermined pattern, spies could pass on a custom piece of fabric and read the secret message, buried in the innocent warmth of a scarf or hat. (Zarrelli 2017: http://www.atlasobscura.com/articles/knitting-spies-wwi-wwii)

All the chapters in this part show how auto/biographically engaged, creative, arts-based practice is political, can have a political, as well as an emotional and intellectual impact. All the chapters in this part highlight the value of positive collaboration and further how collaborative creativity can encourage further play, more creativity.

***

Writing an introduction to three chapters on auto/biographical creativity and collaboration when one is a co-author on one of the pieces inevitably results in a different type of untidiness, of messiness.

Over the last few years, I have been experimenting, both within my academic work and with reference to other non-academic activities (including political activism), with different ways of working. I owe my renewed engagement with this sort of creativity to the experience I had at a conference I went to in 2017—*Thinking Through Things*—organised by Magali Peyrefitte and Carly Guest at Middlesex University. 'Things' are emotionally significant and can be, as Jane Carsten (2000, cited by Smart 2007, 168) suggests, part of the process of identity construction. In one of the sessions during the day, participants were asked to make a collage representative of their 'work self'. I found this activity and the discussion that took place during it both personally enriching and intellectually stimulating. Since then I have initiated, and been part of, collage and zine (*a non-commercial often homemade or online publication usually devoted to a specialised and often unconventional subject matter, sometimes with a political focus*) making in several academic settings and created another zine of my own. This creative *doing* has surprised me and I have amazed at how enjoyable and valuable I, and others I have worked with, found such activity. Although my fiction writing began following some personal loses (see Chapter 4 for more detail) and were separate from my academic work, these writings are embedded in scholarly writings beyond this part. Additionally, I now also run workshops with colleagues and at conferences on fictional writing for academics. Throughout my career, I have always enjoyed and learnt a lot from collaborative working. Newer, creative arts-based collaborations, including with friends and colleagues within this part, across this volume, and more generally, are especially joyful and enriching. For example, see https://collaborations-in-research.org/ which emerged out of, and followed, an Independent Social Research Foundation (ISRF) funded residential (awarded to Julie Parsons and facilitated by Julie and myself). A related and forthcoming issue of *Methodological Innovations* (https://uk.sagepub.com/en-gb/eur/methodological-innovations/journal202509) (guest edited by

2

The Times Are a Changing: Culture(s) of Medicine

A Cone Shell

I was sitting on a beautiful sandy beach, on Nasonisoni Island, Fiji, the day I decided to leave medicine. The Pacific Ocean, sometimes smooth like glass, sometimes a roaring tempest became the backdrop for the biggest decision I have ever made. This part of the Pacific is inhabited by the cone snail, their shells' beautiful chequered swirls, in black and white, but pick up one that is occupied and a sharp barb full of poison will enter your finger. The ultimate defence from predators, the poison is fatal to fish and to humans. Medicine from the outside seemed so beautiful. The inside was a very different story.

Fiji, when I first arrived, gave me little joy. I did not know what to do, but I knew that I had to do something different. I had seen patient after patient approaching retirement with terrific plans for cruises and adventures, only to get a cancer diagnosis and lose the chance to carry out their life's ambition. Since a trip to Amsterdam with my mum aged 11, I had known I wanted to travel, but people discouraged me from this. Sensible practical reasons were always given to prevent me from following my dream. I thought 'one day'. That day came sooner than expected in my fourth year of medical training, when I found myself unable to cope, unable to function. It was something that I and others around me should have (in retrospect) seen coming.

T. Compton (✉)
Plymouth University, Plymouth, UK
e-mail: theresa.compton@plymouth.ac.uk

© The Author(s) 2020
J. M. Parsons and A. Chappell (eds.), *The Palgrave Handbook of Auto/Biography*,
https://doi.org/10.1007/978-3-030-31974-8_2

In this chapter, I tell the story of what happened to me. How my life fell completely apart, but also how I managed, over many years, to put it back together again with the help of creativity and of collaborative support. I reflect too on what I think my story means for medicine and medical practice. I identify the role that emotions had to play in my experiences, the role of the culture within medicine as a whole and how a 'doctor' identity shaped my past, and my present and future.

Becoming and Being a Doctor

In my first week at medical school, the best (in my view) lecture did not provide us with any scientific or clinical facts, but instead described the emotional experience of being a doctor, which was likened to being on a roller coaster. I knew at age 18 that medicine was no picnic, but I am not sure it is possible for junior doctors to be prepared for what faces them in those first few months of medical work. In saying that becoming a doctor 'is stressful', 'difficult', or requires you to be 'the most intelligent person in order to succeed' does medical students a massive disservice. Becoming a doctor is not simply about knowing a lot of bizarre bodily knowledge, but it is **emotionally,** psychologically, cognitively and physically demanding. You will fail multiple times. Patients may suffer or die because of your failures.

I had always wanted to be a doctor, but it was a struggle for me to get there. In 1998, I started medical school in a large London teaching hospital. With around 20–30 applicants per place, getting into medical school was and still is hugely competitive. The first year of medical school was the first time I had been away from home for more than a few weeks. Like most 18-year-olds, I was clueless in how to live independently; from housework to organising my time, my studies and my money. There was very little recognition from the university that new students would face these issues; even less support. I knew I was clever enough to be here, but at the end of the first year, doubt crept in when I failed my exams and had to resit them over the summer holidays. I had partied too hard, studied too little. Next year, I would work harder, and it would be different, except it was not. Over the next five years, I repeated this pattern of trying, failing and repeating exams right up until the end of my medical school training. All this impacted on my university relationships, on my self-esteem and mental health and, after failing my final exams, on my career; losing a job I was due to begin.

Failing. Being 'a failure', made me different from the other students in my year. It was widely known there were some students you would not want to be **your** doctor. Every year I studied harder, worked longer hours, sacrificed more for my work. Every year with the same result. Persistent failure, isolation, increasing amounts of stress, depression. Despite the fact I was a studying in a medical school, not one person noticed my struggles and provided support. In my final year, my gran died of cancer and I began to wonder what I was doing it all for. If I could not save a person I cared about, what was the point of medicine? I became withdrawn, I disengaged from the university. I stopped attending lectures. No one asked me why. In my usual pattern, I failed my final exams and spent the next six months retaking them. But I graduated. I became a doctor living with depression. To start with, I enjoyed my job. I coped. A life in medicine is not without its positives. However, when at the end of your medical school training all your grades add up to your ranking, and students with the best ranking are matched with their first choice of job, students with the lowest will get what is left. That is what I got.

After six months as an old-style house officer, the government changed the model of junior doctor training towards today's foundation scheme approach. I had a choice of finding an unlikely six-month post to complete my pre-registration year or joining the foundation scheme and becoming an F1. I chose to be an F1 in order to get a choice of job, and where I would be working. In my F1 year, I lived in a hospital residence with other doctors. We had our own flats but would cook for each other, go out together. We spent lunchtimes in the doctors' mess, eating chips from the canteen and comparing notes on how things were going, who was enjoying which job, where we were going to go on Saturday night (which always had some poor unfortunate person moaning they were on call). On Wednesday evenings, we went to a local beach to play touch rugby and sink a beer whilst the sun went down. As we were so junior most of the work we did in the hospital was administrative; ordering tests, writing up patient notes, constructing discharge letters. I loved this year. I am still in touch with many of those I worked with and recently we had a reunion. In my second year as an F2, a group of us found a house out in the countryside and moved in for six months. We had some legendary parties, and opportunity to walk for miles or go surfing on days off. The job though was tough.

The competitiveness from medical school continues to play out in the workplace in terms of opportunities for research, audits and publications, mentorship, support **and** time off. In a rota system, when one person has time off, someone else has to cover their role, so one person's home/work life balance is another's overtime. If you are not quite as organised, or struggling to keep your head above water, then your existence is scheduled around the needs of the hospital and other doctors in your department. So the inverse care law (Tudor Hart 1971) applies to doctors too. The ones who need the most support, time off, and opportunities get the least.

A loss of innocence occurs for the junior doctor that is associated with the developing knowledge of ones' own mortality. As an F2, I became more independent in some of the jobs I had, routinely undertaking procedures that patients needed on the ward. I remember the first patient I broke bad news to and how he took it. I was gaining responsibility, but losing my innocence. Every person experiences a friend or relative becoming unwell, and the pain and suffering that might entail. When your every day is punctuated by seeing a person like that every 30 minutes the accumulated experience is overwhelming. An emergency doctor colleague told me to try to remember the one thing in the day that has gone right, the one person you made better. I tried. When faced with all that being a human entails, we shy away, run scared, unable to cope, unable to take it all in. We may become desensitised, make inappropriate jokes, act cynically. I felt this happening to me, and sought support. When I was struggling, I was told by my educational supervisor to 'get some coping mechanisms'. I googled 'coping mechanisms'. Nothing that came up made sense for what I was doing.

There were many days when misery consumed me. I wanted to walk out of the door of the hospital and never come back. It was like I had stared the worst of life in the face, and I wanted no part of it.

After my F2 year, the government brought in another initiative in medical training, and all doctors were to choose their specialty straight after F2. Previously, it was commonplace for doctors to work in a number of different specialities before deciding their further career path, which was much more flexible. I had not really considered what specialty I wanted to go into and had to make a hasty decision. A lot of my colleagues opted for GP training, as this would allow them to continue to rotate through hospital specialties and try things out. As a result, GP places were massively oversubscribed. Wanting to stay near family, I applied for four different rotations in the same place, including GP and obstetrics and gynaecology. I had to visit a test centre and interview for both, with GP rejecting me based on how I decided to prioritise a list of 10 tasks. My test for obstetrics and gynaecology was more successful. I was asked to complete a Lego-based task, timed and blindfolded. Having spent most of my childhood playing with the plastic bricks, I was in my element. Surgery had always appealed to me, but some of the surgeons on my previous placements had put me off.

I would be lucky to get a job, as obstetrics and gynaecology was quite popular, so I was very pleased when I was offered a training post. Yet, I continued to feel slightly ambivalent about it as a career.

At 27 years old, I was working in a local maternity unit, as a specialist trainee in obstetrics and gynaecology. I worked especially hard in this first year of training and sacrificed most of my time off for study. I thought that, however, unplanned my career path was, this might still have been a good choice, because the majority of the patient group is generally young, not ill and simply going through one of life's events: pregnancy and birth. I also needed there to be a positivity to the work that I did, some joy, instead of pain and sadness. But, what I remember from my years in obstetrics is not the happy experience of a family being formed, but rather the near misses and the tragedies, the stillborn babies, never to take their first breath; the terrified expression of a new father as his wife lies pale, haemorrhaging over the bed. In this, we too are distressed and scared. We know practically what to do, but not how to cope with what happens emotionally. What happens if you lose a patient? What happens if that is your fault? Medical school taught me to avoid failing, not how to cope with failure.

When I try to recall positive emotions from this time, it is difficult. They come in flashes, fleeting images like clips in an old movie. A new father, tears flowing silently down his cheeks as a tiny baby, still covered in vernix wails against his bare chest. The relief and surprise of a woman as the shoulders are born, her ordeal is over, and the babe, startled, awkward is placed on her abdomen. The tears cried in joy instead of sadness. The love and awe at a new human life. Witnessing these moments, I felt too like I would cry, or laugh with joy, but felt that it was wrong of me to do so. I was a blank canvas, poker-faced. I thought that this was what being professional meant. More robotic, less human. I never acknowledged my humanity. Suppressing my emotions cost me dearly. I felt sick. I wanted to get off the roller coaster. Seeing another distressed woman who had experienced four miscarriages, I felt empty. I had nothing to give the person whose world felt like it had ended. I offered clinic appointments and investigations, but it sounded hollow. I could not give this woman what she wanted. I could not give her a baby.

I could blame the training, the moving around, the stress of the job, I could externalise it so that it is 'understandable' but this feels like a lie. The truth is more that I did not pay attention to my emotions, especially anger, I did not 'manage' my feelings, I did not know how, and they consumed me. Emotions are not widely discussed in medicine. They are not something the stoic, unflappable doctor is supposed to feel. In learning professionalism, I learned emotional suppression and in suppressing my emotions I had written my own failure.

The ability to identify our emotions, the emotions of others and express or suppress these is seen as a trait prized in medical students and doctors (Mayer and Salovey 1993; Johnson 2015). We are expected to provide empathy for patients, to enable the development of a trusting doctor–patient relationship and an understanding of patients', which in turn enables them to recover (Banja 2006; Chandra et al. 2018). But, there is no 'how to' manual that describes what to do when emotions are overwhelming, or the cost of empathy is too much to bear. There is no doubt that an inability to recognise emotions in yourself or others (alexithymia) is associated with worse psychological outcomes and in healthcare professionals is associated with burnout. Suppression of emotions is also linked with health difficulties, both psychological and physical, including earlier mortality from cancer and cardiovascular disease (Chapman et al. 2016).

Institutions increasingly demand emotional work from employees, yet are oblivious to the consequences of this. The Francis Report on the failings at Mid-Staffordshire hospital details the compassion fatigue experienced by staff, which led to the dehumanising of patients. A recommendation included staff smiling more. A smile costs something to the person that gives it. There is work in expressing and supressing emotions. It takes work to comfort someone who is sick, dying, or inconsolable through loss. Such emotional labour is often invisible, with the majority of occupations and roles requiring high emotional labour being low earning, low status, often female dominated (Hochschild 1979, 2012). Far from being valued and prized, emotional labour is an expected part of occupational role, and as such is uncredited and undervalued.

There are ways to offset these costs and protect healthcare professionals from psychological harm; however, the institutional embedding required for these to be successful is low. In psychological supervision, a counsellor explained to me—there is a difference from being on the roller coaster with the patient, feeling everything they are feeling, than standing on the ground, watching the patient on the roller coaster and seeking to alleviate that discomfort—it is a cognitive shift, away from feeling everything the patient is feeling. Whilst counsellors, police officers and other public service professionals have these mechanisms to reduce the impact of psychological transference, medicine has lagged woefully behind in supervisory practices. Only recently, interventions such as mentoring and Schwartz Centre Rounds have been shown to protect from workplace stress and burnout and therefore may have a role to play in safer emotional regulation. In a Schwartz round, a panel share their stories of working in clinical practice, not from a practical perspective, but from an emotional one. Sharing the stories of what it feels like to be a caregiver reduces work stress by half in regular attendees (Maben 2018). Story sharing has this hidden power that the structure of Schwartz can unlock. Yet, this is something that needs to be learned.

The End

In the end, in expressing my pain I inflicted it on others. Other doctors, junior colleagues, medical students, patients. Relationships with colleagues fractured. When I asked for support, none was forthcoming. I asked a slightly more senior colleague to see a patient for me so I could take a break to eat something. They refused. I asked the nursing staff to not bleep me for things that were not urgent so I could take a 15-minute break. I got bleeped before I had even made the 20 paces to the end of the ward. For four years I was bleeped constantly. I did not pee, eat or talk to patients or their relatives without interruption. I was the lone wolf; the only doctor in the area I was working at my grade. There were no colleagues to hold my bleep for a short time so I could fulfil my bodily needs. I tried to leave my shift every day on time, only to be asked to fill in forms that were 'urgent' at 5 p.m. every day. This led to working about 60–70 hours a week with no breaks. Despite the 'Working Time Directive' limiting working hours and institutionalising breaks, this is not uncommon within the profession (Corrigan and Letherby 2010). Whilst I was sure some colleagues were taking advantage of my situation, the fact I was less organised and could not manage, others were probably just struggling as much as I was. Denying the support I needed was simply just self-preservation for them. I was asked to mentor another doctor, without any training on what this should entail. The ward was busy, and I did not get around to it. As soon as someone struggled the deficit model was applied. If you struggle, it is because you are not good enough, not organised enough, cannot cope, should not be a doctor. Years later and I am mentor for other educators. My understanding of mentoring now is not compatible with the things I was asked to do in the past. From my own (and others) experience as an educator, I know that when enough support is provided, people do reach a potential they never knew they had (Newman 2002). I never experienced this kind of support during my career as a medic.

I felt myself turning into an unhappy, unprofessional cynic and I hated what medicine was doing to me. I was not that person. I became negative towards everything and everyone. I would not become that person. My career became incompatible with my values. My self-esteem suffered. I thought about leaving.

I was tearful a lot of the time. It became harder and harder to leave the ward on time, I struggled to complete all the work that needed doing. In my interactions with nursing staff, I think my stress really showed, but I have no idea if this was ever raised to anyone else to help support me. I felt slow, like I was full of cotton wool. I spent the drive home crying my eyes out for weeks on end. Eventually, an event on the ward brought me to my knees. I was eating my lunch at 4 p.m. One of the only times I had actually made it to the Mess. I got a call from antenatal about an emergency, a patient with dangerously high blood pressure. I asked the midwives to find the labour ward staff. I could not come. I needed to eat. I needed a break. My bleep went off again seconds later. Both labour ward staff were in theatre and unavailable. Patient's blood pressure was 180 systolic. 'Where was I?' In the time I had been on the phone my bleep had gone off about four times. Including from the ward I had just left. I was so angry. I threw my fork across the room. I attended and managed a patient with eclampsia, asking for the consultant on call in the process. I was praised by the consultant in question, but the truth was I felt terrible. I had nearly not done my job. I had nearly cost someone their life because I wanted a plate of chips. I felt like the worse doctor in the world. I felt that if I stayed, I was going to sometime be responsible for the death of a mother or their baby, which was something I could never have on my conscience. The days following the incident, I sought support from a senior member of my department, but it was too little, too late. My memory had completely gone. I couldn't remember the names of people I had worked with for four years. I went off sick for several months with 'work related stress'.

In the days and weeks that I was off sick, I lay on my bed crying, or sleeping. I didn't understand what had gone wrong. My waking hours were punctuated by either resorting to googling 'the answer'. But what was the question? I tried to distract myself with exercise, music or reading, things I had found no time for in the four years I had been working. I looked for career options outside of medicine but found little to inspire me and certainly no evidence of doctors having successful careers after they had left the profession.

In this time, I was I feel heavily stigmatised by the deanery, my friends and colleagues. It never felt safe to talk to my housemate about not going to work. He just did not understand. I think he thought I was lazy slacker. Why could I not just 'get on with it like everyone else?' Emails I received alluded to my absence as a nuisance to the department. I was not fit or safe to be at work. In this state, where I cried every day, I had to decide what to do for the best. I decided to take some time out and applied for an out-of-programme year. The deanery did not want me to do this. I had to campaign to have time out, eventually taking my Dad with me to say the things I could not. I was in a vulnerable state. My cognitive function not enabling me to articulate precisely what was going on in my brain. I was in many ways unreachable. Eventually the deanery saw sense and allowed me a year out, with the proviso I did not apply for an additional out of programme later on in my training. At a dinner with colleagues, I explained my plans. There was much negativity and criticism. It was medical school all over again. Something about my failings, about my struggle was repulsive to others.

When I returned and discussed my experiences with a colleague planning to take time out, I was told 'well of course that's not a proper out of program year'. I do not blame him for his anger, for his annoyance. After all, my leaving directly impacted on others' workloads. But I could not take any more emotional weight. For those that were struggling too, I was probably highlighting something they did not want to see.

There was only one person I blamed for my problems, and that one person was me. I was the one who was not good enough, clever enough, strong enough. I now know that a lot of this was depression talking.

****

So there I was, sitting on the beach in Fiji, running my hands through white sand finding a shell with my fingertips and thinking 'there is more to life than I have had'. I had an opportunity, to see other ways of life. The villagers on the island had relatively little in terms of material possessions, but they had a great joy in life, they laughed long, loud, unafraid of who was watching. I held my life up to theirs and realised that I could choose.

It would be several years before I could finally make sense of what had happened to me. After my out-of-programme year, I resigned to seek a job elsewhere. I knew I could go back. I worked for a charity and for a drug company but none seemed the right fit. Finally, I entered academia, first developing resources for the medical school and now teaching. I am still reflecting on what led me to leave my former career as a doctor.

Rehabilitation and Recovery

The biggest barrier to my recovery was knowledge. I had no knowledge of what had happened to me and trying to figure this out, largely on my own, was a personal journey that was to take years. I could not even give what had happened to me a name. I left medicine in 2009. I started to learn about burnout in 2013.

In 2012, I began work as a lecturer at the Peninsula Medical School in Plymouth, a relatively new medical school having opened just over a decade earlier. Peninsula was different from other medical schools I had visited, a smaller community feel, and having been designed from scratch for today's standards and challenges, it treated its students more supportively than had been my personal experience, with emphasis on holistic education and use of medical humanities. It was initially difficult for me to work as a medical educator. I felt like a fraud, an outsider. 'Those who can't, teach'. Right? A chance encounter with my fourth year medical students was to set something in motion. My students had to complete reflective writing about their experiences on placement. As a 'fun' alternative over the holidays, I suggested a drawing instead. Looking at their doubtful faces, I said I would do one too.

Evidence suggests that using drawing as a method enhances (e.g. Oster and Crone 2004) observational skills and brings emotions to the fore. In our first session after Christmas, we put our pictures up and talked about what we had been feeling when we drew them. The students' pictures were fantastic and had allowed them to think about home/work life balance and what that was going to be like in the future. Mine was altogether darker in nature. The process of drawing enabled me to slow down, to revisit my time as a practising doctor and to explore how I had felt during that period. I think I scared the students with my frankness and honesty. I realised that I could now write about how I had felt based on an image I had drawn, and perhaps unearth some truths that had lain buried, hidden. In April of that year, the university offered me a full-time post and I was permitted to attend an international conference with the medical humanities team. My new role as pastoral lead was weighing heavily on my mind so I went to a number of workshops on student support. In one of them, I started to cry. I was so embarrassed. This was supposed to be a professional conference. The facilitator asked me if I was 'OK', to which I defiantly replied 'fine'.

Later, over risotto and wine, I shared my experience. One kind colleague, a GP, pointed out that perhaps, if there was some emotional release in that workshop, maybe there was something there to explore. Months later and I am presenting at a medical humanities conference. I have followed my colleague's advice, and the result is a series of six reflective paintings about my experiences of 'being a doctor'. I could not initially articulate what I felt in words, but after producing the paintings, I was able to write a small narrative about what was happening in each situation. A narrative that I could later analyse, study and research. I came to the conclusion from this research that a lot of my paintings represented my experience of burnout as a junior doctor. What came through in this writing was not only the elements that make up burnout but also the lack of support I received. Now it is clear that I may have been suffering post-traumatic symptoms (PTSD) as well. Again this is not unusual, as research suggests that a significant proportion of surgeons experience PTSD from purely carrying out their job, not necessarily associated with one isolated traumatic event, with perhaps a smaller number of experiences and events (e.g. Lazarus 2014; Thompson et al. 2015).

In most of my experiences that I found difficult, I felt alone, with little support from family or partner, or work colleagues. The year I really enjoyed whilst practising I was part of a tight-knit group of doctors, who were all experiencing the same troubles. We shared problems, and solutions, mostly over a beer. We had time outside work to play, and enjoy life even with on calls, and the doctors' Mess organised weekly activities for us to attend. I exercised.

In the literature on occupational burnout within the profession (despite some differences), three traits are described as indicators of burnout: depersonalisation, emotional exhaustion, and a low sense of personal accomplishment (e.g. McManus et al. 2002; Graham et al. 2002). The literature though has a few shortcomings. It does/cannot describe how burnout feels, the subjective experience of it in a way that is useful to a healthcare professional. A focus on told experiences of this phenomenon highlights the individuality of it, the risks for it and the context within which it exists.

Burnout, although thought to be associated with elevated stress hormones (Graham et al. 2002), due to lack of scientific evidence is not a clinical diagnosis, and as such is not recognised by doctors as a problem, that patients, **or** doctors, suffer from. Colleagues told me that they have wished they could break an arm or leg so they would not have to go into work the next day. It seems bizarre to me that a broken leg is seen to be more cumbersome than a broken brain, especially amongst doctors, given the extent of medical school teaching that outlines precisely the functions that the brain is responsible for.

Understanding what burnout feels like, enables healthcare professionals to probe, question and therefore identify it in their colleagues. To recognise who is at risk, and to notice when someone is not their normal self and to empathically signpost to resources designed to support doctors' mental well-being. Whilst I attended occupational health, the person I saw was far from empathic. My own GP was much better. I was at higher risk because I already had a history of depression. Above I describe not wanting to see patients, avoiding demands as a way of coping. This was a late sign for me;

discussion of these events with a concerned consultant did not alter the course I took. Had I been given a week off, or counselling support, or had a supportive group or Schwartz round I could go to I cannot say if that would have made a difference. The irony is if doctors were to apply their diagnostic skill to their colleagues, problems could be identified earlier, and support provided earlier, and attrition therefore reduced.

Of the doctors who struggle with mental health issues, access to support is a key problem, reasons for which are quoted as being too busy, or not knowing what support is out there. But I believe the real reason to be our very identity as doctors. We are the fixers, the problem solvers, not the problem creators. The doctor–patient duality is in some ways unhelpful. A disease is something that affects the patient, not something the doctor may also suffer from. Doctors who have at some stage in their careers become a patient describe this as a transformative experience that changes how they practise medicine, how they behave towards patients (Klitzman 2007). As medical students we learn about stigma (Goffman 1963), not least in reference to mental health disorders, but do we truly seek to fight it? It would be a mistake to assume that doctors are above the issues that affect others in society. Indeed, many medical professionals hold firm unhealthy beliefs about their patients. Patients who self-harm may be described as attention seeking, or timewasters. Patients with obesity, as lazy. Anything that reinforces a negative self-image for the patient cannot be construed as helpful or healthy. In my search for support and for answers, I have sometimes felt dehumanised by doctors. This has included some who were responsible for me and my care, and some who had previously been my friends and colleagues. At a conference, I attended recently Dr. Dike Drummond ('Physician Coach and Healthcare Speaker' https://www.the-happymd.com/about) was talking about burnout. The lecture theatre was packed, the conference oversubscribed. As Drummond began his talk, I realised that although I felt so alone in my experiences the fact that 300 people had turned up to a lecture to hear him speak about burnout, meant that I was not the only one.

In reflecting on what the creative process, and what working with supportive others, has given me I realise that I have been given answers, where previously there were none. When you cannot find 'the answer' on Google, where do you look? I looked inside myself. My recovery from burnout and my future in any workplace depended so much on this process. My experience leads me to argue that emotional education for medical students and doctors should be an essential and mandatory part of training, for learning and for protection of students' future well-being. As noted above where emotions are difficult to access, using a visual method can be very effective. In sharing my story with students, I hope they can appreciate that to struggle is normal and know they are not alone. Hopefully, they will enter medical practice armed with strategies to support them in their future careers. In sharing my story, I encourage students to consider a problem, long before they themselves will face it. In doing so, I hope I enable them to identify struggles in others be able to voice the value of support.

In defying the deficit model, I challenge the stigma associated with mental health problems in healthcare professionals. I know now that our relationships with others are key to well-being. When I was alone I struggled, when in a supportive team I thrived. My subsequent recovery, the making sense of it all has involved a large number of trusted individuals from my current workplace, and elsewhere who have supported me and with whom I have worked on various pedagogic and research projects. In short, collaboration works.

Reflecting on Auto/Biography

Thinking auto/biographically gave me space to reflect on all that has happening to me, and once I had that, I could organise support and counselling, be creative, work with others, do whatever might help. Until I understood the problem, I had no solution. In reflecting on the self, we reflect on our relationships with others and acknowledge that others are always present—in both negative and positive ways—in our personal stories (Morgan 1998; Sparkes 2002; Letherby 2014). This is what I have attempted to highlight in this chapter.

Robert Zussman (2000) reminds us of the auto/biographical occasions (job applications, self-assessment documents, criminal and religious confessions, diary writing, etc.) that we all engage in every day. All doctors have a portfolio of their work that they must complete in order to progress to the next stage. With each progression comes more opportunity. After I passed my Part I, I was given my own day case list of procedures to do, which I could manage independently. I was at all times acutely aware of how much I needed to get done and signed off before the next stage, and whilst my training programme director remarked that I was doing all of it, I just felt like I was behind, and that I was never going to succeed in what I was doing. Even though I was achieving something, my perception was of a low sense of personal accomplishment. Perhaps, this was not helped by the fact that no one congratulates you on a job done well in medicine. In four years, I had a handful of 'Thank Yous' from grateful patients, but very little positive from my colleagues to say what they liked about working with me. I did, however, have a collection of criticisms both written and verbal about my practice, dressed up as 'feedback' or 360 appraisals. Perfection is expected, because mistakes cost lives. I was terrified of making any mistake. I suffered all the more at the thought that 'I couldn't hack it', 'I was a failure', 'I was weak'. I blamed no one except myself for my inability to continue in my career. It was the creation of visual 'auto/biographical occasions' and the support of, and collaboration with, others that enabled my reassessment of self.

Conclusion

I do not expect everyone to relate to my story, in fact, I think the telling of it at the many events and conferences I have presented at has made people uncomfortable, upset, angry. I have also been stigmatised here too: I am the one at fault, I am the one that left, that could **not** cope.

As the lead for pastoral care in the medical school within which I work, I see a number of students who are struggling with personal issues. They have what I never did, an extensive support network that could indicate in the early stages that they need support. My experiences have taught me that all students have a right to consider and develop their own well-being as a key factor to their success in life. Learning to be independent and achieve your career goals is never an easy task. A focus in the curriculum on well-being enables students to learn how to be successful, how to communicate and how to get what they want out of life. With a colleague, considering our similar past experiences, I designed a teaching session on well-being for medical students. I first gave it to students who wanted to come, but very soon I was asked to talk to tutors, other healthcare students, at other universities and departments in local hospitals. I had to decide whether to share the very reason I was doing this; my own experiences. I stood up in front of my work colleagues and friends and told them a very small part of my story as presented here. I had feared further stigmatisation, but what I got was interest, enthusiasm, passion, and support. I was later invited to speak to obstetric trainees about well-being including several consultants I had been working with years earlier. So this is the work I have just started: work where I hope to change the paths of the students with similar experiences to me, to provide my students with careers that they love and to enhance the safety of patients, by supporting the well-being of future healthcare professionals. Doctors should be treated as holistic individuals for, as Caroline Elton (2018) rightly notes they are also human.

References

Banja, J. D. (2006). Empathy in the Physician's Pain Practice: Benefits, Barriers, and Recommendations. *Pain Medicine, 7*(3), 265–275.

Chandra, S., Mohammadnezhad, M., & Ward, P. (2018). Trust and Communication in a Doctor Patient Relationship: A Literature Review. *Journal of Healthcare Communications, 3*(3), 36. http://healthcare-communications.imedpub.com/trust-and-communication-in-a-doctorpatient-relationship-a-literature-review.pdf.

Chapman, B. P., Fiscella, K., Kawachi, I., Duberstein, P., & Muennig, P. (2016). Emotion Suppression and Mortality Risk Over a 12-Year Period. *Journal of Psychosomatic Research, 75*(4), 381–385.

Corrigan, O., & Letherby, G. (2010, September). *'Running Around Like a Headless Chicken': F1 Doctors' (Lack of) Time and Emotion Management.* Medical Sociology Conference. BSA, Durham University.

Elton, C. (2018). *Also Human: The Inner Lives of Doctors.* London: William Heinmann.

Goffman, E. (1963). *Stigma.* London: Penguin.

Graham, J., Potts, H. W. W., & Ramirez, A. J. (2002). Stress and Burnout in Doctors. *The Lancet, 360*(9349), 1975–1976.

Hochschild, A. R. (1979). Emotion Work, Feeling Rules and Social Structure. *American Journal of Sociology, 85*(3), 551–575.

Hochschild, A. R. (2012). *The Managed Heart: Commercialization of Human Feeling.* Berkeley: University of California Press.

Johnson, D. (2015). Emotional Intelligence as a Crucial Component to Medical Education. *International Journal of Medical Education, 6,* 179–183.

Klitzman, R. (2007). *When Doctors Become Patients.* New York: Oxford University Press.

Lazarus, A. (2014). Traumatized by Practice: PTSD in Physicians. *Journal of Medical Practice Management, 30*(2), 131–134.

Letherby, G. (2014). Feminist Auto/Biography. In M. Evans, C. Hemmings, M. Henry, H. Johnstone, S. Madhok, A. Plomien, et al. (Eds.), *Handbook on Feminist Theory.* London: Sage.

Maben, J. (2018). *How Can We Support Healthcare Staff to Care Well? A National Evaluation of Schwartz Center Rounds.* National Institute for Health Research. https://www.nihr.ac.uk/blogs/how-can-we-support-healthcare-staff-to-care-well-a-national-evaluation-of-schwartz-center-rounds/7765.

Mayer, J. D., & Salovey, P. (1993). The Intelligence of Emotional Intelligence. *Intelligence, 17*(4), 433–442.

McManus, C., Winder, B. C., & Gordon, D. (2002). The Causal Links Between Stress and Burnout in a Longitudinal Study of UK Doctors. *The Lancet, 359*(9323), 2089–2090.

Morgan, D. (1998). Sociological Imaginations and Imagining Sociologies: Bodies, Auto/Biographies and Other Mysteries. *Sociology, 32*(4), 647–663.

Newman, P. (2002). Valuing Learners' Experience and Supporting Further Growth: Educational Models to Help Experienced Adult Learners in Medicine. *BMJ, 2002*(325), 200.

Oster, G. D., & Crone, G. (2004). *Using Drawings in Assessment and Therapy: A Guide for Mental Health Professionals* (2nd ed.). New York: Routledge.

Sparkes, A. (2002). *Telling Tales in Sport and Physical Activity: A Qualitative Journey.* Leeds: Human Kinetics.

Thompson, C. V., Naumann, D. N., Fellows, J., Bowley, D., & Sugett, N. (2015). Post-traumatic Stress Disorder Amongst Surgical Trainees: An Unrecognised Risk? *The Surgeon Journal of the Royal Colleges of Surgeons of Edinburgh and Ireland, 15*(3). https://www.researchgate.net/publication/283049832_Post-traumatic_stress_disorder_amongst_surgical_trainees_An_unrecognised_risk.

Tudor Hart, J. (1971). The Inverse Care Law. *The Lancet, 297*(7696), 405–412.

Zussman, R. (2000). Autobiographical Occasions: Introduction to the Special Issue. *Qualitative Sociology—Special Issue: Autobiographical Occasions, 23*(1), 5–8.

3

Seventeen Minutes and Thirty-One Seconds: An Auto/Biographical Account of Collaboratively Witnessing and Representing an Untold Life Story

Kitrina Douglas and David Carless

Introduction

Auto/Biography carries with it elements of privilege as certain kinds of lives are narrated while other lives remain untold. As Frank (2004) has observed, those lives that are storied are rendered worthy of notice, while untold lives are implicitly rendered absent or insignificant. In our research, we have seen how these processes can conspire to further marginalise individuals and populations whose lives are already marginal. This is the sharp edge of social exclusion. In this chapter, we explore one particular instance of a creative and collaborative process we have used in an effort to avoid perpetuating exclusion and marginalisation in research. We use a layered storytelling approach which allows four individuals (Kitrina, David and two research participants) to, at different times, take their turn as first-person narrator.

Flat Tyre

Do you believe in telepathy? I'm not sure I do, but sometimes, like when you've been working with someone for years, perhaps you feel as if you know what he or she is thinking. It was like that during our first steering

K. Douglas (✉)
University of West London, London, UK

D. Carless
Visiting Research Professor, Queen's University Belfast, Belfast, UK

© The Author(s) 2020
J. M. Parsons and A. Chappell (eds.), *The Palgrave Handbook of Auto/Biography*,
https://doi.org/10.1007/978-3-030-31974-8_3

group meeting prior to starting a research project looking at the needs and experiences of people over 55 living in urban-supported housing.

There were eight of us crammed around a board room-type table and while it was cordial, we all had our roles. Opposite and to my right were two representatives from the local council. Sitting next to them to my left was someone from the Trust. At the head of the table sat George, director of the charity who had commissioned us to do the research and in middle there was us, sipping instant coffee from white china mugs. We had an agenda, and we hoped for some conversation, to get a handle on what had been happening. We wanted to learn from them—about the problems and challenges—and we were striving to be open-minded.

As we began to talk through how we wanted to approach the research, one of the city council representatives jumped in: 'That won't work!' We'd suggested an ethnography and invitations to residents to take part in interviews or focus groups. She continued: 'And we tried having a consultation but no one came to that either'. I did not turn to look at David but I knew he'd be thinking, *'I'm not surprised they won't talk to you with that attitude! I wouldn't either!'* But he did not say that. He sat there quietly and all I could see were his hands making notes on the pad in front of him.

There was little resolution and the meeting was brief. We thanked everyone for their thoughts, but it was not the kind of start we had hoped for. An air of negativity seemed to hang in the space between us. We left but didn't really speak until we got in the car. Then, David sounded like a car tyre going flat as a long exhale of air seeped from between his lips. He looked over and silently shook his head. He didn't need to say, *'What in the hell were they on?'* But he did. I didn't need to say, *'I can't believe those two!'* But I did. He started the engine, slightly deflated, and we were off.

Silences

How do you act respectful, when you are in someone else's home? By that I mean, how do you notice and *not* notice things. We were making our first visit to a housing scheme the local authority had labelled 'elderly preferred housing'. As we wandered through the corridors, we chatted with the housing support advisor (who was showing us round), and through glances and facial expressions we shared our awkwardness and discomfort over the less pleasant things we noticed.

'Oh yes', said the former warden, former mental health nurse, now resident and gatekeeper. 'What you smell in this corridor is urine'. She was not overemphasising or being overdramatic. She was just stating things that we didn't like to notice in someone else's home. 'He pisses in the corner there', she said, pointing. She paused, momentarily then added, to alleviate any doubt, 'just to annoy us'.

I didn't want to register the stench, but it was acrid, impossible to ignore. We exchanged another glance, this time David screwed up his face. The smell stung my throat at each intake of breath. We walked on in silence, me longing for the double doors to bang shut, to climb the stairs to something less potent. A slow realisation began to register that it was so much easier for us to say nice things than talk about what we were feeling, noticing, smelling.

'These are OK', she said, as we entered the second corridor, 'quite nice even'. Then pointing to Number 23: 'he's not here anymore'. I raised my eyebrows and smiled at David—an empty flat and one less resident to interview. 'And he's died', she said as we passed 27, 'so you won't be able to speak to him either'. Then, a little mischievously added, 'unless you got some connections you haven't told us about!' David's eyes were now dancing and he smiled. We all shared the joke and walked on.

Success

Success is meeting your targets, right? And maybe we had at the back of our minds those two people from the council who said no one would speak to us. But here they all were, coming down to coffee mornings, agreeing to one-to-one interviews, agreeing to focus groups, and seeming to enjoy the opportunity to talk. Of course, we were learning, heaps, and people were so different, some funny, many appreciative, often generous.

The West Indian man in Number 21 talked about his GP: 'If it wasn't for her', he smiled through missing teeth, 'I'd be a gonner m'luv, a gonner'. He was serious and funny in showing recognition for the influence of his doctor in stopping his excessive consumption of strong alcohol.

Another Jamaican man described his roller-coaster life, being thrown out of the navy for something he wasn't responsible for, then buying a gun, going to prison, time passing, trying to make a go of a business, and finally his family, ageing and illness. He reflected on his life: 'I go through a lot of tribulation here', he said, 'but I have learned that if you cannot learn to forget, learn to forgive, right? Because if I couldn't forgive I wouldn't be here talking to you now, alright, 'cause we are talking about *things*. So this is why I need my freedom, because if I don't have that I can't do anything'.

We wondered, what were those tribulations? Why would he not be 'here'? What were those '*tings*' as he pronounced it? Maybe it was what

Jane was getting at when she said: 'This place I just hate. I hate the smell. It doesn't smell as much at my end, it just smells down there. I just feel trapped really. I think quite a lot of people here feel that too. It's dead. I mean this room, you used to be able to smoke in here and things and make tea and coffee and all of that stopped. And people don't want to get involved, you know, we've got people with problems here. We've got one resident … in Number 26…' she paused. '…there was a lot of…' she paused again and then seemed to change track: 'but he has quietened down now. I think a couple of the other residents went down there and threatened to beat him up'.

What *wasn't* she saying? What *couldn't* she say? Why the silences?

As the number of people we had yet to interview reduced, our curiosity about the man in Number 26 continued to intensify.

The Man at Number 26

I left Kitrina drinking coffee in the community room hoping that maybe I could find at home one of those 'elusive' residents we had not managed to interview yet, give it one more try. Or *we* thought *we* needed to give it one more try. Partly I still had those council housing folks' voices in my head, telling us people wouldn't talk to us, and partly because I was motivated by our own ethical standards: we *did* want to hear everyone's story. It is a matter of duty, a moral accountability, we hold ourselves, to at least try to gain every resident's perspective, to avoid writing about *them* without including *all of them*.

So, there I was once again, walking the corridors, turning corners, and once again knocking on the door with the beaten-up paintwork. I had heard a lot about this door already. How it had been knocked down by the police late one night when he refused to open it following disturbance complaints from neighbours.

After a brief pause, the door opened and there he was: the 'he' who was feared and avoided by many of the other residents; the 'he' whose noise late at night had become a curse for his neighbours; the 'he' who residents said would urinate in the corridors, was frequently drunk, high or both; the 'he' rumour had it, had been electronically 'tagged' and required, by the courts, to be in his flat between the hours of 6 p.m. and 6 a.m.

I suddenly felt like I was in a scene from *The Fisher King* and was looking at Parry, the Robin Williams character, complete with ragged dirty clothes and hair and bushy, unkempt beard long and dishevelled.

'Hello', I said. His reply seemed more of a grunt than a word so I continued: 'My name is David and I'm here as part of a team who are doing research into the residents' experiences of living here. I wonder if you might have some time to talk to me?'

Another grunt noise was followed by a pause as his body moved out of the way and the door opened further. 'Mayswell', mumble, 'lucky', mumble, 'catchmem usyou'.

While my feet responded to the door opening, it took me a while longer for my head to work out what he had said. I think he said something like: '*You may as well come in. You're lucky to catch me—I'm usually out*'. But his voice was so rough anyone would struggle to understand what he was saying. My attention was fully on trying to work it out and I didn't notice, as he closed the door behind me, him slipping the chain across. The *gottcha* sound of the chain in the catch startled me and as my eyes met his I wondered if he could read my fear. I wondered if could feel the tremor splitting through my body, an electric bolt. Trapped.

He waved me on and I felt compelled to walk through to, well, it might have been the bedroom or the living room or—it was hard to tell. There was none of the furniture I would expect to see in either. No bed, no sofa, no dining table. No desk, no bookshelves, no TV, no stereo. But, at the same time the room was completely full of, well, *stuff*. If I'm honest it looked like a small municipal waste disposal site. Negotiating my way through used tins, empty bean cans, old newspapers and magazines, I picked my way across little bits of clear floor, eyeing dirty cushions, greying maybe once white clothing, and knee-high piles of empty *Special Brew* beer cans in the corner, some crumpled and crushed. In another corner, there was a pile of grubby duvets which might have been a bed. A bowl of food—a runny red vegetable stew it looked like—sat on a small side table. Flies buzzed around the room.

'Schit dawn', he said, 'sch'anywhere's fane'. There were only two chairs—two old, broken office chairs. I picked the nearest—backless and piled with of crumpled newspapers. I could see the ripped blue fabric of the chair between the papers. I went to move the papers out of the way before thinking better of it. He disappeared from view into what sounded like a kitchen while I perched on the edge of the chair. Feeling uncomfortable. My hands were wet, and I had to stop myself wringing them, I could feel my heart beating faster and heavier, my mouth was dry and I was unable to swallow. I did not feel safe in this man's flat—I worried about being trapped, locked and bolted in. I worried about how it would look if he became violent: me a younger physically strong-looking man, him an older frail-looking man. He looked and talked like he was wild. And I thought about the unhygienic conditions in the flat, imagined the bacteria and germs that inhabit a room like this. I wanted to get up and leave but felt obliged to stay.

After a couple of minutes, he returned with a large mug. I think he said he would make me a drink later but was relieved he did not bring me anything as I wouldn't have risked drinking it. He sat on the other chair, set down the mug on the floor, picked up the bowl of food and took a spoonful. Then, he started talking: 'Donbescarothem. I've goawholelotoclearupodo. Y'know whathat is?'

I had no idea what he had said. 'What was that?' 'Pardon?' 'Can you say that again?'

He spat words and food, saliva and venom: 'Fruit flies!'

All this—the physical environment, my inability to decipher much of his speech, his physical appearance, actions and demeanour, the chain across the door—was increasing my discomfort. My anxiety.

I decided to begin the interview as I had with the other residents: 'How long have you lived here?'

Instantly, he replied, 'Toooofackingloong'.

'Yeah?' I pause a beat before continuing. 'Where were you…' but he cuts me off: 'Sfars rehab's concerned, inaway yar barkingupthe wrong tree cause' then increasing the volume and leaning in 'I's nata fackingjunkie. But, havingsaydthat', he paused, kicked a beer can across room, and eyeballed me again, 'everywan's a lickle facking…' His eyes drifted sideways for a second. Then back they came staring right at me: '… lickle weed! Remember Bill and Ben? At th'end o' tha day we'rrre flob flob flob, alobalob. Weeeeeed! And weed alwaseems to hatheanswer, come upasun-time, said time to go sleepienow. And that was hypnotic for the', he makes a noise. Then: 'Wasn't it?'

'OK', I respond, having again failed to understand any of what he said. Was he toying with me? Playing a game? Might he become violent? I tried to be calm, but I was also preparing to take evasive action. I found myself looking for an escape, but was also trying to keep the conversation going, to do my job. It was torture, he was in control and I felt he could take this where he wanted.

'Y'know', he continued 'at that point imylifeIwasgoinoschoola 9 o'clock at 9 yearold andfivepassnineawafucking off anclimbinguptrees'.

I tried to keep the conversation going, making guesses as to what he was saying, clinging to a few words and trying to sound as if I knew what he was talking about. He'd mentioned school right? And climbing trees and came out with: 'Cause it was more fun than being in the classroom?'

'Yep. Yeah. Butahactualllearnta lot morathe university of life, climbing trees and playinwicatsndogs. But TV, in those days there weren't no

TV'snowhere. I remember when I were 9 year old I used to go up to my mate Geoff Harley, godbleshimman, 9 and 10 year old, anuhIhadngota fucking clue, I justhouit was meunmemate, ah hadn'tgota fucking clue. And get this one fera crack—is that running?' He points at my audio recorder; 'You're gonna fucking lovethisun!'

'Do you want me to stop it?' I ask, not knowing where he is going next.

'No!' he replied laughing; 'The first time heevertasteddeath. And what comes with it. The coffin, the tears, the black clothes'. He paused. 'The wake. Sangndancedngodrunk with the dead'.

I just didn't know what to make of it all—almost too stunned to speak. This is not like any other interview I've ever conducted. More to myself than to him, I settle on: 'Oh God'.

'No, God ain'tgotnothingtodow'it. We were Pagan, nifyou lookaitthatway'. He muttered something. 'Is God around? Is Jesus around? Is thisnthatntheother?'

What should I say? I go for: 'Yeah?'

'Thastoofuckinho. Don't worry, don't panic, just don't fucking panic whatever you do. Don't make any sudden movements, whatever you do. Do you know what happened to me a long time ago? Pete and Jonny, either one of them, you wouldn't want to box off. Pete was a retired boxer but being a fucking vodka head, don't blame the drink, blame the head. Being a vodka head he's likely by the time he's had the second bottle of vodka', he halts and stares at me, intensely. 'He could it like that. I'm doing this on purpose, one minute he'd talk, he'd be looking at you like that, lit a cigarette, y'alright, y'alright, what football team d'you support? And he'd be on your case then, and he'd just duel with you for ages. And he's like a bear mauling something that he's gonna kill in a minute. Playing with it, nudging it and then *Bam*!' He smacked his left fist into his right hand.

By now I'm starting to feel more than just anxious. From the few words I grasp at the moment I'm feeling threatened. *Is this a direct threat from him to me?* Hoping otherwise, I try to clarify: 'And did he do this with you?'

But it does anything but bring clarity: 'Naw!', another pause. 'It don't really matter if you get m'meaning'. He pauses again to crack open a can of *Special Brew*, takes a swig and continues. 'People in the fightgamedotendta hit people' he says with an emphasis on the *HIT*. 'And I don't know ha'many timeser- why you've ever been hit', another dramatic pause, 'buusually whenyoubeen hit, you either know whatitsfor or you don't. There'snotwoways about it. And the otherslike, how s e r i o u s l y whereyou hit. You eitherknowyouwere- hit or youwahalf fucking hit, whacked. N'thenthere's the thing about, there's somany sides. I's like, what d'you call it, a dodecker-fucking-hedron. Its an itchy angle that one. N'alsowhatgoesroundcomesaround, know what I mean?'

He answers his own rhetorical question with a mumble. 'And the root of all evil isn't money, it's the wanting. The wanting and needing. Ss'the loveodesire. In Arabic wacalltha *naff*. S'inlike naff, i's naff. But naff means desire in Arabic'.

'Alright', I reply.

He doesn't pause. 'Soslike you want it. Naff means want'.

'Yeah, OK'. I'm just saying something to avoid saying nothing now.

'IsnoghtlikeIwannasandwich or I wannacupotea. slike I *desire* something. And it's usually something that's *eeeeevil*'.

My digital audio recorder indicated that we are 6 minutes and 2 seconds into the interview—what is going on? I want to get out. I *need* to get out. But my inner voice of practicality kicks in, *maybe you're being overly sensitive*, it whispers. Then, it begins to reason with me: *you do have a job to do.* And reminds me: *You did ask him to let you interview him and he said yes. He is in his 70s, unfit. He invited you into his home.* I look down at my notes, try to clear my head. OK, yes that's right, be respectful, honour his story. I look up and now he has a knife in his hand. A big theatrical-looking knife. *Shit! Where did that come from?* Is it real? Fake? He's just sat there playing with what looks like something Captain Jack Sparrow would wield. But this is not Hollywood—the blade is steel and the end looks sharp.

At 8 minutes 11 seconds, I am still watching him toy with his knife. *How long do I need to stay here to do that? How quickly can I leave without being rude or insulting?* Time is dragging and my stomach is turning. I get a sharp pain in my side. My heart is racing and thumping to get out of my chest, and now too my headaches. I try once more the question I'd begun, faking confidence: 'Have you been living here for long?' And I try to ignore the knife.

'S'leven years'. He replies. 'S'mad. Naw, thatsjustnobtuse remark. While yaw're recordin' I dan't wannna sound like a facking luunatttic'.

'OK'.

'Buironically, I'm a…' I can't make it out. Then he continues: 'S'tookfuckingten yearst'finallygeta fucking place. And really, n'mattawhatah-said, rightly or wrongly about the buildingn'bout therulesn…' something else I am unable to discern. 'It's an indoor prison only I gat the key not you the screws. Bu'thescrew'soutside that door! You coming in here like a vicar havin' aninterview'nI'sdoin' facking life here now'.

Then, he shouts, loud: 'FUCK YOU!'

I jump, startled at the volume and intensity. 'Would you like me to leave?'

'Nat you, ya dick!' He laughs. 'Did I make you jump then?'

'Yes you did, yeah'.

'Well good!' He spits onto the floor. A gob of saliva that slaps the ground. 'Because'tha's wha I did wi'them'.

15 minutes 58 seconds. OK, I've talked with him for quarter of an hour I tell myself. Not long, but respectable. A decent effort under extreme circumstances. I decide then that I'm going. Now. But how to leave safely and without incident? The knife, the lock, how am I going to get out?

I announce, 'Alright', and stand. 'I'm going to make a move. I've got some other people I've got to call on as well'.

'Nah!' he says.

My heart literally misses a beat and thumps hard in my chest. Did I hear him right? *Is he going to try to keep me here?* He doesn't. Instead, he says: 'Ivegottogo on but thank you fa'talkin' tome. Y'er alright man'.

I am now shocked in a completely different way, not sure how to take this late and unexpected vote of confidence but manage, 'I appreciate that'.

He hands me the front door key. I had not notice that he had locked us in as well as putting the chain across. 'A'least you'reno'a Jehovah's Witness!' He laughs as I hurriedly undo the locks.

'That's true', I say. 'Thanks a lot'. I unlock and open to door to leave, but my unsteady hand drops the key. I bend to pick it up, feeling exposed and vulnerable, and hand it back to him.

'D'youseetha'there?' he asks, pointing at a splintered hole in the door. 'Watch! I didtha'onpurpose'. I prepare myself for him to repeat the damage but he doesn't. Instead, he says something—although I can't make it out now or when I listen back to the recording. I hear voices outside in the corridor. Safety. Relief. Relief that I am no longer alone with him in his flat.

'Thasthe police fo'ya', he adds. G'night'.

I go to say, 'Cheers now', but he has already slammed the door.

Shock

I wandered into the corridor, all was quiet. I had visited Number 14 as we agreed, had a coffee and chatted with a couple of the housing support officers in the lounge, then popped my head out into the corridor wondering where David was. There was no one around. I got the sense he should be there by now, but then again, if he had begun an interview, it would take an hour or so. So, I wandered back in, sat down, got on with some work until I heard footsteps. I looked up. I have seen this man lean back casually on two legs of a chair and ask a question that would pull the rug from under me. I have watched him negotiate with some of the most obstreperous members of our mental health group over the rules of golf, when anyone else would have lost their temper or patience or both. I have seen him take on huge ocean waves that can render a person unconscious, rise up and paddle out to the next wave. I have seen him deal with arrogant and ignorant sportspeople in some of our research and CPD. I have heard him sing when a bar is full of drunks and sing when a bar is full of his fans. But I had never seen his eyes so dark before, his whole spirit suddenly old, ill, pale, shaking and unable to talk.

Debrief

'Shit!' was what David said as he sat down. Then a long pause before a flurry of words began to unravel. 'Shit! What a bastard! He was drunk, fucked up, when I arrived—and opened a *Special Brew*. He swore, F-ed and blinded continually and spat on the ground and eye-balled me, and then played with this dagger as he…'.

'Slow down', I urged.

'I'm so glad it wasn't you in there! Christ, I…'

'You're safe now'.

'He had to tell me about violence, boxing, all the time eyeballing me, and something about being "murdered twice", then he said, "but I wasn't there". What does that mean?'

David was still shaking. Almost incoherent. Troubled.

'I really didn't think I was going to get out of there for a while. Thought he might turn on me. With that knife. Or swing at me with his right hand, the one with the sovereign ring on it. I think him putting the chain across after I entered started me worrying. But what could I do by then? Leave straight away? I felt like I had to stay for a while, to give him chance to speak having asked. How long would be enough? I kept glancing at the recorder. I managed 17 minutes 31 seconds. It felt like two hours. Look, I'm still shaking. What must it be like for those who live with him, next door, down the corridor?'

Telling the Untellable

It was only once we had transcribed the interview that we could begin to piece together what the man in Number 26 had said. Slowly, going over and over little bits of the interview, we got most of it. True, there were still words and sounds we couldn't identify, but the recording made some sense. We sat on the sofa playing the recording, reading along with the transcript. It isn't fun reliving bad experiences, or listening to a friend who was clearly struggling, but at least it was over quickly. I hadn't even finished my coffee. But what to do with it? We sat in silence staring at the recorder on the table as if it were a deadly plague, neither of us wanted to touch it. We each looked at the words on the page. There were not many. But both of us sensed in each other that we had to come up with something. But what? We couldn't leave this out of the report. We could not leave *him* out of the research. But how to include it? How to include *him*? How could we represent what David had heard and witnessed in a way that would illuminate what life was like for some in this 'elderly preferred' supported housing scheme?

'Fruit Flies'

[Voice of man in no. 26]

[Voice of housing support advisor]

Some of the residents say
"This place never sleeps!"
There's always someone coming in
and out
Making a noise, causing a disturbance,
but what do you do?
We've got one guy whose been tagged…

Fruit flies
Acrid stench
No fucker gonna fuck with me
I'm not a junkie
You're barking up the wrong tree

…should be gagged

But at the end of the day
Aren't we all a little fucked?

I try to steer clear of him
his language, every other word

And I've tasted death, the coffin and the tears
Black clothes and a wake
I sang with the dead and got drunk
I don't know how many times

but when you've been hit
You either know what it's for
or you don't
You know how hard you were hit

That's the thing, there's so many sides
and what goes around comes around
know what I mean?
The wanting and needing
The crave in your soul
It travels in your carcass
and you push it to the edge
You push – further than the SAS

It's taken ten years to get this fuckin' place, and

and yes I know they need to live
to somewhere
and we all use bad language
on occasion

No matter what I said about the rules, the building
It's an indoor prison
Only I've got the keys
not you, you screws

some do it coz they've never read
a dictionary

You comin' in here like a vicar, having an interview
And I'm doing life here

some to shock or for attention

I don't want to be in here
I'm the ASBO fucker, I've been tagged
6pm to 6am and I can't handle it

but maybe its also help me

I don't want to live with these beep BEEP systems!

And you know what?

From the little fuckin' squirrel

Comes the old fuckin' acorn

And this is the nut:

I'm my granddad's age

That's why I got this place,

Cause I'm OLD

And they're getting on my nerves

She's getting on my nerves

> *even though they will*
> *fight you*
> *every inch of the way*

So I go and rattle her cage

> *and knock your head off,*
> *you know*

And I'm wild and they come and they knock down the door

> *there is a cry for help there.*

But I know the system

I been out in the cold

So I thought fuck it!

Become a little hamster

Live in a cage.

Reflections

Research for us has, it seems, always been a collaborative project. During our doctoral research, Kitrina suggested forming a research team and, although we had very different topics, we got together with another student (Lucy Foster) to read each other's transcripts and reflect on what we each were learning. Although we did not at the time, now we would call it collaboration. Later, in the final year of David's doctoral research, we raised funding for a golf and mental health project. We enjoyed, and gained a lot from, working closely side by side right from the outset of the study—from planning and preparation, through fieldwork, doing joint interviews and focus groups, working up our analysis and stories and interpretations, feeding back to participants, right through publication and presentation at conferences. Throughout the journey, we would communicate with each other with the more usual forms of written and spoken word. We would meet to plan things together, debrief after spending time doing fieldwork, make and share notes together, sometimes one of us speaking while the other wrote, sometimes writing separately. But we would also often find ourselves communicating so much through a look, a facial expression or a nod. And—sometimes—it was all about just being there side by side with and for each other.

These relational ways of working and being have been and are critical to our work, offering us a way to care with and for each other, to be on the lookout for each other. Our particular ways of collaborating are, of course, intimately tied to the process and products of our research. Through working in these ways, we do better research. But they are also entirely bound up with our own well-being—safety even—as qualitative researchers who must sometimes navigate the challenging waters of alienation, marginalisation, trauma, abuse and distress (see, e.g., Carless and Douglas 2010, 2016, 2017; Douglas and Carless 2009, 2014, 2015a, 2018).

This has, perhaps, never been more important than during the events we have recounted in this chapter. The minutes of the interview were such an obvious fracture to our normal pattern. I (Kitrina) had never previously considered that David's safety could be at risk when I wasn't there. *What could have happened with the chain across the door, alcohol consumed and that knife pulled out?* While I (David) was relieved that it had not been Kitrina alone in that man's flat. *What could have happened to a lone woman locked inside his home?* Once those 17 minutes were up, however, our interdependent collaborative way of working—being there with and for each other—came to the rescue and perhaps saved the day. 'Debrief' is an inadequate word in this context. Rather, David was able to find solace—be reassured, witnessed, soothed, calmed—through Kitrina's caring presence. David was able to begin processing his experience of meeting this participant and hearing his story. Later, as we continued our more usual ways of working, we were able to *co-elaborate* on David's experiences of the interview and what the participant had said and done. Drawing also on Kitrina's interview with a housing support advisor, we created the above poetic/lyrical performance piece 'Fruit Flies' to help build a rich, inclusive and dialogical answer our research question.

While we both feel assured of the value and importance (for the research and for ourselves) of working in these kinds of interdependent, caring, relational ways, we have less resolution concerning the complex ethical issues that arise from the events we have recounted here. On the one hand, this concerns sociopolitical questions such as: Which stories count and/ or are counted? What kinds of experiences are allowed to come to the fore and which ones are suppressed? How might we speak up for those who cannot speak in their own name through fear of reprisal? When do the human rights of one person impinge so greatly on another that they must be denied? On the other hand, it concerns practical questions like: How can researchers be tolerant of someone who is verbally and/or physically threatening or abusive? *Should* researchers tolerate someone who is overtly threatening? And, finally, it concerns perhaps the biggest questions: What are the costs (for researchers) of including the most challenging voices in our research? What are the costs (for society) of *failing* to include these voices?

Conclusion

Our focus in this chapter has been on creatively responding to questions of how to access, witness and represent elements of an otherwise untold—and potentially untellable—life: the kind of life that is more often omitted from academic writings, the kind of story that rarely makes it into print. To tell (moments of) this kind of life story here, we have had to delve deep into our own lives, our own stories, our own subjectivities. We have had to remember, reflect, write, rewrite and share critical moments from our own biographies: moments riddled with vulnerability, doubt and emotion and moments which intersect—and sometimes clash—with others' lives. And to take up this challenge, we have had to draw on the arts: here, it has been storytelling and poetry; elsewhere, it has been songwriting and film-making (e.g. Douglas and Carless 2015b). In all this work, our story is ultimately about how, through arts-based methods and creative collaborations, we may begin to reanimate our own and others' lives through including the kinds of life stories, experiences and voices that are typically omitted from social research.

References

Carless, D., & Douglas, K. (2010). *Sport and Physical Activity for Mental Health*. Oxford: Wiley-Blackwell.

Carless, D., & Douglas, K. (2016). Narrating Embodied Experience: Sharing Stories of Trauma and Recovery. *Sport, Education and Society, 21*(1), 47–61.

Carless, D., & Douglas, K. (2017). When Two Worlds Collide: A Story About Collaboration, Witnessing and Life Story Research with Soldiers Returning from War. *Qualitative Inquiry, 23*(5), 375–383.

Douglas, K., & Carless, D. (2009). Exploring Taboo Issues in Professional Sport Through a Fictional Approach. *Reflective Practice, 10*(3), 311–323.

Douglas, K., & Carless, D. (2014). Sharing a Different Voice: Attending to Stories in Collaborative Writing. *Cultural Studies<=>Critical Methodologies, 14*(4), 303–311.

Douglas, K., & Carless, D. (2015a). *Life Story Research in Sport: Understanding the Experiences of Elite and Professional Athletes Through Narrative*. Abingdon: Routledge.

Douglas, K., & Carless, D. (2015b). *The Blue Funnel Line*. https://www.youtube.com/watch?v=cftAy_SaurY. Accessed 8 Feb 2019.

Douglas, K., & Carless, D. (2018). Engaging with Arts-Based Research: A Story in Three Parts. *Qualitative Research in Psychology, 15*(2–3), 156–172.

Frank, A. W. (2004). *The Renewal of Generosity: Illness, Medicine, and How to Live*. Chicago: University of Chicago Press.

4

Reflections on a Collaborative, Creative 'Working' Relationship

Deborah Davidson and Gayle Letherby

Introducing Our (Academic) Selves

Keynote speeches for the 2018 *Qualitative Methods Conference* in Banff, Canada focused on the importance of networks. Discussing the conference and her interest in creative methods, Nicole Brown recalls:

> Many speakers referred to the process of 'finding your people.' Indeed, the principle of having a close network of colleagues working on and through similar issues and concerns chimes with me. But as yet, I still feel isolated within the world of qualitative research. (Brown 2019: 1)

Unlike Brown, and despite there still being some resistance to the methodological and epistemological choices we each make, we do not feel isolated in our endeavours. The collaborative work we do with others and together is **absolutely** significant here. Meeting in a toilet at a conference (again in Canada) in late 1997 we quickly realised that we shared similar substantive and epistemological research concerns. Substantively—alone and together—we have

D. Davidson (✉)
York University, Toronto, ON, Canada
e-mail: debd@yorku.ca

G. Letherby
University of Plymouth, Plymouth, UK
e-mail: gayle.letherby@plymouth.ac.uk

© The Author(s) 2020
J. M. Parsons and A. Chappell (eds.), *The Palgrave Handbook of Auto/Biography*,
https://doi.org/10.1007/978-3-030-31974-8_4

63

researched and written on issues relating to non/parental identity; reproductive disruption; loss and grief and working and learning in higher education. With reference to epistemological and methodological interests, we each have a commitment to feminist and auto/biographical approaches. With the latter in mind, along with others, we agree that:

> [auto/biography is not] … simply a shorthand representation of autobiography and/or biography but also [a] recognition of the inter-dependence of the two enterprises…. In writing another's life we also write or rewrite our own lives; in writing about ourselves we also construct ourselves as somebody different from the person who routinely and unproblematically inhabits and moves through social space and time. (Morgan 1998: 655)

Further to this, in her work Gayle argues for a position she calls theorised subjectivity, which requires the constant, critical interrogation of our personhood—both intellectual and personal—within the production of the knowledge, which starts by recognising the value as in worth (rather than moral value)—both positive and negative—of the subjective (Letherby 2003, 2013). Similarly, Deborah argues that not only is the personal political, it is also theoretical (Davidson 2007). This helps us to reflect meaningfully on the research experience and to take responsibility for the 'knowledge' we produce.

We have always been impressed by Mills' (1959: 204) view that: 'The social scientist is not some autonomous being standing outside society, the question is where he (sic) stands within it…'. And further agree with his advice to sociologists to: '… learn to use your life experience in your intellectual work: continually to examine it and interpret it' (Mills 1959: 216).

In recent years, in addition to our auto/biographical approach, we have each become increasingly interested in creative ways to both collect and present data, which opens up new ways for both respondents and researchers to engage issues and concerns. One example includes our engagement with visual research. We agree that 'visual material created specifically for the purpose [of research], can be used as a stimulus that not only provides a way into talking about particular topics but can also generate different kinds of talk and conversation' (Harper 2002, cited in Bragg 2011). Spencer (2011: 1) reminds us that the visual predates language and 'affects our emotions, identities, memories and aspirations in a most profound way' and thus visual imagery is a channel through which social life and lived experiences can be observed. Similarly, Pauwels (2011: 13) suggests that visual research is a 'cross-cutting field of inquiry, a way of doing and thinking that influences the whole process of researching (conceptualising, gathering and communicating)'.

As researchers and more generally, we have also explored different types of writing to tell our sociological stories:

> I consider writing as a *method of inquiry*, a way of finding out about yourself and your topic. Although we usually think about writing as a mode of "telling" about the social world, writing is not just a mopping-up activity at the end of a research project. Writing is also a way of "knowing" – a method of discovery and analysis. By writing in different ways, we discover new aspects of our topic and our relationship to it. Form and content are inseparable. (Richardson 1994: 515)

Exploring different ways to telling academic stories is not new. Frank (2000) suggests that stories, devoid of academic jargon, can be used to reach broader audiences, and she and others (e.g. Diversi 1998; Sparkes 2002) suggest that fictional representation of data encourages readers to experience emotions—their own and others' emotions—and understand them in relation to contexts in which the emotions arise. Similarly, Tierney (1998: 313) argues that fictional accounts might portray a situation more clearly than standard forms of representation for: 'we rearrange facts, events and identities in order to draw the reader into the story in a way that enables a deeper understanding of individuals, organisations, or the events themselves'. And Lackey advocating sociological creative writing argues:

> What a better way to show one understands a discipline and a society than to use sociological knowledge to create a context in which characters interact, reflect, and observe their social context. (Lackey 1994: 169)

Together, and apart, then, we have adopted an auto/biographical approach to the work that we do and continue to engage with new (to us at least) and different ways to collect, present and archive data. Our relationship as close friends as well as colleagues is relevant here, in that not only do we support each other in our work, but we also provide each other with a safe space to make mistakes, to share ideas, to experiment.

Our research experiences, including the methods and approaches we employ—collaboratively and individually—to collect and present data tells us much about ourselves as social, political beings as it does about our respondents and their experiences (Sparkes 2002; Pelias 2008; Douglas and Carless 2013). This chapter provides further insight into our individual and collective selves. In what follows, we focus on some of our projects to further highlight our collaborative, creative approach and reflect on our challenge to, rather than compliance with, 'expected' approaches and practices within the academy.

Creative Auto/Biographical Examples from the Field

Here we provide three examples of our creative auto/biographical methodological approach. One relates to a project led by Deborah, one by Gayle, and one on which we have worked together. As we show here, each of these projects includes both of our touches.

Deborah—The Tattoo Project: Creating a Digital Archive for Commemorative Tattoos[1]

My relationship with academia over the last 18 years from my Master's Degree through tenured associate professorship has been mentored by Gayle. As friend and colleague, she has encouraged creativity, intellectual risk-taking and has validated use of my life experience in my scholarly work (referring to Mills 1959: 216), and The Tattoo Project is no exception. Following is how, with Gayle's mentorship, collaboration, and friendship, I found myself where I am today.

In my earlier research on grief and bereavement, which evolved from my own experience, I noted that the work to achieve and maintain 'good grief' is successful when the experience of love and loss is integrated into one's life in meaningful ways that continue bonds with the deceased. Good grief is achieved through the social support seen in 'griefwork',[2] where the work of grieving is shared and negotiated between and among grieving persons and supportive others (Davidson 2007, 2008, 2010, 2011; Davidson and Stahls 2010). From this, whilst volunteering for a bereavement group, I noticed that persons I had not expected to have tattoos have them in memory of

---

[1] All interviews for the project received ethics approval from York University.

[2] Griefwork as a social science concept differs from grief work as the psychological concept where the work is done by the grieving person alone.

their deceased loved ones. Tattoos, for memorialisation and later for commemoration more generally, became another direction for my research.

Tattoo research offers critical insight into highly significant aspects of culture, discourses within it and social relations. As one of the most persistent and universal forms of body modification, tattoos have long been recognised, not only as marks of deviance, but also for their use in spiritual and sacred art and ceremony, as well as marks of social position, power and strength of character. Because of the increase in social acceptance of tattooing, we see 38% of Millennials having at least one tattoo and 19% having more than one (Beasley 2012). Moreover, since the death of Princess Diana and following 9/11, public displays of commemoration have also proliferated. Similarly, we are not surprised to see more tattoos specifically for the purpose of commemoration. For those of us with commemorative tattoos, these tattoos are more than body art. We modify our bodies through this practice so as to embody that which we commemorate. Tattoos, then, help us narrate our stories.

> We are our stories and our tattoos are how we remember never to forget. (Isaac Fitzgerald in *Pen and Ink*, 2014: x)

Indeed, as a tattoo bearer myself, after hearing stories of love, life, laughter and loss by persons with tattoos, I became motivated to create a digital archive as an online resource for particular sets of storytellers—persons with tattoos, researchers, tattooists and curious others (Photograph 4.1). I knew this was a project I did not want, nor could I do, alone. Gayle is among a team of international interdisciplinary researchers and community members participating in *The Tattoo Project: Creating a Digital Archive for Commemorative Tattoos*. As a collaborative effort, its purpose is fourfold: (1) to provide a repository for commemorative tattoos and their contextualising narratives, empowering users to make the project a tool of their own, (2) to serve as a cultural heritage site, acknowledging important memories and sharing them publicly, (3) to provide scholars with a digital database of commemorative tattoos and narratives for analysis, and (4) to develop relationships between academics and the public.

Both tattoos and archives share key features. Commemorative tattoos store information, the meaning of which has been made by the bearer; conserve memory—protecting it from harm or decay; allow retrieval at a glance, touch or thought; and invite dialogue. Similarly, archives, store, retrieve, filter and communicate data, with the potential to pass it along generationally. Digitisation of the archive will 'provide an almost infinite set of

"As a tattoo bearer myself, after hearing stories of love"

Deborah's tattoo is also the logo for The Tattoo Project. Elephants are intelligent, sentient and emotional beings who encode experiences into long -term memory, form strong social bonds, and have a highly developed sense of empathy, altruism, and social justice. They mourn their dead and their herds do not rush them through their grief.

Photograph 4.1   Deborah's tattoo

possibilities for the retrieval, filtering and organisation of data' (Miller 2011: 20). Furthermore, like for the bearer of a commemorative tattoo, the user of the archive creates meaning from the data. Commemorative tattoos as well as archives create space for comfort and discomfort through memories collected, recollected and shared and serve as testaments to the intimate relationships between our memories and the media through which they are expressed and made public. Commemorative tattoos, and why we choose to preserve the memories they represent through embodiment and digitisation, are shaped by and continue to shape culture.

Representing our project and tattooing for commemoration more generally, *The Tattoo Project: Visual Culture and the Digital Archive* (Davidson 2017), also with contributions from Gayle (Letherby and Davidson 2017a, b), is a book bridging academics, lay audiences and practitioners. As well as our personal collaboration, by putting a public face on social research, our project is an act of scholarly and community collaboration. The book is about *'our* project' and is directed at both the co-production and mobilisation of knowledge. Together we crowdsource in real and virtual space to produce the online digital archive.

The act of preserving, sharing and honouring memory and maintaining bonds is a key aspect of commemorative tattooing. This act of sharing and preservation has also been described in the use of online support groups (Davidson and Letherby 2014). More information on the digital archive is available at: http://thetattooproject.info/.

Gayle: Doing Griefwork Through Fiction and Memoir

I started writing fiction after my husband John's death in 2010 and began to write more and also to pen some memoir following the death of my mother, Dorothy, in 2012. I write, not only about the loss of them, but of other losses and of happy times also. Deborah was one of the first people I shared this writing with just as I had shared with her my fears and feelings during John's and my mum's illnesses and following their deaths. So, Deborah is one person who I do griefwork with. Bereavement and grief for me were, and is, like a long walk up a hill and I have found writing of all types, but most notably 'creative' work especially comforting and enriching during my journey. My health and well-being are better for it I am sure. What follows is a piece written in 2017 that combines memoir and auto/biographical fiction (see Letherby 2015 for further discussion and examples).

> **Life in the Shadowlands https://www.abctales.com/story/gletherby/ life-shadowlands (Abridged)**
>
> In the run up to a BIG birthday in January next year I find myself spending a deal of time in reflection... My memoir writing ... is mostly focused on what has already been... [Recently] I have spent a little time in 'What If?' ruminations.
>
> **What If?**
>
> In an alternative universe, a different life, my daughter or son would be well into her/his thirties by now with likely, maybe, possibly, perhaps, beautiful children of their own ..... *There was never any more babies. I wanted to try but it had taken us so long to conceive you and the pregnancy was stressful and precarious and your dad made it clear that for him, if not me, enough was enough. Sick of the arguments—there were more, on other issues, but they came later—I gave up, gave in and lavished my love and my time on you*

my precious boy. After the inevitable divorce (we married too young and our hopes and ideals were just too far apart) your father and I got on better than we had for years and you and I found happiness and fun as part of a new blended family. Despite a few teenage tantrums, that I know you won't want me to share, and I'm sure plenty of adventures that I know nothing about, you thrived. As you grew in stature so you did in character. I hid my distress when after college your chosen career took you (too) far away. Whilst studying you'd return regularly with a full laundry bag and an empty stomach but I was sure that this was the real break for us. A belief, I felt, confirmed when one particular colleague's name kept cropping up in your telephone calls and emails. How does the saying go? 'A daughter's a daughter all of her life, but a son is a son until he takes a wife'. I feel stupid, stupid and ashamed, for thinking this now for it was your marriage and the pregnancy that quickly followed that brought you all back home.

As I sit on the garden swing chair, my youngest grandchild on my lap, the other two either side of me I count my blessings but dwell too on the things I have missed. My own career abandoned for full-time motherhood I never managed to return to the teaching job that challenged and thrilled me in equal measure. A part-time occupation or two here and there but nothing so fulfilling or stretching. Loving you beyond measure there was never regret but what if you had never been born? What might I have done? I'll never know. And I do know how much I'd have missed. Never satisfied, never truly grateful, don't we always wish for what we have not? I'm glad though that it's easier (at least in terms of expectation if not always practically, financially or emotionally) for my daughter-in-law and granddaughters to be more than 'just' mother.

Deborah and Gayle: Stepford Academics

Having contributed, in various ways, to each other's individual work we have also worked together on various projects. Separately we have each written auto/biographically about working and learning in higher education (HE) (e.g. Letherby and Shiels 2001; Langan and Davidson 2005; Langan et al. 2005; Davidson and Langan 2006; Cotterill et al. 2007; Langan et al. 2009; Brown et al. 2015). A few years ago, we do not remember quite how anymore, we had the idea of using the written and visual representation of *The Stepford Wives* (written by Ira Levin [1972], original film 1975) as an analogy for our own, and others' work within higher education. This was prompted, we think, by our growing interest in auto/biographical creative practices, but also by many, many discussions we have had about our roles as educators.

In the book and the 1975 version of the film, Joanna Eberhart is a young amateur photographer with two children who moves to the suburban town of Stepford with her husband, Walter. There is something strange about

Stepford for despite a once healthy, now disbanded women's group, most of the married women in Stepford are positively obsessed with personal appearance and housekeeping. The town seems to be under the control of the 'Men's Association' and its ominous leader, Dale 'Diz' Coba (who once worked for Disneyland). When Walter joins the Men's Association, things begin to turn sinister for Joanna who becomes convinced the wives of Stepford are actually look-alike gynoids. In the final scene, it is clear that Joanna has become yet another Stepford wife shopping in the local super-market, whilst the female half of the first Black family to move to the town appears to be on track to become the next victim.

The popularity of *The Stepford Wives* is reflected not least in the clas-sification of Stepford as an adjective—'Relating to a person who has an unthinking, conformist, and uncritical attitude' www.wordspy.com/words/Stepford.asp. With reference to the increased surveillance of the academic job through, not least, student evaluation and peer review in the context of increased and increasing attention to performativity and the audit culture within the corporate university, we wonder just how far academics have become 'victims' of an academic 'Stepford Lobotomy'.

The concept of 'good motherhood' was significant in Stepford and also within the university. Expectations of women as GOOD moth-ers are well rehearsed. Women are expected to fulfil their 'true' feminine identity (motherhood) albeit in the 'right' economic, sexual, social, etc. circumstances (e.g. Letherby 1994; Woodward 2003; Davidson and Langan 2006). Once mothers, women are expected to follow their instincts and at the same time listen and observe (often male) expert advice (e.g. Letherby 2009). Furthermore, mothers are expected to always put their children first and engage in 'intensive mothering' (e.g. Hays 1998). GOOD academics are similarly expected to put the needs of others before their own. Academics are expected to do it all, teach, research, publish, adapt to and embrace change (e.g. technological, institutional, national) and be enterprising and outward facing (Menzies and Newson 2007; Vostal 2014). Moreover, aca-demics should respond to the needs and demands of various internal and external stakeholders and submit and respond to various kinds of audit (from students, from peers, from managers) in order to earn a 'good' posi-tion in league tables (e.g. Tudiver 1999; Lee 2005; Sparkes 2007; Santiago and Carvalho 2008).

In addition, it is widely acknowledged on 'both sides of the pond' that HE is perceived as a product and HE institutions represent a 'service indus-try' and are thus corporate bodies in their own right. For example, in the UK universities and the departments within them have business plans;

both research and teaching are quality assured (e.g. Research Assessment Exercise, Teaching Quality Assessment), and this external moderation and review has encouraged the development of a particular management focus within institutions to ensure improved performance on the criteria valued by the producers of league tables which appear in the media (Marchbank and Letherby 2001). Similarly, in Canada, Polster and Newson (2015) describe ways in which universities have become more corporatised and education more commodified, highlighting profits over teaching, research and service.

Writing with the Canadian university in mind, but relevant more broadly, Tudiver (1999) argues that the process of corporatisation of the academy has been accomplished in such a way as to obscure its presence. Tudiver documents the incursions of business into the HE sector through a process of 'piecemeal' privatisation: in other words, acquisition of assets without assumption of expenses or liabilities. Unlike other instances of privatisation, Tudiver (1999: 7) notes that university privatisation 'is more subtle, and managed without formal changes in ownerships. Rather, value is transferred through licensing arrangements and partnerships'. Terms like 'partnership', 'sponsorship' and 'stakeholder' occlude this fact (Murray 2002). Thus, the intrusion of corporate interests in universities, and thus on the academic, has been insidious (Tudiver 1999) and is aided and abetted by government under-funding.

The development of a 'charter' mentality, with students as customers, in HE education is significant, for although we as staff may still want to encourage students to develop as people, to think differently about the world and to be excited by knowledge acquisition, increasingly students' concerns are with service provision. Thus, the Stepford Academic is created, promoted and held to account. Reading the book, with the images of film in our heads we were struck again and again by the useful comparison. For example: as Stepford wife Carol to Joanna when Joanna asks if Carol gets out much: '*There's always something or other that has to be done*' Carol said '*You know how it is. I have to finish [cleaning] the kitchen now*' (Levin 1972: 8). Similarly, Stepford wife Mary Ann replies to Joanna's question about the possibility of joining a women's group: '*No, I don't think I'd have any time for anything like that. There's so much to do around the house. You know*' (Levin 1972: 20).

Read this extract from the novel:

The first snow fell on a night when Walter was at the Men's Association.

She watched it from the den window: a scant powder of glittery white, swirling in the light of the walk lamppost. Nothing that would amount to anything. But more would come. Fun, good pictures - and the bother of boots and snowsuits.

Across the street, in the Claybrooks' living-room window, Donna Claybrook sat polishing what looked like an athletic trophy, buffing at it with steady mechanical movements. Joanna watched her and shook her head.

They never stop, these Stepford wives, she thought.

It sounded like the first line of a poem.

They never stop, these Stepford wives. They something something all their lives. Work like robots. Yes, that would fit. They work like robots all their lives.

She smiled. Try sending that to the Chronicle.

She went to the desk and sat down and moved the pen she had left as a placemark on the typed page. She listened for a moment-to the silence from upstairs-and switched the recorder on. With a finger to the page, she leaned toward the microphone propped against the framed Ike Mazzard drawing of her. "Taker. Takes. Taking," she said. "Talcum. Talent.

Talented. Talk. Talkative. Talked. Talker. Talking. Talks." (Levin 1972: 73–74)

And now our rewrite:

The first snow fell on an afternoon when Joanna was at a Faculty Board. She watched it whilst the middle managers all around her talked of ensuring the quality of the student experience. The snow might make it hard to get home; she watched it as it swirled in the walk of the light lamppost. It could fall harder. More would come. She couldn't leave now. She couldn't leave yet.

Across the room the dean of another faculty, was busy polishing his stats on student dis/satisfaction. Pointing at his PowerPoint slides and wowing them with graphs and quotes. Joanna watched and shook her head. They never stop; these Stepford academics, she thought.

It sounded like the first line of mission statement.

They never, stop these Stepford dons. They something, something all their lives. Work like robots. Yes, that would fit. They work like robots all their lives.

She smiled. Try sending that to the university newsletter.

After the meeting she went to her office and sat down and opened the file she had been working on previously. She thought for a moment – listening to the students file out of the nearby lecture theatre. With her fingers on the keyboard she began to type: quality assurance, student support, academic review, student evaluations, budget, cuts, reorganisation, redundancy.

Bryman (2004) argues that the contemporary world is increasingly converging towards the characteristics of the Disney theme parks. This is revealed in: the growing influence of themed environments in settings like restaurants, shops, hotels, tourism and zoos; the growing trend towards social environments that are driven by combinations of forms of consumption: shopping; the growth in cachet awarded to brands based on licensed merchandise; and, particularly relevant for our analysis, the increased prominence of work that is a performance in which the employees have to display certain emotions and generally convey impressions as though working in a theatrical event.

Corporatisation/Disneyisation has consequences for myriad aspects of university culture including on what research is funded, what is taught, which departments and programmes receive university funding. Thus, the Stepford Academic is a creation of both the 'Ivory' and 'Corporate' Towers. Diz would be proud of us.

Instead of the Stepford wife ensuring that her lipstick is colour matched to her frilly, yet innocently provocative frock and the children are happy and all pillows well fluffed, the Stepford Academic, in a similarly circumscribed and managed role, is increasingly forced to maintain and feather the corporate nest. Our gendered analysis is of course no accident, for as Meg Maguire (1996: 27–28) argues women who work in HE 'are concentrated in subordinate positions within an occupation which is organised and managed by dominant male workers from the same occupational class and education background.' Men are much more likely to hold higher positions—both administratively (e.g. head of department and dean) and in relation to research (research professor, director of research centre) and conversely women are much more likely to hold short term contracts and to be located in areas that are considered 'softer' and have less status: i.e. administration and pastoral care rather than research and publications (Letherby and Shiels 2001; Morley 2003). The reasons for this may include the fact that women do not adopt the traditional **male** linear HE career path (e.g. see Cotterill et al. 2007) as they often enter late and are more likely to have a 'broken' career due to family responsibilities (Weiner 1996). And yet, as Aiston and Jung (2015) argue, structural and systemic discrimination in the academic workplace are obscured:

> … we have seen that family is not in all cases operating as a form of negative equity in the prestige economy of higher education. An over-reliance on an explanatory framework which positions family-related related variables as central with respect to the gender research productivity gap has the potential to draw our attention away from other, equally as significant structural and systemic discriminatory practices. (Aiston and Jung 2015: 217)

Furthermore, the academy, like the home, is a 'greedy' institution (Acker 1980) and again gender is significant here. Evidence suggests that whilst women academics are much more likely to be challenged by students (and colleagues) especially when concerned with feminist issues (e.g. Lee 2005; Cotterill et al. 2007), at the same time they suffer from expectations that they, like women in general, are seen as responsible for others' emotional needs where men are not (e.g. Perriton 1999; Davidson and Langan 2006; Cotterill et al. 2007; Flaherty 2018). It is worth noting too that academic women without children might like similar women workers in other occupations and institutions, be considered a resource in that they are seen to have less responsibilities than mothers but similar 'qualities' (Ramsay and Letherby 2006). So:

> Numerous studies have found that female professors shoulder a disproportionate amount of service work compared to their male peers. Research also suggests that students hold female instructors to a different standard than they do male faculty members, especially when it comes to personality. Women are expected to be more nurturing and are perceived harshly when they're not, for example. (Flaherty 2018: n.p.)

Stepford lives on.

Conclusion (Doing It Differently)

Traditionally, autobiographers regarded themselves as autonomous individuals in control of themselves, their lives and their stories (Watson and Kimmich 1999: 1). Yet, increasingly just as those researching the lives of others recognise the interplay between the self and the other in auto/biographical writing so do those writing about themselves:

> … "autobiography[ical]," writing mediates the space between "self" and "life". One definition suggests that autobiography is an effort to recapture the self…This claim presumes that there is such a thing as the "self" and that it is "knowable". This coming-to-knowledge of the self constitutes both the desire that initiates the autobiographical act and the goal toward which autobiography directs itself. Thus the place to begin our investigation of autobiography might be at the crossroads of "writing" and "selfhood". (Benstock 1999: 7)

The creative process and practices we have described depend on visual and written stories told by ourselves—individually and collaboratively—and include our reflections on the stories of others by others. Deborah's research on, and archiving of, commemorative tattoos shows that as visuals, tattoos facilitate storytelling to continue bonds with the deceased and form new bonds with interested others (Davidson and Duhig 2017). Gayle's memoir and academic storytelling challenges tenuously constructed boundaries between fact and fiction and between the academic and the personal. Our 'playing about' with Stepford and Stepfordisation demonstrates how previously written and visual stories can be applied to contemporary scholarship (and life more generally). Think here, for example, of just about anything written by George Orwell, Charles Dickens or Margaret Atwood which are all similarly ripe for reworking. One example of this, written by Gayle:

Bless Us Everyone | Tales of Halloween Past, Present and Future https://arwenackcerebrals.blogspot.com/2016/10/bless-us-everyone-tales-of-halloween.html (Abridged)

A story for Halloween written with apologies (and thanks for the quotes in italics) to Charles Dickens.

*****

Last night I had the strangest dream.

It was All Hallows Eve…. Usually I sleep undisturbed so can only put the dreaming down to the especially tasty piece of rich Stilton that accompanied my port following my lunchtime steak pudding and treacle tart and custard. The *Members Dining Room* at the House does a great range of nosh and I dine there frequently. I was back in my seat just in time to vote against the latest suggested hike in disability benefits. Well the incentives to work really do need to be clear don't you think?

So anyway, I'm asleep—not just in reality but in the dream itself—and I'm woken by a large, but somewhat translucent, bloke, standing at the foot of the bed and introducing himself as the ghost of Halloween past….

The ghost's aim, so he said, was to remind me of Halloween back in the day. I'd forgotten what fun my twin brother and I had curled up with mum under the bed sheets telling scary stories and making spooky shapes on the wall with our torches. Dad was usually at work in the pub, following his day job at the docks. The games stopped when we moved up from primary; me to the grammar and Paul to the secondary modern. Things were never the same between us after that. He still lives close to mum, who's a widow following dad's early death, which is good because I'm too busy to get down much. I offer to help financially but they both shun my generosity. Stupid, really stupid. After all I've got enough. I claim more in expenses than Paul earns in a year. There's a rumour going round that there are going to be some restrictions on what we request in future. *Bah, humbug*, I say….

The next thing I know I'm being woken from another deep slumber by a second apparition, this time promising me an insight into the most significant events in the All Saints' Eve of the moment…. More than ever I'm convinced now that this experience must be diet related; *may be an undigested bit of beef, a blot of mustard, a crumb of cheese, a fragment of underdone potato*.

The final… [visitor's focus] is Halloweens to come and before I know it we are in the centre of my constituency. We pass the local NHS hospital although it appears derelict with boarded up windows and doors. The high street is some-what changed too with every other property either a food or clothes bank. Spoils the look of the place rather and surely not necessary for *if they want to die, then they had better do it and decrease the surplus population.*

I'm left alone for the remainder of the night thank goodness, and my rest is peaceful. On waking I'm refreshed for all is well with my world. *Bless us everyone.*

In our auto/biographical work, we attempt to provide space to explore not only the value of creative practices but also the value of collaboration (at all levels) and of co-construction. There has been some writing about collaborative working in the academy (e.g. Cotterill and Letherby 1997; Davidson and Letherby 2015). More than 30 years ago Fox Keller and Moglen (1987: 505) wrote that such practices be 'tremendously difficult to implement in the real world situation of the academic market'. Furthermore, although collaboration and collegiality on the surface appear to be more (women) friendly than competition and individualism, so-called collegiality in the academy sometimes disguises individual self-interest (Morley 2003). These tensions clearly continue. Yet, there are other ways. Rogers (2017) and Rogers and Tuckwell (2016) argue that 'care-less spaces' and 'care-less-ness' in the academy can create and reproduce animosity and collusion which is damaging not only for academics but also for academic work and knowledge production. We agree and like them we attempt to adopt an 'ethics of care' in our working relationships, with each other and with other others. We cannot know how our work would be different without the influence and the support of the other. We cannot know how our work would be different if our relationship was more 'professional', less 'personal'. What we do know, or at least believe, is that our work is richer for the influence of the other, and that which we do together is some of the most enjoyable that we do. Ellis (1999) writes of attempting a 'heartful autoethnography'. For her this includes:

- the inclusion of researchers' vulnerable selves, emotions, bodies and spirits;
- the production of evocative stories that create the effect of reality;
- the celebration of concrete experience and intimate detail;
- the examination of how human experience is endowed with meaning and a concern with moral, ethical and political consequences, an encouragement of compassion and empathy;
- the featuring of multiple voices;

- the seeking of a fusion between social science and literature;
- and the connecting of the practices of social science with the living of life.

In our auto/biographical collaborative, creative working (and personal) relationship this is what we aim for and constantly, continually revisit and reflect on. No time then to be 'deeply concerned about whether pink soap pads are better than blue ones or visa versa?' (*The Stepford Wives*, Levin 1972: 17).

References

Acker, S. (1980). *Women, the Other Academics*. Equal Opportunities in Higher Education EOC/SRHE Conference, Manchester Polytechnic.

Aiston, S. J., & Jung, J. (2015). Women Academics and Research: An International Comparison. *Gender and Education*. https://doi.org/10.1080/09540253.2015.1 024617.

Beasley, M. (2012). Who Owns Your Skin: Intellectual Property Law and Norms Among Tattoo Artists. *Southern California Law Review, 85*(4), 1137–1182.

Benstock, S. (1999). The Female Self Engendered: Autobiographical Writing and Theories of Selfhood. In M. B. Watson & A. B. Kimmich (Eds.), *Women and Autobiography*. Wilmington: Scholarly Resources Inc.

Bragg, S. (2011). "Now It's Up to Us to Interpret It": Youth Voice and Visual Methods. In P. Thomson & J. Sefton-Green (Eds.), *Researching Creative Learning: Methods and Issues*. London and New York: Routledge.

Brown, N. (2019). Emerging Researcher Perspectives: Finding Your People: My Challenge of Developing a Creative Research Methods Network. *International Journal of Qualitative Methods*. https://doi.org/10.1177/1609406918818644.

Brown, G., Davidson, D., Harvey, J., & Letherby, G. (2015). HE(R)tales: Reflections on Some Auto/Biographical Inter/Multi-connections in Academia. *Auto/Biography Yearbook*. British Sociological Association, Auto/Biography Study Group.

Bryman, A. E. (2004). *The Disneyization of Society*. London: Sage.

Cotterill, P., Jackson, S., & Letherby, G. (2007). *The Challenges and Negotiations of Lifelong Learning for Women in Higher Education*. Dordrecht: Springer.

Cotterill, P., & Letherby, G. (1997). Collaborative Writing: The Pleasure and Perils of Working Together. In M. Ang-Lygate, C. Corrin, & M. S. Henry (Eds.), *Desperately Seeking Sisterhood: Still Challenging and Building*. London: Taylor and Francis.

Davidson, D. (2007). *The Emergence of Hospital Protocols for Perinatal Loss, 1950–2000*. Ph.D. Dissertation, York University, Toronto.

Davidson, D. (2008). A Technology of Care: Caregiver Response to Perinatal Loss. *Women's Studies International Forum, 31*(4), 278–284.

Davidson, D. (2010). Grief, Child Loss. In A. O'Reilly (Ed.), *Encyclopedia of Motherhood* (pp. 466–469). Thousand Oakes: Sage.

Davidson, D. (2011). Reflections on Doing Research Grounded in My Experience of Perinatal Loss: From Auto/Biography to Autoethnography. *Sociological Research Online, 16*(1). http://www.socresonline.org.uk/16/1/6.html.

Davidson, D. (Ed.). (2017). *The Tattoo Project: Visual Culture and the Digital Archive*. Toronto, ON: Canadian Scholars Press.

Davidson, D., & Duhig, A. (2017). Visual Research Methods: Memorial Tattoos as Memory-Realization. In D. Davidson (Ed.), *The Tattoo Project: Visual Culture and the Digital Archive*. Toronto, ON: Canadian Scholars Press.

Davidson, D., & Langan, D. (2006). The Breastfeeding Incident: Teaching and Learning Through Transgression. *Studies in Higher Education, 31*(4), 439–452.

Davidson, D., & Letherby, G. (2014). Griefwork Online: Perinatal Loss, Lifecourse Disruption and Online Support. *Human Fertility, 17*(3), 214–217.

Davidson, D., & Letherby, G. (2015). Embodied Storytelling and Other Work: Loss and Bereavement, Creative Practices and Support. *Illness, Crisis and Loss, 23*(4). https://doi.org/10.1177/1054137315590745.

Davidson, D., & Stahls, H. (2010). Maternal Grief: Creating an Environment for Dialogue. *Journal of the Motherhood Initiative for Research and Community Involvement, 1*(2), 16–25.

Diversi, M. (1998). Glimpses of Street Life: Representing Lived Experience Through Short Stories. *Qualitative Inquiry, 4*(2), 131–147.

Douglas, K., & Carless, D. (2013). An Invitation to Performative Research. *Methodological Innovations Online, 8*(1), 53–64.

Ellis, C. (1999). Heartful Autoethnography. *Qualitative Health Research, 9*(5), 669–683.

Flaherty, C. (2018, January 10). Dancing Backwards in High Heels. *Inside Higher Ed*.

Fox Keller, E., & Moglen, H. (1987). Competition and Feminism: Conflicts for Academic Women. *Signs, 12*(3), 493–510.

Frank, K. (2000). "The Management of Hunger": Using Fiction in Writing Anthropology. *Qualitative Inquiry, 6*(4), 474–488.

Hays, S. (1998). *The Cultural Contradictions of Motherhood*. New Haven: Yale University Press.

Lackey, C. (1994). Social Science Fiction: Writing Sociological Short Stories to Learn About Social Issues. *Teaching Sociology, 22,* 166–173.

Langan, D., & Davidson, D. (2005). Critical Pedagogy and Personal Struggles: Feminist Scholarship Outside Women's Studies. *Feminist Teacher, 15*(2), 132–158.

Langan, D., Sheese, R., & Davidson, D. (2005). Beginning with Values: Constructive Teaching and Learning in Action. In D. Vlosak, G. Kielbaso, & J. Radford (Eds.), *Appreciating the Best of What Is: Envisioning What Could Be. Proceedings of the Sixth*

International Conference on Transformative Learning (pp. 267–272). East Lansing: Michigan Center for Career and Technical Education.

Langan, D., Sheese, R., & Davidson, D. (2009). Beginning with Values: Constructive Teaching and Learning in Action. In J. Mezirow, E. Taylor, & Associates (Eds.), *Transformative Learning in Practice: Insights from Community, Workplace, and Higher Education* (pp. 46–56). San Francisco: Jossey-Bass.

Lee, D. (2005). Students and Managers Behaving Badly: An Exploratory Analysis of the Vulnerability of Feminist Academics in Anti-feminist, Market-Driven UK Higher Education. *Women's Studies International Forum, 28*(2–3), 195–208.

Letherby, G. (1994). Mother or Not, Mother or What? Problems of Definition and Identity. *Women's Studies International Forum, 17*(5), 525–532.

Letherby, G. (2003). *Feminist Research in Theory and Practice*. Buckingham: Open University.

Letherby, G. (2009). *Educated for Motherhood: Natural Instincts Versus Expert Advice*. ESRC Seminar—Changing Parenting Culture, University of Kent.

Letherby, G. (2013). Theorised Subjectivity. In G. Letherby, J. Scott, & M. Williams (Eds.), *Objectivity and Subjectivity in Social Research*. London: Sage.

Letherby, G. (2015). Bathwater, Babies and Other Losses: A Personal and Academic Story. *Mortality: Promoting the Interdisciplinary Study of Death and Dying, 20*(2). https://www.tandfonline.com/doi/abs/10.1080/13576275.2014.989494.

Letherby, G., & Davidson, D. (2017a). Creative Methodologies. In D. Davidson (Ed.), *The Tattoo Project: Visual Culture and the Digital Archive*. Toronto, ON: Canadian Scholars Press.

Letherby, G., & Davidson, D. (2017b). Tattooing as Auto/Biographical Practice. In D. Davidson (Ed.), *The Tattoo Project: Visual Culture and the Digital Archive*. Toronto, ON: Canadian Scholars Press.

Letherby, G., & Shiels, J. (2001). Isn't He Good, but Can We Take Her Seriously? In P. Anderson & J. Williams (Eds.), *Identity and Difference in Higher Education*. London: Ashgate.

Levin, I. (1972). *The Stepford Wives*. New York: Random House.

Maguire, M. (1996). 'In the Prime of Their Lives?' Older Women in Higher Education. In L. Morley & V. Walsh (Eds.), *Breaking Boundaries: Women in Higher Education*. London: Routledge.

Marchbank, J., & Letherby, G. (2001). Offensive and Defensive: Feminist Pedagogy, Student Support and Higher Education. In G. Howie & A. Tauchert (Eds.), *Gender, Teaching and Research in Higher Education: Challenges for the 21st Century*. London: Ashgate.

Menzies, H., & Newson, J. (2007). No Time to Think: Academics' Life in the Globally Wired University. *Time and Society*. https://doi.org/10.1177/0961463X07074103.

Miller, V. (2011). *Understanding Digital Culture*. Thousand Oaks: Sage.

Mills, C. W. (1959). *The Sociological Imagination*. London: Penguin.

Morgan, D. (1998). Sociological Imaginations and Imagining Sociologies: Bodies, Auto/Biographies and Other Mysteries. *Sociology, 32*(4), 647–663.

Morley, L. (2003). *Quality and Power in Higher Education.* Maidenhead: SRHE/OU Press.

Murray, H. (2002). Universities for Sale: Resisting Corporate Control Over Canadian Higher Education by Neil Tudiver. *University of Toronto Quarterly, 72*(1), 308–314.

Pauwels, L. (2011). An Integrated Conceptual Framework for Visual Social Research. In E. Margolis & L. Pauwels (Eds.), *The Sage Handbook of Visual Research Methods.* Los Angeles: Sage.

Pelias, R. (2008). Performative Inquiry: Embodiment and Its Challenges. In J. Knowles & A. Cole (Eds.), *Handbook of the Arts in Qualitative Research* (pp. 185–193). Thousand Oaks, CA: Sage.

Perriton, L. (1999). The Provocative and Evocative Gaze Upon Women in Management Development. *Gender and Education, 11*(3), 295–307.

Polster, C., & Newson, J. (2015). *A Penny for Your Thoughts: How Corporatization Devalues Teaching, Research, and Public Service in Canada's Universities.* Ottawa: Canadian Centre for Policy Alternatives.

Ramsay, K., & Letherby, G. (2006). The Experience of Academic Nonmothers in the Gendered University. *Gender, Work and Organisation, 13*(1), 25–44.

Richardson, L. (1994). Writing: A Method of Inquiry. In N. Denzin & Y. Lincoln (Eds.), *A Handbook of Qualitative Research* (1st ed.). Thousand Oaks: Sage.

Rogers, C. (2017). "I'm Complicit and I'm Ambivalent and That's Crazy": Careless Spaces for Women in the Academy. *Women's Studies International Forum, 61,* 115–122.

Rogers, C., & Tuckwell, S. (2016). Co-constructed Caring Research and Intellectual Disability: An Exploration of Friendship, Intimacy and Being Human. *Sexualities, 19*(5–6), 623–640.

Santiago, R., & Carvalho, T. (2008). Academics in a New Work Environment: The Impact of New Public Management on Work Conditions. *Higher Education Quarterly, 62*(3), 204–223.

Sparkes, A. (2002). *Telling Tales in Sport and Physical Activity: A Qualitative Journey.* Leeds: Human Kinetics.

Sparkes, A. (2007). *Embodiment, Academics, and the Audit Culture: A Story Seeking Consideration.* https://doi.org/10.1177/1468794107082306.

Spencer, S. (2011). *Visual Research Methods in the Social Sciences: Awakening Vision.* London: Routledge.

Tierney, W. (1998). Life History's History. *Qualitative Inquiry, 4*(1), 49–70.

Tudiver, J. (1999). *Universities for Sale: Resisting Corporate Control Over Canadian Higher Education.* Toronto: James Lorimer and Company Ltd., Publishers.

Vostal, F. (2014). *Academic Life in the Fast Lane: The Experience of Time and Speed in British Academia.* https://doi.org/10.1177/0961463X13517537.

Watson, M. B., & Kimmich, A. B. (Eds.). (1999). *Women and Autobiography*. Wilmington: Scholarly Resources Inc.

Weiner, G. (1996). Which of Us Has a Brilliant Career? Notes for a Higher Education Survivor. In R. Cuthbert (Ed.), *Working in Higher Education*. Buckingham: Open University.

Woodward, K. (2003). Representations of Motherhood. In S. Earle & G. Letherby (Eds.), *Gender, Identity and Reproduction: Social Perspectives*. Houndmills: Palgrave Macmillan.

Part II

Families and Relationships: Auto/Biography and Family—A Natural Affinity?

David Morgan

There would seem to be an almost natural affinity between auto/biography and family. A life begins with birth and in the majority of cases this birth takes place within a set of family relationships. These family configurations (Widmer and Jallinoja 2008) may be extended or truncated, and they may frequently include significant others who are not related by birth or through marriage. They change in size and composition over time. Where such configurations do not exist, this will be a matter for extended comment and speculation.

Certainly, in modern times there is a strong expectation that any published biography or auto/biography will contain at least one chapter devoted to the subject's family of origin. In some cases, these accounts may go back over two or more generations. Although the subject is usually of interest because of her or his current status within sport, entertainment, politics or the arts, the published account would seem to be incomplete if it excluded all accounts of childhood and growing up. At the most simple level, such accounts of childhood provide points of connection between the reader and the subject, connections which may become lost as the subject enters into the more public realms. But these accounts are also seen as important in that they help the reader to place the subject in a variety of ways.

First, such accounts serve to 'place' the subject socially, showing family connections and the ways in which these connections identify, give solidity to, class, ethnic, national or religious backgrounds. To read such accounts is to gain some sense of social and geographical mobility and of the degrees of continuity or rupture between the families of origin and the lives and experiences of the subject in adult life. At one extreme, the subject seems to be embedded into a particular social milieu and the subsequent career a continuation, extension or modified version of these early configurations. At the other extreme, there is a clear sense of rupture, of distance travelled between the early worlds of family and childhood and later achievements.

Second, accounts of early childhood and the family configurations within which childhood is lived, place the subject psychologically. In a post-Freudian world, it is customary, almost mandatory, to look to childhood experiences in order to discover clues to the subject's adult character. In some cases, these may be major family dramas dealing with neglect, abuse, separation or divided claims and loyalties. In others, it may be more a matter of certain traits being, it is supposed, carried over from one generation to another. A mother's interest in amateur dramatics may be believed to be a clue to a daughter's Oscar award. Diffused, and frequently unexamined, ideas about genetics and psycho-analysis help to account for the abiding fascination of accounts of early childhood in published auto/biographies. This fascination. Is reflected, for example, in the popularity of programmes such as '*Who Do You Think You Are?*'. (A popular BBC television programme in which celebrities, with the aid of archivists and historians, explore their genealogies.)

Finally, such accounts of early family life help to place the subject historically. Even the most minimal pieces of information such as date and place of birth can provide strong hints as to the historical events and changes that the subject passed through. If the reader, the author and/or the subject have some points of overlap in terms of historical experience, this may give rise to a kind of sharing and an understanding of commonalities and differences. Even where there may be decades or centuries between the subject and reader—say between a reader of today and Samuel Pepys for example—there will still frequently be that sense of an appreciation of the links between biography and history that Mills saw at the heart of the 'sociological imagination' (Mills 1959). The historical appreciation, it must be stressed, is not simply to do with major events such as The Great Fire of London (1666, recorded, among other sources, in Samuel Pepys' diaries) or the UK General Strike of 1926, but to do with the very character of everyday life and its points of difference from or overlap with the everyday life of later times.

Thus, the links between family life and auto/biography can be seen most clearly in these accounts of childhood that frequently, almost inevitably, are to be found in the first chapters of published works. These accounts, it has been argued, help to 'place' the subject socially, psychologically and historically. These accounts are often vivid and frequently provide points of connection between readers and subject.

But, of course, family life does not cease once the subject has left home. Not only do old and existing relationships persist in their influences and significance but new relationships are established and add to existing family configurations. If these later relationships sometimes lack the immediacy of these earlier accounts it may be partly due to a desire to preserve privacies (or to avoid legal action) and partly due to the fact that personal relationships are now competing with public lives and public roles. In studying the backgrounds of Anglican bishops, I frequently discovered relatively sparse references to the subjects' marriages and later family lives. Wives might be sometimes named and placed, socially, and described as 'helpmeets' but as little more. (Morgan 1981). Clearly, some sense of the divisions between public and private was at play here as well as, perhaps, some patriarchal assumptions. The way in which public lives tend to eclipse private lives can sometimes be evidenced in the obituaries published in newspapers or other outlets. Here it is not unusual for the account to focus almost entirely on the public achievements of the subject, simply noting, at the end, marriages and children.

Auto/Biographical accounts, published or unpublished, may provide valuable source material for scholars, especially sociologists, interested in family life (Summerfield 2019). But it should be clear from what has been said so far that such material does not imply or unambiguously provide data about everyday family living. As the bishops' example in the previous paragraph demonstrates, sometimes absences may be as significant as what is actually printed or published. More generally, it can be recognised that what we have before us in these accounts are representations or constructions of or discourses about family. Such accounts need to be interrogated for the way in which family is presented or displayed (Finch 2007).

Over the past twenty or thirty years, family researchers have made clear moves away from writing about *the Family* as if it were some relatively stable system or structure performing clearly identifiable functions for societies and individuals and towards addressing something more fluid and open (McKie and Cunningham-Burley 2005; Morgan 2011; Widmer and Jallinoja 2008). In some cases, family relationships may be seen as part, often an important part, of some wider set of relationships such as intimacy (Jamieson 1998) or personal life (Smart 2007). An example of this increasing fluidity in understanding family relationships is provided by discussions of family boundaries (McKie and Cunningham-Burley 2005). Who is included or excluded in a particular family? How do these inclusions or exclusions vary according to external events or changes over the life course? How far do family configurations include persons not formally related by birth or marriage?

These questions clearly connect to discussions of social networks and personal communities which frequently, but not necessarily, include family ties (Spencer and Pahl 2006).

This stress on openness and fluidity in our understanding of 'family' would seem to enhance the affinity between auto/biographical enquiry and family life. The everyday 'messiness' of family life and relationships frequently becomes apparent in our readings of the early chapters of auto/biographies. Put simply, family life rarely conforms to some pre-ordained script of the kind found in some social science models as well as in ideological and cultural representations. This simple insight can be enhanced and enriched by a study of auto/biographical accounts. The emphasis shifts from a search for illustrations of some essential nature of family relationships to, for example, a study of how family gets 'done' (Morgan 2011) or 'displayed' (Finch 2007). There is, in other words, an affinity between family practices and auto/biographical practices. Thus, for example, everyday accounts or presentations of 'family troubles' are both accounts of particular troubles that affect individuals and also presentations of 'family' and the ways in which family relationships are constituted and reconstituted on a day-to-day basis. Auto/Biographical accounts frequent force the readers to take the messiness of everyday family life seriously and not just as some kind of aberration.

One way of exploring the relationship between family practices and auto/biographical practices is to view family living as a 'nexus of stories'. It is likely that any collectivity—a community, a workplace or whatever—can be seen in this way (Morgan 2005). The everyday life of any collective arrangement is constituted and reconstituted, given a sense of reality, through the stories that members tell each other. These stories may be latent or manifest, formal or informal, big or small. They form part of everyday experience and part of the way in which these wider collectivities are reproduced.

Families provide one example of this way of viewing social collectivities but it is likely that the role of story-telling is frequently both more likely and more significant in family configurations. This is because of the co-presence (in actual awareness if not always in terms of physical presence) of people of different ages and generations. Moreover, some of these people are constructed as having responsibilities for others (Finch 1989; Finch and Mason 1993). Further, many of life's most dramatic experiences to do with sickness, abuse, disability and death occur in and are amplified by the family constellations within which they take place. The stories within families may constitute links between siblings, between partners and across generations. Such stories may unite or divide. They can provide links between the living and the dead and between the absent and the present. A family without such stories is barely deserving of the name.

To talk of a 'nexus of stories' is not to imply equal participation. Some may be listeners or observers rather than key narrators and such differences may reflect power differentials (to do with age or gender) within families. These positionings will, of course, vary over time and today's listener may become tomorrow's narrator. The development of new media of communication means that such storytelling does not always require the bodily co-presence of all participants. Further, some of the key practices of social enquiry such as qualitative interviews or oral histories may provide further occasions for the presentation of family through stories.

It is important to note that although these stories involve family members, past and present, and play a role in the reproduction of family connections and identifications, they are rarely just about families. They are also about times past, the times and the contexts within which family practices were played out, how things have changed and how they have remained the same. Thus, family life and family stories provide important mediators between individual autobiography and history and hence are an important constituent of the 'sociological imagination' (Mills 1959).

A key feature of family life, and one that is often marginalised in some accounts, is intergenerationality. Public concerns about divorce, co-habitation, lone-parents and so on tend to lose sight of the fact that, whatever happens to our adult marital or relational ties, individuals remain connected to family others over time and over generations. Paul Thompson's demand that we should see family as 'an intergenerational system of interlocking social and emotional relationships' (Thompson 2005: 27) expresses this clearly. Indeed, it may be argued that as ties within generations sometimes appear to be becoming more threatened, ties across two or more generations become the more important. Such ties may be of practical importance as when we consider the wealth and property that may be handed down across generations (Finch and Mason 2000). But of at least equal importance, from the point of view of this part, are the family scripts and myths and secrets that are passed down and which are woven into the stories that family members tell to each other (Brannen 2015; Thompson 2005).

The term 'generation', as has frequently been pointed out, has at least two meanings. One is more closely related to the individual and to his or her placement in family relationships over time. Thus, an individual may make references to 'my father's generation' or 'my grandmother's generation'. But even here, although it is an individual making this placement, there are strong suggestions of larger groupings. To refer to 'my father's generation' is to look beyond a particular individual and to see that individual in relation to sets of others, related or un-related, who enjoy a rough commonality in terms of being born at around the same time. Even here, we are making some kind of linking between individuals and history.

The other meaning of 'generation' confronts this question of history more directly. Conventionally, there may be references to decades; the 'nineteen sixties', the 'nineteen seventies' and so on. But frequently, these rather artificial designations may be replaced by something more historically descriptive. Thus, people may talk of 'the baby boomers', 'Thatcher's children', the 'inter-war generation' and so on. These designations are often fluid and overlap with each other, providing only a rough sense of commonality. But their use also highlights the ways in which ideas of generation serve to locate individuals and to provide the links between individuals and history. Thus, the stories which link family members are stories of particular individuals who have undergone particular historical experiences. It is here, in generations, that we see the link between family practices and auto/biographical practices.

In this focus on the stories told and the way in which these provide links across generations, it is important to recognise that these links, and the experiences which go with them, are never uniformly positive. Intergenerational relationships are frequently characterised by degrees of ambivalence (Brannen 2015: 35). This may reflect differences in perceived power, gender or, sometimes social class, as individuals move away from their families of origin, socially and geographically. They may reflect conflicting or competing obligations or contradictions between ideal, imagined families and everyday realities. But more generally the idea of ambivalence here indicates the fluctuating mixtures of the positives and the negatives in encounters between the generations.

The theme of generation, which so clearly links family and auto/biographical practices, is clearly to do with the location of individuals in time. Equally, we must see these individuals as being located in space. Here we are principally dealing with the idea of 'home' and the actual spatial location of many family practices. As with the term 'generation', the idea of home brings together many different themes and meanings. Most directly, there is the physical location, the meanings that attach to the rooms, surrounds and entrances, the material and economic significance of the home as property and as an investment (Holdsworth and Morgan 2005; Richards 1990). There are the ideological meanings of the idea of home with the links to notion of personal property and individual achievement. There are the emotional meanings of home, both positive and negative, ideas of home as a refuge or a prison.

It is the more material aspects of home that sometimes gets missed in sociological accounts of family living. Yet this is of considerable importance, providing links between family, the economy, the state and the local community. Further, this materiality does not end with the actual physical construction of the house or the apartment. It continues with the material items that individuals bring into the home and which become as much part of the home as the actual dwelling. These are the pots and pans, the items of furniture, the personal effects which, in the past were often detailed in wills and inventories. We are also talking about the pictures on the walls, the items on the mantelpiece (Hurdley 2013), the paint or the paper on the walls. These material items, with their own histories and provenances, also combine to construct the emotional space of the home.

Of course, people do not always live in family-based households. They may live on the streets, in temporary accommodation or in total institutions such a prisons or hospitals (Goffman 1968). In these cases, there may be a gulf between imagined or ideological constructions of home and the current reality. But ideas of the physical and emotional basis of home may exist in memories or in imaginations and become part of individuals' locations in social space.

Introducing the Three Chapters

Julia Brannen begins her chapter with an introduction to some of the many strands in biographical research and indicating their relevance for family studies. As with much family research, life stories can either be grand narratives or they may deal with the experiences of everyday life. Narrating stories is not simply the provision of valuable source material for researchers; it is also a key element in the continuous construction of personal identities. She considers three key figures in the development of biographical research -Thomas and Znaniecki, C. W. Mills and G. Elder—and it is important to note that family relationships over time are central concerns for the first and the third of these researchers. She indicates the links with developments in oral history and focuses on one particular approach: the 'biographic-narrative interpretive method' or BNIM (Wengraf 2001).

Issues of methodology are at the heart of this, and other, biographical approaches. These deal with questions of memory, the interactions between the interviewer and the subject, the way in which stories are constructed in the course of an interview and the links between these stories and wider narrative conventions. A key distinction is between the 'lived life' and the 'told story' and this highlights the hard work that is required in teasing out the differences between them. Thus, it may be easy to discover that, say, an individual migrated to England in 1950. But to contextualise this movement, to come to an understanding of the part this move played in the construction of a life requires considerable interpretive skill.

Brannen chooses as an extended illustration the stories of an Irish migrant grandfather, Connor, and his adult son, Murray. In so doing, she reflects and develops the growing interest in inter-generational research. In some ways, these are highly contrasting stories. Connor loses both parents and breaks his back as an infant and spends some time at an Irish industrial school. His is a story not only of a geographical move but a social move to a position as a foreman in a major building site. His son, has wholly different experiences, seeing his life as a 'playground' and having a well-paid position in finance in the City. As might be expected, there is evidence of continuities (Murray acknowledges the formative influence of his father) and difference. (It is possible, for example, to see marked differences in fatherhood practices).

Wider analysis, of course, would link these stories to other intergenerational accounts, painstakingly building up sets of stories which are not simply memorable stories of individuals but which also provide accounts which point to wider historical changes. Further, by considering the very processes by which these stories are generated we come to an appreciation of their significance in the construction of personal identities and understandings of family life.

Elizaveta Polukhina's chapter focuses primarily on housing, specifically inequalities in housing in Post-Soviet Russia. Housing can be seen from two perspectives. At the more macro-level, inequalities in housing are the outcome of the complex exchanges between State, market and family. In this particular account, the story is one of a move from a context where the State played the dominant role to one where greater importance was assumed by the market and family relationships. At the more individual level, housing provides the framework for the lived experiences of much of family life. Polukhina's account moves from the large-scale historical changes to the more experiential level where housing interacts with family relationships and self-identities.

Polukhina's discussion is concerned mainly with the methods of enquiry into housing inequalities and experiences across the life course. While large-scale surveys and censuses clearly have an important part to play in exploring inequalities in housing life chances, there are also limitations in these approaches. There is a need, even within quantitative research, for more complex, compounded measures to recognise and explore diversities.

Similarly, more complex understandings of social class are required in this exploration (Savage 2015). Research needs to be alert to the complexities of meanings attached to apparently everyday (in the Russian context) words such as 'barracks' or 'cottages'.

Polukhina's account demonstrates the important role that can be played by qualitative ethnographic research with a strong auto/biographical emphasis. Such approaches can explore the changing meanings and experiences over time and can alert the reader to differences within (in terms of gender and generation) as well as between households. Such an approach may provide a more complex understanding of the very different significance of the role of family and intergenerational ties within different social classes. The better-off may, as in the UK, benefit from financial help from the 'bank of mum and dad'. Less well-off may find themselves sharing accommodation with members of different family generations. Hence, everyday talk (say to an interviewer) about housing may take on a particular sensitivity (other family members may be listening) or may provide an opportunity for a more elaborate presentation of self. Here, as elsewhere, the processes of social enquiry may be just as important as any actual findings.

An account of housing inequalities in Post-Soviet Russia is, of course, of considerable interest in its own right. But here, it provides an insightful case-study into the interplays between housing, family and auto/biography. This discussion clearly demonstrates the roles of gender, generation and class in shaping access to and use of housing in a particular historical context.

In the third paper by Aidan Seery and Karin Bacon, the close connections between auto/biography and family life are explored directly. There are two distinctive features of their discussion. The first is the distinctive source material, a set of letters written on a school exercise book and circulated between a set of siblings. This correspondence not only provides insights into what individuals are experiencing and feeling on a shared basis but also continuously reaffirms a particular set of family ties. It is a form of family display (Finch 2007) although one largely for internal consumption.

Second, these exchanges take place at a very distinctive period of Irish history, one which includes the Easter uprising of 1916 and the subsequently civil war. All auto/biographical practices take place in a historical context but here we see a particularly powerful meeting of history and individual lives. Not only are these young correspondents increasingly and actively caught up in these wider struggles but some of them went on to play an active part in the politics of the new Irish state.

Using the lives of three of these siblings (there were 12 in all), Seery and Bacon elaborate some key ideas about the relationships between auto/biographical and family practices. The first is the idea of the family being both 'networked and internalised'. Family is always more than a collection of individuals; it is best seen as a fluid set or network of relationships that change over time. This complex, networked family is the one that individuals internalise and live with. The stories that are shared, told and retold, serve to recreate and reaffirm the family ties within which these exchanges take place.

The second key idea is that 'changes in narrated family relations over time are a reflection of individual life changes'. The authors were fortunate enough to have access both to accounts of events and feelings close to the time that they actually happened and to accounts, recounted in interviews, several years later. How individuals view particular events and their part in them varies according to their own life trajectories as well as the occasions and audiences for the presentation of particular recollections. Over time, of course, these individual siblings entered into relationships and had children themselves. They remained siblings but their shared sense of family would change over time.

The final idea deals with 'family narrative as distributed autobiographical knowledge'. This emphasises the essentially relational character of family and auto/biographical practices. We see in this chapter accounts of events and encounters which do not simply reflect the fact that their recounting takes place between family members but which also constitute those family relationships. The authors write of a 'familial self' which reflects the strong links over time between family members and which impact upon individual selves. In this case, we have a family self which is middle-class, educated and which, perhaps unusually for the time, is strongly supportive of the aspirations of women. Sometimes, this distributed family self may over-ride deep political divisions such as those which accompanied the Irish civil war.

As part of this process, we read of the role of the family farm, a 150 acre estate at Tomcoole. This played an important role in shared family experiences and subsequent holidays for young generations. This shared space, with all its memories, to some extent transcended possible divisions. More generally, it demonstrates the importance of place and space in the construction of family identities albeit, in this case, ones associated with a relatively privileged group of individuals.

Concluding Remarks

This part has been designed with the aim of demonstrating the close connections between the practices of auto/biography and family life. There can be no auto/biography without some reference, positive or negative, to family life and family life itself is constituted and reconstituted through stories and narratives. This can be seen in the way in which accounts of family life, especially but not exclusively of childhood and early years, serve to 'place' individuals. These accounts can place individuals socially. We can see this clearly in the accounts of the educated Irish middle-class in Seery and Bacon's chapter and in the accounts of social and geographical mobility in Brannen's presentation of Connor and Murray. This kind of social placing is also present in the quotations provided by Polukhina who clearly demonstrates the key importance of social class in the housing careers in post-Soviet Russia.

Psychological placing is clearly present in the accounts we have of Connor's childhood and the contrasting fathering practices between Connor and his son, Murray. Psychological placing of a different, perhaps more gentle, kind is shown in the relationships between siblings presented in the final paper. This kind of placing is, initially, less apparent in Polukhina's account until we consider the enforced family density experienced by some of her subjects and the concerns about who might be listening to the exchanges between interviewer and subjects.

Historical placing is evident in all three accounts. Thus we have the dramatic experiences of the struggles for Irish independence and the moves to a post-Soviet Russia. Connor's story, in Brannen's paper, begins post-Irish independence although it is likely that stories of the earlier struggles continue to have their influence. Instead, we have the changing relationships between the British and Irish economies and the experiences of migration. The close relationships between auto/biography and history are clearly apparent in the three papers.

A key element in the linking of family and auto/biography is the idea of generation. This is itself a complex and multi-stranded theme, playing out at both individual and more collective levels. In terms of individual experiences, generations provide the basis for intra-familial exchanges and, with them, ambivalences. This is clearly demonstrated in Polukhina's account where it is frequently the case that members of the working classes are required to share accommodations with members of other generations. In the other two accounts, we see how the various capitals (economic, social and cultural) are passed on across generations and how these exchanges solidify the links between family living and social class.

At a more macro-level, generations provide links between individual life chances and experiences and historical change. Individuals do not simply, and passively, experience historical change but they are part of cohorts which move through history, which respond in different ways to these changes and, sometimes, can be seen as having an active part in shaping these changes. This last point can be seen most clearly in the case of the Ryan family, discussed in the paper by Seery and Bacon. The story of Connor is both an individual story and an illustration of wider patterns of migration between Ireland and Britain. In the Russian case, historical change is given physical shape in the accounts of the barracks and cottages that provide accommodation for members of different social classes and different times.

Polukhina's account is the one that focuses most directly on the physical settings of family relations, the ideas of and the aspirations for home. Her photographs of exteriors and interiors are not just illustrations but are demonstrations of places and spaces as convergences of meanings. The same meetings of meanings can also be seen in the account of the family farm at Tomcoole, a place of shared memories and shared family practices. Themes of home are not directly developed in Brannen's account but there are hints of a more fluid understanding as when Connor describes Britain as his 'second home' and Murray refers to the 'bomb-site' that was his childhood playground and around this, the general background of post-war urban renewal.

The key terms in family analysis—generations, home and place and stories—are, it has been noted at several points in this part, never just about individual families or more general notions of family. They are also about the contexts within which family practices are performed. Migration, civil war and social reconstruction provide some of the contexts for the family stories presented in this part. In reading these stories, we can enhance a more general understanding of how historical contexts can impact upon individual lives lived out within family constellations.

Family life, it was suggested, might be seen as a 'nexus of stories'. These are stories which not only take place within and across generations and within locations often described as 'homes' but which also serve to constitute these homes and generations. The stories might be the stories which, frequently well-rehearsed, that individuals tell to interviewers or researchers. Or they may be stories directly but artfully included in correspondence that is shared between family members. These stories, short or more elaborated, vary with the time of their telling and the audiences to which they are presented. However, and whenever the stories occur, they provide potent illustrations of the close relationships between auto/biography and family living.

References

Brannen, J. (2015). *Fathers and Sons: Generations, Families and Migration.* Basingstoke: Palgrave Macmillan

Finch, J. (1989). *Family Obligations and Social Change.* Cambridge: Polity.

Finch, J. (2007). Displaying Families. *Sociology, 41*(1) 65–81.

Finch, J., & Mason, J. (1993). *Negotiating Family Responsibilities.* London: Routledge.

Finch, J., & Mason, J. (2000). *Passing On: Kinship and Inheritance in England.* London: Routledge.

Goffman, E. (1968). *Asylums: Essays on the Social Situations of Mental Patients and Other Inmates.* Harmondsworth: Penguin.

Holdsworth, C., & Morgan, D. (2005). *Transitions in Context: Leaving Home, Independence and Adulthood.* Maidenhead, Open University Press.

Hurdley, R. (2013). *Home, Materiality, Memory and Belonging: Keeping Culture.* Basingstoke: Palgrave Macmillan.

Jamieson, L. (1998). *Intimacy: Personal Relationships in Modern Societies.* Cambridge: Polity.

McKie, L., & Cunningham-Burley, S. (Eds.). (2005). *Families in Society: Boundaries and Relationships.* Bristol: The Policy Press.

Mills, C. W. (1959). *The Sociological Imagination Oxford.* Oxford: Oxford University Press.

Morgan, D. (1981). Men, Masculinity and the Process of Sociological Enquiry. In H. Roberts (Ed.), *Doing Feminist Research London* (pp. 83–113). London: Routledge.

Morgan, D. (2005). Revisiting 'Communities in Britain'. *Sociological Review, 53*(4), 641–657.

Morgan, D. (2011). *Rethinking Family Practices.* Basingstoke: Palgrave Macmillan.

Richards, L. (1990). *Nobody's Home: Dreams and Reality in a New Suburb.* Oxford: Oxford University Press.

Savage, M. (2015). *Social Class in the Twenty-First Century.* London: Pelican.

Smart, C. (2007). *Personal Life Cambridge.* Cambridge: Polity.

Spencer, L., & Pahl, R. (2006). *Rethinking Friendship: Hidden Solidaries Today.* Princeton: Princeton University Press.

Summerfield, P. (2019). *Histories of the Self: Personal Narrative and Historical Practice.* London: Routledge.

Thompson, P. (2005). Family Myth, Models and Denials in Shaping Individual Biographies. In D. Bertaux & P. Thompson (Eds.), *Between Generations: Family Models, Myths and Memories* (2nd ed., pp. 13–38). Oxford: Oxford University Press.

Wengraf, T. (2001). *Qualitative Research Interviewing: Biographic, Narrative and Semi-Structured Methods.* London: Sage.

Widmer, E. D., & Jallinoja, R. (2008). *Beyond the Nuclear Family: Families in a Configurational Perspective.* Bern: Peter Lang Publishing.

5

Life Story and Narrative Approaches in the Study of Family Lives

Julia Brannen

Introduction

The term biography refers to a record, spoken or written, of a person's past life and the life course transitions and events that make it up; biographies are examinations of people's experiences and life course trajectories relating to family life and other social domains. But biographies are also more than this: they are stories that people tell about themselves or about others' lives. Life stories are therefore narrative accounts. However, they represent only one end of the 'narrative spectrum' and are typically referred to as 'grand narratives'. At the other end of the spectrum, narratives refer to accounts about the present or recent experiences and practices of daily life many of which constitute 'family practices' (Morgan 2011). Bamberg (2006) terms these narratives 'small stories' or partial narratives. Narratives of this latter variety provide a means by which social actors construct their identities over time, '[they are] constructive means that are functional in the creation of characters in space and time, which in turn are instrumental for the creation of positions vis-à-vis co-conversationalists…. [they] are aspects of situated language use, employed by speakers/narrators to position a display of situated, contextualized identities' (Bamberg and Georgakopoulou 2008: 2).

J. Brannen (✉)
UCL Institute of Education, London, UK
e-mail: j.brannen@ucl.ac.uk

© The Author(s) 2020
J. M. Parsons and A. Chappell (eds.), *The Palgrave Handbook of Auto/Biography*,
https://doi.org/10.1007/978-3-030-31974-8_5

Sociology is by definition about the inseparability of 'individuals' and 'society'. In this context it is relevant to highlight linkages between family members, in particular the significance of family history. Little attention has been paid by sociologists to families as they are constituted over time and across generations. Rather more attention has been given to the study of contemporary family life or as it is practiced in the everyday. However, in the context of the growth in longevity and growing generational fissures in society, for example, concerning voting patterns and geographical location as reported by the Intergenerational Foundation (2016), relations across family generations are attracting increased interest. From a sociological perspective, as Smart suggests, family members are part of lineages and each family member carries with them 'echoes of the past':

> It is impossible to imagine a family without the sense that it is part of a lineage; that the people who are the current parent generation are the children of the previous generation and that they carry with them some sense or aura (not to mention genes) of those who have gone before. Being part of a lineage carries with it echoes of the past, plus an embeddedness in what went (or who went) before. The past and the present are therefore intertwined and each gives meaning to the other. (Smart 2011: 543)

If we are to understand family life as both the reproduction of the past and as the engagement with and transformation of the present, biographical and narrative approaches are apposite in recording and interpreting the accounts and experiences of several generations in a family. In the rest of the chapter, I will draw upon my research on the study of multi-generation families in which biographical and narrative methods were applied. As an exemplar of the application of these approaches I will take a case of a migrant grandfather and his adult son. The case will offer insight into how family and other practices (Morgan 2011), in the sense of both meanings and actions, are negotiated and are subject to change and continuity across time and family generations. But first the chapter will begin with a very brief history of the development of biographical approaches and a discussion of some of the differences between biographical and narrative research.

Biographical Methods: A Little History

Among the key figures who have shaped the development of biographical methods are William I. Thomas and Florian Znaniecki, members of the Chicago School in the early twentieth century. Their book *The Polish Peasant in Europe and America* is considered to be the first biographical study in sociology.[1] At the time Chicago was the fastest growing North-American city with a huge immigrant population that had more than its share of social problems. These researchers set out to study the families, communities and social ties of the Polish migrants both before and after migration, drawing on personal documents, such as life histories, letters, diaries, and other first-person material. This work had a major influence on the urban sociologists in the Chicago School[2]; they treated the biographical material they collected as individual 'cases' in the sense of the term employed in social work (Nilsen and Brannen 2011) while analysing these in the relation to the communities in which they were situated.

A second key figure typically cited in the history of biographical approaches is C. Wright Mills whose insistence that equal attention be paid to history and biography left an indelible mark on sociology. Like those in the Chicago school he too drew on American Pragmatism. Although Mills did not carry out biographical studies, his influence on the field was significant especially in contributing to the revival of biographical research in the 1970s: in particular his insistence that research questions should be located at the intersection of individual biography and society (Nilsen and Brannen 2011).

A third key figure is Glen Elder. His cohort studies were groundbreaking for the way in which he analysed the ordering of phases in the life course and their relationship to historical processes, social structure and social institutions. Here, the life course is seen as 'consisting of age-graded patterns that are embedded in social institutions and history… a view that is grounded in a contextualist perspective and emphasises the implications of pathways in historical time and place for human development and ageing' (Elder et al. 2006: 4). In his study of children who grew up in the Great Depression, Elder was inspired by Mannheim's 1928 essay, *On the Problem of Generation.* His aim was to examine how historical context and economic deprivation

---

[1]See Nilsen and Brannen (2011). Thomas and Znaniecki collected an impressive amount of data of various kinds: newspaper articles, personal letters, archive material and personal stories. Volumes I and II in the original edition concern the peasant primary groups in Poland and their experiences of the rapid industrialisation at home and rising rates of migration to America and Germany. Volume III is an autobiography of an immigrant of peasant origin (Wladek). Volume IV is about the development and reorganisation of peasant communities in Poland under the new regimes of agriculture and modernisation, and Volume V explores the situation of Polish immigrants in the Chicago area and the disorganisation of communities in their new surroundings. There is also a long Methodological Note in the original Volume I, that Thomas explained later was written after the study had been completed (Blumer 1979: 83).

[2]Members of the Chicago School were associated with Hull House, a social settlement founded by Jane Adams.

shaped individuals' lives as they unfolded (Elder 1999); and he showed how the wider context and the individual life course intersected so that the effects of the Depression on deprivation depended also on the point in the life course in which the individual experienced it.

From the late 1970s, biographical methods not only have become commonplace in social science but also have diversified considerably. A broad interest in what have since come to be termed narrative approaches began in the early 1980s with the work of Bertaux (1981). As Bornat (2008) suggests, these methods thrive on invention and have successfully entered the repertoires of those working in a variety of disciplines and fields of sociology, including the field of family studies.

Life Story and Narrative Methods

Biographical and narrative methods are umbrella terms that refer to data available in a variety of forms including data produced for research and data collected for other purposes. Such data can be spoken, written or visual in form. There is only partial agreement about what constitutes a narrative although most would agree that it refers to an account of experiences and/ or events that are connected in an ordered or arranged pattern, constitutive of a plot and structure. Like plays and novels, narrative is also characterised by dramatic devices. Story telling is the building block of narrative (Franzosi 1998). Different types of narrative have been distinguished; those that are based around events and those around experiences. Event-based narratives often characterise life story or life history accounts and therefore cover long periods of the past. In analysing such material there is an assumption that the events of a life happened in actuality although how they are recalled by the narrator may not relate to a single version of the 'truth'.

Narratives that are more associated with experiences may relate to either recent or distant experiences. As with life stories, such representations are likely to vary over time and may be brief or lengthy recollections. However, the boundaries between types of narrative and between life story and briefer narratives are in practice often porous. Increasingly, fuelled by the 'discursive turn' in the social sciences, researchers' attention is being paid to the contexts in which narratives are co-produced, to the occasioning of stories, and to stories as sites in which individuals perform and construct identities (Phoenix 2013).

The methods employed to make sense of life stories and narratives depend upon the researcher as well as the form of the narrative: the ways in which the researcher organises and interprets the material.

For example, biographical and narrative methods can equally be used in the analysis of variable-based quantitative data from surveys or cohort studies that record events and social transitions in people's life course, as they can be applied to qualitative material. As Elliott (2006) observes, statistical stories can be created by thinking 'along cases rather than across them' (148). Such narrative analysis can capture aggregate change while taking account of change at the micro level.

Qualitative methods depend more heavily upon the interpretations of research participants than those of the researcher although the researcher's role in interpretation is critical. Some qualitative biographical approaches are more concerned with issues of accuracy and the reliability of 'evidence', assumptions that underlie statistical research, notably oral history methods (Thompson 2017). Oral history was founded on the idea of 'history-making': to record the lives of those whose voices were silenced or marginalised in 'official' history. Oral historians employ methods of participatory engagement with their research participants in what are political projects but they draw also on other sources of data in order to verify participants' accounts. Many oral historians are eclectic in their methodological approaches. However most tend to place importance upon the following methodological issues that others who espouse a more interpretive stance also adopt: interactivity with an audience, typically the use of direct questions as a means of story elicitation; a priori organising frameworks as in the case of the life course, its social transitions, events and structure; the contextualisation of lives in time and space; and conceptualisations of the interviewee as an active agent in creating their own biography (Bornat 2008).

Researchers who place more importance upon an interpretive stance are less interested in the actual events and experiences that are narrated and give more attention to the meanings of events to the narrator and the narrative form of the data. For these reasons, biographies have increasingly been considered and examined as social constructs. Schütze has been credited with developing the biographical-interpretative method (1983), an interviewing and analysis method refined by Rosenthal (see Rosenthal 2004), and later adapted in the UK by Wengraf in the biographic-narrative interpretive method (BNIM) (Wengraf 2001). Rosenthal's work was critical to the development of methods that analyse biographical meaning through examining the dialectical inter-relation between experience, memory and narration.

Biographic-narrative approaches often involve interviews as their main method. In BNIM, an initial question is posed to an interviewee, one that aims to provoke a life story. The first tenet of the approach is to treat the life story as a gestalt and to consider the genesis of its creation and construction.

A second key tenet is the analytic approach that is applied namely to explore both the subjective perspective of the narrator, the course of action taken, and the contexts in which both reflection and action take place. In practice, BNIM involves the codification of a life story into two parts: the 'lived life' and 'told story' (Wengraf 2001). These distinctions are reflected in the first analysis of the interview in which lived life and told story are separately analysed.

The 'lived life' focuses attention on the shape and chronology of the life course—the timing and ordering of life events and social transitions, irrespective of how the individuals interpreted them. It thus enables analysts to open themselves to frame hypotheses concerning other life course directions the informants may have followed and the choices they may have made. Setting aside the life story narratives is an important step; stories are not histories. Stories are told with hindsight and recounted from the vantage point of the present and are shaped by and during the interview encounter (Schiff 2012). In this method, the researcher takes a critical realistic approach by identifying the biographical data in the interview and also in documentary and historical material external to the interview. The researcher is thereby cautioned against being 'over-persuaded and implicitly seduced by the interviewee and by their story-telling' (Wengraf and Chamberlayne 2013: 64).

The 'told story' is understood as temporally unfolding in relation to the past, present and the future. Memory-based narratives of experienced events are constituted through experiences of the past but refer both to the current life and past experience. Narratives therefore offer insight into the narrator's present as well as about his/her past and perspectives for the future (Rosenthal 2004). Bruner's approach to narrative has many similarities in its emphasis on a 'historically-evolving' self. He writes, 'we constantly construct and reconstruct a self to meet the needs of the situations we encounter, and we do so with the guidance of our memories of the past and our hopes and fears of the future... resulting in the stories we tell about ourselves, our autobiographies' (Bruner 2003: 210). A defining feature of a narrative-interpretative approach therefore is the recognition that there is no 'objective' past that is accessible from story-telling, an assumption shared by many narrative researchers (Andrews et al. 2013 [2008]; Bamberg 2006). As Polkinghorne (1988) comments, 'Research investigating the realm of meaning aims rather for verisimilitude, or results that have the appearance of truth or reality' (Polkinghorne 1988: 183).

Narrative approaches are generally seen as separate from the field of biographical research although it is all a question of degree. Narrative approaches are driven to a greater extent by attention to language, symbolic representations and cultural forms. As already noted, they go beyond conventional ideas of a story in that they encompass habitual narratives, topic centred narratives and hypothetical narratives (Riessman 1993). Moreover, they are not allied with any one set of methods of data collection or analysis.

An Intergenerational Lens in the Study of Families

Family generations are distinguished by their boundedness, while at the same time they are integrated in a cross-generational succession and relationship (Lüscher and Hoff 2013). Each generation is divided by the timing of its birth, by life course phase and by its historical experience at each phase, with consequences for meanings and practices. Looking at families intergenerationally alerts us to differences in historical context but it also draws attention to the multitude of different resources that are transmitted across generations. It moreover shows the dynamism and openness of transmission so that what is passed on only becomes a transmission when it is received by a family member (Bertaux-Wiame 2005 [1993]). As Bertaux and Bertaux-Wiame (1997) argue, it shows the ways in which a younger generation makes its own mark upon what is passed on to it. Intergenerational family relations may also result in generational breaks and ambivalences, as well as continuities. Drawing on Mannheim (1952), as new generations come forward and old generations withdraw, a new generation may employ what Mannheim calls 'fresh contacts' as it engages with the social and cultural heritage of a given society. Ambivalences between generations may be enacted different levels, for example, structurally, inter-personally and at the level of feelings (Nielsen 2016). For example, when people migrate to a new country, an intergenerational focus can show which cultural resources migrants bring, those they act upon and transmit to younger generations, and which transmissions are rejected or not taken up by younger generations.

Grandfather and Son: An Intergenerational Case Study

The case I have selected for discussion is from an ESRC-funded study of three family generations of men—grandfathers, fathers and sons (Brannen 2015). Its aim was to understand changes in fatherhood across family generations including among men who had experienced migration.[3] The case selected is that of an Irish migrant grandfather and his adult son who is also a father of a son (the latter was also interviewed). In this analysis, I will first present a brief account of their life histories and through their comparison demonstrate the importance of setting biographies in their historical contexts. I will next go on to illustrate the ways in which their life stories unfolded, and how their performance situated the self in ways that were not necessarily intended or self conscious (Bamberg 1997). In this sense what the narrator is saying is not so much consciously hidden but needs deciphering in analysis (Josselson 2004). By that I do not mean imposing some external interpretation upon a life story. Rather it is about examining the whole interview and the jigsaw of material that the interviewee recounts, paying attention to its performance and the silences in the account. The case will also identify what family members seek to pass on and the ways in which transmission is negotiated by the next generation.

Life Histories

Connor was born in Ireland in 1933, the seventh child of seven sons. Both parents died shortly after his birth. He spent much of early life in hospital because of suspected tuberculosis and then, following an accident in the hospital, he spent several years in a convalescent home. When he was fit enough to be discharged, he was sent to one of Ireland's industrial schools. These institutions were set up in the mid-nineteenth century to care for neglected and abandoned children and were intended to offer children practical training for employment. Aged 17 in 1950, Connor went to England and worked in a colliery. He soon returned to Ireland where he found work on a building site and went to night school to learn carpentry. Aged 25 he returned, this time to London, with several friends. He continued to work in the construction sector and made his way up to the position of site foreman. Aged 27, he married an Irish woman (many Irish men of his

---

[3]The ESRC study (2010–2012) sought to examine how different generations and 'ethnicities' engage in fathering and the experience of being fathered; how migration influences fatherhood; and the processes by which fathering is transmitted. Three generational chains of men were selected mainly from London and Southern England; eight chains of first generation Polish (migrant) fathers, their fathers (living in Poland), and their sons (plus two chains of second generation Polish fathers); ten chains of second generation Irish fathers, their fathers (born in Ireland) and their sons; ten chains of white British fathers, their fathers (born in the UK) and their sons who had no history of migration in recent generations in their families. The youngest generation was aged 5–18.

generation did not marry) and the couple was granted a local authority flat. His three children were born in the 1960s/1970s. At some point, the family moved to a council house which, in the early Thatcher era (1980s), they were able to purchase under the right to buy scheme. Connor extended the house drawing on out-of-hours labour from his workmates. He remained in construction for the rest of his life and at interview had recently retired.

Connor's son, Murray, had a very different life. Born in London in 1970, he went to the local Roman Catholic primary school and then to the local Catholic secondary school where his mother worked, first as a cleaner and later as its school secretary. Murray failed his GCSEs but retook some a year later. Aged 17 he left school. It was 1987 and Murray easily found a job in a finance company. Aged 19 in 1989, following a tip-off from a friend, he obtained a job as a clerk with a futures trader in the City of London. It was a period when the finance sector was booming. Within a year he was working on the floor of the London Stock Exchange and was moving in the high living world of city traders. Aged 27 he married a 'non-Catholic' and had three children. By 2000, trading was computerised. Murray was offered a trader job in New York but 7/11[4] happened. By the mid-2000s, the boom was over and Murray was no longer making money. The family was living off his savings. His wife took a full-time job and a friend of Murray's offered to back him financially to set up his own financial operation.

Comparing the life histories of father and son, we can see how their biographies reflect the times in which they lived, especially in their formative years, and the stark contrasts between them. A key generational change is the upward mobility and affluence of the younger generation. Connor's life was marked by the harshness of life in Ireland in the first half on the twentieth century that resulted in spending his childhood and youth in institutions; by a lack of educational opportunities; and by migration to the UK that typified his generation. His employment prospects in Britain, as they were for most Irish men at that time, were limited to hard manual jobs in construction; and his family had access to council housing that he was able to purchase during the Thatcher years. By contrast, Murray enjoyed a family life in the affluent climate of 1980s London albeit his father was a manual worker. He had access to education at secondary school level and gained a few qualifications; he entered the labour market at a time and place when the financial sector was booming and found work in the City of London. Murray's trajectory into the world of finance thereby represents

---

[4]The bombing of the twin towers in New York.

both a rise and fall in fortunes: due to the rise of financial capitalism in the 1980s/1990s and its decline following the computerisation of finance and the banking crash in 2008. There are some similarities between the life course of father and son as well as contrasts: both had three children (a sharp reduction in number compared with the generation before) and both their wives attained white collar jobs. Both sent their children to Roman Catholic schools and brought them up as Catholics.

Life Stories

The way informants begin their narratives is often significant. Some but not all informants quickly indicate in their opening words that they have stories to tell. In this instance story telling is prefaced by the interviewee deciding to adopt the narrative turn while the interviewer acts as a mere prompt or catalyst. It has also been argued that a life story has the markers of a narrative when it contains the experience of a rupture or turning point. As Burgos wrote in the 1980s (unpublished paper), following Ricoeur (1985), the narrator who offers a story typically is seeking to make 'a coherent entity out of heterogeneous and often conflicting ideological positions, experiences, feelings, and events which create some kind of disjunction in the life. In that sense the narrator in their story is trying to "transcend" the rupture and to make sense of it herself'.

The Irish migrants we interviewed came to Britain in the 1950s and 1960s and so looked back over more than 50 years in the UK and at a late point in the life course. Their stories focussed less on the 'functional present' (Mead 1932) and more on memories of the past. Typically they positioned themselves as survivors and in some cases as heroes in their own stories, as having struggled more or less successfully to overcome the obstacles in their paths. Their stories demonstrated their pride in having managed to stay in a job throughout their working lives; their sense of pride in having a family of their own, given that many Irish of their generation did not marry; and satisfaction in owning their homes. Above all, they attributed 'success' to a driving commitment to hard work, a quality, they said, inherited from their fathers many of whom had struggled to make a subsistence living in Ireland in the troubled first half of twentieth century Ireland or had themselves migrated.

Connor was an exemplary raconteur. He employs the employment of time to tell a dramatic story. His opening narrative presages what is to follow. Connor recounts his life as a set of turning points that he neatly condenses. His early life in poverty-stricken 1930s Ireland was one of great misfortune; it is emblematic and heroic, the stuff of Irish fiction.

> And the dad (his dad) went to America and then came back …, I was the seventh son. … I'm the last of them by the way. But anyway, father and mother died when I was only 2, And the mother said like you know 'I won't be dead a year, and he'll be behind me' like you know. Which he was… Well anyway … (pause) I didn't know them like you know what I mean, so I don't (pause) in fairness to everybody else like – I didn't miss my mum and dad because I didn't know them. So how can you miss your mum and dad, you know? But you know when you're a baby everybody likes to pick you up, don't they? …Well I'm getting to the story, but everybody likes to pick you up. Well I didn't know this till years and years and years after that what happened to me was (pause) one of the nurses picked me up and let me fall… Yeah, let me fall and broke my back.

In this narrative, there are strong elements of performativity in the way Connor tells the story with an audience in mind. We see how Connor seeks to foreshadow a sense of inevitability about the misfortune of his father's death in his quotation of his mother's words; '*I won't be dead a year, and he'll be behind me*'. He then builds towards the climax of his story, drawing the audience in, setting a scene of seeming normality—'*when you're a baby everybody likes to pick you up, don't they?*' before coming to the 'crisis' in the story ('*Well I'm getting to the story*') when a nurse picked him up and dropped him, breaking his back. What is also clear from the start of his narrative is that Connor is appealing to his audience suggesting that, despite the apparent enormity of losing both parents so young, this misfortune can be overcome, '*I didn't miss my mum and dad because I didn't know them. So how can you miss your mum and dad, you know?*' He then further downplays the loss of his parents in the rhetorical question '*How can you miss your mum and dad?*' Despite the recent adverse publicity given to industrial schools in Ireland where he spent most of his youth, from his current vantage point Connor minimises the effects of this experience, notably stressing that he was not subject to any sexual abuse, which is now known to have been common in such institutions.

Connor employs considerable narrative skill in telling his story and in the selections he makes in the interview. Furthermore, Connor's positive gloss on his unfortunate early life is suggestive of a 'break' or turning point. In Turner's terms (Turner 1974), this is a phase of redressive action in which follows a state of liminality that contains the germ of future developments in which an individual turns his life around. The upward turn in Connor's life course trajectory takes place after his second migration when he is eventually offered a promotion to site foreman in a large building firm. Thus in the way that Connor tells his story the goodness of the present is magnified against the misfortune and poverty of his past (McAdams 1993: 104). Connor's description of being given a company car on his promotion is metonymic, symbolising or standing for the sense of pride Connor takes in his success and the enhanced status his new position bestows, both at the time and in the interview. Again, success is made vivid through the re-enactment of the moment as he employs direct speech.

> So I said (pause) 'well that was a big job for me' and it meant I could get a company car then you see. (Oh) I said 'This is great' … it was a big company like. Gs was the name of them.., and then I went from them to a proper really big crowd, you know – it was in the '50s. And then I said to (wife), I said 'You can have a go at this now' I said 'with this car' I said – it was only an Escort you know. Because when you're higher than a general foreman you get a bigger car… So of course naturally, what did I do? – I got higher. So I run the job then like you know, I was just sitting behind a desk and everybody would come in 'Could I see Mr …' you know whoever it is, and I felt (pause) I felt great.…But anyway, I never looked back, I really never looked back from then on. I carried on and carried on.

The transformative aspects of Connor's story are present later in his narrative in which the interviewer asks him whether he experienced any discrimination when he first came to England. In response, Connor again uses a narrative voice employing what may be termed 'small stories'. While acknowledging the existence of overt discrimination towards Irish people in general, Connor is reluctant to admit to any, exempting himself on account of his status—his power to hire and fire personnel. In this next quotation, we see that when asked about his ethnic identification he draws on the resources of both his family's history and Ireland's colonised past—claiming that members of his family had fought for Britain in two world wars. Thus he seeks to present a multi-faceted ethnic identity integrating his identification with both Ireland and Britain; in looking back from the present vantage point (a 'successful life') Connor demonstrates strategies of resistance and thereby distances himself from the experiences of other Irish migrants whose biographies may be deemed less successful.

I'm saying, 'I'm Irish, but my people were British Army', and I was delighted. I love Britain, to be honest with you I love Britain, and I've never run down Britain – I would never run down Britain. My second home don't forget – you know what I mean? I've got nothing against – they gave me anything I wanted like you know – and that's exactly I mean. I have no compunctions about any of the, what the Brits are – you will get the ignorant type that say 'Oh they shouldn't be in this country' – but now they don't, but at that time they did. At that time they definitely did. But you must remember now, you've got to remember this what I'm saying now – I was in a position on a job that no one would say anything to me, otherwise I'd get rid of them – you know what I mean?

It is therefore clear from Connor's narratives that what is also important in determining the ways in which he engages with the narrative mode at interview are the current purposes of telling the story for the teller.

Undoubtedly Connor's stories have been rehearsed, refreshed and modified over the years. The stories are a performance drawing on strategies of direct quotation to re-enact the moment. The self-conscious manner of this 'presentation of self' is confirmed at the end of his interview when Connor offers a summative account of his life, calling on the interviewer to affirm that he has, after all, made a success of it, '*I think I've gone from the top to the bottom like you know. Really and truly, I think I've done well for you today anyway like. At least you can put something down now can't you?*' In short, Connor's narrative demonstrates how identity is constructed and meaning made in the interview.

Given the focus of the study was on fatherhood, what Connor does *not* choose to talk about spontaneously in his opening life story is significant. Under questioning about his fathering practices it transpires that Connor worked exceptionally long hours including Saturdays and Sundays when his children were young. His role in the family as he saw it was to '*bring in the money*' and '*make sure there's plenty on the table*'. His relatively brief responses to questions about his involvement with his children suggest a traditional model of fatherhood that was common for the time especially with sons—playing football with them and taking them to matches. On the other hand, he offers a reflective response to a question about whether there was anyone he could think of who acted as a role model for fatherhood; his response says a great deal about his own lack of a family life when he was young,

He also supplements his father's picture of his own experiences of being parented as a child, describing how his parents prioritised their own social life over their children, '*we were sort of (pause) don't know, weren't really central to their social life. Yeah, we could just be fitted in*'. By contrast, Murray and his wife tend to organise their leisure around their children. On the other hand, Murray expresses regret that his children lack the freedom that his parents gave him as a child, even though as a father he would not allow them to roam free in the neighbourhood as he used to do.

Thus Murray's story suggests through his life story, other narratives and responses to direct questions that his identity is complex and multi-faceted. He sought to reconcile his present and his future self with different aspects of his past—his Irish ancestry and his relationship with his father as well as defending the choices he made in creating his own very different path in employment and fatherhood in Britain the late 1990s and early twenty-first century.

This case of father and son gives, I hope, some sense of how a biographical perspective and narrative approach, when they are applied to a family intergenerational research design, provides a 'thick description' of the multiple dimensions that create continuity and change across generations in relation to family life and other social domains, and the ways in which subjectivities are made in different eras and contexts—Murray's in 1990s London and Connor's in the mid-twentieth century world of Irish migration. The aim has also been to identify some of the more invisible processes of transmission that take place successfully (or not) across family generations. In this case, Connor was unable to transmit to his son the strong work ethic that he had lived by. Murray for his part had taken on some of the personal qualities and interpersonal skills of his Irish father. The two men also share some of the same practices of fatherhood in having been the main breadwinners but they differ in their involvement with their children, and in Murray's case in the emphasis he places on emotional display of affection to his children. The case also shows how parents negotiate with their adult children and manage intergenerational inequalities resulting from Connor's migration history and the differences created by the upward mobility of the succeeding generation.

Discussion and Conclusion

Biography and autobiography as they relate to childhoods, education and family practices, while they are based on subjectivity, are situated in historical times and places. This requires researchers to engage in processes of contextualisation. It means putting lives in historical perspective and not being overly reliant on informant testimony. As Hammersley (1989) argues, research participants are not necessarily best placed to define or even adequately know fully the contexts in which they live. It is necessary to problematise the Romantic notion of narrative and move beyond the idea of bearing witness to what actually happened as a simplistic reflection of lived experience (Atkinson 2009). Just as, in a parallel way, we need to see quantitative data as products of the methods used and questions posed and not as 'facts'. As Giddens' (1993) concept of the 'double hermeneutic' suggests, it is necessary to leave space for the researcher to produce a sociological narrative.

Biographical research that focuses on a small number of cases has much to contribute to the development of ways of bringing different methods and data together. In a rapidly changing world, the demand to understand across time and space how family life trajectories and practices are lived and narrated by social actors is growing alongside a demand for trend data and comparative analysis at global, national and regional levels. Therefore, small scale life story research means turning to more than one data source. In the past, there have been some important studies in which different types of data have been brought together including biographical data, for example, in the work of Elder. However, researchers who use a mix of methods need to be explicit about data integration.

One of the ways I have discussed in the chapter for the analysis of life story data is the BNIM. This method separates out in the initial analysis the events and life course transitions from the interviewee's interpretations, thereby enabling the researcher to look at the features of an individual's life trajectory in relation to other similar cases and in relation to the societies in which they lived. Filling in the broader historical contexts of informants' lives is an important part of the process of contextualisation which involves researching a wide literature concerning the lives and times of those under study and comparing and interrogating the life trajectories of informants with other cases.

Life stories are generated when people are explicitly invited to tell their life stories provided they are given the space to do so. It is important, however, to note that many interviewees do not necessarily take up the narrative mode (Brannen 2013). In these cases contextualisation processes come into their own. It is also important to bear in mind that life story telling is often provoked by 'having a story to tell'—often related to a break or turning point, or rupture of canonical expectations (Riessman 2008) that the narrator is seeking to 'transcend'. As I have suggested in the case of Connor and Murray, even though the researcher (in the initial invitation to tell a life story) signalled clearly that the study was about fatherhood, the two men (and others in the study, especially the oldest generation) chose not to speak about it in their life stories. BNIM and similar methods need therefore to be supplemented by more conventional forms of interviewing if they are to address a study's objectives and research questions. While such silences on the part of the study's fathers may signify the lack of centrality of fathering in the men's identities this does not mean that they did not have relevant things to say about family life when asked specific questions.

The chapter has shown that the analysis of life story interviews affords insight into the resources that research participants draw upon and transmit to other generations and the strategies by which they construct identities in family life and other social domains. Connor and Murray largely told stories about childhood and their lives in the world of work. They re-presented these identities in their interviews. In Connor's narrative he builds towards the climax of his childhood misfortunes in a way that intimates that a turning point is to follow bringing repair and redemption. In Murray's case, he begins with, and returns to, the central trope of his life which is the idea of life as a playground; in his narrative he begins with childhood and returns to the same idea in his employment as a successful City trader. What are missing from these central narratives are stories that speak to their identities and practices as fathers. Murray is also unforthcoming about his subsequent more mundane working life after the financial bubble burst. Perhaps this is because he had not yet reached the end of 'the story'.

The case of father and son also demonstrates intergenerational transmission in family life despite the differences between the two men. Here we see 'echoes of the past' (Smart 2011: 543) in the way both men displayed their considerable story telling skill that has passed down the generations. Both men employed dramatic devices and performativity in the ways that they engaged with their audience and affirmed by Murray when he suggested his inheritance of his fathers' considerable social networking competencies.

Both men's stories are similar in their current representations of their lives as 'successful' even though the canons of success differ; for Connor, an Irish migrant in the 1950s, success meant never being out of a job and his elevation to site foreman, while for Murray it was about making money in the heady days of the London Stock Exchange in the 1990s. However, stories tell us not only about how informants experienced and continue to experience the past, they also tell us how they see and experience the present and how they envision their lives in the future. Yet Connor's redemptive story—rising above early misfortune through a mix of hard work and luck and Murray's account of his life as a playboy—is more than a positive gloss, they are ways of living. Memories are not mirrors that reflect the past. They are subject to restoration, refracted through contemporary time frames and lenses that are shaped by a multiplicity of factors to do with subjectivities, the nature of researchers' questions, the particular research method employed, the cultural resources and repertoires of the teller, the structure of the life course and its crises and turning points, the wider historical context, and the societal canons concerning what 'success' means. Researchers' interpretations in understanding the meanings that stories have for individuals are also temporal and reflect our own vantage points.

Life stories that combine narrative and biographical approaches suggest the complex interplay between the way people speak about their experiences and the structures against which such talk needs to be understood (McCleod and Thomson 2009). This requires both the art of re-presentation and rigorous analysis. It requires the researcher to bring together the critical elements of a life in a convincing and rigorous way to make an argument or to offer an explanation; to identify presences and omissions; to develop disciplined systematic analyses of how biographies are produced, shared and transmitted. Such endeavours are more likely to produce a rich and multi-layered analysis. This is a difficult feat as Bertaux observes, 'It takes some training to hear, behind the solo of a human voice, the music of society and culture in the background' (Bertaux 1990: 167–168). However, as those writing about the genre of literary biography recognise, there is no one method of doing this (Lee 2009: 18).

References

Andrews, M., Squire, C., & Tamboukou, M. (Eds.). (2013). *Doing Narrative Research*. London: Sage.

Atkinson, P. (2009). *Knowing Selves: Biographical Research and the European Traditions*. Invited Plenary Paper European Sociological Association, Lisbon.

Bamberg, M. (1997). Language, Concepts and Emotions: The Role of Language in the Construction of Emotions. *Language Sciences, 19*(4), 309–340.

Bamberg, M. (2006). Stories: Big or Small: Why Do We Care? *Narrative Inquiry, 16*(1), 139–147.

Bamberg, M., & Georgakopoulou, A. (2008). Small Stories as a New Perspective in Narrative and Identity Analysis. *Text and Talk, 28*(3), 377–396.

Bertaux, D. (Ed.). (1981). *Biography and Society: The Life History Approach in the Social Sciences*. London: Sage.

Bertaux, D. (1990). Oral History Approaches to an International Social Movement. In E. Øyen (Ed.), *Comparative Methodology* (pp. 158–170). London: Sage.

Bertaux, D., & Bertaux-Wiame, I. (1997). Heritage and Its Lineage: A Case History of Transmission and Social Mobility Over Five Generations. In D. Bertaux & P. Thompson (Eds.), *Pathways to Social Class: A Qualitative Approach to Social Mobility* (pp. 62–97). Oxford: Oxford University Press.

Bertaux-Wiame, I. (2005 [1993]). The Pull of Family Ties: Intergenerational Relationships and Life Paths. In D. Bertaux & P. Thompson (Eds.), *Between Generations: Family Models, Myths and Memories* (2nd ed., pp. 39–50). Oxford: Oxford University Press.

Blumer, H. (1979). *Critiques of Research in the Social Sciences: An Appraisal of Thomas and Znaniecki's The Polish Peasant in Europe and America*. New Brunswick: Transaction Books.

Bornat, J. (2008). Biographical Methods. In P. Alasuutari, J. Brannen, & L. Bickman (Eds.), *Handbook of Social Research* (pp. 344–357). London: Sage.

Brannen, J. (2013). Life Story Talk: Some Reflections on Narrative in Qualitative Interviews. *Sociological Research Online, 18*(2), 15. http://www.socresonline.org.uk/18/2/15.html.

Brannen, J. (2015). *Fathers and Sons: Generations, Families and Migration*. Basingstoke: Palgrave Macmillan.

Bruner, J. (2003). Self-Making Narratives. In R. Fivush & C. A. Haden (Eds.), *Autobiographical Memory and the Construction of a Narrative Self* (pp. 209–225). Mahwd, NJ: Erlbaum.

Burgos, M. (Unpublished Paper). *Some Remarks on Textual Analysis of Life Stories; Prolegoma to a Collective Hermeneutic Approach*.

Elder, G. (1999 [1974]). *Children of the Great Depression: Social Change in Life Experience*. Oxford: Westview Press.

Elder, G., Johnson, M., & Crosnoe, R. (2006). The Emergence and Development of Life Course Research. In J. Mortimer & M. Shanahan (Eds.), *Handbook of the Life Course* (pp. 3–22). New York: Springer.

Elliott, J. (2006). *Using Narrative in Social Research*. London: Sage.

Franzosi, R. (1998). Narrative Analysis—Or Why Sociologists Should Be Interested in Narrative. *Annual Review of Sociology, 24,* 517–554.

Giddens, A. (1993). *New Rules of Sociological Method*. Stanford: Stanford University Press.

Hammersley, M. (1989). *The Dilemma of Qualitative Method; Herbert Blumer and the Chicago Tradition*. London: Routledge.

Intergenerational Foundation. (2016). *Generations Apart: The Growth of Age Segregation in England and Wales*. London: Intergenerational Foundation.

Josselson, R. (2004). The Hermeneutics of Faith and Suspicion. *Narrative Inquiry, 14*(1), 1–28.

Lee, H. (2009). *Biography: A Very Short Introduction*. Oxford: Oxford University Press.

Lüscher, K., & Hoff, A. (2013). Intergenerational Ambivalence: Beyond Solidarity and Conflict. In I. Albert & D. Ferring (Eds.), *Intergeneratonal Relations: European Perspectives on Family and Society* (pp. 39–63). Bristol: Policy Press.

Mannheim, K. (1952 [1928]). The Problem of Generations. In *Essays on the Sociology of Knowledge* (pp. 276–322). London: Routledge and Kegan Paul.

McAdams, D. (1993). *The Stories We Live By; Personal Myths and the Making of the Self*. New York: The Guilford Press.

McCleod, J., & Thomson, R. (2009). *Researching Social Change*. London: Sage.

Mead, G. H. (1932). *The Philosophy of the Present*. Chicago, IL: University of Chicago Press.

Morgan, D. H. J. (2011). *Rethinking Family Practices*. Basingstoke: Palgrave Macmillan.

Nielsen, H. B. (2016). *Feeling Gender: A Generational and Psychosocial Approach*. London: Palgrave, Open Access Ebook.

Nilsen, A., & Brannen, J. (2011). The Use of Mixed Methods in Biographical Research. In A. Tashakorri & C. Teddlie (Eds.), *The Handbook of Mixed Methods Research*. London: Sage.

Phoenix, A. (2013 [2008]). Analysing Narrative Texts. In M. Andrews, C. Squire, & M. Tamboukou (Eds.), *Doing Narrative Research* (pp. 72–88). London: Sage.

Polkinghorne, D. E. (1988). *Narrative Knowing and the Human Sciences*. Albany: SUNY Press.

Ricoeur, P. (1985). *Oneself as Another*. Chicago, IL: University of Chicago Press.

Riessman, C. (1993). *Narrative Analysis: Qualitative Research Methods Series 30*. London: Sage.

Riessman, C. (2002). The Analysis of Personal Narratives. In J. Gubrium (Ed.), *Handbook of Narrative Research* (pp. 695–710). Thousand Oaks, CA: Sage.

Riessman, C. (2008). *Narrative Methods for the Human Sciences*. Thousand Oaks, CA: Sage.

Rosenthal, G. (2004). Biographical Research. In C. Seale, G. Gobo, J. Gubrium, & D. Silverman (Eds.), *Qualitative Research Practice* (pp. 48–65). London: Sage.

Schiff, B. (2012). The Function of Narrative: Towards a Narrative Psychology of Meaning. *Narrative Works: Issues, Investigations and Interventions, 2*(1), 33–47.

Schütze, F. (1983). Biographieforschung und Narratives Interview. *Neue Praxis, 3,* 283–293.

Smart, C. (2011). Families, Secrets and Memories. *Sociology, 45*(4), 539–543.

Thompson, P. with Bornat, J. (2017). *Voice of the Past*. Oxford: Oxford University Press.

Turner, V. (1974). *Dramas, Fields and Metaphors: Symbolic Action in Human Society*. Ithaca, NY: Cornell University Press.

Wengraf, T. (2001). *Qualitative Research Interviewing*. London: Sage.

Wengraf, T., & Chamberlayne, P. (2013). Biography-Using Research (BNIM), Sostris, Institutional Regimes, and Critical Psycho-Societal Realism. In J. D. Turk & A. Mrozowicki (Eds.), *Realist Biography and European Policy: An Innovative Approach to European Policy Studies* (pp. 63–92). Leuven: Leuven University Press.

6

The Research Methods for Discovering Housing Inequalities in Socio-Biographical Studies

Elizaveta Polukhina

Housing as a Sociological Question

Sociological approaches to housing are based on Marxist and Weberian traditions and principally focus on studying the structures that form inequalities in the distribution of housing and the rights of ownership (Clapham 2015: 10). Social-housing groups have been the subject of sociological studies as far back as the 1930s (as part of the Chicago School framework) (Anderson 1923: 302). Research in this area fundamentally reveals the structural mechanisms which create disparities when it comes to the distribution of housing (Rex and Moore 1967). Scholars within this field have introduced the concept of a 'housing class' to describe a group with the same housing status, a concept which is determined through key structures in the urban social structure. Two different criteria lay at the heart of their classification: the type of habitation and the ownership of the habitation.

A productive frame for the study of the housing question is the capital that results from the inter-relationship of social and physical spaces (Bourdieu 1984). The dwelling, being a permanent and habitable place for living, reflects the status and lifestyle of the person who lives there. The experience of living in a certain type of housing largely shapes the standards

E. Polukhina (✉)
National Research University Higher School of Economics (HSE),
Moscow, Russia
e-mail: epolukhina@hse.ru

© The Author(s) 2020
J. M. Parsons and A. Chappell (eds.), *The Palgrave Handbook of Auto/Biography*,
https://doi.org/10.1007/978-3-030-31974-8_6

and perceptions of social life. A predisposition to certain behavioural patterns and the perception of certain situations are intrinsic to persons of similar housing experiences and spatial socialisation. Thus, the housing unit reflects the social status of an individual and, at the same time, affects his/her subsequent choices in life (Bourdieu 1984: 517–518). These inhabitants retain and use their homes both through every day practices and through social relationships in the dwelling itself and in the area of residence (Bech Danielsen and Gram Hanssen 2004).

The Context of Post-Soviet Housing in Russia

The social significance of the housing problem in the Russian context, as well as of the mechanisms of obtaining housing units, has historically undergone many changes. During the Soviet period, the State provided its citizens with housing. Housing units were mainly granted by the organisation for which a person worked. The quality of the dwelling depended on the length of service, the person's professional status and family size. Residential districts were built for certain professional groups (housing districts for workers, scientists, etc.). Both the individual's professional and residential statuses were consistent and stable, and housing mobility patterns and opportunities could accordingly be predicted.

In post-Soviet Russia, the housing problem was basically brought down to the levels of family and the individual, which, in turn, accounts for the different nature and dynamics of Russia's current housing status and housing mobility. For example, the main reason why contemporary Russians move within their city or town is the desire to improve their living conditions or to move into a housing unit which is more appropriate for their lifestyle and family needs (Balakireva et al. 2017).

The changed housing policy and housing sector commercialisation have resulted in increased social differentiation. According to Rosstat, in 2012, 83.5% of the *Housing Fund of the Russian Federation*[1] is owned by the tenants.[2] Thus, there is the appearance of the *rentier class* who obtain their income from rented property and are not required to participate in labour relations. At the same time, *urban nomadism*, i.e. those who deliberately

---

[1]The Housing Fund of the Russian Federation is the general registered aggregate of living quarters located within the territory of the Russian Federation. It includes all territories and types of owners.

[2]The Housing Economy and Household Services in Russia. Available at: http://www.gks.ru/bgd/regl/b13_62/Main.htm [Accessed 25 May 2018].

avoid living in a permanent place of residence, is becoming increasingly typical (Brednikova and Tkach 2010). Often it is young people who opt for *nomadism*, frequently moving to different housing units and leading a two-dwelling or more life. The lack of stability, volatile employment, and the trend towards *precarisation* cannot help but affect housing preferences. At the same time, a recent study on leased housing units has shown that leasing is regarded as a 'transitional phase', whereas owning an apartment is considered a norm (Karavaeva and Cherkashina 2015). However, this norm has changed for a portion of Moscow's young people: some of them prefer frequent moves to different housing units and show no inclination towards establishing a permanent dwelling of their own.

In times of economic crises, the scale and number of *socially disadvantaged groups*, such as *hoodwinked-housing investors* or *dollar-denominated mortgage payers*, increase as a result of the instability of market institutions.[3] For example, according to a 2015 survey of middle-class representatives, the problem of housing conditions was named the second-most important inequality problem, with income inequality ranking first and inequality in the healthcare service ranking third (*The Russian Middle Class in the Context of Stability and Crises*, 2016: 23).

The issue of housing inequality in post-Soviet Russia is most crucial for young and multi-child families. Studies show that for many young families, the basis for housing well-being is the inherited privatised Soviet-era housing units (Zavisca 2012). In most cases, the post-Soviet generation of young families is deprived of allocated housing by the government, which is why they must continue to live in an 'inherited' dwelling or instead buy new housing units—often raising the necessary money, partially or completely, from selling such inherited buildings. An analysis of statistical data and surveys on living conditions show that

> …households with children under the age of 18 are most deprived. The housing problem is faced by multi-generation families, where adult children live in their parents' households. The best-housed individuals are those who are either at the beginning or at the end of their life, living alone or with a spouse. (Burdyak 2015: 288)

---

[3]These terms refer to the people who became victims of unreliable developers ('hoodwinked-housing investors') or those who bought an apartment with a mortgage in dollars, and the dollar rate subsequently increased sharply ('dollar-denominated mortgage payers').

The Research Project and Empirical Data

This chapter employs material from the project *Intergenerational social mobility from the XX to XXI centuries—four generations of Russian history* (www. smxxi.ru). The cultural turn (Bennett et al. 2009) has been essential in the research of social mobility, significantly expanding its scope. From that, it became possible to consider mobility not only movements between classes or professional groups, but also the changes that occurred and continue to occur in the auto/biographies outside the sphere of employment. In the field of study of mobility, some variables previously had a subordinate status and became measurable—the choice of 'non-obligatory' qualifications, activities and housing (*Social Mobility in Russia: The Generation Aspect*, 2017: 27).

This chapter is concerned with the distribution of housing and the rights to own it; the principal objective of this research is to identify, on a larger scale, the structures which create inequalities within the housing sector. A more specific sub-question asks what are the living conditions and opportunities for people of different social classes[4] and generations in post-Soviet Russia. In analysing the collected data for this chapter, I will also attempt to discover the mechanisms that created this housing inequality, by using various methods of data collection.

The empirical base for this research was collected within the framework of the 2015 project (*Social Mobility in Russia: The Generation Aspect*, 2017). It consisted of two parts: the nationwide door-to-door survey, with the participation of 5081 respondents from the ages of 25 to 70 years, and 35 in-depth biographical interviews with 19 female and 16 male respondents ranging in age from 25 to 50 years, living in Moscow or Yekaterinburg.[5]

The Russian nationwide survey contained questions about the fixed social changes of the individual, including the housing trajectories of respondents' living conditions, and about property and income from property. The selection of participants for biographical interview was carried out according

---

[4]In our project, the middle-class representatives are holding senior positions with the income above average and higher education; the working class is made up of people without higher education, manual labor with incomes below average.

[5]Yekaterinburg is a city in Russia which was founded around a factory on the Iset' river in 1723 and is located east of the Ural Mountains. It currently has a population of 1,460,000 people (2015 figures). The average monthly income is 40,000–50,000 rubles or ~700 euro (2014). These figures are taken from the official website екатеринбург.рф and 2015 reports from the leaders of the city. In this chapter, quotes from interviews in Moscow and Yekaterinburg will be presented. The author of the chapter has lived in these cities and knows their social spaces, which makes the process of data analysis and the interpretation in the geographic context more credible.

to the criterion of their positions in the professional hierarchy: leading specialists with a higher education were middle class, while those who were involved with physical labour without a higher education were considered as worker class. Study participants were divided into two groups: (1) a cohort of 45–50-year-olds, the 'parent' generation (born between 1965 and 1970) and whose biographies were created during the Soviet and post-Soviet periods and (2) a cohort of 25–30-year-olds, the generation of 'children' (born between 1985 and 1990), and at the start of their educational and professional careers.

Features of the Survey Data, the Experience of Piloting and the Scale of the Types of Housing

The developed questionnaire contained questions about the individual's biography (family, housing, education, work history) and was divided into different age intervals: from childhood to 15 years of age; 25 years of age; 35 years of age; 45 years of age; 55 years of age; and the present time. Thus, the questionnaire made it possible to measure the changes in the status of the individual, including housing, at different periods of their lives. The question about the respondents' housing status took the following form: '*In what kind of housing did you live in at this particular moment?*' and proposed a nominal scale with different types of housing. This question was repeated for each age period and allowed for measurement of changes in the individual's housing status.

While carrying out the questionnaire, we encountered some difficulties in getting answers to some of the housing questions. It was found that when answering the retrospective questions which return to past experiences, the respondents tended to answer in present-day terms. For example, many respondents described their first wooden homes as *cottages,* even though they were actually of the *barracks* type (see Photograph 6.1). Cottages—a more prestigious type of housing than barracks—only appeared in post-Soviet times (see Photograph 6.2). It would appear that in the interview situation, an individual was inclined to 'embellish' and describe his former home as being more prestigious than it actually was. In reality, there is a huge social distance between living in a barracks and a cottage in modern Russia. The residents of the former type are more likely to be at the bottom of society (they want to move, or live in social housing, and hope for the demolition of their current dwelling and the provision of new housing), while the latter are closer to the elite (they are building a comfortable private house as

Photograph 6.1 Preserved houses of the barrack type, built in the early twentieth century. Several families would have lived in each of these barracks. These are historical, but residential, buildings that will be demolished in the near future. Yekaterinburg, 40th of the Anniversary of the October Revolution Street; May 2018 (Photo by the author. To illustrate different types of housing, photographs from the recent expedition *Post-Soviet everyday life of an industrial neighborhood: social practices and identities* [the case of Yekaterinburg City, the Uralmash neighbourhood] were used. The dates of the field expedition: 28.04.2018–10.05.2018)

Photograph 6.2 A contemporary city cottage (a home with amenities), in which separate families live. Cottages are built as individual projects. Kirovogradskaya Street, Yekaterinburg, May 2018 (Photo by the author)

a personal project). In the actual interview descriptions, the barrack and cottage are similar—in that they are both two-storey houses—but their market values, like the quality of housing, vary greatly.

In determining the home-dweller's status in our questionnaire, we allocated him or her to a limited '*type of housing*'. In my opinion, a multidimensional understanding of housing status should generally take several factors into account: first, the *role of housing in personal well-being, as well as in income structure* (housing can either add opportunities or it can limit chances in life, e.g. the lessor can earn money by leasing out extra housing, the tenant must pay the lessor); second, the *status of the place of residence* in the city area (in the suburbs, or the centre); and third, the *type and characteristics of the principal place of residence* (house/building/apartment, the year it was built, the type of accommodation, construction materials, the landscaping of the house/building and its premises, the spaciousness of the housing unit measured by net worth of floor space per person, the ratio between the number of rooms, the number of dwellers and the number of registered dwellers). On the basis of the totality of these parameters, a hierarchy can be built that would reflect either a higher status (an upward housing mobility trend) or a lower status (a downward housing mobility trend). These criteria can be combined with such concepts as 'housing conditions', 'housing relations', 'housing groups', and 'housing status' (Polukhina 2017).

Many respondents taking part in the survey only recalled details of their previous habitations with difficulty and did not know into which survey category their dwelling belonged. We wanted to initially use in our project a scale of the types of housing with reference to the Russian names in the referent language—'*stalinist*', '*khrushchyovka*', '*brezhnevka*', etc. (Attwood 2010). However, only a few respondents understood and employed this terminology. As a result, we decided to discard such names. In the final version of the questionnaire, we included the names of housing, taking into account the period of construction of the housing, its appearance and its materials. However, after conducting the nationwide door-to-door questionnaire, we realised that the sample in our data would be biased. Since the survey is concerned with types of housing, and a residence is a marker of the social status of the individual, then a representative survey would be one which portrays housing resources and its occupants in all its diversity and corresponding proportions. Traditionally, residents of cottages are not included in our door-to-door surveys because this type of resident has been a hard-to-access group, just like residents of apartment buildings with intercoms, residents of the remote private sector, and other hard-to-reach settlements.

The cognitive potentialities of the mass-housing quarters that were real-ised in the study of housing mobility turned out to be rather meagre. The bias in the sample and imperfect current instrumentation make it difficult to study the multidimensional housing question. The most reliable informa-tion on housing status concerns housing availability. Over time, I realised that the most productive scale of types of housing is the visualisation of dif-ferent types of housing, and areas that had already been undertaken in an online survey, such as the *BBC Great British Class Survey* (UK Data Service). However, the development of a survey on such a scale for the Russian reality is a task for the near future.

Biographical Interviews: From 'Own' Field Materials to the Work with Secondary Data

Quantitative methods of data collection do not take into account the ambiv-alent nature of housing status, especially household and family interac-tions (Winstanley et al. 2002). The understanding of the housing status is too simplified in the questionnaire used in this research. The emphasis on the individual does not allow for the obtaining of information concerning all of the cohabitants. The assumption is that the position of all members of the household is the same. However, we understand that the owner or the recipient of income from housing may be specific individuals, and not all members of that household. Moreover, the position of some members of the household may be less privileged. The interpretation of the changes in housing status requires attention to detail. What is often obvious to the researcher is the act of upward housing mobility, i.e. the change of housing to a more privileged one, but which nonetheless the respondent perceives as a 'loss'. Usually, this happens when an individual moves to improved hous-ing conditions (from a room in a dormitory to a separate apartment, for example), but loses touch with the previous environment or neighbours.

Let us turn to the conducted interviews in order to attempt to answer the question concerning the structures that form the inequality in the distribu-tion of housing and the rights to own it. What social structures determine housing conditions and opportunities? Within the framework of this project, I worked with two types of qualitative data.[6] The first are those interviews that

---

[6]All the data were collected based on the ethical standards of social sciences in Russian Federation. The informants of the studies signed the informative agreements and allowed the use of their quotations and pictures for publications.

I collected in Yekaterinburg in October 2015. There were six, and each of them was held at the home of the project participant and usually lasted more than two hours. According to the interview guide, I discussed with the respondent his/her life path and the trajectory of social mobility, his/her childhood, his/her parents' family, changes in living conditions, and his/her professional biography. I considered each interview as a separate case, enriching it with diary entries, taking photos and making constant case comparisons among the subjects. I made an analytical comparison of cases, generated new topics and singled out the social types of project participants to make a general typology. It was these first six interviews that allowed me to develop the basic ideas about differences in housing inequality through the prisms of three important dimensions—*generational, social class and gender*. Further, I supplemented my thematic analysis with data that was collected by other researchers on our team. The analysis involved 35 interviews in total, 19 males and 16 females. The analysis of the secondary data was often of a reduced nature, and the interview materials focusing on housing are difficult to interpret, although working with this type of data is becoming an increasingly common research practice.

By collecting and analysing data on the different housing experiences and the status of the respondents, three distinct features were identified. First is the *sensitivity of the housing theme*. In multigenerational families living in a common house/apartment, housing issues were discussed rather sparsely. This is due to the fact that the interview itself occurred in their home, usually in cramped housing conditions, with people who are merely listening, and sometimes even the participants in the interview become 'members' of the family living together. It is in multigenerational families that this topic creates tension (Burdyak 2015). The topic of housing is often perceived as a topic close to the subject of money; during an interview, a question could have been answered with actual silence or a delicate departure from the answer, and occasionally even bitterness—especially if it concerned issues of inheritance, housing solutions or problems with relatives. Therefore, it seems to me, that it makes sense that the future collection of empirical materials is done through multiple interactions with the respondents, based on trusted and established long-term relations.

The second feature of housing materials is their *contextuality*. As we must try not to proceed from the sub-textual meanings and inter-subjectivities of respondents, it is important to understand the broader personal context of each individual—where she/he is coming from, and where her/his house, district and professional positions lie in relation to her/his current housing stratification. It is accordingly important that the researcher is aware of the social space of the study area.

The social context of housing is *dynamic*. Over time, once esteemed houses lose their prestige because of wear and tear (brick houses of the early '90s, for example) and, conversely, older houses are becoming more prestigious (houses in the Stalinist style or in the Bauhaus style). In this regard, it is difficult to interpret housing stories from the past since no back-story exists for the dwelling, as the researcher is removed from the social context of the territory. For example, the barrack-type house in Photograph 6.1, taken in sunny summer weather, may at first glance be perceived as a unique, perhaps even prestigious, historic building. It is also possible that those who carry out secondary analysis from such photo data could interpret these houses on the basis of visual images and information about the years of construction. In fact, however, these barrack-type dwellings, located in the factory area on the outskirts of Yekaterinburg, are in a run-down condition and extremely uncomfortable for living. Their residents, not having the financial opportunity to buy other housing, live in them as 'hostages' of a difficult housing situation and await the demolition of the dwellings (see Photograph 6.3). The illustrations in Photographs 6.1 and 6.3 show how important it is to look 'closer', since it is with a more detailed consideration that we can more precisely read the social meaning of housing.

Another feature appearing from the home interviews was *'showiness'*. The staging of the interview at home revealed how a guest was received: the

Photograph 6.3 Windows of a barrack-type dwelling with posters advertising free help for drug addiction and homelessness. Yekaterinburg, May 2018 (Photo by the author)

participants were specially prepared, clean, dressed up, food was offered, and the interviewee played the role of a 'hospitable host'. This situation is not unusual for participants and shows the sensitivity of housing issues for many individuals. Quite often in the interview, cohabitants of the respondent, as well as cats and dogs, were present. At the same time, the researcher's experience of her findings—such as visual information and an interpretation of the house—is important and was placed in the researcher's diary. For example, before an interview, the middle-class representatives presented the whole apartment in the format of an excursion, leading a tour of the rooms and describing the contents and furnishings. In contrast, the working-class women with whom I happened to visit, and who lived in the multigenerational families of their parents/grandparents, were extremely modest. They returned to live with their parents after their marriages had broken down. These women did not really feel that they were 'hostesses', but rather understood that they were 'guests' of the apartments. Finding a free space for interviews was difficult and requests for photos proved stressful for them.

Housing Inequality of 45–50-Year-Olds, Based on the Material of Biographical Interviews

In the interviews' data set, I'm here dealing with those who belong to this age group but who have different social and housing statuses. The discrepancy is due to the difference in capital (cultural, social and parental) and personal principles of movement in the social field. An analysis of piloted interviews shows that their current success is the result of adaptation to the changes which occurred during the 1990s after the collapse of the USSR.

One of our respondents, a 45-year-old Yekaterinburg resident, works at a factory as a moulder and is without a higher education. Her personal life did not work out; she is not married, and she does not have children. The 1990s was the period of her youth, and the point at which she realised that, for her, 'there is no time and no reason to study further'. Then, in the late 1990s, her de facto husband suddenly died tragically and she returned to her parents' house. In the absence of a higher education, she was forced to work in a factory. In recent years, she has been changing factories in search of more 'comfortable' working conditions, but her position remained at the same level. Now her income is 'modest', so she is forced to buy the cheapest goods, and in many ways, denies herself many creature comforts. Her current employer does not provide housing, and there are also no means of acquiring it.

At the moment, she lives with her parents, who are pensioners, in a two-room apartment built in the Khrushchev era, and which her parents received from the factory where they had worked all of their lives. She does not have her own room, which meant that our interview took place in the cramped kitchen of about 6 square meters. Tales of housing were laconic and not very desirable, and photographing the interiors of the dwelling caused tension. The respondent constantly stressed her position as a '*victim*' of economic reforms and political instability.

> I don't have a plan of my life…. I became a victim of the numerous economical crises: in 1998, 2008, and 2012. How I can plan if I have nothing to plan with? (Female, 45, factory moulder, Yekaterinburg)

So, let us turn to the case of one of the respondents in Yekaterinburg, the head of the local branch of a Chinese trading company. He received an economic education in one of the most prestigious higher-education universities in Yekaterinburg, and '*was a visitor, and lived in a dormitory*'. During his academic years, foreign firms initially 'came' to the domestic market, and with the help of acquaintances in the university, he became the manager of an international company. As time went by, his professional career dynamically developed; he moved up the corporate ladder through several jobs and became the head of the regional office of an international company. Simultaneously with these professional changes, the respondent moved regularly and had the experiences of living in a variety of housing types (a dormitory, a movable trailer and an old '*odnushka*',[7] or rental flat). Several years ago, he bought himself ('*with his earnings*') a two-room apartment in a prestigious new housing complex situated in the centre of town, where he lives with his wife and child. He was at ease throughout the interview and habitually made a 'tour' of the apartment, as he usually shows his accommodation to first-time guests in his house. His family plans in the future to purchase a second, suburban house:

> Well, of course we want also another house – a suburban home, because my wife wants to go outside the city and to be able to breathe fresh air, have our own walls, etc. (Male, 45, head of the local branch of a Chinese trading company, Yekaterinburg)

---

[7]'*Odnushka*'—bedsit, flat with one room.

Photographs 6.4 and 6.5 The apartment of one of the respondents, 45 years old, head of the local branch of a Chinese trading company, Yekaterinburg, October 2015 (Photo by the author. All interviewees signed informed consent for participation in this project and allow the use of pictures and quotations for publications)

In general, the 45–50-year-old respondents are heterogeneous, have different patterns of mobility and a mixture of capital, which is why their professional trajectories and housing status are so conditioned (Photographs 6.4 and 6.5). Many from this group of respondents have families with young children and live separately from their parents. However, there are those in this group who have already provided housing for their children and talk about the consequences of those benefits:

> Perhaps it was a mistake that everything was given to them at once. We have achieved everything and cherish and appreciate it. We have given our children everything, so it is simple for them like this. They do not need to work to pay for an apartment, they do not need to work for a car, so they do not have to think of where to live, or what to drive. (Female, 50, management position, Yekaterinburg)

The Housing Problems of 25–30-Year-Olds, Based on the Material of the Biographical Interviews

The housing problem is one of the most significant problems facing this generation of young Russians. One of the young participants in the study talks about his '*successful*' experience in buying an apartment and starting an independent life. He was helped by his grandmother, having been given money from the sale of her former apartment. He was able to pay for two-thirds of the cost of the apartment and borrowed the remainder. Now, being a civil servant heading a department, he is experiencing financial difficulties due to the loan, and he has no way to pay for the repairs that the apartment requires. He thus described the possibilities for the purchase of an apartment:

> *In our country, to buy an apartment* [based] *on their own financial abilities … is unreal. It is necessary to kill someone or steal something!* (Male, 28, civil servant, Yekaterinburg)

In the cohort of young people between the ages of 25 and 30, families with children are unrepresented in the interviews' sample (Photograph 6.6). Those who live with an older generation want to live separately, but do not have any opportunity to do so. One such example is a young 26-year-old

Photograph 6.6 Photo of a respondent's dwelling. Male, 28, civil servant, Yekaterinburg, October 2015 (Photo by the author)

manager of a café, who has received a higher education but is currently working at her mother's business. She lives in a two-room apartment with her grandparents, who received their apartment many years ago from their factory employer. '*I lived with one set of my grandparents, then the other, then I lived with my dad when mom left for another town*' (Female, 26, café manager, Yekaterinburg).

She has taken out several loans and is experiencing financial difficulties. Independently buying housing does not seem to be a possible scenario given her current situation. The only option she sees for changing her place of residence, that is, moving to her 'home', is marriage. However, due to the lack of variety of available leisure activities and a limited circle of acquaintances, i.e. cultural and social capital, she has no idea how she can establish a personal life and meet a future partner. In general, the group of respondents aged 25–30 years is heterogeneous, but has already developed certain patterns of mobility in the professional environment and in the private sphere. Some of the respondents of this group live with their parents, and only those who have large capital, mostly of the parental variety, are able to live separately.

Class and Gender: Housing Inequalities in the Optics of the Biographical Interviews

Certain housing patterns for individuals of different classes and gender have been established through study of the interviews. The working-class houses are mainly of Soviet heritage. Some of them live in their parents' apartments, and a percentage of them moved back to their parental homes because of financial difficulties. The group, in general, is characterised by a low level of housing ownership. Parental assistance in the purchase of housing is almost non-existent, since their parents (working class or having already become pensioners) have more modest incomes than the other respondents. For this group of workers, settlement in a separate apartment is difficult. The working class has mostly no involvement at all in the real estate market, since mortgage lending and direct purchases are not available to those on low or volatile incomes. Women are more likely to change residence due to their marriage. Women do not demonstrate the desire to pursue a personal educational or career 'base'. They are oriented to the creation of their own family, moving to their husband's dwelling directly from their parents' home.

For working-class men, the resettlement from their parents is difficult and done through moving to a hostel, renting a home or sometimes taking out a mortgage to buy an inexpensive apartment from the Soviet housing stock. That is why several generations living together is common. In this situation, a young family living under one roof with their parents faces the problem of building their own lifestyle in limited living and housing spaces. Having a child and a family, working-class men are more rational when choosing jobs and guarantees and begin to develop a 'housing strategy' (the exchange of the parental apartment or taking out a mortgage). There is a particularly prevalent practice of returning to the parental home in times of crisis (divorce, separation, inability to pay rent or the death of a spouse).

For the middle classes, some of whom are descendants of the working class of past generations, parental capital in the form of a purchase, or assistance in the purchase of housing, is an important factor to achieving independence. In addition to making financial investments in the direct purchase of an apartment, parents are also eager to invest in the education of their children, considering education as a factor that increases the chances of upward mobility. The middle-class appreciates having their own housing, objectifying the concept of 'their apartment' with such values as material well-being, family happiness and independence.

> But at the same time I understood … that without some personal base, I cannot build a normal relationship, I need to have an apartment that is permanent, because I have moved from many apartments. That I should have one all my own and the best, that's it. I believe that at this moment I, in principle, have achieved all this. I believe that I basically tried. (Female, 30, managerial position, Moscow)

Women from the middle classes receive significant support from their parents in the matter of buying real estate. Men tend to feel responsible for the acquisition of an apartment for their future families, and as a consequence, they take out a mortgage or earmark a significant amount of money from their budget for the purchase of housing, even if this forces them to lower their level of current expenses (Table 6.1).

Data from our study illustrates the trend of housing inequality. However, analysis of material from the biographical case-studies, along with data from the survey concerning the dynamics of housing mobility, does not allow us to talk about generational inequality within the context of post-Soviet Russia as the main mechanism. The data indicates that the individual, his environment, family and availability of capital (cultural, human, social, family) determines the trajectory of social mobility, which is objectified in his housing status. Individuals possessing this capital, or even striving to achieve this capital, demonstrate mobility through changing their social and housing status. In turn, those who do not have capital (parental, social, cultural or economic) find themselves stagnating, thus creating immobility.

Thus, in the era of individualised welfare responsibility, the housing question is strongly connected with family. Generally, the housing status of the young generation depends on the social class of the parental family: if the family belongs to the middle class, the parents usually support their adult children in the housing sphere (either with financial support or an exchange of flats). This contrasts to working-class families who don't have the patterns and financial opportunities to help the younger generation's housing issue. Moreover, the housing issue could be investigated in terms of discrimination inside the family: How do people share the home space and who is more privileged in terms of gender, age, etc.?

Table 6.1 Housing pathways of the working classes and middle classes[a]

	The parental capital	Multigenerational housing	Involvement in the housing market	Drivers of housing mobility	Gender patterns	Level requirements for housing
Working class	Parental housing	Popular, no way to move	Low	Family, children, widespread multigenerational cohabitation	Women moved to husband's dwelling at an early age	Low: 'happy to have any separate housing'
Middle class	Financial support, buying an apartment	Not popular, orientation for separate living	High	Significant step in life course. Separate residence from parents is the norm	Women are more supported in buying an apartment	Rather high, and want to have spacious, comfortable, and even luxury houses

[a]The analysis was extended until 35 interviews were completed, and the data was put in INVIVO 10. The analysis was conducted with the help of my student, Nina Chukina

Conclusion

Current housing studies trace the interactions between housing and other aspects of society and provide the context for the examination of housing through such issues as space, society, welfare and the environment (Clapham et al. 2012: 528). Our data showed how gender's patterns in family and availability of different forms of capital (cultural, human, social, family) determine the trajectory of social mobility, objectified in housing position of individuals. Individuals possessing this capital or even striving to achieve this capital demonstrate mobility through changing their social and housing status. In turn, those who do not have capital (parental, social, cultural or economic) find themselves stagnating, thus creating immobility.

The scope of housing studies is cross-disciplinary and multi-methodical (see Table 6.2). A modern array of data collection methods can be classified by such properties as contextualisation, generalisation and types of gathering data ('subjectified' and 'objectified'). The analysis of the data presented in this chapter shows that the problems of housing inequality are partly based on such macro-structural mechanisms as changes in the labour and housing market, or the family and housing policies of the state and employers. This is indicated by the quantitative data from polls, statistics and housing data, characteristically used when seeking to generalise and obtain an 'objectified' picture. In turn, the analysis of our qualitative data has shown that the problems of housing inequalities are particularly expressed through aspects of gender and class.

A trustworthy source for housing studies is the *housing stock data* (the total of all housing units located within a certain area). This data represents a conditional general totality. The housing stock data is used to form the groups that further represent a hierarchy and a basis for the classes.

Mass interviews conducted at the place of residence, without reference to the housing type quotas, and developed from the housing stock data, lead to incorrect data or data inconsistencies. There are many physically hard-to-reach housing units that are not traditionally covered by nationwide samples. Examples are guarded elite housing or those kept under surveillance, or housing units which are remote from the major public transportation nodes. However, the economic, social and housing classes are interrelated, and therefore, the category of high-status and (most likely) highly mobile groups has not traditionally been covered by household surveys.

Census data is relevant, because it tends to be representative and is more large-scale. It provides for a greater respondent outreach because the citizens are informed on a mass level. However, a census also has such limitations as have been outlined above, i.e. it is impossible to get access to hard-to-reach

Table 6.2 Capabilities of the main data collection methods in the housing study

Research methods/ strategy	Contextualisation	Generalisation	Data about subjective experience	'Objectified' data
Data of housing stock	±	+	−	+
Quantitative survey/ door-to-door polls of residents/census/online survey	±	±	−	+
Biographical interviews	+	−	+	−
Ethnographic case-studies	+	±	+	±

guarded and remote houses or buildings with *concierges*. Nor it is possible to reach mobile respondents who are often not at home. A research response to this problem of respondent availability may be a set of mobile methods, which would enable the respondent to be followed, and to track him/her down using a variety of devices and research techniques (an online survey, for example). However, the visualisation of housing types is required for the development of a valid questionnaire.[8]

The listed method of data collection allows us to see the general picture of housing conditions and inequalities. These materials can be a useful tool—a database of secondary data that allows one to understand the social field, generate research questions and design sampling. Unfortunately, this data does not allow us to fully disclose the mechanisms that form housing inequalities, that is, accessibility and the quality of an individual's housing conditions. Rather, it is necessary to turn to methods that allow the study of subjective experiences such as *biographical interviews*, and hence the reconstructing of the social and housing experience of individuals. In order to extend the data gained from interviews concerning home-making as process, it is possible to use a 'visual narrative' methodology in which informants shaped the understandings of the home and their biographies at the housing scheme, and researchers are combining architectural and social-scientific methods (Lewis et al. 2018: 2).

Cultural turns (Bennett et al. 2009) have played significant roles in housing study. Therefore, making detailed studies of the housing stratification

---

[8]To visualise each type of dwelling means to give a visual image for each type of dwelling. This visualisation scale can be used for further online surveys.

and housing classes of a local territory are implemented in the format of *ethnographic case-studies* (Polukhina et al. 2017; Fusch et al. 2017). This type of design involves a multi-method strategy for data collection through statistical data, interviews using a variety of projective techniques and mapping of the area, and the researcher's personal observations during long-term residence in a particular area. As a result of data collection, a detailed reconstruction of the territorial context takes place. A rapport is built with informants through closer, personal connections, as more time is spent with the participants, and several contacts are made. This gives such opportunities as, for example, discovering the gender aspect of housing inequalities—at the level of family members (home interviews, observations) and at the level of neighbours (mapping, go along interviews, observations, visual data). Regular field diaries should be kept. Such a research format is promising from the point of view of constructing theories, since it allows 'objectified' and 'subjectified' data to be obtained within the studied location. So, for example, the study of the housing classes and mechanisms that create them, at the extreme points of the housing hierarchies—*lower* (such as barracks, see Photograph 6.1) and *higher* (such as cottages, see Photograph 6.2), offers promising results. It is noteworthy that both of these photos located at the beginning of the chapter are residential spaces within the same district. Therefore, within the framework of ethnographic case studies of neighbourhoods, there is a possibility to 'localise' respondents in the space of social differences (Bourdieu 1985: 724–725) and to analyse their attitudes to representatives of other social groups, attitudes which are actualised in their social practices and communications (Bottero and Irwin 2003: 467). In this sense, some aspects of housing inequality can be expressed through the articulation of the informants' feelings and sensations, both in relation to people like themselves and to those who are socially different.

References

Anderson, N. (1923). *The Hobo: The Sociology of the Homeless Man*. Chicago: University of Chicago Press.

Attwood, L. (2010). *Gender and Housing in Soviet Russia: Private Life in a Public Space*. Manchester and New York: Manchester University Press.

Balakireva, M., Goriainova, A., & Polukhina, E. (2017). Intraurban Movings in Moscow: How the Type of Household and Lifestyle Determine a Place of Residence. *INTER, 13,* 82–95. Available at http://jour.isras.ru/index.php/inter/issue/viewIssue/357/22.

Bech Danielsen, C., & Gram Hanssen, K. (2004). House, Home and Identity from a Consumption Perspective. *Housing, Theory and Society, 21*(1), 17–26.

Bennett, T., Savage, M., Silva, E., Warde, A., Gayo-Cal, M., & Wright, D. (2009). *Culture, Class, Distinction*. Abingdon: Routledge.

Bottero, W., & Irwin, S. (2003). Locating Difference: Class, 'Race' and Gender, and the Shaping of Social Inequalities. *The Sociological Review, 51*(4), 463–483.

Bourdieu, P. (1984). *Distinction: A Social Critique of the Judgement of Taste* (R. Nice, Trans.). Cambridge, MA: Harvard University Press.

Bourdieu, P. (1985). Social Space and the Genesis of Groups. *Theory and Society, 14*(6), 723–744.

Brednikova, O., & Tkach, O. (2010). Dom dlya nomady [Housing for Nomads]. *Laboratorium, 3,* 72–95.

Burdyak, A. Y. (2015). Obespechennost' zhil'em v postsovetskoi Rossii: neravenstvo i problema pokolenii [Housing Well-Being in Post-Soviet Russia: Inequality and the Issue of Generations]. *Zhurnal Issledovanii Sotsial'noi Politiki [Journal of Social Policy Studies], 13*(2), 273–288.

Clapham, D. (2015). *The Meaning of Housing: A Pathways Approach*. Bristol: Policy Press, Bristol University Press.

Clapham, D., Clark, W., & Gibb, K. (2012). *The Sage Handbook of Housing Studies*. London, Thousand Oaks, CA, New Delhi, and Singapore: Sage.

Fusch, P. I., Fusch, G. E., & Ness, L. R. (2017). How to Conduct a Mini-Ethnographic Case Study: A Guide for Novice Researchers. *The Qualitative Report, 22*(3), 923–941. Retrieved from https://nsuworks.nova.edu/tqr/vol22/iss3/16.

Karavaeva, E., & Cherkashina, T. (2015). Housing Relations, Policies and Condition. *Monitoring of Public Opinion: Economic and Social Changes, 6,* 118–135.

Lewis, C., May, V., Hicks, S., Santos, S. C., & Bertolino, N. (2018). Researching the Home Using Architectural and Social Science Methods. *Methodological Innovations, 11,* 1–12.

Polukhina, E. (2017). Housing Mobility: Approaches for Sociological Analysis. *The Journal of Social Policy Studies, 15*(4), 589–601.

Polukhina, E., Strelnikova, A., & Vanke, A. (2017). *The Transformation of Working-Class Identity in Post-Soviet Russia: A Case-Study of an Ural Industrial Neighbourhood*. Moscow: NRU Higher School of Economics. Series SOC 'Sociology', No. WP BRP 77/SOC/2017.

Rex, J., & Moore, R. (1967). *Race, Community and Conflict: A Study of Sparkbrook*. Oxford: Oxford University Press.

Social Mobility in Russia: The Generation Aspect [Sotsial'naya mobil'nost' v Rossii: pokolencheskiy aspekt]. (2017). A. V. Vanke, V. V. Semenova, & M. F. Chernysh (Eds.). Institute of Sociology, Russian Academy of Sciences.

The Russian Middle Class in the Context of Stability and Crises [Rossiyskiy sredniy klass v usloviyakh stabil'nosti i krizisov]. (2016). Institut Sotsiologii RAN, Moscow. Available at https://goo.gl/RjdvkW. Accessed 25 May 2018.

UK Data Service. (2011–2013). *BBC Great British Class Survey*. Available at https://discover.ukdataservice.ac.uk/catalogue/?sn=7616. Accessed 25 July 2016.

Winstanley, A., Thorns, D. C., & Perkins, H. C. (2002). Moving House, Creating Home: Exploring Residential Mobility. *Housing Studies, 17*(6), 816.

Zavisca, J. R. (2012). *Housing the New Russia*. Ithaca, NY: Cornell University Press.

7

Auto/Biographical Research and the Family

Aidan Seery and Karin Bacon

Introduction

This chapter can act only as a brief indicator of the dimensions, networks, forces and relations that the experience of family (or its lack) has on the stories and narratives that human beings relate in their autobiographies. It is clearly not possible even to survey the way in which the experiences of family life and the memories that are made of these experiences contribute to and shape life narratives and their understanding. We will, however, attempt to cast some light on a small number of aspects of the connectedness of family and personal biography using a case study of a biography or biographies written consciously within the framework of a family network and reflecting that network in individual lives.

The example of biographical writing within an explicit familial network that we will use here is somewhat unusual. The network that is portrayed is not the more familiar one of parent and child or even grandparent and grandchild, but that of the set of relations that foreground relations between siblings, though clearly these stand in the light of the relationship

A. Seery (✉)
Trinity College Dublin, University of Dublin, Dublin, Republic of Ireland
e-mail: seerya@tcd.ie

K. Bacon
Marino Institute of Education, Dublin, Republic of Ireland
e-mail: karin.bacon@mie.ie

© The Author(s) 2020
J. M. Parsons and A. Chappell (eds.), *The Palgrave Handbook of Auto/Biography*,
https://doi.org/10.1007/978-3-030-31974-8_7

with parents that illuminates the backdrop. The example also does not belong to those that describe crisis families or non-traditional families that have attracted the attention of researchers in recent years. Of course, only those lives and families that leave material traces can be re-constructed and interpreted and most family stories fade and disappear quickly. This family is, however, by the standards of its time and even in a culture of the educated middle-class, distinct by virtue of the large amount of biographical and autobiographical materials that its members left behind. It could be surmised that this is due in part at least to the significance that the family assumed in the history of Ireland in the early twentieth century, but as we shall see the recording of their lives began long before any visible political activity. So, this family (that of my grandparents-Bacon) is not typical of a class or group and shows idiosyncratic features that give insight into individuality, personal autonomy and creativity. However, despite these structural constraints but especially conscious of them, it is still possible using this example to examine a number of research-theoretical aspects of family and auto/biographical writing and research to bring these ideas to a concrete form. The approach taken in the chapter to develop some of these ideas is twofold: first we argue that family narratives are always relational, internalised, change over the life course and are distributed, or shared, across individuals in families. We then take Roland's idea (1988) that it is possible to identify an 'I-self' and a 'we/familial-self' in auto/biography and cultural narrative and use these constructs to understand the connection between family and self.

The Family Narrative as Relational and Internalised

The first idea to be explored, but not for any reason of hierarchy, and proposed by Laing and other psychoanalysts (Laing 1969; Pincus and Dare 1978; Nicolo et al. 2014) is that the family within an auto/biographical narrative is both *networked and internalised*. It comprises of a set of relations, not isolated elements, and this system of relations is brought together into some kind of narrative coherence in the mind, memory and imagination of the person writing their own biography or the one writing the biography of another. Therefore, the family as it appears in auto/biographical research is different from the immediate bodily experience of family in real time and immediate settings. Investigations and inquiries that seek to assess and measure immediate experiences of, for example, children or older people in abusive family situations are subject to a very different set of ethical and behavioural demands and research methods than those associated with research into family in biography. Our concern is solely with the latter, though as biographical and narrative researchers it is important to remind ourselves that the internalised family of memory and imagination is connected in some way that we do not fully understand, to immediate, bodily experiences of the past and that some of these were and can still be traumatic and painful.

In our example, the internalised network of relations is formally constituted by the biological connection of two sisters and one brother. The three were part of a larger family of 14 individuals, two parents and 12 children in relatively economically prosperous conditions in Ireland at the close of the nineteenth century. They were the son and daughters of the Ryan family from Co. Wexford. Their parents, John (1844–1921) and Eliza Ryan (1848–1930) (my great-grandparents-Bacon) had a large farm of 150 acres at Tomcoole near Taghmon and had twelve children. Remarkably for the time, all twelve children received a second-level education and eleven of them continued to university or further studies, and several went on to have remarkable careers in science and the arts. In addition to their engagement with their education, several of the daughters took a prominent role in revolutionary politics and some were interned or imprisoned in the aftermath of the 1916 Rising, during the War of Independence, and the Civil War. In the years thereafter, they would also go on to play political roles in the new Irish Free State. As a result of their political involvement and later social prominence, quite an amount is known about the family and its members and a large archive of primary writings exist in the National Library of Ireland, the archives of University College Dublin and in the family.

Even from this very brief introduction, it is clear that this family has characteristics that are both common to those of others at the time but also distinctive and particular features which we will return to later. What is of interest in this first section is the fact that when the children were in early adulthood, and either continuing their education or entering the world of employment for the first time, they wrote an unusual set of letters that circulated between them and a number of other siblings in the period from 1912 to 1915. The unusual form was a school exercise book that they passed from one to the next so that all could read each other's writing. The network of relations established in this way is one, therefore, that has a distinct spatio-temporal dimension that clearly influences the writing and the construction of relations in the mind of each of the narrators. The correspondence includes entries from six of the sisters: Min, Chris, Nel[ly], Kit, Agnes and Liz and one brother Jim. Our focus in this chapter, however, will be on three of the siblings in this correspondence, Josephine Mary, Jim and Phyllis who was the youngest of the Ryan siblings and not part of the letters but who became politically active later on. It was these siblings in particular who became closely involved in the events of the Easter Rising in 1916 and who later were most prominent in Irish public life in the new republic.

Josephine Mary (Min) (grandmother of the second author of this chapter) was born in 1884 and, following her older sisters, was educated by the Loreto nuns and then took the examinations of the Royal University in Dublin where she took a degree in French, German and English. She went from there to the University of London in 1911 to do a post-graduate teaching qualification. While at the University of London, Min formed a branch of Cumann na mBan, the women's auxiliary of the Irish Volunteers. Following graduation, she then taught in Germany and it was during this time that the siblings communicated with each other by writing letters in an exercise book which was then passed from one to the next. She returned to Dublin at the outbreak of the First World War and taught German at the Technical College in Rathmines.[1] During this time, she renewed her acquaintanceship with Seán MacDiarmada (MacDermott) whom she had known also before leaving from London and they became close. MacDiarmada was one of the seven leaders of the Easter Rising and one of the signatories of the Proclamation of the Irish Republic that was read from the steps of the General Post Office (GPO) on Easter Monday. During the Rising, Min acted as a courier between the different groups of rebels in the city and moved freely in and out of the GPO during that week and visited MacDiarmada who was in the GPO. As we will see further on, it was assumed that MacDiarmada and Min would have married had he not been executed following the Rising. Min eventually married Richard Mulcahy, Commander in Chief of the Irish Free State Army following the death of Michael Collins, on 2 June 1919 and they had six children: Padraic, Elisabeth, Risteárd, Máire, Neillí, (my mother—Bacon) and Seán. Of these children, Elizabeth is still alive.

Phyllis the youngest child was born in 1895 and followed in the footsteps of her sisters. She attended university in Dublin, by then established as University College Dublin, graduating in chemistry in 1916. Together with Min, she acted as a courier during Easter Week and was in the GPO with the rebels. She was present with her sister Min when they visited

---

[1]A suburb in the south of Dublin.

Seán MacDiarmada at Kilmainham Gaol Dublin on the night before his execution.

Subsequent to the Rising she completed a Masters by research, graduated as only the fifth woman scientist in Ireland and then went to London to train as a public science analyst, later establishing her own chemical analysis business at Dawson St in Dublin. In 1936, and following the death of her sister Kit, she married Sean T. O'Kelly,[2] Kit's widower, at the age of 43. Later when O'Kelly became President (of Ireland) in 1945, Phyllis gave up her scientific career but in her own words 'I didn't really enjoy my stay in the [Phoenix] Park [the President's residence in Dublin]... I was happy when it was all over. I had to give up my job on becoming First Lady. However, I am happy to have had the experience' (*Sunday Independent*, 2 March 1980). They lived later at Roundwood in Co. Wicklow and then she lived in Donnybrook in Dublin in the years after her husband's death in 1966. She died in 1983.

James (Jim), the third party in the correspondence was born in 1891 and joined the Irish Volunteers in 1913. 'At the outbreak of the Rising in 1916, he was a medical student. He made his way up to Dublin early on Easter Tuesday and was appointed chief medical officer to the GPO. After the surrender, he was imprisoned in Stafford, England, and finally in Frongoch Internment Camp, in Wales. He was released during the summer of 1916. After qualifying in March 1917, he went into medical practice in Wexford, and also became commandant of the Wexford battalion of the Irish Volunteers. His work in the town during the 1918-1919 Flu epidemic ensured his victory in the 1918 general election in South Wexford. He married Máirín Cregan, an author of children's literature in 1919, the same year that Min married Richard Mulcahy' (National Library of Ireland 2010: 6).

He was present at the First Dáil and later was one of the founding members of Fianna Fáil and would go on to hold posts of Minister for Agriculture, Minister for Health and Social Welfare, and Minister for Finance. He remained in politics until his retirement in 1965.

The letters of these three siblings reveal the biographical family as a map of relations that are clearly networked and internalised over a period of time that was marked by their own growth and development into adulthood but

---

[2]Sean T. O'Kelly (1882–1966) was a founding member of the political party Sinn Fein. He took part in the Rising of 1916 and was subsequently arrested and imprisoned. Elected to Westminster in 1918 he did not take his seat but did take part in the first meeting of the new Irish parliament (the Dail) in 1919 at which he was elected speaker. He held a number of ministerial posts before being elected President of Ireland in 1945.

crucially and influentially in the specific historical context of revolutionary Ireland between 1912 and 1915. Min Ryan, in a witness statement that she gave to the Bureau of Military History many years later in 1965, provides a description of the context in which the letter correspondence took place. In this statement, she outlines the gradual immersion into revolutionary thought under the influence of her eldest brother Martin in the following terms:

> I remember my brother coming home on holidays [from Maynooth University where he was studying to be a priest]. He was one of those people who always had a new idea. He would come home at holiday time and talk tremendously about the language movement and Sinn Féin, We started to read papers about every single thing in connection with the Sinn Féin movement…We used to read every paper [Griffith] was connected with, from cover to cover. That was the origin of our coming into the movement. (Ryan, M. Bureau of Military History: WS 399)

There is an interesting dynamic in the letters that marks the strong influence of external affairs on family life and their relationships but it is also clear from the letters that they were occupied also by very 'normal' matters such as social engagements, money, sibling rivalry and other themes that one might expect under the rubric of family in biographies. So, for instance, in a letter from Agnes to the wider family group of Da, Mother, Aunt Kate, Chaps and Liz, she comments on Nell and Kate who were sharing accommodation in Dublin, writing… 'I suppose they are doing what they like up there… must have a shocking lot of money saved by this- but shure as the fellow said it would be easier for a camel to go through the "knee of an idol" than for a rich man escape, as such – from Tomcoole'. It is clear that the writer has a construct in her imagination of the relations between herself and her sister but also of the sisters between themselves that includes a strong sense of freedom enjoyed by others. In 1912, Jim records of the situation in the shared house 'we're after give[ing] up eating off of the boxes. We're behaving like Christians now again, except we are not very particular about washing ourselves every morning. Kit got a few presents setting up, a bowl from Sean [T] O'Kelly, and a table cloth from Chris. The cloth was all holes' (Ryan Family Letters). These brief quotes reveal further interesting aspects the internalised and imagined relations among the siblings. For one, they demonstrate an openness, intimacy and sense of collective lives and biographies that do not feature often in relations outside of families. Families and members of families among themselves construct collective narratives and, in a sense write each other's lives. The manner in which one sibling takes up the themes, concerns and stories of the previous writer in the shared copy-books and writes them into their own narratives demonstrates this collective narrative where the voice of the individual is certainly accompanied by others if not an echo of others.

In their written recollection for one another of events in the past too, either those that they have experienced together or those which the one or the other have simply heard related by others, there is a clear sense of writing the past for each other. It has been claimed that parents write the past for their children in the sense that much of what children hold in memory, particularly about family history, is what and how it has been related by parents. In the letters of these siblings, there is a similar sense of them writing their history for each other. Not only are family relationships and their imaginaries closely networked and internalised, they also often have these special qualities that can reveal much to the biographical researcher.

Family Narratives in the Trajectory of Individual Lives

A second dimension of the appearance and importance of family in auto/biographical research lies in the investigation of how *changes in narrated family relations over time are a reflection of individual life changes*. The way in which families appear to individuals at different times of their lives says much about the individual and can be a rich source of biographical data. The way in which one relates one's childhood as a twenty-year old who has just experienced the first freedoms of adulthood and the loosening of childhood home constraints will probably be very different from the way in which this 'same' childhood is related and narrated as a sixty- or seventy-year old. Family narratives shift over time. In the case of our example of the three siblings in close contact in their early twenties, the parents rarely, if ever, feature in their correspondence and if so, then not by name or as individuals. The pre-occupations of these years are twofold, their own induction and introduction to adult social life and, at the same time, their growing politicisation and the seduction of revolutionary ideas. For Min this growing politicisation culminated during the week of the Easter Rising when she returned to the home place of Tomcoole. However, on arrival there she reports her saying to the family gathered in the breakfast-room:

I am certain it will come off. I have to go back. I must go back to Dublin. They said "You should take someone back with you". So Phyllis [her younger sister] came with me. (Ryan, M. Bureau of Military History: WS 399: 11)

Later Min says of her attempt to get back into the GPO (a place that was central to the action) on the Wednesday.

We were determined to get back. It would be absolutely idiotic not to; if the men were to die, we would too; that is the way we felt. (Ryan, M. Bureau of Military History: WS 399: 18)

Their writings can be considered as what has been termed 'culturally canonical biographies' (Habermas and Bluck 2000) in the two senses of the wider culture of their time but also the culture of youth at that same time.

In later life, perspectives have been changed by events and the way in which certain events either opened or closed life possibilities and even the course of a whole life. This is clear, for instance, in our example of Min Ryan. She threw herself into a carefree life of social gatherings, visits to theatre and cinema, and card playing with her rebellion-planning contemporaries in 1915, but her memories and later narrative of that time when recorded in the 1960s are starkly different. Min, in 1915–1916, was a politicised, independent active member of Cumann na mBan (Women's division of the Irish Volunteers) and also had a 'sentimental attachment', to Seán MacDiarmada (one of the signatories of the Proclamation of Irish Independence). Just a week before the Easter Rising in Dublin a ceillí[3] was arranged on Palm Sunday that was as a cover for a meeting between Seán MacDiarmada and the volunteer leaders, and Kathleen Clarke[4] recalled that MacDiarmada had Sorcha MacMahon[5] on one side of him and Kathleen on the other. 'three of the Misses Ryan passing, Miss Kit, Miss Min and Miss Phyllis; I am sure they would have [liked] to speak to him but he waved them on' (Clarke, K., WS 564). From Min's writings and interviews,

---

[3]A ceilí is a dance gathering at which traditional Irish dances are played and performed. They became fashionable among the urban middle classes at the turn of the last century as an expression of the revival of Gaelic culture at the time. Always popular in rural Ireland, they played an important role in bringing communities together but particularly couples who would not have had a chance to meet otherwise.

[4]Kathleen Clarke was a founder member of Cumann of mBan (the women's wing of the Irish Volunteers). She was the wife of Tom Clarke and sister of Ned Daly, both of whom were executed for their part in the 1916 Rising.

[5]Sorcha MacMahon (1888–1970) was an early member of Cumman na mBan and a friend of Kathleen Clarke. She acted a as courier during the Rising in Easter Week 1916 and later worked for Michael Collins.

it is evident that she was disappointed at the lack of attention from MacDiarmada and her relationship to him was characterised by all of the contemporary mores of middle-class Irish Catholicism and late Edwardian culture. In an interview conducted in 1965 in preparation for the 50th Anniversary of the Rising her internal conflict and frustration is well articulated as she recalls these events herself:

> The last time that I saw him really I'd say, the Saturday after Holy Thursday, there was a ceilí, that would happen very often and I think that was a sort of preparation ceilí for everything. Seán MacD was there but he was bustling around the place and not sitting very much and I didn't know exactly… I didn't know at all that there was going to be such a thing as a Rising. I never let my mind dwell on that. I was in the movement and really it was just a part of my life. I think and Seán didn't come into the ceilí at all much. He was standing in the hall, holding up people to see what they were doing and so on. He was talking to Mrs. Clarke a lot in the outer hall. So when I came out I felt vexed with him rather, I was vexed with him and I just walked out you see. (RTE interview, 1965)

This descriptive narrative of a young life must, however, be read also in the context and narrative of later life and the way in which the past is always discursively constituted from a particular perspective. Thus Min also writes:

> He loved his country with a passion that at times I scarcely understood. I think he is one of the few young men whom no personal passion could ever have turned away from the work he had set before himself….he worked and planned for the independence of Ireland ever since his boyhood.' (Ryan, M. 1916: 377)

Meanings and interpretations and the narratives that we write of our lives depend on when they are written and the experiences that lie between narratives. The family narratives of Ryans and their relations with each other, their friends and social circle, written before the Easter Rising were transformed by this event. From the viewpoint of narrative and auto/biographical research, this event changed not only the future of these family members but also their past. Major life events reveal the past, or better, reveal the meaning of the past in a transformed way that supersedes all earlier interpretations. It is this realisation and its consequences for reading biography and narrative that is also at the core of Badiou's theory of the event and the central role of the event in the process of subject formation (Badiou 2009).

In a theory of the possibility of political change that can also be applied to other fields, Badiou distinguishes between four kinds of change and newness; modification (which does not bring about any significant change at all), weak singularities (which result in change but having no lasting consequences), strong singularities (which bring existential change but which remains measureable), and finally *events*, which are strong singularities whose consequences are virtually infinite (Badiou 2003: 132). A definition of an event can therefore be given as 'the unpredictable and unexpected irruption of a destructive, transformative singularity of newness of truth whose consequences are virtually infinite' (Seery 2016). Such events can, of course, be on a scale that transforms whole societies and cultures but they can also be found in the individual experience. In the case of Min Ryan, there is an interesting conflation of the large and small scales. Certainly the Easter Rising, and her late knowledge of it despite being very close to its source, transformed the way in which she understood her experiences but equally, she has a deeply personal story, that she kept privately all of her life, of spending a number of hours during last night of MacDiarmada's life with her sister (Phyllis) in Kilmainham Prison before he was executed on 12 May 1916. She recounts this in the RTE interview in 1965 saying:

> We had three hours with him. We talked about everything under the sun... and we talked about how other places had fared in as much as he knew the last week and all that...Then the priest appeared at three o'clock...We stood up promptly when the priest arrived and felt a great jerk, all of us. I was the last to say goodbye to him and he kissed me and just said we never thought that this would be the end....and that was the end of that. (RTE interview, 1965)

Either or both of these events would surely suffice to transform the way one sees and writes self and others.

Family Narrative as Distributed Auto/ Biographical Knowledge

The third aspect that we consider with regard to the way in which family is a shaping factor in life narratives and therefore an important object of investigation in narrative and biographical research is that of what Bietti (2010) refers to as 'distributed auto/biographical knowledge'. This knowledge is a set of shared memories and stories that can be used strategically by family members and also used to maintain feelings of connection. It has also been argued that the connection between shared knowledge and memory and identity is strongly constructive and that shared narratives in families are performative and not just reflective of the social life of a family (Abell et al. 2000). This aspect brings to focus a central question concerning family and the construction of the self. To what extent does or can auto/biographical research cast light on the status of the morally autonomous, self-transparent liberal subject and its possible emergence from the 'family' and from its own history?

For the auto/biographical researcher, this suggests engaging with the relationship and relative status of what has been termed the 'I-self, we-self and the real-self' (Roland 1988). Roland posits that these three 'selves' are in reality three aspects of the individual and that all individuals have all three components. Of some relevance and perhaps even some utility to narrative researchers is his argument that the relative dominance of these aspects differs between individuals within societies and also between cultures. It is perhaps worth describing briefly each of the aspects and then examining them in the context of our example of family and self-narrative. Within the category of the 'we-self', it is possible to mark out a sub-category of the 'familial self' which Roland claims is characterised by a strong emotional connectedness between members but also a well-defined orientation towards empathy and tolerance of others, if it finds the conditions and decisions for its development. Clearly, the necessary conditions are not always present and the relative status of the three aspects of self differ greatly in individual lives and narratives.

In summary, the 'familial self' features a developed sense of communal self-regard and connectedness and the importance of family honour, family traditions and reciprocal obligations between members. The aspect of the 'I-self' in psychoanalytical terms refers to the ability of individuals to be self-contained, self-reliant and a mobile autonomous agent with reference to family ties and obligations. Finally, the 'real' or spiritual self refers to the aspect of individuals' lives experienced in seclusion, in contemplation and in pure artistic creation, or religious experience.

Taking this frame to the narratives and lives of the three siblings in our example family, we can gain a number of further insights into the individuals, the family, and the performativity of their narratives. First, with regard to the question of the relative dominance of each of the aspects suggested by Roland, this family group seems to show an interesting balance of these. The emotional connectedness of the 'we-self' in this family is clear from the intimacy of the letters that they shared in the time before the Easter Rising. However, this connectedness came under severe strain in the time after the revolution when Irish society and Irish families, including the one under discussion here, were divided over the issues of independence. Min Ryan, as was indicated earlier but without comment, married Richard Mulcahy who following his own involvement in the Easter Rising and the struggle for independence was a key figure in the pro-Treaty[6] grouping while most of the Ryan family were anti-Treatyists. Indeed at later stage, Min's sister Kit wrote to her urging her to leave her husband, because he was pro-Treaty. When Min's sister Nell and Brother Jim were both arrested and Nell went on hunger strike Mulcahy refused to intervene as he could not be seen to give preferential treatment (Gillis 2014: 156). The pro- and anti-Treatyists famously fought a vicious and hugely divisive Civil War that split families and Irish society for decades to follow. It is interesting to note of this family, however, that the pro- and anti-Treatyists made a decision as a collective, that the bitterness and division caused by the Civil War should not carry on into the next generation and the children of the Ryans spent holidays together in Tomcoole, the home of their grandparents.

The aspect of the 'I-self' in these individuals is well pronounced in the way that was not usual for the time, at least among the female members of the family. We have noted that almost all of the family enjoyed what we would call a 'third-level' education, including the women. The women particularly were unusual in the way in which they continued to be strongly independent throughout their lives, even though they remained within the social conventions of their time, so that the independence was evident mostly within the lives of their families and friends. Jim's independent live was, of course, lives in a much more public manner but in each case, the confidence and strength of the individual that support autonomy and the ability to distance oneself from family, even within the family, are evident.

Of the 'real' or spiritual aspect of the self as lived by our exemplary family members, we know little at all. This aspect is not present in their writings and interviews, in keeping with the culture of the times that did not include the 'confessional' dimension of narratives that are a feature of a later time. Overall, however, it would seem that the individualised or 'I-self' and the familial or 'we-self' aspects found a particular symbiotic and cohesive form in the lives of our protagonists. A bold conjecture states that this feature of their lives makes a statement about the culture of middle-class Ireland of the

---

[6]The Irish War of Independence from Britain ended with a Treaty that saw 26 counties on the island becoming a Free State while 6 counties (now Northern Ireland) remained part of the UK. The Treaty was not accepted by all political parties in Ireland and it became the origin of a brutal Civil War 1922–1923.

time, where individual assertion and a certain self-promotion that was the result of revolution and education was tempered by the traditional value and importance of family cohesion, reputation, responsibilities and obligations. Viewing their lives and narratives with this somewhat psychoanalytic-anthropological frame does seem to help understand how family and individual are connected in a way that is probably deeper than most sociological analyses can penetrate. Once again, the power and importance of auto/biography are made clear in understanding the human condition.

Conclusion

This chapter has attempted both to tell a story of a family in time and place and to theorise somewhat about it. Or seen conversely, it has proposed some theory on family in biography and narrative and has applied it to a specific story. It does not seem important in which way one views the structure but what is important is the attempt to make clear the way in which family shapes and informs individual lives but also the way in which life events also rewrite family stories. We have attempted to address just a few dimensions of the relationship between family, family stories, individuals and their stories and we hope to have shown the power of internalised imaginative constructions of familial networks in individual life stories. Also, we hope to have shown that changes of perspective on self and family emerge from live experiences and, as a result, family and live narratives change over the life-cycle and finally, that identity in narrative can be seen as an interplay of a familial, liberal individual and inner-held self. In each of these attempts, the role of the family is highlighted and thus offers a continuing source and object of interest and inquiry for auto/biographical researchers. 'We are family', as Sister Sledge[7] proposed in 1979, reflects both a deep truth and the influence of powerful structures of self and identity perhaps not anticipated or intended in the song.

---

[7]An American music group of the disco era who had a hit with the song 'We are Family' in 1979.

References

Abell, J., Stokoe, E. H., & Billig, M. (2000). Narrative and the Discursive (Re) Construction of Events. In S. Sclater (Ed.), *The Uses of Narrative*. New York, NY: Routledge.

Badiou, A. (2003). Philosophy and Truth. In O. Feltham & J. Clemens (Eds.), *Infinite Thought: Truth and the Return of Philosophy*. London: Continuum.

Badiou, A. (2009). *Theory of the Subject*. New York, NY: Continuum.

Bietti, L. M. (2010). Sharing Memories, Family Conversation and Interaction. *Discourse and Society, 21*(5), 499–523.

Clarke, K. (1950). Bureau of Military History: WS 564.

Gillis, L. (2014). *Women of the Irish Revolution*. Cork: Mercier Press.

Habermas, T., & Bluck, S. (2000). Getting a Life: the Emergence of the Life Story in Adolescence. *Psychological Bulletin, 126,* 748–769.

Laing, R. D. (1969). *The Politics of the Family*. London: Routledge.

National Library of Ireland. (2010). *Seán T. Ó Ceallaigh and The Ryans of Tomcoole* (MS 48,443/1–MS 48,503/2). Compiled by Maria O'Shea. Dublin: Author.

Nicolo, A. M., Benghazi, P., & Lucarelli, D. (Eds.). (2014). *Families in Transformation: A Psychoanalytical Approach*. London: Karnac Books.

Pincus, L., & Dare, C. (1978). *Secrets in the Family*. London: Faber and Faber.

Roland, A. (1988). *In Search of the Self in India and Japan*. Princeton, NJ: Princeton University Press.

Ryan, M. J. (1916). Sean McDermott. In M. Joy (Ed.), *The Irish Rebellion of 1916 and Its Martyrs: Erin's Tragic Easter* (pp. 372–379). New York: The Devin Adair Company.

Ryan, M. (1950). Bureau of Military History: WS 399.

Ryan Family Letters. (1912–1915).

Seery, A. (2016). The Educational Encounter as Event. *Journalism, Media and Cultural Studies, 10,* 54–65.

Sunday Independent. (1980, March 2). Interview with Phyllis Ryan, Dublin.

Telefís Éireann [RTE Television], (1965) Portraits 1916. A. O'Gallachoir (Producer), RTE, Dublin.

Part III

Epistolary Lives: Fragments, Sensibility, Assemblages in Auto/Biographical Research

Maria Tamboukou

Letters are important 'documents of life' (Plummer 2001) in revealing meaning about socio-historical practices, and there is an interesting body of literature about their use in auto/biographical research in the humanities and the social sciences, as well as different trends and evaluations within this literature (see Barton and Hall 2000; Stanley 2004; Jolly 2008; Tamboukou 2016).

'Many of us came to letters through an interest in autobiography', Margaretta Jolly has noted (Jolly and Stanley 2005: 1) highlighting and theorising the many entanglements between epistolarity and auto/biographical analyses. Plummer (2001) has maintained however, that the overwhelming, fragmentary, unfocused and idiosyncratic nature of letters cannot provide useful sources for sociological analyses in life history research. Liz Stanley has taken issue with Plummer's (2001) reluctance to recognise letters as useful 'documents of life', arguing instead that letters and particularly correspondences can create rich fields of auto/biographical insights in sociological research and chart innovative methodological approaches in biographical research and the sociological imagination (see Stanley 2011, 2015, 2016; Stanley et al. 2012, 2013). In this context, she has outlined three analytical planes on which epistolary narratives can be deployed: the dialogical, the perspectival and the emergent (2004: 202–204). Letters are dialogical, argues Stanley, opening up channels of communication and reciprocity not only between the correspondent parts, but also between the writer of the letter and any reader (Stanley 2004: 202). Their perspectival aspect means 'that their structure and content changes according to the particular recipient and the passing of time' (Stanley 2004: 203). Finally in having emergent properties, letters evade 'researcher-determined concerns' (ibid.) and instead display 'their own preoccupations and conventions and indeed their own epistolary ethics' (ibid.). In this light, Stanley has argued that the narrative value of the letter could only emerge as an effect of the exploration and indeed juxtaposition of a wider collection of letters and bodies of correspondence, what she has theorised as 'the epistolarium'. As Stanley (2004: 218) has configured the concept:

> The idea of the epistolarium can be thought about in (at least) three related ways, with rather different epistemological complexities and consequentialities: as an epistolary record that remains for *post hoc* scrutiny; as "a collection" of the entirety of the surviving correspondences that a particular letter writer was involved in; and as the "ur-letters" produced in transcribing, editing and publishing actual letters (or rather versions of them).

Stanley has performed a meticulous examination of 'the different epistemological complexities and consequentialities' emerging from the analysis of the three versions of the epistolarium as delineated above. What is interesting in her theorisation is her ultimate conclusion that despite the epistemological, ontological and ethical problems emerging in their analysis, collections of letters do have a narrative structure and offer useful and rare insights into the life of the auto/biographical subject (Stanley 2004: 221).

But how much can letters 'reveal' about the auto/biographical self? Do they have any privileged position as auto/biographical documents? Letters are only fragments of lived experiences: they cannot be brought together by any Aristotelian coherence of beginning, middle and end and they absolutely lack the closure of canonical narratives. Indeed, letters 'reveal' as much as they conceal: they leave traces of ideas, discourses and action, but they can never encompass any 'truth' about who their sender or addressee, 'really were' or how they felt. Then why are letters important in auto/biographical research?

While Stanley (2011) has urged for a robust analytical approach to the use of letters in auto/biographical research in the social sciences, MacArthur (1990) has turned her attention to the analysis of the dynamics of the epistolary form in revealing meaning about subjects and their entanglement in the web of human relations, as well as in the sphere of action. While written to the moment and of the moment, letters 'privilege the energy that propels them' (MacArthur 1990: 25) and create meaning by narrating the present without knowing what the future of this narrated present will be, how it will ultimately become past. However, as MacArthur (1990) notes, a present that unfolds is narrated differently than a present that has already 'chosen its course' (08).

There is indeed a significant difference between lives, unfolded in letters and 'the retrospective teleology' (Brockmeier 2001: 252) of auto/biographical research. Whenever we tell or write a story, including our own life history, the contingencies of life retreat and what emerges is a constructed linearity, an auto/biographical design that was mean to unfold the way it did from the beginning. This difference however and particularly the inability of the epistolary mode to orient the story towards 'the end', deploys a series of 'technologies of autobiography' (Gilmore 1994), a matrix where narratives of truth and experience are knitted together.

Thus, rather than imposing an overarching meaning derived from a central character, letters open up a diversity of perspectives and reveal multiple layers of meanings. Auto/Biographical sense in this context emerges as an agglomeration of epistolary stories that are incomplete, irresolute or broken. Yet when brought together, these fragmented stories create a milieu of communication where the silenced, the secret and the unsaid release forces that remind us of the limits of human communication, the inability of language and representation to express the world. But how can these fragmented epistolary stories be brought together in an auto/biographical design and understanding?

When writing letters, correspondents inevitably become components of an epistolary assemblage, they enter 'storyworlds' (Herman 2002) and start creating plots and characters, of unfolding auto/biographies. But since letters are always fragmented, interrupted and dispersed, who can have access to the overall auto/biographical design in the making?

This is where the role of the researcher becomes crucial: as 'an external reader' (Altman 1982), the researcher can have access to bodies of correspondences and consequently the overall design that they have generated. In this light, letters can be analysed as auto/biographical narratives. Their narrativity, however, can only emerge if they are theorised 'as units, within a unity' (Altman 1982: 167). Auto/Biographical sense emerges as an effect of the exploration and indeed juxtaposition of wider collections of letters and bodies of correspondences, what Stanley (2004) has theorised as 'the epistolarium', as already noted above. However, the consideration of the context should not override the analytic attention to each individual letter, subsuming its singularity into the demands of a supposedly overarching structure of the whole. Altman is very careful in keeping the balance between the unit and the unity:

Each individual letter enters into the composition of the whole without losing its identity as a separate entity with recognisable borders. Each letter is defined by the blanc space that surrounds it; each has its characteristic shape and coloration. The letter retains its own unity while remaining a unit within a larger configuration. (1982: 167)

As I have argued elsewhere in my work (Tamboukou 2011), it is precisely the singularity of each letter that can carry traces of thoughts, affects, passions and actions that ultimately create the epistolary author as an *assemblage*, a cartography of multiple subject positions. It is in the process of how a subject crystallises as an *assemblage* that the Foucauldian self as an effect of the interweaving of certain historical and cultural practices or *technologies* (Foucault 1988) has made connections with the Deleuzo-Guattarian conceptualisation of the self as a threshold, a door, a becoming between multiplicities (Deleuze and Guattari 1988). In this sense, each letter becomes a graph of the wandering self, and a part of the wider cartography of the correspondence and its epistolary figures. Further, drawing on insights from Hannah Arend's take of the political as uniqueness and plurality (1998), what I have also argued throughout my work is that letters carry traces of 'deeds and words' and become 'portraits of moments' that condense political action, expose the existential uniqueness of their protagonists and reveal multiple meanings of action and thought (Tamboukou 2016).

It goes without saying that working with letters as 'documents of life' (Plummer 2001) in auto/biographical research raises a quite complex spectrum of questions around representation, context, truth, power, desire, identity, subjectivity, memory and ethics, questions that are now well identified and richly explored in the field of auto/biographical narratives (See Smith and Watson 2001). However, epistolary narratives have their own take on these questions and indeed demand ways of analysis that are particularly oriented to the specificities of their ontological and epistemological nature. It is, I suggest, by working within specific contexts that methodological problems in analysing epistolary narratives can best be addressed as the three contributions in this part lucidly show.

Reflecting on her rich experience of reading letters in archives all over the world Liz Stanley persuasively maintains that the majority of extant letters in archival collections are written by ordinary people dealing with daily activities and 'the business of life'. Stanley is interested in dissecting epistolary practices about the mundane and the ordinary and she does so by looking into white South African letter-writers in the nineteenth and twentieth centuries. The primary concerns of these letters are to keep family relations alive, but also to support and sustain, economic, cultural, political and religious bonds, Stanley argues, but she also notes that each of the three epistolary collections that she considers in her chapter, develops its own writing traits and practices that have to be taken seriously and followed in any form of epistolary analytics. Epistolary writing is not just about the dialogics of the I/you relation, Stanley argues, but much wider and complex when the 'we' is added to create a tripartite schema in the configuration of the epistolary pact.

Erla Hulda Halldórsdóttir is also interested in the ordinariness and situatedness of nineteenth-century family letters in Iceland in her research with the epistolarium of Páll Pálsson. Drawing on Cavarero's (2000) theorisation of the unpredictability of life histories Halldórsdóttir looks into the importance of context in shaping the historical evidence of letters and correspondences, particularly considering the role of different spatialities and temporalities in their analysis. Multiple narratives and the gendered nature of epistolary writing are two important themes that emerge from Halldórsdóttir's analysis, her argument being that the auto/biographical element of letters and correspondences emerges and unfolds in the process of reading and understanding letters as unforeseeable relational narratives in becoming.

Drawing on the epistolaria of two middle-class women in nineteenth-century Greece Dimitra Vassiliadou theorises epistolary lives through the lens of 'autopathography' (Couser 1991), epistolary writing about bodily, mental and emotional passions and ailments in the form of sadness and melancholia. In doing so, she shows how women's letters offer glimpses not just of their personal emotions and suffering, but also about family histories and gender relations of their times and geographies. Moreover, in expressing their emotions through writing letters to their husbands these women articulate their feelings and respond actively to the social and cultural forces that oppress and torture them. Apart from being textual expressions of auto/pathographies, their letters can also be read in the light of scriptotherapy (Smith and Watson 2001), self-healing writing, or writing to become other.

What brings the three contributions together in this part of the Handbook on *Epistolary Lives*, is what I want to call 'epistolary sensibility', an attempt that goes against the dominant trend of using letters as mere 'sources' or 'data' in socio-historical research and analysis. All three contributions recognise the evidentiary value of letters, but they are deeply engaged with pertinent ontological, epistemological and ethical questions revolving around what it is exactly that we do when using letters and correspondences to derive meaning about subjects, their lived experiences and their relation to the world and others. How is this 'epistolary sensibility' to be configured? Drawing on the rich methodological insights that the three contributions offer I will draw a preliminary sketch that can be taken as an initial plane for more epistolary methodologies to emerge and unfold. Thus, epistolary sensibility includes amongst other practices:

a. striving for understandings that are driven by the letters and collections under investigation;
b. considering the content, form and context of letters and analysing them in their interrelation;
c. taking seriously the I/you/we epistolary relation;
d. considering the problematics of language and translation;
e. avoiding the use [and abuse]of letters as illustrations of auto/biographical analyses, interpretations and theorisations or as captions of images or other visual auto/biographical artefacts and objects;
f. making connections between and among letters and collections;
g. re-imagining the extant letters alongside those that were, burnt, lost or destroyed;
h. acknowledging the epistemological gaps of the absent side of correspondence;
i. challenging and interrogating existing archival ordering of letters and correspondences, as well as edited collections of letters and
j. keep excavating the archive for more unearthed, hidden and forgotten letters and correspondences.

Apart from their attentiveness to what I have called epistolary sensibility, the three contributions of this part respond differently to gender questions in epistolary analyses. Stanley insists that we should not impose contemporary gender binaries in past epistolaria, arguing instead that 'there are no significant differences between letters by males and by females when involved in the same kinds of activities or having the same kind of views'. For Halldórsdóttir, the experiences of nineteenth-century epistolary writers in Iceland are 'highly gendered', particularly in the context of their ordinariness, while Vassiliadou argues that emotions as expressed in nineteenth-century bourgeois women's letters in Greece 'operate across gender lines'. Despite their differences, what all three contributions persuasively show is that the gendering of epistolary writing needs to be problematised, contextualised and situated. Simply put, it should not be taken for granted that 'women' write differently than 'men' or that 'women' are more drawn to the epistolary genre. Gender differences within epistolary writing and indeed within epistolary lives should be mapped within specific social, cultural and political conditions, if our analyses are to add something substantial in the field of auto/biographical research.

'We think in generalities, but we live in detail' (Whitehead 1948: 26) Alfred North Whitehead has famously noted, importantly adding that 'to make the past live we must perceive it in detail, in addition to generalities' (ibid.) It is precisely the perception and understanding of 'the detail' that letters generously offer in auto/biographical research. But in order to receive and appreciate this gift we need to tend to the reading and analysis of letters with sensibility, patience and attentive care, particularly recognising the need to see them as 'units within a unity' (Altman 1982), 'documents of life' in their own right and yet entangled in the multiplicity of diverse 'epistolaria' (Stanley 2004), becoming components of 'narrative assemblages' (Tamboukou 2015). What such a nuanced, detailed, but also situated analysis can offer is a feeling of the infinitesimal and incessant processes of life that keep going on, 'the events' that leave traces behind them in novellas, stories, as well as epistolary fragments of lives, the topic of our reflections and discussions in this part.

References

Altman, J. G. (1982). *Epistolarity: Approaches to a Form*. Columbus: Ohio State University Press.

Arendt, H. (1998). *The Human Condition*. Chicago: University of Chicago Press.

Barton, D., & Hall, N. (Eds.). (2000). *Letter Writing as a Social Practice*. Philadelphia: John Benjamins.

Brockmeier, J. (2001). "From the End to the Beginning": Retrospective Teleology in Autobiography. In J. Brockmeier & D. Carbaugh (Eds.), *Narrative and Identity: Studies in Autobiography, Self and Culture* (pp. 247–280). Amsterdam: John Benjamins Publishing.

Cavarero, A. (2000). *Relating Narratives: Storytelling and Selfhood* (P. A. Kottman, Trans.). London: Routledge.

Couser, G. T. (1991). Autopathography: Women, Illness, and Lifewriting. *a/b: Auto/Biography Studies, 6*(1), 65–75.

Deleuze, G., & Guattari, F. (1988). *A Thousand Plateaus: Capitalism and Schizophrenia*. (B. Massumi, Trans.). London: The Athlone Press.

Foucault, M. (1988). Technologies of the Self. In L. H. Martin, H. G. Patrick, & H. Hutton (Eds.), *Technologies of the Self* (pp. 16–49). London: Tavistock.

Gilmore, Leigh. (1994). *Autobiographics: A Feminist Theory of Women's Self-Representation*. Ithaca and London: Cornell University Press.

Herman, D. (2002). *Story Logic: Problems and Possibilities of Narrative*. Lincoln and London: University of Nebraska Press.

Jolly, M. (2008). *In Love and Struggle: Letters in Contemporary Feminism*. New York, NY: Columbia University Press.

Jolly, M., & Stanley, L. (2005). Letters As/Not a Genre. *Life Writing, 2*(2), 75–101.

MacArthur, E. (1990). *Extravagant Narratives: Closure and Dynamics in the Epistolary Form*. Princeton: Princeton University Press.

Plummer, K. (2001). *Documents of Life 2*. London: Sage.

Smith, S., & Watson, J. (2001). *Reading Autobiography: A Guide for Interpreting Life Narratives*. Minneapolis: University of Minnesota Press.

Stanley L. (2004). *The Epistolarium: On Theorising Letters and Correspondences. Auto/Biography, 12,* 216–250.

Stanley L. (2011). The Epistolary Gift: The Editorial Third Party, Counter-Epistolaria: Rethinking the Epistolarium. *Life Writing, 8,* 137–154.

Stanley L. (2015). The Death of the Letter? Epistolary Intent, Letterness and the Many Ends of Letter-Writing. *Cultural Sociology, 9*(2), 240–255.

Stanley L. (2016). Settler Colonialism and Migrant Letters: The Forbes Family and Letter-Writing in South Africa 1850–1922. *The History of the Family, 21*(3), 398–428.

Stanley L., Dampier, H., & Salter, A. (2012). The Epistolary Pact, Letterness and the Schreiner Epistolarium. *a/b: Auto/Biographical Studies, 27,* 262–293.

Stanley L., Salter, A., & Dampier, H. (2013). Olive Schreiner, Epistolary Practices and Microhistories: A Cultural Entrepreneur in an Historical Landscape. *Journal of Cultural and Social History, 10,* 577–597.

Tamboukou, M. (2011). Interfaces in Narrative Research: Letters as Technologies of the Self and as Traces of Social Forces. *Qualitative Research, 11,* 625–641.

Tamboukou, M. (2015). Narratives as Force. In M. Livholts & M. Tamboukou, *Discourse and Narrative Methods: Theoretical Departures, Analytical Strategies and Situated Writings* (pp. 93–103). London: Sage.

Tamboukou, M. (2016). The Autobiographical You: Letters in the Gendered Politics of the Labour Movement. *Journal of Gender Studies, 25*(3), 269–282.

Whitehead, A. N. (1948). *Essays in Science and Philosophy*. London: Rider and Company.

8

Letter-Writing and the Actual Course of Things: Doing the Business, Helping the World Go Round

Liz Stanley

Introduction: Letters, Auto/Biography and the Course of Things

It is often supposed that letters are private exchanges concerned with personal and sometimes intimate matters, or literary productions requiring considerable skill to write, or written by people of public fame and importance, with *published letters* seen as of note in these respects. However, casting an eye around *archive collections* in different parts of the world, and doing so without cherry-picking just the 'important' letters, something very different can be seen (Lyons 2012; Whyman 2009; Whites Writing Whiteness 2019). This is that the large majority of the letters in archive collections when considered *en masse* are in fact not by people who are important or famous, nor are they of great literary or artistic skill, and nor are they concerned with private matters.

What the general run of letter-writing shows is that most have been written by ordinary people, often with few formal literacy skills, and they consist largely of exchanges about the mundane aspects of life, or in extremis ones of war and other cataclysmic events, have little literary merit, are often part of wider epistolary exchanges and face-to-face meetings, and are by no means confined to intimacies. A well-known example here concerns the letters

L. Stanley (✉)
University of Edinburgh, Edinburgh, UK
e-mail: liz.stanley@ed.ac.uk

© The Author(s) 2020
J. M. Parsons and A. Chappell (eds.), *The Palgrave Handbook of Auto/Biography*,
https://doi.org/10.1007/978-3-030-31974-8_8

of Polish migrants to America researched by Thomas and Znaniecki (1958 [1918–1920]). These were produced by people who were mainly only functionally literate or else were written for them by third parties; when these were read by the addressees back in Poland, this similarly often involved third parties who read them out to people who were not literate, and the contents were concerned with humdrum matters of keeping in touch, maintaining relationships and social bonds. These letters also witnessed over-time departures from then prevailing Polish polite conventions, concerning such things as appropriate forms of address and suitable content to include, and these things were a sign of many social changes occurring at the time (Stanley 2010).

Within an auto/biographical framework (Stanley 1992), this chapter discusses letter-writing by people who were not famous or important, who wrote letters engaging with the actual course of things as part of facilitating relationships with the people they wrote to, and thereby helped make everyday life happen (see also Stanley 1999, 2004; Stanley et al. 2012). These letters are in collections that are part of the Whites Writing Whiteness project, which is researching the epistolary writing practices of white South Africans over the two hundred years from the 1770s to the 1970s, in investigating the processes of change and particularly the complex racialising process that occurred there (Stanley 2017; Whites Writing Whiteness 2019).

The idea of the 'actual course of things' is discussed in Treva Broughton's (2000) thoughtful exploration of the relationship between people's lives and auto/biographical accounts of these, starting with how the term was used by Thomas Carlyle. In writing about 'Biography', Carlyle (1898 [1832]) points out that the business of everyday life involves the production of many different forms of autobiography and biography so that, for instance, conversation and all the things this includes are a more fruitful source for auto/biography than seeing the subject entirely in terms of subjectivity and interiority. Then, in *Sartor Resorts* (1987 [1836]), Carlyle expanded on these ideas by playing with the boundaries between facts and fictions around the reflexive presence of the—fictitious, and tedious—editor of this book.

Broughton points out the relevance of these ideas to the programmatic aspects of today's auto/biography scholarship, which has rejected over-simple genre separations and instead turned attention to the complex overlaps between everyday forms of auto/biography and the interpretive role of the researcher. Here she uses the idea of 'the business' of everyday life to highlight the importance of recognising that mundane forms of auto/biography are essential to how the wheels of social life turn, for people are interested in others and routinely report on and debate their conduct, character and intentions. As a consequence, the activities and characteristic *practices* which produce different forms of auto/biography should be a focus for auto/biographical investigation, and not just the *products* of such practices.

These ideas are explored in what follows by reference to letter-writing by ordinary white people in South Africa. What was the 'actual course of things' for those concerned? What was 'the business' that their letters are expressions of? Did the different letter-writing practices involved result in letters that were different in kind, and not just degree? Letters by people from different backgrounds, living in different parts of the country, and writing at varied points in time, will be discussed. Although living different kinds of lives, they were in their own ways all 'ordinary', with their letters being representative of a type, and were chosen for this and not any out-of-the-ordinary characteristics. The letters are those of a missionary wife living in the north-west of what later became South Africa (Mary Moffat letters, written 1820–1870), a civil service and academic family in Pretoria (Voss family letters, written 1880–1965), and an Eastern Cape businessman who was a printer and newspaper-proprietor (Robert White letters, written 1850–1876). They can all be seen as family letters and will be briefly compared with letters written by members of a large Transvaal farming and entrepreneurial family (Forbes family letters, 1850–1935). Archival information for all the collections discussed appears following the References.

The focus in this discussion is on the 'writing laboratory' aspects of these different letters. This is Michel de Certeau's (1984) term for the practices involved and which are shaped by the particularities of 'the business', that is, the actual course of things that the different letter-writers experienced and were part of. As an aspect of this, the 'I', 'You' and 'We' relationship inscribed in these letters is considered, for a writing laboratory is part of a wider 'scriptural economy' and the business involved among other things connects a network of people writing letters and related documents, with their pronoun uses importantly indicating relationality (Stanley 2002, 2015; Stanley and Sereva 2019). Consequently, how the relationship between these letter-writers and the people they wrote to is inscribed needs taking into analytical account.

Doing the Business

Mary Moffat Letters

A starting-point is provided by the letters of Mary Moffat (1795–1871), half of the Moffat missionary partnership with her husband Robert (1795–1892), and part of a network of missionary letter-writing that also encompassed her parents, missionary-supporters in Britain, her brother John Smith (also a missionary), and later various of her sons, daughters, and daughters- and sons-in-law (which latter group included David Livingstone). All the extant letters are dated from 1820 on. This is when the then Mary Smith left the north of England, arrived in southern Africa and married Robert, and so they were written in circumstances of migration and absence where she did not expect to see any family or friends in Britain again (although in the event she later returned twice for visits). In this sense, they have the archetypical characteristic of letter-writing, of being communications across complete absence and great distance.

Mary Moffat's letters are in two collections (55 in the Cory Library in Grahamstown and 20 in the National Archives of Zimbabwe) and reflect somewhat different aspects of her activities. The Cory Library letters span the period from 1820 to 1870. There are three main groups: to her parents, and after her mother's death in 1826 to her father; to her children and particularly youngest daughters Bessie and Jane when at school in Britain; and to people in evangelical Congregationalist circles in northern England who were supporters of missionary work, with these latter links melding into ties of epistolary friendship persisting even a generation on from the people she had known face to face. These letters have many concerns, but there is an emphasis on relating in detail the actual course of things being experienced at the point she wrote. The National Archives of Zimbabwe letters are all dated in the 1820s; they are mainly to her father, and they focus more on missionary work.

As this indicates, the surviving letters are primarily concerned with maintaining the fabric of relationships across absence and distance, and built into them are notions of reciprocity and accepting the over-time continuation of these relational exchanges as an ethical requirement. While the letters to Mary Moffat's missionary-supporter connections could be seen as written to maintain networks of religious and potentially also financial support for the Moffats and their work, they actually include too many problems and complaints to have been intended for instrumental purposes and come across as letters intended to maintain bonds and provide points of connection for her. In a number of these letters, she comments that few opportunities for friendship were present in and around the Kuruman mission-station the Moffats headed. The Moffats were its leaders, and relationships between the different missionaries carrying out different kinds of tasks at Kuruman were sometimes fraught or occasionally openly hostile, around both religious and interpersonal differences. And as an 1829 letter to Mrs. Graves, a missionary-supporter friend in Britain, puts it, 'It is one of the severest of our private trials that as our old Friends die away we acquire no new ones' (20 October 1829, MS 6030).

In Mary Moffat's very first letter to her parents after arriving in Southern Africa (actually a combined Journal and letter), she describes the evolving pattern of things. This was on the basis that 'nothing very particular having happened, that I have hesitated to send it... [but then] I recollected that the most trivial circumstances relative to me would be interesting to you' (23 May 1820, MS 6027). This brings to attention what became a characteristic practice, that her letters inscribe the ordinary course of things because the Moffats were carrying out activities of much religious interest to her addressees—who would also be interested because of their affection for her. This first letter has a succession of dates and ends precipitously at the point it was dispatched. This was from the then remote Griqua Town and because of the possibility of 'opportunity', that is, a visitor or passing traveller who would take it to a town with a postal service. Particularly in the earlier period, opportunity happened but infrequently, and anyway when it did Mary Moffat was frequently caught in circumstances where she was unable to devote time to writing letters and could not make use of the chance thus offered.

Many of Mary Moffat's letters start with reasons and excuses for the lateness—sometimes a period of years—of her replying to a letter received, including when eventually writing to her daughters after she had missed sending a birthday letter. Thus, in an October 1849 letter to Mrs. Brown, wife of a missionary working elsewhere, she writes that 'It has been my wish for some time to reply to your interesting communication... but having to write to six of my absent children there remains little time' (27 October 1849, MS 6059), and she mentions never having more than a few minutes to herself before interruptions came from children, house-servants, patients in the out-hospital she ran and many visitors.

As this indicates, her reasons are embedded in the daily round and concern the many pressing domestic demands on her time, such that these pushed out even her desire to engage in mission work, which was the basis of her strong wish to participate in religious activities in Africa when Robert Moffat was sent there by the London Missionary Society. For instance, a letter to Mrs. Graves in November 1826 writes 'when I think you will be looking now for Missionary intelligence, I feel truly gloomy having nothing to communicate' (14 November 1826, MS 6029). Then, almost exactly ten years later and also to Mrs. Graves, she comments that 'My very dear Friend I am very sorry you have been so long neglected but for this last two years have been so variously engaged as to have very little time to write... It seems a little strange to write a letter from this country without a word of missionary intelligence but you must excuse it having so much to say on more private subjects' (13 September 1836, MS 6032).

Mary Moffat was responsible for all daily and domestic aspects of the large Kuruman mission-station, gave birth to ten children and experienced migraines as well as other ill-health around her many pregnancies, factors to be taken into account when thinking about the lateness of her replies and reasons given for this. A high proportion of the extant letters were to her daughters Bessie and especially Jane after she had taken them to school in England when aged 9 and 8, respectively. Perhaps surprisingly, these letters like the others deal with the many sometimes difficult events happening in the actual course of things experienced in the Kuruman area at the time, including violent raids by hostile groups and wars as well as more ordinary but still upsetting matters such as illnesses and deaths. Without knowing these letters were addressed to young children, a much older addressee might be assumed. In part, this can be seen as of the times, with notions of childhood not so well defined as now; but in part it is because a strong characteristic of her letter-writing is that it engages in detail with the events occurring at the point of her writing.

Thinking about Mary Moffat's letters overall, they inscribe a strong if sometimes 'late' or deferred 'writing I', one very aware of failing to reply at an earlier more appropriate time. This and the other characteristics identified here certainly evolved over time, but in an early form can be perceived in even her first extant letter. The 'You' of her addressee is by no means absent or just a cipher standing in the shadow of 'I', but in some instances—although not others—it is subsidiary to her practice of writing in detail about current happenings in the missionary context. There is also something to be noted here about the 'We' that is the missionary couple, with 'us' and 'we' often used in writing about the Kuruman mission and ongoing missionary work in Mary Moffat's letters, but not in those of Robert. This is characteristic of other letters by women married to missionaries who had a strong call to the mission-field themselves, with Rebecca Schreiner, writing letters at around the same time, providing another example (Stanley 2017, pp. 123–132). Among this generation (less so the next), however, their husbands seemingly have no hesitation in using 'I' in writing about mission work, while Mary Moffat saw herself in terms of a missionary partnership and a joint calling.

Overall, Mary Moffat's letters involve reciprocity and their content is modulated according to the different people she was writing to and her view of the epistolary pact that these letter-exchanges were bringing about

(Stanley et al. 2012). But at the same time, Mary Moffat's need to express the actual course of things took precedence when she was writing to some people, such as her daughters and Mrs. Brown; but not others, such as her father after her mother's death; and with her laments about not writing more on missionary activities to Mrs. Graves positioning this friend and the other missionary-supporters as transitional figures between these two aspects.

Voss Family Letters

The Voss family letters are typical of much letter-writing, for they result from exchanges between members of a tight-knit family network, including some members in different parts of South Africa, some in Ireland and England, others elsewhere in southern Africa, all living at long distances from each other. The core consisted of two Du Toit sisters born in the Hopetown and Orange River area. They were Hester, who married a cousin, Piet Du Toit, a Hopetown farmer; and Lottie (aka Cottie and other nicknames), who married Thomas Voss, who had moved to the area with his family and was of English background. Voss was an accountant and was later employed by the Transvaal government, whereupon he and his family moved to Pretoria. There are some 600 Voss family letters extant in the National Archives of South Africa (A1967), spanning the period 1880 to the mid-1960s. There are some clusters within this; with the proviso, there are considerable overlaps between them.

The collection includes (i) letters from and to Lottie Voss, in particular involving her sister Hester, Lottie's sons and daughter and cousins of her own generation; and (ii) there are letters from extended Voss family members living outside of South Africa and in particular in Ireland. There were three Voss children, all with letters in the collection. The fewest of these are from various people to (iii) Hettie, who married a cousin. There are (iv) more from various people to George Du Toit Voss, the eldest son, who became a lawyer and later a judge. There are also (v) more to and from the younger son, Vivian Voss, who became a physicist, lectured at the University of Pretoria, and was a strong supporter of Afrikaner nationalism. These latter include letters from various cousins of his generation, also his long-standing friends, and others who married into the wider family, some of whom were also friends of George and Hettie. The three siblings indeed were frequently written to as (vi) 'The Trio', with these letters passed between them.

The Voss family letters are difficult reading because of three characteristic writing practices. The first is the prevalent use of nicknames, coupled with the frequent practice of letters being addressed to and/or signed off in terms of relationship rather than personal names or even nicknames. An example is 'My darling Sister… the children… your loving Sister' (25 October 1907, A1967/1/1). The second is that both Voss and Du Toit components frequently married cousins with the same surnames and did so down the generations, so surnames provide little guide, while personal names are also repeated across the generations. The third is that these letters are highly elliptical. They are focused on the minutiae of family links and small happenings—who has seen whom, had babies, is well or been ill, taken holidays and so on—and with the people concerned typically referred to just with nicknames or in relationship terms. This emphasis on the quotidian of family life and the doings and relationships that compose the actual course of things is a shared characteristic among these letter-writers, both men and women, young and old, those who were born Du Toit and Voss and those who married in.

The difficulties here are compounded because significant numbers of the letters are not dated and nor do they include the places where they were written from or the addresses they were sent to. As a consequence, even basic information cannot be worked out regarding some aspects of the lives, births and deaths of various of the letter-writers and their addressees. It is also rare to come across letters concerned with wider topics and outside events, even when it is clear from date and address that the writer and/or their addressee was in contexts involving such things.

The result of these characteristic practices in the Voss-Du Toit scriptural economy is that it is easy to become immersed in the unfolding details of the actual course of things regarding the minutiae of extended family happenings being reported on by the letter-writers, and to bracket that who many of the letter-writers, recipients and people mentioned are remains opaque. However, what the contents and flows add up to is a very tight-knit extended family network in which letter-writing kept the wheels of family relationships turning across distance and absence and also generations. Writing about complicated matters or explaining people or connections was not needed, for the epistolary pact here rested on the more basic matter of maintaining family contact, with reporting the humdrum actual course of things being what the business of this letter-writing is concerned with. While couched in terms of 'I' and 'You', what results is a 'We' in a strong sense, with much of the 'who and what' resistant to an outside readership. And interestingly, this 'We' results from family letter-writing practices and does not come across as particularly gendered, for these practices are equally shared by the male and female contributors.

The features outlined here add up to a set of characteristic writing laboratory practices, rather than problems. That is, they raise issues only for outsiders. For those who were part of this letter-writing network, they were how letters should be within the family exchanges, and the things that seem mysterious to outsiders now were part of their knowledge-base of things known in common. The result challenges a key assumption about what letter collections are like—that it is possible with close attentive reading to get to know them in an in-depth way. However, in spite of sustained work on this collection, the Voss family letters are not 'known' in this sense, with 'We' remaining largely intact and outsiders cordoned off.

There is also another feature to be added here. It unfolded over time and is concerned with the 'We' of Afrikaner nationalism. The Voss letters show changes over time in the language medium used and the increasing use of Afrikaans (which had originated as a combination of local patois and Dutch), something that was central to the growth of cultural nationalism. In the earlier period, there are just occasional letters wholly or in part in Dutch, with an example being a letter by 'Sister' in English on one side of a sheet of paper and on the other a letter by 'Papa' in Dutch (13 December 1880; A1967/1/59). By the 1910s and early 1920s, Dutch vanishes and there are a few letters which mix early Afrikaans and English, mainly by including idiomatic Afrikaans phrases amidst a letter otherwise in English. The number solely in Afrikaans then markedly increases over the 1930s. An example is a 1937 letter to Hester Du Toit from a long-time friend, Annie Rothman; this is entirely in Afrikaans, although she had earlier written in English (20 November 1937, A1967/1/38).

In spite of their name, the Voss family was from England and migrated to South Africa in the 1870s. However, they and their then adult children strongly supported the Boer republics during the South African War 1899–1902. Relatedly, one exception to the general rule of not commenting on 'external' matters is a July 1915 letter from Lottie Voss to son George expressing her passionate 'national or patriotic feeling' (26 July 1915, A1967/1/63). Also, Vivian Voss's role in nationalist-promoted activities at the University of Pretoria has already been noted. While the 'We' of Afrikaner nationalism does not usually appear in an overt 'we' form, by implication through the growing frequency of Afrikaans-medium letters in the collection, it becomes an increasingly palpable presence and takes a very material form.

Robert White's Letters to Robert Godlonton

The next letters were also written as part of a wider family network. This centred on Robert Godlonton (1794–1884), a printer and publisher, member of the Cape Legislative Assembly, and a high-profile and very divisive figure in political life of his time. The letters concerned were written by his nephew and business partner Robert White (1819–1894), who was relatedly an intelligence-gatherer for Godlonton. However, for reasons now not known, at some point they became separated from the rest of Godlonton's letters and through auction-room sales entered different archives, with just two of his letters remaining in the Godlonton collection (which has nearly 2000 letters and is a Cullen Library collection). There are around 80 White letters to Godlonton in the Bodleian Library, Oxford, and an interconnected set of 40 more in the Cory Library, Grahamstown; the dates of these letters significantly overlap, so it is difficult to discern why they were divided up as they were.

The two sets of White letters to Godlonton also cannot be told apart in respect of the occasions of writing and the kind of content included. They were sometimes written when White had information to impart when he was at home in Grahamstown, although most were written on the regular occasions when he travelled to various small Eastern Cape frontier towns where he and Godlonton had outposts of their printing and publishing business. This was part of White's very hands-on management practices, with Godlonton a sleeping partner largely in Cape Town because of his political involvements, and with the same kinds of letters being sent when Godlonton was in Britain and White remained in South Africa. And while later White removed to Britain for a period, the letters he wrote then have the same kind of origins, that is, when he had been attending to matters of shared business concern, or when something particularly interesting to Godlonton had occurred.

In White's letters, family members and happenings are mentioned (promising young Durban, Godlonton's son; White's wife and her breakdown in mental health and then confinement in an asylum; the education and social life of White's daughters; his meticulousness in requesting his regards be passed on to 'Mrs G' and other Godlonton connections). In addition, they contain much on the political matters that Godlonton was involved in or was something of a leader on, like separation/federalism regarding the Eastern Cape, and the conduct of the ongoing Frontier Wars between settlers and Xhosa there. Contents also show their business interests were not solely in printing and publishing. There is, for example, much about shared interests in banks, insurance companies and share prices. Also, on occasion White acted as an agent for Godlonton in other business matters, for example the purchase of farms and property to rent, although overall their finances were separate.

However, it is regarding their detail on business and political aspects of frontier life that these letters stand out. They are filled with accounts of people, events and the actual course of things in Grahamstown, spreading out to business and political circles in other towns, including King William's Town and Bloemfontein, where White and Godlonton had business partnerships in printing and publishing ventures and also interests in local banking and other commercial concerns. In addition, White's writing practices place Godlonton in a superior position, where they are partners but not equal partners, with this connected more with Godlonton's political role and perhaps that he was Robert White's uncle, than it was with their business relationship.

Given how White's letters to Godlonton are written and the thoroughness with which information is imparted (for none are short or perfunctory), they come across as a cross-genre form of writing, combining a letter and a report of intelligence-gathering which is being passed on. An example from 1852 covers many topics, including: 'I have waited until the last moment before answering yours of the 24th… it is possible Sir Harry is detaining it [the post]… he said to send it by his bullock waggon… your note to Irving… the ballot took place… Solomon, Bowker, Eckley, William and myself… I think you ought to speak to Mr Montagu about it… I hear 200 Burghers are going to turn out from Somerset under Bowker… I closed with Norden for Jarvis's house… last evening from General Somerset' (25 February 1852, Mss Afr s2/245).

The result is that these letters provided Godlonton with immense detail about a range of happenings in the places that White wrote from, as he travelled about expediting their shared business concerns. His letters were also usually written and dispatched as quickly as possible from the places he was visiting, and were posted at the last moment possible in order to include up-to-the-minute information. There is a clear sense of Godlonton being sent information 'hot off the press', or rather hot off the pen, and from there into the press, given that White was also encouraging contributions for the high-profile journal and newspaper publications that their business owned.

Aside from the publication aspect, White's letters to Godlonton share their 'intelligence-gathering and reporting' features with various other letters in the same collection as White's (Mss Afr s1, s2), in particular those by John Montagu, Cape Colonial Secretary until 1852; by the Eastern Cape politician Thomas Philipps; and by Richard Southey, secretary to the Cape Governor and then Attorney-General. These too provide descriptions of the course of things happening that the writers consider important to convey to Godlonton, sometimes indeed providing political information that should have been kept secret. Also, Philipps's letters in particular bear signs of being written when he was on the move and in the immediacy of just leaving situations which he wanted Godlonton to know about. This suggests that Godlonton had a number of 'client' correspondences with people who fed him privy information about what was occurring as the course of things unfolded.

There is, however, a notable difference between White's letters and these others, a difference all the more interesting given Godlonton's well-known retrograde views on matters of race. There is a general prevailing silence in White's letters about both race in general terms and more specifically the everyday presence of black and coloured people in acting as domestic and manual workers or as traders and agriculturalists. Many of Godlonton's correspondents, and certainly the other men who were intelligence-gatherers for him, shared his political views with regard to race. That White's letters should be largely silent on such matters is slightly curious, although it should be noted that those written during the period of the Eighth Frontier War (1850–1853) letters do comment on some aspects.

These latter letters are focused in 1852 to mid-1853. They mention race matters in largely descriptive and non-pejorative terms of opposing forces and invasion, with this happening off-stage as it were, not close to or involving Grahamstown and its everyday course of things in any direct way. They comment on the troops and volunteers away fighting; the Xhosa enemy being duplicitous, in agreeing to peace then breaking truces and ceasefires; and members of the Khoi-composed Cape Corps soldiery deserting even after the proclamation of peace in 1853. While at the time relatively few black people had been incorporated into carrying out labour for white communities, there was still a sizeable group living on the outskirts of Grahamstown and other frontier towns who did so, so White's silence apart from about the Frontier War is difficult to interpret.

Standing back from the detail of White's letters to Godlonton, a number of things come into view. The actual course of things that White writes about involves both business and political life, and is also shaped by his intelligence-gathering purposes in provisioning Godlonton with up-to-the-minute information. These practices did not so much evolve over time as are present even in the early (1850) letters, so possibly there were earlier letters still, although there are no signs of such in the relevant collections.

Are there ways in which White's letters are gendered? Certainly, they were written by a man and addressed to another man, and they deal with business and political matters. However, there are letters and business papers in the Pringle Collection concerning an Eastern Cape businesswoman, Harriet Townsend, who was living in the same area and writing letters and business documents just a few years before White. These too are preoccupied with economic life and indeed focus in an even more fine-grained way on the minutia of commercial activities than do White's letters. While some spheres of activity were organised in ways that excluded women, in particular political life, the economic and business sphere was not one of them, with women visible in a range of commercial activities in the frontier towns of the day, as shopkeepers, jewellers, blacksmiths, pharmacists, owners of lodging houses and hostelries, school-keepers and more. In addition, White's characteristic writing practices led him to write in a descriptive and conversational way, filled with people and their doings and what these might add up to given the interests he shared with Godlonton, and in which Godlonton is indeed often invoked as an active presence and sometimes interlocutor. In this respect, they bear comparison with the letters of Mary Moffat. Gender matters are by no means binary, then, and indeed, in some respects there are traversals of the conventions.

What and how he wrote positions 'I', 'You' and 'We' in interesting ways in Robert White's letters. Clearly, he has a very active 'writing I', in the sense that his letters report on places he has been, things he has done, people he has seen, things they have told him. But at the same time, it comes across strongly that this was for Godlonton and that White is writing what and how he does in order to fit Godlonton's interests, so this 'I' is writing at the behest of 'You', his addressee. Although in a literal sense 'I' predominates, then, it is 'You' who dominates. Certainly, there is also a 'We' in these letters, the we who shared many business interests. However and interestingly, it was here that clashes of interest were raised on a number of occasions across White's letters. In the later 1850s, White became unhappy with some of the personnel employed by Godlonton, he had to manage Godlonton's many business concerns as well as those they shared, the Eastern Cape economy was in severe difficulties and Godlonton had left to him to deal with this, and anyway he wanted to leave the daily round of ordinary business life. They reached a later accommodation, however, and retained many business and commercial interests in common, and the intelligence-gathering aspects of White's letters continued.

The Writing Laboratory and the Scriptural Economy

The idea of a writing laboratory brings together the points discussed so far. For Michel de Certeau (1984), a writing laboratory collects, inscribes and transforms. Writing is a constitutive as well as representational medium, with a resulting text—a letter, diary, Will, memoir, note…—being constituted around (if not always adhering to) the conventions for its kind or type, including how it references back to a lived reality and claims referential force concerning the things that actually happened. It is often an element within a wider scriptural economy (Stanley 2015). Central to it are the specific writing practices people engaged in.

Thinking about this in connection with the Forbes family letters, the letter-writers here include parents, offspring, sisters, brothers, uncles, aunts, cousins, friends, neighbours, business connections, shop owners, merchants, tax inspectors, magistrates and many more, producing some 5000 extant letters of a performative, everyday course of thing—'I am well and send you cheese, here is some news, send me pins, galvanised iron or a horse'—kind. Their letters circulating in South Africa are mainly ongoing communications in circumstances of interrupted presence, where people expected to meet each other again, perhaps fairly soon, and the activities expedited by letters were part of ongoing relationships. Those between South Africa, Scotland, South Australia and elsewhere are surprisingly similar, with these exchanges too being marked by their performative character concerning shared activities. The women Forbes letter-writers are as much involved in this as the men, and write as much or more, with economic and social life complexly overlaying each other and all family members from a young age playing a part in this.

For the Forbes and others in this network, what comes over is an across-the-board getting on with shared matters in hand, with these being literally as well as figuratively 'the business'. The actual course of things here was overwhelmingly business in an economic sense, with family connections and business ones overlaying. The contents are mainly about expediting shared economic interests around farms, crops, stock, gold- and coal-mining, share prices, property-rental and more; and are characterised by focusing on exteriority (things, people, activities) rather than interiority, and performativity rather than reflection or retrospection.

How are the letters in the Forbes scriptural economy to be understood? Writing not only permits communication across time and space, but it also reorders and thereby redefines meaning. The letters consequently have a complex ontological basis as both a representational order and one predicated upon the referential assumption that the things written about were indeed part of the actual course of things that had actually happened. They do not provide unmediated access to everyday lived experience but follow, however loosely, the conventions of genre codes about how as well as what to represent. But at the same time, they are the product of the letter-writers endeavouring to represent aspects of the actual course of things that would be appropriate to the person they are writing to. This returns attention to the particular writing practices involved and which have been discussed earlier concerning the letters of Mary Moffat, the Voss family and Robert White.

These letters, as well as those in the Forbes network and by Harriet Townsend, were written by people who were ordinary in the sense of being representative of their kind. Their letters are performative in various ways, such as materially embodying the good wishes expressed in them, making the payments required and oiling the wheels of social relationships. The letter-writers make use of widespread writing practices, with varying degrees of proficiency. However, the letters that result are not ordinary in the sense of being repetitious or humdrum, but were written in and concerned with what was ordinary *in the circumstances* that each of the letter-writers was part of.

The 'course of things' should not be thought about, then, as though a flat featureless ever-spreading plain with no landmarks; but instead, to continue with the topographical metaphor, as varied landscapes with diverse climates and different geographical features, and which could change over time. The 'course of things' might be circumstances of war or death, might be the weather or fluctuations in share prices, might be office disputes or buying sheep, might be discovering gold or a relative dying, might be planning to meet family members or conveying a local scandal, or could be all these in one letter. The course of things is what *actually happens*, and it implies a claim to referentiality: with whatever representational complexities, the content is indeed concerned with things that actually happened and which could be dull or unique or extraordinary or terrifying or routine…

The letters of Mary Moffat, the Voss family, Robert White, the Forbes family and Harriet Townsend are all part of wider scriptural economies, as indicated earlier. Sometimes practices in these writing laboratories were shared by other contributors, something that is clear regarding the Forbes family (Stanley 2015), and has been discussed here also regarding the Voss family letters, where it exists in an extreme form. Perhaps more typically, the characteristic writing practices of Mary Moffat's letters were not shared by others in the scriptural economy she was part of, and those that are characteristic of Robert White's letters were not generally shared by others in the Godlonton network, although their intelligence-gathering aspect does mark the letters by Montagu, Philipps and Southey, because they had a similar client relationship with Godlonton.

Of course, all of the letters discussed were written either by women or by men, and it is tempting to impose contemporary gender binaries on how they do so. As already indicated, this should be resisted! There are no significant differences to be found between letters by males and by females when involved in the same kinds of activities or having the same kind of views. This comes out regarding the Voss family letters and in a different way concerning the 1840s frontier entrepreneur Harriet Townsend. It also comes out strongly regarding some letters not discussed thus far, which are part of the Gallagher collection. These are 1880s and early 90s letters from many customers purchasing items in letters making orders for goods, which were sent to the Embusheni trading station in the then Pondoland. The letters by women here are exactly the same as those by men, in being to the point, extremely performative, and also well versed in letter-writing's polite conventions, including by signing their names followed by '(Mrs)' or '(Mr)'. The main difference is that its black customers, women as much as men, are more literate than its white ones, with the black/white difference indicating levels of education (and social position) prevalent among a mission-educated group compared with white migrants.

Conclusion: The Business of 'I', 'You' and 'We'

What are the consequences of the letter-writing practices used across these letters with regard to 'the business' of how 'I', 'You' and 'We' are inscribed? This is clearly an important matter because such things are central to auto/biographical practices of oral as well as written kinds and open up relationality for consideration. The letters discussed here provide illuminating examples of how the ways in which 'I', 'You' and 'We' are deployed to convey the different relationships involved, with the letter-writers situating themselves in relation to their addressees, and thereby shaping the terms of the emergent epistolary pact involved (Stanley 2011).

Mary Moffat's characteristic writing practices suggest a kind of mediated need to describe the course of things, so that although the 'writing I' is strongly indicated, even more so it is the unfolding course of things that predominates in her letters. The reiterations of reasons and excuses for not replying 'in good time' when taken at face value suggest the overwhelming character of her responsibilities and working tasks, with letter-writing yet another requirement, but one which perhaps helped her to put perspective on the actual course of things by writing them down. Regarding the Voss letter-writers, much of the 'who from' and 'to whom' of these exchanges remains opaque. But what does come through is that, while they are written in terms of 'I' and 'You', there is an almost agentic 'We' that emerges from how the things that were happening are being expressed. Although only infrequently named, this 'We' nonetheless dominates the writing practices involved. The writing practices that characterise Robert White's letters are very different, for 'You', their addressee, becomes a kind of interlocutor or reference point around which content is chosen and organised. No other letters by White have been traced, so whether this is a wider feature or something specific to his letters to Godlonton cannot be told. However, the result is certain and it is that 'You' the addressee is situated as the motor-force propelling the practices White engaged in.

Did the characteristic writing practices that do 'the business' for Mary Moffat, the Voss family and Robert White come about by happenstance and so almost accidentally produce their particular takes on what the actual course of things is in their letters? Or did these letter-writers have a view of how they saw the actual course of things, and then settle on particular writing practices that would best represent this? The letters in all three cases are very engaged with the actual course of things that were happening, but they do so in different ways and to different effects, and the writing practices concerned are most likely to have evolved in an iterative way because in each case the circumstances prevailing were very different ones.

It is important here to remember a point made earlier that there is no single 'actual course of things' happening, and the terrain over which things happened was varied, and so it is by no means surprising that these different letter-writers used different writing practices in responding to the different things unfolding. What is notable about this is that, in doing so, 'I', 'You' and 'We' and the relationship between them is configured and positioned differently, so that the biography and autobiography aspects take a distinctive form in each set of letters. Auto/Biography is indeed the crucially relevant concept in understanding them.

Acknowledgements My grateful thanks to the ESRC (ES J022977/1) for funding the 'Whites Writing Whiteness' research drawn on here. All the letters discussed are fully in the public domain and no ethical issues arise.

References

Broughton, T. (2000). Auto/Biography and the Actual Course of Things. In T. Cosslett, C. Lury, & P. Summerfield (Eds.), *Feminism and Autobiography* (pp. 243–246). London: Routledge.

Carlyle, T. (1898 [1832]). *Essay on Biography: Little Masterpieces*. New York: Doubleday.

Carlyle, T. (1987 [1836]). *Sartor Resartus*. Oxford: Oxford World's Classic.

De Certeau, M. (1984). *The Practice of Everyday Life*. Berkeley: University of California Press.

Lyons, M. (2012). *The Writing Culture of Ordinary People in Europe*. Cambridge: Cambridge University Press.

Stanley, L. (1992). *The Auto/Biographical I: Theory and Practice of Feminist Auto/Biography*. Manchester: Manchester University Press.

Stanley, L. (1999). Is There Life in the Contact Zone? Auto/Biographical Practices and the Field of Representation in Writing Past Lives. In P. Polkey (Ed.), *Women's Lives into Print: The Theory, Practice and Writing of Feminist Auto/Biography* (pp. 3–30). London: Macmillan.

Stanley, L. (2002). "Shadows Lying Across Her Pages": Epistolary Aspects of Reading the Eventful I in Olive Schreiner's Letters 1889–1913. *Journal of European Studies, 32*(4), 251–266.

Stanley, L. (2004). The Epistolarium: On Theorising Letters and Correspondences. *Auto/Biography, 12*(4), 216–250.

Stanley, L. (2010). To the Letter: Thomas and Znaniecki's *The Polish Peasant* and Writing a Life, Sociologically. *Life Writing, 7*(2), 139–151.

Stanley, L. (2011). The Epistolary Gift the Editorial Third Party, Counter-Epistolaria: Rethinking the Epistolarium. *Life Writing, 8*(3), 137–154.

Stanley, L. (2015). The Scriptural Economy, the Forbes Figuration and the Racial Order. *Sociology, 49*(5), 837–852.

Stanley, L. (2017). *The Racialising Process: Whites Writing Whiteness in Letters, South Africa 1770s–1970s*. Edinburgh: X Press.

Stanley, L., Dampier, H., & Salter, A. (2012). The Epistolary Pact, Letterness and the Schreiner Epistolarium. *a/b: Auto/Biographical Studies, 27*(3), 262–293.

Stanley, L., & Sereva, E. (2019, under consideration). Researching and Theorizing with Norbert Elias: Pronouns, Figuration and the Theory/Method Nexus. Submitted to a named journal.

Thomas, W. I., & Znaniecki, F. (1958 [1918–1920]). *The Polish Peasant in Europe and America, Volumes I and II*. New York: Dover Publications.

Whyman, S. (2009). *The Pen and the People: English Letter Writers*. Oxford: Oxford University Press.

Websites

Whites Writing Whiteness. (2019). Available at http://www.whiteswritingwhiteness.ed.ac.uk. Accessed 1 January 2019.

Archives

Cape Colony Letters, Accessions Afr s1, Afr s2, Bodleian Library, Oxford.

Forbes Family, Accession A602, National Archives of South Africa, Pretoria.

Gallagher Papers, Accession GAL 95/11, Killie Campbell Library, Durban.

Mary Moffat Letters, Accession MO5-6, National Archives of Zimbabwe, Harare.

Mary Moffat Letters, Cory Library, Rhodes University, Grahamstown.

Pringle Collection, Townsend Papers, Cory Library, Rhodes University, Grahamstown.

Robert Godlonton Correspondence, Accession A43, Cullen Library, University of Witwatersrand.

Robert White Letters, Cory Library, Rhodes University, Grahamstown.

Voss Family, Accession A1967, National Archives of South Africa, Pretoria.

9

The Unforeseeable Narrative: Epistolary Lives in Nineteenth-Century Iceland

Erla Hulda Halldórsdóttir

Introduction

"Life cannot be lived like a story, because the story always comes afterwards, it results; it is unforeseeable and uncontrollable, just like life", argues the Italian philosopher Adriana Cavarero in her book *Relating Narratives* (Cavarero 2000: 3). While some auto/biographical texts are written as a narration of past life (memoirs, autobiography, biography), or to comprehend life as it happens (diaries), letters reflect the "unforeseeable and uncontrollable" life as it passes by. This is the case with the letters that Páll Pálsson (1806–1877), a nineteenth-century Icelandic man, received from his closest family members for more than half a century.

By using Cavarero's theorisation of an "unforeseeable and uncontrollable" (life) story I am not denying people of the past their agency, of being able to make their choices and control their lives within respective societies and times. Nor am I contesting that there are examples of correspondences in which signatories and addressees are consciously reflecting on life, contextualising and controlling it. However, I do find Cavarero's theorising helpful when thinking about the fragmented life stories derived from letters, and how these stories unfold as we read a life in retrospect already knowing how it ended. This is, I believe, important when studying letters written by "ordinary" people, whose letters are not easily categorised in literary terms,

E. H. Halldórsdóttir (✉)
University of Iceland, Reykjavík, Iceland
e-mail: ehh@hi.is

© The Author(s) 2020
J. M. Parsons and A. Chappell (eds.), *The Palgrave Handbook of Auto/Biography*,
https://doi.org/10.1007/978-3-030-31974-8_9

as is increasingly acknowledged and discussed by scholars (Lyons 2014; Stanley, this collection).

The focal point of this chapter are the epistolary lives of Páll Pálsson's closest family, as unfolded in their letters to him, the ordinariness and situational aspects of these letters. Páll's collection is well known in Icelandic historiography and has been used to study, among other things, the growing nationalism, the emerging nation state and political and intellectual endeavours in the 1820s to the 1840s. The actors in these histories were, needless to say, young men studying in Copenhagen. My interest has been on more mundane issues, the ordinariness and situational elements of these letters, that is, the ordinary life and temporality they reflect, as well as the network and epistolary and literacy practices of Páll Pálsson's family.

My point of departure is thus the everyday nature of these letters. This calls for epistemological and theoretical considerations on the value of these stories and experiences, on how to turn fragmented letters, with their different life stories and experiences, into "history", to a concise narrative of a life (or lives). How to weave together the macro, the grand narratives of history (whether it is national, global or both) and the microaspect: the personal experiences? Furthermore, these experiences, as they are represented in letters, are gendered.

The themes chosen to be discussed are the theoretical and epistemological aspects of letters; literacy (in particular writing) from an historical perspective; the ordinariness and everyday issues of letters confronted with the grand narratives; and letters as a multi-layered, and highly gendered, venue of self-expression, representation and performance. First, the background and key actors must be introduced.

People and Historical Context

Nineteenth-century Iceland was a poor and sparsely populated rural society, with 47,000 people in 1801 and increasing to 78,000 by 1901. In comparison with Great Britain or the Nordic countries, a middle class or bourgeoisie hardly existed in Iceland until the late nineteenth century through growing urbanisation and education. Iceland was under Danish rule, which meant that the ruling class consisted of both Danish and Icelandic officials. The majority of the population lived by farming throughout the nineteenth century (Hálfdanarson 2008; Magnússon 2010; Róbertsdóttir 2014).

All children were taught to read and to know their catechism before confirmation (Lutheran). This was first and foremost religious teaching which took place within the household, supervised by the parish priest. Writing was much less common and not an obligatory subject until 1880. Evidence indicates that in 1839 about 10–30% of adult women and 20–50% of adult men were able to write (or scribble, as it was often described). In Páll Pálsson's childhood parish in eastern Iceland one-third of adult people could write in 1839, 60 men and 35 women. Hence, being able to write was a privileged skill in the first half of the nineteenth century, especially for women. Women, and poorer men, who could write were either self-educated or taught within the household. This was non-institutionalised but practical learning. It enabled people not only to keep in touch with friends and relatives but also to strengthen networks and social relations, and to perform and construct their epistolary identity (Halldórsdóttir 2015).

Those who could write utilised this to correspond with family or friends living in other parts of the country or in Copenhagen. Some of these connections lasted a lifetime, even though correspondents seldom expected that to be the case and many of them rarely met or never saw each other during their years of correspondence. Their lives, their friendships, family relations, and relationships, were thus interpreted and represented in letters. Moreover, their lives were being narrated without their knowing or foreseeing how they would develop or end.

Páll Pálsson was born into a socially and culturally well-set family of county magistrates in the east of Iceland, the eldest of five brothers and sisters. When his father died in 1815, his mother had to manage both the farm and household and seek ways to secure the prospects of her children, especially the three boys, whose education was the key to their future. In 1817, Páll left home to be fostered and educated by a friend of the family in southern Iceland. Páll's departure marks the beginning of an extensive correspondence between him, his family and friends in his home region. As years passed, his collection expanded when new friends and acquaintances became his correspondents for shorter or longer periods. Páll was an enthusiastic collector. Not only did he keep the letters he received but also collected old books and manuscripts that are now preserved at the manuscript department of the National and University Library of Iceland.

After finishing his exams at the age of seventeen, Páll became a secretary to the district governor of western Iceland, living at Arnarstapi and later in Reykjavík. Contrary to most of his friends, Páll never left Iceland to study at the University of Copenhagen but lived all his life within the household of his employer. Páll never married and died in 1877.

There are about 1600 letters from 165 signatories in Páll's collection, 155 men and 10 women. All but three of the women are relatives. The collection covers Páll's life from when he left home at the age of eleven in 1817 until he died 60 years later, in 1877. If taking the whole family's epistolarium (Stanley 2004) into consideration, Páll's entire life is covered in letters. Both his birth and death are announced in letters.

Almost one-third of the letters are written by his closest family: his mother Malene, his grandmother Sigríður Ørum and his younger siblings: The two sisters, Sigríður and Þórunn, and the two brothers, Stefán and Siggeir.[1] There are 480 letters in all, as demonstrated in the chart below. All but one correspondence started in 1817, the year of departure, and almost all lasted as long as both correspondents lived. This is a fascinating family network that enables a study of various aspects of writing practices and family relations, how they develop in time (or cease to exist), the importance of the knowledge of writing and how it is utilised (Table 9.1).

Páll's grandmother Sigríður Ørum (b. 1753) was widowed in 1788 and lived thereafter with relatives in Reykjavík, e.g., with her brother, who was the Bishop of Iceland 1797–1823. She became a qualified midwife in the early 1800s. In 1806, Sigríður Ørum moved from Reykjavík, along with her daughter Malene, to eastern Iceland, where she lived until her death in 1828. Sigríður Ørum was a determined and witty correspondent, asking her grandson to continue writing letters to her until he received news verifying her death.

Páll's mother, Malene Jensdóttir (b. 1786), was raised by her mother in Reykjavík, had her first child (Páll) in 1806, and moved to eastern Iceland where her husband Páll Guðmundsson became a county magistrate (as generations of men in his family before him). Malene was widowed in 1815 with five children from the age of 3 months to 9 years old. She wrote letters to her son, embracing him with love and encouraging words. Malene seems to have met Páll only once during the years after he left home in 1817 to her death in 1824.

Þórunn (b. 1811) had a more placid temperament than her sister, judging by her own letters and according to other family members. She never left her home county and never met her sister Sigríður again after her departure in 1829. Þórunn married twice, had three children and died in 1880.

---

[1]I refer to Icelandic names according to Icelandic tradition, that is, by the first name, not surname. Furthermore, most often a family does not share surname as a woman is the daughter (dóttir) of her father but a man is the son of his father. That is why the five siblings are either Pálsson or Pálsdóttir, the son of Páll or the daughter of Páll—Páll Guðmundsson, their father. And their mother is the daughter of Jens.

Table 9.1 Time span and number of letters written to Páll by his closest family

Name	Letters	Time span	Relation	Lifespan
Sigríður Ørum	38	1817–1828	Grandmother	1753–1828
Malene Jensdóttir	17	1817–1824	Mother	1786–1824
Sigríður Pálsdóttir	250	1817–1871	Sister	1809–1871
Þórunn Pálsdóttir	44	1817–1866	Sister	1811–1880
Stefán Pálsson	59	1817–1840	Brother	1812–1841
Siggeir Pálsson	72	1824–1864	Brother	1815–1866
In all	480			

Sigríður Pálsdóttir was the second eldest of the siblings, born in 1809. With her 250 letters, covering half a century, she is the most extensive writer in Páll's collection. She moved to Reykjavík in 1829 and married the love of her life in 1833. After he died in 1839, she spent several years farming as a widow but married again in 1845. Sigríður died in 1871. She had six daughters, three of whom lived to adulthood. Judging by her letters she was a strong-minded person who chose to leave her home county as soon as she could, always longing to be nearer to her beloved brother (Halldórsdóttir 2014, 2015, 2016; Sigmundsson 1957).

Stefán, the second youngest (b. 1812), was fostered in another household but at the same farmstead as his mother, grandmother and sisters, but was eventually sent away to be educated. Stefán attended the Latin School in Iceland and went for further studying at the University of Copenhagen. He married in 1840, against his will, and died in 1841. He had no children.

Siggeir was the youngest (b. 1815), and was, after the death of his father, fostered and educated in another household until he was twelve when he moved to his brother Páll. Siggeir finished exams at the Latin School as Stefán had, but did not leave for Copenhagen. He married and had five children, divorced, lived in Norway for a time in the 1850s and learned daguerreotype photography. Siggeir, who his grandmother once lovingly described as a "boisterous stallion", became a priest in the early 1860s. He died in 1866.

The three brothers, especially Stefán and Siggeir, regularly travelled between different parts of the country, their home county in the east, the west of Iceland, where both Páll and Sigríður lived for a time, and the south, mainly Reykjavík, an expanding but still small town and centre of administration, commerce and education. Both of them stayed with Sigríður and Páll for longer or shorter periods of time. Their frequent travels reflect gender differences when it came to mobility. While the brothers travelled freely their sister Sigríður did so in close relation to her social and marital status: a housemaid, wife and widow.

Consequently, these letters reflect different experiences and different realities and are as such a fascinating yet also challenging source about past lives. Hence, it is necessary to view these letters in relation to theoretical and epistemological discussions on letters and correspondences.

Letters and Correspondences

There is a vast literature on letters and correspondences as venues of thought and literary expressions, as providers of facts about the past, particular events and individual lives, and, not least, for biographies of so-called great men (Ellis 2002; Stanley 2004: 202, 223). But letters are more complicated than that. As William Merrill Decker argues in *Epistolary Practices*, "letters do not really provide transparent access to history" but "tell stories centred in the experience of historically real individuals", which "depend on the context in which they are read" (Decker 1998: 9).

Therefore, instead of being studied as the "truth" about the past, letters are now seen as a complex form of communication and a creation of identity. Letters do *reflect* life, argues Stanley, they are "traces" of a person (Stanley 2004: 223). Furthermore, a letter is an expression, a representation, and even a deception (Gerber 2005). Letters are shaped by the relationship of the signatory and the addressee; they are based on reciprocity and answers were expected; problems were solved in letters; questions were asked (Stanley 2004; Decker 1998; Gerber 2006). This reciprocity is one of the main characteristics of correspondence and distinguishes it from other forms of auto/biographical writing (Altman 1982: 17).

Letters have been called a "conversation on paper" and quite often signatories write as if they are speaking to the addressee. For instance, Sigríður Pálsdóttir in a letter to her brother, on New Year's Eve 1828 in which she begins "the blessed new year by talking to you". She is well aware that this is not a real conversation but an incomplete substitute and writes that although she is not so far away from Páll "in her mind the body is too heavy to go along with" (1 January 1828, Lbs. 2413 a 4to).

Distance and time are discussed in letters, the time it takes for a letter to reach its destination, and for a reply to be received in turn. As Stanley has argued, the period that passes between when a letter is written and when it is read creates a rupture in time. Letters are, she argues, always written in the present. When they reach their destination this moment is long gone even though the letter itself is still there. Letters are situated in space and time, are like "flies in amber", to use Stanley's apt phrasing (Stanley 2004: 208). A letter may thus sound "as a dying echo" when it reaches its destination, as Sigfús Jónsson expressed it in a letter to his sister Jakobína in 1864 (3 April 1864, Lbs. 3180 4to).

Furthermore, correspondences are fragmentary. Often only one side of a correspondence has been preserved and there are gaps and silences. Months or years could pass between letters. Letters were deliberately destroyed, have vanished in time, others never reached their destination. Someone dies or simply stops writing. Sigríður Pálsdóttir, for instance, does not correspond with her brother for six years (1833–1839), during her first marriage. Her husband, however, an old friend and correspondent of her brother, continued his writing, for both of them as it seems. More often than not, only one side of the correspondence has been preserved. That is the case in Páll's collection because the letters he wrote to his family have not survived. However, his presence is very strong in these letters. His family constantly refers to him and what he has said in previous letters; and, as time goes by, his siblings seek his advice on various matters. He gives them advice, criticises them, and occasionally they challenge him.

The storyline of collections as these, where there are decades of lives in letters, is formulated by those reading the collection in retrospect, knowing who lived and who died. As an example, knowing that Stefán died of tuberculosis (probably) at the age of 29 in 1841 and was recently married to a woman he did not love and did not want to marry, I have detected sadness, a kind of an omen of what is to come, in his letters. This may be my imagination, but it is there nevertheless, the story of an unhappy, sensitive young man who cannot choose his own path in life but is bound to repay his benefactor, an old priest, by marrying his daughter and becoming his chaplain.

Letters are more than texts, they are artefacts from the past and, as such, tell stories about social practices as networking, family relations, and about the act of writing letters. They reveal how letters were written (privately or collectively); how people learned to write; how letters were sent over long distances, with post and/or travellers (Gerber 2006; Halldórsdóttir 2015; Barton and Hall 2000; Whyman 2011). In 1817, when the correspondence of Páll Pálsson and his family began, there were three official postal deliveries between eastern Iceland and the south. Unexpected journeys, where a traveller was asked to carry a letter in his pocket, were also an important way of sending letters. This, as I have argued elsewhere, influenced what was being written and placed restrictions on the signatory, who quite often was writing in haste (Halldórsdóttir 2015).

How then to fashion a story, a narrative of past lives and events, from a collection of correspondence like Páll Pálsson's? What "reality" does it reflect? How has it been used and how can it be used?

Snapshots of Everyday Life

A selection of Páll Pálsson's correspondence was published in 1957. Its aim was to present a perception on Páll's life and times, how people lived and thought. The letters were edited, and parts were cut out, not necessarily because of sensitive material, but because they were considered unimportant. Annotations helped readers to contextualise what was being discussed in letters, both people and events. This was done, in the apologetic words of the editor, because the letters and the story they told was "all in fractures, snapshots from daily life but not a coherent history" (Sigmundsson 1957: 11). Such incoherent histories and "snapshots" of daily life were once deemed as trivial and unworthy, as Gerber has pointed out, in relation to nineteenth-century immigrant letters. Subjects as "health, family gossip, friendship, personal inquiries and so on" were generally edited out of books containing immigrant letters. Issues like these are now considered important evidence about past lives (Gerber 2006: 55–56).

Furthermore, edited letters are directed to "posterior readership", or "readdressed" to a latter times readership, as Decker has argued (Decker 1998: 09). By selecting letters, editing and annotating, Sigmundsson created the context he believed to be correct but which is, obviously, not the same as when the letters were written. Nor is it the context I see when reading the letters.

Sigmundsson's publication does, of course, include letters from Páll's family, among them letters from his mother, grandmother and sisters, but there is an emphasis on letters written by well-known intellectual men in Icelandic history who corresponded with Páll. Many of those letters were sent from Copenhagen, where the signatories were inspired by new political and literary ideologies, and have been used to illuminate the political and intellectual discourse in Iceland from the 1820s to the 1840s.

As Martin Lyons has argued research on correspondences and other auto/biographical writing have until fairly recently been "confined to the writings of social strata for whom writing came easily". In other words, the educated middle class, in which writing was a familiar cultural practice wherein its members had the technology, the materials, and the instruments (Lyons 2014: 2). This has been changing, as can be seen in this volume (e.g. Stanley) and in recent years in the thriving studies of correspondence and historical literacy in the Nordic countries (Edlund et al. 2014; Kuismin and Driscoll 2013; Liljewall 2007).

One of the challenges of Páll Pálsson's collection is how difficult it is to categorise it. As with so many correspondences, it escapes categorisation or being defined as one particular *genre*. Páll and his siblings were indeed born into and raised in literate households where the practice of writing was highly esteemed; they learned to write at a fairly early age, conquered the technology (the boys earlier than the girls) and had (most often) the materials. It is nonetheless problematic to categorise these letters as "middle class", let alone intellectual, and thus belonging to a particular set or genre of letters. Social class alone is not what defines a letter, or to which genre it belongs.

As Lyons has argued in relation to the writings of European peasants, ordinary letters do "not easily fit the expectations of literary autobiography". These letters are "laconic rather than reflective, pragmatic rather than introverted". Instead of placing these letters as literary texts Lyons suggests exploring them for what they are, being "decidedly non-literary in the hands of peasant writers" and thus a kind of "outlaw genre". Furthermore, Lyons locates "the ordinariness" of these writings "in the social status of the author, rather than in what is going on in the texts" (Lyons 2014: 248–249). While I find Lyons's argumentation on the laconic, pragmatic, and straight-to-the-point letters convincing, and recognise these strands in many of the nineteenth-century correspondences I have studied, I am more interested in the "ordinariness" of the text than the actual social status of the signatory. The reason is that throughout my studies, and now in Páll Pálsson's correspondence, I have seen that ordinariness has less to do with status than the pragmatic and familiar qualities of letters. Moreover, this ordinariness is, in my view, decidedly gendered.

The letters of Páll Pálsson's family, in particular the women's letters, are filled with "ordinariness", that is, information about everyday life. That does not mean that these letters cannot be skilfully or even eloquently written but they do not reflect on life in a philosophical or literary way, just recite everyday events and what was thought to be newsworthy at the time of writing. These letters are first and foremost vernacular writing. Páll's sister Sigríður, for instance, spends considerable space in her letters discussing practicalities concerning the buying and transport of fish for her household. Then there is health, childbirth, death, harvesting hay, the weather. And gossip.

Even the letters of Páll's intellectual friends tend to escape categorisation because they are at once about politics and literature and filled with mundane yet fascinating information. One example is Þorsteinn Helgason (b. 1806), who later became Sigríður's first husband. He sailed to Copenhagen in the summer of 1823, when seventeen.

In the spring of 1824, he wrote a letter of 46 pages to Páll, beginning on April 17 and finishing May 6. It is a summary of his "biography since I wrote to you with the mail boat last autumn" (17 April 1824, Lbs. 2415 b 4to). Signatories often refer to relating their own biographies, but this exceptionally long letter goes further than most because of how long and detailed it is. It describes everyday life and events such as what books he studied at the University; what subjects; stories about his fellow students; entertainment; the short military training Icelandic students were obliged to undertake (as members of the King's guard), etc. The reality it describes is far from the one Páll experienced back home in Iceland. Hence, letters are multileveled, lying at the borders of several genres or frames of narration (Stanley et al. 2012: 264, 269, 276–277; Also, Jolly and Stanley 2005).

There is more in ordinary and ordinariness than just repeated narratives of everyday life. As Stanley has argued, most recently in relation to the vast *Whites Writing Whiteness* project (e.g. Stanley 2017), ordinary letters and their everyday nature can reveal narratives and/or experiences that are hidden in the prevailing historical narrative. Stories at microlevel reveal different aspects of experiences, of history. Furthermore, people do experience events, the times they are living (and history) differently depending on where they are situated (Stanley 2013: 62–63; 2018).

Vernacular writings, such as are found in Páll Pálsson's collection, should not be placed within the frameworks of the literary achievements or gendered aspects of the upper classes, or of ideas about (non)literary correspondents. Instead, they should be read and analysed as they are: multileveled, pragmatic and laconic, but also a formation of a self; performative: a venue for telling news and giving and asking for information on family and friends. Furthermore, they also reveal gendered ideas about men and women, about work and society. However, they also disclose how both men and women were constantly negotiating their status in society. The researcher reading these letters is also constantly negotiating between past and present, between micro and macro, which brings me to the theme of grand narrative and the personal storyline.

The Grand Narrative and the Personal Storyline

When used as evidence of the past, of lives and experiences, letters must be read carefully, contextualised, situated and evaluated, because, as Gerber has argued: "Letters cannot speak for themselves" (Gerber 2006: 227; Also Stanley 2016: 54).

How to contextualise them, however, is not self-evident. When doing biographical research, which often is the case with letters, social and historical contexts can easily become overwhelming, especially when working on the life of lesser known or ordinary people, whose epistolary life most often evolves around their everyday life and familial relationships. The grand narrative of history lurks in the background, so to speak, ready to control what kind of narrative is read into/taken out of the letters.

When exploring the letters of Páll's family it is not only the everyday life that emerges with its discussion on where to buy fish, prices, of knitting and making cheese, haying, farming, childbirth and death, but also a discrepancy between History with a capital H (the grand narrative) and the history told in these letters. This is particularly evident in the letters by the women, for instance, Sigríður's letters that stretch from 1817 to 1871. There is nothing there about the milestones of Icelandic history while she lived—the events we find in history books. She does not talk about politics or the men, the politicians, who were writing and talking about the improvement of Iceland and the emerging nation state. Neither does she discuss the milestones of women's history that took place while she still lived, for instance, equal inheritance in 1850 or unmarried women's full legal age in 1861.

This means that when working on and using letters as these for historical research the scholar must work on two levels at least. On the one hand, there is the "unforeseeable" narrative, preserved in her letters. On the other hand, there is the narrative that the historian constructs from her letters, knowing what actually happened. Depending on in what context the letters are being studied and used, they are intertwined with other sources, such as letters of other family members, memoirs, censuses, parish registries, newspapers, eulogies, and history books.

This brings me to the sociologist Ken Plummer and his apt formulation on life stories:

> Life stories always hurl us into a dual focus on history; into a concern with time in the life – of how it is lived over phases, cycles, stages; and with time outside the life – of how the 'historical moment' plays its role in any life's shape. (Plummer 2001: 39)

Hence, when working on Páll Pálsson's collection, I am "hurled" into "a dual focus on history" where there is a personal life story with inner "phases, cycles, stages" on the one hand, but on the other hand, there is the outer "historical moment", the grand narrative of progression, change and rupture. Weaving these narratives together is challenging because the researcher does not necessarily want to follow that canonised route and nor does the preserved narrative (the letters) automatically follow prevailing paradigms of historical accounts. As Decker argues: "Letters … [do not] generally conform to anything like self-evident story lines" (Decker 1998: 9). And neither does the life of an individual, an ordinary individual.

Multiple Auto/Biographies and Different Experiences

The letters of Páll's collection cover more than sixty years, but when taking into consideration the age of the signatories, as well as their historical and cultural memory, the time frame is expanded. Páll's grandmother was born in 1753 and had experienced, as had a handful of other signatories in his collection, the most dire times in Icelandic history (the Laki eruption in 1783, followed by hunger and diseases resulting in the death of 20% of the nation) but the youngest signatories were almost hundred years younger, born in the 1840s. These differences are evident in the letters, both in the way of thinking (what is written about and how) and technologies (the hand and arrangement of the letters, pens, paper).

Páll and his four siblings never lived all together in the same household except for a couple of months in 1815, when the youngest was a newborn, and their father about to die (as seen by me in retrospect). Their relationship is thus formed in letters, in a correspondence in which Páll is at the centre. All of them correspond with him but not with each other, on a regular basis. As years pass and fewer letters seem to go between the two sisters. Sigríður sometimes asks Páll if he has any news from Þórunn: "I receive no lines from my siblings in the east", she complains in 1842. She is not so attentive herself, however, when it comes to corresponding with anyone other than Páll (19 November 1842, Lbs. 2413 a 4to).

Despite these ruptures, the most prominent theme in this correspondence is the strength of family ties, in particular the bond between Páll and Sigríður, the two eldest. They were old enough to remember the years before the death of their father, while home was still a home for all of them. This is the core of their relationship, which then grows and changes as they themselves become adults. Keeping the letters from his family together, letters that were sent from home, letters that described home and everyday life (some of these had even "Home" written as its location instead of the farm's name, Hallferðarstaðir) have clearly been important emotionally for Páll. Not only did those letters recite what was newsworthy, they also brought love and care to him. As Leonore Davidoff argues in her study of siblings in an historical context, blood relations were of immense importance to people and more important historically speaking than has been recognised, especially as "brothers and sisters are *life's longest relationships*" (Davidoff 2012: 02). Furthermore, correspondence was of great importance to Páll's family, so great indeed that, with the passing of time the next generation stepped in; his nieces, born in the 1830s and the 1840s, felt the need to correspond with him.

Páll Pálsson's family letters are an almost perfect sample for studying how correspondents, in this case family members, develop in time and form their epistolary selves. Not only do we have letters from two grown-up women (the mother Malene and grandmother Sigríður Ørum) but also the four siblings writing to their brother.

Each of the correspondents has his or her own storyline. The first letters written by (actually in the name of) Sigríður, Þórunn and Stefán in 1817 are similarly organised although it seems that their mother, who lends them her hand, tries to give each their own characteristics. But then they go their separate ways. As a boy, Stefán's future prospects depend on his education, and thus his homeschooling has more emphasis on writing properly, as well as other bookish subjects. The two sisters, however, were trained in farm work, as well as in sewing and cooking. This reality is well documented in the letters, in which the sisters excuse their bad writing by saying they have not had time to practise because other things needed to be done: tending the lambs during the lambing season, harvesting the hay during the summer, etc. Moreover, due to a constant illness, their mother could not guide their writing as well as she might have done.

Elsewhere I have pointed out the collective and intertextual features of the letters written within the household of Páll's childhood home by his mother, grandmother and two sisters. At least to some extent his grandmother Sigríður Ørum seems to have acted as an "editor" when it came to writing, directing who should write about what in order to ensure that not all of were reciting the same events. This was particularly important while there still were only three formal postal services each year. And despite them knowing the post was due soon, letters were almost always written in haste and sometimes the whole household was writing at once in a kind of collective enterprise (Halldórsdóttir 2015). However, notwithstanding inter-textuality and collective writing, distinctive features slowly evolve for each signatory. They were forming their identity, both in the real world and in their epistolary personas.

These different storylines are also intertwined and even disrupted by each other's letters when they contradict accounts, or shed a different light on what has already occurred or is still happening. This means that a life unfolded in a series of letters from one signatory looks different when seen from the perspective of the third or even fourth party. Bringing all these let-ters together thus presents a different and more complicated picture than one derived from concentrating on just one correspondent.

One of the most fascinating themes to be investigated in Páll Pálsson's col-lection, a theme that affects the individual stories deeply, are gendered differ-ences, as I have touched upon already.

Gendered Writing

By *gendered writing* I am not referring to the fact that fewer women than men were able to write in the first half of the nineteenth century but the *dif-ferences* in letters written by women and men; differences that are grounded in and can be explained by gendered social and cultural constructions. These can be differences concerning the content of letters and the social and cultural circumstances and ideologies they reflect, as well as grammar, style and rhetoric. Based on extensive reading of women's letters and cor-respondences in the second half of the nineteenth century, I argued in the early 2000s that women wrote mainly about their daily practices, their health, the household and children, and told what was newsworthy of relatives and neighbours.

Although men also wrote about their families, their letters were more, it seemed to me, about farming, politics, literature or whatever was the latest topic in the country at any given time. An example gives a clearer picture of this. One Guðrún Vernharðsdóttir had a letter written in her name in 1852 (she could write herself, but not well enough in her own opinion) in which she speaks about who are given coffee in the morning; in what bed each member of the household slept and with whom (it was common to share a bed); and who did what job. Mundane yet fascinating information, the everyday life with all its ordinariness (13 January 1852, Lbs. 2842 4to). The addressee was her stepson, then studying in Copenhagen, far away from home and perhaps longing to read, and visualise, how home was. Fifteen years later, the stepson, Helgi Hálfdanarson, penned a letter to Guðrún in which he talked about his children, their appearances, how they behaved, and about the household. It is "quite homely to write all this", he writes but, "I imagine that you might like to hear about my small folk" (21 March 1867, Lbs. 2843 4to). His phrasing indicates that this is not how he would write to other correspondents.

Writing about the home and children seems to be what women are assumed to want to talk about. Malene, Páll's mother, in a letter she finishes writing for her husband in 1812, asks herself what she should write about to their learned friend: "People say it is most often the same topic for us women, the children" (27 June 1812, Lbs. 124 fol). In reality, men were also writing about their children, with love and care.

Perhaps, the main difference I detected in the early 2000s, and I still believe is the case, is that men had correspondents from a wider spectrum including relatives, friends and colleagues, while most of the women's correspondents were simply their relatives. In other words, women's correspondences evolved around the family. Furthermore, I argued that women's correspondences in the late nineteenth century revealed women's awareness of receiving less education than men, of being considered less skilled letter writers than men. These differences were closely connected to education and discourse, how thoughts are articulated and expressed on paper (Halldórsdóttir 2003).

Now, while working on Páll Pálsson's collection, especially the letters of his sister Sigríður Pálsdóttir, gender differences in correspondences are once again on my mind. And the lines have become more blurred. I have been seeking ways to theorise this difference, which is at once visible in the letters and difficult to grasp because it has not only to do with words on paper but also a feeling or a sense you get when reading letter after letter: how women styled and phrased their letters, which topics they discussed.

Above I have referred to Martyn Lyons' study on the writing of ordinary people. His research is however mainly concentrated on men, peasants. The fact is that until very recently surprisingly little has been written about the gendered aspects of vernacular letter writing, the writings of ordinary women. Stanley's aforementioned *Whites Writing Whiteness* project is a much-appreciated change, also Maria Tamboukou's studies into the lives and writing of women workers and their gendered aspects (e.g. Tamboukou 2016).

There is a vast literature on "women's writing", "women's letter writing" or "women's life-writing" in early modern times, the eighteenth and nineteenth centuries. However, "ordinary" women are seldom among those studied.

The focus is mainly on upper class/elite women or literary women, that is, women that were either writing what is defined as *intellectual* letters to relatives and friends (either women or men) or women writing *autobiographical* texts and even trying to claim space in the literary world of men. And many of these texts which claim to be on life-writing or autobiographical writing do not address letters in particular. The so-called feminisation of letter writing in the eighteenth-century France is frequently discussed in these works (e.g. Earle 1999; Dowd and Eckerle 2007; Eckerle 2013; Goodman 2009). This feminisation was influenced by romanticism and in particular by such extremely popular epistolary novels as Richard Samuelson's *Pamela* and Pierre Choderlos de Laclos's *Les Liaisons Dangereuses* (Earle 1999: 6–7). One can be almost certain that these are novels an ordinary woman in Iceland would never have heard of, let alone read.

Most importantly, the underlying theory is that women's *life writing*,[2] letters included, was a *conscious* reflection on life and the forming of the self—introspection. Thus the modern self was being shaped and even the modern woman's modernity was not only demonstrated in the ability to write and in self-reflection but also the material needed—writing tools, writing desks (especially designed for women in the eighteenth-century France), and even particular clothes.

There are fascinating studies on the materiality and space of women's letter writing, and how the home became women's place for "intellectual endeavour" (Hannan 2012). However, letter writing in these works is strongly connected to women in the elite classes with plenty of time for leisure.

The intellectual and material world of these women can hardly be applied to the social or cultural circumstances of the sisters Sigríður and Þórunn, nor of their mother and grandmother. Here we have to take notice of cultural, social and geographical differences. In this sense, the letters of Páll Pálsson's family have much more in common with the studies of the Swedish historian Britt Liljewall, who has explored vernacular letter writing in Sweden and theorised the gender differences she detected. Building her case on love letters and letters between a married couple temporarily living apart, in the 1840s, her theorisation offers a way for gendered analysis. These letters shed light on gendered roles; on ideas about femininity and

---

[2] The term *life writing* has in recent years been preferred to autobiographical writing because it offers a wider definition than autobiographical writing and does not necessarily imply reflections on life: I have been using it myself because it offers a space for using different but related narratives when exploring and constructing a life from fragmented sources, letters included. See definition in Caine (2010: 69).

masculinity—what roles the wife, for instance, was ready to take on while the husband was away and those she would not (Liljewall 2007: 31–42). All these themes are to be found in the letters of the women in Páll's collection.

I have tried to categorise some of the differences in the sibling's letters. As mentioned above, one obvious difference lies in the fact that, due to their education, it takes the sisters a longer time to master the skill of writing. Then there is the grammar, which is the most common gender difference discussed in articles and books on letter writing, a difference easily detected. Furthermore, there are several examples of their mother and grandmother, both literate and skilful and effective letter writers, having their letters written for them when they needed to write important letters to officials. Writing such "learned letters" demanded a rhetoric that women had either not mastered or lacked the confidence to use (Halldórsdóttir 2015).

The letters are gendered in content and style. It is difficult to categorise these differences, however, because they are constantly changing during all the years and decades of corresponding. Nonetheless, I perceive several themes in these letters, which although perhaps not clear cut, may yet open up possibilities for further study. There are, for instance, *apologies*, which usually are characterised as a more feminine feature in letters. Apologies are found in the letters of both sisters and brothers, especially for not having anything noteworthy to write about. The sisters do this more frequently, however, and they also comment on a lack of time and practice. This is a continuous theme for them, while the brothers, on the other hand, are gradually entering the world of the adult and formally educated male. This brings me to the *nonchalant style*, which is characteristic of learned young men and becomes apparent when the two brothers have entered the Latin School. There they are trained in classical rhetoric, and thus they use Latin and Danish phrases, which are (almost) never seen in the letters of their sisters.

Emotions, such as love and sorrow, are expressed in the letters of both the sisters and brothers, which is no surprise. This is after all an era affected by romanticism. Both sisters and brothers *gossip* in their letters, the brothers even more so, because while at the Latin School they are within the world of the learned, have stories to tell about who is succeeding or failing, who is the talk of the town, etc.

Family and household are in fact discussed more in the letters of the sisters, most certainly because of the simple fact that both of them married, had children, and both of them were widowed and ran their farms, as such, for a period of time. This does indeed demonstrate the ordinariness or everyday nature of their writing. It reflects their daily reality and experiences.

Finally, letters as a way of *reflecting* on life, being the venue of "introvert" speculation. The brothers are definitely more reflective than the sisters and this, I have argued, has to do with, the endless discussion about their education; how well or badly they are doing in the Latin School; whether they should they sail to Copenhagen; is there any chance of their obtaining public office? The sisters are on the other hand bound by their femininity and their status in life as women in a rural society, which offered them almost no other possibility than marriage, working on a farm, or both (Halldórsdóttir 2018).

To some extent, I have become hesitant about making general assumptions based on the correspondence like this because they emerge from a particular place and space in time and reflect personal experiences and relationships. After all, letters are shaped by the relationship of the signatory and the addressee and their situatedness.

Conclusion

The life stories in Páll Pálsson's collection, his family letters, evolve around class and social status, power and powerlessness. They are about education and not receiving any. About difference and opportunities. How it is possible to become an agent in one's own life, e.g., by writing letters which both establish and strengthen social status and networks. These stories are first and foremost, however, about life. About love and loss, to have and raise children, to survive in harsh circumstances. This is a story of solidarity, love and care. Corresponding with his family was of a great importance to Páll, it enabled him, not only to keep in touch with his beloved ones but also to be a part of the everyday life of his family, to be "home", in some sense while that home existed.

This correspondence consists of familial letters whose principal purpose was to preserve relationships between siblings living apart and to maintain the family network. The letters of Páll Pálsson's family do not tell a consistent life story. Their narratives are thoroughly set in time and space, moulded by their social circumstances in different periods of life. Moreover, there are gaps and silences. For the most part, women's letters are not self-reflective, but pragmatic—they are about everyday life. And, in all their simplicity and "ordinariness" these letters shed light on the gendered roles of society; the letters demonstrate notions about femininity and masculinity; what role the wife takes, for instance, when her husband is away or—as a widow if he dies. All of them narrate their lives in letters, though without realising how this correspondence, how this life story, would eventually end.

A correspondence is not autobiographical in the same sense as are memoirs, autobiographies or diaries. Nevertheless, "it results", to quote Cavarero, in a story that is a narration of life. It is an "unforeseeable" narrative because in spite of agency, performativity or the strategic composition of letters, there is no way for their signatories to comprehend beforehand the storyline's conclusion. The narrative is formed with each new letter, shaped by the time and space of the writing, as well as that of the letter that is being responded to. As Hermoine Lee argues, biography (and I would add auto/biographical writing) is not a true account of a life: "Any biographical narrative is an artificial construct, since it inevitably involves selection and shaping" (Lee 2009: 122). Thus, it is the scholars who study past correspondences who must detect the coherence and the ruptures, and construct the life story that unfolds in letters.

Acknowledgements This study has been funded by Rannís, The Icelandic Research Fund (ref.130811–051). I wish to thank Ann-Catrine Edlund, Susanne Haugen and Lars Erik Edlund for the opportunity to spend time at Umeå University in 2014–2015, thinking and writing about letters and historical literacy. Also Julian Meldon D'Arcy for helping out with the English language.

References

Altman, J. G. (1982). *Epistolarity: Approaches to a Form*. Columbus: Ohio State University Press.

Barton, D., & Hall, N. (Eds.). (2000). *Letter Writing as a Social Practice*. Philadelphia: John Benjamins.

Caine, B. (2010). *Biography and History*. London: Palgrave Macmillan.

Cavarero, A. (2000). *Relating Narratives: Storytelling and Selfhood*. Translated and with an Introduction by Paul A. Kottman. London: Routledge.

Davidoff, L. (2012). *Thicker Than Water: Siblings and Their Relations 1780–1920*. Oxford: Oxford University Press.

Decker, W. M. (1998). *Epistolary Practices: Letter Writing in America Before Telecommunications*. Chapel Hill: The University of North Carolina Press.

Dowd, M. M., & Eckerle, J. A. (Eds.). (2007). *Genre and Women's Life Writing in Early Modern England*. London: Routledge.

Earle, R. (Ed.). (1999). *Epistolary Selves: Letters and Letter-Writers 1600–1945*. Aldershot: Ashgate.

Eckerle, J. A. (2013). *Romancing the Self in Early Modern Englishwoman's Life Writing*. London: Routledge.

Edlund, A. C., Edlund, L. E., & Haugen S. (Eds.). (2014) *Vernacular Literacies—Past, Present and Future*. Northern Studies Monographs 3. Umeå: Umeå University and Royal Skyttean Society.

Ellis, D. (2002). Letters, Lawrence, Shakespeare and Biography. *Journal of European Studies, 32,* 121–134.

Gerber, D. A. (2005). Acts of Deceiving and Withholding in Immigrant Letters: Personal Identity and Self Presentation in Personal Correspondence. *Journal of Social History, 39*(2), 315–330.

Gerber, D. A. (2006). *Authors of Their Lives: The Personal Correspondence of British Immigrants to North America in the Nineteenth Century*. New York: New York University Press.

Goodman, D. (2009). *Becoming a Woman in the Age of Letters*. Ithaca: Cornell University Press.

Hálfdanarson, G. (2008). *Historical Dictionary of Iceland*. Lanham, MD: Scarecrow Press.

Halldórsdóttir, E. H. (2003). Af bréfaskriftum kvenna á 19. Öld. In L. Guttormsson & I. Sigurðsson (Eds.), *Alþýðumenning á Íslandi 1830–1930. Ritað mál, menntun og félagshreyfingar* (pp. 247–267). Reykjavík: Sagnfræðistofnun and Háskólaútgáfan.

Halldórsdóttir, E. H. (2014). 'Don't You Forget Your Always Loving Sister': Writing as a Social and Cultural Capital. In A. C. Edlund, L. E. Edlund, & S. Haugen (Eds.), *Vernacular Literacies—Past, Present and Future* (pp. 181–192). Northern Studies Monographs 3. Umeå: Umeå University og Royal Skyttean Society.

Halldórsdóttir, E. H. (2015). 'Do Not Let Anyone See This Ugly Scrawling'. Literacy Practices and the Women's Household at Hallfreðarstaðir 1817–1829. *Life Writing, 12*(3), 289–308.

Halldórsdóttir, E. H. (2016). A Biography of Her Own: The Historical Narrative and Sigríður Pálsdóttir. In E. H. Halldórsdóttir, M. Leskilä-Kärki, T. Kinnunen, & B. Possing (Eds.), *Biography, Gender and History: Nordic Perspectives* (pp. 81–100). Cultural History—Kulttuurihistoria 14. Turku: Kandh, Turku University.

Halldórsdóttir, E. H. (2018). Beyond the Centre: Women in Nineteenth-Century Iceland and the Grand Narratives of European Women's and Gender History. *Women's History Review, 27*(2), 54–175. https://doi.org/10.1080/09612025.2017.1303888.

Hannan, L. (2012). Making Space: English Women Letter-Writing, and the Life of the Mind, c. 1650–1750. *Women's History Review, 21*(4), 589–604.

Jolly, M., & Stanley, L. (2005). Letters as/Not a Genre. *Life Writing, 1*(1), 1–18.

Kuismin, A., & Driscoll, M. J. (Eds.). (2013). *White Field, Black Seeds: Nordic Literacy Practices in the Long Nineteenth Century*. Helsinki: Finnish Literature Society, SKS.

Lee, H. (2009). *Biography: A Very Short Introduction*. Oxford: Oxford University Press.

Liljewall, B. (2007). »*Ack om du vore här*« *1800-talets folkliga brevkultur*. Stockholm: Nordiska Museets Förlag.

Lyons, M. (2014 [2013]). *The Writing Culture of Ordinary People in Europe, c. 1860–1920*. Cambridge: Cambridge University Press.

Magnússon, S. G. (2010). *Wasteland with Words: A Social History of Iceland*. London: Reaktion Books.

Plummer, K. (2001). *Documents of Life 2: An Invitation to a Critical Humanism*. London: Sage.

Róbertsdóttir, H. (2014). Manufacturing in the Eighteenth Century. *Scandinavian Journal of History, 39*(1), 49–77.

Sigmundsson, F. (Ed.). (1957). *Skrifarinn á Stapa: Sendibréf 1806–1877. Íslenzk sendibréf*. Reykjavík: Bókfellsútgáfan.

Stanley, L. (2004). The Epistolarium: On Theorizing Letters and Correspondences. *Auto/Biography, 12*, 201–235.

Stanley, L. (2013). Whites Writing: Letters and Documents of Life in a QLR Project. In L. Stanley (Ed.), *Documents of Life Revisited: Narrative and Biographical Methodology for a 21st Century Critical Humanism* (pp. 59–73). Farnham: Ashgate.

Stanley, L. (2016). Archival Methodology Inside the Black Box: Noise in the Archive! In N. Moore, A. Salter, L. Stanley, & M. Tamboukou (Eds.), *The Archive Project: Archival Research in the Social Sciences*. London: Routledge.

Stanley, L. (2017). *The Racialising Process: Whites Writing Whiteness in Letters: South Africa 1770s–1970s*. Edinburgh: X Press.

Stanley, L. (2018). *Whites Writing, South Africa and Letters*. WhitesWritingWhiteness. www.whiteswritingwhiteness.ed.ac.uk/overviews/whiteswritingchange/, paragraph 11 and 13.

Stanley, L., Salter, A., & Dampier, H. (2012). The Epistolary Pact, Letterness and the Schreiner Epistolarium. *a/b: Auto/Biography Studies, 27*(2), 262–293.

Tamboukou, M. (2016). The Autobiographical You: Letters in the Gendered Politics of the Labour Movement. *Journal of Gender Studies, 25*(3), 269–282. https://doi.org/10.1080/09589236.2014.957169.

Whyman, S. E. (2011 [2009]). *The Pen and the People: English Letter Writers 1660–1800*. Oxford: Oxford University Press.

Archives

Lbs (Landsbókasafn Íslands – Háskólabókasafn [National and University Library of Iceland]):

Lbs. 124 fol. Miscellaneous. Originated from Páll Pálsson's Collection.

Lbs. 2409–2415 4to. Páll Pálsson's Collection.

Lbs. 2843–2844 4to. Helgi Hálfdánarson's Collection.

Lbs. 3180 4to. Jakobína Jónsdóttir and Grímur Thomsen's Collection.

10

Auto/Pathographies in situ: 'Dying of Melancholy' in Nineteenth-Century Greece

Dimitra Vassiliadou

If the weather or my melancholia does not kill me, it will be a miracle. I feel the same, and the doctor wants me to try iron. Sofia Schliemann to her husband Heinrich, Paris 24 November 1877.

Yesterday I couldn't write you in length, as I was still extinguished from the pains of sorrow. Marigo Makka to her husband Georgios, Athens 2 February 1864.

Melancholy has been a fluid term, with a long and diverse history since antiquity. It has been used to portray a painful emotion, a psychological disorder, a state of mind with no pathological manifestations and a set of symptoms that overlapped a disease (Jackson 1986: 3). It is precisely because of this plasticity that it has been, and still is, a fascinating subject for researchers working on different fields, such as political philosophy, literary criticism, cultural anthropology, art theory and history. In this paper, I draw inspiration out of this theoretical and analytical diversity that privileges an eclectic approach to disrupted emotions of epistolary lives in the past. Firmly grounded on two bodies of correspondence—some 150 letters that two Greek middle-class women, Marigo Makka (182[?]–1877) and Sofia Schliemann (1852–1932), penned to their husbands during the second half of the nineteenth century—I am focusing on autobiographical discourses of melancholy. Both women systematically defined themselves as 'nervous' and 'melancholic'; they had a similar medical diag-

D. Vassiliadou (✉)
University of Crete, Rethymno, Greece

J. M. Parsons and A. Chappell (eds.), *The Palgrave Handbook of Auto/Biography*,
https://doi.org/10.1007/978-3-030-31974-8_10

nosis, and the perceptions of close relatives were comparable. Their surviving letters, this 'nexus of doings and sayings' (Schatzki 1996: 89), urge us to go beyond the narrow description of a single disorder of the past and uncover the emotional cluster of melancholy through the subjects' own voices. Notwithstanding, whenever they talked about their melancholic mood, they did nothing but reflect on their own lives. From this point of departure, I attempt to grasp what is described in their letters as sickness, through the perception and formation of melancholy as psychosomatic disorder. Likewise, I am interested in the dynamics of unruly and unmanageable emotions within private and public realms and the ways they operate across gender lines. Finally, I am curious about daily practices as traced in epistolary narratives back then and their ability to affirm or disorder family ties.

But let me first introduce Sofia briefly and Marigo. In 1869, at the age of sixteen, Sofia married the famous German archaeologist Heinrich Schliemann. Her published biography affirms that she suffered until her death from various psychological disorders, accompanied by innumerable bodily symptoms.[1] Besides Athens, her main residence, she spent several months of her adult life in various other European cities, mostly in Paris, following her husband's wishes, yet generally separated from him and also distanced from her family and close kin. At the beginning of her married life, she tried to kill herself by a desperate leap into the ice-cold water of the river Seine. It is no small wonder that throughout her life, she regularly visited the most renowned European spa cities, seeking an effective treatment for her ailments. Equally adherent to the water cure was Marigo Makka, although our knowledge of her life is, by contrast, extremely limited. Fragments of her story were assembled through the intimate reading of the 93 letters she addressed to her husband throughout the years 1849–1877. The following is, more or less, what is known of her life: Marigo was the wife of Georgios Makkas, a prominent Greek doctor of the second half of the nineteenth century. From an early age (the first epistolary signs date back to 1849), she suffered from unspecific, yet persistent, psychological and bodily disorders. Through her own medical gaze, she recorded her ailments systematically in the letters she addressed to her husband every time he was away, on his rather frequent professional leaves.

The focus of this paper on middle-class female patients is by no means accidental; nor ever is. As many scholars have convincingly argued in past

---

[1]Eleni Bombou-Protopapa published the whole body of correspondence that Sofia addressed to Heinrich, along with biographical data on her life. Here, I am re-reading Sofia's letters from this edited version (Bombou-Protopapa 2005).

decades, since the second half of the nineteenth century a vast range of disorders and/or unruly emotions has been firmly attached to middle-class women, namely 'hysteria', 'neuropathy', 'nerves', 'melancholy', 'depression' and 'sadness' (Cayleff 1988). Given the simultaneous existence of male patients suffering from similar ailments, it was explicitly shown that 'nervous' women were not merely a category of medical statistics, but a culturally constructed legacy of the period (Smith-Rosenberg 1972; Showalter 1993). Melancholic women emerged in abundance for the first time during the nineteenth century, when the word began to lose its fictitious aura, alongside the receding of the (male) melancholic genius of Romanticism (Schiesari 1992). The linkage between this set of maladies and middle-class women, along with the overlapping symptoms and the diagnostic confusion of the physicians of the period, is equally evident within the Greek literature at the time (Karamanolakis 1998: 55, 57; Kritsotaki 2009: 189–190). When it comes to private correspondence, it is palpable that the subjects themselves were deeply immersed in the very same confusing, vague and overlapping vocabulary. Since letters cannot be conceived simply as a private, hermetic dialogue between the sender and the recipient, their writers were equally subscribing to the dominant medical and popular discourses, thus blurring the divide between public and private vocabularies of illness. As far as Sofia is concerned, both her physicians and her family considered her as coping with a chronic disease, specifically with 'nervous system disorder'. She systematically defined herself in her letters as 'melancholic'; however at the age of 39, convinced eventually by her doctors' diagnosis and her husband's emphatic advocacies, she would employ in a dramatic mood the term 'hysterical'. Marigo's correspondence is uninformative when it comes to the possible diagnosis that followed her innumerable upheavals. Yet, she was meticulously describing her condition in her letters.[2] Though it is not clear whether her physicians or her husband considered her as neurologically ill, she was confessing: 'I have become nervous, I, who didn't even know what nerves meant'.[3] Nonetheless, the words that appear time and again in Sofia's and Marigo's letters are predominately 'melancholy' and 'sorrow'. Thus, I will reflect on the emotional vocabulary of melancholia, emphasising—as the two women did themselves—their pluralistic states and declarations of sadness.

---

[2]Unfortunately, as Georgios' replies are missing, I wasn't able to restore the couple's 'dialogue'.

[3]Marigo to Georgios, Athens 16 March 1866.

Letters as Distinct Narratives of Life

The solid grounds that bond together the strands of my analysis are the forceful first-person accounts traced in the family correspondence of Marigo Makka and Sofia Schliemann. Over recent decades, lively discussions occurred in the fields of auto/biographical narratives, autographic poetics and life writings, to name only three out of the many analytical categories that have been proposed for the study of correspondence. Acknowledging the impact of literary theory in the social sciences, historians have also asserted that letters are not simply sources of information about people and facts in the past, but also texts that urged their authors to organise and understand individual and social action and, moreover, that letter writing as a social and cultural practice changes through time and therefore should be placed in its specific contexts. The historical literature on the theoretical and methodological features of epistolarity is vast, as well as the multifaceted aspects of the practice that have been richly explored (indicatively, Chartier et al. 1997; Decker 1998; Barton and Hall 2000; Gerber 2000; Gilroy and Verhoeven 2000; Schulte and Von Tippelskirch 2004; Halldórsdóttir 2007). Be it as it may, today we have moved away from earlier perceptions of correspondence as a distinct genre, as epistolary narratives have been repeatedly addressed as highly flexible (Bazerman 2000; Vassiliadou 2017) and thus do not fall under a particular form. This is a 'problematic and hovering' genre for Panayiotis Moullas (1992: 151), 'hybridic' for Margaretta Jolly and Liz Stanley (2005: 94). And yet, where lies the terra firma for epistolary practices? Here, I will do justice to two core characteristics of epistolary narratives, as essential to the analysis that follows: first, their recognition as routes of interaction and, second, their diverse linkages to the self.

Scholars working with historically situated epistolary narratives agree that despite their diversity in different contexts, time and space, the common elements that bind these texts together are their relational and communicative qualities (Gerber 2000). Letters are attempts to maintain and support social relations that have been disrupted and are efforts to create presence out of absence, both literal and figurative. Epistolarity as a ritual that presupposes and eventually transcends absence turns the spiritual into the material: transforms thoughts and emotions into a written piece of paper. As Christine Haas has firmly put it, 'the relationship between writing and the material world is both inextricable and profound. Indeed, writing is language made material' (cited in Goodman 2009: 9). It has been already mentioned, but now becomes clearer: epistolary narratives are gestures, social actions and thus steadily reveal the writer's relationship to specific others. The writer not only seeks but also promises 'sincere' interaction with the reader and looks constantly for synergy and reciprocity. The element of sincerity and/or truth lies precisely in the relation that connects the sender and the recipient. In other words, people wrote letters that were quite different depending on the recipient and, more importantly, according to the bond that connected the sender and the receiver. Nothing clearer: 'Writing to someone could mean writing for someone, but, at the same time, something much broader: writing along with someone' (Moullas 1992: 166). Therefore, what becomes narrative is the relationship that both parties try to maintain through correspondence (Gerber 2005: 317).

Under Foucault's (1988) influence, private correspondence has been firmly connected with technologies of the self, with the process of fashioning an autonomous yet relational subjectivity (Tamboukou 2011). As Brigitte Diaz reminds us, 'in this lies the paradox of correspondence, that one addresses the other to find oneself' (2006: 9). There is no doubt that writing helped individuals to establish themselves as persons and to make sense of themselves and eventually assisted them to face up to decisions. As the fascinating analysis of Denna Goodman on women letter writers of the eighteenth century shows, these decisions could range from the choice of the proper word in a letter they wrote, to important life choices (2009: 3). However, at the same time letter writers have been equally interested in forming other people's selves (Pearsall 2009: 14). This strategy is evident in epistolary lives, in our case in the correspondences that organised conjugal lives in the past, along with their hierarchical dimensions. When it comes to our leading figures, Marigo Makka and Sofia Schliemann, their epistolary lives are marked by their gloomy mood and the innumerable psychic and somatic symptoms they detected in themselves. It is precisely the thread of melancholy that pierces their writings and defines both themselves and their relation with their husbands.

That said, their accounts constitute for me today, as apparently for them back then, statements of how they felt and consequently about how they lived. I am asserting that Sofia and Marigo, like several other women of their times, did not fabricate their complaints in order to achieve other, specific or obscured, goals. At the same time, I am distancing epistolary analytics from a retrospective diagnosis and the use of modern medical terms to describe the psychological state of my historical subjects. On the contrary, I am interested in their own perceptions, as exposed in their letters (Ferlito 2012: 158). The constant interchange between the state of healthiness and the condition of blurred disorder they were experiencing, along with the periodic loss of self-control, was attached to the need for a reformation of the self, but a self rather confused, fragile and weak. Their letters thus can be seen as auto/pathographies, a term introduced by Thomas Couser for contemporary auto/biographical narratives of illness or disability. The addition of slash in auto/pathography refers of course to Liz Stanley's work (1992) that adds enough plasticity to the term, to fit in epistolary texts as well. Auto/pathographies, as Stanley's auto/biographies, blur the lines 'between self/other, public/private, and immediacy/memory' (1993: 42). Furthermore, Couser considers the emergence of auto/pathography as 'a sign of cultural health – an acknowledgement and an exploration of our condition as *embodied* selves' (1991: 65). These particular auto/pathographies offer rare insights into both women, reflecting on themselves, their connections with specific others and their lives. Marigo's and Sofia's auto/pathographies, the stories their suffering bodies tell and the stories they tell about their suffering bodies (Boon 2015: 3), constitute consecutive self-diagnoses, consistently open to individual interpretations and, therefore, highly negotiable phenomena. No matter what the terms in use, specific disorders are tangible in the letters they each addressed to their husbands. The evidence suggests that conjugal correspondence was the basic framework for the articulation of these detrimental experiences.

Specific, exemplary cases urge us to reflect on the complexity of the big picture in question; by utilising the insights of different fields of study and methodological approaches, the focus on melancholic auto/pathographies contributes to broader academic debates that go beyond the narrow description of a single disorder in the past. First, auto/pathographies form an inquiry into historical perceptions of family life and more specifically of the 'emotional communities' that families formed in the past. Seen as emotional communities, families foster and encourage particular emotional behaviours in their members. They tend to recognise specific emotions, for instance love and happiness, as acceptable, desired and priceless. On the other hand, they criticise other emotional expressions as unwelcome and harmful (Rosenwein 2002: 842). Through an in-depth analysis of letters spilling over with 'undesired' emotions, such as melancholy and sadness, I focus on feelings that were unacceptable according to the dominant domestic ideal of the period. In doing so, I detect both the causes and the effects that disruptive emotions had for family life. Perceiving melancholy as emotion is justifiable: this is how both women describe it in their letters. At the same period, clinical psychiatry equally recognised melancholy as a mood disorder that affected patients' emotions and actions (Katsaras 1898: 439–459).

This last remark leads us to the heart of the history of psychiatry. Although the field mostly privileges severe mental disorders and to a lesser extent milder ailments, such as simple melancholia, several aspects of the specific disorder are today well covered: its nosology and diagnostic fluidity from the mid-nineteenth century until the beginnings of the twentieth century (Jansson 2013); the genealogies of melancholy and their multiple meanings through time (Lawlor 2012; Shorter 2013); and the overlaps and discrepancies between melancholy and the modern clinical disorder called depression (Misbach and Stam 2005). Nonetheless, and despite the early incitement of Roy Porter (1985), who stressed the need to privilege medical history from the 'bottom up', the history of psychiatry until now has been primarily based on sources written 'from above', for instance by physicians and health professionals (Ferlito 2012: 161). The patient's voice is rarely privileged in medical writings, especially outside the medical/bureaucratic context. By contrast, the narratives unfolded in family letters constitute an auto/pathography in situ. In pursuing the chapter's main focus on forceful first-person accounts of the physical and emotional experience of gloom, and the epistolary lives so written, I perceive melancholy traced in correspondences as practice, i.e. as expression, experience, relation and action 'executed by a mindful body' (Scheer 2012: 205). From this point of departure, I expand to a set of related research questions: Which behaviours, thoughts, feelings and embodied reactions, from the diverse geographies of melancholy did these women follow in their auto/pathographies? How did they rationalise their condition and how did they unravel the narratives of their lives? How did the suffering individuals, through their own medical gaze, define familial relations? Given the mass appropriation of 'love' as the prescriptive element of family bliss by the emerging Greek middle classes, alongside the dominant ideal of 'companionate marriage', my concluding argument will be that the vocabulary of melancholy represents a metaphor, extensively used in private correspondence, in order to signify threatened or precarious conjugal and, by extension, family relations. Here, epistolary lives and 'actual' lives are inextricably linked.

The Shackles of Biology and the All-Encompassing Symptomatology

One of the most emblematic figures of early nineteenth-century psychiatry, the French physician Jean-Étienne-Dominique Esquirol, attributed women's melancholy to the seclusion of their lives and their quite distinct biological features. All stages of the female reproductive and life cycle (menstruation, pregnancy, delivery, lactation, puerperium, menopause) were directly associated with multilayered physical, neurological, corporeal and mental disorders. All women notwithstanding seemed victims of their periodical nature (Radden 2009: 48–49; Hock 2011: 452–456). Almost five decades later, by the end of the century, the eminent Greek psychiatrist, Konstantinos Katsaras, would repeat a similar medical opinion:

> Women are seized by melancholy more often than men, as the lack of basic necessities and family anguishes are more frequent and more intense between them. Besides, pregnancies, childbirths and puerperiums, can boost the emergence of melancholy. (Katsaras 1898: 398)

Perceptions of womanhood as primarily reproductive penetrated Marigo's letters; when, for instance, she was linking her menstruation with her 'extinction', a disruptive psychosomatic state, that appeared time and again in her letters. The following was written right after her arrival in the famous spa resort of Carlsbad and her husband's simultaneous departure for Vienna:

> Its is truth that a life and environment change was essential, especially after my last loss of blood, that occurred three days after your departure, and made me suffer a great deal. [...] Whenever my period finds me extinguished, is no good at all for me, and as you remember when you left, I was overwhelmed by stomach ache.[4]

The misty cluster of female reproductive physiology prevented physicians from diagnostic accuracy, especially in the first half of the nineteenth century. Doctor Velisarios' case is rather typical of this obscurity. Examining Marigo's clinical picture, at first he speculates on pregnancy, but immediately expressed a second opinion: 'Doctor Velisarios told me that all these could be also out of nerves, following your absence'.[5] The direct linkage between female reproductive, life cycle, neurological and psychological disorders was eventually leading to thorough diagnostic confusion: Was Marigo Makka pregnant or just 'nervous'?

---

[4]Marigo to Georgios, Carlsbad 1 June 1867.
[5]Marigo to Georgios, Athens 11 May 1849.

Nevertheless, both Marigo and Sofia commented in their letters on the various psychological and bodily symptoms they detected in themselves and on the volatile and ambiguous emotions that overwhelmed them while ill. They each spent a great amount of time in the seclusion of their homes, feeling sick, yet still anticipating their recovery. During difficult times, their doctors would pay visits at home, once or even twice per day.[6] Eventually, even Marigo herself acknowledged the 'comical spectacle' of her relentless maladies, one of the few times she dealt humorously with her illnesses, when she described the family house as an 'actual hospital'.[7] In the same letter, she carried on, with an equally 'factual' diary of sickness. It was not uncommon for the participants in the epistolary exchange to present letters as diaries, acknowledging several common features between the two, namely their 'private' nature, and the detailed everyday experiences:

> Today, must be indeed the very first night after you've gone that I am feeling, and I am referring mainly to my health, content. 21, 22, and 23 of May I was suffering from rheum. As soon as these symptoms subsided, stomach aches returned. 25, 26, and 27 I was suffering from the stomach.[8]

Unfortunately, bellyache was not the only problem she had to deal with. In her letters, she documents, time after time, an extended repertoire of bodily symptoms: excruciating headaches, feebleness, weakness, faintness, dizzy spells and nausea, constipation problems, lack of appetite and, in contrast, incredible hunger, intense heartbeats and extremely strong pain in the lower abdomen. Sofia Schliemann demonstrated a similar abrupt fluctuation between one symptom and another: severe stomach heaviness, blisters around the lips, cephalalgy, gastritis, knee pains, insomnia, anaemia, anorexia and weight loss. We stand at the heart of epistolary narratives as auto/pathographies that shaped body understandings. The link that connected a letter with its writer transformed this written piece of paper into a crucial part of their physical existence—their own body. There was an invisible continuum that correlated the body of the writer with the body of her correspondence (Poustie 2011). In this light, the letter *was* its writer.

---

[6]See, for example, Marigo to Georgios, Athens 18 April 1849; Sofia to Heinrich, Paris 28 February 1885.

[7]Marigo to Georgios, Athens 28 May 1866.

[8]Ibid.

Sofia Schliemann (1852–1932): I Am Dying of Melancholy[9]

Sofia was a part-time wife. According to her own descriptions, feeling a 'straw-widow'[10] and 'eternally apart',[11] since her spouse Heinrich did not care for permanent residency. He used to spend several months every year separated from his family, due, or at least so he claimed, to his demanding profession. Nevertheless, the family correspondence suggests that Sofia was a morally and psychologically abused wife: she had been left alone even during her two difficult pregnancies and her two intervening miscarriages. Yet, in her writings she appears not only to endure hardship, but furthermore to 'adore' Heinrich, a fact that reminds us, once more, the blurred divide between truth and deception, between lives lived and lives written (Stanley 2002). Despite his physical absence, her husband was increasingly tightening his strangle-hold on Sofia's everyday life, supervising her albeit limited outdoor activities. One of the few times she broke the rules, she rushed to apologise:

> My precious and loving husband, you misinterpret my letter, while I was clearly mentioning that despite the fact that all the Greek ladies are coming over to invite me to their evening receptions, I have not accepted a single one of them. It is true though, since I hate hiding the whole truth from you, that I have been visiting the theatre, but my sweetheart, have in mind that I cannot be in bed that early in the evening, and staying in makes me feel terribly melancholic.[12]

Although the family was rich, Heinrich was brutally accusing Sofia of waste, questioning her ability to manage home economics, one of the most acknowledged female capacities at the time. Sofia's disorders seem justified, if attributed to the oppressive family environment in which she spent nearly two decades of her life, until Heinrich's death in 1890. Nevertheless, it is intriguing to consider how she experienced her own illness and rationalised her medical condition and how, in other words, she was unfolding her auto/pathography, letter by letter.

---

[9]Sofia to Heinrich, Paris 29 August 1877.
[10]Sofia to Heinrich, s.l. December 1880.
[11]Sofia to Heinrich, Paris, s.a. [1877].
[12]Sofia to Heinrich, Paris 19 December 1877.

Sofia spent several months during the 1870s in Paris, a city she literally hated: 'The gloomy weather affected my nerves, and everything seems dark to me'.[13] She suffered time and again from loneliness, and she commented bitterly on the compassion her image evoked, as a secluded, melancholic, 'madwoman'. She blamed her psychological disorders on consistent study of foreign languages, the ongoing intensive medical attention and 'melancholia' itself. In this view, melancholia was being substantiated, while maladies, symptoms and causes overlapped:

> You do know really well that I was not harmed by amusements, nor carriages, it is more likely by the doctors, and melancholy, due to [...] constant studying.[14]

Her unpleasant social reality revolved through each twenty-four hours. In daytime, it was experienced as melancholia, while during the nights she was plagued by restless sleep and agitated dreams: 'All day long today it is raining, and I am extremely melancholic. Besides that, I had terrible dreams last night'.[15] Sofia appeared steadily frail, sick, dependent and deprived of her own voice. She attributed her disorders to the weather, her loneliness and her everyday practices. And still, although indirectly, she was aware of a succession of causes, which were immediately linked to her marriage. She cited Heinrich's frequent absences, his parsimony, his judgemental and aloof behaviour, the suffocating control over her everyday activities, the prioritising of his personal and professional interests that harmed his family life. As epistolary bonds reflect human relations and experiences, they are not steadily informed by positive feelings, neither is a letter always written or received with feelings of pleasure. With this in mind, Sofia's letters reveal that the conjugal ideal of companionship had obviously failed for her:

> I am no longer Sofia, the same person I used to be eight years ago, due to my irritated nerves I became more sensitive, and the slightest ache makes me feel the most miserable being in the whole world. You see, my friend, this week, as you already know, I was suffering and [...] despite my efforts I couldn't think of something sweet, to loosen me up.[16]

---

[13]Sofia to Heinrich, Paris n.a [1877].
[14]Sofia to Heinrich, Paris 29 August 1877.
[15]Sofia to Heinrich, Paris 7 September 1877.
[16]Sofia to Heinrich, Paris 8 December 1877.

Her very last line in the same letter opens up a sudden interpretational path, as she states clearly her own panacea, what she thinks of as a remedy for all her troubles: 'Thank God, today I am feeling absolutely fine, *especially when it comes to mind, that I've got a husband, who still loves me, and needs me*'.[17]

Marigo Makka (182[?]–1877): Whenever I Get Sad, I Feel so Wiped Out[18]

If Sofia Schliemann can be viewed as the usual suspect, that is to say, as the incarnation of the submissive, fragile Greek wife of the second half of the nineteenth century, Marigo Makka represents her opposite. Active spouse and housewife, she was fully in charge of a large family (they had eight children at the time) and equally engaged with extended obligations in the public sphere. Well informed on a variety of topics, from medicine to national economy, and from domestic to foreign affairs, Marigo was notoriously prone to interfere in her spouse's professional life. Her correspondence suggests that she definitely had her own, quite distinct voice. The couple's married life seemed harmonious, profoundly 'companionate', in accordance with the dominant ideal of middle-class marriage. Yet, two major issues seemed to spoil the idyllic picture of their marriage: first, Georgios' frequent, long-term absences from home and, second, Marigo's unfailing maladies. Marigo responded to this conjugal 'abandonment' usually with letters of discontent, on occasions with religious stoicism and sometimes with unrestrained rage.[19] In the following passage from a letter she sends on 18 July 1866, two months after his departure from Athens, she is openly threatening him that if he will not come back, as he is stating, within the next five weeks, she will 'let loose to her sorrow, no matter what'.[20] Nevertheless, she attributes her sadness partly to her recurrent conjugal separations:

> They just brought me your letters. You can surely understand the sorrow that, for once more, they provoked me. I was devastated to heart seeing that you set the usual six weeks deadline. [...] Give me your word of honour, that after five

---

[17]Ibid. Emphasis added.
[18]Marigo to Georgios, Athens 29 July [1866].
[19]For example, see Marigo to Georgios, Athens 18 July [1866].
[20]Ibid.

weeks, as you claim, you will be definitely back, and I promise to do whatever it takes to be brave during this time. Or else, I guarantee nothing.[21]

In February 1866, Georgios was on his way to Istanbul, as he would be on professional leave for seven months, in order to attend the 3rd International Sanitary Conference against cholera. During this extended period, Marigo would send him letters on an almost daily basis, expressing in detail the anxieties caused by his long absence. Every time he was away, she was sick. Was this an occasional overlap or, on the contrary, does it urge us to move beyond this 'coincidence'?

Negatively charged emotions, for instance fear or sorrow, were thought at the time capable of causing irreparable damage to those who experienced them. In this light, Marigo's anguish was not perceived as an illness, as a pathological disorder per se. More likely, it was conceived as a condition provoking unhealthy chain reactions. Eventually, the monotonous statement of sorrow in her letters was becoming a powerful tool in her hands, helping her to regain the normality of conjugal living:

> Nonetheless, the unhappiness that has overcome me for so long, will bring along some kind of disease. Initially, I thought of this as the worst evil of all; lately I've started, if not wishing to get sick, at least not feeling sad in case that happens, since I hope that when you find out, you'll have to come back, there would be nothing else you could do.[22]

But how does Marigo herself record the story of her disorders?

> What I am feeling is not weakness, because I do not sense it when I am walking, nor when I'm working; just whenever I am lying down, to get some rest or sleep. Once I am paying attention to see what's going on, at times I think that my heart is beating faster, on occasions not just my heart, but my whole body, as if during [...] an earthquake. Maybe it is not caused by [the unbearable] heat, *maybe it is just my imagination*.[23]

The fact that she attributes her maladies to her 'imagination' at first seems a simple denial. A reverse reading of that phrase, though, is more intriguing. 'Imagination' signifies the starting point and, equally, the cause of her

---

[21]Ibid.
[22]Marigo to Georgios, Athens 18 July [1866].
[23]Marigo to Georgios, Athens 22 June [1866]. Emphasis added.

auto/pathographies, as she describes the psychological and mental tensions she recognises as disorders. Hence, 'imagination' becomes partially disconnected from its fictitious aura; the 'imaginative' is absolutely 'real'. The underlying correlations between body and soul are revealing a different set of symptoms: maladies and symptoms, causes and consequences, are internally intertwined.

The Specialists' View

In a translated French article, published in the *Ladies' Newspaper*, the most influential Greek feminist journal of the nineteenth century, hysteria (and its linguistic equivalents) was presented as an inherited disease, which could emerge if the affected individual was repeatedly exposed to emotional distress, such as fear, rage, deep sorrow and relentless sadness. It is rather palpable that the family unit was the principal domain for the practical application of these disruptive emotions. According to the writer Maria Pierre, 'many hysterical men and women are extremely unhappy in their family life, therefore cure seems impossible, since the cause of evil is always present'. For her, the basic causes of 'hysterism' were prearranged marriages with an 'abhorred person', as well as 'devotion, without a single hope of reciprocity' (Pierre 1892: 03).

Likewise, Miltiadis Venizelos, professor of gynaecology at the Medical School of Athens and one of Sofia's personal doctors, had correctly detected the psychological causes hidden behind her maladies. And he did not hesitate to expose them in two consecutive letters he addressed in June 1870 to his close friend and Sofia's husband, Heinrich. Doctor Venizelos explicitly related their troubled conjugal relations to Sofia's 'nervous system disorders'. To start with, he acknowledged that Sofia was a woman of 'strong morals' and 'good heart'. Additionally, as her doctor, he was reassuring about her 'mental health'. He could detect one single disadvantage: compared to middle-aged Heinrich, Sofia was still very young. On the other hand, this was her husband's crucial obligation when he decided to marry her. From this moment onwards, Heinrich undertook the task to shape her, to guide her and to educate her. Her personal doctor was particularly clear on this: 'She is in need of a skilled rider'.[24] It seems though that her husband was performing other tasks as well:

---

[24]Miltiadis to Heinrich, Athens 23 June 1870.

I am afraid my dear friend, that [by] talking all the time and so intensively about money, you are provoking great sorrow to your wife […]. However, you chose a Greek woman to be your spouse […] and Greek women's mores differ from German or French women's mores […]. Parents are extremely valuable to them, and this is something respected for life.[25]

It is not surprising, therefore, that Greek wives urged their spouses:

[…] not to humiliate their family, as you constantly do, embittering thus and irritating your wife's sensitive heart.[26]

Doctor Venizelos was putting forward to the 'foreigner', Eric, the cultural importance of family and parents in Greece. In fact, he was suggesting, although indirectly, that Eric should reconsider his turbulent relationships with Sofia's parents, whom he was accusing openly for their constant and irrational (in his view) financial demands. Venizelos concluded that Sofia's 'situation' had:

[…] naturally deteriorated due to the circumstances the lady was exposed to […]. Suddenly she felt abandoned by the individual who was bound to protect and support her, and [she felt threatened] by the vagueness of her future life.[27]

In other words, the doctor was attributing the 'disorders of her nervous system, that externalised as intensive irritations'[28] to the failure of the spousal ideal (for which her husband was largely responsible) and, at the same time, to the upheavals of Sofia's present and future family life. Equally important, yet from another point of view, in this case, a gynaecologist undertook a psychotherapeutic role, not exclusively in terms of acknowledging and dealing with the distresses of his female patients, but additionally, in acting as a psychotherapist consultant, almost one century prior to the emergence of 'family therapy'.

Voicing Disorderly Emotional States

Since the letters are sent to significant others, they are firmly connected to the recipients (Tamboukou 2014: 11). Both women addressed the detailed records of their day-to-day ailments to their husbands. It seems that their

---

[25]Ibid.
[26]Ibid.
[27]Miltiadis to Heinrich, Athens 24 June 1870.
[28]Ibid.

letters and the stories they told served as an effective tool of negotiation. Sofia and Marigo repeatedly manifested their physical, emotional and mental states, in the hope of repairing or, at least, salvaging the ideal of companionate marriage, however degraded within their own lives. The ideal-ised couple was constantly lost and found in their daily experiences. The two partners shared the same roof only occasionally. Consequently, they were not able to fulfil their domestic duties through harmonious collaboration and reciprocal support. Whenever conjugality, as a fixed set of daily sup-portive practices that required the physical presence of both spouses failed, both announced urgently in their letters the exacerbation of sorrow and melancholy. However, the following lines offer a shift from auto/pathogra-phy to hetero/pathography, the act of narrating the 'lives of others': Spyros Castriotis, Sofia's brother, who took care of her during Heinrich's very first absence right after their marriage, states in a letter he addressed to Heinrich:

> Soon after the moment of our departure, your wife was overwhelmed with sorrow [...] staying in and crying for three days and nights [...]. Your wife calls me a teacher and a doctor, [teacher] as amid her melancholic days I trans-lated for her several passages from 'Telemachos', and doctor because I send her melancholy away.[29]

Marigo Makka, equally deserted and sad, records in her correspondence a more dynamic reaction, at least verbally. When Georgios suggested she should travel, as a change of environment would rejuvenate her, she responded:

> I am glad to see that as soon as you leave Athens you see everything couleur de rose [...], unfortunately, the exact opposite happens to me, and every time you leave me all alone, something that sadly now happens a lot, I see things d'un rose tellement pale, and therefore I am not in the mood, not only to travel, but I would be very pleased if I could stay constantly inside the house.[30]

The vocabulary of melancholia in auto/pathographies not only legitimates and thus actualises the expression of disorderly emotions, but eventually becomes a crucial tool for negotiating status in marriage (Davis 1989: 112). For both 'abandoned' and 'melancholic' women, their husbands' return home, and consequently, the reinstatement of the imagined, albeit futile, normality of family life, stands as a crucial antidote to their innumerable

---

[29]Spyros to Heinrich, Athens 8 April 1870.
[30]Marigo to Georgios, Athens 1 June 1867.

symptoms, against Marigo's syncope, for instance 'On Friday I fainted once or twice, and just before that, some sort of melancholy overwhelmed me, along with a disposition to cry for no reason', she wrote to Georgios in May 1849 and concluded: 'I hope that the idea that I will meet you soon, will contribute greatly to my overall recovery'.[31]

In my last example, Sofia refers again to her spouse's imagined, idyllic return home:

> Once more I am telling you, every time you leave me it is a shame, the biggest shame of all, is there anything sweeter than us, being together? You do not want it though [...] Ah! Come at last [...] to free yourself from sin.[32]

Several years later, discussing again in a letter she addressed to Heinrich, the countless, albeit unsuccessful medical treatments she went through, she would claim that she never considered him responsible for what she experienced. For all her hardships, she was blaming only her 'bad luck'. But she would override her reservations just a few lines below, adding:

> I want to complain, for you are not giving me the chance to express the love I feel for you [...] i.e. you are doing nice things for me, [but] accompanied with sorrow and disputes that make it just impossible for me to grasp a single moment and thank you.[33]

Although the wider writing culture of the nineteenth century systematically suppressed all voices who questioned the dominant ideals it produced, auto/pathographies persistently penetrated this silence. Melancholic Sofia was, in the end, precise, being able to declare and at the same time quash the prerequisites of conjugal love, in implying that 'love' was living there no more.

Conclusion

Building on the stories that both women told repeatedly in their correspondences and the obscure and fluid terms they used, I argue that within the vigorous domestic ideal of the period that promotes unclouded spousal coexistence and the recognition of 'love' as dominant practice in the emotional

---

[31]Marigo to Georgios, Athens 11 May 1849.
[32]Sofia to Heinrich, Athens 27 September 1878.
[33]Sofia to Heinrich, Ostend 11 August 1886.

community of the family, 'sadness', 'melancholy', 'hysteria' and 'nerves'—whatever the term in use—constitute idioms or communicative gestures, used to articulate disorderly emotional states (Lutz and White 1986: 417). The concept of sorrow—and its equivalents—serves as an indirect yet specific medium for the expression of 'forbidden' feelings. In the cases analysed above, sorrow stands, in particular, for anger, despair, lack of recognition, feelings of abandonment, embarrassment caused by the anxieties of domestic labour and anguish over the burdens of family responsibilities. Since these emotions were negatively charged, they could not be tolerated within the prevalent emotional idiom of spousal love. In this light, the concept of melancholy is discussed here as a marginal, yet forceful outcome of the inherent discontinuities attached to the emblematic emotion of 'love' in/for the family (Vassiliadou 2018) and, equally, as a result of the contradictory tensions that inescapably invaded the daily practices of family life.

The specific physical and psychological disorders involved, as well as the distinct terms the subjects themselves employed to portray them, represent culturally constructed engendered codes, signs or metaphors, extensively used by a wide range of individuals (patients, doctors, close relatives, friends and, finally, 'society' at large), in order to signify threatened or precarious conjugal and, by extension, familial relations.[34] Marigo Makka's auto/pathographies indicate the diversity of this ongoing negotiation. The story that Sofia Schliemann's letters unfold demonstrates, on the other hand, the limitations of this debate for women, the weak link in the gendered power tensions of the Greek nineteenth century. Moreover, the narratives that unravel Sofia's and Marigo's epistolary lives form a binary negotiation. First, they constitute an auto/pathography, an exploration of their disordered reality, along with a strong sense of their embodied selves (Couser 1991: 65). Seen as auto/pathographies letters urge us to think productively on the very small scale, that of the suffering individual who reflects on herself, seeking to be healed. During this writing process, the recognition of the problem comes first, followed by an emphatic quest for its primary causes. Subsequently, both Sofia and Marigo anticipate their mental and physical recovery. To put it differently, with the support of an intentional anachronism, the unfolding of their epistolary lives constitutes a psychotherapeutic practice, nothing less than a narrative self-analysis. With this in mind, these auto/pathographies are, in the first place, addressed to one's own self.

---

[34]Davis underlines (1989: 111–112), the metaphoric qualities of 'nerves', especially in relation to the feminisation of the disorder.

Acknowledgements This work is supported by the Greek State Scholarships Foundation (IKY) and co-financed by the European Union (European Social Fund—ESF) and Greek national funds. Action: 'Reinforcement of Postdoctoral Researchers', Operational Program 'Human Resources Development Program, Education and Lifelong Learning' of the National Strategic Reference Framework (NSRF) 2014–2020.

References

Barton, D., & Hall, N. (2000). *Letter Writing as a Social Practice*. Amsterdam and Philadelphia: John Benjamins.

Bazerman, C. (2000). Letters and the Social Grounding of Differentiated Genres. In D. Barton & N. Hall (Eds.), *Letter Writing as a Social Practice* (pp. 15–29).

Bombou-Protopapa, E. (2005). *Sofia Egastromenou-Schliemann: Letters to Heinrich*. Athens: Kastaniotis (in Greek).

Boon, S. (2015). *Telling the Flesh: Life Writing, Citizenship, and the Body in the Letters to Samuel Auguste Tissot*. Montreal: McGill-Queen's Press.

Cayleff, S. E. (1988). "Prisoners of Their Own Feebleness": Women, Nerves and Western Medicine. A Historical Overview. *Social Science and Medicine, 26*(12), 1199–1208.

Chartier, R., Boureau, A., & Dauphin, E. C. (1997). *Correspondence: Models of Letter-Writing from the Middle Ages to the Nineteenth Century*. Princeton: Princeton University Press.

Couser, G. T. (1991). Autopathography: Women, Illness, and Lifewriting. *a/b: Auto/Biography Studies, 6*(1), 65–75. https://doi.org/10.1080/08989575.1991.10814989.

Davis, D. L. (1989). George Beard and Lydia Pinkham: Gender, Class, and Nerves in Late 19th Century America. *Health Care for Women International, 10*(2–3), 93–114. https://doi.org/10.1080/07399338909515844.

Decker, W. M. (1998). *Epistolary Practices: Letter Writing in America Before Telecommunications*. Chapel Hill: University of North Carolina Press.

Diaz, B. (2006). Avant-Propos. In B. Diaz & J. Seiss (Eds.), *L'épistolaire au féminin: Correspondances de femmes XVIIIe-XXe siècle*. Caen: Presses Universitaires de Caen.

Ferlito, S. (2012). Hysteria's Upheavals: Emotional Fault Lines in Cristina di Belgiojoso's Health History. *Modern Italy, 17*(2), 157–170.

Foucault, M. (1988). *Technologies of the Self: A Seminar with Michel Foucault* (L. H. Martin, H. Gutman, & P. H. Hutton, Eds.). Amherst: University of Massachusetts Press.

Gerber, D. A. (2000). Epistolary Ethics: Personal Correspondence and the Culture of Emigration in the Nineteenth Century. *Journal of American Ethnic History, 19*(4), 3–23.

Gerber, D. A. (2005). Acts of Deceiving and Withholding in Immigrant Letters: Personal Identity and Self-Presentation in Personal Correspondence. *Journal of Social History, 39*(2), 315–330.

Gilroy, A., & Verhoeven, W. M. (Eds). (2000). *Epistolary Histories: Letters, Fiction, Culture*. Charlottesville: University of Virginia Press.

Goodman, D. (2009). *Becoming a Woman in the Age of Letters*. Ithaca: Cornell University Press.

Halldórsdóttir, E. H. (2007). Fragments of Lives: The Use of Private Letters in Historical Research. *NORA—Nordic Journal of Feminist and Gender Research, 15*(1), 35–49.

Hock, L. (2011). Women and Melancholy in Nineteenth-Century German Psychiatry. *History of Psychiatry, 22*(4), 448–464.

Jackson, S. W. (1986). *Melancholia and Depression: From Hippocratic Times to Modern Times*. New Haven and London: Yale University Press.

Jansson, Å. (2013). *The Creation of 'Disordered Emotion': Melancholia as Biomedical Disease, c. 1840–1900*. Ph.D. thesis, Queen Mary, University of London.

Jolly, M., & Stanley, L. (2005). Letters as / Not a Genre. *Life Writing, 2*(2), 91–118.

Karamanolakis, V. (1998). Dromokaitio Asylum: 1887–1903: Views of the Establishment of a Mental Institution. *Mnimon, 20,* 45–66 (in Greek).

Katsaras, M. (1898). *Pathology of the Nerves and Psychiatry: Diseases of the Brain, Diseases of the Cerebellum, and Phrenitis*. Athens: Alexandros Papageorgiou (in Greek).

Kritsotaki, D. (2009). *Mental Illness and Psychiatric Hospitalisation: The Social Perceptions and Functions of Psychiatry and Psychiatric Hospitals in Greece and Scotland in the Beginning of the Twentieth Century*. Ph.D. thesis, University of Crete (in Greek).

Lawlor, C. (2012). *From Melancholia to Prozac: A History of Depression*. Oxford and New York: Oxford University Press.

Lutz, C., & White, G. M. (1986). The Anthropology of Emotions. *Annual Review of Anthropology, 15,* 405–436.

Misbach, J., & Stam, H. J. (2005). Medicalizing Melancholia: Exploring Profiles of Psychiatric Professionalization. *Journal of the History of the Behavioral Sciences, 42*(1), 41–59. https://doi.org/10.1002/jhbs.20133.

Moullas, P. (1992). *Discourse of Absence. Essay on Epistolarity, with 40 Unpublished Letters of Fotis Politis (1908–1910)*. Athens: MIET (in Greek).

Pearsall, S. M. S. (2009). *Atlantic Families: Lives and Letters in the Later Eighteenth Century*. Oxford University Press.

Pierre, M. (1892). The Nervous. *The Ladies Journal, 282,* 3–4.

Porter, R. (1985). The Patient's View: Doing Medical History from Below. *Theory and Society, 14*(2), 175–198.

Poustie, S. (2011). "That Is Supposed to Be My Foot": Letters, Bodies and Epistolary Co-Presence. In L. Stanley (Ed.), *Olive Schreiner and Company: Schreiner's Letters and 'Drinking in the External World'* (pp. 139–167).

Radden, J. (2009). *Moody Minds Distempered: Essays on Melancholy and Depression*. Oxford and New York: Oxford University Press.

Rosenwein, B. H. (2002). Worrying About Emotions in History. *The American Historical Review, 107*(3), 821–845.

Ruberg, W. (2010). The Letter as Medicine: Studying Health and Illness in Dutch Daily Correspondence, 1770–1850. *Social History of Medicine, 23*(3), 492–508. https://doi.org/10.1093/shm/hkq012.

Schatzki, T. R. (1996). *Social Practices: A Wittgensteinian Approach to Human Activity and the Social/Theodore R. Schatzki*. Cambridge: Cambridge University Press.

Scheer, M. (2012). Are Emotions a Kind of Practice (and Is That What Makes Them Have a History)? A Bourdieuian Approach to Understanding Emotion. *History and Theory, 51*(2), 193–220. https://doi.org/10.1111/j.1468-2303.2012.00621.x.

Schiesari, J. (1992). *The Gendering of Melancholia: Feminism, Psychoanalysis, and the Symbolics of Loss in Renaissance Literature*. Ithaca: Cornell University Press.

Schulte, R., & Von Tippelskirch, X. (2004). *Reading, Interpreting and Historicizing: Letters as Historical Sources*. Florence: European University Institute.

Shorter, E. (2013). *How Everyone Became Depressed: The Rise and Fall of the Nervous Breakdown*. Oxford: Oxford University Press.

Showalter, E. (1993). Hysteria, Feminism, and Gender. In S. L. Gilman et al. (Eds.), *Hysteria Beyond Freud* (pp. 286–344). Berkeley: University of California Press.

Smith-Rosenberg, C. (1972). The Hysterical Woman: Sex Roles and Role Conflict in 19th century America. *Social Research, 39*(4), 652–678.

Stanley, L. (1992). *The Auto/Biographical I: The Theory and Practice of Feminist Auto/Biography*. Manchester: Manchester University Press.

Stanley, L. (1993). On Auto/Biography in Sociology. *Sociology, 27*(1), 41–52.

Stanley, L. (2002). Mourning Becomes …: The Work of Feminism in the Spaces Between Lives Lived and Lives Written. *Women's Studies International Forum, 25*(1), 1–17.

Tamboukou, M. (2011). Interfaces in Narrative Research: Letters as Technologies of the Self and as Traces of Social Forces. *Qualitative Research, 11,* 625–641.

Tamboukou, M. (2014). The Autobiographical You: Letters in the Gendered Politics of the Labour Movement. *Journal of Gender Studies, 1*–14. https://doi.org/10.1080/09589236.2014.957169.

Vassiliadou, D. (2017). The Idiom of Love and Sacrifice: Emotional Vocabularies of Motherhood in Nineteenth-Century Greece. *Cultural and Social History, 14*(3), 283–300. https://doi.org/10.1080/14780038.2017.1312190.

Vassiliadou, D. (2018). *The Tropic of Writing: Family Ties and Emotions in Modern Greece, 1850–1930*. Athens: Gutenberg (in Greek).

Part IV

Geography Matters: Spatiality and Auto/Biography

John Barker and Emma Wainwright

Introduction

Starting an argument can often be troublesome for us as academics, and deciding where to begin this part of the handbook was no exception. Inspiration came whilst reading Daniels and Nash's article *Lifepaths: Geography and Biography* (2004) which begins with the well-known rhyme:

> The art of Biography
> Is different from Geography
> Geography is about Maps
> But Biography is about Chaps. (cited in Daniels and Nash 2004: 449)

Geography matters, and in this part of the handbook of auto/biography, we build an argument which (aside from a much-needed feminist critique of 'chaps', a term symbolic of a more misogynistic historical period implying the world of Geography and maps was only accessible and understandable by men) systematically challenges the above statement. This part focuses on the theme of spatiality, exploring interconnections between geography and auto/biography, exploring how auto/biographies draw upon and can be navigated in geographical ways, we bring together academics from a range of disciplines, including Human Geography, Youth Studies, Sociology and Education. The first part of this part introduction considers four interrelated key concepts at the heart of Human Geography: space, place, scale and flow, exploring the relevance and use of these four concepts within auto/

biographical research. Following an introduction to each of the subsequent chapters in this part, linkages between geography and spatiality are identified, discussed and theorised, illustrating some of the diverse interconnections between auto/biography and spatiality.

Geography Matters: Connecting Geography and Auto/Biography

Space is at the heart of geographical analysis. The social and the spatial (i.e. landscapes, places, spaces, regions) are inseparably interconnected, in a process referred to as spatiality (Keith and Pile 1993). The rhyme we began our discussion with implies that whilst geographers accord primacy to the spatial, those interested in auto/biography have focused more attention (either implicitly or explicitly) on the temporal. Auto/biographies are situated within historical *time* periods, and are classically seen to have (significantly in a *temporal* sense) a beginning, middle and end (McGeachen et al. 2012).

However, such distinctions between geography and auto/biography are becoming increasingly blurred. Auto/Biography often considers mundane, ordinary lives (Garner 2004), exploring the experiences and identities of a diverse range of subaltern, marginalised social groups (Gale and Garnder 2004; Schur 2002). Identity is constructed partly through space, and therefore *'identity is a profoundly geographical concept'* (Horton and Kraftl 2014: 160). Baena's (2007: vii) assertion that *'life writing must be located within specific historical and social contexts'* needs to be extended with the additional recognition of *spatial* contexts.

A range of Geographers (see Roche 2011) and others (Hipchen and Chansky 2017) have begun to consider intersections between spatiality and auto/biography, for example, in exploring health (Milligan et al. 2011), mobility (Rau and Sattlegger 2018) and urban life (Valentine and Sadgrove 2014). Historical geographers have adopted auto/biographical approaches to explore a range of historical time periods and experiences (see Philo et al. 2015; McGeachen et al. 2012; Naylor 2008) as well as the contested historical auto/biographies of academic geographers (Wainwright et al. 2014) and geography itself (Johnston 2005; Driver and Baigent 2007). The spatial has been implicit in many auto/biographical projects—for example Hipchen and Chansky's (2017) article *'Looking forward: the futures of auto/biography'* uses the word 'space' 48 times, though arguably the term is rather fuzzy and undefined. Greater recognition of the links between spatiality and auto/biographers is beneficial, since *'the arts of geography and biography appear closely connected: life histories are also, to coin a phrase, life geographies'* (Daniels and Nash 2004: 450). We now outline some ways in which this endeavour has begun, though due to limited space, we can only briefly allude to a range of complex debates (e.g. Cameron 2012 explores radically different post-structural and post-human connections between geography and auto/biography). Whilst geographers have long explored a range of spatial-related concepts (see Johnston and Sidaway 2015), this chapter briefly explores four key interrelated and often hotly contested concepts—*space, place, scale* and *flow*.

Space

In the middle of the twentieth century, quantitative geographers (influenced by positivist, scientific approaches) conceptualised space as an inert, physically measurable, politically neutral and bounded landscape or container for social action (Johnston and Sidaway 2015; Horton and Kraftl 2014). Since the 1970s, a long, diverse tradition of geographers, including feminist, critical, cultural, post-structural and post-humanist geographers (for more exploration of these wide-ranging distinct viewpoints, see Johnston, and Sidaway 2015; Cameron 2012) have critiqued this assertion (Thrift 2009; Gibson-Graham 2008). Rather, space is *generative*, helping to produce personal experience, social life and culture (Horton and Kraftl 2014; Haraway 2008; Fuchs 2002). For example, Foucault's work on institutions (Foucault 1977) has been re-analysed by geographers to show how spatial configurations within prisons help to shape and generate behaviour (Philo 2001; Philo et al. 2015), whilst more recent post-humanist theorisations consider spatial relations between the human and non-human, and how 'matter matters' in the production of space and social life (Cameron 2012; Haraway 2008; Barad 2007).

Thus, a geographical perspective can map the role of space(s) within the production of auto/biographies. Fuch (2002) prompts us to consider this through two questions:

> in what ways do land, ocean, and therefore space, shape our lives and our memories? In what ways do our narratives about land, ocean and space impact our other narratives, our autobiographies and biographies? (p. v)

Given our earlier assertion that space is not simply inert, telling the *'spatial stories of lives'* (McGeachen et al. 2012: 170) can help to explore how auto/

biographies can be laden with a range of spatial dynamics, contradictions, tensions and socio-spatial inequalities, enabling us to think through the workings of power. For example, Schur's (2002) analysis of Patricia Williams' 1991 autobiography links her individual account to structural processes of discrimination, ethnocentrism and racism within the very public spaces of retail shops and advertising billboards. However, some post-human approaches critique connections between personal accounts, space and broader social issues of power, discourse and inequality (Gibson-Graham 2008). Rather, these focus on interactions and assemblages between the human, materiality and space in the generation of auto/biographies (Cameron 2012; McGeachan et al. 2012; Naylor 2008). For example, Jackson's (2010) life history interviews with food producers and retailers note the significance of non-human 'materialities' (such as animal flesh, production lines, packaging) which help to shape auto/biographies around food production and retail spaces.

Place

Place has gained increasing prominence amongst geographers. Places are neither natural nor given—they are generated through social processes. Places can be real (i.e. a mappable point in space), virtual or imagined (Holloway and Hubbard 2001). Places are usually characterised by their locality, particularness and uniqueness, producing distinctive meanings and 'a sense of place' (Massey 1994). In an age of plural and hybrid identities (Plummer 2003), discussions around place(s), either as directly experienced or as sites for meaning, are often central in/to the production of distinctive auto/biographies. As Cresswell 2004 states:

> place is also a way of seeing, knowing and understanding the world. When we look at the world as a world of places we see different things. We see attachments and connections between people and places. We see worlds of meaning and experience. (Cresswell 2004: 11)

Since 'life writing is invariably place writing' (Fuchs 2002: vi), stories and identities are always 'placed'—we talk about places and attach meaning to them as (e.g.) places of violence, fear, love, conflict, safety, oppression and liberation. For example, Philo et al. (2015) discuss how Scottish Highlands residents construct their rural communities as places of surveillance (particularly around who sees, who is seen, what is concealed or denied), specifically in relation to mental health issues.

Post-humanist attention goes beyond how places are given meaning by individuals, to incorporate how the non-human also generates place-making (Barad 2007). By following 'things and their stories', we can explore how the *material practices and relations through which "things" matter* (Cameron 2012: 578) and become productive in generating experiences of place, and *'biographies of objects and places'* (Naylor 2008: 269). For example, Wylie (2005) analyses his walk along England's South West Coast Path, discussing how physical landscape combines with his own human experience, generating a range of affective senses and emotions (e.g. exhilaration, anxiety) to create a sense of place whilst walking.

Scale

Geographers have, in an increasingly globalised world, also shown great interest in the concept of scale. This concept provides an opportunity for geographical analysis to go beyond individual places and spaces, to explore other scales of experience, from focusing upon the small scale spaces of the body, home, school and local, to consideration of the larger scale of the urban, regional, national, supranational and global (Cresswell 2004; Herod 2009). Scale is an essential geographical analytical tool for three reasons: firstly, for investigating human agency, power and relations between people and places at a range of different levels (Horton and Kraftl 2014); secondly, for linking together different local places (Cameron 2012); and, lastly, for exploring whether and how relations between people and places at one scale might be influenced by processes occurring at other scales, such as globalisation (see Holloway and Hubbard 2001). Different metaphors have been used to conceptualise relationships and connections between spatial scales, including ladders, concentric circles, nesting dolls and networks, each offering different ways of thinking about scale, connections, power and agency (Herod 2009).

Scale also helps us to rethink other key geographical concepts; rather than envisioning space and places as bounded, the interconnections suggested by scale leads to a re-conceptualisation of space and place as more open, porous and connected (Thrift 2009; Castree 2009). For example, Massey's (1994) classic 'Progressive sense of place' describes Kilburn in North London as a unique place precisely because of its interactions and connections with other places and processes at a variety of spatial scales.

The geographical concept of scale illuminates how auto/biographies assign meaning to personal experience, social life, power and agency at a variety of levels of social life. For example, at the intimate, minute and small scale, bodies can be seen as significant places through which accounts are generated, especially for those who experience illness/ disability (Philo 2001; Milligan et al. 2011). Embodied accounts can re-authorise one's own subjectivity and contest and challenge professional, public and oversimplified notions of difference and (dis)ability (see, e.g., Mintz 2016; Young 2016 on AIDS memoirs). Working at a larger spatial scale, auto/biographies often highlight the importance (and often complexity) of national identity and the significance of territory, and auto/biographies are often inscribed with broader processes such as globalisation and post-colonialism (Hornung 2016).

Flow

As well as focusing upon space, place and scale, geographers and others have become more interested in flow, movement and mobility in an ever-mobile world. This concern is manifest in many forms (Urry 1999): the flow of commodities; the rapid exchange of ideas, information and news via social media and the Internet; the day-to-day mobility of individuals (Massey 1994; Urry 1999) and longer migration and movement (Hornung 2016); and whether flow and mobility is chosen or forced (Hipchen and Chansky 2017; Fuchs 2002).

Flow, mobility and movement increasingly feature as central to auto/ biographies (Hipchen and Chansky 2017). Migration generates accounts replete with metaphors and experiences of flow and mobility, including around displacement, '(extra)territoriality' and feeling 'out of place' (Hornung 2016). Valentine and Sadgrove's (2014) research focuses upon the significance of mobility and immobility, illuminating issues around power and socio-spatial inequality (particularly around ethnicity, disability and sexual identity). The contemporary prevalence of flow and circulation leads Hipchen and Chansky (2017: 145) to see mobility as a key future trend within auto/biography, commenting to how the '*the future is in motion*'. With this in mind, this part of the Handbook responds to Hipchen and Chansky's (2017: 153) urge for auto/biography to incorporate space and time:

> We are now talking in auto/biographical studies about the movement of people as transit, a concern at first glance about space (the nation space, the space of an ocean, the border space). What if it were treated as concerning time? What if in looking at the spaces of life narrative, we thought about them

as spacetime… but imagine too, the effect of rethinking spacetime in/as narrative, or compressing what we see as the space of the self into what we see as the time of the self?

As this suggests, thinking about space, as well as time, can be a powerful analytical tool to make sense of auto/biographical accounts.

Introduction to the Chapters

Cullen et al.'s chapter focuses on the geography of care and caring within student carers auto/biographies. In doing so, they offer new ways of thinking about intersections between time, space, care and identity. Using Lefebvre's rhythmanalysis and a range of feminist work exploring gendered dynamics of care, they map the spatial and temporal rhythms of women students who have caring responsibilities. These are explored both in terms of everyday and longer-term rhythms. The chapter explores how participants' auto/biographies identify how carers skilfully negotiate the complex, shifting and multiply-intersecting rhythms across space and time to undertake care and also to construct identities as both carer and student. Student carer auto/biographies replete with notions of juggling care, study, care across time and space operate in contradistinction to dominant neoliberal discourses which produce University spaces for and identities as 'autonomous', 'independent' learners. Whilst Lefebvre offers insight into exploring the spatial rhythms of care, a more critical feminist analysis reminds us of the great stress, burden and cost that many student carers face in engaging in their responsibilities within contemporary late modernity and broader economic realities.

Wainwright et al. draw on two different research projects with social housing residents to explore the spatialities implicit in auto/biographical narratives of encounter. They argue that any focus on auto/biographies is inherently relational; auto/biographies are shaped in relation to things, people and place. They argue that auto/biographies are shaped by embodied personal encounters and relationality—to our homes and families; to social housing agencies and officers; and to wider discourses of welfare, dependency and individual responsibilisation. Auto/Biographical accounts are impacted by *where* we are and *who* we are, with the urgency of place experienced through the threat of displacement, loss and dislocation. Through this chapter, the immediacy of the spatial is highlighted, allowing the everyday complexities and intricacies of research participants' lives to emerge.

Hayes' chapter focuses the auto/biographical debate on ethical and moral tensions implicit in the doing of research. Here, the focus of the encounter is between researcher and researched and the auto/biographical narrative of the former. The research project that this argument forms around relates to young people's use and experience of public space, notably their relationship with nature. The power of the research and the researcher underpins this chapter, and Hayes argues that recognition of the *powerful* requires the need to be *careful*. That is, in writing about ourselves and our experiences, we must pay attention to the complex ways in which thinking, seeing and hearing shape auto/biographical research.

Emerging Themes: Spatiality and Auto/Biography

Each of the three chapters in this part offers distinct contributions to an understanding of intersections between space, Geography and Auto/Biography, illustrating how life writing is indeed interlinked with place writing (Fuch 2002). In doing so, the chapters employ a wide range of different epistemological and theoretical approaches (including critical realism, post-structuralism, feminism and post-humanism) and disciplinary insights (from education, geography, youth work) that can be used to further analyse space and auto/biography.

In different ways, each of the chapters illuminates the importance of space. Each chapter maps how auto/biographies are situated within, draw upon and become embodied in/about/through different kinds of spaces (primarily those of home, education, employment and public space). Auto/biographical accounts construct these spaces as important places, with significant meanings and attachments (Cresswell 2004). The chapters link individual accounts to broader social processes at a variety of spatial scales. For example, each paper considers social identities within space (as carer, student, social housing resident, young person) and explore connections, relations and interactions with others (between researcher and participants, student carer and professionals, and social housing tenants and officers). The accounts also connect to a range of broader socio-economic processes and policies, for example, those shaping higher education, housing and welfare. Thus, each chapter explores how auto/biographies always involve belonging, connection and enmeshment between the self and other people, processes and places (Hipchen and Chansky 2017).

Building upon these insights, each chapter also plots spatial expressions of emotion and affect; whilst Cullen et al. explore the stress and burden of student carers' juggling responsibilities and identities, Wainwright et al. consider the vulnerabilities of housing and accommodation, and Hayes reflects on challenges and anxieties around researching public space. Similarly, each chapter considers spatial expressions of agency, inequality and power. Whilst Cullen et al. debate the agency of student carers who are clearly also experiencing inequality and oppression, similarly Wainwright et al. explore inequality and struggle experienced by social housing residents. Furthermore, the papers highlight complex configurations of the relatedness of social life; relationality is not just simply between humans, but also between the human and the non-human. Space, material and matter (as University spaces, homes, public space) are not simply the backdrop for social action, rather, reflecting post-humanist approaches, each chapter prompts further consideration of the generative effects of space (Fuch 2002).

Thirdly, each paper offers insight into methodological and reflective engagements with space and auto/biography and how reflection and writing ourselves back into our accounts constructs 'space' for thinking about auto/biographical research. Hayes firmly focuses upon the reflective spaces created by auto/biographical research. By talking through their own care experiences, Cullen et al. discuss how auto/biographical analysis can be simultaneously shaped by and help to shape (as writers) our own positionalities, academic interests and current engagements. Wainwright et al. reflect on the physical dislocation of researcher and research participant in the conducting of research that draws on the very details of lived experience and embodied relations.

Therefore, we end this introduction with a hopeful note that this part prompts further deliberation, discussion and critical consideration of the multiple intersections between space and auto/biographies. In so doing, we find a more comprehensive understanding of auto/biography that necessarily combines the temporal with the spatial for more critical inquiry.

References

Baena, R. (2007). Introduction: Transculturing Auto/Biography: New Forms of Life Writing. In R. Baena (Ed.), *Transculturing Auto/Biography: Forms of Life Writing* (pp. vii–xii). Abingdon: Routledge.

Barad, K. (2007). Meeting the Universe Halfway: Realism and Social Constructivism Without Contradiction. In L. Nelson & J. Nelson (Eds.), *Feminism, Science and the Philosophy of Science* (pp. 161–194). Dordrecht: Kluwer Academic.

Cameron, E. (2012). New Geographies of Story and Storytelling. *Progress in Human Geography, 36*(5), 573–592.

Castree, N. (2009). Place: Connections and Boundaries in an Interdependent World. In N. Clifford, S. Holloway, S. Rice, & G. Valentine (Eds.), *Key Concepts in Geography* (pp. 153–172). London: Sage.

Cresswell, T. (2004). *Place: A Short Introduction*. Oxford: Blackwell.

Daniels, S., & Nash, C. (2004). Lifepaths: Geography and Biography. *Journal of Historical Geography, 30*(3), 449–458.

Driver, F., & Baigent, E. (2007). Biography and the History of Geography: A Response to Ron Johnston. *Progress in Human Geography, 3*(1), 101–106.

Foucault, M. (1977). *Discipline and Punish: The Birth of the Prison*. New York: Pantheon Books.

Fuchs, M. (2002). Autobiography and Geography: Introduction. *Biography, 25*(1), iv–xi.

Gale, M., & Gardner, V. (2004). Introduction: Women, Theatre and Performance: Auto/Biography and Performance. In M. Gale & V. Gardner (Eds.), *Auto/Biography and Identity: Women, Theatre and Performance* (pp. 1–8). Manchester: Manchester University Press.

Gardner, V. (2004). The Three Nobodies: Autobiographical Strategies in the Work of ALMA Ellerslie, Kitty Marion and Ina Rozant. In M. Gale & V. Gardner (Eds.). *Auto/Biography and Identity: Women, Theatre and Performance* (pp. 10–38). Manchester: Manchester University Press.

Gibson-Graham, J. K. (2008). Diverse Economies: Performative Practices for "Other Worlds". *Progress in Human Geography, 32,* 613–632.

Haraway, D. (2008). *When Species Meet*. Minneapolis: University of Minnesota Press.

Herod, A. (2009). Scale: The Local and the Global. In N. Clifford, S. Holloway, S. Rice, & G. Valentine (Eds.), *Key Concepts in Geography* (pp. 217–235). London: Sage.

Hipchen, E., & Chansky, R. (2017). Looking Forward: The Futures of Auto/Biography. *a/b: Auto/biography Studies, 32*(2), 139–157.

Holloway, S., & Hubbard, P. (2001). *People and Place: The Extraordinary Geographies of Everyday Life*. Harlow: Pearson.

Hornung, A. (2016). Out of Place: Extraterritorial Existence and Autobiography. In R. Chansky & E. Hipchen (Eds.), *The Routledge Auto/Biography Studies Reader* (pp. 183–187). London: Routledge.

Horton, J., & Kraftl, P. (2014). *Cultural Geographies: An Introduction*. London: Routledge.

Jackson, P. (2010). Food Stories: Consumption in an Age of Anxiety. *Cultural Geographies, 17*(2), 147–165.

Johnston, R. (2005). Learning Our History from Our Pioneers: UK Academic Geographers in the *Oxford Dictionary of National Biography*. *Progress in Human Geography, 29,* 651–667.

Johnston, R., & Sidaway, J. (2015). *Geography and Geographers: Anglo-American Geography Since 1945 Seventh Edition.* London: Routledge.

Keith, M., & Pile, S. (1993). *Place and the Politics of Identity.* London: Routledge.

Massey, D. (1994). *Space, Place, and Gender.* Minneapolis: University of Minnesota Press.

McGeachan, C., Forsyth, I., & Hasty, W. (2012). Certain Subjects? Working with Biography and Life-Writing in Historical Geography. *Historical Geography, 40,* 169–185.

Milligan C., Kearns, R., & Kyle, R. (2011). Unpacking Stored and Storied Knowledge: Elicited Biographies of Activism in Mental Health. *Health and Place, 17*(1), 7–16.

Mintz, S. (2016). Transforming the Tale: The Auto/Body/Ographies of Nancy Mairs. In R. Chansky & E. Hipchen (Eds.), *The Routledge Auto/Biography Studies Reader* (pp. 130–138). London: Routledge.

Naylor, S. (2008). Historical Geography: Geographies and Historiographies. *Progress in Human Geography, 32*(2), 265–274.

Olney, J. (2016). Autobiography and the Cultural Moment: A Thematic, Historical and Bibliographical Introduction. In R. Chansky & E. Hipchen (Eds.), *The Routledge Auto/Biography Studies Reader* (pp. 5–14). London: Routledge.

Philo, C. (2001). Accumulating Populations: Bodies, Institutions and Space. *International Journal of Population Geography, 7*(6), 473–490.

Philo, C., Parr, H., & Burns, N. (2015). The Rural Panopticon. *Journal of Rural Studies, 51,* 230–239.

Plummer, K. (2003). *Intimate Citizenship: Private Decisions and Public Dialogues.* Seattle: University of Washington Press.

Rau, H., & Sattlegger, L. (2018). Shared Journeys, Linked Lives: A Relational-Biographical Approach to Mobility Practices. *Mobilities, 13*(1), 45–63.

Roche, M. (2011). Special Issue: New Zealand Geography, Biography and Autobiography. *New Zealand Geographer, 67*(2), 73–142.

Schur, R. (2002). Critical Race Theory and the Limits of Auto/Biography: Reading Patricia William's *The Alchemy of Race and Rights* Through/Against Postcolonial Theory. *Biography, 25*(3), 455–476.

Thrift, N. (2009). Space: The Fundamental Stuff of Geography. In N. Clifford, S. Holloway, S. Rice, & G. Valentine (Eds.), *Key Concepts in Geography* (pp. 85–96). London: Sage.

Urry, J. (1999). *Sociology Beyond Societies: Mobilities for the Twenty-First Century.* London: Routledge.

Valentine, G., & Sadgrove, J. (2014). Biographical Narratives of Encounter: The Significance of Mobility and Emplacement in Shaping Attitudes Towards Difference. *Journal of Urban Studies, 51*(9), 1979–1994.

Wainwright, E., Barker, J., Ansell, N., Buckingham, S., Hemming, P., & Smith, F. (2014). Geographers Out of Place: Institutions, (Inter)Disciplinarity and Identity. *Area, 46*(4), 410–417.

Wylie, J. (2005). A Single Day's Walking: Narrating Self and Landscape on the South West Coast Path. *Transactions of the Institute of British Geographers, 30*(2), 234–247.

Young, H. (2016). Memorializing Memory: Marlon Riggs and Life Writing. In R. Chansky & E. Hipchen (Eds.), *The Routledge Auto/Biography Studies Reader* (pp. 139–144). London: Routledge.

11

'Trying to Keep Up': Intersections of Identity, Space, Time and Rhythm in Women Student Carer Auto/Biographical Accounts

Fin Cullen, John Barker and Pam Alldred

Introduction

Geographies of care and caring are a burgeoning area of geographical thought, although auto/biographical caring accounts have (with exceptions such as Parr and Philo 2003; Milligan et al. 2011; Philo et al. 2015) been less explored. This chapter seeks to understand how time and space are central to how 'student carers' narrate their caring responsibilities. Firstly, we trace understandings of space, place and time in care and educational contexts, including work on emotional labour and the 'second shift' (domestic labour undertaken by women following a day in paid employment, see Hochschild 1989). We then present three vignettes (drawn from a study involving 19 carers), unpacking concerns with space, time, rhythms, identity and transition. Our engagement springs from our analysis as feminist

F. Cullen (✉)
St Mary's University, Twickenham, UK
e-mail: fiona.cullen@stmarys.ac.uk

J. Barker
Middlesex University, London, UK
e-mail: j.a.barker@mdx.ac.uk

P. Alldred
Nottingham Trent University, Nottingham, UK
e-mail: pam.alldred@brunel.ac.uk

© The Author(s) 2020
J. M. Parsons and A. Chappell (eds.), *The Palgrave Handbook of Auto/Biography*,
https://doi.org/10.1007/978-3-030-31974-8_11

scholars and practitioners and our prior research on care, spanning mothers' care responsibilities (Barker et al. 2010), young mothers' views about their education (Alldred and David 2010; Alldred 2011), university students' care roles (Cullen and Alldred 2013) and how mothers make decisions about paid work and childcare (Duncan et al. 2004).

Whilst data are not always routinely recorded in UK universities regarding the numbers of registered carers or student parents, estimates suggest 5.3% of 18–24-year-olds have regular care responsibilities for an ill or disabled relative (Becker and Becker 2008). Since this estimate does not include student parents or parents and carers amongst the mature student population, the proportion of UK Higher Education (hereafter HE) students with care responsibilities is likely to be higher. Clearly, this often overlooked and diverse group needs further study.

Using an auto/biographical approach, we explore how participants have multiple intersecting rhythms and identities across time and space, for example as students, parents and carers for partners or parents. We note the gender and generational features of the participant accounts from what was almost an exclusively female study group. We explore how student carers juggle and negotiate space, time and identity in complex ways. As Bhatti (2014) identifies, one of the benefits of the auto/biographical turn is that it helps raise awareness of ordinary lives, and from our perspective, shines light into ordinary spaces, times and spatial and temporal processes.

Conceptualising Care

Care has been defined and understood in a diverse range of ways (Horton and Pyer 2017). It is often referred to as a particular form or type of personal relation and exchange, undertaken in either the short or long term, within a cultural context and reflecting human vulnerability and interdependence (Philip et al. 2013; Weller 2013). Care can refer to an abstract concern ('caring about') or a social practice ('caring for'), though it is often marginalised, invisible and undervalued (Horton and Pyer 2017). It is provided by individuals, families, voluntary groups, public institutions and private companies and is also often the subject of vociferous debate within the media and political arenas (Rogers and Weller 2013). The notion that caring is unidirectional (between a 'care giver' and 'care receiver') has been critiqued for being oversimplified—caring can be conceived as a more multi-directional, versatile and fluid process (Rogers and Weller 2013; Lithari and Rogers 2017).

Prior studies of non-traditional students have included research about mature students, mothers, parents and women students (Leathwood 2013; Hinton-Smith 2011; Gonzales-Arnal and Kilkey 2009). The limited existing work on students with caring responsibilities explores the experiences of student parents (Alsop et al. 2008; Marandet and Wainwright 2010) or mature students (Edwards 1993; Baxter and Britton 2001; Reay et al. 2002; Schuetze and Slowey 2002). These studies have traced motivations, learning trajectories, the significance of gender, class and intergenerational relationships and the impact of educational routes for 'non-traditional' learners. Key challenges faced by students with care responsibilities include: the emotional upheaval in transitions to student life; the challenges of balancing work-life-study; timetabling issues; difficulties accessing educational and financial resources; and identity challenges (Edwards 1993; Alsop et al. 2008; Marandet and Wainwright 2009). Dearden and Becker (2002) argue that the specific and enduring challenges facing young carers in school settings often lead to educational disadvantage, including absence and punctuality issues, a restricted peer network in school, difficulties in participating in extracurricular activities, poor attainment, tiredness, anxiety and bullying (2002: 5). Similarly, disadvantaged students experience substantial financial and social disincentives to participation in HE and are over-represented in vocational courses at less prestigious institutions (Forsyth and Furlong 2003). Such issues highlight how issues of care are important factors when considering HE as a right and the gendering of broader structural levels of educational disadvantage (Burke 2013).

The value, expectations and experiences of care vary across social classes, societies, cultures, generations and ethnic groups (Rogers and Weller 2013; Horton and Pyer 2017). Furthermore, many carers—both young and older—may not recognise themselves as such. Instead, bonds of reciprocal care with kin and community are narrated as part of expected ties of belonging (Song 1999) and 'helping out' (Smyth et al. 2011) or 'being/having family' (Alldred and Cullen 2012). Moreover, expectations of traditional 'feminine' roles carve out such temporal and relational dynamics as ordinary and part of everyday family life. Earlier work on mature women students (Edwards 1993) and young mothers (Harris et al. 2005; Alldred and David 2010) notes how mothers' views about and visions for their own education were notably secondary to their children's care needs and priorities. Their sense of responsibility for others reflected particularly gendered, classed and intergenerational understandings of who ought to care for whom and at what personal 'cost' (Reay et al. 2002; Harris et al. 2005; Alldred and David 2010).

Theorising Space, Time and Care

A range of academics from a variety of disciplines (including geography and sociology) has begun to map the significance of space in care and the caring relationship (Weller 2013; Rogers 2017). Space is not simply an inert container of social action, and 'care and caring are thoroughly social activities and always constituted by aspects of places in which they occur' (Parr and Philo 2003: 472). The geographies of care have begun to consider everyday caring practices and different spaces and scales of caring, including bodies, homes, streets and institutions (Parr and Philo 2003; Johnsen et al. 2005), as well as mapping the 'micro-politics of care negotiation' (Dyck et al. 2005: 174). Space is central to the production of these everyday 'carescapes' (Bowlby et al. 1997), emphasising the relationality between places and people (Weller 2013). Moral landscapes of care and local cultures of parenting identify how spaces of care are contested and imagined differently by specific localities by different social groups, cultures and individuals (Holloway 1998; Johnsen et al. 2005; Barker et al. 2010) and how place is important in configuring care arrangements, support networks and caring policies (e.g. the re-centring of care from public institutions to privately owned corporations and domestic spaces, see Milligan 2003).

A range of recent work has theorised how institutional spaces, such as universities (Rogers 2017), secondary schools (Lithari and Rogers 2017) and prisons (Philo 2001), are fundamentally (at least in a formal sense) 'careless' spaces. Drawing upon prior work on feminist ethics of care, Lithari and Rogers (2017) identify how in institutional spaces, despite day-to-day informal and often invisible caring practices (see, e.g., Wood and Taylor 2017 on 'caring classrooms'), 'love and care are psycho-socially questioned' (Rogers 2013: 132). Rogers (2017) thus calls for a deeper critical and political exploration of the social relationships bound up in the lived realities of those inhabiting 'care-less' spaces.

Lefebvre argues that space is produced through three interconnected processes referred to as the 'trialectics of space' (Lefebvre 1991). Firstly, 'representations of space' refers to how space is conceived (that is planned, designed and documented) by formal, legitimate and powerful authorities, such as planners, architects, property developers, politicians and policy makers (see Lefebvre 1991; Shields 1999; Elden 2004). Often referred to as 'discourse *on* space', these often elite and privileged voices hold 'legitimate' claims to how spaces are planned and shaped, at least abstractly but often realised in/through physical and actual space (Lefebvre 2013). Secondly, 'representational space' refers to how everyday spaces are lived (Shields 1999). Often referred to as 'discourse of space', it includes the meanings given to space by people as they move around cities and environments (Elden 2004). Thirdly, 'spatial practices' refers to everyday practices that are perceived to structure social life, including daily rhythms (Lefebvre 1991). These three elements which combine to produce space do not always intersect collaboratively or productively: everyday spatial practices may sometimes contest commonly held meanings or perceptions about space and resist more formal attempts by elites to control space (Lefebvre 2013; Shields 1999).

Whilst Lefebvre keenly focused on space, he also criticised analyses which separated space, time, meaning and materiality, since each is co-constituted (Shields 1999; Edensor 2010). Time has long been a feature of academic study, from time-and-motion studies of the early twentieth century (Taylor 1911) to feminist analysis of women and time within the division of labour (Edwards 1993; Bowlby et al. 1997; Dyck et al. 2005). Lefebvre argued time is not experienced as linear but rather has rhythms (Elden 2004). Rhythms are lived interactions between place, time and energy, punctuating social life: 'rhythms imply the relation of a time to a space' (Lefebvre and Regulier 2013b: 104). Using the example of sensations in a busy Paris street (sights, noises and smells, sensations of moving, speeding up, slowing down, being stationary) produced via traffic light changes to consecutively allow passage of road traffic and pedestrians, Lefebvre highlights how social life is saturated with a multiplicity of rhythms (Lefebvre 2013). Rhythms are not inherently natural but are socially produced and calibrated (even the 'natural' heartbeat rhythm is measured through human concepts such as 'minutes'). Whilst rhythms 'of the self' focus inwards (e.g. rhythms such as eating, sleeping), rhythms 'of the other' refer to outward, formal, public-facing rhythms (Lefebvre and Regulier 2013b).

Lefebvre's rhythmanalysis focuses upon micro-level, everyday rhythms. Rhythms can remain steady, but are rarely constant or static (Lefebvre and Regulier 2013a; Edensor 2010), rather 'the question of rhythm raises issues of change and repetition, identity and difference, contrast and continuity' (Elden 2013: 5). There is never a perfect repetition of a rhythm—new rhythmic cycles spiral out from and reconfigure previous ones, and difference always appears, even within established patterns (Lefebvre 2013; Lefebvre and Regulier 2013a). Moreover, rhythms are not singular—rather they are multiple, and overlapping (polyrhythmia) and/or discordant or dissonant (arrhythmia), generating struggle, tension and conflict (Shields 1999; Edensor 2010).

Feminist scholars argue that time is fundamentally a gendered phenomenon and note the patriarchal dimensions of the ordering of time in society (Leccardi 1996; Tronto 2003; Sayer 2005; Maher 2009). The oppressive 'double burden' and Hochschild's 'second shift' (1989) focus on time pressures within women's juggling of domestic labour and paid employment (Maher 2009). Contemporary labour market changes, such as increased precarious, flexible and casualised employment practices (such as the gig economy and zero-hours contracts, see Standing 2016), and the rise of new technologies and home working has begun to erode and fray existing rhythms and temporal and spatial boundaries between work and home (Reay et al. 2002; Jurczyk 1998; Maher 2009). Similarly, a diverse range of changes within UK HE, such as the massification of HE, increasing numbers of women entering university (Burke 2013) and moves towards blended and distance learning and the use of new technologies have all helped to reconfigure spaces of HE (Rogers 2017; Macdonald and Stratta 2001). Whilst rhythms of the academic year (terms, semesters, deadlines and formal taught sessions) remain largely unchanged, trends towards online learning blur the edges of institutional spatial boundaries, with focus shifting towards students' self-determination of how, when and where to study. As well as creating financial pressures, changes to HE funding within England (the demise of grants, introduction of tuition fees and student loans) have also led to *temporal* and *spatial* tensions, with the increasing need for students to combine study with paid employment—with many students attempting within one day to work a paid shift and undertake a day studying at university (Leathwood and O'Connell 2003; Marandet and Wainwright 2010).

These changes have impacted upon women, particularly those with dependents and/or caring responsibilities, in distinct and disproportionate ways (Leathwood and O'Connell 2003). Many mothers undertake a range of roles contemporaneously and concurrently (Maher 2009), producing different temporalities that repeat, overlap and collide, often in discordant ways, to (re)produce and (re)shape family life. Reconfiguring Hochschild's second shift, increasingly student carers combine *triple* shifts (of paid work, study and care). Moreover, even when not on 'shift', women's apparent free time is still dominated with concerns about care (Jurczyk 1998). Such fraying of discrete zones of practice has implications for how education inequalities might be reproduced or challenged. Whilst the massification of HE has seen calls for Widening Participation for disadvantaged groups and a 'right' to education, such developments rarely consider the oppressive gendered institutional space–time logic. Such moves have clear implications for how carers navigate and narrate their aspirations and experiences of post-compulsory education. Therefore, temporal and spatial processes are thus centre stage in relation to identity and what it *means* to be a student and/or a carer.

Situating the Research

This research originated in a small-scale commissioned study on young carers and educational trajectories by one English university's Widening Participation Office in 2012. The twin agendas of Widening Participation and Life-Long Learning have shaped much recent post-compulsory education policy in the UK over the past two decades (Macdonald and Stratta 2001; Schuetze and Slowey 2002; Leathwood and O'Connell 2003; Wainwright and Marandet 2010). Widening Participation is seen as a way of increasing social mobility, diminishing social inequalities including those relating to race, disability and class by addressing 'barriers' to HE entry, raising aspirations and increasing levels of participation of under-represented social groups. Groups often the focus of Widening Participating initiatives include: young carers, mature students, students with disabilities, care leavers and those from low socio-economic groups and areas of disadvantage.

This small-scale qualitative exploratory study (undertaken in a large multi-ethnic and economically diverse English city) comprised six focus groups, with a total of 19 participants. Three focus groups were undertaken with young carers aged 16–23 attending young carers'/parents' groups (funded and run variously by local authorities and schools) who were considering further study. Recruited via the support groups and local publicity, interviews aimed to explore young carers' prior experiences and future aspirations. Three further focus groups were conducted with university students who were parents and/or carers. Recruited by the Widening Participation Office and university course tutors, we sought to explore student carer experiences, barriers to and enablers for participation in HE. We followed BERA guidance and secured ethical approval from our university's Ethics Committee. All locations and individual identities have been anonymised. The focus groups included case study scenarios enabling participants to reflect on but not needing to disclose their own experiences. All groups were audio recorded and transcribed with participants' details anonymised.

Transcripts were later coded and analysed for emerging narrative and key themes. Auto/Biography focuses on placing the storytelling of life histories within the academy (Chansky 2016), enabling individuals to 're-authorise' their own subjectivity and experience (Mintz 2016), producing a particular range of personal experiences that no other form of telling can access (Olney 2016). In discussing their lives, roles and responsibilities, carers produce retrospective auto/biographies. Feminist and other scholars have long discussed how auto/biographies are often not linear, but often fragmentary, disrupted and dislocated (Stanley 1993; Chansky 2016). Narratives never 'reflect' or 'represent' a true 'insider' record of history, but rather produce a storied reworking of self which is situated, contextualised and contestable, blurring boundaries between self/other, public/private, etc. (Sheridan 1993). Texts become the focus as 'generative' or 'fictive', requiring creative acts to interpret, which therefore construct reality rather than reflecting it (Bhatti 2014).

Thus within auto/biography, there is no clear hierarchy between self and other, nor narrator, text and reader (Chansky 2016; Olney 2016), recognising 'a complex dynamic of cultural production' and research as a 'conscious artistic and literary exercise' (Baena 2007: vii). Reflecting this, as authors, we cannot remain silent and invisible, and we are 'active readers' (Stanley 1990). Haraway (2008) notes the 'materialisation of new realities'—in writing others' lives, we rewrite our own lives. Indeed, our own auto/biographies of 'care' and embodiment are deeply implicated in/through the production of this chapter. We come to this project with shifting identities as we navigate the challenges of combining academia with care (see Rogers 2017 for more) and are moved and reshaped by the writing process. For example, early meetings between the authors corresponded with Fin's maternity leave. In busy cafes, John and Fin had hurried discussions, Fin with notebook in one hand and feeding baby in the other. For Fin, the writing of this chapter created a cerebral challenge and a 'break' from expected domesticity and nurture. John's contributions were mostly written during recovering from surgery—juggling rehabilitation and writing whilst also struggling (with a heavily bandaged arm in a sling) to carry laptop and books to cafes, generating unique writing rhythms within space and time. As an example of the difficulties of synchronising rhythms, Pam (a full-time academic and mother of three) found it impossible to make the café meetings—so was marginal to constructing earlier drafts of the chapter and instead edited the full draft (drawing upon her earlier close involvement in the material in the bid writing, data collection, analysis and report writing processes). Thus, the act of writing this chapter generated new social processes, materialities and rhythms of juggling care, space and time in ways eerily reminiscent of those stories told by our participants.

Furthermore, our distinct interests and disciplinary backgrounds led to us to explore different analytical strands. Drawing upon her work on gendered inequalities and identity, Fin was drawn to how participants produced gendered subjectivities through their discussion of care and study. John's main interest centred on a geographical analysis focusing upon the significance of space in carers' accounts. Pam's preoccupation was with the neoliberal university's construction of (and conditions for) the student or staff subject and the stigma expressed by student carers. Thus, the vignettes presented in this chapter draw upon these diverse analytical strands. Whilst feminist geographers have brought such theoretical insights together in powerful ways (see Bowlby et al. 1997; Holloway 1998), that we focus on different elements of narratives demonstrates how researchers bring different perspectives to an encounter or a transcript.

Vignette One: Space, Time, Rhythms and Auto/Biography

Our first vignette focuses on student carer spatial and temporal rhythms. Aysha was in her mid-40s and a mother of four grown-up children and a carer for her disabled partner. At the time of the interview, she was studying for a B.A. Social Work degree, whilst caring for her partner and providing support for her four grown-up children: 'it's like a global thing I'm doing' she explains and then adds 'I'm trying to be this superwoman, but I'm not a superwoman. I realised that'. She was recently made redundant from her job (which had sponsored her to study). When asked specifically about timing of teaching sessions, Aysha speaks more broadly about the challenges of juggling schedules and roles/responsibilities:

> Timetabling is… not right… a mature student working full time, (and) caring responsibilities, you don't have enough time. There's not enough time in the 24 hour clock to that little extra mile that you need to do. And then you stay up all night having that little extra time to do that. And then you… have an hour sleeping, do your caring role and then go back to work. And then come back and go to University (45 minutes away). Go back into your caring role and prepare yourself for work the next morning and you do your coursework as well.

She explains how the different elements of her caring role (as partner, as mother) impacts upon her study:

> The carer role is quite physically exhausting and psychologically exhausting. You're exhausted, you can't, you don't have the time to do (good) quality work or reading as you would have done if you didn't have that role. If I was put there on my own, I would hopefully get straight A's.

Aysha's daily life is produced through and subject to a tightly organised and finely tuned set of rhythms, both temporal ('stay up all night', 'have an hour sleeping', 'do your caring role') and spatial ('go back to work', 'go back to University'). Against a backdrop of contemporary late modernity, Aysha's account is but one example of how individuals, social groups and institutions produce diverse and complex rhythms—each with their own different experiences, spatialities and challenges. In Aysha's auto/biographical narrative, time is scarce ('there's not enough time in the 24 hour clock'). Through increased expectations and demands relating to parenting, caring and employment and careers, mothers have particularly been subject to time–space compression, leading to 'temporal conundrums' (Maher 2009: 232) and indeed spatial ones, in attempting to successfully undertake these responsibilities. These conundrums (although configured differently at different points in her history) are narrated as constant:

> (before I came to University) I needed to do night work, so I could look after my kids during the day time and support them financially… My Mum used to support me but I had to take the kids across to my Mums, leave them, put them into bed and go to work, come back, pick them up. Bring them home, bath and dress them, go and drop them off to school, have a couple hours sleep with my baby there as well. I used to have to get up to change him and feed him and it was just chaotic I don't know how I did it.

As well as the significance of the amount of time available, the notion of being 'harried' also reflects the character of time (Carrigan and Duberley 2013) and the 'lived experience' of intense temporal and spatial caring practices and schedules. That these are experienced and narrated as challenge and struggle is reflected in Aysha describing her 'global' undertaking and her attempts to be 'superwoman'. Aysha's auto/biographical narrative clearly presents a neoliberal subject—she alone has the responsibility for such events, questioning the notion (Stanley 1990) that women are positioned within capacious, resourceful social networks. However, Aysha herself challenges the feasibility of the neoliberal carer and her narrative clearly realises the vulnerability of such finely tuned rhythms ('but I'm not a superwoman, I realised that') reflecting how such rhythms, rather than representing a neoliberal subject skilfully undertaking a range of identities and responsibilities, can often be intractable, conflict-ridden (Lefebvre 2013; Carrigan and Duberley 2013) and, as highlighted by feminists across a range of disciplines, also represent struggle, oppression and 'traps' (Hochschild 1989).

Significantly, these rhythms are not discretely segmented, compartmentalised and sequential—Aysha's auto/biographical narrative results in overlapping, multiple and plural rhythms, experienced contemporaneously through a range of public and private spaces. Aysha's experiences of rhythms as complex, unstable and fragile echoes Lefebvre's (2013) notion of discordant or dissonant (arrhythmia) rhythms. However, as Maher (2009) comments, these potentially conflicting rhythms are unified 'by a focus on the accumulation of care' (p. 231). Furthermore, our example also illustrates how spaces are planned with particularly ideological expectations, reflecting Lefebvre's 'representations of space' (Lefebvre 1991), in this case illuminating normative expectations (or discourse on space) which conceive universities as coherent, bounded and protected spaces, times and rhythms for studying. In our example, there is no commitment-free student (Walkerdine et al. 2001) who can easily embed and immerse themselves into the pre-existing required rhythms and spaces of campus life. Therefore, just as traditional distinctions between home and work become more blurred (Maher 2009), student carers resist the normative rhythmic production of educational spaces, creating porous, fluid, study spaces, rhythms and times which incorporate caring responsibilities.

This resonates with Lefebvre's notion of 'spatial practices' and how space is experienced differently to planners' expectations (Lefebvre 1991), suggesting that student carers are able to (at least partially) contest dominant spatio-temporal rhythms. Whilst research identifying these experiences of mothers juggling care and other tasks is long established (Hochschild 1989), this analysis enables us to see how student carers construct highly spatialised, temporally fluid and plural, overlapping rhythms. However, as Aysha herself notes, the ability to juggle these rhythms comes at a great cost to herself and her studies ('you don't have the time to (good) quality work or reading as you would have done if you didn't have that role. If I was put there on my own, I would hopefully get straight As')—reflecting much feminist research which explores how the lived experience of juggling caring with other roles can be characterised by missed opportunity, mental health concerns, exploitation and social exclusion (Hochschild 1989; Carrigan and Duberley 2013).

Vignette Two: Identity, Auto/Biography and 'Coming Out' as Carer

Focusing upon the experiences of a young carer from a different generation and ethnic group, our second example centres on the significance of identity. Tina (a 16-year-old, school-attending, White British carer) talked about how in school she came to identify as being a young carer:

> because I didn't know I was (a young carer) for quite a while. And when I first found out that I was, I sort of didn't really get it. And then I remember just one day being really tired and had done (hardly) any work. And a teacher was like "oh", you know, "why are you like this?" I was like, "I was looking after my brother" [teacher replied with] "And now you've got this (studying). Oh, so you weren't just being rude and bad in my lesson?"

This is an auto/biography of identity, beginning with Tina not identifying as a carer ('because I didn't know I was [a young carer])'. She then talks about a moment of clarity where she 'first found out', although her account also suggests that this 'coming out' (Plummer 2003) as carer was not an immediate process, but one which required time and reflection ('I sort of didn't really get it'). Of particular interest here is the spatiality; this is not only a neoliberal account of self-realisation drawing upon agency and identity through their domestic caring experiences. It is also an account involving external scrutiny, surveillance and intervention of an educational professional in the public space of school (Smyth et al. 2011). The initial reaction ('you weren't just being rude and bad in my lesson?') shows how the teacher initially brings to the encounter inappropriate and unhelpful generational expectations. Being a student carer is seen as 'out of time'—in relation to life stage (the stereotype that caring is undertaken by older adults) and is 'out of space', as secondary school spaces should be for learning rather than spaces influenced by other responsibilities (Shaper and Streatfield 2012). Following the disclosure, the education professional quickly revises their understanding of Tina's identity. Tina also identifies moments of realisation whereby she links her own personal and private experiences to a much broader collective social and public identity as carer: 'Oh, I thought it was just (in my) school… it's not just in school. It's like all over the country and all places, so I've been registered (as a young carer) with my brother for like a year'. The account ends with a clear, coherent identification in the interview, linked to Tina's legislative registration and declaration as carer, which makes this identity formal and public.

When discussing a hypothetical example of whether a young student carer should disclose their caring responsibilities to their educational establishment, Tina provides a different way of considering the relationship between private, caring responsibilities and a more public identity:

> I think it's your choice, because you don't always want people to know. Because sometimes it doesn't gain that (much) anyway. Sometimes, you can manage it. I think that initially, it seems like it's unnecessary. It's just you don't want everyone to know what goes on in your home, unless you want them to, because at the end of the day, if you can cope, you can cope. If you just need the help there, you can say, like "I'm behind because of this".

The discussion here clearly places the carer in control as the neoliberal agent '*managing*' their own lives. Although a position problematised by many (see Maher 2009; Philip et al. 2013; Walkerdine et al. 2001) for obscuring exploitation, oppression and exclusion, this stance represents a discursive framework of the young student carer as productive, in control and 'coping'. Within this 'idealised learner', carers are presented as having autonomy, control and '*choice*' to decide whether to disclose, in effect a process of 'coming out' and claiming a public identity (Plummer 2003). Whilst some thought there were benefits to disclosing (e.g. in coursework extensions), the focus group conversation continued to discuss disadvantages of disclosing caring responsibilities, particularly around the shame of having a public identity of carer. Another young woman in the focus group says 'I would feel kind of extremely awkward' if disclosing to the college and this was a strong theme in the interviews, even amongst those studying healthcare subjects. The two identities of 'student' and 'carer' were perceived as conflicting, 'awkward' and socially and spatially incompatible. Publicly identifying as carer might be stigmatising—one participant was conscious of being seen as 'needy' rather than 'able' and had tried to hide their responsibilities for fear of judgement by peers and tutors and being seen as 'pleading special case'.

Once again, these accounts resonate with Lefebvre's notion of 'representations of space' (Shields 1999), that is the dominant ways in which spaces are conceived by those with authority, privilege and power. The formal, legible and legitimate identities imagined within places of HE are framed around particular kinds of gendered, classed and 'raced' bodies, identities and activities. The student carer identity spatially and temporally disrupts the notion of student identities as 'carefree' and autonomous (Wainwright and Marandet 2013). Participants within our accounts frame themselves as deficient and/or incompatible in relation to 'bachelor boy' normative gendered and generational framings of identity. Leathwood (2013) notes gendered visual representations of identity within HE's self-produced media representations. Rarely do promotional materials include images of older learners or students with dependents. Where such students' identities are acknowledged, it is seen as within discourses of need or as recipients of paternalistic help from the benevolent university, rather than as positive, legitimate and feasible identities for student life (Leathwood 2013).

Vignette Three: Auto/Biography and Longer-Term Narratives of Care and Study

Aysha (the focus of vignette one) constructs a lengthy auto/biographical narrative through which she explains the influences that have helped shape her long journey towards university:

> I used to get good marks at school. B plus and As. I was 16 (leaving school), I did my O levels then left. I wanted to continue studies but my grandparents had found this partner and I had to get married… I felt my brothers were supported more. I faced that conflict of Asian families- it doesn't matter if girls study or not- that attitude. My Dad wanted me to continue study and he had really good hopes that I would be something, I would be recognised as something. I wanted to be a police officer because there was an opportunity to get into the force. Then my grandparents intervened- "Asian girls don't do that". And then I got married and then if it wasn't for my Dad I don't think I would be alive today. He got me out of that marriage….

> I had a business first. That got repossessed because I was ill for three months, I ended up in hospital after having my baby… six months to recover… and then I didn't get much support from my partner. He was helping himself on the business hence why the business collapsed. He was gambling. My shop got repossessed and the accommodation was above it, so we had to leave the shop. As soon as we moved into rented accommodation, all the benefits were in his name, but he left us and went abroad for a year. I was stuck with having no income, and the landlord demanding rent. I started doing odd jobs for a factory across the road. Sometimes they didn't give me work and I said this is not good enough… So this is how I got into a caring role from that point, doing night shifts in the residential home. Then I just progressed further as the children grew, went to school. So I started doing day jobs as well…I was doing temporary work. They obviously liked my work and there I was quite passionate. They asked me if I would apply for a permanent position. A year after,

they said 'oh there is a senior position going', I got that. I was just going up the ladder all the time, I thought 'I don't want to stop here…'

That's what is has been throughout my life, other people's expectations of being a daughter, of being a mother, of being a wife. It's…you know, I'm an individual, I've got feelings, I've got dreams. I want to be somebody. I want to be recognised. I have brilliant context in life but that's not enough, I want to do it (studying) for me.

The account here is expansive, identifying a broad range of events (leaving school, marriage, motherhood, housing crises, casual jobs and professional employment) within both the private and public spheres, which have helped to shape, influence and give meaning to her life. Her interview also touches upon familial and generational relationships, culture and economic contexts, presenting these as ultimately (if slowly and a non-linear way, a pattern also found by Reay et al. 2002) leading to deciding to train at university to be a social worker. A number of 'critical moments' of transition (Thomson 2002) are mentioned, such as being made homeless, as well as longer-term rhythmic changes, for example evolving relations with family members, engagement in romantic partnerships and changing participation in the labour market. A focus on longer-term auto/biographical narrative enables us to explore how rhythms are not fixed and permanent, but rather are 'spiralling' or rhizomatic as their rhythmic composition changes and evolves over longer periods.

In different times in her often 'messy' and non-linear life story, Aysha constructs herself as powerful and agentic, for example, at key points in her employment history ('I didn't want to stop there'), whilst at other points constructs a story which places her within positions of powerlessness (vis-a-vis family members, partners and financial collapse). Powerlessness requires her to rework her spatial and temporal rhythms (e.g. in her changing childcare regimes) and also forces movement through space (Hipchen and Chansky 2017), for example the necessity to move as the result of being made homeless. The slow movement towards the spaces of HE has significant meaning for Aysha ('I've got *dreams*', '*I want to do it [studying] for me*'). This reflects the second process identified in Lefebvre's 'trialectics of space', that is the notion of 'representational space', that is how space is produced and lived through the meanings attached to it. Clearly, gaining a place at university is a huge goal for student carers and the achievement of access to this space and to this identity has significant meaning (generating a discourse of space). She also constructs a shifting sense of self vis-a-vis her other responsibilities and illustrates how her move to university generates complex intersections between individuation ('for me') and her other commitments (Smith 2016). Entry into HE is seen as something of a shift from an identity of responsibilities to a more ego-driven (Stanley 1990) and neoliberal subjectivity ('I'm an individual, I want to be somebody. I want to be recognised'). She constructs a powerful, agentic account where she constructively finds resistance to adversity and develops procedures to succeed. However, despite narratives of individuation and self-motivation, Aysha's responsibilities to family members remain unchanged. Recognising that auto/biographical accounts are always socioculturally located, much focuses on what is happening around her and her responses to this. As we discussed earlier, it is clear that Aysha is also located and subject to broader familial, social, gender and class-based structural factors which shape her experiences and narrative.

Conclusion

These vignettes cast light on how care, as an embodied and enacted lived reality, is narrated across different generations as entailing complex spatial and temporal rhythms. In an age characterised by the acceleration and compression of time, student carer narratives reflect new challenges as well as highlight traditional gendered norms and expectations. Student carers skilfully navigate overlapping and hybrid rhythms across time and space. Highlighting the complexity of spaces and flows of care, our analysis identifies competing, intersecting and concurrent temporal and spatial rhythms. Navigating these intersections through a range of spaces is reported as complex, difficult and stressful. Throughout the accounts are the difficulties of combining or synchromeshing different polyrhythmic rhythms (Elden 2004). Auto/biographical analysis has enabled us to explore these (often discordant) intersections between study and care rhythms and highlight the nuanced and complex ways in which the rhythm and flow of study and caring folds experience, time and space together.

These auto/biographical accounts of care also shed light on new ways of thinking about the complex intersections between time, space and identity construction. Dominant and ideal notions of autonomous learners (in neoliberal education policy) are recast within these accounts by/through deep ties of belonging, interdependence, responsibility, love and care. Whilst universities might formally be careless institutions (Rogers 2017), they are inhabited by those with deep duties of care and loyalty. The accounts show the tensions constructing identities which bridge such divides, and the losses—physical and emotional—borne by these student carers. Student carers' 'caring' experiences and identities are always contingent on time, place and legibility and are interwoven with and co-constructed by other identities (such as gender, class, ethnicity and generation) and identity transitions (Thomson 2002; Thomson et al. 2003) (e.g. the non-linear pathways between pupil, partner, employee, businesswoman, student, mother identities experienced by participants).

This chapter illustrates how student carers are (through their everyday practices and/or identities) constructed as out of time or out of place. Auto/biographical narratives of student carers resonate with all three elements of Lefebvre's (1991) threefold conceptualisation of space. The power of institutions such as universities to mould and define identity, space and place resonates Lefebvre's representations of space (how space is conceived by formal and legitimate authorities, see Lefebvre 1991; Shields 1999; Elden 2004). That HE is accredited with status, meaning and longing by our participants reflect the second process identified by Lefebvre, that of representational space. That our participants carved out identities and spatial practices which engage with formal institutional rhythms prescribed by 'legitimate' authorities yet also achieved caring responsibilities/identities reflects how spaces are never unproblematically perceived or experienced in ways that planners or policy makers have conceived.

An auto/biographical approach highlights the strengths in feminist analyses of the temporal and spatial, to provide insights into new economic realities, traditional gendered expectations and the navigation of the spatial and temporal logics of combining care and study. Attempts to juggle complex and often competing rhythms come at great personal cost to student carers (Hochschild 1989; Smyth et al. 2011). This re-enforces the need for continued feminist analysis of structural disadvantage to problematise and challenge dominant policy narrative of neoliberal individual 'choice' and meritocratic opportunity.

We call for more focus on analyses which explore intersections between identity, the temporal and spatial within an analysis of feminist auto/biographies. Whilst we have been able only to touch on this in this chapter, we recognise the necessity of developing deeper intersectional analyses that explore how discourses of gender, generation, class and ethnicity inform and shape these auto/biographical narratives. We also call for further development of a geography of care and caring, to map the complex spatialities of care, which traverse diverse geographies across a range of spaces (Horton and Pyer 2017). In particular, we urge for more exploration of the complex and overlapping ways in which formally 'care-less spaces' such as universities might be considered differently by individuals (e.g. planners, teachers, students) who conceive, perceive and experience them.

One last cautionary note concerns the need to challenge stories which emphasise hegemonic, universal narratives (Baena 2007). Recognising that text is 'generative' and 'fictive', in endeavours such as this chapter we are engaged with creative, interpretive acts rather providing the truth. There are 'multiple layers of fictive paradigms of selfhood with the result that a multiplicity of speaking positions weaves through… texts' (Smith 2016: 87). As authors, we recognise that our narrative analysis is simultaneously shaped by and helps shape our own positionalities, interests and engagements in various forms of care and academic work, as well as reflecting those of Aysha, Tina and other participants.

Acknowledgements The authors wish to thank Dr. Michael Whelan, Dr. Craig Johnston and Dr. Leonie Kindness for conducting focus groups for this project. Interviews with university students were with P. Alldred, with young carers with F. Cullen (see Alldred and Cullen 2012).

References

Alldred, P. (2011). "How Come I Fell Pregnant?": Young Mothers' Narratives of Conception. *International Journal of Adolescence and Youth, 16*(2), 139–156.

Alldred, P., & Cullen, F. (2012). *How Do Responsibilities for Caring for Others Create Practical and Psychosocial Obstacles to University Study, and What Might a University Do to Minimise Such Obstacles? Widening Participation Among People with Care Responsibilities.* A Research Report to the Widening Participation Office (WPO) (university identity withheld).

Alldred, P., & David, M. (2010). "What's Important at the End of the Day?" Young Mothers' Values and Policy Presumptions. In S. Duncan, R. Edwards, & C. Alexander (Eds.), *Teenage Parenting: What's the Problem?* London: Tufnell Press.

Alsop, R., Gonzalez-Arnal, S., & Kilkey, M. (2008). The Widening Participation Agenda: The Marginal Place of Care. *Gender and Education, 20*(6), 623–637.

Baena, R. (2007). Introduction: Transculturing Auto/Biography: New Forms of Life Writing. In R. Baena (Ed.), *Transculturing Auto/Biography: Forms of Life Writing* (pp. vii–xii). Abingdon: Routledge.

Barker, J., Alldred, P., Watts, M., & Dodman, H. (2010). Pupils or Prisoners? Institutional Geographies and Internal Exclusion in UK Secondary Schools. *Area, 42*(3), 378–386.

Baxter, A., & Britton, C. (2001). Risk, Identity and Change: Becoming a Mature Student. *International Studies in the Sociology of Education, 11*(1), 87–103.

Becker, F., & Becker, S. (2008). *Young Adult Carers in the UK: Experiences, Needs and Services for Carers Aged 16–24 Princess Royal Trust for Carers.* Available at https://www.sussex.ac.uk/webteam/gateway/file.php?name=young-adult-carers-uk-full-report-dec.pdfandsite=271. Accessed 1 May 2018.

Bhatti, M. (2014). Garden Stories: Auto/Biography, Gender and Gardening. *Sociological Research Online, 19*(3), 1–8.

Bowlby, S., Gregory, S., & McKie, L. (1997). Doing Home: Patriarchy, Caring and Space. *Women's Studies International Forum, 20*(3), 343–350.

Burke, P. (2013). The Right to Higher Education: Neoliberalism, Gender and Professional Mis/recognitions. *International Studies in Sociology of Education, 23*(2), 107–126.

Carrigan, M., & Duberley, J. (2013). Time Triage: Exploring the Temporal Strategies That Support Entrepreneurship and Motherhood. *Time and Society, 22*(1), 92–118.

Chansky, R. (2016). Introduction. In R. Chansky & E. Hipchen (Eds.), *The Routledge Auto/Biography Studies Reader* (pp. 1–4). London: Routledge.

Cullen, F., & Alldred, P. (2013, April 25). *"If That Was Me, I Would've Probably Given Up by Now": Widening Participation, Care Responsibilities and Becoming a Higher Education Student, Gender and Education Association Conference.* South Bank University, London, UK.

Dearden, C., & Becker, S. (2002). *Young Carers and Education.* London: Carers UK.

Duncan, S., Edwards, R., Reynolds, T., & Alldred, P. (2004). Mothers and Child Care: Policies, Values and Theories. *Children and Society, 18*(4), 254–265. ISSN: 0951-0605.

Dyck, I., Kontos, P., Angus, J., & McKeever, P. (2005). The Home as a Site for Long-Term Care: Meanings and Management of Bodies and Spaces. *Health and Place, 11*(2), 173–185.

Edensor, T. (2010). Walking in Rhythms: Place, Regulation, Style and the Flow of Experience. *Visual Studies, 25*(1), 69–79.

Edwards, R. (1993). *Mature Women Students: Separating or Connecting Family and Education.* London: Taylor and Francis.

Elden, S. (2004). *Understanding Henri Lefebvre: Theory and the Possible.* London: Continuum.

Elden, S. (2013). Rhythmanalysis: An Introduction. In H. Lefebvre, *Rhythmanalysis: Space, Time and Everyday Life* (pp. 1–10). London: Bloomsbury.

Forsyth, A., & Furlong, A. (2003). Access to Higher Education and Disadvantaged Young People. *British Educational Research Journal, 29*(2), 205–225.

Gonzales-Arnal, S., & Kilkey, M. (2009). Contextualizing Rationality: Mature Student Carers and Higher Education in England. *Feminist Economics, 15*(1), 85–111.

Haraway, D. (2008). *When Species Meet.* Minneapolis: University of Minnesota Press.

Harris, J., Howard, M., Jones, C., & Russell, L. (2005). *Great Expectations: How Realistic Is the Government's Target to Get 60 Per Cent of Young Mothers into Education, Employment and Training.* Oxford: YWCA Report.

Hinton-Smith, T. (2011, September 5–8). *Lone Parent Students and the Bachelor Boy Ideal of University Participation.* Symposium: Student Parents in Higher Education: Equity and Policies. British Educational Research Association Annual Conference, 2011, Institute of Education.

Hipchen, E., & Chansky, R. (2017). Looking Forward: The Futures of Auto/Biography. *a/b: Auto/Biography Studies, 32*(2), 139–157.

Hochschild, A. (1989). *The Second Shift: Working Parents and the Revolution at Home.* New York: Viking Penguin.

Holloway, S. (1998). Local Childcare Cultures: Moral Geographies of Mothering and the Social Organisation of Pre School Education. *Gender, Place and Culture, 5*(1), 29–53.

Horton, J., & Pyer, M. (Eds.). (2017). *Children, Young People and Care.* Abingdon: Routledge.

Johnsen, S., Cloke, P., & May, J. (2005). Transitory Spaces of Care: Serving Homeless People on the Street. *Health and Place, 11*(4), 323–336.

Jurczyk, K. (1998). Time in Women's Everyday Lives: Between Self-Determination and Conflicting Demands. *Time and Society, 7*(2–3), 283–308.

Leathwood, C. (2013). Re/presenting Intellectual Subjectivity: Gender and Visual Imagery in the Field of Higher Education. *Gender and Education, 25*(2), 133–154.

Leathwood, C., & O'Connell, P. (2003). 'It's a Struggle': The Construction of the 'New Student' in Higher Education. *Journal of Education Policy, 18*(6), 597–615.

Leccardi, C. (1996). Rethinking Social Time: Feminist Perspectives. *Time and Society, 5*(2), 169–186.

Lefebvre, H. (1991). *The Production of Space.* Oxford: Blackwell.

Lefebvre, H. (2013). Elements of Rhythmanalysis: An Introduction to the Understanding of Rhythms. In H. Lefebvre, *Rhythmanalysis: Space Time and Everyday Life* (pp. 11–80). London: Bloomsbury.

Lefebvre, H., & Regulier, C. (2013a). The Rhythmanalytical Project. In H. Lefebvre, *Rhythmanalysis: Space, Time and Everyday Life* (pp. 81–92). London: Bloomsbury.

Lefebvre, H., & Regulier, C. (2013b). Attempt at the Rhythmanalysis of Mediterranean Cities. In H. Lefebvre, *Rhythmanalysis: Space, Time and Everyday Life* (pp. 93–117). London: Bloomsbury.

Lithari, E., & Rogers, C. (2017). Care-Less Spaces and Identity Construction: Transition to Secondary School for Disabled Children. *Children's Geographies, 15*(3), 259–273.

Macdonald, C., & Stratta, E. (2001). From Access to Widening Participation: Responses to the Changing Population in Higher Education in the UK. *Journal of Further and Higher Education, 25*(2), 249–258.

Maher, J. (2009). Accumulating Care: Mothers Beyond the Conflicting Temporalities of Caring and Work. *Time and Society, 18*(2/3), 231–245.

Marandet, E., & Wainwright, E. (2009). Discourses of Integration and Exclusion: Equal Opportunities for University Students with Dependent Children? *Space and Polity, 13*(2), 109–125.

Marandet, E., & Wainwright, E. (2010). Invisible Experiences: Understanding the Choices and Needs of University Students with Dependent Children. *British Educational Research Journal, 36*(5), 787–805.

Milligan, C. (2003). Location or Dis-location? Towards a Conceptualization of People and Place in the Care-Giving Experience. *Social and Cultural Geography, 4*(4), 455–470.

Milligan, C., Kearns, R., & Kyle, R. (2011). Unpacking Stored and Storied Knowledge: Elicited Biographies of Activism in Mental Health. *Health and Place, 17*(1), 7–16.

Mintz, S. (2016). Transforming the Tale: The Auto/body/ographies of Nancy Mairs. In R. Chansky & E. Hipchen (Eds.), *The Routledge Auto/Biography Studies Reader* (pp. 130–138). London: Routledge.

Olney, J. (2016). Autobiography and the Cultural Moment: A Thematic, Historical and Bibliographical Introduction. In R. Chansky & E. Hipchen (Eds.), *The Routledge Auto/Biography Studies Reader* (pp. 5–14). London: Routledge.

Parr, H., & Philo, C. (2003). Rural Mental Health and Social Geographies of Caring. *Social and Cultural Geography, 4*(4), 471–488.

Philip, G., Rogers, C., & Weller, S. (2013). Understanding Care and Thinking with Care. In C. Rogers & S. Weller (Eds.), *Critical Approaches to Care: Understanding Relations, Identities and Cultures* (pp. 1–12). London: Routledge.

Philo, C. (2001). Accumulating Populations: Bodies, Institutions and Space. *International Journal of Population Geography, 7*(6), 473–490.

Philo, C., Parr, H., & Burns, N. (2015). The Rural Panopticon. *Journal of Rural Studies, 51,* 230–239.

Plummer, K. (2003). *Intimate Citizenship: Private Decisions and Public Dialogues.* Seattle: University of Washington Press.

Reay, D., Ball, S., & David, M. (2002). "It's Taking Me a Long Time but I'll Get There in the End": Mature Students on Access Courses and Higher Education Choices. *British Educational Research Journal, 28*(1), 5–19.

Rogers, C. (2013). Intellectual Disability and Mothering: An Engagement with Ethics of Care and Emotional Work. In S. Weller & C. Rogers (Eds.), *Critical Approaches to Care: Understanding Caring Relations, Identities and Cultures* (pp. 132–143). London: Routledge.

Rogers, C. (2017). "I'm Complicit and I'm Ambivalent and That's Crazy": Care-Less Spaces for Women in the Academy. *Women's Studies International Forum, 61,* 115–122.

Rogers, C., & Weller, S. (Eds.). (2013). *Critical Approaches to Care: Understanding Caring Relations, Identities and Cultures.* London: Routledge.

Sayer, L. (2005). Gender, Time and Inequality: Trends in Women's and Men's Paid Work, Unpaid Work and Free Time. *Social Forces, 84*(1), 285–303.

Schuetze, H., & Slowey, M. (2002). Participation and Exclusion: A Comparative Analysis of Non-Traditional Students and Lifelong Learners in Higher Education. *Higher Education, 44*(3/4), 309–327.

Shaper, S., & Streatfield, D. (2012). Invisible Care? The Role of Librarians in Caring for the 'Whole School' Pupil in Secondary Schools. *Pastoral Care in Education, 30*(1), 65–75.

Sheridan, D. (1993). Writing to the Archive: Mass Observation as Autobiography. *Sociology, 27*(1), 27–40.

Shields, R. (1999). *Lefebvre, Love and Struggle: Spatial Dialectics*. London: Routledge.

Smith, S. (2016). The Impact of Critical Theory on the Study of Autobiography: Marginality, Gender and Autobiographical Practice. In R. Chansky & E. Hipchen (Eds.), *The Routledge Auto/Biography Studies Reader* (pp. 82–88). London: Routledge.

Smyth, C., Blaxland, M., & Cass, B. (2011). "So That's How I Found Out I Was a Young Carer and That I Actually Had Been a Carer Most of My Life": Identifying and Supporting Hidden Young Carers. *Journal of Youth Studies, 14*(2), 145–160.

Song, M. (1999). *Helping Out: Children's Labor in Ethnic Businesses*. Temple University Press.

Standing, G. (2016). *The Precariat: The New Dangerous Class*. London: Bloomsbury.

Stanley, L. (1990). Moments of Writing: Is There a Feminist Auto/Biography? *Gender and History, 2*(1), 58–67.

Stanley, L. (1993). On Auto/Biography in Sociology. *Sociology, 27*(1), 41–52.

Taylor, F. (1911). *The Principles of Scientific Management*. New York and London: Harper and Brothers.

Thomson, R. (2002). Critical Moments: Choice, Chance and Opportunity in Young People's Narratives of Transition. *Sociology, 36*(2), 335–354.

Thomson, R., Henderson, S., & Holland, J. (2003). Making the Most of What You've Got? Resources, Values and Inequalities in Young Women's Transitions to Adulthood. *Educational Review, 55*(1), 33–46.

Tronto, J. (2003). Time's Place. *Feminist Theory, 4*(2), 119–138.

Wainwright, E., & Marandet, E. (2010). Parents in Higher Education: Impacts of University Learning on the Self and the Family. *Educational Review, 62*(4), 449–465.

Wainwright, E., & Marandet, E. (2013). Family Learning and the Socio-Spatial Practice of 'Supportive' Power. *British Journal of Sociology of Education, 34*(4), 504–524.

Walkerdine, V., Lucey, H., & Melody, J. (2001). *Growing Up Girl: Psycho-Social Explorations of Gender and Class*. London: Palgrave/Red Globe Press.

Weller, S. (2013). Who Cares? Exploring the Shifting Nature of Care and Caring Practices in Sibling Relationships. In C. Rogers & S. Weller (Eds.), *Critical Approaches to Care: Understanding Relations, Identities and Cultures* (pp. 160–170). London: Routledge.

Wood, B., & Taylor, R. (2017). Caring Citizens: Emotional Engagement and Social Action in Educational Settings in New Zealand. In J. Horton & M. Pyer (Eds.), *Children, Young People and Care*. Abingdon: Routledge.

12

Spatiality and Auto/Biographical Narratives of Encounter in Social Housing

Emma Wainwright, Elodie Marandet and Ellen McHugh

Introduction

This chapter explores auto/biographical narratives of encounter in social housing, arguing that such an approach foregrounds the spatial and enhances our understanding of the everyday and institutionally shaped lives of social housing residents. In taking an auto/biographical approach, we argue that narratives are always relational, emplaced and embodied, and this relationality, emplacement and embodiment are central to the retelling and retracing of the everyday. We do this by drawing on research with social housing residents as they moved into a financial education and capability programme run by a large housing association (HA) operating in London and the South East.

The chapter is framed by the now sustained geographical and sociological scholarship on 'encounter' and 'narratives of encounter'. 'Encounter' is a conceptually charged construct, historically coded as a meeting of opposites

E. Wainwright (✉) · E. McHugh
Brunel University London, London, UK
e-mail: emma.wainwright@brunel.ac.uk

E. McHugh
e-mail: ellen.mchugh@brunel.ac.uk

E. Marandet
University of Brighton, London, UK
e-mail: E.Marandet@brighton.ac.uk

© The Author(s) 2020
J. M. Parsons and A. Chappell (eds.), *The Palgrave Handbook of Auto/Biography*,
https://doi.org/10.1007/978-3-030-31974-8_12

(Wilson 2017) and collision of difference, and has become widely used in work on urban diversity. As Wilson (2017: 452) argues, 'encounters are fundamentally about difference and are thus central to understanding the embodied nature of social distinction and the contingency of identity and belonging'. In this chapter, we use the term in relation to the encounters residents have with their social housing landlord and, notably, in relation to mentors on a financial capability programme aimed at educating residents out of debt.

Methodologically, we draw from Valentine and Sadgrove's (2014) work on 'narratives of encounter', an approach that allows individuals to be recognised as both agents and subjects in any given encounter. They stress there has been a 'general neglect of how individuals approach and experience encounters and their subjective reflections on the meaning of such moments for them' (Valentine and Sadgrove 2014: 1981). Encounters can only be understood when they are analysed within the context of an individual's life history, with auto/biographical narratives enabling this as they enhance 'understandings about the situated and relational nature of people's identities, attitudes and values' (Valentine and Sadgrove 2014: 1982). We take this forward through our focus on the auto/biographical narratives of welfare from social housing residents, highlighting the moments of encounter with social housing staff that shape, structure and puncture these.

Encounter is both a spatially and temporally charged term. In terms of spatiality, it requires a bringing together of different parts into some type of dialogue. This requires an embodied and physical location and coming together requiring some sort of presence, whether in person or at a distance. Wilson (2017) highlights that writing on encounter is frequently worked through geographical concepts such as marginality, boundary making and breaking and relationality. This spatiality is implicit in our use of the term and is underpinned by social housing residents' sense of emplacement in and threat of displacement from their home and thus vulnerability that their narratives of welfare and financial uncertainty expose.

Temporality too is writ large in understandings of and use of the term encounter. The literature commonly presents encounters as casual, fleeting and happening 'by chance' (see Wilson 2017 for overview of this work). However, calls for research on more sustained forms of encounter (Matejskova and Leitner 2011) have grown with multiple and more routine encounters in spaces such as community centres, neighbourhoods and schools gaining interest (see, e.g., Slatcher 2017; Mills and Waite 2018). This chapter builds on this extended and more sustained temporality to focus on encounters that include a dimension of planning, organisation and regularity through a programme of meetings and mentoring, as explained below.

Marrying the spatial and the temporal is movement and mobility which are also central to conceptualisations of encounter, whether a movement into or away from an encounter or whether the encounter itself precipitates a movement into or out of something. This is both a spatial movement and location and a temporal one inferring a past and future self. An emphasis on movement has informed recent welfare reform (Wainwright et al. 2011; McDowell 2004), and this chapter adds to the literature on HAs in contemporary urban governance by focusing on their role in attempting to move residents out of financial precarity and into financial independence. Focusing on encounter in this way offers the possibility for change to occur, and this movement to, in and through encounter is particularly resonant to work focusing on welfare, as we explore later.

The HA-run programme this chapter draws on is called Debts, Overheads and Savings Help (DOSH) which aims to: increase social housing residents' confidence; improve their money management; and enhance their knowledge and ability to take control of their finances. It works primarily through targeting residents 'in need' of support with their finances and then encouraging them to participate in a programme of 'therapeutic mentoring'. Therapeutic mentoring is an approach to working with service users that merges mentoring with therapeutic services and has emerged from practices associated with health and clinical sciences. Adopting a therapeutic mentoring approach, DOSH mentors work with residents to support them with and educate them about their finances. Mentors' work also incorporates wider aspects of resident well-being, through advice on a range of health and welfare issues (e.g. mental health and benefits) and referrals to other organisations. This mentor support and financial education is mobilised through face-to-face meetings and email and telephone conversations and includes mentors providing anticipatory guidance, using role-plays and behaviour referrals and enhancing problem-solving and social skills in everyday situations. We suggest that a focus on residents' retelling, through their auto/biographical narratives, of encountering the DOSH programme enables the complexities and intricacies of social housing residents' lives to emerge and highlights the spatial determinants and constraints of everyday living that exist for many. In so doing, we highlight the different temporalities and spatialities that these encounters take and their impact on everyday narratives of welfare.

The chapter begins with an appraisal of social housing and welfare and the contemporary role and framing of HAs as place-based community settings. This is firmly embedded in wider discourses of welfare, dependence and responsibilisation that have emerged from contemporary political debate. From this, we highlight the particular substantive focus of this chapter—that of financial capability—up to and through which narratives of encounter emerge. We then outline the projects from which our data comes and highlight the centrality of an auto/biographical approach for understanding the everyday lives of social housing residents. Here, we also offer a methodological reflection: how we were physically dislocated from our research participants in the conducting of research, and why this is important to note. From this reflection, we frame our findings round two themes: 'auto/biographies of welfare' and 'encounter and relationality'. By way of conclusion, we consider the role of spatiality—of emplacement and displacement—that weave through these auto/biographical accounts.

Context

Social Housing and Local Welfare Intervention

In recent years, there has been a rescaling of the state downwards, with an emphasis on local public service provision. With a proliferation of agencies operating at and through the local level, emergence of a 'new localism' has tallied with critique and rollback of the welfare state (Jacobs and Manzi 2013a). In the UK, rather than a welfare state we have a welfare society operating through organisations at the local scale (Jacobs and Manzi 2013b) and which emphasises the responsibility of citizens and communities to address their own 'problems' and deprivation.

Fiscal austerity has led to the mobilisation of the voluntary and community sectors, with decentralisation of employment and welfare policies giving rise to the production of new 'welfare spaces' (Cochrane and Etherington 2007). This focus on localism, active citizenship and new welfare spaces brings to the fore the role of HAs as significant social housing agencies and their re-imagining as 'community anchors' (McKee 2015). Though notionally independent and non-profit organisations, the prominence of HAs has grown in recent years (Walker et al. 2003). At the end of 2015/2016, HAs in England owned 2.67 million below-market affordable homes, housing some 5.87 million people (NHF 2016). In spite of the current challenging funding context, HAs have been mobilised as key instruments for developing active citizenship and responsible community through close connection to the people and places they serve and through neighbourhood renewal and local service provision. Conceptualised as forms of intermediate social control (Atkinson and Flint 2004), they continue to play a strong role in their operating localities and, as the term 'community anchor' suggests, are tasked with providing local 'support' and 'stability' through depth and weight of their service provision.

Social housing providers have always exercised urban governance over the residents they house (Flint 2004; Saugeres 2000; Mullins 2000), but in recent years, this governance has been extended in new and concerted ways:

> The emerging role for housing agencies reflects wider trends in urban governance towards the responsibilisation of individuals and the use of community as a territory and process of government. (Flint 2002: 635)

As Flint argues, social housing governance has been reconfigured with 'a range of new technologies aimed at reshaping the conduct of tenants and practitioners' (Flint 2004: 152), and this has strongly traded on the responsibilisation of residents.

Social housing infers a dependency and reliance on another and is the antithesis to the current responsibilising agenda. Residents have increasingly been constructed as a social problem (Flint 2004; Manzi 2010), marked out and defined by their relationship to national policy imperatives, key examples being labour market participation (Wainwright and Marandet 2019) and financial independence (Wainwright et al. 2018). By actively pursuing a government determined, market-led agenda at the local level through creating spaces for resident identification and welfare intervention, HAs have become part of a 'shadow state' (Malpass 2001). This is driven by government rationalities based on market prioritisation (Flint 2004) and, as we argue, is ripe for exploring residents auto/biographical narratives of welfare and encounter based on HAs need to identify, target and reform residents to ensure they pay their rent. One way that this is being pursued is in relation to residents' financial well-being and capability.

Welfare Reform and Financial Capability

The UK's Financial Capability Strategy (Fincap.org.uk 2015: n.p.) focuses on individuals 'taking control of their finances' while recognising that people have different needs at different stages in their lives. It emphasises the need for 'improving people's ability to manage money well, both day to day and through significant life events, and their ability to handle periods of financial difficulty' (Fincap.org.uk 2015: 6). This is particularly pertinent to the social housing sector as research has shown that social housing residents are more susceptible to lower levels of financial capability (Atkinson et al. 2006) than others. A large proportion of social housing residents are in no or part time and precarious forms of employment and therefore rely on welfare provision. Changes to this welfare provision in terms of mode of receipt (most especially the roll-out of Universal Credit) and amount given (with benefits capped) are significant for both social housing agencies and residents. As has been argued, these welfare reforms mark an important opportunity to renew efforts to address the high levels of financial exclusion among social housing residents:

> welfare reforms should be viewed as an opportunity for landlords to review their current practice and put in place policies and practices that will deliver financial inclusion, as this will help to mitigate the risk of rent arrears and evictions. (Williams, n.d.: 3)

Over the past decade, the social housing sector and individual agencies have given increasing attention to the financial capability of residents (National Housing Federation and Toynbee Hall 2008) with a proliferation of financial skills/education programmes implemented at local level (e.g. Collard et al. 2012). Such programmes are important as social housing agencies benefit from lower rent arrears and cost savings as a result of fewer failed tenancies (Chartered Institute of Housing 2011). Directly related to the roll-out of Universal Credit, recent research evidences that many residents are experiencing difficulties with direct payment and landlords' arrears are rising markedly (Hickman et al. 2017; Tanner 2018).

Financial capability is a broad concept that encompasses knowledge and skills, along with the motivation to take action. As HM Treasury (2007: 19) explains: 'Financially capable consumers plan ahead, find and use information, know when to seek advice and can understand and act on this advice, leading to greater participation in the financial services market'. However, financial capability is a controversial area of public policy. The academic literature is particularly critical of the increasing financialisation of everyday life of which financial inclusion and financial capability are parts. Financial capability can be seen as a form of advanced liberal governmentality with financial capability a substantive governing project. For example, in the discourse of financial capability it is the individual who should be rational and self-interested, prudent, knowledgeable, as HM Treasury's definition above suggests. Within this discourse, it is the individual that needs to realign to fit with this. As Berry (2015: 518) argues, financial capability is about 'displacing ultimate responsibility for welfare to the individual level', and, following a behavioural economics approach, 'individual rationality is besieged within the context of the market and believed in need of some kind of intervention' (Marron 2014: 506). In this sense, financial capability deepens neoliberalism forming one part of a free market project to hollow out the welfare state and turn people into 'investor-subjects'.

In these critical terms, Finlayson (2009: 407) discusses how the interventionist welfare state, having been delegitimated and 'rolled back', finds a way to reinvent itself, 'intervening into and acting upon new objects in new domains' with financial capability programmes being a good example of this. In terms of social housing, we can see this quite clearly with a reconfiguring of the role of social housing agencies to fit with the broader responsibilisation agenda. For HAs, this requires knowing and encountering their residents and then managing and changing their behaviour and conduct so they become a financially capable and educated resident-subject. The next section discusses in more detail the research projects that explored these formalised spaces of financial capability created and operated at the local level by social housing agencies.

Researching Social Housing

This paper stems from funded research projects[1] with two HAs located and working across London and the southeast of England. Both projects linked to the extended role HAs now have in relation to their localities and residents as a provider of welfare services and support. The projects had a different focus but both incorporated discussions with residents engaged in the financial education and capability programme called DOSH. In particular, the projects focused on the dynamics through which residents are engaged in the wider services offered by HAs, the various encounters that led them to the DOSH programme and then their more sustained encounters with DOSH mentors. In particular, we were interested in residents' auto/biographical narratives of welfare and how these led to them accessing the DOSH programme.

---

[1]Projects were funded by the British Academy (SG152101) and the Money Advice Service What Works Fund.

The fieldwork for both projects was undertaken between 2016 and 2018. While the broader projects drew on a range of methods including questionnaires and focus groups, this chapter draws on the narrative interviews which were framed by an auto/biographical approach. We were interested in residents' experiences and understanding of their everyday lives linked to their identity as social housing residents, rather than a presumed reality (Bruner 1990). We recognise that the way people narrate their lives and the auto/biographies they provide are a specific performative encounter between the interviewee and interviewer and linked to subject and situational context of each interview. As Somers (1994: 606) notes, 'it is through narrativity that we come to know, understand and make sense of the social world, and it is through narratives and narrativity that we constitute our social identities'. For us, this approach was especially important for engaging with social housing residents many of whom are in receipt of state benefits and have been cast in current political discourse as 'other' and so commonly written about rather that heard from. Valentine and Sadgrove (2014: 1982) describe narratives as the 'complex and shifting processes through which individuals narrate themselves, and their experiences in relation to multiple (structural) narratives provided by society'. An auto/biographical narrative approach gives prominence and relevance to social actors in the research process (Lincoln and Denzin 2000) and, in particular, enables, '[i]mportance [to be] … given to honouring the voice of those who are socially excluded' (Suárez-Ortega 2013: 190).

For us, in our focus on everyday experiences and encounters which, as we argue, requires a consideration of relationality, the interviews we draw on here were all conducted 'at a distance' and by telephone. Interviewing is a relational enterprise, a dialogue and encounter between at least two people (Fujii 2017), and the use of telephone interviews configures this differently to the usual face-to-face positioning. Telephone interviews were used for various reasons including project timeframe, participant availability and preference and researcher restrictions. We were thus physically dislocated from our research participants during interviews, yet by asking about their everyday lives and struggles, their experiences of being a social housing resident, of being on welfare and in a financial precarious position were focusing on issues of relationality and encounter. These conversations also exposed dimensions of risk and vulnerability and required an opening up and trust on the part of the participants. On reflection, we were surprised at the richness, extent and depth of our data and the fluency and length of some of the interviews.

Previous research (e.g. Ward et al. 2015) has found that telephone interviews give participants more freedom and confidence to disclose personal or sensitive information without feeling judged or inhibited. The distance is a mechanism through which auto/biographies are prised open and participants are encouraged to talk as anonymity is further enhanced (see, e.g., Greenfield et al. 2000), and this was certainly our experience in the interviews we draw on here. Participants can also choose to locate themselves in a safe and comfortable space where they feel free from 'surveillance' (Holt 2010), confident to speak about themselves and can exert control over this dimension of the research process. Therefore, while we remained disembodied researchers and displaced from the interviewees, the assembled auto/biographies effectively enabled a retelling of embodied and emplaced residents' lives.

The four residents we include in this chapter consist of 2 men and 2 women and from across different age ranges living in different areas of London and the South East. Table 12.1 provides an overview of each as context for the auto/biographical narratives in the proceeding section where we draw on verbatim interview excerpts. Residents are identified by use of a pseudonym.

In the next section, we present and analyse our auto/biographical data around two themes. First, auto/biographical narratives of welfare and second, encounters and relationality.

Table 12.1 Overview of research participants

Lisa is a female resident in her late 50s who lives in Spelthorne with her four children and has been an HA resident for more than 14 years. Although she has no formal qualifications, she has recently completed an employment training course and is hoping to return to work shortly. The breakdown of a relationship and changes to her benefit entitlement resulted in Lisa falling behind in her rent payments
Dominic is a male resident in his early 40s, who currently lives in Oxford and has been an HA resident for 18 years. Currently long-term unemployed due to a mental health condition, Dominic has been receiving support and guidance from the HA about his financial situation and changes to his benefits
Susan is a female resident in her early 30s and currently lives in Ealing with her five young children and partner. She has been an HA resident for three years. After her husband passed away last year, Susan found herself falling into rent arrears and was contacted by the HA about rent repayments
Joel is a male resident in his early 20s and, after a period of homelessness, currently lives in an HA-provided home in Ealing. Due to a long-term mental condition, he has been unable to work for sustained periods of time. With the switch from Employment and Support Allowance to Universal Credit, he began experiencing financial difficulties, causing him to fall behind with his rent payments

Auto/Biographical Narratives of Welfare

Plummer (2013) argues that everyday life is where complexity unfolds, and hence it is vital that we study it. The auto/biographical narratives of welfare that we present here show an unfolding of everyday lives—both temporally and spatially—as experienced and retold by participants and are linked to complex forms of class and gender experience (Back 2015). With welfare recipients, including those in social housing, so frequently spoken of and about, we argue that auto/biographical accounts can disrupt and undermine prevailing narratives of dependency that reproduce negative stereotypes of irresponsibility.

The auto/biographical narratives start with an event or series of events that interviewees used to explain their reason for being on benefits. These are then frequently marked by coming to a 'crossroads' where support was sought from or offered by their social housing provider. For Lisa, this begins with recounting her school days, moving through training and employment and then explaining her identity as a mother and her day-to-day caring responsibilities:

> Lisa: Yeah, didn't do very well at school. I spent most of the time jumping around instead of in books and things. I left school early. I got an apprenticeship and left school. I did three days at work and then two days at school. Then I left at 16, not with the grades that I wanted, I must admit. After that, I had a baby, and then I decided to go back to college. So went back to… in between that I had a job, a part time job as a gymnastics coach, then when my little boy got a bit older, I went back to college, and did a full time hairdressing course. Got them qualifications, worked part time for a little bit of hairdressing, realised that this really isn't for me. Then had some more children, and then I stayed at home, I was a stay at home mum for a long time. And now my boys are a little bit older, I decided to do a personal training course, which I absolutely loved. Like sports and gymnastics being my… it's been my everything, ever since I've been little, it's all I know. Then once I qualified with that, suddenly my relationship broke down, and I was a single mum again, which was fine, it was fine, but it just meant a lot of… a lot of money worries, a lot of… which just brings a lot of stress onto you. So therefore I decided that you know, I need to now think about me and try and better myself for my children as well, really.

With four children aged between 16 and 4, the breakdown of her relationship and an injury, Lisa found herself struggling financially, as she recounts:

Lisa: … my relationship broke down, then I had… I got hit with the benefit cap. Unfortunately, I never received my letter to say that they'd… my benefit cap went in on a certain day, so obviously I didn't even know any different. I was just carrying on as normal, then two months later I get a letter saying you're in like £2,000 rent arrears on your rent. And I was like what?

For Dominic, it was towards the end of his undergraduate studies at a London university that he suffered from considerable mental ill health which changed and disrupted his planned trajectory:

Dominic: I had a breakdown when I was a student, just before finals, so I did three years, and then… so I've only got A levels, so I was educated up to A levels. And so I moved… I've… I had… well I worked… I haven't worked since I've been here, since the breakdown. So that's a very long time. And well, just been on benefits ever since.

Dominic spoke vividly about his now long-term mental health diagnosis and the challenges of his day-to-day being:

Dominic: …depression and schizophrenia; the treatment, the injection I'm on is for schizophrenia, you know, so I don't hear voices, you know, start hearing voices, and… yeah, depression really, but it's very difficult to you know, treat. I don't feel better after you know, after each thing really.

These health challenges have been coupled with financial difficulties stemming from not being able to work. The anticipated move to Universal Credit and benefits freeze led to anxieties about paying his rent to the HA and meeting other daily expenses:

Dominic: I'm on housing benefits, so that… that goes through quite clearly, so I've never been in arrears…benefits are stagnant, so I'm… I've lost… you know, I'm sort of going down in my balance, but not… but everything… everything else has gone up, as you know, like gas and all the bills… You know, even food and clothes and things. So it's quite difficult.

Similarly, Susan began by recounting her education and work, but the fluency of her retelling is punctured by her current poor mental health:

Susan: Yeah, I have worked in the past. Education wise, I'm a college graduate or whatever you want to call it, Business admin and IT. That was a good few years ago. Yeah, that was… so at the moment, I can't really remember much about dates. I was Operations Manager for a company, and then gosh, what can I say? Yeah, I done that for a while, and then… sorry, I'm just trying to… I'm just trying to concentrate on it, because I've got a lot of like memory problems, then I left that, and then I became a housewife. I stayed at home to look after my kids, yes.

Susan has five children aged nine, seven, five, three and two. As the excerpt below describes, she has considerable caring responsibilities as a recently widowed parent. Emotional struggles have been compounded by very real financial challenges caused by changes to the benefits system:

> Susan: Because I'm currently in rent arrears, because I've been put on a benefit cap, after the death of my husband last year - he died of cancer last year, a cancer related illness actually. And he was on disability, considering he died, so that was taken away, so what happened is, is that I… because I was on Widow's children's allowance, that's actually been put under the benefit cap, so that had affected me. I don't understand why I was under the benefit cap, but you know, it's… that's just how the government… the government has obviously blanketed everything under the same thing. But what I found is actually literally it's put me in a tight spot, and this has made my mental health deteriorate further.

Falling behind in rent arrears led to the tenancy sustainment team of the HA to get in touch with Susan.

Our last narrative comes from Joel, the youngest of those interviewed, who focused on explaining where he came from and where had been home:

> Joel: I've lived in the area my whole, well I say lived in the area, I've lived everywhere if I am honest but I mean I grew up in this area so I've lived here my whole life. I've also lived all over the country really. At the moment I've been here since February with [HA]. … I was homeless for a long time and I got given my place to live … and then when I was there I had to switch over from ESA [Employment Support Allowance] to Universal Credits and then I started experiencing loads of problems.

As highlighted in Joel's account, and as runs through the accounts from Lisa, Dominic and Susan, recent and ongoing changes to mode of welfare receipt and amount of welfare payments have triggered and precipitated immense challenges and difficulties in everyday lives. Continued governmental economic objectives have focused on extensive welfare reforms with the aim to 'make work pay'. As Wiggan's (2012) articulates, these changes have marginalised the structural aspects of, for example, persistent unemployment, poverty and ill health and transformed them into individual pathologies of benefit dependency, irresponsibility and worklessness. The auto/biographical welfare narratives above demonstrate that challenges of welfare reductions are compounded by other serious difficulties.

Social stratification is implicit in social housing, though the diversity of residents in terms of, for example, education and employment status often gets hidden. In the examples above, everyday narratives of welfare are framed and shaped by the immediacies of mental and physical ill health, family life and caring responsibilities, bereavement and other significant struggles. For Susan and Lisa, their auto/biographical accounts are located within their caringscapes. Informal caring, critical to human flourishing and evident across many aspects of women's lives, is captured in the notion of caringscapes (McKie et al. 2002; Bowlby et al. 2010). For Susan and Lisa, benefits, housing and employment are all parts of their caringscapes and enable or hinder the informal caring they provide and which are central in their auto/biographical narratives of welfare.

Encounter and Relationality

Consideration has been paid to the role of housing professionals in operationalising national policy imperatives (Parr 2009; McKee 2015; Dobson 2015; Robinson 2000). Here, we argue that a relational understanding, focusing on relations between housing professionals and residents, is both useful and important for recognising that the enactment of national policy requires a focus on day-to-day practice and residents' everyday experiences. The relationality of encounter between social housing residents and professionals is always forming, fluid and dynamic and takes shape across different social housing spaces—through neighbourhoods, homes, offices, community centres, support services and so on.

Governance and control are mobilised through this embodied relatedness of individuals within institutional space (Dobson 2015). This embodied personal relationality, so critical to the work of HAs, is based on comings and goings, of noticings and movements, as relationships are forged. Social reality is always in movement, processual and fluid and constitutive of and through dynamic and unfolding relations, networks and bonds (Dobson 2015) as auto/biographies demonstrate:

> Dominic: I got this letter through [about the move to Universal Credit]....
> And I rang the number.

After initially getting through to the switchboard, Dominic explains how he was put in contact with a financial capability mentor and a series of meetings was set up. For Lisa, she telephoned the HA when she received a letter informing her of her rent arrears:

> Lisa: So obviously I phoned them, and said like I don't understand, and then they explained it to you, and then I was like 'oh my God, how am I going to get out of this now?' So literally then I had to start paying my rent, like, which was absolutely fine, but then paying my rent arrears off on top of that, which then led me to more worry, strain, and stress, 'cause obviously all this… at the time I'd had an operation on my leg, so they put me in touch with [mentor].

As we read these auto/biographical narratives, there is a need to consider how these encounters can be viewed through a lens of governmentality and biopolitics whereby power is productive and can produce positive and negative effects. Encounters of this kind have become central to a neoliberal logic and demand critical scrutiny. Certainly initially, notably in relation to income officers and tenancy sustainment teams, encounters were fraught with anxiety and stress as residents were faced with the burden of debt and worries over loss of income and, potentially, their home.

Discussions of encounter enliven these auto/biographical narratives of welfare as they are affective and emotive. As Susan recounts, from the initial letter she received she felt abandoned to her problems:

> Susan: …and then I've been told to just get on with it, and pay my rent, which is £140 something a week. But with the arrears, I had to pay like minimum £150, and then I'm… and then I'm… you know, housing benefit's only paying 50p a week, which to me is an insult. I don't see the point, what's £2.00 a month, going to do?

In the excerpts above from Dominic, Lisa and Susan, whether through a letter or phone call, this was an initial encounter of suspicion and unequal power. There exist complex positionings of residents and staff evident through the 'conflicting' roles of HAs (Wainwright and Marandet 2019) as rent collector and provider of tenancy sustainment and support. With HA staff responsible for ensuring rents are paid on time, individual auto/biographies can get lost within institutional practices that require compliance in the form of rent payment.

It was from these initial encounters that Joel, Lisa, Susan and Dominic became engaged in a programme of financial capability, and as both

Dominic and Lisa explain below, this is an engagement that requires a sustained encounter between residents and staff.

> Lisa: He [the mentor] came round and like obviously helped me out and he advised… that's how I got onto this course. And now I've managed to… now I've managed to help out, like my rents up to date, you know, and everything… everything's going good.

> Dominic: I've been to two meetings and it was just really, really it was what, sort of what I thought already. But she suggested a couple of… a couple of things, like volunteer, sort of volunteer work, but it's not the whole day. It's just a short programme, which would be useful you know. She mentioned a place called [name] as well, which is allied to mental health services. So I've been there before, and I actually found it quite difficult doing the whole day, you know. So I'm not doing that.

In the extended narrative below, from the initial letter she received, Susan met with her mentor who she found listened and understood:

> Susan: she was very sympathetic actually, it was really good talking to her, so she was like… she was like, in my case there's not really much that can be done, because the government doesn't really… there's a blanket of people in my circumstances, which they really shouldn't. She was like if there was a way that you know, she could… if there was someone that she could go to about my situation, for me to get like you know, preferential treatment or something, she would do it, but she was like there's not really much that can be done.

> … she knows that I'm a young mum, I'm 33, I've got five children, I've recently lost my husband from a disease that just came out of nowhere. So on top of it, you know, I've just been thrown into this poor financial situation where you know, my benefit's been cut to under £500 a week, and then I've been told to just get on with it…

> … I feel it's a positive thing, because I get a light… like she makes me feel comfortable and I can talk to her, because she's under… she's very understanding. So I would prefer to deal with her, than anyone else or organisation… It's just… she just understands… she's got kids herself, so she can understand, she can relate as a mother, to what I'm going to through. She understands how the system works, she knows that it's unfair at times to people who are in dire situations, because she's seen it herself. And she's just… I guess it's just experience making her more understanding to what I'm going through.

This experience of 'supportive' power (Robinson 2000) between individuals within the institutional context requires a tailored personal one-to-one approach which, in many cases, involves several hours of discussion which is key to building trust and allowing mentors to get to know individuals. For Susan, this support came from her mentor both 'knowing' the welfare system and understanding her day-to-day caring work. Engaging in conversation and offering practical assistance, this account suggests a seeming mutuality of staff-resident relations with the later observed and enticed to participate in forms of self-governance. In spite of potentially disparate class locations and socio-economic status between staff and residents, this particular encounter was forged through a common gender position to nurture and sustain conversation and scrutiny.

For Joel, he could not clearly recall how he was put in touch with his mentor but relayed the importance of this encounter:

> Joel: I can't really remember who put me in touch with him,… oh I don't know but someone else put me in touch with him and then I started speaking to him from there really.

> …well to be honest with you, [mentor] sort of saved my life man. He's a good geezer. He was only supposed to help me with a few things but it pretty much ended up being like, well like I said, I don't want to sound drastic and that but I don't have no family to help me with anything and I don't really have anyone else. So without him I don't know, I honestly couldn't tell you where I'd be like.

These sustained encounters narrated by Susan and Joel are very positive, at least initially, with a retelling of the support and reassurance they were given.

As highlighted above, it is important to be cognisant of power in and through encounters; encounters can produce anxiety and resentment, and they can harden and affirm unequal power relations and existing concerns and antagonisms (Wilson 2017). This came to the fore as difficulties emerged in the sustaining the encounter. Here again we get a glimpse of the affective and emotional impact when encounters are frustrated or cut short:

> Dominic: The trouble with that is if you look at [HA name], you still only get one number, so if you ring up, like about a repair or anything, you actually only get one line. … I know I'd have to be put through to her, and the… I think the last time I tried, she wasn't there.

Lisa: I phoned him last week, sometime last week, and left a message for him to call me back, but he hasn't, so I'll give him a ring this week. No, I haven't spoken to him.

For Susan, from her initial warm retelling of her relationship with her mentor, a later interview indicated a shifting of the relationship:

Susan: I'll tell you now she is really difficult now to get hold of, and I've certainly been trying to call her, and she's never at her desk, on the Friday she's not in. And she never returns my phone calls now, it's kind of like you know, I kind of feel differently now.

With the talking and perceived friendship of the encounter now at a distance, the unequal positioning of staff and resident is reinstalled through remoteness and lack of contact with Susan left struggling.

Conclusion: Emplacements and Displacements

In bringing this chapter to a conclusion, we want to highlight two inter-related points linked to taking an auto/biographical approach to research. First is the usefulness of focusing on encounter and auto/biographies of encounter for elucidating everyday lives. Second, we highlight the need to interrogate the geographies that are shaped by and shape these encounters, and why these matter. An auto/biographical approach that focuses on spatiality and encounter is vital for understanding everyday lives, especially so when researching marginalised groups whose voices are often unheard or ignored, such as the social housing residents discussed here.

As Valentine and Sadgrove (2014) attest, encounters can only be understood when they are analysed within the context of an individual's life history. The narratives of welfare retold in this chapter are done so through a lens of encounter between residents and housing professionals and within the context of an identity linked to social housing. Auto/biographies are always relational to other people and other things; in this chapter, we have begun to highlight just some of these relations for residents: to homes and families, to social housing agencies and officers, and to wider discourses of welfare and dependency. A retelling of encounters, through a primary focus on resident experiences of a financial education and capability programme, enables some of this relationality and complexity of the everyday to be made visible.

These auto/biographies of encounter also demonstrate that geography matters in a very real sense for social housing residents. Individuals are always placed and located and have a relationship to particular places and locations. The term 'emplacement' describes the way in which individuals narrate their experiences as a product of placed and 'solidified configurations' (Valentine and Sadgrove 2014). This is foremost for social housing residents, and running through their auto/biographies of encounter is the ever-present threat of displacement—of losing their home—as these final interview excerpts vividly highlight:

> Lisa: I didn't even realise I was in so much debt, because I didn't realise they'd sent me the letter out, starting from this date, you need to get this done. And there was just no other letter, no follow up. But literally they just let it go on and on and on, until they sent me a final warning, and eviction. And I was like what's this all about, because I didn't even… and it wasn't until I spoke to them, and then a week later, I can't afford this, we need to come to some sort of agreement. … I don't think I'd be where I was today, I don't think they would have put me through to [mentor] and ended up getting all these opportunities.

For Lisa, initial meetings with her mentor allayed these fears and anxieties of eviction and displacement. However, for Susan, with an eviction notice having been served, it was a real and present threat as she was preparing to go to court over rent repayments:

> Susan: with this pending court date coming up, I do feel, I don't know, I just feel extremely depressed about it. And I've got five children, I don't want my children to go through all this, which is why I've been wanting to try and sort this out. But I don't need to have to go to court, because I don't know if anyone can actually come with me that day. 'Cause like I said, I have difficulty going out alone. And what I need the [HA] to understand, it just seems like they're not getting it.

As this excerpt highlights, fear of displacement disrupts Susan's sense of home and belonging. Sense of place refers to how people feel and think about places and is used by geographers to emphasise that places are significant because they are the focus of personal feelings (Rose 1995). It is an important concept because it is linked closely to identity and how we make sense of ourselves and our lives. For Susan, the threat of eviction means losing her home and the home of her five children. As these final interview excerpts remind us, auto/biographical accounts are shaped by structural inequalities linked to *where* we are and *who* we are, with the urgency of place experienced through the threat of displacement, loss and dislocation.

As a final point, auto/biographies of encounter highlight how residents are positioned as both agents and subjects (Valentine and Sadgrove 2014). HAs have a critical role in constructing 'identities of agency, self-regulation and responsibility amongst their tenants' (Flint 2004: 151) and operating close and personal forms of governance and regulation in order to do this. Control and self-control filter through institutional structures, professionals and residents. Residents are variously the subject of wider welfare discourses that have shaped HA rules and regulations, and in relation to the financial capability programme discussed here, they are subject to programme and mentor support or lack of support. But the auto/biographies of encounter also highlight varying degrees of resident agency—agency in precipitating, shaping and reflecting on the encounter and agency in changing personal trajectories of welfare. It is through the lived experiences and developing relationships between residents and professionals, as retold in the auto/biographies of encounter we present here, that this more complex story emerges.

References

Atkinson, R., & Flint, J. (2004). Reconfiguring Agency and Responsibility in the Governance of Social Housing in Scotland. *Urban Studies, 41,* 151–172.

Atkinson, A., Mckay, S. D., Kempson, H. E., & Collard S. B. (2006). *Levels of Financial Capability in the UK: Results of a Baseline Survey (Consumer Research 47).* Financial Services Authority.

Back, L. (2015). Why Everyday Life Matters: Class, Community and Making Life Liveable. *Sociology, 49,* 820–836.

Berry, C. (2015). Citizenship in a Financialised Society: Financial Inclusion and the State Before and After the Crash. *Policy and Politics, 43,* 509–525.

Bowlby, S. R., McKie, L., Gregory, S., & MacPherson, I. (2010). *Interdependency and Care Over the Lifecourse.* London: Routledge.

Bruner, J. (1990). *Acts of Meaning.* Cambridge: Harvard University Press.

Chartered Institute of Housing. (2011). *Improving Financial Inclusion and Capability in Social Housing.* Coventry: CIH.

Cochrane, A., & Etherington, D. (2007). Managing Local Labour Markets and Making Up New Spaces of Welfare. *Environment and Planning A, 39,* 2958–2974.

Collard, S., Finney, A., Hayes, D., & Davies, S. (2012). *Quids in: The Impact of Financial Skills Training for Social Housing Tenants.* Bristol: Personal Finance Research Centre.

Dobson, R. (2015). Power, Agency, Relationality and Welfare Practice. *Journal of Social Policy, 44,* 687–705.

Fincap.org.uk. (2015). *Financial Capability Strategy for the UK.* https://www.fincap. org.uk/uk_strategy.

Finlayson, A. (2009). Financialisation, Financial Literacy and Asset-Based Welfare. *British Journal of Politics and International Relations, 11,* 400–421.

Flint, J. (2002). Social Housing Agencies and the Governance of Anti-Social Housing Behaviour. *Housing Studies, 17,* 619–637.

Flint, J. (2004). Reconfiguring Agency and Responsibility in the Governance of Social Housing in Scotland. *Urban Studies, 41,* 151–172.

Fujii, L. (2017). *Interviewing in Social Science Research: A Relational Approach.* New York: Routledge.

Greenfield, T. K., Midanik, L. T., & Rogers, J. D. (2000). Effects of Telephone Versus Face-to-Face Interview Modes on Reports of Alcohol Consumption. *Addiction, 95,* 277–284.

Hickman, P., Kemp, P., Reeve, K., & Wilson, I. (2017). The Impact of the Direct Payment of Housing Benefit: Evidence from Great Britain. *Housing Studies, 32,* 1105–1126.

HM Treasury. (2007). *Financial Capability: The Government's Long Term Approach.* London: HM Treasury.

Holt, A. (2010). Using the Telephone for Narrative Interviewing: A Research Note. *Qualitative Research, 10,* 113–121.

Jacobs, K., & Manzi, T. (2013a). Investigating the New Landscapes of Welfare: Housing Policy, Politics and the Emerging Research Agenda. *Housing, Theory and Society, 13,* 213–227.

Jacobs, K., & Manzi, T. (2013b). New Localism, Old Retrenchment: The 'Big Society', Housing Policy and the Politics of Welfare Reform. *Housing, Theory and Society, 30,* 29–45.

Lincoln, Y., & Denzin, N. (2000). The Seventh Moment: Out of the Past. In N. Denzin & Y. Lincoln (Eds.), *Handbook of Qualitative Research* (pp. 1047–1065). London: Sage.

Malpass, P. (2001). The Restructuring of Social Rented Housing in Britain: Demunicipalization and the Rise of 'Registered Social Landlords'. *European Journal of Housing Policy, 1,* 1–16.

Manzi, T. (2010). Promoting Responsibility, Shaping Behaviour: Housing Management, Mixed Communities and the Construction of Citizenship. *Housing Studies, 25,* 5–19.

Marron, D. (2014). Informed, Educated and More Confident: Financial Capability and the Problematization of Personal Finance Consumption. *Consumption Markets and Culture, 17,* 491–511.

Matejskova, T., & Leitner, H. (2011). Urban Encounters with Difference: The Contact Hypothesis and Immigrant Integration Projects in Eastern Berlin. *Social and Cultural Geography, 12,* 717–741.

McDowell, L. (2004). Work, Workfare, Work/Life Balance and an Ethic of Care. *Progress in Human Geography, 28,* 145–163.

McKee, K. (2015). Community Anchor Housing Associations: Illuminating the Contested Nature of Neoliberal Governing Practices at the Local Scale. *Environment and Planning C, 47,* 1–16.

McKie, L., Gregory, S., & Bowlby, S. (2002). Shadow Times: The Temporal and Spatial Frameworks and Experiences of Caring and Working. *Sociology, 36,* 897–924.

Mills, S., & Waite, C. (2018). From Big Society to Share Society: Geographies of Social Cohesion and Encounter in the UK's National Citizen Service. *Geografiska Annaler: Series B, Human Geography, 100,* 131–148.

Mullins, D. (2000). Social Origins and Transformations: The Changing Role of English Housing Associations. *Voluntas: International Journal of Voluntary and Nonprofit Organisations, 11,* 255–275.

National Housing Federation. (2016). *Key Statistics Briefing: How Many Affordable Homes to Housing Associations Own?* Retrieved from http://s3-eu-west-1.amazonaws.com/pub.housing.org.uk/KSB2_2016_How_many_affordable_homes_do_associations.

National Housing Federation, & Toynbee Hall. (2008). *A Guide to Financial Capability for Social Housing Tenants.* London: National Housing Federation.

Parr, S. (2009). The Role of Social Housing in the 'Care' and 'Control' of Tenants with Mental Health Problems. *Social Policy and Society, 9,* 111–122.

Plummer, K. (2013). Epilogue: A Manifesto for a Critical Humanism in Sociology: On Questioning the Human Social World. In D. Nehring (Ed.), *Sociology: An Introductory Textbook and Reader* (pp. 489–517). Harlow: Pearson.

Robinson, J. (2000). Power as Friendship: Spatiality, Femininity and 'Noisy' Surveillance. In J. Sharp, P. Routledge, C. Philo, & R. Paddison (Eds.), *Entanglements of Power: Geographies of Domination/Resistance* (pp. 67–92). London: Routledge.

Rose, G. (1995). Place and Identity: A Sense of Place. In D. Massey & P. Jess (Eds.), *A Place in the World?* (pp. 87–132). Milton Keynes: Open University.

Saugeres, L. (2000). Of Tidy Gardens and Clean Houses: Housing Officers as Agents of Social Control. *Geoforum, 31,* 587–599.

Slatcher, S. (2017). Contested Narratives of Encounter from a Bridge-Building Project in Northern England. *Space and Polity, 21,* 191–205.

Somers, M. (1994). The Narrative Constitution of Identity: A Relational and Network Approach. *Theory and Society, 23,* 605–649.

Suárez-Ortega, M. (2013). Performance, Reflexivity, and Learning Through Biographical-Narrative Research. *Qualitative Inquiry, 19,* 189–200.

Tanner, B. (2018). *Housing Related Arrears Reveal 'Dismal Failure' of Universal Credit.* https://www.24housing.co.uk/news/housing-related-arrears-reveal-dismal-failure-of-universal-credit/.

Valentine, G., & Sadgrove, J. (2014). Biographical Narratives of Encounter: The Significance of Mobility and Emplacement in Shaping Attitudes Towards Difference. *Urban Studies, 51,* 1979–1994.

Wainwright, E., & Marandet, E. (2019, early online) Housing Associations as Institutional Space: Care and Control in Tenant Welfare and Training for Work. *Area.*

Wainwright, E., Marandet, E., Buckingham, S., & Smith, F. (2011). The Training-to-Work Trajectory: Pressures for and Subversions to Participation in the Neoliberal Learning Market in the UK. *Gender, Place and Culture, 18,* 635–654.

Wainwright, E., McHugh, E., Gilhooly, K., & Hills, L. (2018). *What Works? Evaluation of the DOSH Financial Capability Programme.* London: Brunel University London.

Walker, R., Mullins, D., & Pawson, H. (2003). Devolution and Housing Associations in Great Britain: Enhancing Organisational Accountability? *Housing Studies, 18,* 177–199.

Ward, K., Gott, M., & Hoare, K. (2015). Participants' Views of Telephone Interviews Within a Grounded Theory Study. *Journal of Advanced Nursing, 71,* 2775–2875.

Wiggan, J. (2012). Telling Stories of 21st Century Welfare: The UK Coalition Government and the Neo-Liberal Discourse of Worklessness and Dependency. *Critical Social Policy, 32,* 383–405.

Williams, S. (n.d.). *Increasing the Parity of the Pound for Social Housing Tenants: How Systematic Financial Inclusion Can Help Mitigate the Impact of Welfare Reform.* London: Toynbee Hall.

Wilson, H. (2017). On Geography and Encounter: Bodies, Borders and Difference. *Progress in Human Geography, 41,* 451–471.

13

'I Thought… I Saw… I Heard…': The Ethical and Moral Tensions of Auto/Biographically Opportunistic Research in Public Spaces

Tracy Ann Hayes

I Thought… I Saw… I Heard…

Laughing, I lower myself down the steep section on my bottom, thinking to myself that I am polishing the rocks as I go. It's been a good walk, up and over the hill. I'm looking forward to reaching the bottom and the final stretch of relatively flat walking to reach our car (visions of a cold drink waiting for me at our favourite pub spur me onwards). Glancing up I see a youngish couple (possibly late twenties/early thirties, he looks a bit older than her, although I can't quite see from this distance) with a girl of about 10 or 11. They are approaching this steep section of the path. The man and the girl are in sports-wear and trainers. The woman is not. She looks like she was expecting to go for a stroll in a park, not a hike over a hill. In a few shuffling slides, I will be alongside them. I pause as I hear a voice, exasperated, saying "*That's it. I can't go on, there's nothing left in me. Go on without me. Leave me behind.*" She is speaking to the backs of the other two who are already giddily leaping up the path, racing to the top, skipping surefootedly from rock to rock. Gazing up at them as they pass, I admire their youth, their fitness, their ability to stay on their feet, whilst I have resorted to an awkward downward shuffle. Looking ahead, I see the woman sit down and remove her phone from her handbag. She resolutely stares down at it, ignoring the other two. She does not appear to

T. A. Hayes (✉)
University of Cumbria, Carlisle, UK
e-mail: tracy.hayes@cumbria.ac.uk

© The Author(s) 2020
J. M. Parsons and A. Chappell (eds.), *The Palgrave Handbook of Auto/Biography*,
https://doi.org/10.1007/978-3-030-31974-8_13

have noticed me yet. As I draw level, she looks up. I smile, and say, "*it's tough going isn't it? Especially on such a warm day.*" I hear her sigh as she nods, agreeing without words, then looks back down at her phone. She looks exhausted. I carry on with my walk. Hearing voices again (I can't quite make out the words), I glance over my shoulder and see that the man and child have turned around and are making their way back to where the woman is waiting. They seem exhilarated by their walk, joking and laughing as they skip back down together. I wonder who they are—is the man the father of the girl (they do look alike)? Is the woman a new partner navigating her way into this family unit? I wonder how the woman will react to their arrival. Conscious that I am staring, I make myself look away and allow them their privacy as they regroup as a three rather than a two. I walk on. Over a cold drink, the moment lingers in my consciousness, stirring memories from my recently completed doctoral research. I recall the words of a young woman called Lexi telling me, "*You should think about people's abilities when planning activities, when I can't do something that others can, I think they're going to laugh at me, it makes me upset and not want to go out.*"[1] Her voice blends in with those of others I have listened to over the course of my study: Liz who told me that given the choice, he would "*go where the moon is rising, just sit there and look at the surroundings.*"[2] Jack who thought that disconnected from nature might mean you were scared of sheep.[3] The young woman, whose name now escapes me, who refused to attend a residential experience at an outdoor education centre, expressing embarrassment at her inability to do all the activities on offer and her reluctance to admit she needed extra support. The sense of achievement expressed by those who had made it to the top of a mountain and had then returned to the centre for a game of hide and seek in the woods. The challenges of addressing the needs of different abilities and preferences.[4] I find myself questioning, not for the first time, where does the 'research' begin and end, what counts as research, how do we address the messiness of research? When we are using methods such as auto/biography, boundaries can become more blurred, transcending more traditional methodologies. I sip my drink, lost in thought.

*   *   *

---

[1] Pseudonym; informed consent gained (Hayes 2017).

[2] Pseudonym; informed consent gained (Hayes 2017).

[3] Pseudonym; informed consent gained (Hayes 2017).

[4] Hayes (2014).

Introduction

This chapter opens with a short story, presented in the form of an auto/ethnographic vignette (after Humphreys 2005) that provides a present-tense, reflexive, first-person narrative with embedded retrospective thoughts. This is designed to enhance the authenticity of the account, which will be utilised to exemplify, and reflect upon the ethical and moral tensions of 'auto/biographically opportunistic research in public spaces'. I use this term to refer to those times when we find ourselves in a public space, observing (seeing and/or hearing) something that has relevance to/with a topic we are studying, which we want to share with other people, for example through a story. It may be that the 'something' we observe will help us provide a context for our research or to show the potential impact of what we have found.

When constructing a story, the observational moment(s) chosen for inclusion may be relatively insignificant, part of the mundane or every day (after Silverman 2007) that goes unnoticed by others or if noticed does not have the same meaning and, if it was retold in a story by someone else, would take a very different form. Humphreys highlights there are a number of closely related terms used to categorise stories like the one used here, citing '...narratives of the self (Richardson, 1994), self-stories (Denzin, 1989), first-person accounts (Ellis, 1998), personal ethnography (Crawford, 1996), reflexive ethnography (Ellis and Bochner, 1996), and ethnographic memoir (Tedlock, 1991)' (Humphreys 2005: 841). Like him, for the purpose of this chapter, it is Reed-Danahay's (1997) concept of autobiographical ethnography that has both more resonance and more use for the issues being explored. However, I use it in the form 'auto/biographical ethnography', with a slash between 'auto' and 'bio' to show that they stand in a dialectical relationship (see Roth 2009) with the inclusion of ethnography to show that this approach has a specific aim of understanding social and cultural experiences. It also allows me to highlight that sometimes there may be more of a focus on the auto (personal experience), other times more on bio (life story), both of which are considered in relation to the ethno (culture), whilst at all times the aim is to be critical and analytical (graphy) about/with the relationship between them (see Ellis et al. 2011). This conceptual framing places the self within a story of a social context and recognises that the story is both a method and a text.

The auto/biographical ethnographic approach creates a reflective space whereby I can make use of my 'sociological imagination' (after Mills 1959) to analyse the experiences encapsulated in the vignette that started this chapter.

> The sociological imagination is the practice of being able to 'think ourselves away' from the familiar routines of our daily lives in order to look at them with fresh, critical eyes. Mills, who created the concept and wrote a book about it, defined the sociological imagination as "the vivid awareness of the relationship between experience and the wider society." (Crossman 2018: n.p.)

Defined and applied in this way, it provides a useful concept for analysing apparently disparate moments (e.g. from planned and unplanned observations) that enables explicit and reflexive self-observation, sensitivity and awareness of the relational nature of research.

However, this concept is not limited to sociology; as Mills himself argued, it provides a 'common bond for all the social sciences' (Mills 1959 cited in Harvey 2005: 211), and we can extend this imaginative approach to embrace our geographical imagination or what Harvey refers to as 'spatial consciousness' (ibid.). As a transdisciplinary researcher (explored in more detail later in the chapter), I extend this to using my imagination in a multifaceted, transdisciplinary way to develop criticality from my understanding of a range of knowledges—geographical, historical, anthropological and philosophical—using this broad range of different lenses to develop understanding without becoming 'muddle-headed' (Harvey 2005: 237). We can avoid this 'muddle-headedness' by using physical and social 'maps' to guide our thinking in a way that allows us to distinguish between unreasonable prejudices, masked by adherence to outdated traditional methods and a perceived need to defend disciplinary boundaries. I propose that we view the process of gaining ethical clearance from a university review panel as a way of developing a useful map to guide us through our research studies. Furthermore, this approach allows us to consider the spatial and temporal dimensions of ethics, viewing them as agentic, active, lived, embodied, reflexive and retrospective as well as the more predictive. To do this, we need to ask some fundamental questions about where research begins/ends and what we mean by 'data', so that we can begin to answer questions about the ethical and moral issues/tensions of opportunistic research in a public space.

Opportunistic research is more open, less planned than other more formal research approaches; Andrew (2017) refers to this as 'accidentalism' rather than intentionality. As a result, less anticipated/more unanticipated ethical issues may arise, making it difficult to predict what may happen and to address this within the customary ethical procedures. Indeed, as a result, many refute that this is even a form of research (Andrew, ibid.), seeing it as more like auto/biographical research or journalism, and as such exempt from formal ethics review (discussed by Tolich 2010). Similarities may be found with internet-based forms of research, particularly those involving participation in public fora, such as chat rooms and online communities (see Roberts 2015; Eysenbach and Till 2001), in that the methods may be deemed to fall outside of formal ethical review procedures. Some researchers may even choose these methods in an attempt to avoid ethical review and consent procedures, which Roberts (2015: 318) argues 'is a disturbing trend, particularly when dealing with vulnerable populations such as children and youth in relation to a sensitive topic'. I do not follow or approve of this trend. I have always been honest and open, in academic publications and in the applications for ethical approval that precede them, about the epistemological connections I make between my personal and academic experiences. In doing this, my epistemological approach is similar to that taken by Letherby (2015), and like her, I openly reflect on my use of creative methodologies and alternative ways to share research findings, or she phrases it 'to tell academic stories' (2015: 128).

As I have written elsewhere (e.g. see Hayes and Prince 2019), for research to be demonstrably ethical and responsible, we need to acknowledge our position of power, explain the approach we have taken and take great care with our words, to avoid being inadvertently harmful. Davies (2012: 744) refers to this as being 'self-conscious methodologically', and she argues that 'Narrative accounts, auto/biographies and ways of writing that "tell of the telling", allow tensions, nuances, complexities, confusions and unclear thoughts to remain...' (ibid.: 747). However, we have to recognise that when we write about ourselves and our experiences, we also expose those around us, and in the process, things that may have been private are made public. I find it troubling that Davies (ibid.) does not attend to this issue. Whilst her paper openly and honestly analyses her experiences of being subject to a child protection investigation, the emotional impact this had on her and the challenges she encountered in her attempt to combine experiential knowledge in an authorised, academic account, there is no mention of the invasion of the privacy of her children, partner or other family members that was inherent in writing her story. As a reader, we have to trust that she had their consent to publish this very personal account of an intrusive, distressing experience that occurred in the private space of their family home. With opportunistic research in public spaces, naturalistic observations happen without the participants' consent; indeed, unless they read the finished product, it is without their knowledge. As argued by Roth (2009), it is therefore not a surprise that this reporting of events from our lives is a contested research approach and that some may not view this as a valid or appropriate form of research.

This level of critique is familiar to auto/ethnographers and auto/biographical ethnographers, who regularly encounter claims that their work is narcissistic, a form of self-therapy or arguably worse, a process of self-transformation. Atkinson (2006: 403) demands we remember that:

> "Others" remain infinitely more interesting and sociologically significant than the majority of sociologists who document their own experiences rather than analysing social action and social organisation.

However, how can we maintain this focus on 'others' in an ethical and moral way, whilst embracing auto/biographical ethnography? To address this question, I first provide a summary of my doctoral research, briefly explaining the methodology used and outlining the findings this generated. Drawing on these findings, I then move on to explore ethical and moral tensions in relation to the opening story, focussing the discussion around three key research methods: theoretical and philosophical perspectives (what we think); observations (what we see, through both planned and naturalistic observations); and aural and oral (what we hear and say).

The chapter will conclude with a concise overview of storied approaches in research, highlighting the place of auto/biographical ethnography within this. Extending Letherby's argument for 'a position of theorised subjectivity (Letherby, 2003, 2013)—which requires the constant, critical interrogation of our personhood—both intellectual and personal—within the production of the knowledge' (Letherby 2015: 133), I argue that there is a way to navigate the moral and ethical tensions of auto/biographically opportunistic research in public spaces. And that we can do this in a responsible and responsive way, so that the resultant discoveries are both valid and appropriate. The chapter closes by providing guidance for others who want to utilise a similar approach.

My Doctoral Research: Making Sense of Nature

My doctoral research was a creative exploration of young people's relationship with nature, titled 'making sense of nature' (Hayes 2017). I looked at a range of facilitated programmes that offered outdoor learning opportunities and explored what young people (11–25 years) thought of their experiences. The aim of my study was to find a way to research and analyse how experiences such as these can enable young people to develop a positive, personally meaningful relationship with nature and then to make use of this learning to inform policy and practice. I utilised an innovative transdisciplinary methodology, which blended hermeneutics, auto/ethnography and action research (Hayes and Prince 2019) and used a range of data elicitation/collection tools to capture and '… make the most of the information available' (Tracy 2013: 26). This included using documentary data, observational and focus group data, with a mix of semi-structured and naturalistic interviewing, depending on the participants involved. To this, I added stories, anecdotes, memories and reflections, which I used to highlight and explore themes/issues in more detail as they emerged and to provide context within the broader aims of my study. Tracy refers to this process as 'bricolage' and highlights it enables a researcher to creatively and flexibly '…create an interesting whole' (ibid.: 26). She further asserts '…*qualitative researchers find meaning by writing the meaning into being*' (ibid.: 275; her original emphasis in italics).

I add to this by stating that a storied approach provides additional data in the form of stories and allows flexibility for emergent insights into refine methods, enabling us to respond to context and, most importantly, to participants. The stories created and shared within my study are more than mere artefacts: they form part of the data set and are based on specific incidents within my research. I refer to these as 'magic moments': the moments when things seem to fall into place. A more conventional academic term for this is crystallisation; as Robson explains, 'Such crystallisations range from the mundane to the "…earthshattering epiphany" (Fetterman, 1989: 101) after which nothing is the same' (Robson 2002: 488–489).

Although there has been movement in recent years towards adopting a more inter- and/or transdisciplinary, creatively interpretive approach to research, this is still seen as controversial, arguably undisciplined, and is not generally accepted by policymakers as a credible method. There is still a political preference for more traditional, quantifiable and, in my opinion, simplistic methods, which ignore, or at the very least limit, the complexity, the nuance and the messiness of what we are studying. I find this unethical and, more to the point, unkind to those we are studying. I argue that this is an area that warrants further research: we have a responsibility to keep up the momentum of challenge and to promote more caring, humane ways to conduct and present research. We also have a responsibility to do our best to ensure this is perceived as valid and ethical research, so that we can enable others to follow our approach.

Throughout my study, there were two concurrent processes: (1) data elicitation through primary and secondary research and (2) employing writing inquiry as a research method. When planning my methods for data elicitation and analysis, I was aware of ethical considerations, as highlighted by Anderson (1999: 65): 'Researchers have the power to misrepresent and abuse subjects when they interpret, selectively report and publicise the data' (see also Lounasmaa 2016). Therefore, I endeavoured to represent participants' views as accurately as possible, whilst maintaining their anonymity and respecting their privacy. Key themes that emerged included the importance of playfulness (Hayes 2016a/2015), kindness (Hayes 2016b), responsiveness (Hayes 2013), comfort and belonging—themes that will be drawn from when exploring the opening story.

I Thought…

In the story, I am thinking to myself as I slide over the rocks, finding humour in the way I have chosen to navigate my way down the hillside. I am self-conscious, I feel the rock through my clothes and am aware that I am not as young, fit or agile as other walkers; however, although I notice this, I am not perturbed by it. My research over the last four years has enabled me to understand that we all experience outdoor spaces and activities in subjective, personalised ways. Through participating alongside others with a wide range of differing abilities, and analysing this through a number of alternative theoretical and philosophical perspectives, I discovered the importance of playfulness (I am polishing the rocks), kindness (to myself and others), responsiveness (to the rocky environment and other people around me) and I feel a sense of both comfort and belonging. I have chosen to come and walk here and have carefully chosen my walking companion. He understands me, and although he is a more experienced walker, he is very patient and encourages me when I need it. I cannot help but compare this to the family I encounter. They are having a different shared experience. It reminds me of one of my early conference presentations (Hayes 2014), near the start of my doctoral journey, when I used Aesop's Fable, The Tortoise and the Hare, to explore how we can facilitate outdoor learning in a way that helps to develop connections with nature. For many, especially young people and those experiencing physical and/or mental ill health, stepping outside into a natural environment can be a real challenge. What I see in front of me brings that academic exercise to life: as I argued then, hares may be happier and more comfortable walking with other hares, as may also be true of tortoises. Thinking about this can help us to ensure that we do not inadvertently intimidate or discourage others from joining us in activities. My thinking about it now is filtered through my research encounters, and the voice in my head is joined by the remnants of conversations with young people over the last four years. Their voices are still loud and clear, as if I heard them yesterday, probably as a result of having listened to them so many times as I painstakingly transcribed and then analysed their words. However, their faces have become blurred in my memories; I am not sure I would recognise them if we met again.

I Saw…

I saw lots of things on that walk, some of which are mentioned in the story. Observation was one of the main methods I used for my doctoral research and is something I have found comes quite naturally to me: I notice things, someone who in everyday language may be called a 'people-watcher'. During my studies, I took on the role of participant observer at a number of rural and urban locations, capturing my thoughts and observations in my field notebook, along with initial reflections and analysis in the form of short stories and anecdotes. All references to individuals, organisations and locations were anonymised to respect confidentiality and/or privacy. There was also ongoing dialogue with practitioners by email and phone, which were incorporated into my reflective journal. Utilising these methods, data was continually being collected, elicited and analysed, not through separate stages, but through an iterative, reflexive process. This helped me to develop my understanding through ongoing analysis of my data and is an example of how writing formed part of the process of my inquiry (Richardson 2000).

As a result of my analysis, I felt able to confidently answer my research questions in a particularistic way (after Maxwell 2005). From my observations and our conversations, I can explain how the young people and practitioners I spent time with appeared to make sense of their experiences, and I can explain and justify how I subsequently interpreted and made sense of that, through analysis with academic literature. I can even apply evaluator criteria to assess the quality of my work, to help me decide if it is ready for the examination that is integral to the doctoral process. However, my findings will only ever be partial and subjective, that is the nature of this type of research.

I Heard…

The title of this chapter comprises the three notions of thinking, seeing and hearing; however, it is also important to consider what is said and what is left unsaid. Anecdotes, informal, naturalistic conversations—words said in passing in open, public spaces—may offer a stark contrast to those said in planned, managed spaces such as research interviews, where the words are more considered, more thought-through. In my doctoral study, I conducted individual interviews, with practitioners and with young people, and I had many more naturalistic conversations which inveigled their way into my thinking. Some of the young people I participated alongside were unable to speak due to their complex disabilities (Hayes and Prince 2019); others were reticent as a result of their previous experiences (Hayes 2016b). Pausing now to think about the things I heard and did not hear highlights the importance of using all our senses in research, drawing on observations, being mindful of body language and other non-verbal methods of communication. This helps us to build a more holistic picture of what is happening and can lead to greater understanding of why this may matter.

Navigating the Moral and Ethical Tensions

As asked within the story, where does the 'research' begin and end, what counts as research, how do we address the messiness of research? Reflecting on my choice to include an apparently trivial, unplanned moment, like the encounter on the hillside, I agree with Maxwell (2005: 79) that there '… is no such thing as inadmissible evidence in trying to understand the issues or situations you are studying'. This is reinforced by Thomson (2016: n.p.) who reminds us:

> Data is created when you actually sit down, back in the office, away from the everyday busyness of field work, to work out what you have that will actually help you answer your research question(s) (…) In a very real sense, the researcher creates the data.

It is important to consider the ethics of this, to respect the privacy, confidentiality and safety (emotional as well as physical) of participants and researcher (Kafar and Ellis 2014). When we are using methods such as auto/biography and auto/biographical ethnography, boundaries can become more blurred and indeed may even transcend the constraints of more traditional methodologies. This needs to be accounted for within the overall design of the study, by being explicit about axiology, as well as epistemological and ontological perspectives. Axiology refers to the internal valuing systems that influence our perceptions, decisions and actions and includes our ethical and moral stance.

Atkinson (2006: 400) concerned about this blurring of boundaries, argues for more analytical and theorising research approaches which '… are too often lost to sight in contemporary fashions for subjective and evocative ethnographic work'. He emphasises that the autobiographical has always been a key aspect of ethnographic work and that the '… very possibility of social life and of understanding it ethnographically depends on an elementary principle: the homology between the social actors who are being studied and the social actor who is making sense of their actions' (ibid.: 401–402). However, it is possible to embrace all of this. For example, we can follow Letherby's advice to '…start with the subjective, and make our position throughout the research *process* and in the research *product* clear, our work is not only more honest but also more useful' (2015: 137; my emphasis added in italics). Creative research methods, especially storied approaches, can offer an effective and ethical way to do this.

Storied Approaches in Research and the Place of Auto/Biographical Ethnography

Storied approaches are a creative way to capture the essence of research findings and present them in a way that aims to show, rather than to tell, what has been found. As identified by Ingold (2000: 21) '… the idea of showing is an important one. To show something to somebody is to cause it to be seen or otherwise experienced – whether by touch, taste, smell or hearing – by that other person.' Hence the descriptive language used within the opening story. This is an approach advocated by both Pelias (2004: 1) as a way of inviting 'identification and empathetic connection' and Sparkes (2007: 522), in that in this format, the story '…simply asks for your consideration' without lingering on methodology or theoretical concepts. This can come afterwards, as exemplified by this chapter.

For the purpose of exploring ethical and moral tensions inherent in auto/biographically opportunistic research in public spaces, three key research methods were identified (thinking, seeing, hearing) to provide a focus for the discussion. However, these are not distinct, separate methods: they are interwoven, relational and interconnected, and my choice to apply them this way is subjective—someone else could choose to do this in a different way. Therefore, it is important we remain conscious that our interpretation and subsequent presentation of what we think, see and hear has been filtered through our own prior experiences (Denscombe 2002/2008). Mason (2017: 22) asserts that scrutinising our:

'…own changing perspectives and assumptions should become almost a habit of active reflexivity' whilst avoiding becoming self-obsessed in the process. In my case, my experiences of conducting research into how we make sense of nature inveigle its way into all my encounters in outdoor spaces, and it is not something that I can simply switch off. As elucidated by Maxwell (2005: 79), I have been a research instrument, my 'eyes and ears are the tools…' that I use to make sense of what is going on. I notice things more than I used to, I am more aware and conscious of what is happening around me. Moreover, as Cotterill and Letherby (1993: 74) argue:

> we draw on our own experiences to help us understand those of our respondents. Thus their lives are filtered through us and the filtered stories of our lives are present (whether we admit it or not) in our written accounts.

We can also draw on the responses of our respondents to help us understand our everyday, lived experiences. There is no actual temporal and/or spatial divide between our academic research and personal experiences, much as it may appear more professional to pretend there is. The reality is much more complex and, indeed, messy than that. Transdisciplinarity provides us with a holistic approach that enables us to more effectively understand and solve contemporary issues (problems) by placing the topic/issue at the centre of the process.

Transdisciplinary Research

Transdisciplinarity goes beyond involving academics (or literature) from different disciplines, to include practitioners and other non-academic stakeholders. Leavy (2016: 24) explains transdisciplinarity '… has emerged in order to meet the promise of transcending disciplinary knowledge production in order to more effectively address real-world issues and problems'. Leavy (2016) cautions it is important to recognise that taking this approach does not necessitate abandoning individual disciplines; indeed, there need to be disciplines for transdisciplinarity to exist, as they provide the foundations, the building blocks for a methodological approach. Transdisciplinarity draws on knowledge from disciplines relevant to specific research issues or problems, whilst ultimately transcending disciplinary borders and building a synergistic conceptual and methodological framework which is irreducible to the sum of its constituent parts. Transdisciplinarity views knowledge-building and dissemination as a holistic process that requires innovation and flexibility. However, it still needs to be ethical.

I have constantly questioned if I am just seeing/hearing/thinking what I want/expect to and not seeing/hearing/thinking, or worse, choosing to ignore things I do not like or agree with (Bassot 2016). I do not believe I have done this and have openly admitted where I have been troubled or found the research 'messy'. Leavy asserts, 'Reflexivity is necessary in order to be able to "see" the big picture from multiple vantage points' (2016: 78). Wickson et al. (2006) also emphasised the importance of reflection, to enable the researcher to be conscious and aware of how our own '…frames of reference/values/beliefs/assumptions etc. have shaped the conceptualisation of the problem, as well as the development of the method of investigation and the solution' (ibid.: 1053–1054). However, it is challenging to balance the need for reflection, for an auto/biographical stance, against the need to be perceived as a cutting-edge academic rather than a self-indulgent, egotistical, navel-gazer (Gutkind 1997).

Transdisciplinarity thrives on creativity, on looking at and thinking about things in a different way, with the purpose of doing things differently. Yet, as Leavy (2016: 14) reminds us: '… the modern academy has been based on the creation and maintenance of disciplinary borders. Therefore, the recent growth in transdisciplinary approaches to research signifies a major turn in how social research is conceived and conducted'. Being part of this movement, whilst concurrently establishing an academic identity, which is measured by quantifiable impact as part of the current audit culture, is not easy (see McCoy 2012; Sparkes 2007; Humphreys 2005). Creative processes can be used '… both as tools of discovery and a unique mode of reporting research' (Brady 2009: xiii), enabling us to explore, gather/elicit and interpret in a more holistic and empathically connected way (McCulliss 2013). However, these are not separate processes; they are symbiotically intertwined: creative, transdisciplinary methods can make visible the geographical, social, cultural, political, moral and ethical nature of these issues.

With regard to data collection and analysis processes, Van Maanen urges ethnographers to '…continue experimenting with and reflecting on the ways social reality is presented' (2011: xiv–xv). He refers to this as 'intellectual restlessness' and highlights '…the distinction between literature and science in ethnography is shrinking … newer voices are audible, new styles are visible, and new puzzles are being put forth'. As a researcher looking to be informed by both natural science and social science, whilst working within a practice-research-pedagogy nexus, this restlessness is something I recognise. Creating a blended methodology enabled me to find new ways to address old problems (e.g. the relationships we have with young people and with nature) and to be intellectually daring. I recommend this approach to other researchers. However, to be successful with it, to be judged to have made a substantial contribution to knowledge, this approach must involve scholarly caution, respect for process and academic rigour.

So, when does a research study begin and end? In my doctoral thesis (Hayes 2017: 292), I wrote:

> …my study draws from a wide range of theoretical constructs, which have been carefully applied to my experiences and observations from my time in the field. Formally this time is recognised as the four years of registered doctoral study; however, my reflexivity has made the most of the 45 years preceding this, taking a blended approach to life/work, as advocated by Ellis (2004/2014).

If we accept that data is spatially and temporally distributed, there is a shift in focus of responsibility, on to the researcher, to be overt and honest about the purpose, the rationale for this approach. Spatial and temporal boundaries are imaginary as much as material, and as a result, the data extends beyond that boundaried by the method(s) approved by the ethical review board. Creative researchers like me may struggle with formal structures, such as review boards, which are often comprised of those from distinctively different epistemological and ontological perspectives; equally, our questions and challenges may be perceived as disruptive to the status quo. The fluidity of data elicitation/collection necessitates ongoing ethical thinking, which is responsive, creative, considerate and contextualised. Careful, considered scrutiny which makes full use of ethical processes in a dialogical and dialectical way allows us to be clear about what we are doing and why—enabling creative, responsive and responsible research by opening up a space for critical transdisciplinary and ethical inquiry.

I am advocating for a more dynamic ethical process, grounded in the relationship between research processes and outputs, which is explicit about what it is we want our research to achieve and how we want it to be applied within everyday life (if indeed that is the aim). My aim is to revitalise conversations about research ethics as a useful and creative part of the process. My analysis of the story which opened this chapter has included identification of key themes and ideas that emerged, weaving them together and interpreting them in a process of evaluation. Ely et al. (1997: 223) explain that as interpreters '...we could be likened to filters through which we sift data in the process of making meaning'. The filtering process involves reflecting on what I have found, comparing it with other studies and relevant theoretical literature, before deciding what to include/exclude. There are choices to be made, for example, which stories to tell and which to leave until another day. This is an active process of writing to discover what it is I am doing, what it is I am saying, rewriting, rethinking, finding meaning and clarifying understanding. This is all part of writing as a method of inquiry. I am aware that each time I (re)listen to an interview recording, (re)read a transcript, (re)view entries in my field notebook and/or (re)interpret the data, I find something new, different, another point of interest.

With regard to my doctoral study, how do young people (and other ages) make sense of nature? To answer this, it is necessary to consider how we/they encounter nature, through the recognisable processes of mediated, direct and indirect contact with nature—and how these are facilitated/accessed. There is no 'one size fits all' or most effective approach: for most people, it is a complex blend of all three processes, with socio-cultural and political influences determining the nature of this relationship. And it is a fluid relationship, like a river it ebbs and flows, gaining/losing significance within our lives, depending on what else is demanding our attention. For some people, at times within their lives, nature may go unnoticed: something that is just there, in the background—perhaps even an annoyance when encountered in a form that is more challenging than anticipated (the reluctant walker in the opening story); at other times, it provides a place of refuge, fun, adventure, solace, peace or escape. For me, it has been all these, at different times during my doctoral studies. I have valued the many walks with my dogs, friends, family and research participants in and with nature and have found special places where I have been able to process and make sense of my observations and thoughts—to think about thinking (Nixon 2013).

When I reflect on the research relations established with those I have studied—the way I have carefully selected the projects, the sites, the participants, the young-person-centredness, the ways I have chosen to collect and analyse data—I can see the importance of story. It is a golden thread weaving throughout. Some decisions I have taken were conscious, planned and methodical; others were more instinctive and intuitive—in response to my encounters. There are inherent philosophical, ethical and political issues within these decisions. It is crucial to remember that what to me is a research project may be perceived as an intrusion into the lives of others. Consideration, care and kindness are vital.

Conclusion: Bringing This to a Close

Researching in a moral and ethical manner goes beyond ethics panels and their procedures: it demands ongoing ethical processes of self-awareness, empathic skills and a creative imagination—in this chapter, I extend that to embrace a transdisciplinary imagination. We have to stop, put ourselves in the 'other's' position and consider how we would feel about what has been said about us—a very familiar position for auto/ethnographers and auto/biographical ethnographers. The three named young people in the opening story provided informed consent for me to include them in my doctoral study. Their identity and right to privacy are protected through the use of pseudonyms and through anonymising any references to specific places. This follows guidance provided for the procedural, anticipatory ethics of qualitative research. In contrast, I do not have consent from the unnamed young woman mentioned in the story, nor from the family I encountered in the public space of a hill. Does this mean these accounts cannot be considered to be of value within a research study? No, it does not; however, it does demand careful consideration of the purpose for including them and highlights my responsibilities as an author to consider the ethics of autoethnography (Tolich 2010).

Tolich (2010) provides a critique of the use of retrospectively gaining consent, arguing that this can lead to potentially coercive situations, where someone feels obliged to consent to being included in an autoethnographic account. Moving on with his critique by reviewing the work of well-known autoethnographers, Tolich (2010: 1602) further emphasises that:

> …some of the leading autoethnographers, often held up as experts in their craft, did not appear to anticipate ethical issues or recognise boundaries within their collection of ideas. They did not know how to answer the question: Do others mentioned in the text also have rights?

I agree with Tolich (2010) that we need to be able to answer this question with conviction and, like him, am unconvinced by arguments for assumed or apparent consent. For me, it is not enough to be able to say someone did not object to being included within a story, or that they wanted me to tell their story. I feel the need to be able to evidence that. However, that is impractical with auto/biographically opportunistic research in public spaces: if I had stopped the family on the side of the hill to ask them if they would consent to the possibility, that one day in the future, I may remember our encounter and want to write about it in relation to something I was studying, they would quite understandably have thought me very strange. We cannot walk around with consent forms, just in case we see something that may be relevant and interesting, that we think may add depth to a topic we are writing about. And if we did, then by the nature of the process, I would have acquired their names and increased the risk of violating their right to privacy. This serves to highlight the need for clear, practical guidance for research of this type, combined with open, honest reflexive practice.

References

Anderson, P. (1999). Disturbed Young People: Research for What, Research for Whom? In S. Hood, B. Maynall, & S. Oliver (Eds.), *Critical Issues in Social Research: Power and Prejudice* (pp. 54–67). Buckingham: Open University Press.

Andrew, S. (2017). *Searching for an Autoethnographic Ethic*. New York: Routledge.

Atkinson, P. (2006). Rescuing Autoethnography. *Journal of Contemporary Ethnography, 35*(4), 400–404.

Bassot, B. (2016). *The Reflective Practice Guide: An Interdisciplinary Approach to Critical Reflection*. Oxon: Routledge.

Brady, I. (2009). Foreword. In M. Prendergast, C. Leggo, & P. Sameshima (Eds.), *Poetic Inquiry: Vibrant Voices in the Social Sciences*. Rotterdam: Sense Publishers.

Cotterill, P., & Letherby, G. (1993). Weaving Stories: Personal Auto/Biographies in Feminist Research. *Sociology, 27,* 67–79. https://doi.org/10.1177/0038038593 02700107.

Crossman, A. (2018). *Definition of the Sociological Imagination and Overview of the Book: How You Can Use It to See the World Anew*. Available at https://www. thoughtco.com/sociological-imagination-3026756. Last viewed 3 November 2018.

Davies, P. (2012). 'Me', 'Me', 'Me': The Use of the First Person in Academic Writing and Some Reflections on Subjective Analyses of Personal Experiences. *Sociology, 46*(4), 744–752.

Denscombe, M. (2002/2008). *Ground Rules for Good Research: A 10 Point Guide for Social Researchers*. Maidenhead: Open University Press.

Ellis, C., Adams, T. E., & Bochner, A. P. (2011). Autoethnography: An Overview. *Qualitative Social Research, 12*(1), 273–290.

Ely, M., Vinz, R., Downing, M., & Anzul, M. (1997). *On Writing Qualitative Research: Living by Words*. London: The Falmer Press.

Eysenbach, G., & Till, J. E. (2001). Ethical Issues in Qualitative Research on Internet Communities. *British Medical Journal, 323,* 1103–1105.

Gutkind, L. (1997). *The Art of Creative Nonfiction: Writing and Selling the Literature of Reality*. New York: Wiley.

Harvey, D. (2005). The Sociological and Geographical Imaginations. *International Journal of Politics, Culture and Society,* 211–255. https://doi.org/10.1007/s10767-006-9009-6.

Hayes, T. A. (2013). Seeing the World Through Their Eyes. Learning from a 5 ½ Year Old, a Rabbit and a Boat Ride with Aunty. *Horizons, 63,* 36–39.

Hayes, T. (2014). The Challenges of Social Inclusion in Outdoor Education: Can Tortoise and Hare Learn Together? In Dr. P. Varley and Dr. S. Taylor (Eds.), *Being There: Slow, Fast, Traditional, Wild, Urban, Natural…Proceedings from the 2nd International Adventure Conference*, Sabhal Mòr Ostaig, Skye, May 2013 (pp. 43–54). Fort William: University of the Highlands and Islands.

Hayes, T. (2016a). A Playful Approach to Outdoor Learning: Boggarts, Bears and Bunny Rabbits! In J. Horton, B. Evans, & T. Skelton (Eds.), *Play, Recreation, Health and Well Being, Vol. 9 of Geographies of Children and Young People*. Singapore: Springer.

Hayes, T. (2016b). Kindness: Caring for Self, Others and Nature—Who Cares and Why? In J. Horton & M. Pyer (Eds.), *Children, Young People and Care*. London: Taylor Francis.

Hayes, T. (2017). *Making Sense of Nature: A Creative Exploration of Young People's Relationship with the Natural Environment*. Unpublished doctoral dissertation, Lancaster University, UK.

Hayes, T. A., & Prince, H. (2019). Shared-Story Approaches in Outdoor Studies: The HEAR (Hermeneutics, Auto/Ethnography and Action Research) 'Listening' Methodological Model. In B. Humberstone & H. Prince (Eds.), *Research Methods in Outdoor Studies*. Oxford: Routledge.

Humphreys, M. (2005). Getting Personal: Reflexivity and Autoethnographic Vignettes. *Qualitative Inquiry, 11*(6), 840–860.

Ingold, T. (2000). *The Perception of the Environment: Essays in Livelihood, Dwelling and Skill*. London: Routledge.

Kafar, M., & Ellis, C. (2014). Autoethnography, Storytelling, and Life as Lived: A Conversation Between Marcin Kafar and Carolyn Ellis. *Przegląd Socjologii Jakościowej, 10*(3), 124–143.

Leavy, P. (2016). *Essentials of Transdisciplinary Research: Using Problem-Centered Methodologies*. Oxon: Routledge.

Letherby, G. (2015). Bathwater, Babies and Other Losses: A Personal and Academic Story. *Mortality, 20*(2), 128–144.

Lounasmaa, A. (2016). *Lessons in the Calais Jungle: Teaching Life Stories and Learning About Humanity*. Available at https://theconversation.com/lessons-in-the-calais-jungle-teaching-life-stories-and-learning-about-humanity-67095. Last viewed 25 November 2018.

Mason, J. (2017). *Qualitative Researching*. London: Sage.

Maxwell, J. A. (2005). *Qualitative Research Design: An Interactive Approach*. London: Sage.

McCoy, K. (2012). Toward a Methodology of Encounters: Opening to Complexity in Qualitative Research. *Qualitative Inquiry, 18*(9), 762–772.

McCulliss, D. (2013). Poetic Inquiry and Multidisciplinary Qualitative Research. *Journal of Poetry Therapy, 26*(2), 83–114.

Mills, C. W. (1959). *The Sociological Imagination*. New York: Oxford University Press.

Nixon, J. (2013). Thinking About Thinking with Hannah Arendt. *Prospero: A Journal of New Thinking in Philosophy for Education, 19*(4), 1–4.

Pelias, R. J. (2004). *A Methodology of the Heart: Evoking Academic and Daily Life*. Walnut Creek, CA: Altamira Press.

Reed-Danahay, D. (1997). *Auto/Ethnography: Rewriting the Self and the Social*. Oxford: Berg.

Richardson, L. (2000). Writing: A Method of Inquiry. In N. K. Denzin & Y. S. Lincoln (Eds.), *Handbook of Qualitative Research* (pp. 923–948). London: Sage.

Roberts, L. (2015). Ethical Issues in Conducting Qualitative Research in Online Communities. *Qualitative Research in Psychology, 12*(3), 314–325.

Robson, C. (2002). *Real World Research*. Oxford: Blackwell.

Roth, W. M. (2009). Auto/ethnography and the Question of Ethics. *Forum Qualitative Sozialforschung/Forum: Qualitative Social Research, 10*(1). Available at http://nbn-resolving.de/urn:nbn:de:0114-fqs0901381.

Silverman, D. (2007). *A Very Short, Fairly Interesting and Reasonably Cheap Book About Qualitative Research*. Los Angeles: Sage.

Sparkes, A. (2007). Embodiment, Academics and the Audit Culture: A Story Seeking Consideration. *Qualitative Research, 7*(4), 521–550.

Thomson, P. (2016, November 24). 'Rack Ratting – A Common or Garden Field Work Practice', *Pat Thomson's Patter Blog*. Available at https://patthomson.net/2016/11/24/pack-ratting-a-common-or-garden-field-work-practice/. Accessed 2 December 2019.

Tolich, M. (2010). A Critique of Current Practice: Ten Foundational Guidelines for Autoethnographers. *Qualitative Health Research, 20*(12), 1599–1610.

Tracy, S. J. (2013). *Qualitative Research Methods: Collecting Evidence, Crafting Analysis, Communicating Impact*. Oxford: Wiley-Blackwell.

Van Maanen, J. (2011). *Tales of the Field: On Writing Ethnography* (2nd ed.). London: The University of Chicago Press.

Wickson, F., Carew, A. L., & Russell, A. W. (2006). Transdisciplinary Research: Characteristics, Quandaries and Quality. *Futures, 38*(9), 1046–1059.

Part V

Madness, *Dys*-order and Autist/Biography: Auto/Biographical Challenges to Psychiatric Dominance

Kay Inckle

Introduction

This part introduces three authors—Alyssa Hillary,[1] Brid O'Farrell and Phil Smith—who draw from different aspects of the auto/biographical tradition in order to flesh out challenges to psychiatric knowledge and power as they are lived and experienced first-hand. In the first chapter, Hillary extrapolates a critique of the ways in which the autobiographies of autistic people, or autist/biographies, are read primarily for diagnosis and consequently deny the personhood and even the authorship of the autistic writer. Thus, psychiatric dominance is re-inscribed upon the subjectivity of the autistic person, despite the very act of autistic self-narration contradicting the psychiatric perspective. Following on, O'Farrell employs a polyvocal auto/biography using poetry, journal extracts and collective recall to reveal the limitations of psychiatry in understanding and supporting those with eating dys-order. Her account highlights, instead, a family drawn into confusion, fear and pathologisation and left ultimately without the promised resolution. This part closes with an auto/biography of Mad identity and Mad Studies in poetic form which embodies the painful and sometimes terrifying beauty of madness. The narrative structure of Smith's poetry not only encapsulates the multilayered dimensions of madness but also does so via a medium which calls out to the humanity of reader and author alike.

---

[1]When citing Hillary please use pronoun "they" e.g. non-binary/gender neutral.

All of these chapters emerge from the intertwined disciplines of Mad Studies and Survivor Research, disciplines which share many of the principles, practices and ethics of the feminist research movement which gave birth to auto/biographical practice. Here, by way of introduction to the chapters I offer a brief contextualisation of the Mad and auto/biographical traditions and explore their intersecting politics and practices. The subsequent chapters in this part demonstrate how crucial these approaches are in challenging the failings, abuses and inequalities of psychiatric practice and in giving voice to alternative ways of knowing and being.

The concept and practice of auto/biography is widely credited to Liz Stanley and her work in challenging the traditional binary structure between author and subject in biographical studies (e.g. 1990, 1992, 1993). Stanley's work emerged within a wider context of feminist research, theory and activism which challenged the dominant patriarchal structures of knowledge production (e.g. Ramazangolu and Holland 2002; Ribbens and Edwards 1998; Roberts 1981). Feminists highlighted the power imbalances inherent to concepts such as objectivity, science, truth and facts which privileged normative masculine positions (i.e. biases) and concurrently devalued the work and knowledge of women (and other minoritised groups) as the binary opposite—i.e. as subjective, emotive, unempirical and partial. As such, feminist work has centred on critical reconsiderations of the epistemological conventions underpinning social research, as well as exploring new methods for conducting and representing research which promote equality and the critical self-awareness (reflexivity) of the researcher (Griffiths 1990; Reinharz 1992).

This critical analysis of the inequalities embedded in knowledge production and the power relations it reproduces has also been integral to Survivor Research (e.g. Faulkner 2004; Faulkner and Thomas 2002; Rose 2014; Russo 2012) and the more recent development of Mad Studies (Faulkner 2017; Landry 2017). Survivor Research and Mad Studies emerged from the activism of survivors of psychiatry and their organising to produce evidence of the failings and abuses inherent with in the psychiatric system. Here, the use of "survivor" denotes being a survivor of psychiatry, *not* a survivor of "mental illness" as diagnosis itself is called into question. As such, survivor research and the discipline of Mad Studies embody an ethics, politics, practice and knowledge in direct opposition to psychiatric norms, values and practices. And, similar to feminist and auto/biographical work, subjectivity, identity and experiential knowledge are at the forefront of Mad Studies and Survivor Research. The shared (or similar) identities and experiences of Survivor Researchers create an alternative dynamic to the power inequalities which are integral to psychiatric practice and research and thereby embodies, as well as espouses, an egalitarian mode of being and knowing (Faulkner 2004, 2017). This not only enables a robust critique of psychiatric power, research and practice, but also gives rise to viable—and vibrant—alternatives for knowledge production and in providing support for those in distress.

Here, I tease out three themes which are shared by feminist auto/biographical approaches and Mad Studies/Survivor Research and discuss them in the context of the three chapters which follow. These themes are, firstly, the critique of objectivity and the recognition of the ways in which identity and locatedness are inevitably bound up in knowledge production. Secondly, the political significance of the "auto/biographical 'I'" (Stanley 1992) and the importance of the reflexive presence of both author and reader when engaging with a text. This centring of the I is integral to the development of autoethnographic practice as a challenge to conventional structures of research and connects with the third theme, namely alternative forms of engagement with, and representation of, knowledge production. Non-traditional/non-scientistic modes of representation are fundamental to producing a thorough and complete alternative to psychiatrised, patriarchal ways of knowing and being.

Stanley argued that "scientism has been at the heart of the academic mode" and "it's dominant motifs are the separations between the knowers and what/who is known, subjectivity and objectivity, science and nature" (1992: 11). This approach creates a binary in which the female (or mad person) is always the object of knowledge and the male (psychiatrist) the creator/author of it—indeed, historically, masculinist psychiatry has positioned all women as mad by virtue of being female (Ussher 1991). Survivor researchers and Mad Scholars have highlighted that this scientistic dualism means that "the mad can never have credibility in science" (Rose 2014: 155), and therefore, experiential knowledge is devalued and excluded all in subservience to scientific objectivity. For Stanley, objectivity is always an operation of power, "a set of intellectual practices for separating people from knowledge of their own subjectivity" (1992: 11). This separation produces "alienated knowledge" which bears "no apparent trace of the conditions of its production or the social relations that give rise to this" (1992: 11) and thereby reproduces power inequalities while espousing objective, value-neutral rationality.

Hillary's chapter "Autist/biography" draws from these classic themes in feminist auto/biography and illustrates practices of separation and power at work in the interpretation of autobiographies of autistic people, e.g. autist/biographies. Hillary highlights that integral to the diagnosis of autism is the assumption that those so labelled have no "theory of mind", something which is theorised as essential to an inner life, and thus rendering autistic people devoid of subjectivity, identity and even personhood. This denial of personhood informs both the medical and social oppression of autistic people. However, the very existence of autist/biography rests uncomfortably with this diagnosis: if an autistic person has no inner life or subjectivity, how can they construct an autobiographical text? Nonetheless, notwithstanding the evidence of inner-life presented in autist/biographies, they continue to be read by "experts" in ways which shore up the diagnosis by separating the writer from their own subjectivity in precisely the way Stanley describes (above). In contrast, and positioning themself in the text, Hillary explores how autist/biographies present a multidimensional challenge to the neurotypical/diagnostic—or "scientistic"—practice of reading and interpreting autist/biographies and autistic people. Hillary highlights the ways in which the locatedness, purpose and motivations of the reader inherently skew the meaning that is discovered—echoing Stanley's assertion that "knowledge production does indeed differ systematically by social location" (1993: 50). This assertion has been evidenced in the findings of survivor researchers which have contrasted dramatically with, and called into question, the assumptions and practices that psychiatric research is based upon, reinforcing Stanley's position: "changing the knowledge producers changes the knowledge" (Rose 2014: 152). Thus, Hillary highlights the fundamental flaws of the diagnostic reading and the importance of autist/biography in challenging medical power. Moreover, like other critical auto/biographical works, Hillary's self-location in their writing disrupts the normative diagnostic reading of autist/biographies and challenges the reader to engage, listen and understand in non-objectifying, self-reflexive and egalitarian modes (see also Kruger and DasGupta 2018).

Central to auto/biographical writing and reading, then, is the politics of the "I". "The auto/biographical 'I'" is a political identity, which "recognises that knowledge is contextual, structural and specific and that it will differ systematically according to social location" (Stanley 1993: 49). This position contrasts sharply with the "modernist" values of psychiatric/medical research which deems distant, linear, singular, non-experiential "objective" knowledge as the only credible authority (Faulkner and Thomas 2002). Thus, as Hillary has challenged diagnostic power in reading and writing of autist/biographies, O'Farrell's polyvocal, experiential, family autoethnography of eating *dys*-order and recovery draws attention to the ethical imperative behind the auto/biographical I and the dysfunctional nature of psychiatric knowledge and practice.

The practice of autoethnography, where the researcher's self becomes the vehicle for the research analysis emerged directly from the practice of auto/biography. In "classic" auto/biography, an "intellectual autobiography" (Davis 2018; Stanley 1992) is employed to address the locatedness of the researcher as they construct knowledge: "the 'auto/biographical I' signals the active, inquiring presence of sociologists in constructing rather than discovering knowledge" (Stanley 1993: 44). This presence not only draws attention to the constructed nature of all knowledge, but also renders the author visible and accountable to the reader. This emphasis on visibility and reflexivity as political and ethical practices encourages researchers to be open about their relationship with their research in a context where, congruent with feminist practice and in parallel to survivor research, a connection or insider status is more credible than distant, detached "neutrality".

Once separation and distance have dissolved, the self as research subject comes into play in both feminist autoethnography and survivor research. In survivor research, experiential knowledge is essential to the ethics of equality, accountability and social change that motivate the work (Faulkner 2017; Russo 2012) as well as providing "ecological validity" to the research questions, methods findings and recommendations (Faulkner and Thomas 2002: 2). In O'Farrell's polyvocal account, which draws from journal extracts and collective recall, and which is expressed in a poetic, nonlinear form, the paradoxes and failings of psychiatry are made visible as diagnosis moves from O'Farrell herself to her entire family, without ever delivering the promised resolution or "cure". Instead, she and her family are left to navigate their own journey, sometimes together and sometimes apart, through fear, confusion, love and pain.

In writing a polyvocal autoethnography, O'Farrell draws attention to the intersubjective nature of knowledge and experience and in the inseparability of self from other. In autoethnography, "reflexivity … is located in treating oneself as subject for intellectual inquiry, and it encapsulates the socialised, non-unitary and changing self positioned in feminist social thought" (Stanley 1992: 44). The understanding of the self as non-unitary, as co-constructed in relation to others, social context, discourses, structures and practices is crucial to O'Farrell's account of eating dys-order and her dissonance with psychiatric norms, values and perspectives. The purpose of her account, then, is similar to the auto/biographical Testimonies of indigenous activists whose simultaneously individual and collective narratives function "to make something that has been suppressed known, to break the silence, to reveal, to uncover, to encounter Otherness through words" (Gregorčič 2018: 70). For O'Farrell, this desire to use autoethnography "to reach beyond the auto" is an ethical and political gesture intended to release herself, her family and others from the bondage of the psychiatric pathologisation and its impossible linear trajectory from bad/sick to good/well which ultimately only dashes hope and leaves blame in its place.

Overall then, both the content and the forms of writing and representation that O'Farrell employs—the use of multiple voices, collective recall, poetic and nonlinear structures—embody a challenge to scientistic writing and demand an intimate and emotive rather than a distant and objective engagement with the text. This practice whereby the subjective presence of the author calls for alternative forms of representation has stimulated an exploration of new approaches to auto/biographical writing and representation. Likewise, in Mad Studies normative, "rational", scientistic forms have no value and, instead, self-narration, creativity, artistry, innovation and experimentation are embraced (see, e.g., Sweeney et al. 2009 and Smith in this volume). Indeed, since the challenges to the objectivity have revealed it to be nothing more than a fiction which shores up the binary positionings of power and authority which underpin patriarchy and psychiatry, it is an oxymoron to remain wedded to the norms/forms of writing and representation (e.g. "scientific reporting") which are inextricably bound up with it.

Thus, just as the autoethnography emerges from the auto/biographical imperative, then these two together inspire new forms of representation. As Stanley describes it, auto/biography has provided "a set of tools which can be differently used by writers and readers, each intent on their own aims and purposes" (1992: 244). Auto/Biographical tools have enabled the jettisoning of traditional, normative forms of academic writing and fuelled a surge of "new writing" in the social sciences (Denzin 2003: 118). Unleashed from the confines of maintaining "neutral" "factual" language and attempting to remove the self/author/subject from the work, feminist social science and Mad Studies have begun to take shape in first-person-based research projects (autoethnography, above), and in poetic, dramatic and literary formats. This creative outflow has not only repositioned the traditional power relationships between the knower and the known but also the hierarchical relations between the author as the all-knowing expert and the reader as the passive recipient of their wisdom. In creative texts, the author invites active readership, empathic engagement and embodied, experiential encounters with the author(s) as they re-present and re-embody their experiences—and the reader is left with thinking and feeling questions rather than a simple set of finite, "proven" truths (Inckle 2007).

Creative, arts-based and evocative forms of representation are essential to survivor research and Mad Studies. A two-dimensional text, stripped of subjectivity, emotion and the embodied and sensory registers can never capture or communicate experiences of madness and distress which are, by their very nature, often beyond words (Inckle 2017). Smith's chapter "[R]evolving Towards Mad: Spinning Away from the Psy/Spy-Complex Through Auto/ Biography" closes this part in precisely this way. Smith employs the poetic form throughout his chapter to both represent his experiences of madness and also to present his "academic argument" around the positioning of such knowledge. He traces his own madness along with the developments of firstly, a disability studies-oriented perspective, and latterly Mad Studies critique of sanism. Like Hillary, O'Farrell (and Rose) (above) his work highlights and challenges the ways in which "Because Mad people are crazy // they are by definition // unreliable knowers. // Their knowledge is literally unknown". In response, he describes his work as "deliberately and oppositionally defiantly" challenging to normative conventions. In doing so, he (deliberately) re-uses and re-orientates words which are used by psychiatry to indicate pathology and to invalidate the experiential knowledge, credibility and personhood of the mad (e.g. deliberate in the diagnosis of deliberate self-harm, and oppositional and defiant in the diagnosis of oppositional defiant disorder). This rebuttal of psychiatric values and meaning is also central to his evolving relationship to his own madness which he comes to recognise as both "a function of what society does to me" and yet also something which has intensified his life and experiences and which can be expressed and represented with beauty.

Overall then, Smith's non-normative experience, perspective and politics are embodied in the structure and content of his writing. The text is insight-full and meaning-full despite it being nonlinear, irrational, and subjective. Indeed, it is precisely this way of being and knowing, its vivaciousness, its richness, its intersubjective, provocative emotionality which elucidates the barrenness of the psychiatric project and the vacuousness of an objective perspective. Smith's chapter, then, exemplifies what happens when "conventional dichotomies or binaries are refused" (Stanley 1993: 44) and when auto/biographical tools are brought to the service of Mad Studies. Indeed, all of the chapters in this part serve such a purpose, highlighting how auto/ biographical ethics, politics and practices resonate with Mad Studies and Survivor Researchers' challenges to the oppressive power of psychiatric paradigms. Each of the chapters engages with both Mad Studies and auto/biography in multiple dimensions, only a few of which I have elucidated in this brief introduction. Here, I have highlighted some of the "classic" themes of auto/biographical practice: the identity and locatedness of the author and reader, the ethics and politics of the "auto/biographical 'I'", and the new forms of representation that these positions give rise to. I invite the reader to approach the following chapters with an open mind—and an open heart—ready to be moved into new dimensions of experience and understanding which, by their very existence, give lie to the dogmas of psychiatry which (attempt to) diagnose and constrain the lives expressed here.

References

Davis, K. (2018). Auto/Biography—Bringing in the 'I'. In H. Lutz, M. Schiebel, & E. Tuider (Eds.), *Handbuch Biographieforschung* (pp. 633–646). Frankfurt: Springer.

Denzin, N. K. (2003). *Performance Ethnography Critical Pedagogy and the Cultural Politics of Culture.* Thousand Oaks: Sage.

Faulkner, A. (2004). *The Ethics of Survivor Research.* York: Joseph Rowntree Foundation.

Faulkner, A. (2017). Survivor Research and Mad Studies: The Role and Value of Experiential Knowledge in Mental Health Research. *Disability and Society, 32*(4), 500–520

Faulkner, A., & Thomas, P. (2002). User-Led Research and Evidence-Based Medicine. *British Journal of Psychiatry, 180,* 1–3.

Gregorčič, M. (2018). Silenced Epistemologies: The Power of Testimonies and Critical Auto/Biographies for Contemporary Education. *Andragoška Spoznanja, 24*(1), 61–75.

Griffiths, V. (1990). Using Drama to Get at Gender. In L. Stanley (Ed.), *Feminist Praxis* (pp. 221–235). London: Routledge.

Inckle, K. (2007). *Writing on the Body? Thinking Through Gendered Embodiment and Marked Flesh.* Newcastle-upon-Tyne: Cambridge Scholars Publishing.

Inckle, K. (2017). *Safe with Self-Injury: A Practical Guide to Understanding, Responding and Harm-Reduction.* Monmouth: PCCS Books.

Kruger, S., & DasGupta, S. (2018). Embodiment in [Critical] Auto/Biography Studies. *a/b: Auto/Biography Studies, 33*(2), 483–487.

Landry, D. (2017). Survivor Research in Canada: 'Talking' Recovery, Resisting Psychiatry and Reclaiming Madness. *Disability and Society, 32*(9), 1437–1457.

Ramazangolu, C., & Holland, J. (2002). *Feminist Methodology: Challenges and Choices.* London: Sage.

Reinharz, S. (1992). *Feminist Methods in Social Research.* Oxford and New York: Oxford University Press.

Ribbens, J., & Edwards, R. (1998). *Feminist Dilemmas in Qualitative Research.* London: Sage.

Roberts, H. (1981). *Doing Feminist Research.* London: Routledge.

Rose, D. (2014). Patient and Public Involvement in Health Research: Ethical Imperative And/Or Radical Challenge? *Journal of Health Psychology, 19*(1), 149–158.

Russo, J. (2012). Survivor Controlled Research: A New Foundation for Thinking About Psychiatry and Mental Health. *Forum: Qualitative Social Research, 113*(1), art 8.

Stanley, L. (1990). Feminist Praxis and the Academic Mode of Production. In L. Stanley (Ed.), *Feminist Praxis* (pp. 3–19). London: Routledge.

Stanley, L. (1992). *The Auto/Biographical I.* Manchester: Manchester University Press.

Stanley, L. (1993). On Auto/Biography in Sociology. *Sociology, 27*(1), 41–52.

Sweeney, A., Beresford, P., Faulkner, A., Rose, D., & Nettle, M. (2009). *This Is Survivor Research.* Ross-on-Wye: PCCS Books.

Ussher, J. (1991). *Women's Madness: Misogyny or Mental Illness?* New York: Harvester Wheatsheaf.

14

Autist/Biography

Alyssa Hillary

Introduction

It may surprise you to learn that Autistic people write books, but we do. Similarly, it might surprise you to learn that we write autobiographies, but we do (Baggs 2013). As autism becomes better known, and as more autistic adults *know* we're autistic, more of us write autobiographically. "Where are all the autistic adults?" audiences ask, in good faith and bad. "Right here!" we answer, writing our stories.

However, these stories are typically read and interpreted by people accustomed to more normative autism narratives, which show the importance of autism more so than autistic people (Yergeau 2010). Autism itself must be introduced, typically including a reference to "theory of mind", which is used to assert that autistic people can not empathise, understand their own mental state, or develop identities (Harvey 2016; Yergeau and Huebner 2017). Our narratives are then assessed diagnostically, with searches for specific symptoms used to determine just how autistic we really are (Happé 1991).

That's not how auto/biography studies usually works, and I'd like to see us do something else. We can centre the autistic writers, discussing representation, expertise, and flipping the script. We can throw poetry into the

A. Hillary (✉)
University of Rhode Island, Kingston, RI, USA

© The Author(s) 2020
J. M. Parsons and A. Chappell (eds.), *The Palgrave Handbook of Auto/Biography*,
https://doi.org/10.1007/978-3-030-31974-8_14

mix—I've broken up my own piece, "Monsters in the Mirror", including stanzas throughout this chapter. We don't *have* to be bound by what's been done before.

This is the point where I have a confession. That one famous autistic autobiography you've heard of? I probably haven't read it. I own copies of *Emergence: Labeled Autistic* (Grandin 1996) and *Born on a Blue Day* (Tammet 2006), the two most commonly recommended to me. I haven't read them. They're staring down at me as I write. But maybe, since the point of this chapter is *avoiding* typical readings of Autist/biography, I'll keep skipping the expected sources. Sorry, Dr. Grandin. Sorry, Daniel.

A History of Autist/Biography

Thirteen years ago, Rose (2005) compiled a history of autistic autobiography in English, finding 54 books by 42 authors, and coining the term "autie-ethnography". Grace calls much the same practice "autistethnography" (2013). I prefer "autist" to "autie", which feels diminutive, but I also like having punctuation to break up the word. Mostly, though, I want to respect the language choices of the Autistic authors I cite. Regardless of word choice, disability experiences matter in our autobiographies, so we can consider them as autoethnographic accounts (Couser 2009). We're writing about our experiences *as Autistic people* and about realisations based on those experiences (Ellis et al. 2011). We reference our communities or how reading each other's experiences helped us understand our own (Rose 2005). I resemble this remark! I have an official diagnosis, but I first recognised my own autism from a story about an autistic child who sounded like me.

Of course, these books are not the only auto/biographical practice (Stanley 2000), and so autistic autobiography, sometimes called autie-biography (Couser 2009), is not all of Autist/biographical practice. While Rose restricts her 2005 study to autobiographies proper, she notes the importance of anthologies containing autistic personal narratives and "the myriad of life writing available in other media, be it the internet, art, music, animation or oral testimony" (Rose 2005: 2). I will cite our Internet presence, because far more autistic people write Autist/biographical narratives, discuss disability and representation, and generally have ideas I want to talk about than get publishing contracts or peer-reviewed publications. And even those of us who do both those things? Some of us (like me) still write online. Blogs tend to be more accessible, both in terms of how they're written and in terms of paying money to read things. Not everyone has a university affiliation or the money to subscribe to journals individually. If we want autistic people leading conversations about autism, we have to have those conversations in places we can get at, and academic publications don't always fit that bill.

Common Interpretations of Autist/Biography

Autist/Biography isn't interpreted in a vacuum. Interpreters who have heard of autism or read typical autism essays are influenced by the norms of autism writing. The typical autism essay starts with statistics—how many of us are there and how much does it cost. It defines what autism is, including diagnostic criteria, common stereotypes, or both (Yergeau 2010). Even auto/biography scholars aiming to present autism through our perspectives provide these typical definitions (Vuletic and Ferrari 2005). I'm not going to. Typical autism essays ensure readers understand why *autism* is important, but showing why *autistic people* matter is optional and often neglected (Yergeau 2010). So I'll neglect the standard right back. If you really want criteria, read the DSM or the ICD. I'd rather read the humans these texts diagnose and ignore.

Theory of Mind

Interpretations of all things autistic have been heavily influenced by something called *theory of mind*. People are said to have a theory of mind if they can infer the mental states of others—and themselves. The term originated with the question, "Does the chimpanzee have a theory of mind?" (Premack and Woodruff 1978). These scientists said yes. Seven years later, Simon Baron-Cohen, Alan M. Leslie, and Uta Frith asked the same about autistic children (1985). *They* said no.

Both assertions have since been qualified: Chimpanzees struggle with some parts of this nebulous skill (Call and Tomasello 2008), and autistic people usually get better at it as we get older. We don't always have more trouble with it than neurotypicals do (Scheeren et al. 2013). We've also questioned the theory of mind tests (Emma et al. 2015). For example, tests to determine our ability to realise that someone else has incorrect information use *complicated* language constructs, and we have language disabilities (Harvey 2016). Besides, if I were unable to infer anything about what my readers know, I wouldn't know to introduce theory of mind!

These qualifications haven't prevented theory of mind from being treated as a "core deficit" of autism. Philosophers discussing theory of mind continue to assert autism "as an inability to understand other minds and a corresponding inability to genuinely empathise" (Yergeau and Huebner 2017: 273). Rhetoricians do the same: "Rhetoric is about audience and autism is not" (Yergeau 2013). This causes problems.

Can autistic people have identities? Not if you believe that our "core deficit" is in theory of mind. Sam Harvey puts together the disturbing logic on identity formation and theory of mind:

1. You need to know what other people are thinking to develop an identity (Erikson)
2. You need to have a theory of mind to know what other people are thinking (Baron-Cohen, Frith, and Leslie)
3. Autistic people do not have a theory of mind (Baron-Cohen, Frith, and Leslie)
4. Therefore, Autistics cannot develop an identity because they do not have a theory of mind (2016: 49).

So, we don't get identities. That's going to make it tricky to write autobiographies. Maybe that's why we're expected to write "textbooks, which happen to be about ourselves", rather than autobiographies as they are usually understood (Baggs 2003). The problems continue. Simon Baron-Cohen asks if autistic children have a theory of mind and says *no* (1985), then calls theory of mind part of what makes us human (1997).

> In other words: The whole point of theory of mind is that autistic people do not have it.
> In other words: The whole point of theory of mind is that humans do have it.
> In other words: The whole point of theory of mind is that autistics are not human. (Yergeau 2013)

Sure, this is a bit subtler than Lovaas, the pioneer of applied behavioural analysis, the supposed gold standard therapy for autistic children. He straight up *said* we weren't people (Chance 1974). I'm not convinced that helps—Baron-Cohen's subtlety adds plausible deniability without changing the denial of our humanity. Theory of mind means we don't get to be people.

Autistic Autobiography as Anomaly

> In 1986, a quite extraordinary, unprecedented, and, in a way, unthinkable book was published, Temple Grandin's *Emergence: Labeled Autistic*. Unprecedented because there had never before been an "inside narrative" of autism; unthinkable because it had been medical dogma for forty years or more that there *was* no "inside," no inner life, in the autistic, or that if there was it would be forever denied access or expression; extraordinary because of its extreme (and strange) directness and clarity. (Sacks 2006: xiii)

Despite the quantity of auto/biographical writing Rose discussed in 2005, Autist/biographical writing is often treated as rare or unique. Magazines call *The Reason I Jump* (Higashida 2013) rare for its inside, first-hand description of autism. *Carly's Voice* (Fleischmann and Fleischmann 2012) is called one of the first first-hand accounts of the challenges of living with autism. Tammet's *Born on a Blue Day* (2006) is supposed to be virtually unique, because the author can describe what's happening in his own head. Grandin's *Emergence* really was one of the first autistic autobiographies published when it first came out in 1985, so it makes sense for her writing to have been treated as unique or unusual, but *why* are we still calling each new autistic autobiography unique or nearly so, 20+ years later?

I look at the conclusions drawn from theory of mind. If autistic people aren't human, and if we don't form identities, then clearly whatever Autist/biographical texts we manage to produce must be anomalies. Is each individual Autist/biography considered an anomaly in order to avoid challenging the idea that autistic people can't write autobiography? To avoid having to challenge other common assumptions about autism? Or maybe both?

If each individual Autist/biography is taken as an anomaly, then each is written by *one* exceptional person, so what they have to say doesn't generalise. If you've met one autistic person, you've met one autistic person, after all. This is tautologically true. Reading Temple Grandin's autobiographical work would tell me quite a bit about Temple Grandin (1996, 2006), and less about autism in general. The same goes for David Miedzianik (1986), Donna Williams (1992), and any other single person whose autobiographical work I could read. And if each one is taken as an anomaly, I don't need to make connections, do I? The text is just a curiosity. This seems a clever way to ignore patterns: demand each individual narrative generalise to the whole, as an inside look at *autism* rather than *an autistic person*, when we wouldn't demand the same of a neurotypical autobiographer (Hacking 2009). Grandin is supposed to be an inside view of autism, but she thinks in pictures, and I don't. This part of her narrative doesn't apply to me, and I'm autistic too, so her work isn't an inside view of all autism. But my experiences as an autistic person with no minds eye at all won't apply to her, so anything I write won't be an inside view of all autism. No one's work can be, which lets readers dismiss each isolated autobiography when autistic people inevitably fail to be a monolith. Rinse and repeat. The text is just a curiosity.

> Monsters have no reflections in the mirror,
> Is this who you want us to be?
> Invisible, unreal, if extant ignored,
> Till we learn to reflect your kind back.[1]

Autistic Autobiography as a Diagnostic Document

Presented with autobiographical writing by autistic adults, some researchers choose to learn what they can—about our autism, not about us. In conversations about autism, "experts" usually means ableist non-autistic researchers, to the extent that autistic people who know quite a bit about autism may not want to identify as "autism experts" (Grace 2012). I don't usually call myself an autism expert, and calling myself one wouldn't grant me the power in autism conversations the non-autistic experts get. Against a background where autistic people are, by and large, assumed not to even have an inner life, let alone the ability to describe it, Francisca Happé, among the first prominent non-autistic autism researchers to examine autistic autobiographies, is initially surprised by the apparent normality of Temple Grandin's story, finding her work "surprisingly well written" (Happé 1991: 209). However, she notes it odd that readers do *not* find descriptions of the autistic traits which must have been present for Grandin to have been referred to clinicians or labelled as autistic. Where is the diagnostic information she seeks from Grandin's text? A reviewer of Donna William's (1992) first autobiography makes a similar comment: he initially wanted to see more description of autism (Bass 2016). We're not expected to write autobiographies, but rather textbooks, which happen to be about ourselves (Baggs 2003). It's not enough to tell readers who *we* are: we must tell them what *autism* is, too.

---

[1]"Monsters in the Mirror", the poem I won first prize for at Autistic Pride Reading 2018, appears stanza-by-stanza at the beginnings or endings of some sections. I didn't realize festival meant competition until the organizers told me I'd won. Oops for the win?

Not that explaining our neurotype will save us. If we write about autism as we understand it, but our ideas don't line up with common expert opinions, then our judgement is still called into question (Baggs 2003). Grandin pays attention to cognitive styles and sensory differences in her discussion of autism, and Happé (1991) finds this odd—why is her focus not on social difficulties?

Discussing social difficulties may not be enough, either. I'll talk about social difficulties, but I like to think of communication between autistic people and non-autistic people as resembling cross-cultural communication. Prahlad (2017), a black autistic man, notes that with white people, his social misunderstandings could relate to Asperger's or race, and it's usually *both*. Studying in China, I got to watch the *same* conversation about 直接 (directness or bluntness, approximately) and 委婉 (indirectness or subtlety) that I heard as an autistic person in the USA. This time, my part was played by my neurotypical American classmates, whose ideas of 委婉 communication were still "太 (too) 直接!" for our academic director. If you translated their conversation into English, it matched what I heard from counsellors and psychologists trying to "fix" my social skills (Hillary 2018). I kept quiet as I watched, having no illusion that I could contribute any suggestions 委婉 enough for our academic director. After class, I told her about my observations, yet she denied holding the same role in two plays. She never explicitly said my autism was the reason I couldn't understand the supposed difference, but she also never said what the difference was. It's implied; how dare I conceptualise my social difficulties as cultural without dependence on my clearly impaired theory of mind?

So, let's read Autist/biography for discussion of impairments, shall we? Happé (1991) certainly does. Grandin, like many autistic people, has sensory needs that don't match neurotypical expectations. She designed a squeeze machine as a source of controlled deep pressure, to meet one of those needs. She discusses this squeeze machine several times in her work. Happé (1991) thinks Grandin's discussion of the squeeze machine is noteworthy, because of the difficulties with touch that prompted her to design the machine, and because, unlike her teachers and family, Grandin does not feel a "perhaps irrational, but nonetheless intuitive, unease" about the machine (Happé 1991: 211). Are neurotypical intuitions, then, the baseline for all intuitions? I think a squeeze machine sounds like a *great* idea, though a friend of mine who tried it says Grandin's doesn't squeeze hard enough.

Happé says Grandin perseverates on the squeeze machine, returning to it again and again. Her use of the same words and phrases again and again, to make the same point in different contexts, too, is called perseveration

(Happé 1991). Dr. Melanie Yergeau (2013) points out the same pattern in her own writing: she explicitly *hopes* to engage her audience perseveratively and echolalically, repeating her topics and phrases. And I have some 15 different posts on my blog making a single main point: I'm an Autistic person, not a person with autism. I respect people's right to decide how they want to refer to their neurological wiring, and I *will* have that same respect (Hillary, n.d.). When will I learn to let it rest? (When will parents and professionals learn to let me say I'm Autistic? Who is perseverating, now?)

Maybe the diagnostic discussion is about speech abilities. Sure, I might be trying to tell you about what sorts of considerations are important when I choose alternative communication methods as a teacher who can't always speak (Hillary and Harvey 2018). I might be trying to tell you what it's like to be in a class *about* augmentative and alternative communication (AAC), the umbrella term for communication tools and strategies people use when speech is either unavailable or insufficient to meet their needs, while using AAC part-time myself. Or I might be trying to give advice about what *you* can do if and when you have a student, classmate, or colleague who uses AAC (Hillary 2017). But do we care what my point was if we're reading for impairment?

No. In this reading, we want to know the particulars of my speech differences and how well they match the speech differences you expect from your working definitions of disorder. I can't always speak. That's the important bit, here. Will you diagnose me with selective mutism? Would it matter if I explained, point by diagnostic point, why selective mutism *doesn't* describe my intermittent speech (Sparrow 2017), where sometimes I can talk and sometimes I can't? I can explain. Selective mutism is a consistent failure to speak in certain environments (American Psychiatric Association 2013), and there is no environment where I am *consistently* unable to speak. There are environments where, 90% of the time or more, I'll be able to speak, and there are other environments where I'll only be able to speak about half the time. Selective mutism is also classified as an anxiety disorder (American Psychiatric Association 2013), and my anxiety barely correlates with my ability to speak. Would it matter if two psychologists who actually saw me agreed selective mutism isn't an appropriate description? We're reading for impairment, and I can't always speak.

Not only can anything we say be used to prove impairment, but what we *don't* say can also be used diagnostically. Happé (1991) questions Grandin's awareness of what readers might think because she doesn't provide excuses or show remorse for wrecking her teachers garden and lying about who did it, even as she says pulling off the lie required social understanding.

When Yergeau (2013) tells us about her involuntary commitment to the psychiatric ward of her university hospital in her second week as a new faculty member, she never actually says *why* she was committed. She does, however, consciously note that failing to share the excuse given for her commitment could be read as a failure in her theory of mind.

We can look at the meta-characteristics of my writing, too. I don't focus on the fact that I can't always speak. Since that's what the diagnostic reader wants to know about, this must mean I lack theory of mind. The particulars of my speech differences are what *they* want to know and I have failed to read my audience. Never mind that autism professionals weren't my intended audience. I have no illusions that they'll listen, so I don't write for them. I'm sure specifically *trying* to do something different and choosing an audience that might listen is a failure of my theory of mind too, somehow.

Back to perseveration! Just like the person reading for impairment notes Grandin's "perseveration" on the squeeze machine or Yergeau's "perseveration" on theory of mind, a reader could say I "perseverate" on AAC. Who cares that I focus on AAC for a reason? Who cares that I know I'm the first student at my university to get AAC use as an accommodation? Who cares that most people don't think of AAC as an option for autistic people who can speak? Who cares that I think AAC could help other people like me? The reader focusing on impairment doesn't care what my reasons are—repetition means perseveration. (Is that a failure in the reader's theory of mind, or does it only count when someone fails to intuit what a neurotypical thinks?)

> Monsters have no reflections in the mirror,
> For we're made as a mirror to you.
> Find what you are from all we are not,
> Leave only lacking to us.

Autistic Autobiography and Functioning (or Faking): Not Like My Child/Student

If autist/biography is being read diagnostically, in search of autistic "symptoms", then what happens when a given trait does not appear in the text? Or even if it does, what happens if the person doesn't demonstrate it to the extent a reader wants to see? What happens if someone shows abilities the reader believes (or, in bad faith, claims to believe) are always dependent upon some other skill the writer lacks? The author must be at fault, whether it's our judgement or the "extent" of our autism that is questioned (Baggs 2003).

When the extent to which we are truly autistic is questioned, professionals assign functioning levels to our autobiographies. Happé (1991) calls the autistic autobiographers she reads "able autistics" or "Asperger syndrome adults". She uses the terms interchangeably, applying them to "autistic individuals with fluid language and normal intelligence" (Happé 1991: 207). Is my language still fluid when it's not spoken? How are we defining intelligence? Does Happé know how thoroughly defining and testing intelligence is tied to eugenics (Ryan 1997)? Would she care? Probably not. (I care.)

Reading like Happé (1991), Grandin's writing reveals a remarkably intelligent and articulate woman. Would Happé make this comment about a non-autistic writer? Probably not, but we need to rate autistic people's functioning. David Miedzianik's autobiography shows some awareness of what his readers do and don't already know—some *theory of mind*, that is. In some ways, Happé (1991) says that makes him the least autistic of the three authors. She's explicitly saying some writers are more autistic than others.

Happé (1991) compares the authors she reads to autistic people in general, too. The authors show some insights into their own thought processes, which surprises her because professionals assume we lack an inner life, and that even if we have one, we can't understand or articulate it (Sacks 2006). However, this is only taken as evidence that particularly *able* autistic people can understand their own inner experiences (Happé 1991). Whatever insights Happé gains, she limits them explicitly. Adults who can write about their experiences must be inherently different in their autism from children who presumably can't understand the experiences they aren't writing about. They're articulate, so you don't have to listen (Bascom 2011).

As for me? I'm in graduate school, studying for a Ph.D. in neuroscience. I have an MS in maths and a job teaching it. I'm not like your child (except when I am). I'm also not four or five or six. Nor am I much like I was at four or five or six, or even ten or twelve. I *shouldn't* be just like your child. And I'm not. I might have met your daughter in the self-contained classroom, when some members of my lab used smartwatches to collect data from children with autism. The first time the public announcement system turned on, there was a terrible noise. I covered my ears. The second time, I bit my lip. The third time, I almost fell over. Your daughter kept working like nothing was wrong. I'm not like her. Learning to hide my reactions was never my highest priority. I sin openly "against the holy gods of ABA and

Ivar Lovaas,[2] and every other methodology that aimed to extinguish autism" (Gardiner 2017: 12). She doesn't get to. That leaves me with the energy to devote to academics, which proves I'm not like her. I get to be a successful *autistic person*, not a poor imitation of a neurotypical person. My path to success is exactly the opposite of the path enforced when apparent neurotypicality is the optimal outcome (Hillary 2019).

All this is just the ranking of perceived functioning based on *given* information. Remember that we can be punished for our omissions. Not only can our audience awareness and judgement be called into question for what we don't say, but if we decide not to say enough about "symptoms" or "impairments", *our autism itself can be called into question for what we don't say* (Baggs 2003)—never mind that admitting to certain "symptoms" isn't safe. Yergeau (2013) never tells us why she was involuntarily committed— maybe someone who found out would try to do it again. But if we don't say it for the public eye, it doesn't exist, and we're not autistic (enough).

The same goes if, in order to survive, we've worked to pass as well as we can. It's assumed that if we can hold a job and do some things that others do, we must be normal; if we're not children, then we can't be autistic. Now we're not just unlike your child, unlike your student, unlike your patient. If we don't match the popular idea,

> Autism=(white male-presenting) toddler wearing a Thomas the Train t-shirt; autism=(white male-presenting) quirky teen gamer; autism=(white male-presenting) geeky computer programmer; autism=(white male-presenting) adult rocking and staring off into space … a ready scapegoat for all of their caregiver's life disappointments; (Onaiwu 2017a: xv),

then we're not really autistic. Not just in the eyes of the public, who would never have guessed, but sometimes even our own doctors, who "don't know what it took for [us] to get here" (Ellis 2017: 24). We are, instead, liars. Does my presence in graduate school mean I'm faking the times I cannot speak and need to type instead? What about my sometimes-functional speech? Or a cyclic statement that I'm not really autistic, so my speech

---

[2]ABA, or applied behavioural analysis, is typically billed as the "gold standard" way of treating autism, with the claim that it will make 47% of students indistinguishable from their peers (Lovaas 1987). ABA therapists tend not to like it when we point out its shared roots with conversion therapy (Rekers and Lovaas 1974), but the same researchers tried the same techniques on both groups, and we're starting to get academic evidence that autistic people get PTSD from our version of the treatment, too (Kupferstein 2018).

issues are fake, so I'm not really autistic (Hillary 2013)? Is my lab mate's knowledge of *which* table to look under if they want to find me in the lab irrelevant in the face of my being part of a lab?

Self-Narrating Zoo Exhibits

> If you are asking someone else to share personal information about himself, only for the purpose of educating you and without reciprocal sharing on your part, this is what I have often referred to as a "self-narrating zoo exhibit". (Sinclair, quoted in Ellermann, n.d.)

Autistic communities use the phrase "self-narrating zoo" for one way autistic narratives are exploited. Observers demand very personal information about us, generally without reciprocal sharing, and often in the Q and A for presentations on *completely different topics*. A friend of mine starts presentations with a social story for the audience: we don't get physically violent over what she's saying, and we don't ask about her poop (Asasumasu 2017). There's seriously a (neurotypical) parent and professional obsession with autistic poop (Yergeau 2018). Why are y'all asking about this? I don't care this much about my faeces, and I'm a bit creeped out if you do!

Being expected to share private details, without reciprocity, isn't unique to autism. Any time there's a power gradient, people may be expected to share otherwise private details about their lives, and it can become a tiresome task (Stanley 2000). "Acceptable Autistics" are expected to have our words turn tricks on why we act as we do "until the tape runs out" (Bascom 2011). If we're going to insist on speaking, parents and professionals will parade us at conferences and speaker series that pay their neurotypical "expert" speakers real honoraria, while we're often lucky to find our transportation costs reimbursed (Costa et al. 2012).

We're asked to share stories of how we overcame our disabilities. (We're not asked to question what overcoming or recovery would mean. I do it anyways.) We are asked to share how some intervention or other, such as taking our medications, listening to professionals, and generally being a "good patient" saved our lives or let us recover (Costa et al. 2012). Temple Grandin will tell us of the success of her intensive therapy as a child, and her first book is called *Emergence* (1996). The idea of recovery or overcoming is even in the title. Maybe that's why the cure and recovery folks like to bring her to speak, rather than someone who'd tell BCBAs to fuck off and let autistic kids be awesome *autistic* kids. They don't want me throwing myself into walls as an act of protest against indistinguishability and the elimination of autism as the optimal outcome. And yes, I've done that (Hillary 2019).

> Monsters have no reflections in the mirror,
> Illusionists fuelling gas lanterns,
> Brighten their words, darken our worlds,
> Show deception to our eyes.

Theory of Mind Returns

Theory of mind never really left. It backs up treating Autist/biographies as ignorable anomalies. A famous, but unnamed autism researcher, tells students who just found *Thinking in Pictures* (a Dr. Grandin [2006] book I know of, but haven't actually read),

> That's fun and interesting, but it won't tell you anything. You remember what we learned about Theory of Mind, don't you? By definition, a person with autism does not know what it means 'for life to be like something for someone,' so she cannot possibly get the concept of what it is like to be herself. (Grace 2012: 142)

Each story is an outlier, and even if the ability to write such a story were common, it wouldn't matter.

And the story may not even be true! Under normal (neurotypical) circumstances, autobiographers agree to tell the truth as they understand it and readers look for that truth (Watson 1999). If a reader's belief that we all lack theory of mind makes them assume Autist/biographers can't understand what it's like to be ourselves, our understood truth becomes irrelevant and the agreement fails.

Happé (1991) directly questions one of Grandin's stories because it would require a strong understanding of other's minds, asking how much of this story is Grandin's own and how much is added or changed by her co-author. She similarly casts doubt on David Miedzianik's ownership of his writing: "The question of parroting cannot, of course, be ruled out – but if David's remarks are his own they are surprising and challenging" (Happé 1991: 217). Is our writing even ours?

Then, when we agree to narrate our own zoo exhibits, the conversation is one-sided. We are self-absorbed, providing all sorts of information about *ourselves* but not asking similar questions in return. Not that you'd answer them, if we did! Clearly, this is evidence that we don't think of other people as *people*, because we lack theory of mind. If we do ask in return, we are criticised for not realising just how private these topics are. Even simply answering could "reveal" this lack of understanding, which is also a sign that we lack theory of mind.

Even if we're saying what professionals want to hear, that just means we're taking their autism theories unquestioned (Baggs 2003), supporting our supposed permanent lack of theory of mind, rather than discussing the difficulties just about everyone has understanding people who are very different from themselves. Not questioning professional perceptions means not considering the cultural differences that intertwine with our communication differences (Hillary 2018; Milton 2014; Prahlad 2017). Our theory of mind can't exist, so in some very important ways, neither can we.

> Monsters have no reflections in the mirror,
> No images prove who we are,
> Hide us from the world, say we are not there,
> Convince us of our non-existence.

How Else Could We Read Autist/Biography?

Clearly, we've got a problem. Standard ways of viewing and reading autism narratives mean we do not get to exist as people, which would make it hard to write autobiographies. So, if we cannot write auto/biographies, does it even make sense to talk about Autist/biography as an object of study? If we want Autist/biography to be a sensible concept, we're going to need to sit outside these standard readings.

Autistic People Writing Ourselves Reflected, or Reading for Representation

> Monsters have no reflections in the mirror,
> No view through the looking glass.
> Where are we from, and where are we going?
> Who imagines what we could be?

We write where we've been, and *we* imagine what we could be, where we could go. In an exercise of collective meaning-making, Autistic people write ourselves. This is especially important for those of us who don't, or only rarely, see ourselves in the public's ideas of autism, because we're not white and male-presenting, nor are we Temple Grandin. So: We're not alone. We exist. It's been argued that rather than merely recording their lives, women write themselves into existence (Watson 1999), and I say autistic people do the same.

Rather than merely recording our history, we're creating the language and concepts needed to describe autistic experiences (Hacking 2009). It's interactive. We don't just write for neurotypical audiences—we write for each other, too. Cynthia Kim, an Autistic blogger, is explicit in selecting her autistic, or possibly autistic, audience in *I Think I Might Be Autistic: A Guide to Autism Spectrum Diagnosis and Self-Discovery for Adults* (2013). Kim mixes advice for adults who think they might be autistic, perhaps because they've recognised themselves in other Autist/biographical writings, with an account of her own journey of recognition and diagnosis (2013). Not only does she combine her own experiences with information for others, reflecting on both, but she addresses her work to others in her former situation. Here is the collective meaning-making that makes Autistic autobiography into autie-*ethnography* (Rose 2005).

And once we've written, possibly for each other and quite probably building off what's been written before, we read each other's narratives. When *I* read Autist/biography, I look for the reflections of myself I may not find elsewhere. Temple Grandin is not the only autistic person to have sensory processing differences, sometimes including synaesthesia, nor is she the only one to write about them. I have. *Aquamarine 5*, an anthology of Autistic writing, is named for one contributor's synaesthetic association between the colour and the number (Baggs 2013). Tammet's *Born on a Blue Day* (2006) is another synaesthetic title. My synaesthesia connects sounds to relative temperatures, so I, too, have crossed sensory wiring. Prahlad tells us how he "can't stop hearing all the conversations around [him], or the patterns of silverware striking glasses and plates" (2017: 7). What would Happé have said about that? I'm happy enough not to find out—I'd rather recognise a piece of my own experience in Prahlad's.

In some ways, reading for representation resembles reading Autist/biography diagnostically. After all, reading other autistic people's autobiographical writing is sometimes how we recognise that *we* are autistic (Rose 2005). We must be recognising shared autistic traits in those narratives to do so. Consider my examples above. Couldn't those be interpreted diagnostically? I know Happé (1991) thought even Grandin's decision to discuss sensory processing issues was some sort of autistic symptom.

Reading for representation is also worlds apart from diagnostic readings. In diagnostic readings, readers search for evidence of the writer's autism, as a checklist of impairments. When seeking reflections of ourselves, the writer's neurotype isn't in question. (The reader's might be.) We're looking for connections and confirmations of our own perceptions. Isn't that part of how most people read autobiography (Watson 1999)? If autism is supposed to mean an absence of connection to others, then an autistic audience reading for connections inherently challenges what autism is supposed to be. Simply treating Autist/biography like the rest of auto/biography can challenge dominant ideas of autism as an exceptional lack of connection, empathy, and humanity.

It is no accident that my first alternative for reading Autist/biographies centres autistic readers. Common (mis)interpretations of Autist/biography centre neurotypical readers, so the biggest shift I can think of is to centre the autistic reader first. Doing so recognises an Autistic sociality, even if we're not following the same rules the neurotypicals do. We interact with each other, and it's real.

Autistic Expertise

Here, too, like reading for representation, I'm centring autistic people. It's just the writers, now, and the fact that we can know things, both about ourselves by default and autism generally if we work for it. Autistic expertise is, in fact, a thing (Milton 2014). Go ahead! Learn from us! Just…learn what we're actually teaching, instead of what deficits you think our lives/biographies imply.

We argue against theory of mind discourse because it means we don't get to have identities (Harvey 2016) or even be human (Yergeau 2013). We talk about how neurotypicals aren't any better at guessing our thoughts than we are at guessing theirs but *we* learned to guess *their* intentions to survive. We introduce alternative hypotheses to explain social difficulties, too. Milton (2014) talks about a "double empathy problem" where autistic and non-autistic people can *mutually* misunderstand each other, and he discusses interactions with Autistic cultures. I use the language of cross-cultural communication, reminded of my experiences in China (Hillary 2018). You could consider our hypotheses.

We want you to know that AAC can make a huge difference for autistic people, even if we can speak. A respected researcher in autism and AAC estimates that 10–25% of autistic people will require AAC, due to not having "functional speech" (Mirenda 2013). But "functional speech" is a low bar—it requires a few words or phrases. We might have more to say than we can use mouth sounds to tell you. Typing can help us process what we're thinking, in a way that speaking does not (Wayman and Rothschild 2018). It does that for me.

We have been saying for a long time that we are interested in having friends, but do not always know how to (Grace 2012), and that other people often do not want to be friends with *us*. We will also tell you Autistic ways of socialising exist and that we can connect with each other. Formal examinations of Autistic sociality (Heasman and Gillespie 2018) and experimental confirmation of others judging us negatively (Sasson et al. 2017) are recent. These experiments would not have been *hard* to do earlier, but doing so required scientists to think Autistic hypotheses were worth testing.

Turnabout's Fair Play

> Monsters have no reflections in the mirror,
> That's monstrosity defined.
> But what of the makers, what of the designers?
> They choose what mirrors may find.

Some Autist/biographical writers point out how neurotypical society, as a whole, fails on the same counts we are accused of failing on. But, can you read my body language and guess what I'm thinking? You just might lack a theory of my mind. It's not just Autist/biographical writers who do this, really. The Institute for the Study of the Neurologically Typical (Muskie 2002) is one example: rather than defining autism in terms of how it lacks aspects of neurotypicality, neurotypicality is instead defined (as a syndrome, no less!) in terms of how it lacks aspects of autism. And if you don't like being defined by your deficits? Turnabout's fair play, so maybe don't do that to us. Until then, let's play.

Tell us we have no theory of mind. *Theory of whose mind*, we ask (Harvey 2016; Yergeau 2013). You see, as good as people might think they are at guessing the intentions and inner experiences of others, they're pretty bad at guessing the intentions of those significantly unlike them (Hutto 2012). This applies to non-autistic people assuming they know what autistic people are thinking or feeling—or assuming they know we *aren't* thinking or feeling. Who lacks theory of whose mind, here?

Tell us autistic children do not want friends, because they do not act as *you* would if you wanted friends? It is time to remind you that you are not, in fact, a mind reader. It is possible they do not know *how* to make friends with neurotypical children (Grace 2012). But maybe they have learned that neurotypicals judge us quickly on how we move, how we speak (Sasson et al. 2017) and decide that trying to make friends with people who do not want to be friends with us is not worth it. Who does not want friends, here?

Tell us we need to walk in the shoes of parents and professionals who have the power and/or money to throw around in autism-land? Well, let us remind you that we have shoes (Asasumasu 2013). Have you ever walked in them? If not, who needs to take a new pair of shoes for a spin here?

Tell us we are inconsiderate, when we are late coming in from recess because we are getting junk out of the bottoms of our shoes. *You* did not hear the janitor talking about how much his back hurts and try to make less work for him by cleaning your shoes, that was Lydia (Wayman and Rothschild 2018). You track your mud all over the place. Who is inconsiderate, here?

Tell us we are non-compliant. Fun fact: being unable to do something is not, in fact, "a behaviour", nor is it wilfully refusing to do it, nor whatever else you might want to call it to avoid recognising disability (Asasumasu 2013). But is it really just us? The people in charge don't always follow their own rules. Who's non-compliant, here (Hillary 2016)?

Tell us we are rigid. I say I am Autistic, but if someone calls themself a person with autism, I am not going to argue with them. Autism parents who always, *always* use "children with autism" tell me I am calling myself the wrong thing. Sometimes they ask, but usually, they just tell. Who is rigid, here?

Tell us we are perseverating. Yergeau (2018) points out the parent and professional preoccupation with autistic people and poop. *I* don't care that much about my poop, and Yergeau is more interested in the rhetorical implications of the neurotypical obsession with autistic faeces than with the faeces themselves. Are they just throwing shit at the wall to see that the literal case stuck? Who is perseverating, here?

Every single accusation levelled against autistic people, we can find examples of non-autistic people doing that exact thing to us. Their "preoccupation with social concerns, delusions of superiority, and obsession with conformity", as described in neurotypical syndrome (Muskie 2002), leads to their claiming autistic people alone are responsible for any misunderstandings between us. But it's *not* just us, and we've been showing you exactly how it is you, too.

Intentionally Politicised Narratives: Public Rhetoric

In 1999, Martha Watson published *Lives of Their Own: Rhetorical Dimensions in Autobiographies of Women Activists*. In the summer of 2018, I read it. She told me these women wrote their lives partly to preserve the records of their movements, as they were conscious of their own roles. They sought to show the growth of their movements through their life stories (Watson 1999). Similarly, Autistic life writing can be considered part of the record of the Autistic, neurodiversity, and broader disability rights movements. Just as the life stories of activist women complemented their more explicitly argumentative work, Autistic stories serve to complement more explicitly stated arguments.

In Autistethnographic writing, the two are explicitly combined. Here is the argument: Autistic people are human—why do we even need to argue this? Here is the life event: strap the author to a gurney, which is apparently more material than she is, and attribute her actions to her neurotype but never to *her*. "That's just her—autism talking" (Yergeau 2013). Her neurotype gets more agency as something that can cause actions than she does, because autistic people don't get to be human (Harvey 2016; Yergeau 2013) or have agency (Yergeau 2018). Here, in life details, are the effects of theory of mind theory on an Autistic professor of rhetoric, denied rhetoricity in favour of being a victim of her neurotype (Yergeau 2013). Here, in life detail, is one reason I *didn't* tell my students I'm Autistic for the first three semesters I taught—I'd like to count as a person who can say things and not have it taken as my autism talking, thanks. That's not an exaggeration for effect, by the way. That article was new when I started teaching in fall 2014, and it, along with the reactions my disclosure brought the year I studied in China, scared the shit out of me. Can I hide who I am from my work? I think it would be safer.

But when I need to argue, telling true stories has worked better for me than sticking to the theoretical. Establishing some sort of common ground and building identification can lead to some form of cooperation with the reader. If we advocate for controversial causes, we must work to craft persuasive and appealing stories (Watson 1999). Since we, apparently, write controversial statements, we need the help. I say apparently because some of these things shouldn't be controversial.

For example, I don't think it *should* be controversial to be against parents killing their kids. And yet, when disability comes into play, it suddenly is. Onaiwu, a Black Autistic mother, tells us autism is "a world where our killers can be showered with sympathy and compassion for having had to endure a life with us" (2017b: 30), and I've read enough articles and comment sections to know it is true. I have read the Disability Day of Mourning list, complete with the cause of death and the (often lack of) sentence for the killer, too many times to doubt the frequency with which the legal system also takes the stance that killing autistic people (and especially autistic people of colour) is acceptable. When we complain? We are told to walk in the shoes of the parents. It is never acknowledged that *we* have shoes. So, let us build some common ground, in the language that is used against us.

Sick of being told to walk in the shoes of these parents, one Autistic activist takes the shoes metaphor and runs with it. She provides readers with "an illustrated guide to most of the shoes [she remembers] walking in" (Asasumasu 2013). These literal shoes remind readers of Asasumasu's metaphorical shoes. Here they are! You can walk in them, identify with the person wearing them. Here is the common ground, taking the language and metaphor already in use so as to better convince readers (Watson 1999).

And then, among the shoe metaphors made literal, Asasumasu shares stories of mistreatment. Her kindergarten classmates were mean, and then meaner once they realise she could not tell them apart to tell on them. Here are the shoes she was wearing. She was locked in a locker while teachers watched, then suspended for kicking her way out of it. Here are the shoes she was wearing. A rock-climbing teacher refused to teach autistic students because he was certain we could not understand the risks involved. Here are the shoes she was wearing. Strangers told her, to her face, that they would have understood if her mother killed her, and her disability services office shrugs. Here are the shoes she was wearing (Asasumasu 2013).

The comments on Asasumasu's blog post tell me her rhetoric was effective. Readers are moved. I think Yergeau (2013) is effective, too, though it is harder to know how *other* readers reacted to a journal article without comments enabled. It affected me, certainly. The idea that autistic people can be intentionally rhetorical, in any form, requires challenging common ideas about autism (Yergeau 2018).

> Monsters have no reflections in the mirror,
> Now we set the record true:
> If your mirror refuses our worlds,
> That's on the mirror-maker—That's *you*.

(Not) Concluding

This is not the end. Subverting standard work on autism (on *autistic people*) takes ongoing work, just like it does for any marginalised group. Read the work of autistic people who do *not* match the standard media portrayals of autism: people who are not white and male-presenting, people who are neither geeky programmers nor scapegoats for the disappointments of those around us (Onaiwu 2017a). Consider connections between works from *several* autistic authors. Look for the themes you were taught autistic people could not comprehend that we weave into our narratives. You will find them, and you will find people, with identities and stories to tell. You do not need to follow the patterns of standard autism narratives.

References

American Psychiatric Association. (2013). Anxiety Disorders. In *Diagnostic and Statistical Manual of Mental Disorders: DSM 5*. Washington: Author. https://doi.org/10.1176/appi.books.9780890425596.dsm05.

Asasumasu, K. (2013, September 8). Here, Try on Some of My Shoes. *Radical Neurodivergence Speaking*. Available at http://timetolisten.blogspot.com/2013/09/here-try-on-some-of-my-shoes.html. Accessed 8 August 2018.

Asasumasu, K. (2017, October 21). *More Than Crumbs: Autistics Deserve More*. Autistics Present: A Symposium on Autistic Culture and Identity (For All), Bellevue, WA.

Baggs, A. (2003). The Validity of Autistic Opinions. *Autistics.org*. Available at http://web.archive.org/web/20160205063008/; http://archive.autistics.org/library/autopin.html. Accessed 15 May 2018.

Baggs, A. M. (2013). A Bibliography of Autistic Authors. *Autonomy, the Critical Journal of Interdisciplinary Autism Studies, 1*(2). Available at http://www.larry-arnold.net/Autonomy/index.php/autonomy/article/view/AR7.

Baron-Cohen, S. (1997). *Mindblindness: An Essay on Autism and Theory of Mind*. Cambridge: MIT Press.

Baron-Cohen, S., Leslie, A. M., & Frith, U. (1985). Does the Autistic Child Have a "Theory of Mind"? *Cognition, 21*(1), 37–46. https://doi.org/10.1016/0010-0277(85)90022-8.

Bascom, J. (2011, August 31). On Being Articulate. *Just Stimming*. Available at https://juststimming.wordpress.com/2011/08/31/on-being-articulate/. Accessed 18 June 2018.

Bass, C. (2016, July 30). Review of Nobody Nowhere the Extraordinary Autobiography of an Autistic by Donna Williams. *Ethical ELA*. Available at http://www.ethicalela.com/nobody-nowhere/. Accessed 23 August 2018.

Call, J., & Tomasello, M. (2008). Does the Chimpanzee Have a Theory of Mind? 30 Years Later. *Trends in Cognitive Sciences, 12*(5), 187–192. https://doi.org/10.1016/j.tics.2008.02.010.

Chance, P. (1974). A Conversation with Ivar Lovaas. *O. Ivar Lovaas Interview. Psychology Today, 7*(8), 76–80, 82–84.

Costa, L., Voronka, J., Landry, D., Reid, J., Mcfarlane, B., Reville, D., et al. (2012). "Recovering Our Stories": A Small Act of Resistance. *Studies in Social Justice, 6*(1), 85–101. https://doi.org/10.26522/ssj.v6i1.1070.

Couser, G. T. (2009). *Signifying Bodies: Disability in Contemporary Life Writing.* Ann Arbor: University of Michigan Press.

Ellermann, M. (n.d.). *Interview with Jim Sinclair.* Available at https://www.autism.se/RFA/uploads/nedladningsbara%20filer/Interview_with_Jim_Sinclair.pdf. Accessed 25 June 2018.

Ellis, E. P. (2017). Blood, Sweat, and Tears: On Assimilation. In L. Brown, E. Ashkenazy, & M. G. Onaiwu (Eds.), *All the Weight of Our Dreams: On Living Racialized Autism* (pp. 23–29). Lincoln: DragonBee Press.

Ellis, C., Adams, T. E., & Bochner, A. P. (2011). Autoethnography: An Overview. *Historical Social Research [Historische Sozialforschung]*, 273–290. https://doi.org/10.17169/fqs-12.1.1589.

Emma, Alexis, D., Asasumasu, K., Yergeau, M., & Grace, I. (2015, July 2). The "Reading The Mind In The Eyes" Test: A Collaborative Critique. *Lemon Peel.* Available at https://emmapretzel.wordpress.com/2015/07/02/the-reading-the-mind-in-the-eyes-test-a-collaborative-critique/. Accessed 8 August 2018.

Fleischmann, A., & Fleischmann, C. (2012). *Carly's Voice: Breaking Through Autism.* New York: Simon and Schuster.

Gardiner, F. (2017). A Letter to People at the Intersection of Autism and Race. In L. Brown, E. Ashkenazy, & M. G. Onaiwu (Eds.), *All the Weight of Our Dreams: On Living Racialized Autism* (pp. 11–18). Lincoln: DragonBee Press.

Grace, E. J. (2012). Autistic Community and Culture: Silent Hands No More. In J. Bascom (Ed.), *Loud Hands: Autistic People Speaking* (pp. 141–147). Washington, DC: The Autistic Press.

Grace, E. J. (2013). Autistethnography. In P. Smith (Ed.), *Both Sides of the Table: Autoethnographies of Educators Learning and Teaching With/in [Dis]ability* (pp. 89–101). New York: Peter Lang.

Grandin, T. (1996). *Emergence: Labeled Autistic* (Reissue ed.). New York: Warner Books.

Grandin, T. (2006). *Thinking in Pictures, Expanded Edition: My Life with Autism.* New York: Vintage.

Hacking, I. (2009). Autistic Autobiography. *Philosophical Transactions of the Royal Society of London B: Biological Sciences, 364*(1522), 1467–1473. https://doi.org/10.1098/rstb.2008.0329.

Happé, F. (1991). The Autobiographical Writings of Three Asperger Syndrome Adults: Problems of Interpretation and Implications for Theory. In U. Frith

(Ed.), *Autism and Asperger Syndrome* (pp. 207–242). Cambridge University Press. https://doi.org/10.1017/cbo9780511526770.007.

Harvey, S. T. (2016). *A Rhetorical Journey into Advocacy*. Masters thesis, St. Cloud State University. Available at https://repository.stcloudstate.edu/engl_etds/54/. Accessed 24 August 2018.

Heasman, B., & Gillespie, A. (2018). Neurodivergent Intersubjectivity: Distinctive Features of How Autistic People Create Shared Understanding. *Autism*. Online First. https://doi.org/10.1177/1362361318785172.

Higashida, N. (2013). *The Reason I Jump: The Inner Voice of a Thirteen-Year-Old Boy with Autism*. New York: Random House.

Hillary, A. (2013, March 13). Not Really Autistic. *Yes, That Too*. Available at https://yesthattoo.blogspot.com/2013/03/not-really-autistic.html. Accessed 20 August 2018.

Hillary, A. (2016). Who is Noncompliant Now? In N. I. Nicholson & M. S. Monje (Eds.), *The Spoon Knife Anthology: Thoughts on Compliance, Defiance, and Resistance* (pp. 140–150). Fort Worth, TX: NeuroQueer Books.

Hillary, A. (2017, October 22). Disabled in Grad School: Augmentative and Alternative Communication Awareness Month. *Gradhacker*. Available at https://www.insidehighered.com/blogs/gradhacker/disabled-grad-school-augmenta-tive-and-alternative-communication-awareness-month. Accessed 20 August 2018.

Hillary, A. (2018). Who Is Allowed? In A. Reichart & N. Walker (Eds.), *Spoon Knife 3: Incursions* (pp. 172–184). Fort Worth, TX: NeuroQueer Press.

Hillary, A. (2019). I am a Person Now: Autism, Indistinguishability, and (Non)-Optimal Outcome. In C. Bobel & S. Kwan (Eds.), *Body Battlegrounds: Transgressions, Tensions, and Transformations* (pp. 110–113). Nashville, TN: Vanderbilt University Press.

Hillary, A. (n.d.). Don't Call Me a Person With Autism. *Yes, That Too*. Available at http://yesthattoo.blogspot.com/p/dont-call-me-person-with-autism.html. Accessed 18 June 2018.

Hillary, A., & Harvey, S. (2018). Teaching with Augmentative and Alternative Communication. In M. Jeffress (Ed.), *International Perspectives on Teaching with Disability: Overcoming Obstacles and Enriching Lives* (pp. 219–234). New York: Routledge.

Hutto, D. D. (2012). *Folk Psychological Narratives: The Sociocultural Basis of Understanding Reasons*. Cambridge, MA: MIT Press.

Kim, C. (2013). *I Think I Might Be Autistic: A Guide to Autism Spectrum Disorder Diagnosis and Self-Discovery for Adults*. Narrow Gauge.

Kupferstein, H. (2018). Evidence of Increased PTSD Symptoms in Autistics Exposed to Applied Behavior Analysis. *Advances in Autism, 4*(1), 19–29. https://doi.org/10.1108/AIA-08-2017-0016.

Lovaas, O. I. (1987). Behavioral Treatment and Normal Educational and Intellectual Functioning in Young Autistic Children. *Journal of Consulting and Clinical Psychology, 55*(1), 3–9. https://doi.org/10.1037/0022-006X.55.1.3.

Miedzianik, D. (1986). *My Autobiography.* Nottingham: Childhood Developmental Unit, Nottingham University.

Milton, D. E. (2014). Autistic Expertise: A Critical Reflection on the Production of Knowledge in Autism Studies. *Autism, 18*(7), 794–802. https://doi.org/10.1177/1362361314525281.

Mirenda, P. (2013). Autism Spectrum Disorder: Past, Present, and Future. *SIG 12 Perspectives on Augmentative and Alternative Communication, 22*(3), 131–138. https://doi.org/10.1044/aac22.3.131.

Muskie. (2002, March 18). Institute for the Study of the Neurologically Typical. *Autistics.org.* Available at http://web.archive.org/web/20160510135505/http://isnt.autistics.org:80/. Accessed 24 August 2018.

Onaiwu, M. G. (2017a). Preface: Autistics of Color: We Exist … We Matter. In L. Brown, E. Ashkenazy, & M. G. Onaiwu (Eds.), *All the Weight of Our Dreams: On Living Racialized Autism* (pp. x–xxii). Lincoln: DragonBee Press.

Onaiwu, M. G. (2017b). Autism Defined: A Poem. In L. Brown, E. Ashkenazy, & M. G. Onaiwu (Eds.), *All the Weight of Our Dreams: On Living Racialized Autism* (pp. 30–32). Lincoln: DragonBee Press.

Prahlad, A. (2017). *The Secret Life of a Black Aspie: A Memoir.* Fairbanks: University of Alaska.

Premack, D., & Woodruff, G. (1978). Does the Chimpanzee Have a Theory of Mind? *Behavioral and Brain Sciences, 1*(4), 515–526. https://doi.org/10.1017/S0140525X00076512.

Rekers, G. A., & Lovaas, O. I. (1974). Behavioral Treatment of Deviant Sex-Role Behaviors in a Male Child. *Journal of Applied Behavior Analysis, 7*(2), 173–190. https://doi.org/10.1901/jaba.1974.7-173.

Rose, I. (2005). Autistic Autobiography: Introducing the Field. In *Proceedings of the Autism and Representation: Writing, Cognition, Disability Conference.* Available at https://case.edu/affil/sce/Representing%20Autism.html. Accessed 23 August 2018.

Ryan, P. J. (1997). Unnatural Selection: Intelligence Testing, Eugenics, and American Political Cultures. *Journal of Social History, 30*(3), 669–685. https://doi.org/10.1353/jsh/30.3.669.

Sacks, O. (2006). Foreword. In T. Grandin (Ed.), *Thinking in Pictures* (Expanded ed., pp. xiii–xviii). New York: Vintage.

Sasson, N. J., Faso, D. J., Nugent, J., Lovell, S., Kennedy, D. P., & Grossman, R. B. (2017). Neurotypical Peers Are Less Willing to Interact with Those with Autism Based on Thin Slice Judgments. *Scientific Reports, 7,* 40700. https://doi.org/10.1038/srep40700.

Scheeren, A. M., de Rosnay, M., Koot, H. M., & Begeer, S. (2013). Rethinking Theory of Mind in High-Functioning Autism Spectrum Disorder. *Journal of Child Psychology and Psychiatry, 54*(6), 628–635. https://doi.org/10.1111/jcpp.12007.

Sparrow, M. (2017, November 13). Coping with a Crisis When You Have Unreliable or Intermittent Speech. *Thinking Person's Guide to Autism.*

Available at http://www.thinkingautismguide.com/2017/11/coping-with-crisis-when-you-have.html. Accessed 24 August 2018.

Stanley, L. (2000). From 'Self-Made Women' to 'Women's Made-Selves'? Audit Selves, Simulation and Surveillance in the Rise of Public Woman. *Feminism and Autobiography: Texts, Theories, Methods* (pp. 40–60). London: Routledge.

Tammet, D. (2006). *Born on a Blue Day*. London: Hodder and Stoughton.

Vuletic, L., & Ferrari, M. (2005). A Transfer Boy: About Himself. In J. Rak (Ed.), *Auto/Biography in Canada: Critical Directions* (pp. 129–143). Waterloo: Wilfrid Laurier University Press.

Watson, M. (1999). *Lives of Their Own: Rhetorical Dimensions in Autobiographies of Women Activists*. Columbia: University of South Carolina Press.

Wayman, L., & Rothschild, C. (2018, June 26). *AAC and Verbal Individuals: How AAC Impacted Our Lives*. AAC in the Cloud. Available at https://presenters.aac-conference.com/videos/UVRJd1FURTQ=.

Williams, D. (1992). *Nobody Nowhere: The Extraordinary Autobiography of an Autistic Girl*. New York: Times Books.

Yergeau, M. (2010). Circle Wars: Reshaping the Typical Autism Essay. *Disability Studies Quarterly, 30*(1). Available at http://dsq-sds.org/article/view/1063/1222.

Yergeau, M. (2013). Clinically Significant Disturbance: On Theorists Who Theorize Theory of Mind. *Disability Studies Quarterly, 33*(4). Available at http://dsq-sds.org/article/view/3876.

Yergeau, M. (2018). *Authoring Autism: On Rhetoric and Neurological Queerness*. Durham: Duke University Press.

Yergeau, M., & Huebner, B. (2017). Minding Theory of Mind. *Journal of Social Philosophy, 48*(3), 273–296. https://doi.org/10.1111/josp.12191.

15

Reaching Beyond Auto? A Polyvocal Representation of Recovery from "Eating Dys-order"

Bríd O'Farrell

Introduction

The reflections of/on life (bio) and culture (ethno) offered in this chapter[1] are aligned with contemporary critical feminist approaches to "eating dys-order"[2] (e.g. Malson and Burns 2009; Riley et al. 2008) and the process of recovery (e.g. Garrett 1998; Malson et al. 2010; Moulding 2016), as well as the social construction of the "madness of women" (Ussher 2011; Showalter 1987) and the broader field of Mad Studies in which a critique of psychiatric discourse and practice is developing. Critical feminist approaches to "eating dys-order" undermine the psychiatric positioning of these embodied experiences as individualised psychopathology by continuously pointing up the broader historical and sociocultural context in which "eating dys-order(s)" materialise as embodied experience. Care is taken to avoid the

---

[1]Auto/bio/graphy is the self (auto)/life (bio)/writing (graphy); Autoethnography is the self (auto)/culture (ethno)/writing (graphy) (Stanley 1995; Ellis 2004).

[2]In my work, I have adopted the term "eating dys-order", both as a way of refusing psychiatric medicine's illness categories and as a means of signalling, via Drew Leder's (1990) thesis on bodily dis/dys-appearance, the relations between embodied dys-order, and the prevailing form of social order (see also Williams 1998).

B. O'Farrell (✉)
Dublin, Ireland
e-mail: ofarrebm@tcd.ie

© The Author(s) 2020
J. M. Parsons and A. Chappell (eds.), *The Palgrave Handbook of Auto/Biography*,
https://doi.org/10.1007/978-3-030-31974-8_15

positioning of "eating dys-order" subjectivities as either a socially inscribed reproduction of gendered norms or on the other hand as resistance to such norms. Rather "eating dys-order" is understood here as:

> A plural collectivity of embodied subjectivities, experiences, and body management practices embedded in and constituted by the contemporary discourses and discursive practices of late 20th Century postmodern culture and the gender/power relations that cut across this socio-historically specific context. (Malson 1999: 137)

Perceiving "eating dys-order" subjectivities in this way leaves room to listen for the manifold and multi-level (often contradictory) meanings that are embodied in the living through of "eating dys-order" and the process of recovery.

Yet, in studying my and my family's "eating dys-order" and recovery experiences, one of the dilemmas I face is finding a way to represent how such meanings are lived as feeling, emotion and intersubjectively constituted affect (see Probyn 2009; Tillmann-Healy 1996; Kiesinger 2002). I cannot make my work seem life-like, cannot ask of it to contain and convey feeling and emotion, to vibrate with dissonance, or ring out with joy without a creative methodology that makes lived experience seem alive (Inckle 2010). I find my answer to this representational dilemma within the creative analytical method of evocative autoethnography (Richardson 1999; Ellis and Bochner 1998).[3] Emerging out of a threefold crisis in qualitative research around issues of representation, legitimation and praxis, and drawing on feminist approaches to auto/biographical theory and praxis (e.g. Jelinek 1980; Lorde 1980; Stanton 1984; Hooks 2009; Stanley 1995), contemporary autoethnographic practice sets out to challenge and subvert those research practices which (re) produce inequitable hierarchies of observer/observed, researcher/researched, object(ive)/subject(ive), which mask the art(ifice) and subjective interpretative modes that are involved in writing up research, and which leave us with life-less and body-less (Csordas 1994), monologically voiced accounts of social life.

My approach to researching my and my family's "eating dys-order" and recovery experience, exploring the relationships between our experiences and the sociocultural context in which these experiences occur, through which

---

[3] I use autoethnography here as a specific development of the auto/biographical tradition, see Inckle (2020) this volume.

they are mediated, takes direction and guidance from pioneers in subversive autoethnographic practice like Carolyn Ellis and Arthur Bochner, who invite authors of social science research accounts to:

> Share interpretive authority by presenting layered accounts with multiple voices and by experimenting with non-traditional forms of representation, including the fictional and the poetic. (Ellis and Bochner 1998: 9)

The polyvocal evocative autoethnography, which follows, allows me to represent both "eating dys-order" and the recovery process as intersubjectively constituted, in a lively manner, i.e. sensorially rich, emotionally vivid. A central aim is to allow the narration of our lives to "not only coexist but intermingle in ways that encourage, not merely permit, active readership" (Stanley 1995: 247). Much as Stanley insisted that "the baseline of a distinct feminist auto/biography is the rejection of a reductionist spotlight attention to a single unique subject" (ibid.: 250), here a polyvocal narrative points up the embodied subjectivity of "eating dys-order" and that of recovery as a "position within, not apart from (our) social networks" (Stanley, ibid.).

My sociological voice, reflexively layered in with these extracts (Ellis 1991; Ronai 1992), allows me to emphasise the personal/political dimensions of my work and the multiplicity of voice(s) in my own self. I write and rewrite in order to craft a more capacious, less stigmatising story for my family and I (and others too), of a circuitous nonlinear process of recovering from eating dys-order. The narrative, I seek to create, troubles the seductive power of the popular "restitution" narrative, which plots itself as: "yesterday I was healthy, today I'm sick, but tomorrow I'll be healthy again" (Frank 1995: 77; Sparkes and Smith 2003; see also Eckerman 2009).

In *The Wounded Storyteller* (Frank, 2005), Frank makes the point that illness narratives are told through the body. Bodies shape narrative (embodied experience gives rise to narrative) and are in turn dynamically shaped by narrative. Shared narrative resources lend structure to the ways in which our stories of embodied experience may be told, including what is admissible to the telling and what is not. Frank examines three narrative forms common to illness experience: the restitution narrative; the chaos narrative; and the quest narrative. Behind the restitution narrative, Frank suggests, is an increasingly technologised medicine, with its veneration of medical expertise, and its belief in a science-led power of cure. Medicine's story of illness, Frank argues, is the story that trumps all others in our time. However, Frank also warns us that some stories are dangerous, or at the very least, may not be the best companions (Frank 2010). In the process of recovery from "eating dys-order" that I attempt to represent below, the restitution narrative was certainly an ambivalent if not a dangerous companion for my family and me, a breeding ground of suspicion and mistrust. I will be suggesting, that the recovery process, for us, was lived somewhat slantwise, or better spiral-wise to our entanglements with both psychiatric discourse and practice and with their particular version of the restitution narrative.

I do not name myself "recovered", neither do my family members when I ask them, but I am, we are, together, living through a process of recovery which is no longer fixed in place by the diagnostic category of "anorexia-nervosa". The polyvocal autoethnography I have crafted here, through practices such as interactive interviewing, sociological introspection, emotional recall, and the use of personal and fieldwork journaling (Ellis 2004; Ellis et al. 1997), also involves a variety of *selective* "memory work". There is much that is left out, partly for the purpose of narrative structure, partly in the service of the ethic of mutual care that we adhere to. The ethic of care that my family and I employ in both remembering and co-narrating experience, and in their subsequent listening to and further reflecting on my fictionalised and poeticised versions of their accounts, has meant that there are experiences/feelings/thoughts we have not wanted to disclose to each other. Some of the conversations we have about our experiences of "eating dys-order" and the processes of recovery are akin to treading between live tripwires; we tiptoe and at times keep our lips shut tight. I believe that an evocative auto/ethnographic approach allows for the silences and gaps in this research account, to be pointed up. In spite of those gaps and silences, we are still enabled here to speak back to the psychiatric narrative which had engulfed our experiences, and in many ways stopped us from being able to speak with each other without suspicion, shame, and distrust constraining us. The voices that will speak our story in the work that follows are my own (Bríd), my mother's (Mary), and my father's (Liam). Sarah and young Liam are my siblings.[4]

Where Does It Begin?

It is a dull day. Rain sits on the horizon as a possibility. I, however, do not care. I am neat and tidy and precise. I am prim and proper. I am perfectly suited up for the occasion, my younger brother's communion, in a navy,

---

[4]This research was part-funded by the Irish Research Council and underwent ethical review and approval within the Department of Sociology Trinity College Dublin in line with the institutional review procedures of the time.

polka-dotted two-piece. I can feel the breeze catching at bare legs where culottes end and limbs lengthen into patent shiny endings. It catches at the sailor collar draped in an elegant circle over my shoulders, flipping it into my face, teasing my serious lips into the ghost of a smile. I stand straight and tall. I am proud.

I am proud because in this suit I can place my hands around my waist and touch fingers at either side. I am waspish, I am waifish, I am pride of place in the extended family meeting which happens to be going on around me.

"Look at you.",

my Aunts say,

"so pretty, so thin."

"I wish I had a waist like that!"

I am seven or eight maybe, I am looking at women and men around me, I keep touching and holding my waist, sucking myself in, flattening my belly, pinning my wishes to be a "good girl" to my bones. I remember knowing even then, I could never be anything but thin.

....

Years later and it is the first morning that I will attend secondary school. All is quiet in the pink and grey room until the alarm buzzes hoarsely at 7 a.m. to wake me from my dreams. Like a boa constrictor from a tree branch, I slither out of the bunk bed settling my feet with certainty into the plush carpet and stretching and yawning my body into its full length and breadth.

Still in the greyish haze of sleep, I make my way to the bathroom to plunge my roaring mane of curls into a sink full of cold water. I finally begin to wake up. I begin to feel excited. A crisp white shirt, smart green tie, grey skirt, grey jumper and white knee socks hang over the edge of the avocado bath, all new, all labelled clearly, carefully and patiently by my mother. I look long and hard in the small square mirror over the sink, pleased with the fresh freckled face that looks long and hardback at me.

I want you to see my face shining brightly from September freshness. I want to ask you if you can try to feel the heady mix of nervousness and excitement that sprang in my step. I want you to understand how everything changed so quickly when the boys, gathered in their packs, began to shout at me…

"HERE DOGGY".

"WOOF, WOOF, WOOF".

I can still feel and hear the heavy sickening thud as a suffocating, silencing bell-jar of shame fell down around me.

"WHAT A DOG".

I had never heard anyone call a girl a dog before. On this first day at my new school, this is the first problem I had to figure out. Not how to say please and thanks in French, or how to calculate mathematical sets, but how to react when someone assesses you, measures you, judges you based solely upon how you look.

In those years in secondary school, I try everything to change myself, to look different so that when I crunch my way down the gravel to our prefab classrooms the boys will not bark at me.

I leave my hair down, rising an hour earlier so as to style and tease every curl on my head into tamed perfection. In response the boys spit in it, pull at it, laugh at the fuzz it becomes as the day wears on.

Next, I tie my hair up. I flatten and smooth my wildly coiling curls with sludge creams and disappear them into a neat little knot twisted into the small dent at the base of my skull. In response, the boys throw my colourful scrunchies into the trees, laughing, jeering, more spitting.

I begin to do stomach crunches every night, hooking my toes under the rim of my bed, curling up and down over and over till my sweat drips into the worn carpet. Each crunch is a determined effort to improve my chances of escaping the shaming gaze and calls of the boys who line up to hate me.

Whatever I do it is not enough or it is too much. I am too studious, too ugly, and too unfashionable. I am not breasted enough, not funny enough, not attractive enough to avoid the daily teasing, touching, and jokes made at my expense. I am too upset and ashamed to tell my mother and father what is happening.

It goes on for years, it gets worse. Today, I do not want to tell you the whole of how bad it gets.

....

Mary and Liam Some Years Later

Morning smells pervade the forest green kitchen. Burnt toast, freshly brewed coffee, and Liam's first cigarette of the day. He sucks hard on the sand and snow-white stick, taking the smoke deep into his lungs through lips pursed tighter than usual.

"Can you not make her sit down and eat with us?".

There is pleading in his tone, accusation too, she thinks.

Mary puts down the breakfast bowls in the sink and turns around in anger and frustration. She feels like crying.

"Look I just don't know what to do. If I *make* her eat a meal with us she will make herself sick. If I try to get her to sit still or stop her from going for her run she goes mad… I can't keep her in… I can't lock her in her room… She's seventeen for God's sake… And she just keeps saying there is nothing wrong with her … to leave her alone… She won't come home any more if I push her… I'm at my wit's end. I don't know what to do. I just don't know what to do".

Her voice breaks towards the end of this tirade and tears begin to roll down her cheek. Liam is off his chair, arms around her. He doesn't know either. He has never not known before. He is afraid.

"It's all right love, we'll figure something out".
………………………………………………………………………

Hospital No. 1

Sunlight bounces off the polished flooring creating glaring pockets of brightness down the long corridor. Long rectangular rooms shoot off to the side, four beds in each one like peas in a pod. "Patients" spot the long walk to "the consultant's room"… a "professor you know", only the best for me. The "psych" patients mostly cast their eyes to the floor. They don't look very happy. I want them to look at me. I want to make them smile. I want them to know what I know… that this is the cure… this place, this man, these pills we take… this is the cure. My father holds my hand tight. I am full of apprehension but also full of hope.

The professor shakes my father's hand. My father thanks him, bowing a little towards the professor with his handshake. The professor shakes my hand too. Owww, he grips so firm that the ring on my ring finger bruises the knuckle of my middle finger.

"Come inside Bríd, let's have a talk".

I don't want my father to go.

He goes.

I float dizzily inside and sit in the chair the professor assigns me with a wave of his hand.

He is old and carbuncled.

He has the air of one who appreciates fine wines, and Opera.

He is the cure?

He knows how to help me?

"Tell me why you are here, Bríd",

His voice is soft yet persuasive.

I begin to cry. I tell him I can't eat. I tell him I am terrified of putting on weight. I tell him I feel fat but that others tell me I am too thin. I tell him that I can't see I am too thin, that when I look in the mirror I see big trunky limbs and bulky mass.

"Where do you feel fat, Bríd?".

"My stomach my thighs, everywhere, just everywhere. I am too big, there's just too much of me".

"MMMMMMMMMMMMM." He says

He says it often. I grow to hate that. Is he listening to me?

"Tell me about your relationship with your parents"….

MMMMMMMMMMMMMMMMMMMMMM

AAAAAAAAGGGGGGHHHHH !!!!!

…………………………………………………………………………

Mary and Liam

Sarah and young Liam have gone to bed and the fire crackles through its last sticks of the night. Images flicker on the TV screen casting a playful light onto the peachy wall of the sitting room… No one really watches.

"The Professor told me she'll just grow out of it. He said it will be gone by the time she's 21. It's just part of growing up. We just have to stick with this. She knows now what to do. They've given her all the information in the hospital, she has seen the dietician. She sees him every week. What more can we do? It will be fine".

Liam turns back to the cross-word, acting out for her, in this mundane activity, his belief that everything will be ok.

"I hope so Liam". Mary says, but she is furrowing her brow and fidgeting with her hands and as she gets up to throw a lichen patterned log on the fire, she adds

"I am hoping and I'm trying to help, but I don't think she's getting any better, and I don't think those tablets are doing her any good".

Liam looks up from the crossword.

"It will work, Mary".

He says this with a determined fierceness, as if to claim anything else were to endanger the process. "It will work. It has to work. You just have to give it time. We all have to give it time".

....

Bríd

Months pass, long, long months… I talk about "anorexia" for an hour every week, I talk about my family, and I talk about my friends. I talk and talk and talk. I think and think and think. I "do" very little any differently, save for popping some blue and white pills three times a day.

....

Who are we? I, the I who crafts this text, am a straight, white, upper-middle-class woman, and I grew into this specific form of womanhood, with more than its fair share of privilege, in an Ireland which is only of late managing to come out from beneath the mysogynist stranglehold of the Catholic church, with its narratives of shameful bodies and sexual (im)morality. My parents grew up in rural Ireland, in working-class families, faithful to the church and in their education-fuelled-rising-up through the middle class, to notions of "respectability" and "respectable appearances", through which, as Skeggs argues, class boundaries are policed and maintained (Skeggs 1997).

Becoming "dys-orderly" was not a respectable affair but like many Irish people of my parent's generation, ease with placing confessions in the hands of the local priest, and faith in absolution, was mirrored in an ease in confessing all to medicine, and this too with a kind of faith, not only in absolution but in cure. A point of intersecting interest here is the way in which the discovery of "eating dys-order" as a deviant category of "madness" and its ensuant understanding evolved, as Brumberg argues, in response to new developments in the balance of power between the institutions of religion and medicine:

> By the nineteenth century a general decline in faith and the rise in scientific authority had, for the most part, transformed the refusal of food from a religious act into a pathological state. (Brumberg 2000: 7)

Both church and medicine, as Turner (1995) points out, are institutional forms of social control for the management of deviance. Yet, the capacity of the church to organise and order bodies is by far surpassed by the scientifically ratified knowledge/power through which psychiatry, as a branch of medicine, comes to organise "psychological deviance". Nonetheless, much in kind with the catholic church's complicated and contradictory history of image-ing female embodiment and bodily practice, the DSM and ICD categories of "eating dys-orders" emerged "through a particular Mysogynistic configuration of social, political and ideological thinking" (Hepworth 1999: 6) which depended upon the surveillance and stigmatisation of women's bodies, minds and especially their emotions (see Hepworth and Griffin 1990; Hepworth 1999). As many feminist writers argue, these Mysogynistic roots of the "eating dys-order" categories reach all the way back to the discovery and documentation of "eating dysorder" as "mental perversion" in the work of Gull (1997), and Lasegue (1997) in the late nineteenth century, and entangle insidiously with contemporary psychiatric diagnosis and treatment

The above vignettes are part of the story of becoming a woman diagnosed with an "eating dys-order". In this phase of our story, my family and I began to understand our experiences through the mediating knowledge/power of psychiatric medicine. It was also at this point in time that our embodied experiences came to be fixed in certain positions, subjectified, through the reduction and reification of my embodiment to the diagnosis "anorexia", through my baptism into the noun "anorexic" and the turning of my form of embodiment into a psychological problem, series of deficits, and individualised pathology, to be contained and controlled with psy's expert knowledges.

Fixed identities, as McNay suggests, freeze experience (2004: 174). In the West however, the self is predominantly imagined and normatively experienced as unitary and stable. Psychiatric and psychological discourse and practice have been a major support for this phenomena, conceiving of and analysing self-hood as the "psychological attributes and characteristics of an essential self" (Henriques et al. 1998), and coterminously applying diagnostic categories in such a way as to fix psychological deviance as the psycho-*pathological* attributes and characteristics of an equally essential, unchanging self. As Helen Malson argues anorexia and bulimia configured through the psychiatric discourse and practice which conceive of the self in this way, do get frozen into place, and become "as seemingly intransigent as any other aspect of an essentialised self" (Malson et al. 2010: 30). It is difficult to imagine the way out.

Bríd: Back Again

In the library basement, the air is heavy and still and smells like old books and damp. A white trolley loaded with academic tomes awaits my filing skills. Resignation moves through me as I bungle slowly through the stalls replacing books which seem almost as heavy as I am.

It has happened again.

I can't eat.

I can't eat and I am tired and weak and so very frightened.

I push my legs and arms and sometimes my speech into motion with jaw-clenching determination but I am hollow and empty and feel no real connection to anything I am doing…except to not eating.

Sweat beads at my forehead, black fog floats before my eyes, I teeter at the edge of a falling I long for. I could lie down and sleep forever.

……………………………………………………………………

Mary, Liam and Brid: A Homecoming Scene

"Oh my God, what have you done to yourself?" Mary pales as she carefully holds Bríd close. She grips Bríd's wrist, feels at an upper arm, and starts to cry.

"You shouldn't be driving", she says.

"How could you do this again?" she implores, "Why are you doing this?"

Liam walks through to the kitchen to put the kettle on. He is stoic. Young Liam has told him about finding Bríd…

He can't think about that.

He is determined to find her help. He is determined to find her the best help he can. He will bring her to the doctor in the morning, he will get the best advice, he will get the best help, and he will do anything he can do, to help her get better.

"Mum, Dad I'm so so sorry".

Bríd whispers through her tears.

"I don't know why it happened, it just came back and I couldn't eat".

"But you didn't look so awful a month ago. Now you look near death. I don't understand. What happened, what happened to you?"

Liam is genuinely bewildered. Bríd had looked just fine the last time she was home… fine for her that is.

"Daddy, I'm sorry, I don't know what happened, it just got worse, the hating noise in my head, and I couldn't eat, I just couldn't bear it anymore, I had to make it stop".

"This bloody 'anorexia'", Mary spits out, "you have so much, we give you so much, we give you the best of everything. Why are you throwing it all away?"

Flashing words out in anger Bríd shouts,

"You think I want to be this way, you think I'm doing this on purpose?"

Deflating quickly, beginning to ball inwards, she whispers again through her tears, her face and body twisted with pain of guilt.

"I'm sorry, I'm sorry, I'm sorry………….. I want to get better, I really do. Please don't be mad. Please. I'm so sorry. I couldn't help it, it got so hard. Please Mum. Please Dad, I want it to go away, I want to get better".

"We'll get you to the doctor tomorrow- we'll get help".

Liam reinforces his intentions with a gentle hug. Mary holds Bríd's scrawny, yellowed hand, inwardly cringing at the fragility she senses in her daughter. They sit for a long time in silence. Mary is frightened to ask Bríd if she will eat something. Eventually, Bríd gets up professing tiredness and goes to her room. Mary sits alone in the kitchen with her thoughts. Liam sups tea in the living room. Both feel like a devastating bomb has been dropped into the midst of their rebuilt lives. They are too shocked to talk to each other.

………………………………………………………………………………

Bríd's Diary

First day on St. Camillus's ward. Acceptance to Eating Disorder Recovery Programme pending two weeks "weight restoration". Time to leave "disordered eating" behind. Now if only I could sit and write this diary without all the jumbled torturous thinking about food and eating getting in the way.

I couldn't really sleep last night. It will take a while to get used to having a torch shone in my face every hour. They do this, I presume, to make sure we are still here and still breathing. With the sunrise, I hopped out of bed, tried to stretch some life into my limbs, and settled finally for meditation.

A nurse came at 8 a.m., handing me a menu card and urging me to prepare for my first "weigh in". The menu was beyond me, overwhelming me with panic, routing my mind once more into frantic calculations. How could I choose from amongst an array of foods so foreign now to my tastes, an array of foods which had been prepared by someone else?

I didn't have long to dither before the nurse was back and motioning me out of the room for "weigh in". I grabbed my hooded pale blue robe and slipped cold feet into slippers to follow the harried nurse into a dull brown coarse-carpeted room where a giant robotic-looking weighing scale loomed in the corner.

"We have to weigh you for the programme", the nurse explained. "Take your robe off and remove your slippers and step up".

Just like at home, I thought to myself. Weighing, every morning, my infuriatingly stubborn body. Every morning, praying for lower, smaller, lighter numbers, the numbers that sing the highest brightest notes on chords of jubilant victory.

Devilishly, the digits on that grey screen danced between numbers before settling on figures the nurse, her name is Elaine, blocked into her notes with a thick red marker pen. With that pen, she made the numbers fatter and rounder than I could bear.

....

Irene, the nurse in charge of the Eating Disorder Recovery Programme, came to my room after breakfast with contract in hand for me to look over. Irene is short-haired, sturdy, and robust. She reminds me of the farmer's wives in children's stories, wives who were practical and shrewd and who knew what to do with the golden goose or the magic beans. Her voice is quiet and gentle with a subtle lacing of humour barely detectable around the edges. She snips her sentences dead in the air with pursed lips as she reaches the end of her breath.

"We are going to set you a target weight", she explained "and we are going to create a graph which will represent for you the targets you will have to meet on a weekly basis".

She went into detail but it was all a bit confusing and I began to see number ladders in my head and pounds of flesh circling around like flies that I, fat toad, would have to swallow into me. A graph, a chart of me, of mine, of the food I put into me and the flesh it puts on to me. If this is what it takes for me to leave "anorexia" behind, then this is what I will bind myself to. This is why I am here. I will do everything they tell me to do if this is what it takes to get better. Is this what it takes to get better?

....

Mary and Liam: After Family Therapy

At home after a long day in the hospital, Liam and Mary eat in tense silence.

"You think it's my fault don't you?"

Mary serves her words tersely.

Liam chews his food as memories of the day's family therapy flash through his mind-

Bríd finally telling it all through a covered mouth.

"I just wanted you to be proud of me", she had cried; "I disappointed you. I thought you didn't love me".

He measures his response to Mary's question.

"No I don't blame you", he says. There is more to say but he is too tired to say it.

Who else is to blame, Mary thinks to herself. Who else is to blame?

....

These pieces of writing, some of which are taken directly from my journals of the time, are representative of my, and my family's second desperate entanglement with psychiatric medicine's approach to treating "eating dys-order". This time, the psychiatric reach was more thorough. Family therapy formed an obligatory part of the regime (see Gremillion 2003 on the multidimensional treatment approach that is "*de rigeur*" in the inpatient treatment of eating dys-order). In psychiatric medicine's consideration of "eating dys-order", it is not just the diagnosed who is pathological but the entire family system, usually the Mother in particular (Vander Ven and Vander 2003; Gremillion 2003; Moulding 2006). An understanding of "eating dys-order" would be incomplete, one influential proponent of the family therapy approach to "eating dys-order" claims:

> Without reference to their home life. Both the patient and her family form a tightly knit whole, and we obtain a false picture of the disease if we limit our observation to the patient alone. (Minuchin et al. 1978: 12)

In encounters with the psychiatric "experts" who presided over my treatment regimen, our lived experiences of relationality and connection were neatly packaged and handed back to us as an enmeshed family life, as too close, overly protective and overly dependent. The origin of my "dys-order" was traced in this context to the confines of our "anorexogenic" (Palazzoli 1985) family life. If family operates as a social mechanism for producing and regulating normatively healthy embodiment (Rose 1990: 51), then my family had failed, and they too needed to be disciplined. An education in the psychology of "eating dys-order" formed part of my family's disciplining in this regard, but as far as I can tell from speaking with my parents, only lip service was paid to the gendered, sociocultural dimensions of "eating dys-order" beyond my susceptibility to the proliferation of body beautiful imagery in the cultural sphere.

Together, we attended family confessionals, where we were expected to reveal and reflect upon our relations with one another in the light of the information which had been given us about our familial dys-function and pathology. We began to question the form of relationality and bodily practice that bound us together, including our love for each other. Was it too much, too little, not enough? Much talk time was devoted to the fact that our family environment had fostered ambitions and expectations that hinged on the presentation of an acceptable, respectable version of embodiment to the world, achieving academically, getting a job, being sociable, partnered, being "normal". These expectations and ambitions seemed to add to the dys-functionality of our family despite the fact that they are not unique to us and are common values of Western advanced capitalism and the families who must organise themselves in relation to that system.

In this second hospital stay, I find myself all too often on bed rest, a body and behaviour regulating enforcement which differs little from the "rest cure" Silas Weir Mitchell proposed for the hysterics and neurasthenics of the nineteenth century "a combination of entire rest and of excessive feeding".

Bed rest in this lineage of thinking is framed as a benevolent control increasing the likelihood of weight gain and preventing the high levels of "restless activity" (Gull 1997: 500), or "aptitude for movement" (Lasegue 1997: 494) which have been associated with "eating dysorder" since the nineteenth century. Being on bed rest narrows the world to dys-order in an eerie reflection of Lasegue's remark that:

> The disease becomes developed and condensed so much the more as the circle within which revolve the ideas and sentiments of the patient become more narrow. (Lasegue 1997: 495)

This induced narrowing of my world to my experiences of and reflections on my "dys-order" also increased my subjection to the disciplinary, panoptical power which was deemed absolutely necessary because I continued to fail in measuring up to the normative health standard upon which recovery is predicated.

How exactly is such health imagined? What are its terms? As a subject of the disciplinary regimes which aim to treat "eating dys-order", both mind and body are required to measure up to health. Yet, when psychiatric medicine aims to treat the mind that produces "eating dys-order", what it means is to instil or ingrain the logic historically understood to be the possession of the rational individual, an individual who is by no means gender-neutral thanks to the alignment of male-ness with mind and thought, and female-ness with body and feeling. Long an ideal of the Western world, the figure of the rational individual, can be theorised as a specific form of (dis)embodied subjectivity, shaped by principles of bodily transcendence, autonomy, and mastery, that are conjured up and culturally elaborated as the necessary means of escaping the irrationality of the body. A healthy mind, it follows, floats free of its constraining material base, and has full jurisdiction over its various irrationalities. Consider however, that "eating dys-order" may manifest as embodied experience within a similar nexus of hierarchical dualism (Bordo 1993; Malson 1998). For my own part, "eating dys-order" includes the experience of my body as both terrifying and disgusting and the concomitant ongoing necessity of doing everything I can to quiet it, numb it, and make it disappear, efforts which are thwarted by the physiological and affective consequences of eating little, while exercising more.

Yet here in this second hospitalisation, the treatment regime to which I am subjected seems to reproduce this contradictory nexus through which, while I *must* achieve the form of rationality which evinces an ability to transcend the body and it's vagaries, the conditions under which this must occur make transcendence impossible. This is because both the healthy body and the healthy mind are produced via the ongoing micromanagement and microsurveillance of the body, the irrational cognitions and moods it produces, and its fluctuant weight. Indeed, the healthy body that psychiatry wishes to recover from "eating dys-order" is largely the body that measures up to normative weight and hetero-normative (reproductive) fitness (including the restoration of menses), not too little, not too much, nothing in excess. The means of achieving this weight is via variations on the rational practices of counting, measuring and weighing, precisely the practices through which "eating dys-order" comes to manifest as embodied experience in the first place. As Helen Gremillion (2003) has argued (see also Malson et al. 2010), prevailing treatment regimes may in this way reproduce (and further entrench) the conditions of possibility for "eating dysorder".

Besides which, notions of healthy weight are disingenuous since, as Burns and Gavey (2004) argue, weight and the appearance of health belie the potential existence of behaviours which could arguably be considered unhealthy, devoting isolating hours to exercise for example. Burns and Gavey point out that the look of health, a look which is mediated through contemporary sociocultural imaginations of normative femininity and heterosexual attractiveness, may have little to do with lived experiences of wellbeing and vitality. As Susan Bordo remarks in this vein:

Just because a teenager looks healthy and fit does not mean that she is not living her life on a treadmill, metaphorically as well as literally, which she dare not step off lest food and fat overtake her body. (Bordo 2009: xix)

Fortunately for psychiatric medicine, notoriously ineffective treatment regimes have an easy scapegoat, since those living under the sign of the diagnosis eating dys-order are know as most resistant to treatment and recalcitrant (Malson et al. 2010). In fact, I left this programme before I reached my target weight and I was one of those secretive, deceitful, and manipulative women my parents had been warned about, shamming my weight gain by waking at unearthly hours to bloat my body with water. Let me borrow from Foucault, not as explanation but as resonance:

The body is broken down by a great many distinct regimes...through eating habits or moral laws; it constructs resistances. (Foucault 1977: 153)

I am no different leaving than entering the program, though I am a higher weight, my body-hating practices masked behind that, so that now I can be pestered every now and then by someone who is keen to know the secret to staying so trim and looking so well.

Bríd: No More Than

No more than two scooped hands
Eaten with a sparrow's
Chipping beak.

No more than a supplicating sip
Slow as your last breath
Conscious as your last word.

Two scooped hands
Seem solid, seem just
Seem sadder than the wind.

I ushered it in this time
Pushed mother-like
The feckless child upon the stage.

Don't look in the poppies
My mother would warn
But I would stare for hours
In their darkened hearts.

I am hoping for escape.
I am hoping for recognition.
I am hoping to feel something
Dark and deep.

I ushered it in.
To help me play my part
To hide my part
To kill me off…

Mary: The penitential brooch
She is my bright pin of penance
A shard of bone
polished by pain
And humbly worn.

She is my shadow Reflector
My nightmare Projector

Here, a razor blade or glinting knife
Drawn slowly cross her arm to play a screeching note

Or sawing, craven
Teeth biting skin and crying tears of blood.

Closer, starker still, the ghost who walks with faded bones
An effigy of the soft and bonny body we made

We made- with love-with care
Forgetting some vital part

Or making some fatal error
That shrunk my daughter's chances with her bones.

And now I wear her like a pin
That sticks at night in my twisted heart and gut

And though I can't sleep
And though the watchers whisper and judge.
I will keep her with me.

For she is my bright pin of penance
A shard of bone
polished by pain
and humbly worn.

....

Liam: Breaking Bridges

Dependency
Like this word-
Waiting for the next
Is hard to break

We gave time
We gave love
Money and Clothes of course

We gave her a hand when she needed

We built bridges for her
So she wouldn't have to step in the mud
And dirty those shining shoes
Her mother always bought for her

I'll have to break those bridges now
Stamp them through with my builder's boots
Hack through the high nerve suspension
holding her above the earth

What do you do then?
When you see her lift each stone in puzzlement
Wetting the cement with tears of frustration
Turning left and right to see who comes to help

But knowing you can only watch from the half open windows
Of your own firm, four walls
Knowing she will never build her own house
For her own dreams
If she comes to you, if you go to her

....

Some Inconclusive Conclusions

As I have written above, I left hospital that second time at a higher weight but I felt no different. My body still horrified and filled me with disgust, my mind still ran its constant calculations, was sunken by shame. I still made my world as safe and small as I could through the routinised body management practices of food, eating, and exercise. Before long, weight gained was lost and my family and I were returned to the feelings of fear, frustration, and failure that we were becoming accustomed to. What I wish to consider, as I come towards the end of this particular crafting of polyvocal narrative is the way in which the experiences I have come to consider as part of my recovery process were often lived in co-existence with "eating dys-order", a phenomenon which I read as a consequence of the multiplicity of embodied intersubjectivity, and of the cyclical nonlinear quality of recovery when positioned as a process metaphysic (Williams 1998) rather than as teleological. Autoethnography succeeds in representing this teleological disruption in ways that case studies or other research representation methods would fail at.

Undoubtedly, the experiences I am thinking of were not contingent upon measuring up to healthy weights or embodying a rational instrumental approach to my transcended unruly body. In fact, experiences that I would consider part of my recovery process were those in which, rather than apprehending my body as a shameful object to be transcended, I experienced my body as immanence, and these were experiences of intense hope-inspiring feeling, of grounded strength, of peace, and of joy. Some of these embodied experiences were materialised in new relationships, with a therapist who made it clear that she would be working with me and not with my "eating dys-order", by friends who accepted me as I was and did not see madness, by the embrace and caress of love, in the cradling arms of Dublin Bay, bobbing in its seaweed silky waters.

Others were manifested through bodily techniques, which rather than being mired in the Cartesian logic of body management practices such as diet and weight watching, issue from the premise that the carnal body is intelligent in its own right (Sheets-Johnstone 2009, 2011; Noland 2009). I encountered such techniques, in the somatic practices of the Feldenkrais Method, in Authentic Movement, certain forms of modern Yoga and in Body Mind Centring which, as systems of thinking and practice, value, in fact prioritise, the near senses; the kinaesthetic sense (our qualitative sense of ourselves moving), touch, proprioception, interception, and the vestibular system's capacity for sensing and orienting in space. Embodiment shaped from this alternative perspective upsets the prevailing hierarchy of the senses which privileges vision and succeeds, for me, in materialising embodied subjectivity not as a reified image, but as dynamic and relational movement (O' Farrell 2017).

Body techniques that require attention to the sensations and feelings of the self that moves are characterised by relational information generating dynamics that McLeod (2002) describes as the prototypical basis of trust. They allow for the development of listening and feeling skills, which help me in learning, that, in the immanent dimensions of my embodiment, I can experience without fear or shame. These skills of sensing sensation and feeling are invaluable to me in my recovery process, since one of the skills I developed during the years in which "eating *dys*-order" was my way of navigating the world, was not listening to the various sensations and feelings my body was vibrating with. These messages were loud and clear. I could hear them, feel them, but I, resolutely, did not listen.

Reviving the possibility of listening to these sensations was an enormous part of my recovery process. Centrally though, the possibility for that revival was not an abstracted cognitive making peace with basic needs like thirst or hunger. I was not rationalised into understanding that flesh and bone need food and water to live; I knew that all along. The gradual shifting of my way of being in the world, happened from the bottom up, from my flesh, blood and bones upwards, as much as from the top down.

For Miles, there is a form of what she calls "carnal knowing", through which "the intimate interdependence and irreducible cooperation of thinking, feeling, sensing and understanding is revealed" (Miles 1989: 9). Her belief is that such forms of knowing realise or make real in a person's body the kinds of strong experiences that may alter a person's sense of self and may bind them anew to alternative interpretive communities to those they belonged to before (Miles ibid.: 24). Similarly, Crossley proposes that the body can take on new meanings for us as a consequence of the way in which we learn to use it:

> Performing the technique allows agents to experience their embodiment in new ways and, in some cases at least, to take on a role which, in turn, leads them to relate differently to their bodies. (Crossley 2006: 108)

Moving with others, touching others, being touched, feeling my potential strength, learning to balance, learning my limits, these continue to be strong experiences that alter my experience of embodiment such that it is no longer constrained by and riddled with shame and a desire to escape my flesh.[5]

A niggling question remains however, the question of: For whom was/is this auto/ethnography created and can the method reach beyond the Auto/Eating dys-order in women and men, as this continues to rise, and support around these experiences is desperately needed? What I hope for this work, alongside the desire to represent the intersubjective dimension of "eating dys-order" experience, is to point up sprouting, rhizomatic directions in recovery processes that are not teleological and that are un-concerned with the return to normative management of food, weight and eating praxis. The auto/ethnographic approach I have used here allows me to disrupt the positioning of psychiatric discourse and practice as the author(ity) of my eating dys-order and recovery experiences. It also allows me to continue pointing to alternatives.

Bríd: This Is What I Have Learned

This is what I have learned
To stand proud and still as the mountain
Drawing my mind into the crook of its arms
And its great heart.

I have learned
To let the breath be soft
An auspicious guest
Followed gladly through the house.

I have learned
To wait for the bones to settle
And drop their weight, yes weight
Into the earth.

I have learned
That there is value in weight
As in feather light
That both can be balanced without measurement.

---

[5]The gendered nature of "the somatic field" warrants investigation and is perhaps a subject for a research project in its own right.

I have learned
To inhale- exhale-
Jump, step, fold-
Land in Trikonasana
triangle pose.

I have learned
To wait, mind in body
For a pose to unfurl
For it to flower.

I have learned;
To feel, as the flash of sun
On the underbelly of sea gull gliding
Almighty.

I have learned
That there is a way of focusing the gaze
a way of sensing the senses
In this moment moving through my body.

I have learned
Through my body
To feel unafraid

I have learned
I could someday
be free.

References

Bordo, S. (1993). *Unbearable Weight: Feminism, Western Culture and the Body*. Berkeley: University of California Press.

Bordo, S. (2009). Not Just a White Girl's Thing: The Changing Face of Food and Body Image Problems. In *Critical Feminist Approaches to Eating Dis/orders* (pp. 68–82). London: Routledge.

Brumberg, J. (2000). *Fasting Girls: The History of Anorexia Nervosa*. Cambridge, MA: Harvard University Press.

Burns, M., & Gavey, N. (2004). Healthy Weight at What Cost? "Bulimia" and a Discourse of Weight Control. *Journal of Health Psychology, 9*(4), 549–565.

Crossley, N. (2006). *Reflexive Embodiment in Contemporary Society*. Maidenhead: Open University Press.

Csordas, T. J. (1994). Introduction: The Body as Representation and Being-in-the-World. In *Embodiment and Experience, the Existential Ground of Culture and Self*. Cambridge: Cambridge University Press.

Eckerman, L. (2009). Theorising Self-Starvation: Beyond Risk, Governmentality and the Normalising Gaze. In H. Malson & M. Burns (Eds.), *Critical Feminist Approaches to Eating Dis/orders* (pp. 9–21). London: Routledge.

Ellis, C. (1991). Sociological Introspection and Emotional Experience. *Symbolic Interaction, 14*(1), 25–30.

Ellis, C. (2004). *The Ethnographic I: A Methodological Novel About Autoethnography*. Walnut Creek: Alta Mira Press.

Ellis, C., & Bochner, A. (1998). Editor's Introduction. In A. Banks & S. Banks (Eds.), *Fiction and Social Research: By Ice or Fire* (pp. 7–9). Walnut Creek: Alta Mira Press.

Ellis, C., Tillman-Healy, L., & Kiesinger, C. (1997). Interactive Interviewing: Talking About Emotional Experience. In R. Hertz (Ed.), *Reflexivity and Voice* (pp. 119–149). Thousand Oaks, CA: Sage.

Foucault, M. (1977). *Discipline and Punish: The Birth of the Prison*. London: Allen.

Frank, A. W. (1995). *The Wounded Storyteller: Body, Illness and Ethics*. Chicago: The University of Chicago Press.

Frank, A. W. (2010). *Letting Stories Breathe: A Socio-Narratology*. Chicago: The University of Chicago Press.

Garrett, C. (1998). *Beyond Anorexia: Narrative, Spirituality and Recovery*. Cambridge: Cambridge University Press.

Gremillion, H. (2003). *Feeding Anorexia: Gender and Power at a Treatment Center*. Durham and London: Duke University Press.

Gull, W. W. (1997). Anorexia Nervosa (Apepsia Hysterica, Anorexia Hysterica). Paper Read and Adapted from *Transactions of the Clinical Society of London, 7*, 22–28, 1874. Reprinted with Permission in *Obesity Research, 5*(5), 498–502.

Henriques, J., Holloway, W., Urwin, C., Venn, C., & Walkerdine, V. (1998). *Changing the Subject: Psychology, Social Regulation and Subjectivity*. London: Routledge.

Hepworth, J. (1999). *The Social Construction of Anorexia Nervosa*. London: Sage.

Hepworth, J., & Griffin, C. (1990). The Discovery of Anorexia Nervosa: Discourses of the Late 19th Century. *Text, 10*(4), 321–338.

Hooks, B. (2009). Writing Autobiography. In L. Bryant & H. Clark (Eds.), *Essays on Writing* (pp. 29–35). New York: Longman.

Inckle, K. (2010). Telling Tales? Using Ethnographic Fictions to Speak Embodied "Truth". *Qualitative Health Research, 10*(1), 27–47.

Inckle, K. (2020, this volume). Part V: Madness, *Dys*-order and Autist/Biography: Auto/Biographical Challenges to Psychiatric Dominance. In J. M. Parsons & A. Chappell (Eds.), *The Palgrave Handbook of Auto/Biography* (pp. 305–313). Cham: Palgrave Macmillan.

Jelinek, E. (1980). *Women's Autobiography: Essays in Criticism*. Bloomington: Indiana University Press.

Kiesinger, C. (2002). My Father's Shoes: The Therapeutic Value of Narrative Reframing. In A. Bochner & C. Ellis (Eds.), *Ethnographically Speaking: Autoethnography, Literature and Aesthetics*. Walnut Creek: Alta Mira Press.

Lasegue, G. (1997). On Hysterical Anorexia. Archives Generales de Medecin, Adapted from *Medical Times and Gazette*, 6 September 1873, 256–266. Reprinted with Permission in *Obesity Research, 5*(5), 492–497.

Leder, D. (1990). *The Absent Body*. Chicago: University of Chicago Press.

Lorde, A. (1980). *The Cancer Journals*. San Francisco: Aunt Lute Books.

Malson, H. (1998). *The Thin Woman: Feminism, Post-structuralism and the Social Psychology of Anorexia Nervosa*. London: Routledge.

Malson, H. (1999). Women Under Erasure: Anorexic Bodies in Postmodern Context. *Journal of Community and Applied Psychology, 9*, 137–153.

Malson, H., Bailey, L., Clarke, S., Treasure, J., Anderson, G., & Kohn, M. (2010). Un/imaginable Future Selves: A Discourse Analysis of "In-Patient's" Talk About Recovery from an "Eating Disorder". *European Eating Disorders Review, 19*, 25–36.

Malson, H., & Burns, M. (2009). *Critical Feminist Approaches to Eating Dis/orders*. London: Routledge.

McLeod, C. (2002). *Self-Trust and Reproductive Autonomy*. Cambridge, MA: MIT Press.

McNay, L. (2004). Situated Intersubjectivity. In B. Marshall & A. Witz (Eds.), *Engendering the Social: Feminist Encounters with Sociological Theory* (pp. 171–186). Maidenhead: Open University Press.

Miles, M. (1989). *Carnal Knowing: Female Nakedness and Religious Meaning in the Christian West*. Eugene, OR: Wipf and Stock Publishers.

Minuchin, S., Rosman, B. R., & Baker, L. (1978). *Psychosomatic Families: Anorexia Nervosa in Context*. Harvard: Harvard University Press.

Moulding, N. (2006). Disciplining the Feminine: The Reproduction of Gender Contradictions in the Mental Health Care of Women with Eating Disorders. *Social Science and Medicine, 62*, 793–804.

Moulding, N. T. (2016). Gendered Intersubjectivities in Narratives of Recovery from an Eating Disorder. *Affilia: Journal of Women and Social Work, 31*(1), 70–83.

Noland, C. (2009). *Agency and Embodiment*. Cambridge, MA: Harvard University Press.

O'Farrell, B. (2017). "Recovery", "Eating dys-order" and Somatic Practice: An Autoethnographic Exploration. *Journal of Dance and Somatic Practice, 9*(1), 31–46.

Palazzoli, S. M. (1985). *Self-Starvation: From the Intra-psychic to the Transpersonal Approach to Anorexia Nervosa*. Maryland: Jason Aronson.

Probyn, E. (2009). Fat, Feelings, Bodies: A Critical Approach to Obesity. *Critical Feminist Approaches to Eating Dis/orders* (pp. 113–123). London: Routledge.

Richardson, L. (1999). Feathers in Our CAP. *Journal of Contemporary Ethnography, 28*(6), 660–668.

Riley, S., Burns, M., Frith, H., Wiggins, S., & Markula, P. (2008). *Critical Bodies: Representations, Identities and Practices of Weight and Body Management*. London: Palgrave Macmillan.

Ronai, C. R. (1992). The Reflexive Self Through Narrative: A Night in the Life of an Erotic Dancer/Researcher. In C. Ellis & M. G. Flaherty (Eds.), *Investigating Subjectivity: Research and Lived Experience* (pp. 102–124). Newbury Park, CA: Sage.

Rose, N. (1990). *Governing the Soul: The Shaping of the Private Self*. London: Routledge.

Sheets-Johnstone, M. (2009). *The Corporeal Turn: An Interdisciplinary Reader*. Exeter: Imprint Academic.

Sheets-Johnstone, M. (2011). *The Primacy of Movement* (2nd ed.). Philadelphia: John Benjamins.

Showalter, E. (1987). *The Female Malady: Women, Madness and English Culture, 1830–1980*. London: Virago.

Skeggs, B. (1997). *Formations of Class and Gender: Becoming Respectable*. London: Sage.

Sparkes, A., & Smith, B. (2003). Men, Sport, Spinal Cord Injury and Narrative Time. *Qualitative Research, 3*(3), 295–320.

Stanley, L. (1995). *The Auto/Biographical I: The Theory and Practice of Feminist Auto/biography*. Manchester: Manchester University Press.

Stanton, D. (1984). *The Female Autograph: Theory and Practice of Autobiography from the Tenth to the Twentieth Century*. Chicago: Chicago University Press.

Tillmann-Healy, L. (1996). A Secret Life in a Culture of Thinness. In *Composing Ethnography: Alternative Forms of Qualitative Writing*. Thousand Oaks: Alta Mira Press.

Turner, B. (1995). *Medical Power and Social Knowledge* (2nd ed.). London: Sage.

Ussher, J. (2011). *The Madness of Women: Myth and Experience*. London: Routledge.

Vander Ven, T., & Vander, Ven M. (2003). Exploring Patterns of Mother Blame in Anorexia Scholarship: A Study in the Sociology of Knowledge. *Human Studies, 26*(1), 97–119.

Williams, S. W. (1998). "Bodily Dys-order": Desire, Excess and the Transgression of Corporeal Boundaries. *Body and Society, 4*(2), 59–82.

16

[R]evolving Towards Mad: Spinning Away from the Psy/Spy-Complex Through Auto/Biography

Phil Smith

1.

Seventeen thousand eight hundred and nineteen days ago
Madness walked into my room
sat down at the desk
crossed one leg over the other
and smoothed the cowlick in his hair.
He looked at me rather blankly
and asked for a glass of water.
I didn't recognise him
and thought it a bit audacious
that a stranger would come into a place
I let no one else enter.
But being a polite and shy and curious
adolescent virgin white boy
with no experience in such matters
I went out to the kitchen
to get his drink.
The room was empty when I returned.
I remember standing
next to my bed

P. Smith (✉)
National Louis University, Chicago, IL, USA

© The Author(s) 2020
J. M. Parsons and A. Chappell (eds.), *The Palgrave Handbook of Auto/Biography*,
https://doi.org/10.1007/978-3-030-31974-8_16

looking around the room –
at my artistically crooked built-in bookshelves
the high many-drawered bureau
my small desk with shelves above –
wondering where he could have gone.
The windows were all shut and locked.
He would have had to go past me
in the kitchen
to get outside.
I stepped outside the room
looked down the hallway
and saw a dark figure at the far end.
I stood staring, terrified
unable to so much as twitch
looking at whoever it was.
It took me several minutes
of rigid unmoving fear
to realise that what I saw
was my own reflection
in a window.
Almost fifty years later
that image is still present with me
as is the feeling of my body's inability
to move
despite every attempt
by my pathetic little brain
to make it do something.

2.

I have come to know (and be) that

> disability is a historically and culturally specific, contingent social phenome-
> non, a complex apparatus of power, rather than a natural attribute or property
> that certain people possess… disability is not a metaphysical substrate, a natu-
> ral, biological category, or a characteristic that only certain individuals embody
> or possess, but rather is a historically contingent network of force relations in
> which everyone is implicated and entangled and in relation to which everyone
> occupies a position. (Tremain 2018)

Disability is socially constructed (Smith 2018).
This is an essential element –
perhaps *the* essential element –
of the social model of disability.
I say social model, singular
as if it was one thing.
But really there are several social models.
In opposition to this is the medical model of disability.
The medical model posits that some people are broken
and that brokenness is inherent to individual people
part of them.
The medical model asserts that this brokenness –
the thing we call disability –
can be fixed
or at least ameliorated
through a variety of technological, professionalised
practices and tools (Smith 2018).
It is also eminently clear that Madness operates in the same
(but not identical)
kinds of ways.

3.

We've known for a long time –
really, a long, long time –
that   "…insider and outsider positions systematically influence what kind of
            knowledge is produced…" (Stanley 1993: 42).
What we know
depends on
who does the knowing.
Because Mad people are crazy
they are by definition
unreliable knowers.
Their knowledge is literally   unknown
                                meaningless
                                outside of knowledge
                                nonsense
at least to those holding to the dominating psy-complex
ideology of sanism.

Their thoughts and knowledge are "mere anecdote" (Sweeney 2016: 38) at best.
The work I do here
is outside of that psy sanist shit.
It is over dat.
It sez something completely different:
that   Mad
         Made
         Maid
         Mud
         Maud
crazy motherfuckers
are   the real knowers
            the only knowers
of what it means to be   Mad
                               Made Mad

by a   kulchuh
          skullchuh
          skullchuh kulchuh
focused on keeping people who think differently
than the normative bodyminds
of boring white patriarchal middle-class   bodyminds
                                             bawdymineds
                                             maudybinds.
As a result, the work here   intentionally
                               explicitly

disputes the genre distinction between biography and autobiography… between self/other, public/private, and immediacy/memory. (Stanley 1993: 42)

I'll go further father faster fatter future:
      the Made Mad work de-inscribbled here
      disputes the differences
      between   fact/fiction
                     true/false
                     real/imagined
as, at minimum, disputable
and probably without any kind of useful meaning or utility
in this post world.

4.

Saneism is an institutionalised, ideological process
inherent in Western, Eurocentric, hegemonic culture
founded in psychiatrism (the ideology of psychiatry)
and the psy-complex (the set of practices, ideas, research, and social institutions that includes
psychiatry, psychology, special education, social work, and other fields).
Saneism is

> the systemic discrimination, the individualised prejudice, the structural barriers, as well as the fear, hatred, and distrust directed toward psychiatrised people. Sanism impacts negatively on their entire world—socially, politically, economically, physically, personally, intellectually and emotionally. Generally, the impact of sanism is far-reaching and devastating, more devastating than the experiences that bring us into contact with psychiatry in the first place. (LeFrançois 2012: 7)

5.

Dear self,
You're fucked up.
Really.
Really fucked up.
Quintessentially fucked up.
The very definition of fuckeduppedness.
The poster child of fugged ub.
Did you know that?
Just sayin', in case you didn't.
Your friend,
Phil

6.

In the late 1990s, I discovered disability studies, a growing academic field by which

> I want to mean an interdisciplinary, bricolagic exploration of ways in which disability plays out in social and cultural contexts. Here, as elsewhere, I understand disability as a socially constructed enterprise, and the study of it as being intentionally, explicitly, and unabashedly interdisciplinary in approach... This kind of disability studies is multiple, plural, poly—opposed to essentialism. It looks at disability through social model lenses... (Smith 2013: 5)

This way of seeing and understanding the world immediately captured my imagination, and became an essential set of perspectives through which to look at the word-worlds around me—it opened wider the windows through which I critiqued and understood and thought and felt and believe. It was a new kind of onto-epistemology that was palpably exciting, even breathtaking.

7.

This text
like many I've written
for a few decades (Smith 2018)
is deliberately and oppositionally defiantly
against standardised normative
scholarly texts.
it does so because
        "(h)Our   thin   (king)
        not the queen but the king
        down by the old….
        is forced to ride in the slow lane uv
                textual
                processual
                sexual
                {tr}aff°ic {A}
        required by the metaph(l)or (mat) police of so-called
        common(bourgeois)-sense, trans[parent] texts…
        all texts – all special texts – all species (of) all – all species awful offal
        all special education texts hide behind
                trans [parent]
                common
                comMAN
                        sense
                        cents
                        $ and cents
        lan(guage)
        gauging the size of it all
        measuring it out
        speci(es)al rulers and tools
        ruling us, ruling (THEM)

disguising itself in a new   ALL HALLOWS EVE costume

                                ALL GALLOWS EVE

(heh, me and Freddie Kruger)

(never even saw the movie, just heard about it)…

it's all metaph(l)or (mat) then

                the literal

                the limitable

        becoming, through poetic deconstruction

        (tearing it down with a wordy rotten wrecking crane)

                        (talk to me now)

                a process of semiotic unparceling

                                            semiosis

                                            halitosis

                        BECOMING

                        the liminal

                        the illuminatable

                        the illimitable…

ideo-logical = idiot logic

words log[strawberry]

                        jammed

                        jellied

                        jelly roll (rock and morton) into   reified

                                                                commodified

                                                                latinate

                super{MAN} struc   tures

                                        struck chores

filching the   homogenised

                  homophobic

                  enqueered

enfreaked   bawdy

badly

bloody

bodies and   mined

(moth)er {father} lode

minds

of the counter-normate subaltern.
(PHEW) SAY THAT 10 TIMES FAST" (Smith 2018: 78–80).

this text, risen out of madness
rises too out of the
irrational
illogical
unreasoned
soul of anti-scholarship.
and proud of it.
It is a kind of "meaningful meaning-(un)making" (LeFrançois 2016: vii).
It deploys
a performative, poetic narrative
as a way to understand and push back
against the linear, rational discourses
to which Mad people and Mad Studies
are naturally opposed,
understanding that

> dominant ways of writing in academia are not only Eurocentric, heteronorma-
> tive, and ableist, but also sanist. (Eales 2016: 66)

In fact, psy-complex research and practice epitomise this saneist, classist
ideology:

> biomedical psychiatric practices reproduce social inequalities rather than
> address them. (McWade 2016: 66)

offering instead
new ways of knowing-thinking-being-doing
(do-be-do-be-do)

a new kind of onto-epistemological undoing
in a Mad Mad Mad Mad Mad Mad world.

8.

Madness continued to drop by
from time to time
over the years.
Our relationship has never been
whatcha might call cordial
and certainly not
by any stretch of the imagination
friendly.
I would sometimes go for months
without seeing him
and then there he'd be –
his short, unruly hair standing on end
usually dressed in khaki pants
and a rumpled white shirt.
I'd catch a brief glimpse of him
on the other side of a room
filled with people
or sometimes through the trees
at the edge of the field
while I weeded the garden.
Other times he'd sit down next to me
get uncomfortably close
and make himself to home
lean over breathing on my face
smelling of too-much garlic
and start in on a good
long
heart-to-heart chat.
I never really knew who he was
for the longest time
didn't know why he'd come
or what he wanted of me.
I recognised his face
covered with marks from adolescent acne
the scar on his left hand
the blandness of his voice

the way he pointed his right foot
slightly inward when he walked
but I never knew his name
why he kept showing up
or what he needed.
Still, he kept coming.
He was there those months
that I ate only one real meal a day
breakfast at the crack of intolerably frigid dawn
rationing four crackers and a teaspoon of peanut butter
for lunch and dinner.
He was there that night
I slept beside the bed
of the woman with long dark hair
unable to sleep or talk or move.
He was there when I took all the pills
and when I cut myself without skill
and when I pounded my head
not quite endlessly
on the wall or the floor or the door.
He was there that time
when I sat on the floor
of a small bedroom looking blankly
out to the sea
for hours.
The time sitting in a restaurant
unable to eat
or speak
or look
at those around me.
The police. The doctors. The therapists. The psychologists.
The time I sat in the dark
sobbing so long
that stopping seemed
like a dream
a complete impossibility.

9.

In 2005
(give or take –
linear time is, for me, a slippery eel
that swims in the water
of normate reality)
I began to realise that what I'd come to recognise
as my rather odd way of being in the world
could be categorised as psychiatric, or mental, disabilities.
I recognised that these disabilities were not
an innate and essential brokenness that was part of me
but the result of social processes
through and by which I was understood by those around me.
That is
my Madness was a function of what society does to me
rather than some way in which I was messed up.

10.

Although I generally pass as able-bodyminded
in most of my day-to-day encounters
with the normies that surround me
those who know me intimately
know I'm crazy as a motherfucker.
It's easier to pass –
to keep my crazy invisible –
because

there are acceptable and unacceptable ways to cope and be through/in my madness. I continue to fold my crazytraumadepressionbrainbody into itself, knowing that for most of my life it has been easier to perform sane then to live the harder reality of being crazy. (Forfa 2016: 14)

11.

Those visits from Madness
(they've never stopped –
they continue to and through this moment)
have left me disturbed.

I swallowed him
hook, line, sinker, bobber, worm and all.
The whole big thing.
I'm Mad
but not angry, mind you
(at least not mostly)
at other people
(though I am beyond pissed
at the sizdumbs and maytricycles of oppression)
but Mad as in
crayZ as a mudderfugger.
What is Madness?
What does it mean to be Mad?
For me,
being Mad is not the same as mental illness.
I'm not ill; I'm not sick.
What I am can't be fixed –
not with pills or treatments or therapies.
I can't be fixed because I'm not broken.
I don't mean to say that I haven't gone
through some pretty tough times.
I have.
But what's broken is not me.
What's broken is a kill-kulchuh
that sees Mad people as needing to be fixed
because of how they understand
and experience the world:

> …madness has come to represent a critical alternative to 'mental illness' or 'disorder' as a way of naming and responding to emotional, spiritual, and neuro-diversity. (Menzies et al. 2013: 10)

Madness, see, is social constructed (Smith 2018).
And Mad people are neurodivergent; Mad people and those who identify as neurodiverse share common attributes and interests (McWade et al. 2015). That is, Mad people are people who have

> a brain that functions in ways that diverge significantly from the dominant societal standards of 'normal'. (Nick Walker 2014)

The key there is "dominant societal standards."
Mad people think differently from normative bodyminds.
Madness is

  a difference that made a difference…; and thus, a difference that mattered and
  could mean something good. (Aubrecht 2016: 187)

Too often, Madness is defined and created
by psychiatrism – an ideology, not a science.
As such

  whoever has the power determines what it means. (Filson 2016: 21)

So Mad people have taken back our identity
from the psy-complex
and saneism.
We own it, motherfuckers.
It's ours now.
You can't have it.
And get the fuck out of our sandbox.
Not to put too fine a point on it,
                    "mad people are   non-linear
                                             irrational
                                             nonsensical
                                             unreasonable
            in our saneist culture.
            our professional discourse" (Smith 2018: 157).

12.

The ideer of the bodymind has been around for awhile
for at least 30 years (Dychtwald 1986).
Even those within the psy-complex
have long rejected the mind-separate-from-the-body binary (Bracken and
Thomas 2002).
I come to the use of the term body-mind through the work
of the Mad feminist rhetorician Price (2011).
My bodymindsoulheart are inseparable parts
of what it means to be do-re-me.

13.
The chair was red.
The kind of dark red
that looks like dried blood.
I sat in it.
It was night
which it almost always is.
She said to me
"What do you want?"
I thought about that for a while.
Really, what
do
I want?
In this moment.
Right now.
The answer was simple
but pretty hard.
"What I want," I said,
"is to get a knife from the kitchen cupboard
and slit my neck from one side to the other."

14.

Here, as elsewhere and elsewhen, I use

> …language that puts the disability first. This is explicit and intended. Person-first language has become a norm in the field of supporting students with disabilities, to indicate that they are, literally, a person, not the disability… however, I put the disability first, in alliance with the thinking that disability is an identity, one which I seek to assert and reclaim, and also to remind the reader that disability is socially constructed, created to oppress those who are not seen as normal by a dominant, ableist hegemony. (Smith 2013: 13)

Disability is, for me, political—charged with meaning sometimes not understandable to those who see themselves as inhabiting normative bodyminds.

15.

They went out to the tracks one day.
Stood on a cross-tie.
And waited.
Looked one way.
Then the other.

Nothing.
They imagined what it might feel like.
What would happen.
What sounds they might hear.
No whistle, no bell.
Nothing.
No train.
"I guess it wasn't the day for it,"
they said to me later.
And went home.

16.

Mad studies is

> a project of inquiry, knowledge production, and political action devoted to the critique and transcendence of psy-centered ways of thinking, behaving, relating, and being… Mad Studies is an interdisciplinary and multi-vocal praxis. (Menzies et al. 2013: 13)

It is
an umbrella term that is used to embrace the body of knowledge that has emerged from psychiatric survivors, Mad-identified people, antipsychiatry academics and activists, critical psychiatrists and radical therapists. This body of knowledge is wide-ranging and includes scholarship that is critical of the mental health system as well as radical and Mad activist
scholarship. This field of study is informed by and generated by the perspectives of psychiatric survivors and Mad-identified researchers and academics (LeFrançois et al. 2013: 337).
It "centres the knowledges of those deemed mad…" (LeFrançois 2016: v).
And

> "maaaaaad stud tease is, in parterated, about madness (the socially constructed state of being
> crazy, or nutso).
> mad studies reclaims
> declaims
> enflames
> madness as an identitooty.
> mad studies is, in part, about understanding how sanism works."

(Smith 2018: 156–157)
If Mad Studies is to stand in opposition

to psychiatrism's eugenicist hold
on acadoomic, Eurocentric, Northern, patriarchal, heteronormative
understandings of cccccccrrrrraaaaazzzzzyyyyy in the dominating white, middle-class kulchuh,
then it will have to stand outside the onto-epistemological foundations
of traditional quantitative and qualitative research and scholarship.
It will, by definition, have to be   illogical
incoherent
irrational
indefinite
imprecise
fluid
rhizomatic
dynamic
nonsensical
murky
unclear
unreasonable
reasonable
undisciplined
anti-foundational

unreliable

 surreal

unnatural

disordered

inappropriate

unmanageable

incredible

illegitimate.

This kind of Mad Studies is   oppositionally defiant.

Its personality is on the   borderline.

It is   anxious and depressed.

It   listens to voices.

It   wears a tin foil hat

as a sign of strength and determination.

It   works on a spindle as a sign of strength and determination.

It   works on a spindle
connected to the lathe of antirationalism
and explores the bipolarity of body forcibly separated from mind.

It turns

and turns

and   t

                u

                        r

                n

        s

again

toward an approach that   subverts sanism

                             questions reliability

                             defies validity

                             avoids trustworthiness.

It calls for a reliance on   in   too   i   shun

                              e   more   shun

                              re   volu   shun

                              i   magic nay   shun

                              in   vent   shun

                              Mad-as-a-verb.

In doing all this, Mad Studies will have to
constantly examine and re-examine
ways in which it interacts
with issues resulting from
racism, classism, ableism, heteronormativity, and patriarchism
among a host of other concerns (Sweeney 2016).
Additionally, Mad Studies must explore the many challenges
inherent in working within ivory-towered academia,
and to constantly find ways to
"continually seek paths back to the community" (Sweeney 2016: 54).

17.

The study of Mad people
suffused and infused
as it has been
for so long
by the ideology of psychiatrism
and controlled
by the professionalised and dominating psy-complex
has denied
Mad voices
Mad thought
Mad doing
Mad knowing
Mad being (Sweeney 2016).
It is clear that

> academic activities around madness and neurological divergence have failed to include those with lived experience… This is not limited to the big business of pharmaceuticals, or to the biological or genetic research that seeks to identify bio-markers for and eradicate autism, schizophrenia and the like. Indeed, much of social scientific work in these areas may aim, but continually fail, to include lived expertise equally, positioning patients/users/survivors as outsiders, objects for interpretation and research 'on' rather than 'with'. (McWade et al. 2015: 305)

So in response,
I have said elsewhen that

> Mad people need to create, control, and enact research and
> scholarship projects about madness. People who identify as being mad need to create, control, and enact research and scholarship projects about mad studies. Mad studies needs to be accountable to the needs, wants, dreams, and desires of mad people. (Smith 2018: 181)

18.

So.
Being crazy sucks, most of the time.
But, this:

I honestly believe that as a result of it I have felt more things, more deeply; had more experiences, more intensely; loved more, and been more loved; laughed more often for having cried more often; appreciated more the springs, for all the winters; worn death "as close as dungarees," appreciated it – and life – more; seen the finest and the most terrible in people, and slowly learned the values of caring, loyalty, and seeing things through. I have seen the breadth and depth and width of my mind and hear and seen how frail they both are, and how ultimately unknowable they both are. (Jamison 1995: 208)

I'm crazy. And when my head is clear, I love every damn minute of it.

Allusions to the Litritchuh

Aubrecht, K. (2016). Psy-Times: The Psycho-Politics of Resilience in University Student Life. *Intersectionalities: A Global Journal of Social Work Analysis, Research, Polity, and Practice, 5*(3), 186–200.

Bracken, P., & Thomas, P. (2002). Time to Move Beyond the Mind-Body Split. *British Medical Journal, 325,* 1433. https://doi.org/10.1136/bmj.325.7378.1433.

Dychtwald, K. (1986). *Bodymind*. New York, NY: Penguin Putman.

Eales, L. (2016). Loose Leaf. *Canadian Journal of Disability Studies, 5*(3), 58–76.

Filson, B. (2016). The Haunting Can End: Trauma-Informed Approaches in Healing from Abuse and Adversity. In J. Russo & A. Sweeney (Eds.), *Searching for a Rose Garden: Challenging Psychiatry, Fostering Mad Studies* (pp. 20–24). Monmouth, UK: PCCS Books.

Forfa, A. (2016). invite in. go steady crazy. *Canadian Journal of Disability Studies, 5*(3), 12–17.

Jamison, K. (1995). *An Unquiet Mind: A Memoir of Moods and Madness*. New York: Vintage Books.

LeFrançois, B. (2012). And We Are Still Being Psychiatrised. *Asylum, 19*(1), 7–8.

LeFrançois, B. (2016). Foreward. In J. Russo & A. Sweeney (Eds.), *Searching for a Rose Garden: Challenging Psychiatry, Fostering Mad Studies* (pp. v–vii). Monmouth, UK: PCCS Books.

LeFrançois, B. A., Menzies, R., & Reaume, G. (2013). *Mad Matters: A Critical Reader in Canadian Mad Studies*. Toronto, ON: Canadian Scholars' Press.

McWade, B. (2016). Recovery-as-Policy as a Form of Neoliberal State Making. *Intersectionalities: A Global Journal of Social Work Analysis, Research, Polity, and Practice, 5*(3), 62–81.

McWade, B., Milton, D., & Beresford, P. (2015). Mad Studies and Neurodiversity: A Dialogue. *Disability and Society, 30*(2), 305–309. https://doi.org/10.1080/09687599.2014.1000512.

Menzies, R., LeFrançois, B., & Reaume, G. (2013). Introducing Mad Studies. In B. LeFrançois, R. Menzies, & G. Reaume (Eds.), *Mad Matters: A Critical Reader in Canadian Mad Studies* (pp. 1–22). Toronto, Canada: Canadian Scholars Press.

Price, M. (2011). *Mad at School: Rhetorics of Mental Disability and Academic Life.* Ann Arbor, MI: University of Michigan Press.

Smith, P. (2013). Introduction: What Dis Is, Why Itz Here. In P. Smith (Ed.), *Both Sides of the Table: Autoethnographies of Educators Learning and Teaching With/in [Dis]ability* (pp. 3–13). New York: Peter Lang.

Smith, P. (2018). *Writhing Writing: Moving Towards a Mad Poetics.* Fort Worth, TX: Autonomous Press.

Stanley, L. (1993). On Auto/Biography in Sociology. *Sociology, 27*(1), 41–52.

Sweeney, A. (2016). Why Mad Studies Needs Survivor Research and Survivor Research Needs Mad Studies. *Intersectionalities: A Global Journal of Social Work Analysis, Research, Polity, and Practice, 5*(3), 36–61.

Tremain, S. (2018). Philosophy and the Apparatus of Disability. In D. Wasserman & A. Cureton (Eds.), *The Oxford Handbook of Philosophy and Disability.* Retrieved from www.oxfordhandbooks.com; https://doi.org/10.1093/oxfordhb/9780190622879.013.5.

Walker, N. (2014). Neurodiversity: Some Basic Terms and Definitions. *Neurocosmopolitanism: Nick Walkers Notes on Neurodiversity, Autism, and Cognitive Liberty.* Retrieved from http://neurocosmopolitanism.com/neurodiversity-some-basic-terms-definitions/.

Part VI

Prison Lives

Dennis Smith

Introduction

The three chapters of original historical research in this part draw together three instances of imprisoned rebels. They exemplify in practice the challenges and opportunities involved in narrating and analysing the following cases: first, Antonio Gramsci (1891–1937); second, Bobby Sands (1954–1981), and, finally, Nelson Mandela (1918–2013).

Antonio Gramsci

Antonio Gramsci, leader of the Italian Communist Party, was arrested on Mussolini's orders and sentenced to twenty years imprisonment. This study focuses on his struggle, while in prison to maintain his relationship with his wife Giulia Schucht and their sons, who lived in Moscow. Giulia's voice was and always had been absent, and consequently, she has been underestimated and misunderstood. Firstly, by Gramsci and subsequently by biographers whose focus was the political persona and writings of Antonio Gramsci himself, in his roles as journalist, activist and politician before prison, and Marxist theoretician while imprisoned. Here, Jenny Nicholson looks at the separation and its sorrow from Giulia's point of view too. There is little detailed material about Giulia so the chronology is supplied by Gramsci's letters and Tania's, whose information from Russia and critical evaluations of the morbid and suffocating atmosphere within the Schucht family were vital to Gramsci's, and our, understanding of what it was like to be Giulia. This chapter also outlines her situation and ensures that she is brought into the conversation; using Gramsci's Letters from Prison, those of Tania, his sister-in-law and favoured correspondent, and unpublished material from Giulia his wife. Gramsci complained of the 'other prison', the 'unforeseen' one, the loss of control, the isolation, the hostile pressures, the blows from 'unexpected quarters'. Gradually, he began to realise that Giulia suffered similar conditions in an 'other prison' of her own.

Nelson Mandela: Courage and Conviction—The Making of a Leader.

Nelson Mandela (1918–2013) had a long life, just over a quarter of which was spent in prison. He was incarcerated in his mid-forties and released in his early seventies. After his release in 1990, Mandela lived for nearly another quarter of a century. The object of this essay is to assess how Mandela's experiences as a prisoner relate to his life before and after imprisonment. How did he end up in prison and how did being a prisoner shape his subsequent approach to life and politics? How we can discover and interpret the part played by Mandela's long imprisonment in his own personal and political development and in shaping his contribution to the struggle of the African National Congress (ANC) and the townships to overthrow the constraints of *apartheid*? How did the long campaign to 'free Nelson Mandela' and Mandela's own development within the context of his arduous imprisonment combine to build his influence and shape his approach as the ANC's leader and the nation's president after his release? The objective of this chapter is not to arrive at some irrefutable 'answer' to the problems posed here but to identify the agenda of issues that his case presents and to suggest some of the ways in which those issues might be tackled.

Bobby Sands

Bobby Sands was not your usual revolutionary leader, if there is such a thing. Unlike Gramsci or Lenin, he lacked formal training in political theory. Unlike Mandela, he was not bred for leadership. Rather, society itself put Bobby Sands into a position of leadership. His education, rather than in high schools, colleges and universities, was grounded in the community and, especially, the prison. Long Kesh prison, which came to be known by Northern Irish revolutionaries as the 'University of Freedom', *made* Bobby Sands. How did this young man achieve his high status and recognition? The IRA leadership in prison was still an older, conservative generation. They maintained a militaristic structure, with nightly parades, orders and delegation of work. IRA officers avoided menial jobs. They discouraged open debate and held burnings of Marxist books. They held courts of inquiry and encouraged prisoners to spy on each other. Yet a cadre of younger leaders encouraged the prisoners to form 'cooperatives' to make handicrafts, share food and distribute chores. It would be hard to overestimate the importance that such solidarity and radical thinking had on Bobby's intellectual development. This chapter narrates the story of that development and its political consequences.

An implicit issue arising is how accounts of these three prison lives located at three different points in the twentieth and twenty-first centuries are related as narrative, history and auto/biography. A key source is Dilthey who considered hermeneutic techniques for enhancing our understanding of the organisational structures of human lives embedded in history, seeing them in their appropriate contexts and bringing their structural similarities to the fore. This theme emerges in these three chapters which focus on the interplay between the public and private dimensions of lives experienced partly in conditions of incarceration, partly in conditions of relative freedom. More recently, work by Ricoeur in *Time and Narrative* (1984–1988) and by White in *The Content of the Form* (1990) has acknowledged that the immanent dynamics of the person being studied interact with the biographer's own intellectual agenda. That includes attempts to identify and understand the emotional drives at work, shaping and the lives being studied, a feature that is prominent in all three of these chapters on prison lives. The development of this late-named dimension of auto/biography is to be seen in works such as Thomas and Znaniecki's The Polish Peasant (1918–1920), Stanley's *The Auto/Biographical I* (1992) and Banville's *The Untouchable* (1998). Meanwhile, I am happy to acknowledge that the comments in this paragraph have benefited from the scholarship and experience of Michael Erben who is one of the leading British experts and a founding figure within this field in twentieth-century and twenty-first-century social sciences and humanities.

More specifically, this part on historical lives demonstrates how, by deploying historical perspectives, it is possible to locate the high-profile lives of specific writers and political activists in the context of life and death struggles. These were underway over several decades in divided societies where the rights and obligations of powerful interests and those over whom they exercise their dominant influence were in dispute. As will be seen, the general issue explored in all three studies concerns how power resources are and should be distributed and employed, and with what rights and obligations. These themes are considered at both at the macro-historical level and the interpersonal level.

These three chapters all deal with activists located in specific polities (South Africa, Italy and Northern Ireland) that are experienced as manifestly unequal and discriminatory, favouring propertied establishments who use the state to maintain their advantages and repress resistance. In all three cases, there are lateral conflicts (e.g. between Zulu and Xhosa, fascists and communists, republicans and loyalists), which are rooted in a mix of ethnic, tribal, ideological and religious identities. The fact that all three of the prisoners concerned developed an acute awareness and theoretical understanding of the power dynamics, political organisation and class structures of modern capitalist societies means that their understanding of, and reflections upon, their own situation is easily recognised by their biographers who are familiar with such societies as well the theoretical traditions and religious cultures upon which their subjects drew.

In all three cases, the deep political engagement of the central protagonists led to their incarceration, which, in turn, profoundly disrupted their previous existence as members of households, extended families and neighbourhoods. Mandela, Gramsci and Sands each navigated the almost insufferable emotional pressures imposed upon themselves and others as a result of their imprisonment in one or more of three ways. Firstly, they cultivated an intense inner life, undertaking a formidable historical, philosophical and political self-education (Sands), engaging in creative reflection upon Marxist theory (Gramsci) and acquired advanced training in law (Mandela). Secondly, where possible, they engaged in regular dialogue, through work, play and debate, with other political prisoners (something possible for Mandela and Sands, but not Gramsci).

Thirdly, they maintained contact with their relatives and friends outside prison through letters and visits. These letters and the observations of their associates both inside and outside of jail, as well as information about their lives before and, in Mandela's case at least, after their prison terms, provide a body of evidence on which the biographers may build their analytical and empathetic narratives of these lives and their significance. In two cases (Mandela and Gramsci), written evidence of the kind just mentioned provided the main source. In the case of Bobby Sands, the author also had the advantage of residing for a number of years in a working-class Catholic district in Belfast, which gave him access to the broader communal networks from which Bobby Sands came. This enabled him to understand on the basis of a multitude of informal encounters how a specific consciousness of injustice and struggle was sustained within that district, motivating young men such as Bobby Sands.

There is a conversation going on within and between the three chapters about the conflictual relationship between personal lives and public responsibilities: to humankind, to the future and so on. Gramsci's relationship to Giulia Schucht, like Mandela's to Winnie Mandela, is modulated by the shared commitment of husband and wife in both cases to socialist ideals and goals. That, to some degree, salves the pain of separation. In the case of Bobby Sands, his commitment to his own martyrdom claimed a moral and political purpose that offered the partial compensation of pride to those that lost him.

But in all three cases the conflicts, and the pain they brought, were ultimately irreducible. They provided a counterpoint to the broader political and historical conflicts under way, and a dramatic instantiation of them through three suffering lives. In these prisons in South Africa, Italy and Northern Ireland, the weight of oppression and the answering demand for individual freedom were set directly against each other. All three prisoners recorded victories in the struggle: Mandela won his presidency and the abolition of *apartheid*; Sands achieved his political martyrdom and shamed the oppressor; while Gramsci produced his profound political theories. These confrontations tested the strength not only of personal character but also of competing ideologies, interests and sociopolitical alliances. That is why these three biographies matter.

References

Banville, J. (1998). *The Untouchable*. London: Picador.

Gramsci, A. (1994). *Letters from Prison*. (2 Vols, F. Rosengarten, Ed., R. Rosenthal, Trans.). New York: Columbia University Press.

Ricoeur, P. (2001). *Time and Narrative*. Chicago, IL: University of Chicago Press.

Stanley, L. (1995). *The Auto/Biographical I*. Manchester: Manchester University Press.

Thomas, W., & Znaniecki, F. (1996). *The Polish Peasant in Europe and America*. Champaign, IL: University of Illinois Press; originally published 1918–1920.

White, H. (1990). *The Content of the Form. Narrative Discourse and Historical Representation*. London: Johns Hopkins University Press.

17

Nelson Mandela: Courage and Conviction—The Making of a Leader

Dennis Smith

Introduction

Nelson Mandela (1918–2013) had a long life. His auto/biography takes us into the very heart of South Africa's long national struggle for political freedom, civic rights and social justice. Mandela began as the son of an African chief and ended up as the president of South Africa. He was a crucial part of an immense national struggle. As a result, he spent just over a quarter of his life in prison. He was incarcerated in his mid-forties and released in his early seventies. After his release in 1990, Mandela lived for nearly another quarter of a century. The object of this essay is to assess how Mandela's experiences as a prisoner relate to his life before and after imprisonment. He defined and expressed his ambition to rise to the top of the political tree in South Africa at a very young age. Mandela succeeded and became the Africa figure most closely associated in the world's eyes with the indigenous struggle against *apartheid* and with the success of that struggle (see Lodge 2006: 57). But what about the many decades that intervened between Mandela's birth and his presidency? How did they shape and drive the journey towards his desired destination? How did he end up in prison and how did being

D. Smith (✉)
Loughborough University, Loughborough, UK
e-mail: d.smith@lboro.ac.uk

© The Author(s) 2020
J. M. Parsons and A. Chappell (eds.), *The Palgrave Handbook of Auto/Biography*,
https://doi.org/10.1007/978-3-030-31974-8_17

a prisoner shape his subsequent approach to life and politics? In all these respects, this essay takes further the analysis first developed in the chapter on Nelson Mandela in Smith, 2018.

Mandela's case has been very well documented, for obvious reasons (Barnard 2014; Boehmer 2008; Bundy 2015; Carlin 2008, 2013; Gibbs 2014; Lodge 2006; Mandela 2002, 2003a, b; Meredith 1997; Sampson 2000; Smith 2010). This fact allows us to observe some of the tensions and processes that his struggle entailed in the course of his long life. With hindsight, we can gain greater understanding of

> how Mandela *the favoured son* became Mandela *the rebel*,
> how Mandela the rebel became Mandela *the prisoner*, and, finally,
> how Mandela the prisoner became Mandela *the president*.

A Glance at the End Game

But to emphasise why this story is worth telling we can briefly dip into that story at a crucial point towards the end of his sentence before returning to the beginning and his birthplace in the Eastern Cape.

Mandela's last five years in jail brought increasing contacts with the leaders of South Africa's *apartheid* regime. Both before and after his release, Mandela played a pivotal role, along with Prime Minister Frederick Willem de Klerk (1999) in guiding the country through a perilous handbrake turn, reversing its direction of travel.

Before, and for some time after, the mid-1980s South Africa was in a state of low-level civil war, with the white minority fearing for their personal security and the black majority frequently aroused to mass protest. The armed wing of the African National Congress (ANC), known as the MK, short for *uMKhonto weSizwe*, or Spear of the Nation, made frequent incursions into South Africa from bases in neighbouring countries such as Botswana, Lesotho, Mozambique and Swaziland. The South African military responded by attacking ANC bases in these countries. Assassination was a favoured tactic on both sides.

Beginning in the mid-1980s, Mandela spent a decade bargaining with De Klerk and other regime ministers, and with ANC colleagues as—after four dreadful decades—the legal structures of *apartheid* were dismantled. Finally, in 1994 the first South African election took place for all South African citizens from whatever background and Mandela became the national president. See, for example, the special issue of *Current Sociology* edited by the author, to celebrate and interrogate South Africa's first decade since the first free elections in 1994. *Current Sociology* 52, 5, September 2004.

After about two years, Mandela, by then in his late seventies, began to let his deputy and eventual successor, Thabo Mbeki, take more day-to-day executive responsibility (Gevisser 2009; Gumede 2007). This meant that for another decade and a half, or thereabouts, Mandela was able to enjoy a less pressured existence, taking an advisory role not just in South African politics but throughout the continent and beyond.

Public Successes and Private Costs

Those are some of the public successes. However, to get a taste of the personal costs we should track back to the mid 1980s, catching Nelson Mandela at a time when, aged sixty-eight, he had spent three years confined in a claustrophobic rooftop cell shared with four fellow political prisoners in Pollsmoor prison: Walter Sisulu, Raymond Mhlaba, Andrew Mlangeni and Ahmed Kathrada. Mandela and the others in this small group had been transferred to Pollsmoor in 1982.

That was a huge change after eighteen tough years on Robben Island where several dozen other political prisoners had looked to Mandela as their leader and spokesperson (Buntman 2003; Coetzee 2000; Dlamini 1984; Coetzee et al. 2004). In their squalid new home, the five exiles from Robben Island only saw the sky when allowed into the prison yard. Pollsmoor is located in a salubrious southern suburb of Cape Town at the southern tip of South Africa. Surrounded by wealth, it had the reputation of being 'hellish', a place designed to demoralise impoverished, rebellious and law-breaking Black Africans (Mandela 2003a: 267–273, 283–284; Lodge 2006: 147–160). By the time Mandela left Pollsmoor in 1988, he had contracted tuberculosis.[1]

---

[1]Supporting evidence may be found at: 'Exclusive: Inside the hellish prison where Mandela was held', at https://edition.cnn.com/2016/02/25/africa/south-africa-jail-mandela/index.html; see also 'Mandela moved to house at prison farm', *New York Times*, 8 December 1988, at https://www.nytimes.com/1988/12/08/world/mandela-moved-to-house-at-prison-farm.html; on Ahmed Kathrada, 'Mandela's right hand man and prison mate, his elder brother and mentor', *New Statesman*, 6 December 2013, at https://www.newstatesman.com/samira-shackle/2013/12/mandelas-right–hand-man-and-prison-mate-his-elder-brother-and-mentor; and the following files: http://www.sahistory.org.za/sites/default/files/nelsonmandelaswarders.pdf; https://www.nelsonmandela.org/content/page/prison-timelinehttps://www.nelsonmandela.org/content/page/trials-and-prison-chronology; all accessed 17 October 2018.

By contrast, on Robben Island the prisoners had been several miles off-shore. Unlike at Pollsmoor, they made frequent trips across country. Their regular destination was the island's lime quarry, not a pleasant place. Here they laboured under the dazzling sun, in some cases doing permanent damage to their eyesight. The prisoners sometimes collected seaweed on the seashore, a task that reminded them how impossible it would be to escape by swimming.

Mandela was thrown out of his old Robben Island 'home' at very short notice. He left behind a close-knit though fractious community of inmates. They were united in misery, despised and, at times, oppressed by the Afrikaner guards. At Pollsmoor, the food was better and the bedding less spartan. But for Mandela, more closely confined than before and separated from many old comrades, the painful feeling of loneliness surely increased. In 1985, he had prostate surgery. When he came out of hospital, he was given a separate cell. This meant Mandela had more room and privacy but was also isolated from his comrades.

However, 1985 was a crucial year, the year in which Mandela began the long process of negotiation with the South African government. This would eventually lead to the release of the political prisoners in Pollsmoor, Robben Island and elsewhere. This was part of a larger transformation in South Africa leading, as already noted, to the abolition of *apartheid*, free and democratic elections, and the ANC's entry into government with Mandela as the country's first Black president.[2]

In 1985, Mandela could not have known the timing or the details of these momentous changes but he could surely see that things were shifting and that the ANC's long struggle, and his own, were moving towards their conclusion. Perhaps these circumstances explain why in one of his letters written from Pollsmoor Mandela gave rare explicit expression to some thoughts about his lengthy incarceration that had, he admitted, 'crossed the mind' on 'many occasions'.

[2]Beinart and Bundy (1987), Brown (2012), Bundy (2012, 2015), Carlin (2013), Carlson (1977), Filatova and Davidson (2013), Darwin (2011: 217–754), Gevisser (2009), Giliomee (2012), Gumede (2007), Hancock (1962, 1968), Johnson (2015a, b), Koorts (2014), Madikizela-Mandela (2013), Madonsela (2016), Maharaj (2008), Mamdani (2015), Mandela (2002, 2003a, b), Marsh (1994), Mbeki (1964, 1991, 1992), Meredith (1997, 2008), Murray (2016), Nimocks (1968), O'Brien (1979), Packenham (1992), Plaut and Holden (2012), Pogrund (2000), Ross (2008), Rotberg (1988), Russell (2009), Sampson (2000), Schreiner and Cronwright-Schreiner (1896), Schreiner (1989), Sitze (2013, 2014), Smith (2013), Stanley (2016), Steyn (2015), Thompson and Berat (2014), Welsh (2000, 2009, 2015).

He had been looking back to his younger self, to his time as a leading activist in the ANC. During the early 1960s, Mandela was the ANC's principal coordinator leading the team secretly preparing for armed resistance to South Africa's *apartheid* regime. For this crime against the regime, Mandela, along with others, was punished with a life sentence. In a letter written at Pollsmoor to a friend on 17 February 1986, he wrote:

> If I had been able to foresee all that has since happened, I would certainly have made the same decision, so I believe at least. But that decision would certainly have been far more daunting, and some of the tragedies which subsequently followed would have melted whatever traces of steel were within me. (Venter 2018: 484)

Mandela seems to be implying that endurance of the kind he was required to display depends on two things. The first is an outer layer of exuberant optimism combined with an existential sense of personal inviolability, a suit of armour that implicitly declares: the worst will not happen to me, or if it does, it will not touch me fatally. The second factor is a determined stubbornness of character (his inner 'traces of steel'), a stubbornness that is very sturdy but potentially dissoluble.

The optimism and sense of inviolability together act like the crumple zone on a motor vehicle. In other words, they absorb the immediate shock of being stopped in one's tracks and thrown behind bars. In the earliest years of a lengthy incarceration, unrealistic optimism, expecting too much success, too soon, is subject to an immense battering. The experience of getting too little success for too long is likely to transform that optimism into, at best, unalloyed realism. At worst, the prisoner may succumb to the fate that the authorities apparently intend, in this case at least: pessimism and demoralisation.

That 'crumpling' process absorbed the initial shock of being given life imprisonment. It protected the inner stubbornness from being subjected, immediately and unshielded, to the sustained direct assault on the self that results from such a profound reversal of fortune. As the early optimism wore off over a few years, Mandela's steely inner stubbornness was gradually called upon, more and more.

In Mandela's case, the strain imposed upon his spirit of stubbornness was eventually alleviated by two other factors. On the one hand, relations between captive and captor became a little more familiar, allowing some implicit consensual redefinition of those roles in ways that gave both captors and captives an easier life. This was not a smooth or continuous process since shifts in this direction were sometimes sharply reversed, temporarily at least, when changes occurred in the prison management. New prison brooms intermittently swept the inmates' regime clean of such softness (Lodge 2006: 15–49; Mandela 2003a, e.g. 84–92, 124–132, 128–133, 179–183).

On the other hand, shifts also occurred in the wider scene of struggle outside the prison, at several levels: within South Africa itself where the cities were in intermittent revolt; in the wider region of Southern Africa where the ANC was in military confrontation with the armed forces of the *apartheid* regime; across the West where a sustained campaign to 'free Nelson Mandela' was being mounted; and globally as the Cold War fought its way through to a climax which destroyed the Soviet Union, deprived the ANC of Russian aid, and undermined America's support for the *apartheid* regime itself as that government's fate became less strategically vital for Washington.

As news from the world outside improved in the mid-1980s, the future prospects for Mandela and his comrades began to look increasingly bright. Mandela's stubbornness and determination refocused, moving away from self-preservation and turning towards the challenge of reshaping South Africa's government and society. Optimism, blended with realism, kicked in once more. But these bright prospects were still only faint glimmers when Mandela, plagued with threats of serious illness, wrote his introspective letter from Pollsmoor in February 1986.

In his letter is Mandela writing about being absent from the field of battle, so to speak? Is this his 'Song of Roland', echoing the classic text in which the iconic, mythical feudal knight replayed crucial armed combats from his past inside his head? (This twelfth-century epic *chanson de geste* celebrated the brave deeds of Roland, nephew of Charlemagne, in battle against the Saracens in the eighth century. Roland sadly lost that battle but his side won the war. See Glyn Burgess (ed.) 1990, *The Song of Roland*, Harmondsworth: Penguin.) No, the 'Song of Mandela', if we can put it that way, is about the painful fracturing of his civilian life, about being torn out from the middle of a dense personal network. As Mandela puts it in the same letter:

> The death of your beloveds and your intimate friends to whom you are linked by countless ties, some going back for several decades; the wide variety of problems to which your family would be exposed in your absence, are personal disasters which are often difficult to endure and, on most occasions, leaving you wondering whether in this kind of life one should have a family, raise children and make firm friendships. (Venter 2018: 484)

This revelation of his inner conflicts reminds us that one of the sources of the global influence exercised by Nelson Mandela is his evident humanity. This was neither eliminated nor repressed by his revolutionary role as a leader dedicated to overthrowing the *apartheid* regime. Humanity is not the same as charm. Like many people, Mandela could certainly be charming, especially when it was politically or personally useful, or when he wished to make the other feel pleased, irrespective of utilitarian concerns. But humanity involves more than mere charm. It may refer to a person's visible faults and inadequacies—'how very human'—as well as their capacity to get along with the excesses and eccentricities of others: 'how very humane'. Both these things, the raw humanness and the commendable humanity, evoke our empathy and admiration.

But to get a more secure handle on these processes, we need to locate Mandela's prison experience within yet another context: his life and career as a whole. From this broader perspective, it soon becomes clear where his initial exuberant optimism comes from. Ever since birth Mandela was recognised and supported as a child with promise. He was a favoured son. This fed his immense personal ambition. As early as 1952 he was telling ANC colleagues, he would become South Africa's first Black president (Lodge 2006: 57). But what about the many decades that intervened between Mandela's birth and his presidency? How did they shape and drive the journey towards his desired destination? Let us begin at the beginning.

How the Favoured Son Became a Rebel

Young Mandela was born in a *kraal*, a term that refers to a traditional African village consisting of a collection of huts surrounded by a fence. The villagers' cattle or sheep were in many cases also enclosed. In early childhood, Mandela was brought up alongside his three sisters in his village, Qunu in Umtata within the Transkei district of the Eastern Cape.[3]

Mandela was the offspring of a feisty Transkei chief, Chief Mphakanyiswa Mandela, also known as Gadla Henry Mandela. This man challenged the authority of the local English colonial magistrate and was punished for it. His mother, Nosekeni Mandela, a devout Methodist, masterminded the construction of a church in her community. Methodism is well named.

---

[3]See 'Nelson Mandela's childhood' at https://nelsonmandelaresearchcenter.weebly.com/about-nelson-mandela.html; accessed 17 October 2018.

There is method in its holiness: it propagates the systematic pursuit of Godly work in everyday life: being good by doing good in the most effective way possible. (On Methodism, passion, discipline and dissent, see, e.g., Thompson 1966: 350–400; Hattersley 2004). Mandela inherited his father's arrogance and political feistiness along with the self-discipline and moral fervour of his mother.

Here already are the key elements that shaped Nelson Mandela's approach to life: determined self-discipline, a sense of personal authority sometimes bordering on impunity, and great respect for what is right, fair and appropriate in two ways: the implementation of basic human rights and adherence to his people's traditional customs and values.

Six years into his life sentence, Mandela told a correspondent 'I never succeeded in shaking off my peasant background'; he remained 'essentially a rustic'. In prison, he lived off thoughts of 'the veld and the bushes' where, as a boy, he 'tended stock, hunted, played' and attended 'the traditional initiation school' (Venter 2018: 484–485). Mandela's father arranged for him to be brought up in the royal court of the Thembu paramount chief where he spent part of his time acting as one of the shepherds of the royal flock. At other times, he attended court and was allowed to be present when petitions were heard and matters of state debated amongst the elders present.

Mandela was closely related to the heir to the Thembu throne, who at that time was still very young. Thembuland was governed by a regent, Jongintaba, who became Mandela's guardian. Jongintaba's son, Justice, was Mandela's playmate and *confidante*. At the Great Place, as the court compound with its surrounding land was known, young Mandela got to know the etiquette of speech and behaviour required to maintain and respect inter- and intra-tribal hierarchies. The prestige of different interests and individuals went up and down depending on the services they gave to the Thembu royal house and the favours they received.

The key passage rite leading to manhood was the drama of circumcision, which Mandela went through along with a group of other youngsters of the same age. Following this memorable process, the newly emancipated young men, collectively proud of their bravery, heard a speech from Jogintana's brother, Chief Meligqili. The speaker threw cold water over the occasion because he reminded his young audience that, for all their local privileges, they were a conquered people. Many of their brethren were destined to live in squalid city shacks, become alcohol-sodden and destroy their lungs in mines owned by prosperous white men. The chief's words were disappointing to his audience, including Mandela, since they thought Chief Meligqili was spoiling their party (D. J. Smith, 30–31).

Mandela grew up between the two world wars, before the Nationalist party officially installed *apartheid* in 1948 (Welsh 2009). He was living in an increasingly segregated society but one that had not yet acquired its later rigidity. As the child of a Methodist mother, Mandela was greatly influenced by the supportive paternalism of the English missionary tradition. He encountered this at Clarkebury High School and Healdtown College, both elite Methodist institutions.

But the dynamics had changed by the time, Mandela arrived at the University of Fort Hare. On the one hand, he was impressed by an inspiring speech that Jan Christian Smuts, a leading anglophile Afrikaner general and politician, gave at the university. Smuts praised the contribution that the British Empire, or Commonwealth as he chose to call it, was making to world peace. At that time, Mandela was beginning to see his future as a top-flight lawyer conducting cases in the courts set aside for the indigenous African population to which he belonged. With this in mind, he was studying anthropology, native administration, law and politics (Hancock 1962, 1968; Steyn 2015).

But there was a strong pull in another direction, towards the interests and values of traditional African villages. This would later extend towards the concerns of the townships and urban slums where migrants from the countryside typically found places to live. A key figure stimulating these interests was Oliver Tambo, a fellow student in the same dormitory who came from Pondoland, located, like Thembuland, in the Eastern Cape region. Mandela and Tambo, both from the Xhosa tribal group, took part in a boycott organised by the Student Representative Council, protesting at the quality of the food served up to students at Fort Hare.

In this way, Mandela was being drawn into an African oppositional network. The university authorities suspended him as a means of imposing discipline but it did not work. Mandela left the university and did not go back. His career as a rebel had begun. At this point, things began to move very fast. When Mandela got back to the Great Place, he discovered his guardian, the Regent, was planning to tie him down and weave him into the court society by forcing him into an arranged marriage. His friend Justice was destined for the same fate.

The two young men conspired. They purloined some cattle, sold it off to get some escape funds, and headed north to the big city, Johannesburg, with a vague plan to get work in or around the gold mines Chief Meligqili had warned them about. It was 1941. Mandela took a gun with him. He was twenty-two years old. Justice soon changed his mind and went home but not Mandela. He was quickly rumbled as a runaway and sacked from his first job as a night watchman. He moved in with a cousin and before long encountered Walter Sisulu, an influential Xhosa ANC activist. Sisulu got Mandela a job as an articled clerk in a Johannesburg law firm.

How the Rebel Became a Prisoner

Mandela the country boy became Mandela the city slicker. He signed up for a law degree at Witts, the University of the Witwatersrand, the first Black African to do so. The multiracial circle he joined at the university included fellow law students Joe Slovo and Ruth First. Mandela was soon radicalised but instead of being satisfied with belonging to a rather Europeanised elite, exciting though that was, he reckoned his special task was to mobilise the subjugated mass of Black Africans (Mandela 2002: 128–131).

Mandela joined the ANC in 1943 and became very active in its youth wing. In those days, he spoke against close cooperation with either communists or Indians since he considered both un-African. However, he was certainly influenced in the following years by the ideas of Gandhi, with his preference for non-violent defiance of oppressive laws. Paradoxically enough, Mandela was also influenced by the arguments for violent resistance that came from the South African Communist Party (SACP) (Baxter 2017; Fischer 2015; Gandhi 2012).

While Mandela was getting to know the range of oppositional ideologies and activist groups in play, he was also becoming familiar with the different scenes of inner-city, suburban and township life in and around Johannesburg. Mandela was securely installed on the ANC's national executive by the end of the 1940s. He had also discovered and explored his own immense talents as a persuader. Mandela was able to rouse a crowd, certainly enough to alarm the police in attendance. He could also sway a committee. Not least, he knew how to use his good looks and charm to impress others socially.

In 1944, Nelson Mandela married Walter Sisulu's cousin, Evelyn Mase, a nurse. She was a deeply religious woman and later became a Jehovah's Witness. The couple had four children. Those were years during which Mandela was not only increasingly active politically but also working as an attorney and studying for advanced legal qualifications. Since 1953 he had been working with Oliver Tambo in the first African-run law firm in the country, based in downtown Johannesburg, often taking on impoverished clients on a no fee basis. Meanwhile, Mandela took a lead in the defiance campaign pressing for the rights claimed in the ANC's Freedom Charter.

He spoke at many mass protests and was soon placed under a banning order intended to stop him going to any political meetings and gatherings (Lodge 2006: 78–80).

Mandela's first marriage did not withstand the strain imposed by his personal ambition to make a powerful mark on South African society and politics. Evelyn and Nelson divorced in 1958. By the end of that year, Mandela was married to Winnie Madikizela-Mandela, a social worker and ANC member who already had a prison record for political activism. Winnie came from Pondoland and was embedded in traditional African dynastic structures in a similar way to her new husband. She was, likewise, closely related to African royalty. Mandela was to have two daughters by this second marriage (Gilbey 1994; Bridgland 1997).

During the 1940s and 1950s, Mandela threw himself into three major enterprises. One, as we have seen, was marriage and homemaking with Evelyn Mase, with whom he produced a sizable family. By the 1950s, he was also in great demand as a brilliant advocate defending African labourers, house servants and other needy cases against white employers, often with great success. However, after 1948, when *apartheid* was introduced, Mandela could see clearly that his ambition of rising to the very top of the legal profession would be denied him because, being black, he was officially considered to belong to an inferior and inadequate racial group.

This made Mandela's third enterprise, taking a leading part in the ANC's struggle to overcome *apartheid*, his highest priority. He was not prepared to accept being denied the vocational rewards and high sociopolitical position his talents deserved. In other words, his radical political mission was not simply an expression of support for human rights, especially African rights. It was also a demand that he, Mandela, should be treated as a fully emancipated human being deserving the highest honours that he could obtain in a fair context with all others, regardless of colour or background. He might well have been able to bargain with the regime for a top position in a Bantustan, as some others did, but he took another route. By becoming a folk hero to the millions living in run-down townships, Mandela forged a strong and intimate bond with the future electorate, the men and women who would choose the president of a post-*apartheid* South Africa.

The law court soon changed for Mandela from a venue where he defended others to a place where he defended himself. For six years after 1955, he was entangled in a treason trial along with other colleagues. After being acquitted Mandela went underground. He took the lead in building up the newly created *Umkhonto we Sizwe* (Spear of the Nation) or, more briefly, MK intended for violent resistance against the regime.

Mandela became a symbol of that struggle. Journalists labelled him 'the Black Pimpernel'. In April 1964, he ended up in the dock alongside other colleagues at the so-called Rivonia trial, facing a possible death penalty. The trial was so-called because the team planning to set up MK had meetings in a house in Rivonia, which is a suburb of Johannesburg. A number of them were captured in a police raid (Brown 2012; Joffe 2014). Those put on trial in 1963 during the so-called Rivonia trial, accused of treason, were Nelson Mandela, Walter Sisulu, Govan Mbeki, Ahmed Kathrada, Raymond Mhlaba, Denis Goldberg, Elias Motsoaledi, Rusty Bernstein, Bob Hepple, Andrew Mlangeni and James Kantor.

Mandela made a four-hour speech. Basically, he put the *apartheid* regime itself on trial. His basic message was that *apartheid's* legal system and judicial apparatus treated him, an African, as an intrinsically defective and incomplete human being who should not expect to be treated with dignity or granted substantial freedom. In effect, it had forced him to become an outlaw (Sitze 2014, 150–161). At the end of his speech, Mandela told the judge that democracy, equality and harmony were, for him, an ideal for which to live and work. He added: 'if needs be, it is an ideal for which I am prepared to die' (Mandela 2002: 54). Fortunately for Mandela, his very notoriety as a fighter for the people's cause made the judge unwilling to sentence him, and his fellow defendants, to death. The regime did not want to make Mandela a martyr whose memory would inspire other rebels. Instead, it hoped that a very long term of imprisonment would erase him and, hopefully, his cause, from the people's mind.

How the Prisoner Became the President

The political prisoners on Robben Island, where Mandela and his comrades were sent, found that prison life was a microcosm of *apartheid*. For example, the food given to African prisoners was worse than that supplied to Indians. The Afrikaner guards tried to make the prisoners refer to them as *baas*, something they refused to do. Mandela, for one, insisted he would not be forced to wear short trousers, for which he was punished. The attitude of the guards ranged between sneeringly contempt and downright cruelty. Most ANC inmates were crowded into shared cells but members of the leadership were given individual cells. Regular work tasks such as breaking stones in the prison yard brought everyone together.

For his part, Mandela kept up an intense regime of physical exercise in his cell. Occasionally, he was given solitary confinement or got beaten, but he was not subjected to torture or serious physical abuse, unlike Winnie

Mandela who was consigned to jail on the mainland in May 1969 and detained in atrocious conditions for over year. When Mandela heard about this, it caused him intense distress, as did news that a son from his first marriage had died (Madikizela-Mandela 2013).

Slowly, after about a decade of intense toughness, prison life became slightly less rigorous, leading to a lighter work regime with more free time for association. During the 1970s, the prisoners began to hear about the MK's exploits. Also, about the Soweto shootings in 1976 which led to student protests in the townships. This brought another cohort of political prisoners into Robben Island, bringing with them the ideas of the Black Consciousness movement.

The prisoners gained a little more leeway in organising their daily lives. Sporting contests were arranged. Music was played. There were even plays, in which Mandela took part. Govan Mbeki produced a scheme of education for the prisoners. He told them about the long historical background leading up to the struggle against *apartheid*. Policy matters and internal conflicts, including discipline issues, some involving the prison authorities, went to a regular meeting of a council that became known as the High Organ. Nelson Mandela served as the High Organ's chair and became the main communication channel with the prison governor.

These experiences gave Mandela useful preparation for his future life after prison. In particular he got used to finding ways through intense conflict situations that had to be resolved or cooled down without having the option of walking away. Dealing with disputes between prisoners and Afrikaner guards was one example of this. So were his disagreements with Govan Mbeki whose son Thabi later became Mandela's vice-president. Govan Mbeki, a more dedicated Marxist than Mandela, was also a chief's son and looked the part. They often clashed in the High Organ. This helped Mandela burnish tactics and arguments that would come in handy when he was drawn into the middle of the protracted negotiations between the *apartheid* regime and the ANC (Mandela 2003a: 164–167).

Prison kept Mandela alive, safe from assassination attempts, especially since he did not fall for any attempts by the authorities to lure him into escape plots. Another benefit of incarceration was that Mandela was not directly involved in the nastiness of the war being waged within South Africa and beyond its borders between the ANC and the *apartheid* regime. Not least, the fact of being locked away for over a quarter of a century meant that a whole generation of young people grew up who came to think of Mandela as, so to speak 'the king across the water', a person whose name embodied their dream of a free and democratic South Africa.

The Mbeki's father and son were both utterly dedicated communists. For them both, party came before family. By contrast, Mandela's allegiance to the ideals legitimising the ANC's political ideology did not stifle to the same extent his emotional life as a son, father, husband and close friend of individuals both within and outside the ANC. On the contrary, Mandela's letters show that his imagination was full of thoughts about those diverse involvements. This matter is more complex than it seems initially because his links with his extended kin also drew him into political concerns, some of which went beyond the ANC.

Mandela belonged to a network of interlocking high-status Xhosa dynasties wielding traditional authority in the Transkei region of the Eastern Cape. In the Transkei, political disputes sometimes cut across family ties but the other side of that coin was that those same family ties could help to keep those conflicts within manageable bounds.

For example, Kaiser Matanzima, Mandela's cousin, decided to support the *apartheid* government's policy of separate development. As a result, in 1976 Transkei became South Africa's first Bantustan in 1976 with Mantazima as president. Matanzima competed for power with the Thembu king, based in the Great Place near Umtata where Mandela himself had been reared as a youngster. By 1980 the king had been forced to abandon the Transkei and go into exile. But Mantazima did not last long as the Transkei supremo. By 1986 he, too, had been forced out of office, accused of corruption. From jail, Mandela could not make any difference to these events. However, even though he found Mantazima's political stance abhorrent Mandela continued to deal with him as a family member deserving respect and in need of wise counsel (Gibbs 2014).

Another aspect of Mandela's kin network is more widely known. Winnie Madikazela-Mandela had high status within the Pondoland's traditional authority structure. She was eighteen years younger than her husband whom she effectively lost, apart from letters and prison visits, a mere six years after they married. Not surprisingly, she became her own woman, an independent political actor, surviving the best she could in the dangerous townships where gang warfare was rife. She became beset with scandal but, once again, Mandela remained loyal. They finally divorced in 1996 after thirty-eight years of marriage (Gilbey 1994; Bridgland 1997).

To summarise, Mandela's links with his immediate family and his extended kin sustained his sense of who he was and helped to keep his sense of honour and duty alive. For Mandela in prison, letters and visits, both strictly limited, nourished these vital links. So did his imagination, which was less limited.

Useful evidence is contained in the letters exchanged between Nelson Mandela, Winnie Mandela and others from the years 1969 to 1970, a time when for nearly five hundred days Winnie was detained by the security police and treated very cruelly. Mandela's letters are full of requests to hear about his wife, children, uncles, aunts, cousins and in-laws. He had a voracious appetite for apparently mundane details about wanted to know about marriages, births and deaths, who was well, who was ill, health and illness, who needed to be praised and who given words of condolence or commiseration.

Mandela's letters reflect his upbringing. As I have noted elsewhere, they are replete with traditional images and full of Christian feeling. Sometimes, writing to Winnie, he plays the paternalist, at other times the lover. He shifts between a rather paternalistic style and bursts of raw affection and longing. There are pride and strength on both sides (Madikizela-Mandela 2013).

When Mandela began negotiating with the *apartheid* regime in the mid-1980s, he did not immediately consult his ANC colleagues back in Robben Island, although Thabo Mbeki and the ANC leadership in exile were soon also engaged in talks. The point is that Mandela slipped free from Robben Island's High Organ just as, in the 1940s he had escaped from the Great Place. In both cases, Mandela was able to make a major change in his personal circumstances and then negotiate himself into a good working relationship with both his old and new associates.

After about two years in office, Mandela made another escape, this time from the heavily hands-on duties required of South Africa's national president, which he largely passed on to Thabo Mbeki. However, in spite of his newly acquired respectability, Mandela remained on the US terror until he reached the age of ninety in 2008, as reported here: 'Mandela taken off terror watch list', 1 July 2008, *BBC News*, at http://news.bbc.co.uk/1/hi/world/americas/7484517.stm and 'Nelson Mandela's long history of support for Palestine', 30 January 2014, *Middle East Monitor*, at https://www.middleeastmonitor.com/20140130-nelson-mandelas-long-history-of-support-for-palestine/ (both accessed 11 April 2017). Whatever Washington thought, Mandela's role in avoiding widespread unrest and maintaining an optimistic spirit was very important. He was able to transfer the skills of persuasion and negotiation he had burnished in jail to helping ease the transition away from *apartheid*. No-one else commanded trust and respect in three crucial locations at the same time: within the Afrikaner establishment, the ANC leadership and the African townships.

It was Mandela who avoided a bloody confrontation between Xhosa township dwellers and Zulu migrant workers in 1991 at Katlehong, near Johannesburg, when he told his audience that their task was reconciliation: 'as long as I am your leader, I will tell you, always, when you are wrong' (Lodge 2006: 179–180). It was Mandela who went on television after Chris Hani, leader of MK, was murdered, and reminded his angry African audience that an Afrikaner woman had taken the vehicle number of his killer and informed the police. Not least, in 1995 it was Mandela the Black African national president who handed the winning trophy in the Rugby Union World Cup, being held for the first time in South Africa, to the Afrikaner captain of the winning team. Mandela was wearing the national team's rugby shirt when he did it (Carlin 2008).

Conclusion

Mandela's skilful diplomacy during the 1995 Rugby Union World Cup and the need for him to deploy those skills were telling reminders that neither *apartheid* nor the ANC had been defeated by force of arms. Their struggle was ended by the conclusion of the Cold War and the withdrawal of support from both sides by the United States and the Soviet Union, respectively. The ANC put down its arms. The Nationalist party relinquished control of the national government. The legislation enforcing *apartheid* was discarded. Both sides had to live together. Mandela's voice and presence were very important in helping that to happen.

After the first democratic election in 1994, the ANC discovered that the socialist revolution they had fought for was blocked by the tight grip international big business had on the national economy. The ANC's key card was its ability to hold in check the vehemence of the impoverished townships. A pragmatic deal eventually emerged. The ANC would direct sufficient resource to the poor, especially in urban areas, to damp down mass support for aggrieved local leaders. In return, business would support a black economic empowerment programme, introduced in 2003, that co-opted Black African entrepreneurs, many from the ANC, onto lucrative schemes promoting the development of South Africa as a prosperous modern rainbow nation. (On some of the challenges that South Africa has been facing since 1990 see Adedeji et al. 1991; Adonis 2015; Aldana 2006; Asmal 1997; Booysen 2016; Bundy 2014; Johnson 2015b; Leibbrandt et al. 2014; Madonsela 2016; Maharaj 2008; Mamdani 2015; Meredith 2008; Plaut and Holden 2012; Russell 2009; Swilling 2017; Thompson and Berat 2014.)

It is likely that the Nelson Mandela who led the defiance campaign and worked his way up the ANC hierarchy in the 1940s and 1950s would have campaigned ferociously hard to find effective remedies for the disappointment and corruption that followed the implementation of the pragmatic arrangement just described. But by 2003 Mandela was in his eighties. He was a loyalist and a patriot as well as a socialist, a chief and a Christian. In the event, Mandela's biggest contribution to the new South Africa, with its magnificent potential and evident defects—hopefully, just growing pains— was not his pursuit of specific policies. It was the legitimisation he gave to the ANC in the wider world and on the South African streets. The national president acquired a near-saintly reputation as an imprisoned martyr; a man who suffered for his country's cause yet remained totally undefeated. His presence sanctified the regime, especially when seen from abroad. He knew how to combine ambition with empathy for the concerns of others, including his rivals. His successors have a lot to live up to.

References

Adedeji, A., Teriba, O., & Bugembe, P. (1991). *The Challenge of African Economic Recovery and Development*. London: Frank Cass.

Adonis, C. K. (2015). Generational Forgiveness and Historical Injustices: Perspectives of Descendants of Victims of *Apartheid*-era Gross Human Rights Violations in South Africa. *Journal of Psychology in Africa, 25*(1), 6–14.

Aldana, R. (2006). A Victim-Centered Reflection on Truth Commissions and Prosecutions as a Response to Mass Atrocities. *Journal of Human Rights, 5*(1), 107–126.

Asmal, K. (1997). *Reconciliation Through Truth: A Reckoning of Apartheid's Criminal Governance*. Rochester, NY: James Currey.

Barnard, R. (Ed.). (2014). *The Cambridge Companion to Nelson Mandela* (pp. 131–160). Cambridge: Cambridge University Press.

Baxter, P. (2017). *Gandhi, Smuts and Race in the British Empire: Of Passive and Violent Resistance*. Barnsley: Pen and Sword Books.

Beinart, W., & Bundy, C. (1987). *Hidden Struggles in Rural South Africa*. London: James Currey.

Boehmer, E. (2008). *Nelson Mandela: A Very Short Introduction*. Oxford: Oxford University Press.

Booysen, S. (2016). *Dominance and Decline: The ANC in the Time of Zuma*. Johannesburg: Wits University Press.

Bridgland, F. (1997). *Katiza's Journey: Beneath the Surface of South Africa's Shame*. London: Sidgwick and Jackson.

Brown, S. B. (2012). *Saving Nelson Mandela: The Rivonia Trial and the Fate of South Africa*. Oxford: Oxford University Press.

Bundy, C. (2012). *Govan Mbeki*. Athens: Ohio University Press.

Bundy, C. (2014). *Short-Changed? South Africa Since Apartheid*. Athens: Ohio University Press.

Bundy, C. (2015). *Nelson Mandela*. Stroud: The History Press.

Buntman, F. L. (2003). *Robben Island and Prisoner Resistance to Apartheid*. Cambridge: Cambridge University Press.

Carlin, J. (2008). *Playing the Enemy: Nelson Mandela and the Game That Made a Nation*. London: Atlantic Books.

Carlin, J. (2013). *Knowing Mandela*. London: Atlantic Books.

Carlson, J. (1977). *No Neutral Ground*. London: Quartet Books.

Coetzee, J. K. (2000). *Plain Tales from Robben Island*. Pretoria: Van Schaik Publishers.

Coetzee, J. K., Gilfillan, L., & Hulec, O. (2004). *Fallen Walls: Prisoners of Conscience in South Africa and Czechoslovakia*. New Brunswick, NJ: Transaction Publishers.

Darwin, J. (2011). *The Empire Project: The Rise and Fall of the British World System 1830–1970*. Cambridge: Cambridge University Press.

De Klerk, F. W. (1999). *The Last Trek—A New Beginning*. London: Pan Books.

Dlamini, M. (1984). *Hell Hole, Robben Island*. Nottingham: Spokesman.

Filatova, I., & Davidson, A. (2013). *The Hidden Thread: Russia and South Africa in the Soviet Era*. Johannesburg: Jonathan Ball Publishers.

Fischer, L. (2015). *The Life of Mahatma Gandhi*. London: Vintage.

Gandhi, M. K. (2012). *An Autobiography: Or the Story of My Experiments with Truth*. London: Penguin.

Gevisser, M. (2009). *Thabo Mbeki*. Johannesburg: Jonathan Ball.

Gibbs, T. (2014). *Mandela's Kinsmen: Nationalist Elites and Apartheid's First Bantustan*. London: James Currey.

Gilbey, E. (1994). *The Lady: The Life and Times of Winnie Mandela*. London: Vintage Books.

Giliomee, H. (2012). *The Afrikaners: Biography of a People*. London: Hurst.

Gumede, W. M. (2007). *Thabo Mbeki and the Battle for the Soul of the ANC*. London: Zed Books.

Hancock, W. K. (1962). *Smuts: The Sanguine Years 1870–1919*. Cambridge: Cambridge University Press.

Hancock, W. K. (1968). *Smuts: The Fields of Force 1919–1950*. Cambridge: Cambridge University Press.

Hattersley, R. (2004). *John Wesley: A Brand from the Burning. The Life of John Wesley*. London: Abacus.

Joffe, J. (2014). *The State vs. Nelson Mandela: The Trial That Changed South Africa*. London: Oneworld Publications.

Johnson, R. W. (2015a). *Look Back in Laughter*. Newbury: Threshold Press.

Johnson, R. W. (2015b). *How Long Will South Africa Survive?* London: C. Hurst and Company.

Koorts, L. (2014). *DF Malan and the Rise of Afrikaner Nationalism*. Cape Town: Tafelberg Publishers.

Leibbrandt, M., Woolard, I., McEwen, H., & Koep, C. (2014). *Employment and Inequality Outcomes in South Africa*. Cape Town: Southern Africa Labour and Development Research Unit (SALDRU). At http://www.oecd.org/employment/emp/45282868.pdf. Accessed 16 August 2016.

Lodge, T. (2006). *Mandela: A Critical Life*. Oxford: Oxford University Press.

Madikizela-Mandela, W. (2013). *491 Days: Prisoner Number 1323/69*. Athens: Ohio University Press.

Madonsela, T. (2016). *State of Capture: A Report of the Public Protector*. Pretoria: South Africa.

Maharaj, M. (2008). *The ANC and South Africa's Negotiated Transition to Democracy and Peace*. Berlin: Berghof Foundation at www.berghoffoundation.org/fileadmin/redaktion/.../Transitions.../transitions_anc.pdf. Accessed 19 August 2016.

Mamdani, M. (2015). Beyond Nuremberg: The Historical Significance of the Post-apartheid Transition in South Africa. *Politics and Society, 43*(1), 66–88.

Mandela, N. (2002). *Long Walk to Freedom: The Autobiography of Nelson Mandela. Volume One. 1918–1962*. London: Abacus.

Mandela, N. (2003a). *Long Walk to Freedom: The Autobiography of Nelson Mandela. Volume Two. 1962–1994*. London: Abacus.

Mandela, M. (2003b). *Nelson Mandela in His Own Words: From Freedom to the Future* (K. Asmal, D. Chidester, & W. James, Ed.). London: Abacus.

Marsh, P. T. (1994). *Joseph Chamberlain: Entrepreneur in Politics*. New Haven, CT: Yale University Press.

Mbeki, G. (1964). *South Africa: The Peasants' Revolt*. London: Penguin Books.

Mbeki, G. (1991). *Learning from Robben Island: The Prison Writings of Govan Mbeki*. London: James Currey.

Mbeki, G. (1992). *The Struggle for Liberation in South Africa: A Short History*. Cape Town: David Philip.

Meredith, M. (1997). *Mandela: A Biography*. London: Simon and Schuster.

Meredith, M. (2008). *Diamonds, Gold and War: The Making of South Africa*. London: Simon and Schuster.

Murray, B. (2016). Nelson Mandela and Wits University. *The Journal of African History, 57*(2), 271–292.

Nimocks, W. (1968). *Milner's Young Men: The "Kindergarten" in Edwardian Imperial Affairs*. London: Hodder and Stoughton.

O'Brien, T. H. (1979). *Milner: Viscount Milner of St James's and Cape Town 1854–1925*. London: Constable.

Packenham, T. (1992). *The Scramble for Africa*. London: Abacus.

Plaut, M., & Holden, P. (2012). *Who Rules South Africa?* London: Biteback Publishing.

Pogrund, B. (2000). *War of Words: Memoir of a South African Journalist*. New York, NY: Seven Stories Press.

Ross, R. (2008). *A Concise History of South Africa (Cambridge Concise Histories)*. Cambridge: Cambridge University Press.

Rotberg, R. I. (1988). *The Founder: Cecil Rhodes and the Pursuit of Power*. Oxford: Oxford University Press.

Russell, A. (2009). *After Mandela: The Battle for the Soul of South Africa*. London: Hutchinson.

Sampson, A. (2000). *Mandela: The Authorised Biography*. London: HarperCollins.

Schreiner, O. (1989). *The Story of a South African Farm*. London: Virago; Originally published 1883.

Schreiner, O., & Cronwright-Schreiner, C. S. (1896). *The Political Situation*. London: T. Fisher Unwin. At https://archive.org/details/politicalsituat00crongoog. Accessed 19 August 2016.

Sitze, A. (2013). *The Impossible Machine: A Genealogy of South Africa's Truth and Reconciliation Commission*. Ann Arbor: University of Michigan Press.

Sitze, A. (2014). Mandela and the Law. In R. Barnard (Ed.), *The Cambridge Companion to Nelson Mandela* (pp. 131–160). Cambridge: Cambridge University Press.

Smith, D. J. (2010). *Young Mandela*. London: Weidenfeld and Nicolson.

Smith, D. (2013). Forced Social Displacement: The 'Inside Stories' of Oscar Wilde, Jean Améry, Nelson Mandela and Aung San Suu Kyi. In N. Demertsiz (Ed.), *Emotions in Politics* (pp. 60–83). London: Palgrave-Macmillan.

Stanley, L. (2016). *Imperialism, Labour and the New Woman: Olive Schreiner's Social Theory*. London: Routledge.

Steyn, R. (2015). *Jan Smuts: Unafraid of Greatness.* Jeppestown: Jonathan Ball.

Swilling, M. (2017). *Betrayal of the Promise: How South Africa Is Being Stolen*. Johannesburg: Public Affairs Research Institute.

Thompson, E. P. (1966). *The Making of the English Working Class*. New York: Vintage Books.

Thompson, L., & Berat, L. (2014). *A History of South Africa*. New Haven and London: Yale University Press.

Van der Merwe, J. P. (2009). An Anthropological Perspective on Afrikaner Narratives and Myths. *Identity, Culture and Politics: An Afro-Asian Dialogue, 10*(1), 30–50.

Venter, S. (2018). *The Prison Letters of Nelson Mandela*. London: W. W. Norton & Co.

Welsh, D. (2009). *The Rise and Fall of Apartheid*. Johannesburg: Jonathan Ball.

Welsh, D. (2015). Apartheid and the Herrenvolk Idea. In C. R. Browning, S. Heschel, M. R. Marrus, & M. Shain (Eds.), *Holocaust Scholarship: Personal Trajectories and Professional Interpretations* (pp. 187–214). London: Palgrave Macmillan.

Welsh, F. (2000). *A History of South Africa*. London: HarperCollins.

18

The 'Other' Prison of Antonio Gramsci and Giulia Schucht

Jenifer Nicholson

Introduction

Originally, I was to examine Gramsci's decline in prison and his anxiety over the relationship with his wife, and how his attitude to her situation changed, but since I 'write forward' (Kincaid Weekes 2002; Nicholson 2016) following the life or lives as I trace them, so the initial idea sometimes changes as the characters and their thoughts and feelings unfold—developing 'concrete imagination' which Gramsci described in a letter to Giulia as the faculty of being able to recreate 'another life with its needs and requirements… so as to understand it and come into intimate contact with it' (L.P.2: 371).

As I read the letters from Giulia, Gramsci's wife (held in the Fondo Antonio Gramsci at the Fondazione Istituto Gramsci, Rome), and those from his sister-in-law Tania (A.G., T.S.), I realised that Giulia's voice was and always had been absent and consequently she has been underestimated and misunderstood. Firstly, by Gramsci and subsequently by biographers whose focus was the political persona and writings of Antonio Gramsci himself, in his roles as journalist, activist and politician before prison, and Marxist theoretician while imprisoned (Fiori 1965; Davidson 1977; Vacca 2012; D'Orsi 2017). Here I look at the separation and its sorrow from Giulia's point of view too. There is little detailed material about Giulia so the chronology is supplied by Gramsci's letters and Tania's, whose information from Russia

J. Nicholson (✉)
Southampton, UK

© The Author(s) 2020
J. M. Parsons and A. Chappell (eds.), *The Palgrave Handbook of Auto/Biography*,
https://doi.org/10.1007/978-3-030-31974-8_18

415

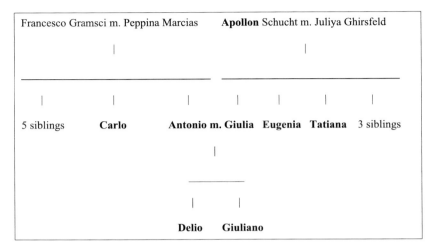

Fig. 18.1 Who's who (those in bold are named in the story)

and critical evaluations of the morbid and suffocating atmosphere within the Schucht family were vital to Gramsci's, and our, understanding of what it was like to be Giulia (see Fig. 18.1).

Antonio Gramsci is known for his prison writings, *The Prison Notebooks*, which contain his theories on hegemony, the role of the intellectuals, and education.

He also wrote the *Letters from Prison* (L.P.1 L.P.2), which chronicle his efforts to stay sane and productive, despite his illnesses, and the erosion of the self in prison and the pain of separation from his wife Giulia and his two sons. The letters are fascinating and moving, but the account is one-sided. It was fifty years before another part of the conversation was published, the letters from Tatiana (Tania) Schucht, his sister-in-law (A.G., T.S.). His wife Giulia's letters have never been published in full; she remains a shadowy figure. Her pre-prison letters have been lost. Giulia's silences tormented Gramsci; biographers have attributed the gaps between the letters to her mysterious illness, but the subtext implies that she was weak, had mental problems or had been swept off her feet by Gramsci and did not really care for him (Fiori 1965; Davidson 1977; Cambria 1976).

There are only thirty-nine letters from her written to him in the archive. Why, ask biographers, did she write so few? Gramsci's letters show that in fact she wrote at least twenty-five letters more than those found, so that her total is at least sixty-four. Still a meagre total for eleven years, but when the correspondence is seen as a whole, Gramsci wrote two hundred and thirty-nine letters to Tania, Giulia's sister, and only seventy-four to Giulia. This begs the question why did Gramsci write so few letters to Giulia?

Antonio and Giulia

They met in 1922, when he was being treated at a sanatorium. Giulia was visiting her sister Eugenia, also ill, with whom Gramsci was involved in a love affair. Enter Giulia, and Gramsci was overwhelmed by her beauty and her political ideals. She was already a party member, an accolade, a Bolshevist veteran of the 1917 revolutions, a professional violinist and a town councillor (Izvestia 6 January 1918: cited Gramsci Jr. 2014: 62). He was her ideal man as described in her girlhood diary (Cambria 1976). They fell passionately in love, he left Eugenia for Giulia, and despite the disapproval of her father Apollon Schucht, they married in autumn 1923. Gramsci later admitted that he had rushed her into sex and the partnership (Gramsci 2014). Eugenia never forgave him; regarded their first child Delio as really hers; usurped Giulia's role with him; and undermined the marriage wherever possible.

Giulia and Antonio never ever had a home and life together. Lenin sent Gramsci to Vienna in December 1923, from whence he wrote passionate letters to Giulia begging her to join him. Apollon prevented this. Gramsci was then sent to Rome to lead the Italian Communist Party and once again the relationship was conducted by letter. The only time they spent together was in Rome from autumn 1925 to summer 1926, but not quite. Eugenia, who accompanied Giulia to Rome, vetoed sharing accommodation with Gramsci. They never had the privacy to get to know each other without interference, to become truly partners. It is clear that this was an intensely physical relationship. Eugenia was revolted by it and summoned her father (Gramsci 2008).

When Apollon arrived from Russia, he wrote to his wife that Antonio had corrupted Giulia; she was addicted to him, he was moulding her to his needs (Gramsci 2008). Giulia had written to him too saying that she had sometimes felt that she was losing herself and that it had taken all her energy to remain autonomous (Gramsci 2008). In other words, she and Antonio had been working out the balance of the relationship, which, unfortunately, they were unable to accomplish in that abnormal context. Much later, in 1932, she was to reflect on this period and her own lack of maturity. The relationship had remained as it had been in Vienna, 'deep down we have not had the time to feel ourselves husband and wife, we have just been lovers on our honeymoon' (Gramsci 2014: 279); each of them still in love with an idealised perception of the other.

They did find the privacy to conceive another child. Eugenia, furious, decreed that Giulia should go back to Moscow for the birth and no one dared oppose her. Giulia was devastated: she wanted Gramsci to defend her against Eugenia, interpreting his silence as an indication he no longer wanted her to work with him (Cambria 1976). Gramsci wanted her to stay of her own volition, he would not press her (L.P.2: 353). Each, it seems, was disappointed in the other's reaction. Giulia left for Moscow in June 1926 and he never saw her or his sons again.

After his arrest in November 1926, he spent eighteen months of detention awaiting trial. He was bored, but he had companions, cash and an unlimited book supply, funded by his friend Sraffa. He had been assured that Giulia and his sons would receive an allowance. He had made the ultimately damaging decision that Tania would be his main correspondent, relaying communications to Giulia in Russia (with a loose arrangement that Tania would also forward all his letters to her, Tania) and sending copies of letters to the party in exile. For Giulia, life had been much harder. Still recovering from the birth of Giuliano and from nursing Delio through scarlet fever, she had collapsed with the shock of his arrest. Over the winter 1926–1927, both children had been ill for months while she went back to work. She had to nurse a sick baby and toddler in a flat shared with other tenants, her elderly parents and an intermittently unwell and resentful Eugenia, while working full time. Both she and Eugenia had Spanish flu, Giulia so badly that it triggered severe clinical depression and possibly a form of epilepsy. These lingered for years without definitive diagnosis. She underwent several different forms of treatment. She recovered in a sanatorium and then went back to work. 1927–1928 saw Giuliano with suspected diphtheria and Delio with bronchitis and followed much the same pattern. In 1928, Gramsci preoccupied with preparation for his defence only wrote to her directly three times.

The prison sentence of twenty years in June 1928 was crushing. They had to find a way to maintain their relationship and bring up their children by letter—a form which Gramsci disliked and had always avoided where possible and Giulia, according to a childhood friend, never wrote more than a page of anything (Cambria 1976). In the past, Gramsci's letters to Giulia had been part passion and part politics, neither would be possible now. All correspondence was censored at the prison, and then, in Giulia's case, probably by the Russian authorities too, so overt politics were out of the question. Gramsci felt too inhibited by censorship to write love letters, so his solution, to begin with, was not to write to her at all directly, begging Tania to do so for him. A process repeated in every new prison until he could accustom himself again to censorship. Only once did he question whether Giulia would be hurt by this—in a letter to Tania (L.P.1).

Sterilisation of the Heart

We pick up their story in November 1929, three years after Gramsci's arrest, after a year in which he had received at least seven letters from Giulia between January and July. All these letters are missing. Then there had been a long gap. Gramsci wrote to Tania that he had not heard from Giulia for four months and saying surely it was not just lack of time (L.P.1). In part it was. Giulia, the family breadwinner, had earned more than anyone else in the family since 1923. Her mother and Eugenia do not seem to have had paid employment. Unknown to Gramsci, Giulia had another demanding year; the children had been ill; the fourth-floor flat was inconvenient and at least one of their co-tenants was drunken and abusive. To protect the children, the family moved to the country which meant that Giulia had to make the long commute daily to work in Moscow, before returning to look after Giuliano, who Eugenia, obsessed by Delio, appears to have disliked and ignored. Giulia became exhausted and her letters were short. She had spent the summer in a sanatorium without telling Gramsci, only returning in November.

Gramsci felt uneasy; he had written twice without an answer, so perhaps she was waiting to hear from him, but he felt he could not write to Giulia a third time without hearing from her in case she no longer wanted to hear from him (L.P.1). He told Tania to send this letter to Giulia. Tania refused. She told him that the poor girl already lived in too much sadness (A.G., T.S.). In December, once again he refused to write to Giulia: his ties with the world are breaking, how was he supposed to interpret the fact, that last time she wrote 'she felt ever closer to me' and then he heard nothing for four months (L.P.1: 297).

As ever with Gramsci, the political and the personal are intertwined; in his political practice and journalism, he had refused to write or decide tactics without the collection of full and accurate data. He was refusing again now. Besides, Giulia's silence corresponded with a change of policy in Stalin's Russia. He had begun to worry that she was at risk and under pressure from work; perhaps letters from him might compromise her. Worse, that as a party member she too regarded him as dissident, so that his letters would be unwelcome. He also suspected that Tania had informed Giulia of her own suggestions to Gramsci to petition for release on grounds of ill-health via one of her medical friends. Gramsci had categorically refused. He would never beg for mercy from Mussolini, he would never agree to any amnesty which required reneging on his political stance, not just because it would be a betrayal of his beliefs and the workers but because Giulia, a committed communist, would think less of him.

In response, Tania sent him news of the family, writing critically of their chaotic lifestyle. She relayed letters from Apollon detailing their lives and that of the children, but this does not fulfil Gramsci's needs. He quoted Spaventa (prisoner of the Bourbons in Naples) as saying that being without news from loved ones is very painful for a man with an affectionate heart. Spaventa, and by implication Gramsci, did not think his family loved him any less, it was his own reaction he feared '… the long imprisonment, the suspicion of being forgotten by everyone, slowly embitters and sterilises my heart' (L.P.1: 305).

Tania reprimanded him saying, you only have to reread one of Giulia's letters, saying what comfort she feels when she receives a few lines from you, especially when you mention the children, to know her state of mind. She told him that in terms of emotional ties, Giulia was infinitely worse off than he. He was physically removed from the world, but he had support. Giulia was 'violently and pitilessly cut off from you… She has absolutely no one who can bring her a real sensation of your existence, of your love' (A.G., T.S: 441–448). Tania suggested it was possible that Giulia also thought like Spaventa about isolation and the sterilisation of the heart. She emphasised her point saying that perhaps it had never occurred to him that, concretely, Giulia had been more cut off from him than he was from her; that his imprisonment and the limits imposed on his writing letters were as much a punishment for Giulia as for him. He had all of the family and Tania here to support him, but who talked to Giulia, who comforted her? The implication is that the Schuchts are not doing so. She continued 'she only has the hope of a few lines from you addressed to her, a bit of news… It's too little in reality to prevent her soul from being in constant pain, always filled with nostalgia, tormented by separation' (ibid.). She will not send on his second letter about Giulia either.

Gramsci was incensed by the idea that he suffered less than Giulia because he received letters from Tania and the family. He wrote that in some situations one person (Tania) cannot replace another (Giulia); furthermore, it was not a question of needing comfort himself but rather of being able to 'give a bit of strength to Giulia' who was struggling and had been 'saddled with so many burdens because of our union'. He reiterates his fear that if he knew nothing, became isolated from her, detached from her world, he would no longer understand or feel anything about it (L.P.1: 307–308).

Nevertheless, he wrote to Giulia on the next writing day, an impersonal letter about books which gave him a pretext to write to her, asking for details of the boys' intellectual development. His letters to Tania also avoided the personal. He seemed resigned to getting whatever news he could of the boys via Tania's letters. Tania wrote, visited and talked to him about Giulia, and described her life: her prostration when he was arrested; her demanding life; her discomfort about the powerful relationship between Delio and Eugenia. She also makes the point that just as Gramsci has to suppress his emotional reactions to defend himself, so Giulia, in order to be a good mother, to cope with the demands of her life, has to suppress hers (AG., TS.). They are both inhibited by the external conditions. So, in May 1930, he wrote to Giulia that Tania had visited and 'drew a dark picture' of her physical and mental health. He reminded her that she had agreed never to hide anything about her health or the children's development from him, this has obviously changed, and he does not know why. She compounds his sense of impotence by keeping him in the dark; bad news is better than no news.

His next letter to Tania enlarged on the theme of imprisonment made worse. He talked of 'the other prison'. He had expected the walls, the bars and so on, what he had not bargained for was

> the other prison, which is being cut off not only from social life but also from family life etc.etc. I could estimate the blows of my adversaries whom I was fighting, I could not forsee that blows would also come at me from other sides, from where I would least expect them (metaphorical blows, of course, omissions too are faults or blows). (L.P.1: 331–332)

Clearly, Giulia is to be counted among those delivering blows.

Tania does not respond to this outburst directly but on 24 May she sends him the translation of two postcards from her father. The first confirms Gramsci's first concern that Giulia is ill which made writing to him more difficult. The second is more ambiguous, if Giulia does not write it is because she cannot. A later letter says clearly that they have not understood. Apollon wrote, 'I did not say that Giulia cannot write because she is ill, I said she writes so seldom because it is hard to do so under the conditions in which she is forced to do it' (AG., TS.: 533). Just as Gramsci had feared, Giulia is ill, under surveillance and political pressure; she too is imprisoned.

Giulia remained silent, and then four letters arrived together in July 1930. Gramsci told Giulia that the effect of only having received one letter between July' 29 and July' 30 had been first obsession, and then, as defence against pain, numbness. Her letters and photo imply she has gone through a serious crisis which she has not yet overcome. She looked 'sorrowful or resigned' which has upset him. He tells her she is stronger than she thinks, and she should write to him and it would help, instead of not writing and then getting distressed about it and so on in a descending spiral. He likes what she has told him about the children but wants more detail about their development as men 'their embryonic conception of the world' (L.P.1: 342). In a later letter, he complained that they have not been able to initiate a dialogue; their letters form parallel monologues (L.P.1: 355).

Over the course of 1930, there was more reliable information from Russia. Piero Sraffa, Gramsci's friend, went to Russia in August. He visited the Schuchts and also went to see Giulia, once again in a sanatorium. Tania relays Sraffa's letter recounting his meeting with Giulia and what she had told him about her health; that Giulia and the family had decided that Gramsci should not be told about her illness; and that she found it difficult to write without revealing the truth.

However, in December, Tania confessed that she had not sent on Gramsci's letters regularly, as agreed. That summer she had sent on *most* of them, not directly to Giulia but to Apollon who would read them and hand them on to Giulia according to his estimation of her health (A.G., T.S.). Sraffa had taken those of Gramsci's letters to Tatiana which she had *still* held back and gave them directly to Giulia (ibid.). For some time, there had been a *double* barrier between Gramsci and Giulia by letters withheld. Tania also copied to Gramsci more of Eugenia's letters to her which she had recently received. They revealed how obstructive, hostile and domineering Eugenia is now and how morbidly possessive of Delio. It becomes clear to Gramsci again how emotionally confined Giulia is; the family have never let her go, or grow up. She too is in receipt of 'blows'—intentionally from Eugenia and unintentionally, 'to protect' her from Apollon and Tania.

Gramsci was appalled, 'what is … disguised as altruism and disinterested tenderness, … is arrogant, pure egocentrism, oppression of another's human personality' (L.P.2: 02). He was distressed he had misjudged Giulia and not realised her situation, that she has endured long periods without letters too. In January 1931, he wrote to them both. To Tania, he says that Giulia has been the chief victim of all the misunderstandings about correspondence; which have now he fears, become past mending and crystallised. He had been concerned about Eugenia's behaviour in Rome but had not intervened, and he should have done. He regrets not protesting much earlier about the silences and avoiding months of despair and distress for Giulia and himself. Now they must both try to bring some order into the moral and emotional muddle of Giulia's life in order to support her (L.P.2).

To Giulia, he says he regrets not hearing from her for a long time and says openly that he is afraid that both their letters occasionally go astray. He has been informed about her health but why haven't they kept their word about telling each other the truth? He thinks she should write not just for him, for her own sake too, 'because it seems to me that you too must be isolated, and … that by writing to me you would feel this inner solitude less' (L.P.2: 4). He wrote a long letter in February, in reply to her January letter, which remains missing. He talks of the expectation they have constructed between them about her strength or weakness for which he takes 'the greater responsibility', which meant that she could not write to him because she did not want to damage the image of the 'strong woman' which they had made for her. That, in effect, they had created a barrier, which prevented her from writing.

Now the important thing is to establish a normal relationship so that she can write to him without feeling 'almost revulsion at appearing different to what you imagine I think you are'. He goes on to say that he is convinced that she is stronger than she thinks she is because, even in her depression, she has maintained her willpower and her control of herself, doing so 'in the social environment that always demands an extremely determined effort of will'. He means her family and her job with OGPU (the security service, forerunner of the NKVD), both of which Gramsci now realises, confine and oppress her. He goes on to try to support her, to persuade her that she does have the power and strength to get better. He feels his inability to do any-thing 'real and effective' help her; should he be tender or tough? Their great-est misfortune is to have spent so little time together, and that little 'under abnormal circumstances, detached from real and concrete everyday life'. He wants to save everything that was good from the past and they must help each other. He wants to help her to overcome her depression; she could help him by teaching him how to help her, and help him to get to know their children and to participate in their lives (L.P.2: 9–12).

When he finally hears from her again in May 1931 and receives another letter that was posted a year before, he is obviously pleased and relieved. He says, however, that he still doesn't know how ill she has been or what the doctors say. He is very happy about her letter and sees it as the beginning of a new period in their relationship. She replies telling him she feels stronger, talking about Giuliano and telling him that Delio will read his gift of Dante with love (Schucht 1931). She includes a note from Delio and Gramsci replies to them in both a humorous and lively letter. The immediate crisis seems to have faded and Gramsci is beginning to grasp how similar their situation and feelings are.

In June, he told Tania that he felt less like writing and that the threads between him and the past are breaking and becoming difficult to re-tie. He reiterated in August, in a miserable letter, rephrasing Spaventa, that both he and his emotional world have now grown accustomed to his imprisonment. '…I feel isolated on the very same ground that in itself should produce emotional ties'. This was probably a rebuke to his political colleagues as well as to Giulia (Rosengarten in L.P.2: 53; Vacca 2012: 81). He used to feel proud to be isolated, and now he felt 'the pettiness, the aridity, the squalor of a life based exclusively on will' (L.P.2: 51). That day he had suffered a serious haemorrhage and a fever. From now on his health deteriorated.

Giulia's next letter, in August, is lucid and humorous. His letter gave her joy because her letter brought him joy; and 'your tone… Professor gave me…a jolt of memory from our former life'. She talked about Delio's concept of time, about the boys catching frogs. She told him that even she does not know her diagnosis—it ranges from epilepsy to hysteria, depending on the doctor; but that doctors sometimes make her laugh. The year before a doctor had diagnosed her as hysteric-epileptic and then said the illness did not exist, but that Gogol and Dostoevsky had it and Napoleon was hysteric! She likes her treatment, which is encouraging her not 'to curl up' but to be assertive, aggressive even, about her needs. She believes that he would help her in this if they were together. She admits that in the past she was intimidated by his learning and had told him they could not work together as she felt unequal. Now she thinks she was wrong, they should have used both their knowledge. Furthermore, she has decided against telling Delio that his father is in prison and explains why (cited, L'Unita, January 1994: 8). This Giulia is not passive, she is a lively person with her own opinions.

Gramsci replies cheerfully with tips on catching and cooking frogs and his interest in the psychoanalytical treatment she is having. He reminds her that he had often said she needed to disentangle her personality and that it has always been his opinion that she suffers from an inferiority complex. She does not reply. Once again there is a hiatus, each assuming that the other has not written, when in fact letters have been lost or delayed. In November, she wrote that she had not received his reply to her long letter in August when she had talked so clearly about her treatment and her feelings; she is nervous about his reaction. She knows he expects her to write and she wants to be more active and to study, but she does not want to tell him the bad things in her life when she writes, because thinking of him makes her feel stronger (Schucht 1931).

Gramsci's response is brutal; his reply to her has been lost, and although he could have written to her on several occasions, he found it difficult to write to her. From her letters, he thinks she feels the same about this disjointed correspondence with long silences, but he cannot find a way to change this. He had expected her to help him to keep in contact with their shared life and that of the children, but she has contributed to his isolation. He feels there is still time to bind themselves together and this letter is a new attempt. He wishes he could shake her to make her feel his anxiety and pain (L.P.2). This was at least an emotional response. A week later he wrote again, having received a translation of Giulia's recent letter to Tania, he almost regrets his outburst. Why doesn't she tell *him* about her illness and the treatment? Even that does not justify her not writing. They are joined by bonds of solidarity as well as affection, and although he could write passionate letters quite sincerely, he does not want to because their letters are not private. Therefore, they must rely on the bonds of political allegiance and their bond as parents and should help each other on both counts (L.P.2). The problem is that while they love each other and share those bonds they have never had time to really know each other and to shed their mutual idealised images. When he wrote again, a warmer letter, he referred to her decision approved by the doctor that she should begin to study. He had a practical suggestion which would help her and interest him. She should choose to research and inform him 'systematically' on the scientific framework within which the school(s) that their sons attend function. She would have to research and present her impressions in an orderly and coherent way, which would help her back into study mode, and he would get the facts about their sons' education which he craved (L.P.2: 115–116).

Moving Towards a Crisis

In 1932, the correspondence between the two is the most connected and positive it will ever be. Giulia makes a real effort to work with the psychoanalysis and to keep Gramsci informed. Through 1932 his health deteriorated as hers responded to treatment, so that their situations gradually reverse. He receives a long letter in January from Giulia about herself and the children—a brave letter, trying to explain her treatment and her personality. She now feels that she does not have to defend her personality (partly from his learning and intellect too) in order to preserve it, but that rather, in parts, she will have to destroy and reconstruct her Self (Schucht 1932).

Delio had also written and Gramsci replies to him; but he told Tania he could not write to Giulia because he was not well and could not marshal a helpful response to her information about her treatment. He knew little about it except to think, in essence, that complicated people create complicated problems for themselves. Giulia had 'unreal problems' which cannot be solved, so she had found an authority figure to do so. In fact, as an active member of society, which as an accredited party member she is, 'Giulia should be and is the best psychoanalytic doctor of herself'. Why does she wish to study? Why is wishing to study, to improve such an issue? He did not accept that she defended herself against his intellect and influence in the past as much as she thinks. He did not defend himself against her influence but was changed and enriched by it. He told Tania to send this dismissive intellectual analysis on to Giulia on as a partial reply (L.P.2: 137–139). She refused point-blank to send his letter and explained how mistaken his perception of Giulia and her illness was, mostly due, she conceded, to lack of information. She refuted all his arguments; Giulia wants to study because she needs another job and different skills, there is nothing complicated about it. She told him that what Giulia needed from him was very simple; treat this like any other illness; show your care and concern about her; ask her questions about the treatment, about her meetings with doctors (AG., T.S.).

In March, Giulia once again tried to explain and reveal herself. She has changed, 'when we were together, I was afraid of feeling like a woman' and so it comforted her to be called 'baby' by the family and be 'so weak and tired in Rome' (Schucht 1932. Giulia's letters from this period are almost all missing. Her letters are noted in Tania's letters to Gramsci until the end of 1934, and to her family in Russia also until 1934. The letters to Russia after that date are being translated and edited by the Fondazione Istituto Gramsci for publication in 2020).

In Rome, Giulia had been caught between remaining Apollon's daughter and wanting to enjoy being Gramsci's wife. She admits that he was right to say that her character was undeveloped. She had been afraid to let it develop, 'I was looking for a way to stay in the same place when I should have grown' (ibid.). Now if she seems preoccupied by these ideas, it is because in the past she had found her strength in being passive and now she wants to understand why and change. She has started to work a bit and should do more, but she had not expected that starting again would be so difficult. She regrets that she has been unwilling to discuss her feelings with him in the past 'I didn't talk to you about so many things that I was almost afraid to feel'. She signs off this letter 'Love me' (ibid.). Finally, at the end of March, Gramsci replied. He said he was finding it difficult to write to her because he was afraid of interfering with her treatment and also that he is aware now how dry, bookish and preachy he has become and how sometimes he talks nonsense. She has taken 'disentangling' too much to heart. He was talking about the fact that she does not devote herself as much to music, that she has focused on practical work, being useful, and immediate interests and this has split her from her artistic core almost like an amputation. She has directed her life towards the practical, 'without being inwardly convinced, as you could not be and rightly so' (L.P.2: 156). This is a very perceptive comment from Gramsci, about her sacrificing her music.

Meanwhile, Giulia had started a letter on several sheets at different times, before she received his March and April letters. It is clear that not hearing from him since December, nor indeed from Tania, has really upset her. 'Write to me Antonio' she pleads 'don't hate me because I couldn't withstand the bad things that in me became an illness… I am picking up a normal life … when we were together…I wasn't right then in my thinking, and … I love you' (Schucht 1932). The letter starts again in May in answer to two of his. He has said that the change of focus away from music has had an effect on her personality. She tells him that even in her music she was afraid to express herself too much, to feel, she needs to discard the old self. Then Gramsci responds with the fable of the man in the ditch and encourages her, tells her she is wise 'It is necessary to burn all of the past and rebuild a completely new life' only keep the good bits from the old, get out of the ditch and fling away the toad from one's heart (L.P.2: 189). Then he received a translated letter from Apollon, sent by Tania, with her comments, which finally convinced Gramsci about the peculiar and suffocating atmosphere of the Schucht family and its effect on Giulia (A.G., T.S.: 980–981, 985–989).

He heard from Giulia several times that summer. The letters are mostly about the boys, Giuliano, who loves mechanical things, having thoroughly examined a car, in every usual way, licked it. Giulia talked of her treatment, of going to a sanatorium, improving, wishing to study and start to work again. But she is not sure what or how; how she feels she must now make her own decisions, but how difficult that is after years of compliance. She says now she feels stronger so she could give up the psychoanalytic treatment (Schucht 1932). He replied in July, telling her he feels unwell, but is glad to hear that she is so much more sure of herself and giving up on the treatment which he has always felt 'to be tainted with charlatanry'. She would do better to listen to her mother and eat more (L.P.2: 191) and another loving letter reminding her about the folktales he told her that made her laugh, and the development of their sons (L.P.2).

He wrote to Tania in August that Giulia really seemed to have reached the shore and had her feet on solid ground. His situation, however, was worse. His health was deteriorating, the noise at night stopped him from sleeping, and the regulations had been tightened so that Tania could no longer send his medication. Within a week, he tells Giulia he could not possibly help her with her 'vague and generic' plans for her future or understand what she wants from him. He has aged terribly, becoming irascible and dissatisfied with everything, and if he was ever stronger than her, he isn't now (L.P.2: 197). Then Giulia wrote for his advice about Italian or French books to read. A week later he wrote to them both. To Tania, he says he is delighted to hear from Giulia so often; but things have changed, and he doesn't know whether he can be the correspondent she seems to want. He is always in a daze, either semi-conscious or frantic. He is unhappy that Giulia has such an unrealistic impression of his life to imagine that he could possibly know about modern publications for her to read. To Giulia, he repeats that he cannot help her either with her project or books. She has a mistaken and idyllic picture of his life, which is in fact 'empty, squalidly and terribly empty of any interesting content…of any satisfaction that makes life worth living' (L.P.2: 198). The fact that other people imagine his life as useful and active makes him feel more cut off than ever. Intellectually, he is genuinely pleased about Giulia's improvement, but as his health deteriorated and the prison conditions became more punitive, he retreated from her. He felt ill and desperate and he had suddenly realised that he had to clarify that he might never again be the man she remembered.

By September 1932, he recovered sufficiently to write a helpful letter to Giulia, suggesting that rather than reading new books, she needed to decide on a direction and some specific goals and that given her talents, experience and knowledge she should become a qualified translator from Italian. Subsequently, he had a row with Tania over arrangements for an independent medical examination, followed by great jolt of hope and disappointment when Carlo, his brother, sent him a telegram about an amnesty and the possibility of freedom. However, this turned out to be only a reduction in sentence. Within all this emotional turmoil and furious letters to Carlo and Tania, he had written several beautiful letters to his sons and two affectionate ones to Giulia. Finally, on November 6, he wrote a philosophical letter to Tania admitting how upset he had been about the amnesty, 'I have always considered myself a dead man on leave… now the holiday may be prolonged' (L.P.2: 224) and a positive one to Giulia on the same date encouraging her, telling her not to worry, she will readjust to work, that her new existence is in reality the continuation of her entire past. Despite their agreements to tell the truth, he did not tell Giulia about his illness, or about the reduction in sentence.

As the true nature of Giulia's situation had emerged and as his health declined, Gramsci had come to realise that she too had been imprisoned, by her love for him and her sons; by Apollon's protectiveness which concealed a need to control; by Eugenia's domination, envy and jealousy; and politically by an increasingly paranoid state. Finally, he feared that in his enfeebled physical state, even were he to be freed, he would become another responsibility for her, rather than the dynamic partner he had been. She is becoming stronger and more independent. He wrote to Tania on 14 November 1932, 'Why should a living being be tied to someone who is dead or almost?' He is taking into account Giulia's life and future. She is young enough to take a new direction and a new phase of life. He wants Tania's help. Please will she ask Giulia on his behalf to divorce him or give him her approval to contact Giulia himself. Tania must forward his letter or write one of her own. Will Tania do this, yes or no? (L.P.2: 229). This is Gramsci's drastic solution to Giulia's predicament and his own deterioration. He has reached a point where he can longer bear any uncertainty or emotion. A divorce will free him too, from emotional suffering, eventually. Tania does not reply to his request for almost a month, and her answer is no.

Aftermath

He continued to write letters of support to Giulia, usually offering an intellectual, theoretical response to her problems and adding a personal note occasionally; he should have been the one to help her to know herself better… that he often thinks what he might have done and didn't that their situations are similar; she has been 'on the margins of life's flow and doesn't know how to plunge in again' (L.P.2: 234). He continued to ask her for more details, of the boys' progress and development, of her health, why should there not be maximum confidence between them? In January 1933, he explains why he needs details, 'I would like to help, but I often think that in the past, since I did not know exactly how you felt I may have contributed to your despair' (L.P.2: 262). It never seems to have occurred to him that she needed details of how he felt in order to write to him. During 1933 in the depths of intense pain and despair, he finally understands that

Giulia's depression and illness are not conducive to intellectual analysis and willpower. He wrote to Tania that he would never have believed that physical being could so overwhelm moral strength. Days later he added that he thought Giulia's illness came from the same causes as his own psychic ailments.

Giulia's letters are mainly about the children that she is not receiving letters either and she knows that he is not well. In spite of pleas for news and more letters from both of them, they each give more detail to Tania, who then relays it. From 1934 when he does not write for a year, this pattern becomes more settled. Only in the very last phase of his life, after prolonged illness so serious that the authorities finally moved him into hospital care, does he begin to write to her simply and from the heart.

> My dear, you have always been one of the essential elements of my life, even when I had no precise news of you or received letters from you that were rare or without vital substance, and even when I did not write to you because I did not know what to write or how to write.

He goes on to say that now, finally, he wants her to come to see him because their states of mind are very similar.

> I do believe that you can do much for me, and I believe that I too can do something for you, not much but something...My dear I pour all my tenderness into what I am writing, though it does not appear so from the written words …. (L.P.2: 353)

She sent him an inconclusive reply.

They were out of step again. In 1934, while he was still ill, she had been determined to come, even Eugenia agreed, but she was told to wait as Gramsci might be exchanged (D'Orsi 2017). He begs her in 1935 and 1936 to come to Italy to see him, not just for his sake but for hers, he feels that her health would improve, and her life would improve if only they could talk. It is a calm and reassuring letter, they are friends, she is not to worry, they will chat about ordinary things the way friends do, but then the longing seeps through 'I wonder whether a caress from me would calm you' (L.P.2: 354). But the moment and her courage have passed. Eugenia has had second thoughts and announced that Giulia was too ill to travel. They will never meet.

Conclusion

The Giulia who emerges from the letters is a strong and loving person, struggling with exhaustion, grief and hostility, which never entirely subdue her. Her letters include expressions of love and hints of physical longing. Too late, her last letters to Gramsci challenge him about his criticism of his sons or the sort of information he demands, in the way he liked.

Why did they write so little to each other? The answer lies in a combination of politics and love. Their idealised images of each other created mental barriers between them, and censorship and illness created concrete ones. Gramsci's writing was restricted by prison regulations; in Turi, he could only write one letter a fortnight to an approved addressee. He circumvented this by writing to another person on the same sheet, and Tania relayed it. Nevertheless, the imbalance of letters between Tania and Giulia is striking. A major cause of this was his decision, within weeks of arrest, to make Tania his main correspondent. It was mainly a political decision, she would send on copies of his letters to the party in exile, and a practical decision, because she alone could offer both medical advice and medication, as well as being able to provide other essentials. It was a bad decision for his marriage. Inadvertently, he had added another layer of inhibition, because Tania read all the letters to and from Giulia. Also, she became a gatekeeper, protecting the partners, withholding letters from both which she thought might upset them. Letters were delayed because she was ill or had moved. Crucially, Tania provided an excuse; she mediated between them and implored them both to write to each other, but they chose to write to her because it was easier. Writing to each other was painful.

Early in their marriage Gramsci had written to Giulia that there must be absolute clarity between them even if they drew blood. But during the prison years, they were never confident enough in each other, or sufficiently informed about the other's circumstances to talk about painful or difficult issues, to be truthful. They concealed problems, tried to avoid giving hurt, suppressed emotions, whether love or anguish, and in so doing so created their own prisons from which they could not escape.

Acknowledgements I wish to thank Dott. Francesco Giasi, director of the Fondazione Istituto Gramsci in Rome for his permission to use archive material from Giulia Schucht. I am indebted to him and to Luisa Righi and Eleonora Lattanza for their interest and useful discussions, and to Giovanna Bosman, Cristina Pipitone and Dario Massimi for their help in negotiating the archives and the library.

Abbreviations for Frequently Used Texts

(A.G., T.S.) Gramsci, A. and Schucht, T. (1997) *Lettere 1926–1935.* Eds. Natoli, A. Daniele, D. Torino: Einaudi.

(L.P.1) Gramsci, A. (1994) *Letters from Prison.* Vol. 1. Ed. Rosengarten, F., Trans. Rosenthal, R. New York: Columbia University Press.

(L.P.2) Gramsci, A. (1994) *Letters from Prison.* Vol. 2. Ed. Rosengarten, F., Trans. Rosenthal, R. New York: Columbia University Press.

References

The translation of the letters from Giulia and Tania Schucht is my own.

Cambria, Adele. (1976). *Amore come rivoluzione.* Milano: SugarCo.

Davidson, A. (1977). *Antonio Gramsci, Towards an Intellectual Biography.* London: Merlin.

D'Orsi, A. (2017). *Antonio Gramsci, una nuova biografia.* Milano: Feltrinelli.

Fiori, G. (1990). *Antonio Gramsci, Life of a Revolutionary* (T. Nairn, Trans.). London: Verso (original published 1965).

Gramsci, A. (1994). *Letters from Prison* (2 Vols., F. Rosengarten, Ed. and R. Rosenthal, Trans.). New York: Columbia University Press.

Gramsci, A. (2014). *A Great and Terrible World* (D. Boothman, Ed. and Trans.). London: Lawrence and Wishart.

Gramsci, A., Jr. (2008). *La Russia di mio Nonno.* Roma: L'Unita.

Gramsci, A., Jr. (2014). *La storia di una famiglia rivoluzionaria.* Roma: Editori Riuniti.

Kincaid Weekes, M. (2002). Writing Lives Forward. In P. France & W. St Clair (Eds.), *Mapping Lives, the Uses of Biography* (pp. 235–252). Oxford: Oxford University Press.

Nicholson, J. (2016). 'How Do You Know How Gramsci Felt'—Thinking About the Methodology of Writing a Life. *Auto/Biography Yearbook, 2016,* 12–26.

Schucht, G. (1931). *Letter,* in Archivio Antonio Gramsci, Epistolario; Sottoseria 21:152. Fondazione Gramsci via Rome.

Schucht, G. (1932). *Letters,* in the Archivio Antonio Gramsci, Epistolario; Sottoserie 22:08 and 84. Fondazione Gramsci Via Sebino 43a Rome.

Schucht, G. (1932). cited in *L'unita.* January 17, 1994. P. 8.

Vacca, G. (2012). *Vita e pensieri di Antonio Gramsci 1926–1937.* Torino: Einaudi.

19

Bobby Sands: Prison and the Formation of a Leader

Denis O'Hearn

When he died in Long Kesh prison after 66 days on hunger strike in 1981, Bobby Sands was one of the most famous people on earth. News of his death spurred protests by thousands in major world cities. Motions of sympathy, minutes of silence, and days of mourning were declared in national parliaments of Italy, India, Portugal, Iran, and several of the United States. Streets were named in his honour. *The Hindustan Times* wrote that Margaret Thatcher 'allowed a member of the House of Commons, a colleague in fact, to die of starvation. Never had such an incident occurred in a civilised country'. And the *New York Times* editorialised that Bobby Sands 'bested an implacable British prime minister'.

How did this young man achieve such status and recognition? Bobby Sands was not your usual revolutionary leader, if there is such a thing. Unlike Gramsci or Lenin, he lacked formal training in political theory. Unlike Mandela, he was not bred for leadership. Rather, society itself put Bobby Sands into a position of leadership. His education, rather than in high schools, colleges, and universities, was grounded in the community and, especially, the prison. Long Kesh prison, which came to be known by northern Irish revolutionaries as the 'University of Freedom', *made* Bobby Sands.

D. O'Hearn (✉)
University of Texas at El Paso, El Paso, TX, USA
e-mail: daohearn@utep.edu

© The Author(s) 2020
J. M. Parsons and A. Chappell (eds.), *The Palgrave Handbook of Auto/Biography*,
https://doi.org/10.1007/978-3-030-31974-8_19

Bobby Sands was born into a Catholic family that lived in a mostly Protestant neighbourhood north of Belfast. Northern Ireland—carved by the British in 1920 out of the northeast corner of the island of Ireland—comprised the largest piece of that corner that contained an assured majority of Protestants over Catholics. Protestants ran the state and were loyal to the Queen of England. Most Catholics and a few Protestants aspired to a united Ireland. In 1922, Northern Ireland's first Prime Minister called the local government 'a Protestant parliament for a Protestant people'. The Prime Minister in 1954, when Bobby Sands was born, told people not to employ Catholics, boasting, 'I have not a Roman Catholic about my own place' (Farrell 1976: 90, 136). Protestants ran the police forces and government offices that controlled housing and education.

Yet the industries that provided jobs for working-class Protestants were rapidly declining. Harland and Wolff shipyard, where Protestant workers built the *Titanic* in 1912, was shrinking rapidly. It was an explosive mix: a dominant population losing its economic advantages and a marginalised population with a history of rebellion.

Perhaps the most immediate social threat was the region's housing. Three out of every ten houses were uninhabitable (Planning Advisory Board 1944). Protestant advantages were only marginal. Protestant and Catholic children alike slept several to a bed, head-by-toe, like sardines packed in a tin. The poorest Protestants always felt under threat of losing these marginal advantages, and many perceived that the biggest threat came from Catholics.

Bobby Sands experienced the results of this division. When he was seven years old, neighbours discovered that his family were Catholics and forced them out of their house. For most of the next decade, they remained in a heavily Protestant working-class neighbourhood. Yet, as Catholics began to mobilise and protest for civil rights in the late 1960s, the Protestant police reacted violently against them and working-class Protestants formed into gangs that aimed to cleanse their neighbourhoods of Catholics.

Society was splitting apart. Bobby's Protestant friends turned away from him. He had to sneak home from work or school to avoid armed gangs. Once, he was caught and cut with a razorblade but escaped. The police supported the gangs, and it was not uncommon to watch police beating civil rights marchers on the nightly news.

The police patrolled Catholic neighbourhoods in armoured cars mounted with Browning machine guns. On the night they shot nine-year-old Patrick Rooney in his bed, police also shot dead one man as he sat in his front room and another as he walked along the road. When the government sent in the British army to control the violence, a bad situation became worse.

The army stood by while Protestant crowds burned hundreds of Catholic homes. The Irish Republican Army (IRA) responded to killings of unarmed Catholics by the British army and police with an escalation of its own war. Then, early in the morning of August 9, 1971, the army swooped on 450 people and put them into internment camps. The anger of the Catholic population—practically every family had or knew someone who was interned—was intense and violence surged. These events had a significant impact on Bobby Sands. Not only did he begin to link the police with violence against his community, he began to view the British army as the enemy.

In early 1972, residents in Bobby's neighbourhood began to notice vigilante 'estate agents', women who took young couples around, pointing out Catholic houses for them to make their choice. Local gangs painted crosses on the chosen doors and the following night rioters trashed them. Catholic residents, frustrated by the apparent indifference of authorities, talked about forming Citizen's Defence Committees. Young people like Bobby Sands joined the IRA.

Every family that was evicted and every police statement that covered up the problem increased Bobby's commitment to the IRA. Yet his thinking was still instinctual, not highly political. Inevitably, the Sands family were intimidated and had to move to a new Catholic neighbourhood (Twinbrook) south of Belfast where the houses were not even finished and there were no sidewalks and few roads. Nonetheless, the family for the first time enjoyed a sense of solidarity among the other refugees trying to survive in their new surroundings.

Solidarity for Bobby meant reporting to the local unit of the IRA. Again, his commitment was instinctual, a response to atrocities committed by the police and the British army against his family, friends and neighbours. The singular force that drew young people into the IRA and kept them there was anger and resentment. Bobby's IRA unit carried out support activities for more experienced units. He robbed cars and money. He stored weapons, most of which were unfireable. Inevitably, his activities drew the attention of the police. In October 1972, the British army raided a house on the word of informants. They found weapons that they associated with Bobby Sands. He was hardly a 'player' as an IRA guerrilla, yet Bobby was arrested, interrogated, tried, and imprisoned. He was about to get his first political education and start on the road to leadership.

After he was sentenced, Bobby Sands was sent to 'Cage Eight' in Long Kesh prison, a series of Nissen huts on a disused airstrip which also housed hundreds of uncharged political internees. Ever restless, Bobby learned the guitar and the Irish language. He became engaged in reading circles and debates about revolutionary theory and history. As the younger prisoners read Marxism and guerrilla histories, they became politically aware.

The IRA leadership in prison was still an older, conservative generation. They maintained a militaristic structure, with nightly parades, orders and delegation of work. IRA officers avoided menial jobs. They discouraged open debate and held burnings of Marxist books. They held courts of inquiry and encouraged prisoners to spy on each other. Yet a cadre of younger leaders encouraged the prisoners to form 'cooperatives' to make handicrafts, share food and distribute chores. It would be hard to overestimate the importance that such solidarity and radical thinking had on Bobby's intellectual development.

As friends outside supplied books, the men built a revolutionary library including Carlos Marighella (*For the Liberation of Brazil*), Regis Debray (*Revolution in the Revolution*), Robert Taber (*The War of the Flea*), Franz Fanon (*The Wretched of the Earth*), and Che Guevara (*Passages of the Cuban Revolutionary War*). They read about guerrilla struggles in Asia, Africa, and Latin America and George Jackson's *Soledad Brother*. Paolo Freire was a favourite, as were classic works of Marxism. As harassment by the authorities intensified, the prisoners began to plan a collective action: burning the prison camp. A dispute between the guards and the prisoners provoked the action. After burning the camp, the prisoners occupied green spaces in the prison, sleeping out under the stars, burning campfires, and eating food that they 'liberated' from the prison shop. While British helicopters buzzed overhead, the prisoners enjoyed a night of relative freedom and kinship with comrades from across the prison camp. Finally, at dawn, helicopters dropped CS gas and the British army came in from all directions. A pitched but uneven battle broke out in which the prisoners were overwhelmed. Yet they shared a sense of victory. As one prisoner recalled:

> We were beaten but not broken; and since the object of the exercise was to break us, it failed. We claimed the victory; and in retrospect, I believe we won. (McCann 1998: 19)

The burning was a key episode in Bobby's political formation. The material weapons were practically all on one side—yet the prisoners had solidarity and common purpose. The more the enemy beat them physically, the more it lost morally. The prisoners used their powerlessness as a weapon. When they created new forms of protest, the authorities responded with physical repression. The prisoners even turned injustices back on the authorities by engaging in *self*-deprivation. The utter confusion and lack of control this imposed on the authorities and the sense of injustice it created among the prisoners, was a great weapon. When they destroyed their very surroundings, refusing to accept imprisonment physically *and* symbolically, they compelled the enemy to use 'chemical warfare' and then leave them in their devastation.

Bobby learned from the confrontation: one could endure seemingly limitless physical and emotional degradations and even turn them to advantage. Was it possible, in certain circumstances, that the more one lost, the freer one became?

Yet he still had a relatively low level of political awareness. He did not have a deep understanding about *why* he and his comrades resisted, apart from a gut-level 'us' and 'them' analysis. After the burning, Bobby and his closest comrades were moved into a new cage (Cage Eleven) along with young leaders like Gerry Adams and Brendan Hughes, who were planning to democratise the IRA and the broader political movement. Bobby had been reading and discussing radical ideas but he never seriously questioned the conservative IRA leadership or their associates in the Sinn Fein political party. Under the mentorship of Adams, he began to consider whether the struggle should be organised on participative principles rather than militaristic orders and punishments. The struggle had to become more politicised; it had to offer something to the communities at its centre if they were to support it over the long haul.

Adams worked to raise the prisoners' political awareness. He introduced new classes that critically deconstructed Republican ideology and policy. The curriculum used Irish history as the context for debating the current conflict and how the movement needed change. As important as the content of the curriculum was its emphasis on participation. Adams had great faith in the potential of these young men. They were in prison, he said,

> for instinctive patriotic reasons or for broadly nationalist reasons or for a sense of national consciousness or because they were confronted with British aggression and responded to it in an instinctive way. They knew they were Irish and they knew they wanted a United Ireland. But they were not politically or ideologically schooled or perhaps even aware of their own awareness. (Adams interview)

Getting them to participate seriously in education was a way to get them to believe in their own political awareness. Adams encouraged the young radicals to synthesise global revolutionary thought with Irish socialists like James Connolly and Liam Mellows:

"You ground your politics in the indigenous," he said, "it's much easier to argue the validity of a position from the perspective of a James Connolly or a Fintan Lalor or a William Thompson or a Liam Mellows or a Pearse."

Bobby threw himself into the new education regime. He organised notebooks on 'guerrilla struggle' and began talking with other prisoners about how they could change life in their communities once they got out of prison.

The debate with the strongest impact on Bobby was about a radical alternative that Adams called 'active abstentionism': abstention from existing structures of governance while actively creating an alternative that combined grass-roots democracy with military resistance to British rule. Presaging what anarchists would later call *prefiguration*, but also adapting experiences from Mao's long march and Fidel's Sierra Maestra campaign, the prisoners discussed how they would build an alternative administration in 'war zones' where the IRA enjoyed widespread grass-roots support *and* where the state failed to provide adequate services.

According to Adams, 'the building of alternatives cannot wait until 'after the war'. It must start now'. This was not just a military war; it was also necessary to fight on economic, political, and cultural fronts. Now was the time to build 'peoples' organisations' because they could harness the energy that 'only a people at war possess' (Brownie 1975).

Bobby Sands was excited by this kind of talk. Here was a revolutionary project that was Irish in character yet reflected the militant politics he was studying. He led discussions on people's councils. In a folder of notes that he entitled 'Development of Community Councils in Local Areas: Proposed Ideas', he argued that IRA volunteers needed to integrate their army activities into the broadest spectrum of political activity in their communities. The community's alienation from the state paralleled their own alienation from the prison regime. Republicans had to become centrally involved in newspapers, co-ops, and tenant's associations. They had to ensure that people had access to basic services like transport and better housing, as well as cultural resources like music and Irish language education.

Bobby addressed these themes in his first-known prison writing. Towards the end of 1975, he wrote a piece for the prison newspaper entitled *Ag bunadh Gaeltachta* ["Establishing an Irish-speaking Community"], entirely in Irish. He related prison life and big political issues to a small Irish-speaking community that had recently been set up close to his neighbourhood, in South Belfast. He wrote:

I think that there are about fifteen houses there, as well as a small nursery school, and the children are learning everything through Irish…They only had one thing and that is a lot of courage, and that is the most important thing, and I know that it is a small school but it is an Irish school at least…It doesn't stop there, a lot of other things are happening…They will be able to set up small factories first and then they will be able to move forward from there… They would be able to make a profit for themselves and with that profit they would be able to establish a new school, or factory, or new houses, or whatever they like.

And it would be without help from the government, too. I know that they wouldn't get any help from any government, north or south, and that is why we must do it ourselves. As I said already, before you do anything you need information as to why and how, as well as strong courage (hope), and then you can do anything. (Sands 1975)

Bobby was released from prison in early 1976. As a close friend put it, he and Bobby were no different from the rest of the people when they went to prison. They certainly were not the vanguard of their people. They weren't even socialists. But when they came out of jail three years later, they were *totally* politicised (Seanna Walsh interview).

Back in his neighbourhood, Twinbrook, Bobby began mobilising activists. He caused a stir because it was still rare for ex-prisoners to get involved in the *political* side of things. He established a newspaper called *Liberty* and encouraged young activists to write articles. He organised a takeover of the local tenants' association, where they built a full schedule of events for elderly and young people, including Irish language classes and dances. The locals soon viewed Bobby as someone to call for help. They came to his door or stopped him on the street, asking for all kinds of help. If they needed the plumbing or heating fixed, a broken window replaced or rats exterminated they came to him to organise 'fixes' through his contacts in the community. He even got the 'black taxi' cooperative to extend transport services to the neighbourhood.

But there was a problem. Bobby believed community action was part of a wider strategy that included armed struggle. Many of the younger activists pleaded with him to concentrate on community activism and to stay out of armed actions. But Bobby could not ask others to do something that he was unwilling to do. After just six months of freedom, he and a group of others were caught following a firebombing operation in a nearby suburb of Belfast. It was part of the IRA's 'economic bombing campaign'. Bobby Sands soon returned to prison.

After trial, Bobby found himself in a newly built cellular section of Long Kesh prison: the 'H-Blocks'. Each block was in the form of an H, with an administrative centre in the crossbar and four wings of cells that formed each leg. Cellular confinement was part of a British government policy of criminalisation. Anyone convicted of an offence after March 1, 1976 was considered a criminal and placed in the new blocks. They were to do prison work, wear a prison uniform, and mix with 'ordinary decent criminals'. When the prison governor told IRA prisoner Kieran Nugent that he was just a criminal and that he would have to wear the prison uniform, Nugent reportedly said that if they wanted him to wear that uniform they would have to nail it to his back. Hundreds of prisoners followed his example. As punishment they were confined in their cells without clothes and only a blanket to wear, with no reading or writing materials. They were only allowed a bible and a few religious pamphlets. The cells were simple and bleak. Heating pipes ran along the back wall and the floors were cold black bitumen. At first, there was simple furniture: a bed, chair, desk, and locker. The locker contained the prison uniform and boots that they refused to wear.

The only people the prisoners saw regularly were their cellmates and the 'screws', or prison guards. In isolation, some of them never even saw the faces of prisoners a few cells away. The screws came on the wing at 7:30 in the morning and left at 8:30 in the evening. At nights, the men could communicate freely without the screws listening in. Without face-to-face contact or writing materials, the prisoners developed a largely oral culture. The only visitors were priests. On Sundays, most prisoners put on their uniform bottoms and went, half-naked, to the unused dining room for mass. If the priest was considered trustworthy, prisoners gave him messages to take out of the jail in his socks or in the rolled-up sleeve of his sweater.

Most 'blanketmen' doubled up two to a cell. They devised ways to communicate and distribute supplies like tobacco. Bobby communicated with others by talking out the windows, through the cracks around the heating pipes and shouting out the door. A note written on a piece of toilet paper could be passed by placing it in a folded religious pamphlet and passing it to the next cell through the crack around the heating pipes. For larger items, a prisoner tore a six-foot strip from his blanket and tied a deadweight on one end. He put his arm out the cell window and swung his 'rope' until the prisoner in the next cell caught it. Then, the item to be passed was tied to the other end and pulled in by the other prisoner.

To get things across the corridor, the blanketmen devised a technique called 'shooting the button'. They unravelled ten to fifteen feet of wool stitching from the tops of their blankets and tied a button to its end for weight. There was a small gap at the bottom of each door and the shooter would flick the button towards the door across the corridor. After a few tries, the shooter usually got it close enough for the other prisoner to fish it in and get the note or tobacco that was tied to it. Button shooting took place at night, after the screws left (Campbell et al. 1994).

> When Bobby met his first cellmate, he noticed that he slept a lot.
> "What do you do all day?" he asked.
> "I sleep," was the reply.
> "It's a waste of your opportunities, isn't it?" (Collins 1986: 57–58)

So, there was Bobby Sands, in a bare cell with no exercise, no clothes and nothing to read. And he spoke about *opportunities!* He spent his first week talking to the others about their situation. He concluded that the authorities were happy to keep them lying around doing nothing. They were isolated and silenced. Bobby decided that the prisoners had to organise an *active* campaign to raise public awareness, sympathy, and support. They needed to make bridges of information to people who would pass it on to others. Everyone should take their monthly visits to open up lines of communication. Once these were established, they could write letters, as many as possible, and smuggle them out through their relatives and friends. They needed pens or pen refills, which they could pickpocket from the screws or take from the priests in mass. They needed writing paper; cigarette papers or toilet paper would do.

Bobby wrote his first article within three weeks of arriving in the H-Blocks. He wrote about life there, the good and bad, depression and comradeship. He wrote surreptitiously, with a ballpoint pen refill on slick prison toilet paper, one ear cocked for approaching screws who would confiscate his writing and send him to the punishment cells if they caught him. When he finished, he took it to his mother on his next visit with instructions to give it to Sinn Fein's newspaper, *Republican News*. After describing their horrific conditions of isolation, he ended with:

> We are all Republican Prisoners-Of-War here, and there is nothing that the Prison Authorities, the Northern Ireland Office, or the British Government can say or do to change this. They can keep us incarcerated and naked, they may use everything and every means at their disposal to try and break us. We have lived in terrible conditions under constant harassment, through a freezing winter and a sweltering summer locked up in our cells like animals. But there

is one thing that we remember always, and those who torment us would do well to listen: "You have nothing in your entire arsenal to break one single man who refuses to be broken". (*Republican News* November 5, 1977: 6)

Bobby continued to write. He took a leading role in education. They relied mostly on memory, which gave him an advantage from his experiences in the cages. Irish was easier than history, since teaching depended on fluency. When Bobby started teaching Irish in the blocks, about three or four others were fluent. Within eighteen months, nearly four hundred blanketmen spoke Irish. The language was taught constantly and spoken constantly. Yet the situation was becoming institutionalised. Things might have continued that way but early in 1978 Bobby's old comrade Brendan (the Dark) Hughes was moved to H5 and Sands was moved into a cell next to him. It was the beginning of an intimate working relationship. From then on, they never shared a cell but every time they were moved, they were put in adjacent cells. Hughes says the importance of Sands' constant location next door is indisputable. 'We discussed everything. *Everything* we done I discussed it with Bobby … I never made a decision without consultation with Bobby' (Brendan Hughes interview).

They discussed strategies to move away from inactive protest, as much to inject life into the failing movement outside of prison as for the men in the prison. Said Hughes:

> What I was doing at the time and Bobby knew it, I knew it, a lot of the people in the jail did not know it … I knew the leadership on the outside were rebuilding. We had an issue here that could give some help to the leadership on the outside. I knew that was the situation, and that's what we were doing.

Bobby's first move was to create a communications infrastructure, to keep in constant contact with the IRA and activists who were beginning to organise a public campaign. Prisoners started taking visits to open new lines of communications and get pens and other materials, even if it meant putting on the prison uniform. The Dark was acutely aware of the difficulties involved.

> It was quite tough at the time to go out of your cell and put on that prison uniform. Initially it was symbolically very very difficult and then it became brutally difficult because obviously they realized what we were doing, bringing in the lines of communication and so forth and bringing stuff in and getting stuff out. So they began to make it tougher for us by physically abusing people. (Brendan Hughes interview)

Most prisoners came to realise that taking visits actually lightened the protest. They got to see their loved ones, *and* they were doing something positive. 'The stuff Bobby used to bring back. Tobacco, pens, papers. It was fantastic', Hughes recalled. Bobby's mother Rosaleen smuggled in tobacco and smuggled Bobby's writings out. She was so good that they called her 'Old Faithful'. Visits were not just a source of communications, but also luxuries.

Smuggling was not easy. The visitors, usually women, had to carry their packages into prison through a rigorous search. Then, they had to pass their message and receive one in return while sitting at a table in a visiting box with a prison warder watching. The passing usually took place during an embrace and a kiss. A small message, tightly folded and wrapped in cling film, could be passed from mouth to mouth. Larger items, such as tobacco and pen refills, had to be passed by hand. Once the prisoner had the package, he discretely slipped it up into his anus through a hole ripped in the uniform trousers. Prisoners often had to swallow comms, hoping to retrieve them later by vomiting or waiting until nature took its course. Visits soon turned from capitulation to *confrontation*. Once the prison warders realised that things were being smuggled, they started strip-searching the prisoners, probing their hair, mouths, and rectums. Forced squatting, bending, and probing became common. Beatings increased as the prisoners resisted. Action and reaction combined in an escalating process of confrontation. Prisoners were brutalised on the way to and from the washroom. The corridors became a battleground for control.

In March 1978, the blanketmen refused to wash, shower, or clean their cells. It was the beginning of a long process that they called the 'no-wash' protest. The authorities and the media called it the 'dirty' protest. 'No-wash' became a tactic because the warders' repressive reactions gave the prisoners a sense that they controlled their jailers. The guards stopped letting prisoners slop out their buckets and refused to take scraps of food away after meals. The prisoners coped in the only ways they could. They urinated into the uniform boots and threw their bodily waste out the windows. When the screws threw it back into the cell, they began smearing it onto the walls. One might expect that such privations would break the prisoners. But every time the screws introduced a new form of repression, the men interpreted it as a sign of weakness, an indication that they were winning.

"Morale was sky high," recalls a prisoner. "We felt that we were winning and for a change that we, not the screws, had control over our lives because we dictated the pace of events. The screws for their part were demoralised because they had no control over what happened next. They dreaded Mondays because that was the day that we kept upping the tempo of the protest by introducing something new". (McCann in Campbell et al. manuscript)

As the mess became unbearable, the authorities started taking the furniture out of the cells. Upon hearing this, the Dark and Bobby told the men to smash it before the screws could take it away. The next day, the warders removed the beds, leaving the mattresses on the floor. Since the cell floors were soaking wet with urine, so were the mattresses and blankets. In these bare conditions, the men invented new forms of entertainment. Their favourite was the 'book at bedtime', where the best storytellers recited books from memory after the screws left the wing at night. There were good book tellers and bad ones. Bobby was regarded as one of the best.

Night-time belonged to the prisoners. Once the warders left, they began their nightly routine of cigarette manufacture, button shooting, news broadcasting, and general entertainment. The last business of the night was the 'book at bedtime'. The storyteller pulled his mattress up to his cell door and shouted out while the rest of the men lay, listening. When the book was good and the storyteller was engaging, everyone got lost in the story. Bobby's speciality was epics. His telling of Geronimo and his Apache guerrillas 'epitomised everything that he thought a human being should be', says an ex-blanketman, 'compassionate but unbreakable, fighting the whole of America on his own' (Richard O'Rawe interview). Other stories were about struggle: *How Green Was My Valley*, about the Welsh miners.

One story became legendary among the blanketmen. *Jet* was about a man who deserted the US marines in Vietnam and achieved his own personal freedom by living an anonymous life on the run back in the United States. To the prisoners, it was a story about them, about how they could achieve an inner freedom even as they lay isolated in their grim cells, surrounded by barbed wire, concrete and hostile screws. For a couple of hours a night as they listened to *Jet*, they were free. Their minds' eyes took them beyond the walls, beyond the razor wire, wherever Bobby chose to take them. Perhaps more than any other aspect of his seemingly tireless efforts to organise the prison struggle, this turned Bobby Sands into their leader. In their own way, the blanketmen were building an ideal world, if one could use such a term in such miserable circumstances. In their interactions with the screws, they resisted. Among themselves, they built a shared community.

Conflict continued to escalate through the summer of 1978. The cells got dirtier. The solution was to clean the wings in rotation, by moving blanketmen in into a wing that had just been cleaned while they steam cleaned the newly vacant cells for the prisoners from the next wing. 'Wing shifts' became extremely violent affairs. The violence overflowed into the cells as warders raided them to find pens, tobacco, and other contraband. Priests at mass began to notice marks on the half-naked prisoners. Nonetheless, morale heightened as the violence escalated. After each wing shift, every-one took stock of each other and, realising that they survived another move without permanent damage, broke into songs and rebellious chants. Brutality rose with morale. In November, the authorities introduced mirror searches, forcing prisoners to squat over a mirror. If they refused, they were physically forced to squat so that the screws could look up their anuses.

The period of escalated violence effected Bobby's writing. Between July and late November 1978, *Republican News* did not publish any of his arti-cles. He concentrated on press releases and coordinating information that was coming in from different blocks. It was not the physical abuse—the wing shifts, beatings, searches, forced washings—that provoked Sands to write again. Rather, it was the threatened loss of his last visual contact with normal life, the free birds in the prison yard and the stars in the heavens above. In the midst of the violent struggle, the prison authorities began something that, to Bobby, was basest:

> Today the screws began blocking up all the windows with sheets of steel, to me this represents and signifies the further torture of the tortured, blocking out the very essence of life—nature!

They had not yet blocked Bobby's window but he knew his turn would come; darkness would prevail over his cell and his life.

> A few words I once read came echoing back to me today—"No one can take away from a person his or her ability to contemplate. Throw them into prison, give them hard labour, unimaginative work to do, but you can never take from them the ability to find the poetry and music in life"—and I realised that they, here, my torturers, have long ago started and still endeavour to block up the window of my mind. (Marcella 1978)

By the end of 1978, the prison authorities were totally bewildered. Despite the prisoners' horrific conditions, their morale kept rising. Every night they organised entertainment. Most had enough Irish to speak freely without fear of being overheard.

Bobby now wrote poetry as well as prose. Articles with titles like 'Alone and Condemned', 'A Break in the Monotony', and 'A Battle for Survival' described the conditions of life on the blanket and the psychological tensions of fear and boredom. A poem, 'A Bright Star', spoke of the loss of physical beauty and the gain of spiritual strength through resistance. 'Modern Times' was a biting critique of what we now call globalisation, in which he connected his own struggle to those of oppressed people around the world. But Bobby had his mind on bigger things. He wanted to write a definitive record of life on the blanket. On a cold and snowy day in December 1978, he began to write what would become his best-known work, a detailed story of life on the blanket that he called *One Day in My Life*. It was an ambitious project: when eventually published, ninety-four pages long. Bobby kept the manuscript, written on dozens of sheets of toilet paper, stuffed up his anus wrapped in plastic seal, carefully folded like an accordion to keep it as small as possible.

One Day is a relentless journey through a 'normal', terrible day on the blanket. It was a 'good day' for Bobby even though it began with a frightening wing shift and a beating that sent a prisoner to the hospital. He received a letter from home and two packets of tissues that he laid on the floor to keep his feet warm for a moment until the urine soaked through them and they disintegrated. It was also the day of his monthly visit with his family, his half-hour of comparative happiness each month.

He had to endure humiliation by the warders before they handed over his letter; an obstacle course of strip searches and insults on the way to and from his visit; abuse when he hugged his mother in the visiting room; intense fear that he would be discovered smuggling back a quarter ounce of tobacco. In between were 'petty' annoyances. He waits in his cell, shivering, for the warders to deliver his blankets while the wind and the snow blow in through the broken window. A warder steals his fish, his only substantial bit of food that day. He tries to clear the urine from his cell floor.

Through it all, Sands punctuates his terrors with small victories. He refuses to beg for his package. He will not bend for the mirror search. He rolls cigarettes and delivers them around the wing. He participates in a hastily organised singsong to recover their morale after a shattering attack by buckets of disinfectant. He shares good news from his visit. Sands ends the book on a hopeful note, reflecting on the events of the day.

> That's another day nearer to victory, I thought, feeling very hungry. I was a skeleton compared to what I used to be but it didn't matter. Nothing really mattered except remaining unbroken. I rolled over once again, the cold biting at me…I rolled over again freezing and the snow came in the window on top of my blankets. "Tiocfaidh ár lá [our day will come]," I said to myself. "Tiocfaidh ár lá." (Sands 1983)

One Day in My Life was published in 1983, two years after his death. If it never achieved the international status of Solzhenitsyn's *One Day in the Life of Ivan Denisovich*, it is less because it has inferior literary value—*One Day in My Life* is doubtless a magnificent piece of jail literature—than because it served the opposite side in the then-raging cold war.

By summer 1979, the prisoners began planning a hunger strike. Gerry Adams was against it, saying that Thatcher would simply let them die. Hughes and Sands told him that if someone had to die for them to win their rights, so be it. Bobby made an impassioned speech to his comrades, saying that at certain points in the struggle it takes a few good men to do a major deed in order to turn fortunes around. When Archbishop Tomás Ó Fiaich, who was sympathetic to the prisoners, was elevated to Cardinal at the end of June, he offered to negotiate with Thatcher on their behalf. Adams used this to persuade the prisoners to postpone their hunger strike, promising in return to intensify the prisoner support campaign outside of the prison.

Sands and Hughes were not long in holding the movement to its word. Bobby led a discussion about mobilising publicity. He developed slogans like 'Smash H-Block' and 'Don't Let My Daddy Die in H-Block', both of which became central to the subsequent campaign. He got the Movement to smuggle in names and addresses of famous people around the world to whom the prisoners could write. Then, he organised a mass smuggling campaign to get in the cigarette papers and pen refills needed to write hundreds of letters and to get them out for distribution. While Bobby organised the communications network inside the prison, women activists coordinated it outside. A team of young women went back and forth into the jail, twice a day, smuggling communications and supplies. On most days, Bobby could smuggle out messages to the movement in the morning and receive replies that afternoon.

Sands used the new communications network as a launching pad to create 'a production factory for comms'. Each prisoner had to write four or five letters a day on toilet paper. Bobby drew up sample letters, explaining the conditions in the H-Blocks and why they had been forced into the no-wash protest. Each letter contained a section where the prisoner introduced himself. Sands customised the templates for different kinds of people. It would take a different message to move an academic or politician than an actor or artist. In time, they wrote to hundreds of trade unionists, actors, writers, and musicians around the world. Jane Fonda, Muhammad Ali, and Jean-Paul Sartre all got letters.

Hunger strike was still on the agenda, but Adams kept persuading them to postpone the action. In October 1979, Bobby gave an interview to a journalist and said that he expected to die. 'I know I'm dying. I'm prepared to die on the blanket. I will never, never accept criminal status. All the prisoners have the same determination as myself, and we will never give up' (Boyd 1979). One day, Bobby got a new luxury. Someone designed small crystal radios, the size of two D batteries placed end to end. Smuggling the radios into prison was hard for the women, who brought them in between the cheeks of their buttocks or taped to the insides of their legs. And it took courage to discretely take the radios off of the women and then slip them through the rip in his crotch and up his own anus.

During the summer of 1980, talk of a hunger strike became more common. Hopes of a settlement were quashed in September when the British side told Ó Fiaich bluntly that they would not change the prisoners' status. After the breakdown of negotiations, Bobby sent documents to each block instructing them to debate the impending hunger strike. This was more about building consensus than debate. The consensus was that it was past time for action (Bik MacFarlane interview).

Sands and Hughes asked for volunteers. They wanted six; they got a hundred and forty-eight. They made a shortlist, ruling out anyone who was physically or psychologically questionable. They agreed that six hunger strikers, one from each county in Northern Ireland, would widen public support. Then, they decided to include a seventh, the number who signed the Proclamation of the Irish Republic in 1916. Symbolism was thick in the air.

Choosing hunger strikers caused the Dark's only real argument with Bobby. When Hughes told Sands that he would not be going on the strike Bobby exploded:

> "I'm on this hunger strike, end of story," he told Hughes.
> "No, you're not," replied the Dark. "I'm the OC and I made my
> own decision. I'm going on the hunger strike and you're taking
> over". (Brendan Hughes interview)

Bobby finally gave in. Coming up to the hunger strike, Bobby raised the level of smuggling. 'You'll have 180 odd visits with centre in December', he wrote to the movement. Then:

> Back to the leaky comms. This is the crux of the matter comrade; men have to swallow 99 percent of all in-coming comms. They vomit them up on arrival back into cell. This has 40 percent success rate. The other 59 percent have to be passed through body. Body acids eat S/S [stretch-and-seal] (sometimes, and, especially, on country men. Ha!). (Dear God.) Anyway, to deflect this, put

two light layers of silver paper around comms followed by the usual amount of S/S. Now you know what I've to go through to get a comm, okay. You wouldn't believe half of it.

Monday morning, October 27, 1980. When the warders came around with breakfast, seven blanketmen announced that they were on hunger strike. On November 6, they were moved to the prison hospital. As the hunger strike wore on, public pressure mounted on the British government to reach a settlement. Supporters plastered the countryside with 'Smash H-Block'. There were daily marches and protests, and constant confrontations between young people and the army/police. As the hunger strikers weakened, the crowds got bigger. An opinion poll conducted by the Irish radio and television network found that half of the southern Irish population wanted the British to grant immediate political status (Clarke 1987: 130).

On December 1, three women from Armagh jail joined the hunger strike. The strike was moving towards its decisive stage.

Some of the men began to have difficulty walking. Hughes made a daily round to check on their physical and mental conditions. One of them, Sean McKenna, was close to death. McKenna had a request: 'Promise me that you won't let me die'. 'You have my word', Hughes replied. 'I won't let you die' (Brendan Hughes interview).

That afternoon, McKenna slipped in and out of a coma. Finally, Hughes shouted to the doctor, 'Feed him'. Hughes told the other five that the hunger strike was over. When Bobby Sands heard that the strike ended without an agreement he was livid. Hughes usurped his authority to end the hunger strike without achieving their objective. Now, he felt, the blanketmen emerged from the strike weaker than they had gone into it. When Bobby returned to his cell, he told the prisoners that he would start a new hunger strike immediately. They felt angry, betrayed, and sad that their leader would start a protest that would certainly cost his life.

In a few short hours, Bobby had learned a vital lesson. You have to control information and you have to control the actions of your key actors. The slightest failure can be fatal. States have tremendous power to control and manage information in order to influence even their most committed adversaries. For several years, the blanketmen had partly neutralised this power with their creative forms of communication. Now, at the most critical moment, they lost control. Bobby wrote to Adams:

So, comrade mor ["boss comrade'], we maintain, and the next part of this comm will be very disturbing… I want to make it quite clear, myself and four others to hunger strike. There is one realisation here, comrade, which rings clear. Someone will die. I know others told you this, but I am prepared to die and no one will call this hunger strike off, comrade… The people, the movement, have taken a blow. We need out of it and if it means death then that is accepted. We stand to be destroyed, comrade…When you're knocked down you get up and fight back. We can do it… I'm not prepared to watch four and a half years of sheer murder be fritted into conformity and respectability. (Marcella [Bobby Sands] communication to Brownie [Gerry Adams], 3:00 P.M., 12/19/80)

Over the next few days, Sands exchanged communications with the movement about a second hunger strike. Adams was against it. He did not think that the movement could generate public support again after the first strike ended in such an unsatisfactory fashion. Everyone was drained.

Bobby shifted the discourse surrounding the new hunger strike to a more political emphasis. It wasn't just about the uniform or the beatings. As political prisoners, they could claim to be engaged in a legitimate liberation struggle; they could take that status to the world as recognition of their right to resist British tyranny. But if they allowed themselves to be criminalised, the whole struggle was criminalised. There was also a practical point. Bobby remembered his personal development in the cages. Prison had made him who he was today, instead of the relatively unaware lad of 1972. Prison was the basis of his identity: his music, his political awareness, his poetry. The vast majority of books he had ever read, he read in prison. Thus, the only way he knew to mould young politically aware Republican activists was in jail. To do it effectively, they had to be free to read, lecture, debate, and write. In short, the *prison struggle was the centre of the struggle*. The key to reinvigorating the IRA was through the prison, which was the centre of political consciousness. The first hunger strike was portrayed as a human rights issue. Now, the second one was an explicit struggle for recognition as political prisoners.

March 1, 1981, began like any other day. The screws left Bobby's breakfast at the door. His portions were much bigger than usual. It was Sunday and the regular staff was off duty. There was no one of consequence to whom Bobby could announce that he was beginning the biggest protest that ever enveloped an Irish prison. Finally, the governor visited. He asked him the reason for his action.

"Political status," replied Bobby.
"Is this for yourself alone?" asked the governor.
"It is for all Republican POWs, both here and in Armagh [the women's prison]". (Sands 1982)

Six days into the hunger strike, Bobby began to feel isolated. Soon, he expected, they might move him to the prison hospital. Although he would be sorry to leave, he was consigned to that fact that 'the road is a hard one and everything must be conquered'. The *Irish News* reported a perceptible rise in public support for the hunger strike. On Sunday, the eighth day of his hunger strike, a screw set Bobby's breakfast on the table while he read. The meals, he thought, just kept getting bigger and better. On the fifth day of the hunger strike, the MP for Fermanagh/South Tyrone Frank Maguire had died of a heart attack. Now, the movement suggested running Bobby for the vacant seat.

Bobby had no expectation that winning the seat in parliament would save his life. And he was too weak to take an active part in the campaign. But when he won the election as a member of parliament, many activists thought that the British government would have to save his life and give concessions to the prisoners. Maggie Thatcher had other ideas. In far-off Riyadh, she emerged from a royal Saudi banquet to insist that the result had changed nothing.

'A crime is a crime is a crime', she said. 'It is not political it is a crime'.

Bobby's election to parliament undoubtedly shortened his life. The doctor said Bobby was 'going downhill very fast' from too many visits and too much talking. When Bobby's family next visited him, his speech was slurred, his hearing impaired and his eyes unable to focus. For some time a rhythmic wobbling of the eyes, indicating that his body was beginning to shut down. He had a severe headache and the fillings began to fall out of his teeth. Each movement caused severe pain. He was practically blind.

His mother Rosaleen was overcome by Bobby's condition.

"Son, I'm thinking of taking you off this," she said.
"Mammy, just get out of here," replied Bobby, raising his arm with effort and waving toward the door.

Rosaleen went home but immediately returned to the prison hospital. She told Bobby that she was behind him all the way (interview with family friend). By Thursday, April 30, Bobby lost all feeling in his mouth and found it harder to speak. On Saturday, his eyesight was gone and one side of his body was numb. When Bobby's family arrived on Sunday, they thought he was already dead. Rosaleen knelt beside him and said an act of contrition in his ear. At this, Bobby nodded. Through it all, a prison warder stood by, writing down everything. On Monday evening, Bobby's bowels burst and he was in excruciating pain. The priest administered Holy Communion and last sacraments and he went into a coma. According to his family, his last words were, 'I love you all. You are the best mother in the world. You stood by me'. Seventeen minutes past one in the morning on May 5, 1981:

> He was in a coma and his breathing was laboured and it just stopped and that was it. (Feehan 1983, 135)

Few British politicians mourned. The Northern Ireland Office released a pathetically terse statement that acknowledged Bobby Sands' death while pointedly ignoring his new-found political status, saying that he took his own life by refusing food and medical intervention. In Westminster, British parliamentarians ignored their customary tribute to a fallen member, simply announcing the death with a terse statement. Thatcher went one better, telling parliament that Bobby Sands was a convicted criminal and, as such, would never be granted political status.

The Catholic Church was hardly more sympathetic. The bishop directed that no public masses would be said for 'a certain person'. It caused anger among the clergy. One wrote in a newspaper that the bishop was practising 'junk theology'. In Republican Belfast, tens of thousands lined the hundred yards or so between the Sands house and the chapel as the body was removed for the funeral mass. Camera crews came from far away countries in Asia and Africa.

On the road to the cemetery, the coffin was removed from the hearse and put onto trestles. Four IRA men in full battle dress emerged from the crowd and fired three volleys over the coffin. They bowed their heads, observed a minute's silence, and melted back into the crowd. Through the summer of 1981, as nine more men died, it became clearer that the Thatcher government would not move. On October 3, the prisoners reluctantly called off their fast.

What did Bobby Sands achieve? What was the meaning of his life? In a personal sense, it was a remarkable story of a young boy who was cursed or blessed by being born into a remarkable place at a remarkable time. Within this context, Bobby Sands repeatedly reinvented himself. He began as the schoolboy trying to fit in among his peers. As his 'peers' changed, he became an enthusiastic but not terribly reflexive IRA volunteer. In prison, he became the radical student, using what he learned from fellow prisoners and books to prepare himself as a grass-roots community leader. Then, back in prison, he met new conditions of extreme deprivation as a teacher, writer, organiser and, ultimately, leader of the Irish prison struggle. Everyone adapts to new situations but Bobby Sands used new knowledge to raise his awareness and his practice in each subsequent period of his life. In doing so, he shaped events; he made history.

Sands also reinvented himself culturally, into propagandist, story-teller, and poet. He progressed from listening to stories, to reading them, to recounting them and, finally, to writing his own story. He went from listening to songs as others sang them, to singing others' songs, to writing and singing his own song. Ultimately, others sang his songs. In the process, he became an international symbol, even an icon of resistance. This, arguably, was not his intention. Yet in the process of leading a relatively small group of protesting prisoners, he built such strong determination and took that determination to such a remarkable end, that the world looked on in admiration. The example of the hunger strikers, concentrated in the image and the name of Bobby Sands, reverberated around the world, giving hope to others who struggled for freedom or liberation. His example inspired thousands to support freedom struggles across the continents.

In Havana, Fidel Castro put the Irish hunger strikers in rather high company, in a statement that would have galled the Irish clergy:

> Tyrants shake in the presence of men who are able to die for their ideals, after sixty days of hunger strike! Next to this example, what were the three days of Christ on Calvary, as a symbol down the centuries of human sacrifice? (Castro 1981)

On Robben Island, Nelson Mandela joined a group of young prisoners from *Umkhonto we Sizwe* on a hunger strike that was directly inspired by Bobby Sands. In Cerro Hueco prison in Chiapas, Arturo Albores Velasco organised the first hunger strike in that prison's history. It was a key episode in the early history of a movement that would soon emerge on the global scene as the Zapatistas. Twenty years later in Turkey, when hundreds of political prisoners went on hunger strike, their secret messages had a code word for the coming hunger strike: Bobby Sands. And, in the United States, a wave of prison hunger strikes was directly influenced by prisoners who read about Bobby Sands and the blanketmen. At its apex, 30,000 prisoners in California went on hunger strike in 2013 to defeat the state's policy of long-term solitary isolation. They were organised by a small group of prisoners in the 'short corridor' of Pelican Bay State Prison. These were men had been isolated without any human contact for twenty years, in windowless 11-by-7 foot cells. They were supposedly the 'worst of the worst', accused leaders of the Black Guerrilla Family, the Mexican Mafia, La Nuestra Familia, and the Aryan Brotherhood. They were supposed to hate each other and were placed together in the expectation that they would be in constant conflict. Instead, they organised a solidary 'Short Corridor Collective', much like the oral community in the H-Blocks. Over five years, after reading the H-blocks experience and combining it with principles from Mayan cosmology and Tom Paine, they organised a mass hunger strike and a court action that forced the state to end its policy of long-term solitary isolation. Similar successful hunger strikes took place in Ohio, Illinois, and even in migrant holding facilities.

In Ireland, the influence of Bobby Sands and the hunger strikers has been most profound. The British government considered the end of the fast to be its victory, yet the Republican Movement grew strong as a result of the hunger strike, both militarily and electorally. Although the British government claimed victory over the hunger strikers, it conceded most of their demands soon after the protest ended. The Republican Movement and, especially, its political party Sinn Féin gained strength during the 1990s by launching a peace process and parlaying its new political strategy into electoral strength in the north and south of Ireland.

One thing is certain. Bobby Sands' determination comes through. One image returns over and over again: a naked man locked up twenty-four hours a day in a cell, without even the most rudimentary comforts like clothes or reading materials. He turns to his cellmate and chastises him for sleeping all day.

It's a waste of your opportunities, isn't it? (Collins 1986: 57–58)

Just as his consciousness was formed by Che Guevara and Franz Fanon, so too are the consciousnesses of thousands of activists around the world informed by the life and death of Bobby Sands. His determination, surely. And his dignity, even grace.

References

Boyd, J. (1979, October 7). Hunger Strike Threat. *Sunday News*.
Brownie [Gerry Adams]. (1975, November 29). The Republic: A Reality. *Republican News*, p. 4.
Campbell, B., McKeown, L., & O'Hagan, F. (Eds.). (1994). *Nor Meekly Serve My Time*. Belfast: Beyond the Pale.
Castro, F. (1981, September 18). *A todos hombres y mujeres que lucharon por la independencia de Irlanda*. Statement to sixty-eight Conferencia de la Union Interparliamentaria.
Clarke, L. (1987). *Broadening the Battlefield: The H-Blocks and the Rise of Sinn Féin*. Dublin: Gill and Macmillan.
Collins, T. (1986). *The Irish Hunger Strike*. Dublin: White Island Book Company.
Farrell, M. (1976). *Northern Ireland: The Orange State*. London: Pluto.
Feehan, J. (1983). *Bobby Sands and the Tragedy of Northern Ireland*. Dublin: Mercier Press.
Marcella (Bobby Sands). (1978, November 25). The Window of My Mind. *Republican News*.
McCann, J. (n.d.). Manuscript for *Nor Meekly Serve My Time*.
McCann, J. (1998). *The Gates Flew Open*. Belfast: Glandale Publishing.
"On the Blanket," *Republican News*, November 5, 1977, p. 6. Sands was never identified publicly as the author of this article.
Planning Advisory Board. (1944). *Housing in Northern Ireland: Interim Report of the Planning Advisory Board* (p. 1944). Belfast: H.M.S.O.
Sands, B. (1975). Ag bunadh Gaeltachta [Establishing a Gaeltacht]. *Ár nGuth Fhéin* (original prison manuscript).
Sands, B. (1982). Diary. In *Skylark Sing Your Lonely Song: An Anthology of the Writings of Bobby Sands* (pp. 153–173). Dublin: Mercier.
Sands, B. (1983). *One Day in My Life*. Cork: Mercier Press.

Part VII

Professional Lives

Jenny Byrne

Introduction

The auto/biographies of certain professional groups, such as teachers, have been explored in depth and for some time (e.g. Connelly and Clandinin 1999; Goodson and Sikes 2001; Goodson 2003). Interest in life history or life story of the working lives of other professionals, such as social workers and healthcare professionals (e.g. Radley 1993; Barnard et al. 2000; Abels and Abels 2001; Reissman and Quinney 2005; Martin 2010), has increased recently and may in part be due to the 'narrative turn' in qualitative and auto/biographical research (Roberts 2002; Denzin and Lincoln 2005). However, the emphasis in these studies is frequently on the therapeutic and empowering effects of auto/biographical narrative for the clients or patients of these professionals rather than the lives of individual professionals. The interest in this chapter lies in exploring auto/biographical accounts of individuals within their social, historical, political and cultural contexts in order to understand their lived experience of being a professional within particular occupational groups (e.g. Bertaux 1981). These personal stories are important because they provide unique insights into the experiences of individual lives that make their auto/biographies a precious record of their selfhood and identity (Josselson and Lieblich 1999). But they also reflect the way in which societal and cultural changes are understood and therefore have wider implications for understanding professional life (Erben 1998; Ricoeur 1988; Plummer 2001). Secondly, in recent decades traditional concepts of a profession have been disrupted in a period of rapid change as a result of technological advances and globalisation that has created uncertainty for individuals' professional identity living in a period of 'liquid modernity' (Bauman 2000). For some, this has led to the deskilling and over-regulation of working practices that lead them to question their sense of professional self (Braverman 1974; Kumar 1978; Sparkes 2007).Thirdly, the increase in neoliberal agendas, marketisation of services, performativity, accountability and the rise of managerialism, calls into question the meaning of a profession and therefore impacts on how individuals may perceive their professional identity and sense of professional self (Sachs 2001, 2003; Day et al. 2006; Shore 2008; Darbyshire 2007; Sparkes 2007; Evetts 2009). Using auto/biographical accounts a reappraisal of professional life is presented in these chapters with the aim of providing an enriched and up-to-date understanding of what it means to be a professional.

Who Is a Professional?

Characteristics of the professions have traditionally included knowledge and expertise, gained as a result of higher education (Freidson 1986), as well as, adherence to a code of ethics for professional conduct, altruism that is manifested in public service and a concern for the community rather than self-interest or material gain (Goode 1960; Barber 1963). The arcane knowledge and expertise that professionals hold is thought to be used for the protection of the public and society as a whole; as a result, prestige and privilege are accorded to those belonging to the professions. Membership of a professional association is also necessary, and adherence to a code of conduct an absolute to maintain standards of the highest order with any disciplinary action undertaken by the professional group rather than through public scrutiny (Elliott 1972). The ability to work autonomously and be responsible for the application of professional judgement are also identified as features of the professional role (Evetts 2009). Those occupational groups embracing all the characteristics described above have been used to denote the higher professions, for example senior civil servants, high ranking officers of the armed services, judges, barristers, solicitors, architects, doctors and dentists, whereas teachers, nurses, social workers and librarians are occupations that do not entirely meet the criteria of a 'full' profession and are regarded as 'quasi-' or 'semi-professions' (Etzioni 1969).

However, the notion of who is a professional has long been a contested issue (e.g. Hargreaves 2000; Whitty 2000; Evetts 2009; Saks 2012). One might consider that someone who can work with resistant materials such as granite or marble using a hammer and chisel to produce an object of functionality or aesthetic beauty might be thought of as either a stonemason or a sculptor. The question is, which of these knowledgeable, capable, talented and creative individuals would be regarded as a professional? Both or only one? And how, depending on their status, would they provide an auto/biographical account of their professional life? Undoubtedly, notions of professional knowledge, professional competence and professional practice are encompassed in the example above and have frequently been regarded as identifying features of a profession (e.g. Carr-Saunders and Wilson 1933; Greenwood 1957; Millerson 1964). Nevertheless, the auto/biography of a high court judge is likely to be quite different in detail and content to a nurse, or teacher but what is highlighted in the following chapters is how the lived experience of these individuals' professional lives with their myriad contingencies influence the narratives, and as a consequence how they might perceive their professional self (e.g. Bruner 1987).

More recently arguments have developed about the loss of autonomy and power within the professions and a de-professionalisation of the professions. Demands from governments and private enterprise alike for greater accountability, improved results, and increased competition have resulted in performance management with specific indicators, standardised criteria for target setting, competency-based pre- and in-service training, audit and inspection (e.g. Whitty 2000; Tomlinson 2001; Evetts 2009). These bureaucratic imperatives have created the need for a larger managerial echelon in public institutions and private corporations. The rise in managerialism, and within the public sector New Public Management, has eroded traditional perceptions of being a professional and a situation could arise where professionals may become little more than skilled practitioners enacting the policies and practice dictated through a managerialist discourse (Sachs 2001, 2003). Exploring the auto/biographies of the professionals in the following chapters will help to elucidate how these changes may have affected their understanding of professional life that appears to be at the behest of external rules and constraints. However, Sachs (2001) offers a more optimistic outlook where the focus is on the agency and power of individuals to define their own conditions of work and construct their professional identity through creative engagement, compliance and at times resistance to managerial demands. The narratives of the professionals in the following chapters may also help to illuminate how they negotiate their professional lives in order to maintain a coherent sense of professional self (MacIntyre 1985; Ricoeur 1988; Taylor 1989; Plummer 2001).

Furthermore, their auto/biographical accounts may help to shed light on other issues brought about by post-industrialisation with regard to understanding professional life. These include the internationalisation and globalisation of professional companies, the increase of service-based industries and with it the rise of new occupational groups that claim professional status such as those working in the financial services or software industries (Abbott 2001).

It is unsurprising then that what we mean by a profession has clearly changed since the first typologies were produced and that professional boundaries are in a constant state of flux (Saks 2012). This dynamic will influence what it means to be a professional and how members of particular occupational groups perceive their professional identity now and in the future.

Professional Identity

When meeting someone new for the first time after an exchange of names one of the first questions a person is frequently asked is, 'What do you do for a living?' This aspect of a person's auto/biography is of interest in these initial conversions because career choice can sometimes be an indicator of someone's personality (Jung and Hull 1991). Therefore, the answer may help to provide a purchase on an individual's personal attributes such as character and attitudes. In addition, a conscious or unconscious appraisal of the individual's social status may also occur. Depending on the reply if the answer is one of the traditional or primary professions, such as a doctor, lawyer, judge, diplomat and so on, the response to the individual may be quite different towards those who say they are, for example, a housewife, a bricklayer or a teacher. These value judgements and subsequent interactions with others in a social context are of crucial importance to the individual's sense of self and their professional identity (Mead 1934; Berger and Luckman 1971). As McAdams (1997: 6) notes having a particular identity enables a person to give 'meaning, unity and purpose' to their lives and shapes their selfhood. Professional identity is therefore a key component to someone's self-concept and can be employed as an auto/biographical resource to explain, justify and make sense of themselves and their occupation in relation to others in social and professional contexts, as well as more widely (MacLure 1993). Therefore, the relationships that individuals have with others and the connections they make with their social, professional and cultural world will shape and constrain their narrative (Dunne 1996). As their story unfolds individuals may also choose to emphasise certain parts of their professional life whilst diminishing others, as part of impression management to provide an appropriate narrative of themselves, which not only influences how they may be regarded but how, through personal reflection, they perceive their professional identity and occupational role (Goffman 1959; Taylor 1989).

Professional identity is an ongoing process developed not only as a result of personal reflections but through interactions and conversations with other similar professionals. The encounters with others in a professional context and inclusion in the particular community of practice creates a joint narrative which reinforces professional identity (Wenger 1998; Sfard and Prusak 2005; Beauchamp and Thomas 2009). As individuals become a valid member of the community of practice, their professional identity develops and is constantly negotiated and re-negotiated throughout their working life as a result of these interactions, including the shared professional repertoires with their particular language, traditions, symbols and values, that will affect their auto/biographies (Mead 1934; Berger and Luckman 1971).

Narratives provide the individual with a sense of self and it is through these accounts that people make sense of who they are, who they were and who they might become (MacIntyre 1985; Taylor 1989). These reflections of the past and projections of the future provide a mechanism to develop a sense of identity, as well as offering coherence and structure to the professional life course (Ricoeur 1988). In recounting experiences of one's professional life, it is time that provides the essential structure of its existence and it is through narrating what has occurred that time is experienced, identity is formed, and the life lived can be comprehended (Erben 1998). As Smith and Sparkes (2008) note it is through the stories individuals tell about their [professional] life that they are able to fashion their autobiography and professional identity. Therefore, taking an auto/biographical approach and listening to the narratives of the professionals presented in the following chapters we hope to offer an understanding of their professional lives and professional identity in more profound ways. That narrative can bestow meaning to professional lives and that it consequently influences, constructs and shapes someone's professional identity suggests narrative is of central importance if we are to understand more generally what it means to be a professional in the twenty-first century.

The Chapters

Irene Selway, Jenny Byrne and Anne Chappell re-examine the lives of academics in higher education that formed part of a larger Ph.D. Study. Re-examining their auto/biographical accounts has enabled further reflections on academic professional life and illustrates how their auto/biographies can be understood in a period of change. Using *Bildung* as a conceptual lens, we illustrate the process of constructing a professional life. In narrating their auto/biographies, these academics have been able to reflexive about the embodiment of the culture of their profession and consciously consider the moral, ethical and political values that shape their educative relationships with students and colleagues. These values appear to be retained by the academics despite the many changes that have taken place in higher education in the past 25 years.

The academics in this chapter have very different autobiographies and they have altered their practices and approach to deal with the changes in the curriculum and student population but reflecting on their narratives they appear to have retained their initial commitment to a set of educational values. Their auto/biographies illustrate that local institutional culture is not a monolithic set of injunctions or absolute directives but it demands that the academics interpret the directives and adapt their professional sense of self in ways that maintain their own moral and ethical stance. We suggest that the stories of academic life indicate that the three academics live in a kind of border country. Whilst the details of the stories may differ, the common theme in these auto/biographical accounts is the academics' attempt to construct a professional life they find acceptable to themselves.

Glenn Stone employs the personal narratives about teaching of early career teachers and examines how perceptions of professionalism are changing based on current expectations for new teachers working in the public sector. Narratives from pre-service teachers illustrate how Initial Teacher Education can involve the enculturation of New Public Management values. This causes conflict when the pre-service teacher has a different philosophy of education and can be conceived as a threat to occupational professionalism when the pre-service teacher willingly adopts practices of organisational professionalism in order to demonstrate the competencies required to pass their initial training. Extracts from the stories in this chapter show how the pre-service teacher negotiates different forms of professionalism, but will also engage in performative practices to appease those that are in more powerful positions. This is seen as necessary in order to succeed. However, when becoming newly qualified and working as a teacher in the induction year, there is a shift in values that may be interpreted as the teacher returning to their original motivations and occupational values. This is not to say that the structures of New Public Management and organisational professionalism have been eradicated for these teachers, but rather that their stories elucidate the transformative power of education and by association, the value of professional work.

Jenny Byrne turns away from the 'caring' public sector and welfare professions to examine the lives of young graduates working in the private sector. She employs auto/biographical accounts of three millennials otherwise known as Generation Y to explore their understanding of their working lives, and thus their perceptions of professional status and professional identity. This generation have often been criticised and stereotyped as self-centred, demotivated and lacking collegiality and only interested in high salaries. The narratives of the three young graduates presented belie these stereotypical notions and it is evident that contrary to these perceptions the stories of their working lives indicate that they are dedicated to their industry, place of work and colleagues. They are hardworking and in spite of managerial requirements they strive to meet expectations and targets, often in difficult and demanding circumstances, behaving with what they consider to be professionalism. The constraints to their autonomy may suggest that they work in a culture of organisational rather than occupational professionalism. Nevertheless, their auto/biographies indicate that they are agentic. They have a self-developed sense of professional identity and they exhibit many of the qualities, attributes and criteria that define a 'traditional' profession. However, their narratives also indicate that they do not fully identify with the notion of a traditional or semi-profession, for example that they did not have a vocation or calling, or any intrinsic motivation to enter a specific occupation, unlike may working in the public sector. However, their auto/biographical accounts of working in the private sector have resonance with those in the public sector particularly in how they negotiate their sense of professional self and re-define their professional lives in their own terms. Therefore, the nature of a professional life in the twenty-first century appears to be a dynamic and evolving concept that is subject to liquid modernity but also contingent upon personal and professional circumstances (Bauman 2000).

As the brief outlines of the chapters in this part indicate the lives of three different groups of professionals at different points in their careers may seem to be quite disparate. Chapter 20 (Selway, Byrne and Chappell) explores the lives of older academics in a higher education institution during a period of considerable change, whilst Chapter 21 (Stone) considers the way in which pre-service teachers negotiate their professional identity within the era of New Public Management and finally Chapter 22 (Byrne) examines the lives of young professionals working in different parts of the private sector. Issues of threats to professional identity and self-hood are apparent in all three chapters as a result of marketisation, accountability and performativity in an era of New Public Management and its associated structures within private enterprise. The narratives explore the dilemmas each individual faces in the light of managerial demands and expectations, changes to working practice, uncertainty and ontological insecurity alongside their personal expectations of what it means to be a professional. Tensions between neo-liberal agendas and managerialism in the workplace as well as these individuals' core professional values mean that at times there is resistance to particular demands, and yet at others resigned acquiescence is apparent.

The auto/biographical accounts of all the participants illustrate in illuminating ways how they negotiate their way through the complexities of their everyday professional experiences and how this affects their professional (and personal) identity. The narratives indicate how these professionals manage the conflicting demands on their selfhood that is contingent upon the specific professional context. Nevertheless, each auto/biographical account highlights the need for the professionals to manage their personal and professional agency, values and attitudes in order to maintain a coherent sense of self. In this respect all three groups of participants live within the interstices of their professional environment, that is neither an entirely occupational nor organisational professional habitat. As Selway, Byrne and Chappell suggest all the participants inhabit, 'a border country'; for example, in Stone's chapter his participants are faced with having to maintain a professional identity that may be at odds with how they perceive themselves as the young teachers they want to be. Whilst the academics in Selway, Byrne and Chappell's chapter juggle demands from managers with their own moral and ethical views of what it means to be an academic and how they perceive their professional role. Byrne's participants are concerned, amongst other things, with how they can maintain their professionalism whilst also seeking the autonomy that enables them to achieve the work/life balance that they desire. The auto/biographical accounts indicate a synergy within and between the individuals in each professional group in their understanding of being a professional, as such these life stories inform us in similar but different ways about professional life in the twenty-first century.

To conclude, the three chapters in this part offer original research focussing on the lived experiences of individuals within their different professional contexts and how they view their working lives, their professional identity and sense of self. From an auto/biographical perspective, the reality of the lives of these professionals is best understood through the scholarly examination of, and imaginative reflection on, the personal accounts of everyday experiences that each chapter provides (Erben 1998). The analysis of their narratives is therefore expected to illuminate the specific lived experiences of these individuals thereby providing insights into the meaning of particular lives, as well as offering more general observations about each occupational group, that enable an enhanced comprehension of the particular features of these professional contexts. In this way, the chapters are expected to add to the theory and practice of auto/ biography in this field of study.

References

Abbott, A. (2001). Sociology of Professions. *International Encyclopaedia of the Social and Behavioural Sciences, 18*, 12166–12169.

Abels, P., & Abels, S. L. (2001). *Understanding Narrative Therapy: A Guidebook for the Social Worker*. New York: Springer.

Barber, B. (1963). Some Problems in the Sociology of Professions. *Daedalus, 92*, 669–688.

Barnard, D., Towers, A., Boston, P., & Lambrinidou, Y. (2000). *Crossing Over: Narratives of Palliative Care*. Oxford: Oxford University Press.

Bauman, Z. (2000). *Liquid Modernity*. Cambridge: Polity Press.

Beauchamp, C., & Thomas, L. (2009). Understanding Teacher Identity: An Overview of Issues in the Literature and Implications for Teacher Education. *Cambridge Journal of Education, 39*(2), 175–189.

Berger, P. L., & Luckman, T. (1971). *The Social Construction of Reality*. Harmondsworth: Penguin.

Bertaux, D. (1981). *Biography and Society: The Life History Approach in the Social Sciences*. London: Sage.

Braverman, H. (1974). *Labor and Monopoly Capitalism*. New York: Monthly Review Press.

Bruner, J. (1987). Life as Narrative. *Social Research, 54,* 12–32.

Carr-Saunders, A. M., & Wilson, P. A. (1933). *The Professions*. Oxford: Clarendon Press.

Connelly, M., & Clandinin, J. (1999). *Shaping a Professional Identity: Stories of Educational Practice*. London: The Althouse Press.

Darbyshire, P. (2007). Never Mind the Quality, Feel the Width: The Nonsense of Quality, Excellence and Audit in Education, Health and Research. *Collegian, 15*, 35–41.

Day, C., Kington, A., Stobart, G., & Sammons, P. (2006). The Personal and Professional Selves of Teachers: Stable and Unstable Identities. *British Educational Research Journal, 32*(4), 601–616.

Denzin, N. K., & Lincoln, Y. S. (2005). *The Sage Handbook of Qualitative Research*. 3rd edn. London: Sage

Dunne, J. (1996). Beyond Sovereignty and Deconstruction: The Storied Self. In R. Kearney (Ed.) *Paul Ricoeur: The Hermeneutics of Action* (pp. 137–157). London: Sage.

Elliott, P. R. C. (1972). *The Sociology of the Professions*. New York, NY: Herder and Herder.

Erben, M. (Ed.). (1998). *Biography and Education*. London: Falmer Press.

Etzioni, A. (Ed.). (1969). *The Semi-professions and Their Organisation: Teachers, Nurses, Social Workers*. London: Collier-Macmillan.

Evetts, J. (2009). New Professionalism and New Public Management: Changes, Continuities and Consequences. *Comparative Sociology, 8*(2), 247–266.

Freidson, E. (1986). *Professional Powers: A Study of the Institutionalization of Formal Knowledge*. Chicago: Chicago University Press.

Goffman, E. (1959). *The Presentation of Self in Everyday Life*. New York: Doubleday.

Goode, W. (1960). Encroachment, Charlatanism and the Emerging Profession. *American Sociological Review, 25,* 902–914.

Goodson, I. (2003). *Professional Knowledge, Professional Lives: Studies in Education and Change*. Maidenhead: Open University Press.

Goodson, I., & Sikes, P. (2001). *Life History Research in Educational Settings—Learning from Lives*. Buckingham: Open University Press.

Greenwood, E. (1957). The Attributes of a Profession. *Social Work, 2,* 45–55.

Hargreaves, A. (2000). Four Ages of Professionalism and Professional Learning. *Teachers and Teaching: Theory and Practice, 6*(2), 151–182.

Josselson, R., & Lieblich, A. (1999). *Making Meaning of Narratives: The Narrative Study of Lives*. Thousand Oaks, CA: Sage.

Jung, C. G., & Hull, R. F. C. (1991). *Psychological Types*. London: Routledge.

Kumar, K. (1978). *Prophesy and Progress: The Sociology of Industrial and Post-Industrial Society*. Harmondsworth: Penguin Books.

MacIntyre, A. (1985). *After Virtue: A Study in Moral Theory*. London: Gerald Duckworth.

MacLure, M. (1993). Arguing for Your Self: Identity as an Organising Principle in Teachers' Jobs and Lives. *British Educational Research Journal, 19*(40), 311–322.

Martin, V. (2010). *Developing a Narrative Approach to Healthcare Research*. Oxford: Radcliffe Publishing.

McAdams, D. P. (1997). *The Stories We Live by*. New York: The Guilford Press.

Mead, G. H. (1934). *Mind, Self and Society*. Chicago, IL: University of Chicago.

Millerson, G. (1964). *The Qualifying Association*. London: Routledge and Kegan Paul.

Plummer, K. (2001). *Documents of Life 2: An Invitation to a Critical Humanism*. London: Sage.

Radley, A. (Ed.). (1993). *Worlds of Illness: Biographical and Cultural Perspectives on Health and Disease*. London: Routledge.

Reissman, C. K., & Quinney, L. (2005). Narrative in Social Work; A Critical Review. *Qualitative Social Work, 4*(4), 391–412.

Ricoeur, P. (1988). *Time and Narrative* (Vol. 3). Chicago: University of Chicago Press.

Roberts, B. (2002). *Biographical Research*. Maidenhead: Open University Press.

Sachs, J. (2001). Teacher Professional Identity: Competing Discourses, Competing Outcomes. *Journal of Education Policy, 16*(2), 149–161.

Sachs, J. (2003). Teacher Professional Standards: Controlling or Developing Teaching? *Teachers and Teaching: Theory and Practice, 9*(2), 175–186.

Saks, M. (2012). Defining a Profession: The Role of Knowledge and Expertise. *Professions and Professionalism, 2*(1), 1–10.

Sfard, A., & Prusak, A. (2005). Telling Identities: In Search of an Analytic Tool for Investigating Learning as a Culturally Shaped Activity. *Educational Researcher, 34*(4), 14–22.

Shore, C. (2008). Audit Culture and Illiberal Governance. *Anthropological Theory, 8*(3), 278–298.

Smith, B., & Sparkes, A. C. (2008). Narrative and Its Potential Contribution to Disability Studies. *Disability and Society, 23,* 17–28.

Sparkes, A. C. (2007). Embodiment, Academics, and the Audit Culture: A Story Seeking Consideration. *Qualitative Research, 7*(4), 521–550.

Taylor, C. (1989). *Sources of the Self: The Making of Modern Identity*. Cambridge: Cambridge University Press.

Tomlinson, S. (2001). *Education in a Post-Welfare Society*. Buckingham: Open University Press.

Wenger, E. (1998). *Communities of Practice: Learning, Meaning, and Identity*. Cambridge: Cambridge University Press.

Whitty, G. (2000). Teacher Professionalism in New Times. *Journal of In-service Education, 26*(2), 281–295.

20

Academic Lives in a Period of Transition in Higher Education: Bildung in Educational Auto/Biography

Irene Selway, Jenny Byrne and Anne Chappell

Introduction

The chapter explores the lives of academics working in higher education, drawing upon the auto/biographies of two male academics undertaken by Irene as part of her unpublished Ph.D. completed at Southampton University (Selway 2008). Using the theoretical lens of *Bildung*, we have re-examined the original auto/biographical data alongside Irene's contemplations of academic professional life which are inevitably intertwined with, and reflective of, the auto/biographies of her participants. As such, Irene positioned herself as the researcher, but she is also one of the researched. The impetus for this re-examination came after Irene had read Chapman's article (2014: 127) who noted:

I. Selway
West Sussex, UK

J. Byrne
University of Southampton, Southampton, UK
e-mail: j.byrne@soton.ac.uk

A. Chappell (✉)
Brunel University London, London, UK
e-mail: anne.chappell@brunel.ac.uk

© The Author(s) 2020
J. M. Parsons and A. Chappell (eds.), *The Palgrave Handbook of Auto/Biography*,
https://doi.org/10.1007/978-3-030-31974-8_20

In a broader sense, anyone undertaking auto/biographical research is able to reflect on the values and beliefs exposed in other's lives and through that greater understanding can also make choices about their ideals and ethics which contribute to the evolution of themselves as moral human beings.

This prompted us to think about the values, ethics and ideals which the academics and she had employed as they narrated their experiences to themselves and others in order to make sense of their professional lives. The narration of experiences creates a reflexive auto/biographical account in which individuals engage in a process of self-discovery, understanding and moral development (MacIntyre 1985; Ricoeur 1984). Narrating our own auto/biographies provides us with opportunities for educative self-formation and the development of our professional identity (Taylor 1989).

The concept of *Bildung* is relevant here as it is also concerned with understanding and transformation of the self through an educative process (Gadamer 2004). In this chapter, we explore the concept of *Bildung* as it pertains to the auto/biographies and educational self-transformation of three academics.

Bildung and Auto/Biography

The German notion of *Bildung* has a long tradition, going back about 200 years in continental education, but has no direct translation into English (Laros et al. 2017). English equivalents include 'formation', 'growth', 'shape', 'training', 'education', 'culture'; and 'higher education', 'higher culture', 'refinement', 'good breeding', which make it difficult to express what is meant by the term *Bildung* (Prange 2004: 502). Although the lack of direct translation makes it difficult to present a precise definition, a broad understanding for the purposes of this chapter follows.

The concept of *Bildung* as simply education is often (mis)used in educational contexts today (Prange 2004). *Bildung* is complex, particularly when considering the current state of Higher Education in the UK (and elsewhere) with its overly prescribed and instrumentalist curricula, and accompanying competencies and performance targets. The notion of *Bildung* is at odds with such a functionalist and neoliberal perception of education, where the purpose is to develop productive citizens for the benefit of the state and thus undermine the potential of education as an instrument for liberation, self-formation and development of people's humanity (Dewey 1916; Freire 1972; Rousseau 1979).

Bildung, on the other hand, crucially encompasses learning and understanding oneself and the social, cultural and historical world rather than education, as defined above. According to Gadamer (2004), *Bildung* is a process in which an individual strives to establish understandings of the world and to edify themselves. Similarly, Hegel, refers to *Bildung* as the formative self-development of mind or spirit (*Geist*), which he regarded as a social and historical process (Wood 1998). In this respect, the general purpose of auto/biographical research resonates with *Bildung* in that it also aims to illuminate the meaning of lives within their social, cultural and historical context (Erben 1998). In exploring the narrative of a research participant, the researcher and the participant both gain a purchase on the meaning of that life, and through reflexivity they learn about themselves and each other.

Here, learning is considered to be much more than the acquisition and accumulation of knowledge or skills but a transformation of knowledge and increased personal understanding (Gadamer 2004). This has both cognitive and affective dimensions, and involves the transformation of the learner's personality, feelings and relationships to others (Fuhr 2017). As an educative process, *Bildung* alters an individual's perceptions of the value, purposes and meaning of life that implies ethical and moral development (Carr 1991). Auto/Biography in this respect is also an educative process as the accounts allow individuals to respond to a life story by considering its moral and ethical implications for themselves and others. In short, auto/biography facilitates the conditions in which an individual can perform moral reasoning (Erben 2000).

Bildung does not occur through a didactical process where information is imparted by a teacher. Instead, it is a conflict-ridden process, that Hegel calls 'experience', in which a spiritual being discovers her/his own identity or self-hood whilst striving to actualise the self-hood it is in the process of discovering (Wood 1998). Bildung is therefore a self-educative process or experience that has a broader compass than mere education and is characterised by transformative and holistic personal development. *Bildung* is fundamentally an inner or self-directed activity that cannot be imposed upon an individual. Rather it is a personal endeavour in which the individual is responsible for their learning and character formation (Prange 2004). Self-discovery is also a central element of any auto/biography, in which the self is understood in the process of constructing its narrative (Bruner 1987). This process is undertaken by a retrospective look at a life in the construction of the auto/biography. Baynes (2010: 449) discusses Taylor's views on whether such accounts are the way of making sense of a life:

…it does seem essential to the narrativity thesis… what I shall call a process of account giving that requires on condition of making oneself intelligible [by] locating one's action in a script that 'makes sense' of one's life (to oneself) at any given time. To be a self or an agent an individual must locate herself and her action within a larger narrative context; and at least part of what it means to be a self or an agent is to engage in (implicit and explicit) acts of self-interpretation or "account giving".

Bildung can be regarded as the cultivation of the self by the self, as well the state of being educated, cultivated, or learned in order to have the capacity to grasp and articulate the reasons for what one believes or knows (Fuhr 2017). Acquiring a rational comprehension of things goes hand in hand with a process of liberating maturation through a struggle involving self-hood and the overcoming of self-conflict (Wood 1998). Bildung is associated with personal liberty, autonomy, human dignity and human experience.

Bildung is a lifelong process of becoming, as is the auto/biographical project of the self, in which Heideggerian notions of 'being-towards-death' are apparent where time is the ultimate referent in the development of the self (Ricoeur 1984). As MacIntyre (1985: 220) notes, the unity of the self 'resides in the unity of a narrative which links birth to life and to death'.

However, the unifying features that create self-hood and identity formation over time, and are central to auto/biography and *Bildung*, are challenged by uncertainties resulting from postmodern notions of reflexive (late) modernity (Bauer 1997), liquid modernity and individualisation (Bauman 2001). The impact of modernity is to disrupt the linear sequential life transitions due to constantly changing societal and individual relationships and other contingent factors, such as professional context, that affect someone's auto/biography (Bauer 1997). Pertinent to this study are the massive changes occurring within higher education where the roles, norms and expectations in academia have become much more fluid and transitional. Considerable adaptation of professional skills and practices was required by the academics presented in this chapter that led them to reflect upon, and to question their professional identity and self-hood. In such circumstances, identity formation becomes more reflexive. As Bauer (1997: 171–172) points out:

The re-evaluation and de-routinisation of vocational [and professional] roles will demand qualitatively new patterns of learning in terms of information production of creative ideas and the ability to respond flexibly to new situations or adjust flexibly when interacting with others.

Learning and working in higher education are regarded by many as an important element of self-transformation which *Bildung* represents. How processes of modernity continue to affect the auto/biographies and development of *Bildung* of those in higher education who have experienced loss of stability and uncertainty is contestable. However, this study goes some way to addressing these issues. The connection between learning, *Bildung* and auto/biography is seen as a way forward for research, as Bauer (1997: 17) says:

> A Bildung oriented study of biographical data might be re-presented... so that the processes of learning and education play a central part in forming a life story, the account or autobiography of the actor is relevant to the study of Bildung. However, such processes neither take place consciously nor are they, as a rule, intentionally controlled. Nevertheless, they become manifest if disturbances and crises arise in the course of a life story which cause the author to refer back to earlier experiences.

How the participants have drawn on *Bildung* (unconsciously and unintentionally) in the course of making sense of their auto/biographies and reflecting on their experiences including specific critical events to facilitate self- formation is discussed below.

The Research Context

In the period that the academics in this study worked at the university, there were many changes in higher education policy and practice. There was enormous and unprecedented university expansion in the period, as a result of two policy documents: *The Learning Age: A Renaissance for a New Britain* (DfEE 1998) and *Widening Participation in Higher Education* (DfES 2006). Many referred to it as the massification of higher education that was meant to transform universities from an 'elite' to a 'mass' and highly diverse system of participation (Naidoo 2003: 30; Reay et al. 2001), the drive for which continues to date.

Barnet and Di Napoli (2007) offer a cogent analysis of these changes and their subsequent ramifications that required changes in the way all universities organised the curriculum, teaching and learning and assessment. Bauman (2001) considers the implications for individual professional lives with his notion of 'liquid modernity' where changes in society and the economy, and in this case Higher Education, preclude planning for long term careers. Other writers, like Thomson (2005: 244) argue that we 'increasingly instrumentalise professionalise, vocationalise, corporatise and ultimately *technologise* education' in ways which prevent a critically reflective approach to learning and being. This is epitomised by Dall' Alba and Barnacle (2007) in their description of the increasingly managerialist and performative nature of the university sector.

Such changes have challenged the approaches taken by the academics discussed in this chapter where each describes changing their practice as well as reflecting on the impact on their professional identity. The shift from an elite to a mass system of higher education led to different types of students accessing higher education, as well as changes to their prospects and financial issues. The purpose of higher education has altered to one which has many of the characteristics of preparing 'human capital' for participation in society and is revealed in contemporary students' references to the outcome of their degree in the labour market when being interviewed. In some cases, the interest in the subject is becoming subservient to its economic value, and this is understandable given the increases in fees and living costs incurred by higher education students. Postmodern society is a fluid one where work and opportunities for graduates have changed markedly (Bauman 2001). Specialised knowledge, previously one of the hallmarks of a profession, is often not directly usable as currency in the labour market, whereas flexibility, and knowing how to change is of greater value (Ball 2012). The state of *Bildung* is helpful here in enabling individuals to reflect on what they value, overcome self-conflict and alter their practice in an autonomous and informed manner (Fuhr 2017). Barnett (2005) speaks of a need for an 'ontological turn' in teaching within higher education, whilst recognising that the nature of knowledge is not entirely displaced. He argues that:

> …instead of knowing the world, being-in-the-world has to take primary place in the conceptualisations that inform university teaching. Knowledge is of course still important, but the focus should no longer be knowledge transfer or acquisition. (Barnett 2005: 795)

Similarly, Dall'Alba (2005) says that rather than accumulating knowledge, learning should be understood as the development of embodied ways of knowing or, in other words, ways of being. In higher education, such transformations Dall'Alba and Barnacle (2007: 12) suggest:

Heidegger's description of Bildung points to one means for achieving such transformation, namely 'removing human beings from the region where they first encounter things'. This would mean creating space and opportunities for students to encounter the familiar in unfamiliar ways. Through the strange and unfamiliar we engage with difference: the possibility that things could be otherwise. In other words, by considering the taken-for-granted from other perspectives, we can develop new ways of dealing with our world.

In a similar vein, Barnett argues for presenting 'awkward spaces to and for students' (2005: 795) in order to enable them to deal with the 'strangeness' they inevitably encounter in an uncertain and unpredictable world. Whilst teaching and learning processes in the university did include critical debate (Miller, cited in Barnet and Di Napoli 2007: 107) it was fairly tightly constrained within the planned curriculum because quality assurance procedures rely on predicted content to design appropriate comparable measures of quality.

The metrics used to measure the 'quality' of a degree course include student satisfaction which incorporates accountability to students in terms of choice and greater democracy that can leave academics feeling vulnerable (Barnett and Di Napoli 2007). Miller (2007) argues that increasing cultural capital has long informed academic opinions about the benefits of higher education and indicates that academics fear that the academic landscape has been shorn of morality except via disciplinary and ethics committees whilst being inculcated with market values.

Contrary to this rather bleak picture of the marketisation of Higher Education, the opportunity to provide students with challenges and opportunities for critical thinking was certainly evident in the narratives of the academics discussed in this chapter. Although the dangers of focussing heavily on skill acquisition in higher education rather than criticality were also mentioned. Blake et al. (2000: 26) argues 'what are commonly called "skills" or "competencies" are not activities to which we give anything of ourselves… a narrow focus on skills undermines skilfulness itself because it fails to integrate knowing and being'. Furthermore, the 'over modularised' degree structure can create confusion for students through a lack of coherence for all (Miller, cited in Barnet and DiNapoli 2007: 107). This landscape of higher education is now explored through the auto/biographical narratives of the academics presented in this chapter.

Ph.D. Focus and Approach

The unpublished Ph.D. completed at Southampton University (Selway 2008) focussed on exploring, recording and understanding the academic lives of five male participants who had worked for 20 years or more at a University, a post-1998 new university, named here as Redpath University. The reasons for focussing on male participants reflected the predominantly male make-up of academic staff at the beginning of the 20-year period. It was also relevant given that male staff were the main instigators of the academic and curriculum changes taking place during that period.

The participants were recruited as volunteers via an email and then a subsequent meeting to explain the purpose of the research with the main requirement from them of having 15 or more years of service in the university. Ethical approval was given by the university. Five different disciplines or subject areas were selected based on who had responded rather than a deliberate selection of subject areas. The participants were interviewed for up to three hours in total on different occasions. Tape recordings and transcripts were made of the interviews.

The ambience of the interviews was collegiate with an informal framework of questions to explore their academic role and practice. A conversational rather than an interrogative style of interviewing was employed to allow key ideas and topics to be discussed but to allow specific topics to be elaborated upon according to the participants' interests as well as those of the researcher.

The Researcher and the Researched

This chapter examines the auto/biographies of two of the male academics, referred to by the pseudonyms of Harold and George. Their teaching disciplines were history and sociology, although during their long careers as lecturers they had added other roles, and both had achieved promotion to senior positions. They were in different faculties at the time of the interviews. Both had worked at the university exclusively for 20 or more years having joined not long after they graduated. The chapter also explores the contemplations of Irene's academic professional life which are inevitably intertwined with, and reflective of, the auto/biographies of the participants. As such, Irene was part of the social world under investigation where she was a dynamic and embedded actor within the study (Lincoln and Guba 2000). Reflexivity and critical self-reflection were therefore crucial throughout the study which enabled the interconnections between the auto/biographies of the professional academic lives of all 'participants' to be illuminated.

As Irene shared some of the period of time in Redpath University with the participants it seemed appropriate to consider her own teaching auto/biography alongside those of the two participants. As Palmer says (2017: 4):

> Seldom, if ever, do we ask the "who" question - who is the self that teaches? How does the quality of my selfhood form or deform the way I relate to my students, my subject, my colleagues, my world? How can educational institutions sustain and deepen the selfhood from which good teaching comes?

Irene felt that she had not fully examined the stories revealed in her own auto/biographical research in this context and revisited the Ph.D. research for the purpose of writing this chapter. Taylor (2004) notes that auto/biographical research heightens practitioner-researchers' reflective awareness of the culture of their professional environment and makes the moral, ethical and political values a conscious part how they form the educative relationships they have with students and colleagues as they develop *Bildung* (Gadamer 2004).

On reflection, this was a process that Irene felt had occurred for her and she was alerted to the values that shaped her own practice as a result of conducting the auto/biographical study. The research could be called 'insider research' in that Irene also taught at the university for the same period, although not all the participants were known to Irene prior to the study. Insider research is used to describe projects where the researcher has knowledge and understanding of the field of the study by virtue of their own involvement in it (Robson 2002). There are potential difficulties with such research but Irene was not directly involved with any of the participants' work in the university whilst the shared knowledge of the culture of the organisation facilitated understanding without compromising the stories they told.

Re-analysing the Professional Identity of Two Academics

The academics interviewed could be seen as part of an academic community but in fact had only one common dimension; they were lecturers in the same university and had worked within the culture of that university for 20 years or more. Their identities were distinct and had very different dimensions which emerged in the interviews.

George

George was a student at Redpath University when it was a Polytechnic and graduated with a B.A. (Hons) in history, French and economics. He had no plans to become an academic but he was giving academic history seminars as an undergraduate and someone suggested that he should apply for a job in the School of Social Studies. He was appointed and achieved his Ph.D. after nine years of part-time study.

George had taken on the identity of an academic in his terms as a kind of 'master identity' around which his whole life revolved. He believed strongly in the traditional academic approach to learning in higher education, with small group work and seminars, and a strong understanding of individual students' learning needs developed through frequent individual tutorials. His approach to the purpose of higher education was to inculcate critical thinking and his most prominent value was rooted in the value of education for individuals and society. Academic work *was* his identity (see, e.g., Barnett and DiNapoli 2007; Stojanov 2012). His scholarly approach was informed by his passionate belief in the value of learning throughout life. He thought that the new modularised degree structures could create a lack of coherence for the students and was concerned that some students saw collecting credit for a module as an end in itself rather than a building block to wider understanding. He was therefore committed to developing ways of teaching that challenged student preconceptions and insisted on having small group seminars for critical discussions and development of ideas between students, even after the university shifted towards larger lectures to cope with increased student numbers. This strategy was criticised by his departmental head on the basis that there was insufficient time to see all the students in this way. He acknowledged that massification of higher education did require adaptation of teaching and learning strategies but managed to incorporate small group learning at considerable personal expense on his time. He wanted the students to learn how to learn and research ideas. He was known as the 'gentleman scholar' always showing respect for students and colleagues, even in meetings where he was under considerable pressure. When Irene went to interview him for the first time she sat on a chair outside his room with one of his students who also wanted to see him. She said to the student, *Do you have an appointment?* and he replied, *Oh no, Dr…. will always see you if he can. If you have an urgent problem go in before me as I can wait.*

George passionately believed in the transformative powers of education, referring to his own experiences as well as those of numerous students with whom he was still in contact. He recalled many stories about his students and, despite the long passage of time, was able to clearly articulate their many characteristics. He also saw his role as having a moral dimension; for example, he noted:

> I am not just a year tutor, I have to look after seventy five people. I'm not just an academic adviser, or spiritual, welfare, moral, financial and bereavement adviser. I am the whole lot.

George felt that kindness should be central to the academic role, however, did not subscribe to a 'soft' approach to learners when it came to effort and responsibility. He mentioned that a student had described himself as a customer and George replied saying:

> You don't have any rights without acceptance of responsibilities. You are not a customer. Let us make this quite clear, this is an institution of undergraduates and postgraduates - we don't have any customers, we have learners.

George talked about the tyranny of time in mass education and his response indicates not only his frustration with the system but again illustrates his professional and moral commitment to his students:

> I mean typical example is our dissertation students who are allocated half an hour a week. I have got fourteen people booking with me and I said to them if you require more than half an hour you will get more than half an hour; I am not having a meter on the table that will ding when your half an hour is up. This idea that you can measure and quantify everything is ridiculous because it's the way bureaucrats look at things. You don't get the best out of people doing that. If we are to be measured at all it should be on how to get the best out of people.

At the end of the meeting, George reflected on his academic life and offered a reasoned and rationale account that described and made sense of his experiences and actions in relation to incidents in his past and his current position. In summing up his academic life what was clear was the moral responsibility George felt about his work and the formative nature of education. He had modelled himself on a past or traditional conception of an academic and felt that these academic values were better than those currently emerging. He articulated a cogent, reasoned moral explanation of his life suggestive of the process of *Bildung* in which through reflecting upon his academic professional life he shared aspects of his discovered professional identity and self-hood. His professional auto/biography was very much part of his own life, indeed it dominated his private life.

Harold

Harold joined Redpath University in 1969 after graduating from a College of Technology in the North of England. He was appointed as a lecturer but initially, did not conduct research or write articles as was expected of an academic. However, he did spend a lot of time planning teaching sessions that he identified as illuminative and original. He began to take in interest in teaching and learning after attending a number of workshops run by a city-based university. He developed an innovative approach which involved making the familiar strange, and challenging taken for granted ideas, which was subsequently acknowledged by the university and his peers, nationally and internationally. He received a significant national teaching award for his work.

Harold described multiple professional identities, rather than a single role and he was a reluctant academic in some ways. Other identities kept coming up powerfully such as amateur dramatics, liaison with the world of industry as ambassador for higher education, staff development, and latterly on the conference circuit promoting his work-based learning model for higher education. None of them seemed to predominate but were integrated into his shared insights on educational issues.

Harold described finding meaning in his academic life by setting his own challenges. He understood and accepted the conditions of working in the changing context of academia by seeing the changes in the curriculum and modularisation as an opportunity rather than a threat to his professional identity. He liaised with industry and other external training organisations in the professions to design a work-based learning degree that could take account of existing skills and knowledge via accreditation of prior learning. Harold's sense of the purpose of higher education was to be outward looking and he envisaged it as perfectly possible to undertake a degree based on the work individuals were employed to do. He had a very strong democratic approach to student learning and access to higher education, and felt that knowledge creation should not be exclusive to higher education. These attitudes reflected his values about opportunity and fairness which, like George indicated the way his self-hood had become understood through the reflection on aspects of his professional life.

Irene

Irene did not set out to include herself in the original Ph.D. study as a result of concern that it would split the focus. However, in setting about writing this chapter Irene reflected on her own professional, and inevitably personal, auto/biography. In her reflections, Irene sought to make sense of her working life in terms of her passion and motivation for education during a dynamic period in education policy. Irene undertook a Postgraduate Certificate in Education (PGCE) and started her career as a primary school teacher prior to the implementation of the National Curriculum, before moving into secondary school teaching, then to a role as a further education lecturer, and latterly 23 years in higher education. Here she taught adults and set up an access course to a higher education degree programme, which she found hugely rewarding. Irene looked forward to going to work every day with students who she described as, *hungry for education*, having made sacrifices to study by giving up work or working part-time. Irene felt that the debates and discussions in class were outstanding and she enjoyed the lively exchanges with and between students. She reflected that she had learned a great deal from the students about social and economic life.

She recalled much debate about the purpose of education with clear differences in students' philosophies. Some stressed the value of academic work, others said their trade and skill was the most important and valuable matter, but all agreed that education had transformed them, and acknowledged that they had changed because of their educational experiences. Many understood that the world was altering with less certainty about jobs and training routes but described that they understood the world more and were enabled to interact with and influence it, as a result of their education. They felt more equipped to adapt and face challenges, and enable their own students to recognise that education is not a 'one off' period in life. Irene also had similar perceptions; having entered higher education as a mature student she acknowledged that education had formed and transformed her ideas about the world.

In terms of *Bildung*, Irene recognised that she had worked with a strong moral purpose, albeit unconsciously, relishing the debates with students about ideas, values, and practices in which she learned alongside them as an equal. The idea of a teacher or lecturer as an 'expert' in a relatively specific area of knowledge was never inspiring to her and she valued the way students could learn for themselves with facilitation and support. Certainly, not all students liked that approach at first, claiming they wanted to be, *told what to do to pass the course successfully* but ultimately most saw the value in finding out things for themselves. This was connected to Irene's world view which she perceived as increasingly uncertain as a result of modernisation and the effect on people being required to deal with the consequences of this uncertainty. Irene reflected that teaching had enabled her to continue to learn about the world whilst becoming less certain about the theories she once took to be valid, as she became increasingly sceptical about constant change, she was nevertheless able to find interest and enlightenment in studying change.

A challenge came when Irene was appointed to a senior position in the Academic Development Unit as an adviser for the curriculum changes connected to modularisation. She was uncertain about the role as she did not consider she had sufficient expertise. However, what surprised her was the shift from open dialogue that Irene had become accustomed to with students and the nature of early interactions she had with some senior academics had undermined her sense of professional self. Not long after she was appointed a senior member of male staff questioned Irene about her role indicating that on the basis of her subject background she could not advise how to adapt teaching and learning in the light of policy change within his subject discipline. He commented that his staff would be *told* about the new policies by him, and *get on with it*.

Despite these difficulties, Irene was determined to make her new role a success and she became interested in transformative learning approaches using learning journals and reflexive writing incorporating reflective practice journals as part of some of the degree courses for staff. These journals sought to encourage critical thinking by bringing myths, images and metaphors from the unconscious through imaginative writing and thinking processes. Whilst difficult to introduce they remained a key part of the degree programme over time.

Holstein and Gubrium (2000) suggest we appropriate past experiences all the time, as people construct their present selves out of what they choose to notice from their immediate and distant pasts so that they can make sense of their professional life. In making sense of hers, Irene identified that she was able to deal with crises and disruptions and actively work to overcome them. However, after six years in the administrative role, she saw classroom teaching as the most rewarding aspect of her professional life, as it offered her the opportunity to debate ideas with people whose minds were open to new ideas. She proactively made the change to return to the classroom. *Bildung* was a very clear theme for Irene's professional life that was underpinned by a strong moral mission concerning the value of education in transforming the lives of her students, as well as her own.

Bildung and Educational Auto/Biography in the Formation of Professional Lives

The auto/biographical accounts of the three academics summarised here illustrate the meaning they gave to their professional lives, particularly their lived experiences of changes in higher education policy and increased managerialism. Despite the changes brought about by the massification of higher education and the concomitant alterations to student intake, academic expectations and the curriculum, the academics revealed a constancy in reasoning about their moral purpose in teaching in higher education, including their responsibility towards students and themselves that has impacted on their sense of professional identity (Erben 2000). A state of *Bildung* is implicit in these auto/biographies in the way these academics gave reasoned accounts of their lives that can be seen as drawing on the ideals of *Bildung* (Gadamer 2004). The academics articulated their ideas about the value and purposes of education, including the importance of their relationships to others, and feelings of justice, integrity and creativity within their professional work (Carr 1991; Fuhr 2017). Even though the academics adopted different teaching and learning strategies they were very aware of the moral and formative nature of educational experiences for themselves and their students. These experiences transformed their ontologies, values and ideals about education and fostered critical and moral reasoning (Gadamer 2004).

Differences in pedagogical approaches were apparent in each of the narratives, George disobeyed managerial directives to manage his time according to a set of metrics and continued to operate with his profound sense of moral responsibility towards his students; generously giving his time according to their needs. Harold's approach did not preclude caring for his students' welfare but he had a more pragmatic view and accepted the changes in academia. He regarded this as an opportunity to be innovative with the curriculum and expand learning beyond the confines of the institution. He used the language of the market to expand higher education in new directions and challenged the exclusivity of higher education qualifications, working in collaboration with industry to produce courses that were beneficial to the students. Irene's approach was similar to Harold's. She accepted the situation despite experiencing severe disruption to her sense of professional self when she changed roles within the institution. She found new ways to transform learning but rather than looking beyond the university she worked with a colleague to develop innovative courses 'in house'. Albeit in idiosyncratic ways by adopting a critically reflective stance the narratives indicate that the academics were able to make sense of what might have been a time of considerable confusion and uncertainty that could potentially disrupt their professional lives and sense of identity (Barnett and Di Napoli 2007). This reflexive approach to their professional sense of self enabled them to adjust to the demands of postmodern academia so that they could work with pedagogic 'dignity' in their attempts to provide creative and innovative learning and teaching (Bauer 1997: 172). Therefore the academics were able to hold on to a deep-seated belief in the moral purpose of education and maintain their professional self-hood and *Bildung*.

Empowering students to pursue routes through higher education that facilitated independent learning and critical thinking by creating 'awkward spaces' was high on the academics' agenda (Barnet 2005: 795). George referred to developing ways of teaching that challenged student preconceptions and provided seminar opportunities that created 'awkward spaces' for students to examine. Irene reflected similarly, as she described working alongside the students to reduce their dependency on the teacher. The narratives of the academics illustrate that learning does not occur purely by the imparting of information but through a conflict-ridden and iterative process of learning. The academics were perhaps unconsciously emulating the conflict-ridden process of *Bildung* by giving their students these 'awkward spaces' in which to learn and strive towards self-actualisation (Wood 1998). They challenged university policy with regard to the modularisation of degree courses that did not encourage or emphasise critical thinking skills and were incoherent in reducing knowledge to packages that were an end in themselves, so that an in-depth understanding of the discipline was at risk (Barnett and Di Napoli 2007).

Empowerment of students within the university included these academics using innovative ways of teaching and learning to enable students to become critically aware of the world in which they live rather than being tied to a prepared curriculum or relying on didactical approaches to accumulate knowledge. They thought that critical discussions and honing the skills of reflection are essential attributes for students to acquire in a university but that they also need to make use of them in the wider world long after the period of study. The learning and teaching approaches adopted by the academics resonate with the development of *Bildung* as a self-educative process of self-discovery and personal endeavour in which the individual is responsible for their learning, cultivation of the self and character formation (Fuhr 2017; Prange 2004).

Empowerment outside the university included recognition of previously achieved knowledge and skills through accreditation of prior learning and very flexible teaching and learning schedules. Harold developed new forms of learning that linked work-based learning and higher education learning, working within and beyond the university to do so. Although he did not directly mention it, his understanding of the conditions of work in post-modern society was evident, as was his sense of liquid modernity (Bauman 2001). These learning and teaching strategies encourage students to develop new ways of being and seeing the world (Dall'Alba 2005; Dall'Alba and Barnacle 2007). In this way, the academics helped to transform the students as learners. Although the academics did not articulate their pedagogical approaches in terms of *Bildung*, it is clear that they were conscious of the value of the formative aspects of higher education and holistic personal development of learners. Hegel considers this as the development of mind (*Geist*) that is a social and historical process occurring throughout life rather than in an academic institution as part of a time-defined period of study (Wood 1998).

What is clear in these narrative accounts is the degree of autonomy available to the academics despite that, over the last two decades, higher education institutions have come under increasing pressure from market and state forces with the result that some individual academics feel they have little or less control (Ball 2012). These academics have worked in an institutional environment where there is pressure to change but in the flux of it all there have been opportunities for a considerable degree of autonomy (Delanty 2007). It is evident that the academics have interpretively constructed their lives in unique ways during this period of considerable structural change and have lived in a kind of 'border country' within the higher education sector in the UK. In some cases, they had outwitted what they deemed unacceptable policy and remade a practice that was acceptable to them to protect their professional identity. As one of the academics in the Ph.D. study said when asked about restrictions on their practices; *we walk the walk, we talk the talk and then do it our way* (Selway 2008). In taking such action they had control over their professional lives and were able to retain elements of their professional academic values. Nevertheless, they took risks, going against the grain in order to fulfil their sense of moral responsibility for their students and preserve their own sense of an acceptable professional identity.

For example, George continued with research and publication despite his hugely increased workload of teaching. This was important to him as he regarded the academic role as one that included research as well as teaching. He taught as if the changes in higher education had not happened and justified this strategy as a defence of higher education in its former sense and his sense of professional self as a scholar. Indeed, George's master identity was as an academic. Harold had a different strategy. He attended many conferences on university change including ones where he proposed a system of accreditation of prior learning which meant that learning attained from life, work and other activities could be incorporated into a bespoke or existing degree programme. He conceptualised this pedagogical approach as emancipatory and democratic. Irene believed in the transformational power of learning and developed courses to include learning journals and reflexive writing in some of her courses. She acknowledged that there were institutional challenges in introducing this style of learning but she persisted because she considered that they would encourage critical thinking and the students' educative self-formation, which was a key aspect of practice that she was committed to retaining.

Reflecting on their professional lives the narratives of all three academics indicated that they believed passionately in developing educationally challenging and creative opportunities for their students. This was coupled with a profound sense of responsibility towards themselves and their students for their moral development and educative self-transformation. In this sense, these academics were operating within a framework of *Bildung*. *Bildung* was their mission for themselves and their students.

Conclusion

The narratives of the academics presented in this chapter demonstrate that their auto/biographies and their unconscious sense of *Bildung* coincide in how they shaped their educative relationships with students, colleagues and themselves. In this respect, their moral, ethical, and political values are of prime and enduring importance to their sense of professional self and identity, despite the many changes that have taken place in higher education in the past 20 years.

These reflections on their professional lives have helped the academics to make meaning of their auto/biographical selves and their sense of *Bildung* in the social, cultural and historical context of changes to higher education. It is in the narrating of their stories that the academics illustrate that the local institutional culture is not a monolithic set of injunctions or absolute directives but that it incites particular interpretations and adaptations that are required to maintain their sense of professional self. That is why, as previously noted, these academics can be thought of as living in a 'border country'. Their auto/biographies indicate the different ways they have negotiated ways through the changes to their roles, the curriculum, student population and policy directives whilst retaining their commitment to a set of moral principles in which humanistic and democratic educational values are prominent (Dewey 1916; Freire 1972).

Whilst the stories may differ, the common theme in these auto/biographical accounts is that of *Bildung* as the academics' reflect socially, culturally and historically upon their negotiations in their ways of being to attain a professional life and identity they find morally and ethically acceptable.

References

Ball, S. J. (2012). Peformativity, Commodification and Commitment: An I-Spy Guide to the Neoliberal University. *British Journal of Educational Studies, 60*(1), 17–28.

Barnett, R. (2005). Recapturing the Universal in the University. *Educational Philosophy and Theory, 37*(6), 783–795.

Barnett, R., & Di Napoli, R. (2007). Identity and Voice in Higher Education: Making Connections. In R. Barnett & R. Di Napoli (Eds.), *Changing Identities in Higher Education: Voicing Perspectives* (pp. 196–204). London: Routledge.

Bauer, W. (1997). Education, Bildung and Post-Traditional Modernity. *Curriculum Studies, 5*(2), 163–175.

Bauman, Z. (2001). *Liquid Modernity*. Cambridge: Polity Press.

Baynes, K. (2010). Self, Narrative and Self-Constitution: Revisiting Taylor's Self-Interpreting Animals. In *The Philosophical Forum* (pp. 441–457). Accessed online from Syracuse University, May 2016.

Blake, N., Dods, J., & Griffiths, S. (2000). *Employers Skill Survey: Existing Survey Evidence and Its Use in the Analysis of Skill Deficiencies* (National Skills Task Force/DfEE, Research Report, SKT30).

Bruner, J. (1987). Life as Narrative. *Social Research, 54*(1), 11–32.

Carr, D. (1991). *Time, Narrative and History*. Indianapolis: Indiana University Press.

Chapman, J. (2014). Auto/Biographical Work as Bildung. In A. C. Sparkes (Ed.), *Auto/Biographical Studies Yearbook, 2013* (pp. 114–130). Nottingham: Russell Press.

Dall'Alba, G. (2005). Improving Teaching: Enhancing Ways of Being University Teachers. *Higher Education Research* and *Development, 24*(4), 361–372.

Dall'Alba, G., & Barnacle, R. (2007). An Ontological Turn for Higher Education. *Studies in Higher Education, 32*(6), 679–691.

Delanty, G. (2007). Academic Identities and Institutional Change. In R. Barnett and R. Di Napoli (Eds.), *Changing Identities in Higher Education: Voicing Perspectives* (pp. 196–204). London: Routledge.

Department for Education and Employment (DfEE). (1998). *The Learning Age: A Renaissance for a New Britain* (Green Paper CM 3790). London: The Stationery Office.

Department for Education and Skills (DfES). (2006). *Widening Participation in Higher Education*. London: The Stationery Office.

Dewey, J. (1916). *Democracy and Education. An Introduction to the Philosophy of Education*. New York: Free Press.

Erben, M. (Ed.). (1998). *Biography and Education*. London: Falmer Press.

Erben, M. (2000). Ethics, Education, Narrative Communication and Biography. *Educational Studies, 26*(3), 379–390.

Freire, P. (1972). *Pedagogy of the Oppressed*. New York: Continuum.

Fuhr, T. (2017). *Bildung*: An Introduction. In A. Laros, T. Fuhr, & E. Taylor (Eds.), *Transformative Learning Meets Bildung* (pp. 3–15). Rotterdam: Sense Publishers.

Gadamer, H. G. (2004). *Truth and Method* (3rd ed.). London: Continuum.

Holstein, J., & Gubrium, J. (2000). *The Self We Live By; Narrative Identity in a Postmodern World*. Oxford: Oxford University Press.

Laros, A., Fuhr, T., & Taylor, E. W. (2017). *Transformative Learning Meets Bildung*. Rotterdam: Sense Publishers.

Lincoln, Y. S., & Guba, E. G. (2000). Paradigmatic Controversies, Contradictions, and Emerging Confluences. In N. K. Denzin & Y. S. Lincoln (Eds.), *The Handbook of Qualitative Research* (2nd ed., pp. 1065–1122). Thousand Oaks, CA: Sage.

MacIntyre, A. (1985). *After Virtue* (2nd ed.). London: Duckworth.

Miller, L. (2007). Scenes in a University; Performing Academic Identities in Shifting Contexts. In R. Barnett & R. Di Napoli (Eds.), *Changing Identities in Higher Education: Voicing Perspectives*. London: Routledge.

Naidoo, R. (2003). Repositioning Higher Education as a Global Commodity: Opportunities and Challenges for Future Sociology of Education Work. *British Journal of Sociology of Education, 24*(2), 249–259.

Palmer, P. L. (2017). *The Courage to Teach; Exploring the Inner Landscape of a Teacher's Life*. San Francisco: Jossey-Bass.

Prange, K. (2004). *Bildung*: A Paradigm Regained? *European Educational Research Journal, 3*(2), 501–509.

Reay, D., David, M., & Ball, S. (2001). Making a Difference? *Institutional Habituses and Higher Education Choice, Sociological Research Online, 5*(4), 1–12.

Ricoeur, P. (1984). *Time and Narrative* (Vol. 1). Chicago: The University of Chicago Press.

Robson, C. (2002). *Real World Research: A Resource for Social Scientists and practitioners*. Malden, MA: Blackwell.

Rousseau, J.-J. (1979). *Emile, or on Education* (A. Bloom, Trans.). New York: Basic Books.

Selway, I. (2008). *Inhabiting Border Country: Auto/Biographies from a Post 1992 University*. Unpublished Ph.D., University of Southampton.

Stojanov, K. (2012, March 30–April 1). *The Concept of Bildung and Its Moral Implications*. Annual Conference of Philosophy of Education, Society of Great Britain. New College, Oxford.

Taylor, C. (1989). *Sources of the Self: The Making of the Modern Identity*. Cambridge: Cambridge University Press.

Taylor, C. (2004). *Modern Social Imaginaries*. Durham: Duke University Press.

Thomson, I. (2005). *Heidegger on Ontotheology: Technology and the Politics of Education*. New York: Cambridge University Press.

Wood, A. W. (1998). Hegel on Education. In A. O. Rorty (Ed.), *Philosophy as Education*. London: Routledge.

21

Narratives of Early Career Teachers in a Changing Professional Landscape

Glenn Stone

The Changing Landscape: New Public Management and Teaching in England

The research presented in this chapter sheds light on a professional teacher training environment that has been shaped by New Public Management. A context, which amongst other things, emphasises product over process (Hood 1995) and is associated with organisational professionalism (Evetts 2009). As such, contemporary education structures in England (and elsewhere) are seen to align teachers' professionalism with high stakes outcomes, over and above the process of learning.

New Public Management has been a feature of education in England for many decades and so the word 'new' has become somewhat of a misnomer. New Public Management was borne out of the policies of Margaret Thatcher's conservative government (1979–1990). Thatcherism was influential in shifting the locus of control from teachers in the classroom to managers, parents, the state and others in a free market model of education and was achieved most notably through the 1988 Education Reform Act. This was the start of 'what may reasonably be called the "new-professionalism" era' (Evans 2011: 851). In the decades since, state schools and teachers in

G. Stone (✉)
University of Chichester, Chichester, UK
e-mail: g.stone@chi.ac.uk

J. M. Parsons and A. Chappell (eds.), *The Palgrave Handbook of Auto/Biography*,
https://doi.org/10.1007/978-3-030-31974-8_21

491

England have found themselves part of a modernising project where professionalism has been used by state actors to reconstruct education in order to fit free-market principles:

> It involved, firstly, efforts to discredit teachers, for instance by portraying the behaviour of some teachers as unprofessional, and... making teachers more effectively accountable to others – especially central government. The second phase... under New Labour ... centred on attempts to construct a new model of teacher professionalism and to win teachers' support for it. (Beck 2008: 122–123)

The result may be deprofessionalisation as power shifts from the occupational group to government and others (Beck 2008; Evans 2008). As a result of New Public Management reforms, teachers are found to be relatively acquiescent in accepting that their professionalism is shaped by the government who have aligned teachers' priorities to the state's intended outcomes (Furlong 2008).

Arguably, the modernisation project seen in England is a desire to make schools and their teachers more accountable through the adoption of private sector values. Consequently, market principles, cost-cutting and the positioning of parents and their children as 'clients' are foregrounded (Hargreaves 2000). New Public Management also places policymakers at a distance from managers whose own entrepreneurial leadership becomes important and disaggregates public services to focus on their basic functions (Osborne 2006). It is here that a neoconservative ideology of returning to the basics of the core subjects, or '3Rs' (reading, writing and arithmetic), become juxtaposed with the neoliberal tendencies towards marketisation of education. As a result, performance against national tests in the core curriculum can be used in league tables to support the market model (Hall et al. 2013). New Public Management therefore emphasises outcomes that can be measured externally and quantified by policymakers and the professional status of teachers is further aligned to these outcomes.

New Public Management is a phenomenon indicative of a Global Education Reform Movement and is therefore widespread in many jurisdictions around the world (Sahlberg 2011). Whilst policymakers argue that such reforms strengthen the professionalism of teachers, it can be argued that an unintended consequence can be a loss in the type of professional autonomy that is associated with the traditional professions. For example, Hall and McGinty (2015: 12) argue that teachers have been reduced through New Public Management to 'compliant operatives' where professionalism is 'a manufactured and managerialist discursive co-option'. Furthermore, New Public Management's emphasis on accountability and performativity causes conflict between 'the professional' and 'the personal' dimensions of teacher identity (Menter 2009). Consequently, new forms of professionalism emerge to typify teachers, and others, working within an ever-changing public sector.

'Organisational professionalism' is one form of professionalism associated with New Public Management and therefore has contemporary relevance for understanding teachers as individuals and collectively as a professional group:

> As an ideal-type organisational professionalism is manifested by a discourse of control, used increasingly by managers in work organisations. It incorporates rational-legal forms of authority and hierarchical structures of responsibility and decision-making. It involves increasingly standardised work procedures and practices, consistent with managerialist controls. It also relies on external forms of regulation and accountability measures, such as target-setting and performance review. Professional discourse at work is used by managers, practitioners and customers as a form of occupational control, motivation and expectation. (Evetts 2009: 248)

Organisational professionalism, as an ideal type, can be contrasted with occupational professionalism, where 'Occupational professionalism represents the ways scholars studying professions and the process of professionalisation have traditionally defined what it means to be in a profession' (Torres and Weiner 2018). Occupational professionalism is associated with autonomy, high levels of trust, collegiate working and what McClelland (1990: 170) describes as coming 'from within' as opposed to organisational professionalism that comes 'from above'. The top-down standards agenda is seen to reinforce an organisational professionalism because it emphasises the need for schools to 'strive' for 'high performance' (Clarke and Newman 2009: 45). In short, organisational professionalism can be seen as placing paramount importance on the success of the school as an organisation over and above the individuals within it.

Research Aims and Approach

Teachers' voices have become important as part of research on teacher identity and professionalism within a changing educational landscape in order to connect the individual self to the wider social context

(Beauchamp and Thomas 2009). The research reported in this chapter derives from one-to-one interviews conducted with pre-service teachers (PSTs) and Newly Qualified Teachers (NQTs). Auto/biographical research can 'reveal the differing ways in which an individual perceives educational situations, issues and changes' (Hitchcock and Hughes 1995: 189). Furthermore:

> To investigate the way the self-consciousness of others is utilised to produce self-formation lies at the heart of the biographical method. The human subject can only interpret itself by interpreting the signs found in the surrounding world. (Erben 1996: 160)

Therefore, the research presented in this chapter connects the identity of the early career teacher as 'human subject' to an interpretation of local and national policy context 'found in the surrounding world'. The aim of the research was to understand how first-hand experiences of teacher training shape conceptions of professionalism. Of importance were PST and NQT responses to New Public Management with a view to establish early interactions with 'organisational professionalism' (Evetts 2009).

Prior to data collection, ethical approval was sought and the research complies with British Educational Research Association (2011) guidelines. There were two phases to the research. First, PSTs were interviewed at the end of their initial teacher training in primary education. In England, there are multiple routes to become a primary school teacher and as MacBeath (2011) notes, teacher training in England is more susceptible to market forces than any other nation. Furthermore, at the time of research, university-led programmes of teacher training were being downplayed by the government who were in favour of school-led courses. This is important contextually as universities' position in professional training may be seen as a hallmark for the traditional professions (Freidson 2001). Despite the plethora of routes into teaching, the participants reported here comprise PSTs enrolled on university-led programmes (seven participants enrolled on three-year undergraduate degrees with recommendation for Qualified Teacher Status [QTS], and five enrolled on postgraduate certificate); a further two participants were enrolled on a school-based route connected to the same university (a programme known in England as School Direct). Most of the participants were female, reflecting the wider workforce of primary school teachers. The interview questions were designed to elicit conceptions of professionalism through their first-hand experiences of training. As Hitchcock and Hughes (1995) suggest, biographical research needs to encourage participants to be introspective. It is through their introspection that the stories of being a PST could be used to ascertain views on organisational professionalism. The following discussion focuses mainly on the experiences of PSTs as it helps to establish the training ground and context through which conceptions of the profession are formed.

In the second phase of the research, three NQTs were interviewed towards the end of their induction year. The NQTs were given an initial question about how they thought their induction year had built on initial training. This enabled a conversation to proceed in the manner of iterative auto/biographical methodology (Wengraf 2001). It is recognised that the NQTs' auto/biographies of initial training would have been influenced by their experiences since training but, nevertheless, interviewing teachers at different stages within their early careers has helped connect individual stories to the wider social phenomenon of becoming a professional teacher in the current educational landscape.

Early Challenges to Occupational Professionalism

Prior to teacher training, young teachers and career changers are motivated typically by a desire to work with young people (Lortie 2002; Hayes 2004; Manual and Hughes 2006; Hobson et al. 2009). Many prospective teachers also tend to believe in progressive, non-didactic, teaching approaches and recognise that learning needs to be adapted for the individual child (Furlong 2013). These conceptions are not taught through initial training and are instead embedded in the PSTs' consciousness as a result of their own experiences of being a learner. As Furlong (2013: 70) asserts, 'Student teachers do not come to initial teacher education value free' whilst Lortie (2002: 61) argues, '[t]hose who teach have normally had sixteen continuous years of contact with teachers and professors'. Therefore, new entrants into professional programmes of teacher education have, in actual fact, been learning about teaching through observation of experienced teachers since their childhood. However, early motivations to teach can be challenged during initial teacher training by sociocultural contexts, threats to autonomy and inadequate support (Yuan and Zhang 2017).

The PSTs presented in this chapter had similar motivations to those reported more widely:

> I wanted to make a difference to the wider community and society generally…I felt that the most change can be given to children of primary school age. … I was of the mindset that once a child has reached secondary school age their personality and attitudes are set …So if they have a good primary school experience they will be better learners as they go forward. I thought I can do the most positive change for someone's life at that age. (David, pre-service teacher)

To an extent, David identified the altruism and service ethic that can be associated with teaching. Such motivations are connected to occupational professionalism (Torres and Weiner 2018). David spoke broadly about having a positive impact on children's lives and this connects him with other PSTs who referred to the holistic development of a child. For David, this was also seen as something that is special to primary education where a teacher can influence a child's personality. However, it is notable how David referred to his motivations in past tense, '*I wanted…*', '*I was…*', '*I thought…*', suggesting that his beliefs may have become dormant as he accommodated new conceptions of the profession. Indeed, this was echoed across the interviews with PSTs. As they experienced the realities of teaching, PSTs acquiesced to the prevailing outcome agenda in their school settings, suspending their initial motivations as they do so. For example, Carl reflected on some of the practice that he had seen and taken part in and concluded:

> I think sometimes there is so much emphasis on [the] academic side of things that the actual person behind the child is forgotten about and that is a very important part in terms of developing a child. If you don't develop the holistic side they are never going to fulfil their full potential. (Carl, pre-service teacher)

Carl explicitly mentioned the holistic development of the child and this remained part of his own personal philosophy and motivation to teach. However, he interpreted England's education system as emphasising other priorities, referred to here as the, '*academic side*'. The tension between children's holistic development and academic imperatives had challenged Carl's professional identity and it is possible to see here an early induction into New Public Management that accommodates organisational professionalism.

Another example of this accommodation was seen through Catherine's auto/biography who, aside from altruism, also drew motivation from her experiences of being a parent and working as a teaching assistant:

As a parent, and as a TA [Teaching Assistant], a lot of what I am and what I do is the pastoral side of working with children. It is not until I have become a teacher that I am able to see why teachers do the prescriptive stuff and don't deviate. I recognise the pressures that they are under. I don't recognise that is the way that it should be but I do get it more now. I think that I [was] seeing primary education through rose-tinted glasses … With a boy who struggled in school, I didn't understand why the teachers weren't doing more to help him. But now as a teacher, I think I do see that getting 30 children through the system at a certain time brings lots of pressure and you can't always do everything you want to. (Catherine, pre-service teacher)

Here we see a shift in values from an occupational professionalism that was conceived, '*through rose-tinted glasses*' and the realities of organisational professionalism: Catherine has understood the organisational imperative to, '*get children through the system*' and she has learnt that this can result in some children not receiving the help that they may need. As a result, Catherine's professional identity has shifted somewhat. Within her professional identity, there has been a trade-off between a belief that teachers should 'help' every child and a realism that the 'pressure' of teaching might make this unachievable.

Learning How to Comply Through the Demands of Organisational Professionalism

Managerialism is key to both New Public Management (Tolofari 2005) and organisational professionalism (Evetts 2009). Wilkinson (2006) explains that managerialism focuses on outputs, internal competition, and deploys 'professional' managers. Managerialism assumes:

> …that efficient management can solve any problems…private sector enterprises can also be applied to be public sector…management is inherently good, managers are the heroes…and other groups should accept their authority. (Sachs 2001: 151)

Managerialism emphasises the authority of managers who use their position to place subordinates under surveillance and teachers in England can be perceived as being under constant scrutiny as a result (Czerniaiski 2011). Troman (cited in Wilkins et al. 2012: 67) suggests that school managers act as 'the ever-present inspector within'. Management becomes 'ubiquitous, invisible, and inescapable' (Ball 2003: 223) and the links to organisational professionalism are foregrounded as school success becomes paramount:

> Increasingly, we choose and judge our actions and [managers] are judged by others on the basis of their contribution to organisational performance, rendered in terms of measurable outputs. (Ball 2003: 223)

This has changed head teachers' roles in schools as they now 'spend more time on managing performance and the outward image of the school' rather than act as a 'teacher that leads a group of teaching professionals' (Tolofari 2005: 85).

Managerialism was experienced and understood by the PSTs as a necessity to comply with expectations of others in a hierarchy. The most illustrative story comes from Andrea whose beliefs about enquiry-based learning were challenged by a head teacher on her teaching placement:

> When I tried to use an enquiry-based approach, I was told that I wasn't allowed because it wasn't the way they did things in this school. I knew that my children would love it from [a previous] lesson I done and the children asked me to do more lessons like this. … I felt really restricted as a teacher … The head teacher did not believe in it. … It was in mathematics and the children normally sit in rows and I wanted them to sit in groups and work in collaboration and there was lots of discussion. He came in and basically told me off in front of the class. It was humiliating. … He wanted them back in rows with a teacher input at the start and modelling how to work out… and the children would copy off the board … That was how I had to teach and it was quite boring really…. I did [enquiry-based learning] up until the point I was humiliated. (Andrea, pre-service teacher)

Andrea associated children's '*love*' for learning with the enquiry-based approach that she espouses. Her initial professional judgement and personal beliefs about teaching led her to adopt a pedagogy that she had implemented successfully in a previous lesson. In this way, it can be interpreted that Andrea values an occupational professionalism as she hoped to be trusted to use her professional discretion when teaching. However, the head teacher is described in a way that illustrates potential consequences of organisational professionalism. Through the authority afforded to him by managerialism, his approach resulted in Andrea being, first 'restricted', and then compliant in her own teaching. As a result, her professional autonomy was significantly eroded within the context of this school.

Equally concerning from Andrea's story was her perception that other teachers working in the school were similarly disempowered as professionals: when asked about the class teacher's response to Andrea's humiliation, the importance of the school hierarchy was further emphasised:

> [The class teacher] didn't challenge it either. The head teacher was not really to be messed with. (Andrea, pre-service teacher)

Hierarchies of decision making are indicative of organisational professionalism according to Evetts (2009). Andrea, similar to other PSTs, felt that she was at the bottom of this hierarchy and this position was perpetuated by other structures that need to be adhered to in order to be awarded QTS. The head teacher who was, '*not really to be messed with*' was also perceived to be instrumental in authenticating the placement during her final appraisal. Therefore, as Andrea's QTS required the head teacher's endorsement, she was unlikely to disregard his authority. Indeed, Andrea went on to explain that once she had complied with the head teacher, she made progress on the placement and ultimately received the highest possible grade for this school placement. Therefore, not only does the school reinforce an outcome-orientated pedagogy for organisational success, the PST is also engaged in being outcome-orientated for herself. In terms of her professional identity, Andrea had become socialised in an organisational professionalism, recognising the necessity to comply with expectations from management. Her professionalism was being directed from above and the only way it manifested itself from within was through her frustration with the situation. She had not yet developed a professional identity where she would be empowered to challenge the status quo and furthermore, she witnessed how other teachers in the school were also reticent to challenge it.

The Strengthening of Organisational Professionalism Through Performative Practices

In the previous example of compliance, we also see how teachers can engage in practices of performativity where teachers position themselves in ways that are expected by others (Ball 2008). For teacher identity, this can be damaging as it leads to 'values schizophrenia' (Ball 2003: 221) where enacted classroom practice may not match intrinsic pedagogic beliefs. Andrea, adopted a pedagogy that was discordant with her own beliefs in order to give an impression of what her head teacher expected, and as a result she succeeded in her performance. In doing so, she suspended her values of occupational professionalism in order to, as she put it, *'play the game'* and her willingness to do this as a PST may suggest that she will again if the need arises. PSTs can therefore be seen as entering the profession already susceptible to performativity as a feature of their professionalism.

The synergy between performativity and organisational professionalism is evident as both focus on 'accountability and externalised forms of regulation, target setting and performance review' (Evetts 2009: 263). Within the research reported here, PSTs articulated a connection between accountability that arises from the external regulator, Ofsted, and the performativity of teachers:

> Are they [schools] playing the Ofsted game? I believe that a school should look at their data, their children and their school and decide what is best to use. If the senior management can't do that, then they are flawed. If the senior management are doing this because it ticks an Ofsted box, then they are also flawed. What they should be teaching is what will help the children meet their full potential. What they shouldn't be teaching is what will get them through an Ofsted [inspection]. However, senior management … have to get the school through the Ofsted because that is what keeps the school busy. That is what gets the children through the door. (Katie, pre-service teacher)

Katie's use of the term 'playing the Ofsted game' is indicative of much practice observed by PSTs in initial training. Ofsted was widely used as a reason for changes to teachers' behaviour in school and this was perceived as being a source of pressure and anxiety for teachers:

> The massive amount of accountability… is put on [teachers] by head teachers and the government and Ofsted. (Lucy, pre-service teacher)
> The teacher is feeling [pressure] because of the head and the head is feeling it because of inspectors. (Catherine, pre-service teacher)
> If Ofsted come in, you have to have all of your books in a certain way, done in a certain way. (Jenny, pre-service teacher)
> We used to use [named website] and you're really not supposed to use [named website], so two days before an Ofsted inspection, we spent the time taking down all of the displays. (Katie, pre-service teacher)

It is clear that schools are keen to 'impression manage' (Cribb 2009: 33) when it comes to Ofsted and this was seen as escalating standardised practices of pedagogy.

Standardised practices (another feature of organisational professionalism) can be defined as teachers adopting the same pedagogic approach in a school, or across schools, and often in response to a belief that the act of teaching can be reduced to a list of features. This was witnessed by Steven, a PST who described a staff meeting where a video of an Ofsted 'Outstanding' lesson was analysed to provide criteria that could be applied in future teaching:

> The lesson was graded outstanding and then for in-service training they picked apart why they thought it was outstanding and picked apart the components that made it Outstanding. (Steven, pre-service teacher)

Here, Steven has been socialised into believing that this is a positive approach to professional development as it helped him to understand how to be 'Outstanding' (the highest category used by Ofsted inspectors to grade lessons at that time). However, he did not question the notion that the criteria for teaching and learning were now being determined by an external regulator situated outside of the teaching profession. Furthermore, his understanding of professionalism led him to believe that teaching is something that can be reduced to formulaic criteria that can be replicated in all contexts. Antonia, another PST, similarly concluded that she must teach in a particular way:

> If I don't have a plenary...I won't get a point towards 'Outstanding'. It gets drilled into you so much... You think that it is the only way to teach. The only way to run your classroom. (Antonia, pre-service teacher)

Antonia's use of the phrases, '*I won't get a point towards "Outstanding"*' and, '*the only way to teach*' was particularly illuminating as it further evidences how PSTs acquiesce to standardised practices and receive metaphorical 'points' for those that teach to the formula.

Inevitably, the practice that Antonia described results in PSTs learning how to, '*play the game*' and similar themes were echoed throughout the interviews:

Sometimes, you do jump through hoops. Sometimes you want to jump through the hoops to get through… you know if your link tutor wants to look for a specific thing, you may have covered it in a university module and you can think about it and include it in your lesson. For example, with maths the focus has been open-ended tasks so a lot of observations have been focused on that. We make sure we include this as we think that is what they want. (Rachel, pre-service teacher)

The amount of marking I had to do was not contributing to personalised learning. It was very prescriptive - I was told how to mark and my books had to tick the boxes for marking. And sometimes that had to take priority over the personalised learning for the next day because I couldn't find time to tick the box and personalise the learning in the way that I would have liked to. (George, pre-service teacher)

For someone like me, I can jump through hoops and I will 'play the game' but I think it does thwart some of the creativity. It comes down to time to a certain degree. Because you are doing all of these things it takes time to do the other things. It is difficult to be creative when you have so many other things to do. There isn't the time to do it. (Catherine, pre-service teacher)

The PSTs have learnt that it is necessary to enact performative practices in order to be seen to be doing the right thing in the eyes of others, particularly those who have the authority to make decisions about progress towards QTS. Their teacher identity has already been shaped in a way that accepts a reduction in autonomy. Rachel had included open-ended maths tasks in her lessons not because she believed in this pedagogic approach but because she thought, *'that is what they want'*. This reduction in autonomy may also be a pragmatic response to time pressures. Specifically, George did not have time to personalise learning in the way that he wanted as he was, *'told how to mark… and that had to take priority'*; Catherine wanted to be more creative but she was preoccupied with playing the game. However, as Troman et al. (2007) point out, the implementation of performativity policy, amongst other initiatives, is complex, and some teachers may even draw what Lortie (2002) terms 'psychic rewards' from seeing their children succeed within this performativity culture.

The experiences of the PSTs indicate that they have shifted their teacher identity to accommodate the values of organisational professionalism. Acceptance of performativity has been found elsewhere, particularly amongst younger teachers (Stone-Johnson 2014) who are likely to have spent 'their entire educational career in an increasingly performatised school (and higher education) system' (Wilkins 2011: 404). It is also possible that the longer the teaching profession has had performativity and accountability, the more acquiescent teachers have become to this aspect of their role (Swann et al. 2010).

Recognising the Importance of Organisational Survival: Teaching to the Test

So far the stories from PSTs elucidate a socialisation into organisational professionalism. The PSTs own survival on their programmes of initial training has emerged as being part of the reason for doing this. However, it is also the case that the school environment is reinforcing the importance of organisational survival against the backdrop of New Public Management and the high accountability, high stakes testing culture that has emanated from this:

> I think it is the whole testing process, working towards Year 6. I can see it building and building. It is no longer pressure just in Year 6; I think that everyone feels it, even a lot further down. (Catherine, pre-service teacher)

The pressure of national tests was seen as resulting in undesirable teaching practice:

> It was so boring. It was just repetitive and every lesson was the same… the children would work through a practice paper and they would just work in silence. It was so dull… because the head teacher felt that they were not meeting their SATs so it was practice, practice, practice…. I have seen more intervention groups; extra maths classes. Year 6 children were doing an extra hour and a half every day for maths just to make their levels… they want to get good results. (Andrea, pre-service teacher)
>
> If it wasn't about passing the SATs we didn't do it. They were a very academic school and everything was about getting the results up… You can try and make it interesting but there is a lot of the curriculum that you don't get to do if you are in Year 6. (Jenny, pre-service teacher)
>
> I have heard that some issues have been overlooked to focus on getting the grade. (Natalie, pre-service teacher)

Teaching on the run-up to national tests was described by the PSTs in negative terms ('boring', 'dull') and focused on organisational outcomes. By describing outcome-orientated pedagogy in these negative terms, the PSTs have alluded to their own dissatisfaction with what they see as a necessity in primary classrooms. This is far removed from their original motivations described earlier and so despite a desire to adopt interesting approaches to the curriculum, the amount of content that needs to be covered and pressure to succeed in national tests has initiated the PSTs into a different view of teaching.

The prevailing 'standards agenda' of the Global Educational Reform Movement (Sahlberg 2011) is a reason for strict performance appraisal and high accountability in teachers' work. Performance management and teacher accountability are processes within organisational professionalism that may lead to the performative practices mentioned previously:

> There are certain things that teachers do, not for the benefit of the children, but are for the benefit of jumping through hoops and admin… it is required because they need the evidence…for their performance management. (Antonia, pre-service teacher)

Whilst the PSTs did not demonstrate a clear understanding of performance management, their interviews did allude to an acknowledgement that individual accountability is a by-product of school-level outcome. Antonia observed how teachers became focused on collecting evidence for performance management purposes and as a result, may have felt it was necessary to suspend their beliefs about what is of most benefit the children. Rather than addressing the children's needs and issues—putting the client's needs first as in occupational professionalism—Antonia recognised the way that school teachers become focused on organisational survival.

The Newly Qualified Teacher: Opportunities for Occupational Professionalism?

By the end of the initial teacher training period, many accounts of teaching and learning can be conceptualised in organisational professionalism terms and the PSTs consider this as being undesirable, yet an inevitable part of the job, for new entrants into the profession. However, the story does not end here. By listening to the experiences of NQTs towards the end of their induction year, it is evident that aspects of occupational professionalism can refocus teachers in the formation of their identity. The teachers in this section have reflected on their journey through their induction year and their auto/biographies elucidate an awakening of altruistic motivations that may have been dormant during initial training.

Elizabeth is a NQTs who has developed her understanding and perceptions of performativity. During her training, she had engaged with organisational professionalism as she was keen to perform in a way that pleased external assessors and this led her to be focused on aspects of her training that she considered were less important than teaching:

> I used to be a perfectionist so my folders would be colour coded and massive. Everything would be typed up and presented beautifully. (Elizabeth, NQT)

She did not believe that her classroom practice was strong enough and this had been reaffirmed through the external grading of her teaching, '*[I was] never getting the "high"*'. The measure used by her external assessors became synonymous with the way she felt about herself and in order to compensate, an organisational professionalism emphasis on bureaucracy became a touch-stone for understanding her identity. However, as an NQT, she noted how her priorities and understanding had shifted. It was a change in her self-perception that returned Elizabeth to her original motivations for teaching:

> My mindset has just switched. Now I am thinking less about me and more about them [the children]. You can't do that until you have got your children in front of you and know that they are going to be yours for the next year.... (Elizabeth, NQT)

As Evetts (2009) suggests, organisational professionalism may prevent the service ethic that has been an important component of professions; Elizabeth had regained this service ethic as she became focused on others and foregrounded the values of occupational professionalism through her relationship with the children. Having her own class was an important moment in her professional development, presumably because she was afforded more discretion in her teaching than she did as a PST who needed to demonstrate her competency through the aforementioned bureaucracy.

Another feature of occupational professionalism is collegiate working practices (Evetts 2009). Elizabeth also found that she had entered a more collegiate professional group of teachers than she recognised or acknowledged as a PST. When training she believed that she was the, '*lowest priority*' for teachers, '*that are already under so much pressure through other things*'. However, as an NQT, she was made to feel like a valued colleague and found that support was offered by other teachers more freely. She described a collective responsibility for the children's education in her school. Most notably, this had resulted in a change to the way that training opportunities were conceived:

> If you asked me [in initial teacher training] to tell you about a task, I would probably have looked at you blankly because I was too busy typing it all up and making it look like something you wanted, rather than actually immersing myself into the task and really experiencing what the children were doing. This year [as an NQT], it has been more like 'you are going to watch phonics, don't take a note pad, sit down with the children, get a white board and do phonics with them. This is the best way to learn'. This was more about understanding how children learn, rather than just box ticking and getting all these tasks written up. (Elizabeth, NQT)

Elizabeth's reflections on the move away from a performativity-focused identity, that she regarded as necessary to pass initial training, towards one that focuses on the children in her class means that her professional identity has been transformed. Furthermore, Elizabeth perceives herself to be a valuable member of the school community rather than at the bottom of a hierarchy and appreciates the collegial authority of occupational professionalism. As a result, she ceased to complete tasks superficially, or for bureaucratic ends and went onto assert that she is now, '*allowed to be me*'. Therefore, not only has occupational professionalism connected her to other members of staff but it has also served to strengthen her own identity as the teacher she wants to be.

Another NQT found greater autonomy and freedoms in her induction year but discovered that autonomy raises new dilemmas:

> Before teaching, I always believed that children should not have work to do over the holidays and that they needed time to be children. Then, just before this Easter, I found myself making packs with books for my readers that are not quite where they should be with a letter to the parents asking them to do things during the holidays. But then I thought, 'what am I doing? I am going completely against what I believe in.' So, I didn't send them home and they are still on my desk. But it was an internal struggle. I could send them home and that's the professional side of teaching coming out; I'd be ticking the box because they have to get to orange level by May half term. But do you know what? These children have made fantastic progress this year so why should they have to do even more just to get 75% progress in reading? Afterwards I regretted it for a while because it is so difficult to keep that side of you and I was worried about the results. But then, I felt proud of myself for not sending it out. But then the head teacher was saying 'oh the percentage is only 63% for reading' and I thought 'they are just percentages to you; just numbers to you. Come into my classroom and see Max, who wouldn't even sit on the carpet in September and see how well he is doing now'. But it was difficult and I worry - will I get swept away with the tide? (Karen, NQT)

When defining performativity, Ball (2008: 67) suggests '[teachers] are mostly left to struggle with the difficult dilemmas involving organisational self-interests being set over and against obligations to... students'. Karen's example above shows how she was faced with difficult decisions about setting work during holidays. She knew that the school, as an organisation, would benefit from this intervention as it would increase the percentage of children reaching national expectations. However, she also believed that, '*they needed time to be children*'. Weighing up the options, Karen decided to remain true to her own beliefs but at the end of this extract from her auto/biography, she leaves a question hanging in the balance—will she, '*get swept away with the tide?*' How long will she remain true to her beliefs when the realities of performance management set in?

Decisions have to be made in the light of the need to perform in a way that improves school-level data. As Karen pointed out, the head teacher remained concerned about targets and evidence and so it was Karen who had exercised her professional discretion in order to mitigate against this, but in doing so, she questioned her own professional judgment. What was also interesting from Karen's story was that, '*the professional side of teaching*' had, once again, been defined in terms of, '*ticking the box*'; she did not seem to recognise that the ability to use her discretion was a professional attribute. Although occupational professionalism was in evidence, Karen had nonetheless framed her professionalism in New Public Management's organisational terms.

One of the consequences of professionalism in the public sector can be that managers appeal to occupational values in order to achieve organisational control (Evetts 2009). For example, professionalism can be constructed in a way that requires high levels of dedication, as in the professional musician who continually practises their instrument. For teachers, this aspect of professionalism can result in an assumption that they will work excessive hours for the children in their class. Indeed, as Evetts (2009) asserts, a discourse of self-control can lead to self-exploitation as any attempt to time-bound professional work can be construed as being illegitimate. However, whilst the NQTs reported that they were willing to put in this time, it was also evident that they were discouraged by colleagues and managers in their school:

> When I was training I marked at home all the time... I've still got that student mind-set where I think that if I do take [work] home then I might feel better about myself in case I do want to work on things at night. But they [teachers and school leaders] are like 'you don't need to take things home; you are not a miracle worker'. (Elizabeth, NQT)

Elizabeth's use of the phrase, '*student mind-set*' was interesting as it suggested that her pre-service training was the place where she developed a belief that being professional meant that she should take work home at the end of the school day. As such, she had complied with the notion that professional work is not time-bound and yet, in her induction year, she was told that she was not a, '*miracle worker*'. This alteration in expectations requires Elizabeth to readjust her professional identity and accept the limitations on the work she is expected to do.

Whilst developing a pragmatism in their approach, the NQTs had returned to the ethical and moral dimensions of teaching that may be associated with occupational professionalism. It was evident from the NQTs' accounts that they felt validated in their work as a result of supporting children in greater need:

> I've got three children with severe health problems. I have an asthmatic child who does not have the maturity to ask for her inhaler. Instead she may have an attack while I am teaching the rest of the class. I need to support her but you take it on because they are your responsibility. I think 'wow, I am doing a good job actually'. (Elizabeth, NQT)

Similarly, they recognised their contribution to society:

> Now I am making such an impact on people's lives. It is a high pressured job. We teach the doctors; we teach the scientists... It should be valued. (Hayley, NQT)

These NQTs had repositioned their professionalism in altruistic terms as they recognised the difference that their profession has in shaping society. They acknowledged the responsibility and pressure but also referred to doing good work and impacting people's lives.

Despite evidence that the NQTs were able to demonstrate aspects of occupational professionalism, organisational professionalism was perceived to remain an issue for the teaching profession more widely. However, this was discussed through a perception of other teachers' workloads and professional expectations, as opposed to their own experience:

> I think I have been lucky with my school. I was on an NQT course the other day and [another NQT] who is at a school that's a bit wobbly was saying that she is working from seven in the morning to seven at night in school. (Hayley, NQT)

Perceived demoralising aspects of New Public Management were therefore understood as reality for others in the teaching profession. The initial teacher training period was similarly described as establishing negative expectations:

> I was always told that your NQT year is harder than your third year at university. The amount of people that said that to me made me scared to start in September. We all had lots of people saying similar things to us like 'Just wait. Enjoy your university experience while it lasts because when you get into your NQT year it is going to be so hard'. Having that negativity thrown at you before you have even experienced it means you go in thinking that you just have to survive each day. But actually, you should ignore all that and just try to be you. (Elizabeth, NQT)

These auto/biographies suggested that teachers' professional identities can be positioned and shaped in response to others. In this example, the pressures of workload were set up as an expectation that early career teachers should be fearful of. On entering the profession, others had suggested that it was going to be challenging. However, the actual experience had turned out differently and a professionalism emerged that these new teachers were more comfortable with. This version of professionalism became a negotiation between the competing demands of organisational and occupational professionalism.

Conclusion

Evetts (2009) notes that New Public Management has consequences for professional trust, discretion and competence and the narratives of the teachers in this study show how these are concerns within the context of their early careers as professionals. Initial teacher training has many hallmarks of organisational professionalism and is a site for being socialised into this form of professionalism. PSTs comply with these demands and believe that experienced teachers are engaged in: standardised practices, performativity and compliance within a hierarchy and are focused on the organisation's survival. Further, as these new teachers enter the profession as post-performative teachers, in which their entire education experience has been within the New Public Management structures borne out of the 1988 Education Act and subsequent education policy, there seems to be an acceptance that this is part of the job (Wilkins 2011). However, it is also evident that the motivation to educate children in a holistic sense and a belief that education has a deeper more transformative power than acquiring particular performance measures remains important to both PSTs and those that are newly qualified.

Competence is at the forefront of initial teacher training because the PST is focused intently on achieving their QTS. The PSTs in this study had limited opportunities to exercise professional discretion in order to counterperformative practices. However, NQTs reported that they had regained professional discretion when they felt validated as a member of staff. Trust is therefore earned and the NQTs in this study may be seen as having a regulated autonomy, similar to that found in other studies on New Public Management and teaching (e.g. Lundström 2015).

Nevertheless, New Public Management and organisational professionalism continue to be experienced by the teaching profession and influence the early stages of a teacher's career. Of particular note is how standardised testing and a standards agenda in England is perceived to be inducing performativity cultures. Initial teacher training socialises early career teachers into an understanding of this and the frameworks and structures (such as keeping files of evidence) also induct new teachers into the externally assessed, bureaucratic importance of their work.

With a backdrop of New Public Management, early career teachers' professional identities emerge from conflicts between their personal beliefs about teaching and real or perceived challenges in the classroom. If New Public Management advances organisational professionalism (Evetts 2009), then it is also evident that occupational professionalism remains important for these new teachers in order for them to make sense of their early careers and professional identity.

References

Ball, S. (2003). The Teacher's Soul and the Terrors of Performativity. *Journal of Education Policy, 18*(2), 215–228.

Ball, S. (2008). Performativity, Privatisation, Professionals and the State. In B. Cunningham (Ed.), *Exploring Professionalism*. London: Bedford Way Papers.

Beauchamp, C., & Thomas, L. (2009). Understanding Teacher Identity: An Overview of Issues in the Literature and Implications for Teacher Education. *Cambridge Journal of Education, 39*(2), 175–189.

Beck, J. (2008). Governmental Professionalism: Re-professionalising or De-professionalising Teachers in England? *British Journal of Educational Studies, 56*(2), 119–143.

BERA. (2011). *Ethical Guidelines for Educational Research.* London: BERA.

Clarke, J., & Newman, J. (2009). Knowledge, Power and Public Service Reform. In S. Gewirtz, P. Mahony, I. Hextall, & A. Cribb (Eds.), *Changing Teacher Professionalism: International Trends, Challenges and Ways Forward* (pp. 43–53). Abingdon: Routledge.

Cribb, A. (2009). Professional Ethics: Whose Responsibility? In S. Gewirtz, P. Mahony, I. Hextall, & A. Cribb (Eds.), *Changing Teacher Professionalism: International Trends, Challenges and Ways Forward* (pp. 31–42). Abingdon: Routledge.

Czerniawski, G. (2011). Emerging Teachers-Emerging Identities: Trust and Accountability in the Construction of Newly Qualified Teachers in Norway, Germany and England. *European Journal of Teacher Education, 34*(4), 431–447.

Erben, M. (1996). The Purposes and Processes of Biographical Method. In D. Scott & R. Usher (Eds.), *Understanding Educational Research* (pp. 159–174). London: Routledge.

Erben, M. (1998). Biography and Research Method. In M. Erben (Ed.), *Biography and Education: A Reader* (pp. 4–17). London: Falmer Press.

Evans, L. (2008). Professionalism, Professionality and the Development of Education Professionals. *British Journal of Education Studies, 56*(1), 20–38.

Evans, L. (2011). The 'Shape' of Teacher Professionalism in England: Professional Standards, Performance Management, Professional Development, and the Changes Proposed in the 2010 White Paper. *British Educational Research Journal, 37*(5), 851–870.

Evetts, J. (2009). New Professionalism and New Public Management: Changes, Continuities and Consequences. *Comparative Sociology, 8,* 247–266.

Freidson, E. (2001). *Professionalism: The Third Logic.* Chicago: University of Chicago Press.

Furlong, C. (2013). The Teacher I Wish to Be: Exploring the Influence of Life Histories on Student Teacher Idealised Identities. *European Journal of Teacher Education, 36*(1), 68–83.

Furlong, J. (2008). Making Teaching a 21st Century Profession: Tony Blair's Big Prize. *Oxford Review of Education, 34*(6), 727–739.

Hall, D., Gunter, H., & Bragg, J. (2013). Leadership, New Public Management and the Re-modelling and Regulation of Teacher Identities. *International Journal of Leadership in Education, 16*(2), 173–190.

Hall, D., & McGinity, R. (2015). Conceptualizing Teacher Professional Identity in Neoliberal Times: Resistance, Compliance and Reform. *Education Policy Analysis Archives, 23*(88). http://dx.doi.org/10.14507/epaa.v23.2092.

Hargreaves, A. (2000). Four Ages of Professionalism and Professional Learning. *Teachers and Teaching: History and Practice, 6*(2), 151–182.

Hayes, D. (2004). Recruitment and Retention: Insights into the Motivation of Primary Trainee Teachers in England. *Research in Education, 71,* 37–49.

Hitchcock, G., & Hughes, D. (1995). *Research and the Teacher.* London: Routledge.

Hobson, A., Malderez, A., Tracey, L., Homer, M. S., Ashby, P., Mitchell, N., et al. (2009). *Becoming a Teacher: Teachers' Experiences of Initial Teacher Training, Induction and Early Professional Development* [Online]. http://dera.ioe. ac.uk/11168/1/DCSF-RR115.pdf. Accessed 24 July 2015.

Hood, C. (1995). The "New Public Management" in the 1980s: Variations on a Theme. *Accounting, Organizations and Society, 20*(2–3), 93–109.

Lortie, D. C. (2002). *Schoolteacher* (2nd ed.). Chicago: University of Chicago Press.

Lundström, U. (2015). Teacher Autonomy in the Era of New Public Management. *Nordic Journal of Studies in Educational Policy, 2,* 73–85.

MacBeath, J. (2011). Education of Teachers: The English Experience. *Journal of Education for Teaching, 37*(4), 377–386.

Manuel, J., & Hughes, J. (2006). 'It Has Always Been My Dream': Exploring Pre-service Teachers' Motivations for Choosing to Teach. *Teacher Development, 10*(1), 5–24.

McClelland, C. E. (1990). Escape from Freedom? Reflections on German Professionalization 1870–1933. In R. Torstendahl & M. Burrage (Eds.), *The Formation of Professions: Knowledge, State and Strategy* (pp. 97–113). London: Sage.

Menter, I. (2009). Teachers of the Future: What Have We Got and What Do We Need? In S. Gewirtz, P. Mahony, I. Hextall, & A. Cribb (Eds.), *Changing Teacher Professionalism* (pp. 217–228). Abingdon: Routledge.

Osborne, S. (2006). The New Public Governance? *Public Management Review, 8*(3), 377–387.

Sachs, J. (2001). Teacher Professional Identity: Competing Discourses, Competing Outcomes. *Journal of Education Policy, 6*(2), 149–161.

Sahlberg, P. (2011). Global Educational Reform Movement Is Here! *Pasi Sahlberg Blog.* Available at https://pasisahlberg.com/global-educational-reform-movement-is-here/. Accessed 4 June 2018.

Stone-Johnson, C. (2014). Parallel Professionalism in an Era of Standardisation. *Teachers and Teaching, 20*(1), 74–91.

Swann, M., McIntryre, D., Pell, T., Hargreaves, L., & Cunningham, M. (2010). Teachers' Conceptions of Teacher Professionalism in England in 2003 and 2006. *British Journal Educational Research, 36*(4), 549–571.

Tolofari, S. (2005). New Public Management and Education. *Policy Futures in Education, 3*(1), 75–89.

Torres, A. C., & Weiner, J. M. (2018). The New Professionalism? Charter Teachers' Experiences and Qualities of the Teaching Profession. *Education Policy Analysis Archives, 26*(19). http://dx.doi.org/10.14507/epaa.26.3049.

Troman, G., Jeffrey, B., & Raggl, A. (2007). Creativity and Performativity Policies in Primary School Cultures. *Journal of Education Policy, 22*(5), 549–572.

Wengref, T. (2001). *Qualitative Research Interviewing.* London: Sage.

Wilkins, C. (2011). Professionalism and the Post-performative Teacher: New Teachers Reflect on Autonomy and Accountability in the English School System. *Professional Development in Education, 37*(3), 389–409.

Wilkins, C., Busher, H., Kakos, M., Mohamed, C., & Smith, J. (2012). Crossing Borders: New Teachers Co-constructing Professional Identity in Performative Times. *Professional Development in Education, 38*(1), 65–77.

Wilkinson, G. (2006). McSchools for McWorld? Mediating global pressures with a McDonaldizing education policy response. *Cambridge Journal of Education, 36*(1), 81–98.

Yuan, R., & Zhang, L. J. (2017). Exploring Student Teachers' Motivation Change in Initial Teacher Education: A Chinese Perspective. *Teaching and Teacher Education, 61,* 142–152.

22

What Does It Mean to Be a Young Professional Graduate Working in the Private Sector?

Jenny Byrne

Introduction

In this chapter, I examine the auto/biographies of three young graduates employed in the private sector to explore their understanding of working life, in order to elucidate their perceptions of their professional status and professional identity. In contrast to professionals working in the public sector, little has been written about the lives of those working for private enterprise organisations. Indeed many of the current issues facing professionals; for example, in education, health and social care, or social justice, such as the increase in auditing, accountability, performativity and marketisation that are associated with New Public Management, as noted in the preceding chapters, may be regarded as such an inherent part of the private sector that they are unremarkable, and therefore there may seem little need for comment. However, over the past three or four decades, the rise of neo-liberal ideology, with its focus on individualisation, has affected everyone, whether working in the public or private sector, and individuals have to deal with these issues and the associated risks within their everyday and professional lives (Beck 1992). Beck (1992), Giddens (1991) and Archer (2007) consider that a person's auto/biography is constructed through reflection

J. Byrne (✉)
University of Southampton, Southampton, UK
e-mail: j.byrne@soton.ac.uk

© The Author(s) 2020
J. M. Parsons and A. Chappell (eds.), *The Palgrave Handbook of Auto/Biography*,
https://doi.org/10.1007/978-3-030-31974-8_22

on their personal and professional decisions and choices. Ironically in late modernity, the state and capitalist enterprise have increased their authority over the professions with a consequent diminishing of professional power, authority, autonomy and ontological security for individuals (Abbott 2015; Sennett 1998). The working life, expectations and professional status for those working in both the public and private sectors have therefore altered in recent decades. The auto/biographical accounts that the young graduates in this chapter tell are not only dependent upon their personal agency but are contingent upon structural influences, including the current changes to the professions and these will inevitably impact on the meaning they give to their professional lives (Erben 1998; Plummer 2001; Polkinghorne 1988; Roberts 2002). Therefore, exploring the young graduates' narratives within their social, cultural, political and historical context will offer a better insight of their professional lives and identity and understanding of professionalism.

The Millennial Generation

The people born between 1979 and 1994 are commonly known as Millennials or Generation Y (Strauss and Howe 2000). The majority of these young people, most notably in the West, have grown up in a period of unprecedented economic expansion and peace. Many have benefitted from these conditions in having a comfortable lifestyle, and with the rise of consumerism, this generation has been able to spend much of their disposable income on goods that are specifically targeted at them. Parental investment in their children has also been high with parents actively engaged in their children's future to ensure they are successful materially and personally. They have provided social and emotional support and financial security to enable their children to take up opportunities to gain higher education qualifications, travel, do volunteering work or work as interns (Myers and Sadaghiana 2010). Millennials therefore expect to be successful and are noted for their high self-efficacy and self-assurance (Twenge 2009).

As a result, the popular press and some popular literature have often depicted this demographic as the 'Look at Me' generation that suggests they are overly self-confident and self-absorbed (Myers and Sadaghiana 2010). Such stereotypical views based on mainly anecdotal evidence have contributed to a negative perception of these young people. A more accurate picture of millennials' attitudes, values and their sense of self, including their professional self, is hampered by a lack of empirical evidence and what little empirical research exists is confused and contradictory (Deal et al. 2010). Marston (2007) considers they lack loyalty and a work ethic. Whereas others (Howe and Strauss 2000; Ng et al. 2010) note that this generation is ambitious and seeks roles and significant responsibility soon after joining an organisation. They are also committed and willing to work hard for those they respect with whom they have a strong professional relationship (Marston 2007). Rather than chasing high salaries by moving from post to post or working long hours in order to gain promotion within an organisation millennials prefer to maintain a more rounded work-life balance so that work is less of a defining aspect of their identity and selfhood (Carless and Wintle 2007). However, this attitude is counter to more normative working practices and older people in the organisation may perceive them to be lazy and unmotivated (Myers and Sadaghiana 2010). Nevertheless millennials have high expectations and want to find work that is meaningful, enjoyable and financially well rewarded, but money is not their only source of happiness (Myers and Sadaghiana 2010). Millennials also are perceived as self-centred, lacking collegiality and favouring the individualistic aspects of a job (Ng et al. 2010). Counter evidence indicates that millennials have high levels of team spirit and are team players preferring team and group work to working alone, although this may result in them being risk-averse (Myers and Sadaghiana 2010). As a consequence, they expect openness and transparency from managers and colleagues including regular and constructive feedback about their performance (Marston 2007). In addition rather than being selfish, they show high degrees of altruism and are civically minded (Myers and Sadaghiana 2010).

These characteristics are generally anchored in Anglo-American capitalist societies similar to the professional characteristics discussed in the introduction to these chapters. It is not my intention to rehearse these here but rather to illustrate through auto/biographical accounts how these features can illuminate and possibly refine our understanding of the professional lives of the millennial generation. A narrative unstructured interview was conducted to explore the participants' experiences of professional life. Informed consent was sought from each participant and a guarantee of anonymity was given prior to the interviews with each participant. The auto/biographies of three Millennials are now examined to illuminate their professional selfhood and identity in order to provide meaning for these specific individuals about their professional lives and others in similar professional contexts (MacLure 1993).

Vignettes of Kate, Tom and Alice

The three participants in this study are all graduates born between 1979 and 1994. None of them had long-held ambitions to enter a particular profession nor did they have any pre-determined ideas about what they wanted to study at university. They were also graduating and trying to enter the workforce at the time of the financial crisis, when graduate unemployment soared. Fortunately, all three found employment when they wanted to, and relatively quickly. They have remained in their respective sectors since being first employed, although both Kate and Alice moved to new employers. Alice works in the financial sector and both Tom and Kate work in market research. A short vignette of each person is provided below.

Kate

Kate studied, Art, Media, Psychology, English Literature and Language at 'A' level. Along with her sister, Kate was the first in her family to go to University and her parents encouraged her to choose a degree that was vocationally orientated so that, '*the money wasn't wasted*'. She didn't know what she wanted to be or do as a career but her 'A' levels in media and English attracted her to how and why advertising works. Kate studied advertising and marketing at university, a choice her parents approved of, although on reflection, she feels that she could have applied for a much more academic degree in a more prestigious university than the one she attended. She went travelling with friends after she graduated. She heard about different jobs her friends were doing but they didn't, '*sound that creative or fun*'. She then met someone who told her about market research, and even though Kate was sceptical about it at the time, she looked at the websites of some companies and liked the look of one. So she applied for an internship that lasted for longer than the usual month and she was subsequently employed, '*it sort of just rolled from there… and then they put me forward for an interview and that was that*'. Since starting work in 2009, Kate has gained promotion in the company where she has responsibility for a small team of colleagues and the recruitment of new personnel. She has since moved to another company, also in market research, that deals with charities rather profit-orientated companies.

Tom

Tom's 'A' levels were in English literature, Sociology and Drama. He was uncertain about what to do for his degree or even whether he wanted to go to university at all. He enjoyed Music and Drama and spends some of his spare time DJ-ing.

Eventually, he did apply to university after discussing possible degrees with his brother who suggested anthropology. This was something new for Tom and he thought it sounded interesting so he applied and went to UCL. After graduating in 2009, he remembers having a very clear sense of freedom and thinking, '*Yes, this is now going to be like, just party, and free for a little bit – certainly over the summer*'.

However, this was short-lived because Tom felt a sense of urgency, alongside some pressure from his parents, to support himself and his lifestyle, as well as more pragmatically to pay his rent. He didn't want to leave London and so started to explore vacancies in the capital. He was attracted to a small advert in *The Guardian* and looked at the company's website. He was surprised that they seemed to be involved with aspects of research that chimed with his degree. He applied for one of the advertised posts and was appointed as a junior researcher. However, the synergy between the research Tom did at university and the company's view is not as compatible as Tom had thought. Tom has had to adjust to a more profit-orientated form of research, and he has found this uncomfortable at times. He has, however, remained with the same company and has gained promotion so that he is now, at times, in charge of his own projects and the team working on it. He has considered leaving the company but to date he has no definite plans to so.

Alice

Alice decided to go to university because she thought it would be fun rather than having any particular desire to study a specific subject or field of study. Alice's choice of degree was based on the subjects she enjoyed at 'A' level as well as, for her, a novel area of study. She also discussed her choices with her parents and took their advice into consideration. She studied Sociology with History. History was her favourite subject at 'A' level, whilst Sociology was an area of study that was new to her but which subsequently she found fascinating. She graduated in 2008 at the height of the financial crisis, a difficult time to be entering the job market. Alice hadn't thought about developing or facilitating a particular career whilst at university; instead, she had spent her summers working in bars until she had enough money to go travelling.

Alice emphasised parental influence on her decisions in a more positive way than Kate, and acknowledges them as significant others in her life describing them as, 'super supportive in whatever I do'. She considers she had a great education and her parents gave her many wonderful opportunities when she was growing up. She now feels that she has a responsibility towards them, as well as her partner, to make them feel proud of what she does in her career.

However, her choice of employment was based on its location in London, rather than the job, in order to achieve her primary goal to live in the city. She wasn't sure what career options were open to her, nor did she know what she wanted to do. Prompted by a friend who informed Alice that the financial sector paid well, she optimistically applied for several positions. Given the climate and without any experience, she was not successful, but the recruitment consultancy saw her potential and employed her. Thus, the move into the world of work was entirely circumstantial and unplanned:

> …completely by chance, not predestined. I didn't grow up wanting to work in the financial industry; I didn't grow up wanting to work for a big firm or investment bank, or anything like that.

Eighteen months later, she moved to the company she has worked for ever since. Her position in the company has altered as a result of a number of promotions, and she now has responsibility for a small team of people. The micro-politics within her company have caused her to question her position, and she is considering whether her future lies with the company or not.

Stories of Professional Life

Kate, Tom and Alice were aware that they were fortunate to be employed, as Tom notes, 'I mean out of my graduate friends, Sean was the only other person to get a full-time job, at the time'. None of them had thought about their future careers whilst choosing their degree course, nor had they planned for, or sought opportunities to work towards a particular profession as undergraduates. They accepted the first post they were offered. Those professions that are defined by their arcane knowledge and specific skills may suggest that these young graduates cannot be considered as part of the professional class (Freidson 1986). However, like many millennials they had studied at higher level in university but the proliferation of higher education; for example, in the UK during the turn of the last century has meant that for many their qualifications have been somewhat unrelated to the career they enter post-graduation. Instead a degree is regarded as a passport to professional employment.

This is not necessarily unusual for many young people going to university but it does contrast with those individuals deciding to study degrees where the qualification will enable them to enter a specific profession. Many of this latter group have made the decision early in their lives about their future profession, and some may regard their choice as a vocation with intrinsic rather than extrinsic rewards that echo some of the more virtuous characteristics of the professions such as altruism and working for the public good, exemplified by the teachers in Glenn's chapter (e.g. Roness and Smith 2009).

In this respect Kate, Tom and Alice may not be thought of as professionals who are dedicated to a particular profession such as teaching, nursing or the law. Instead it could be perceived that they have a more hedonistic view and their career choice is based on the financial and other extrinsic rewards it offers to enable them to achieve the lifestyle they want to achieve, as Kate says:

> …then some things are just nice to have, and you know, influences on your working life are the need to sort of live somewhere that you want to live…. does it pay enough money to kind of afford a comfortable lifestyle?

Work-life balance is an important consideration for them all. For Kate, this meant that she would not consider a job if it entailed a long commute as this would impact negatively on her life beyond the working day and desired lifestyle. Whilst Alice negotiates her office hours to ensure work does not encroach on her social life and personal time, '*I like having an evening with my partner, and I like being able to do things with my friends in the evening*'. Tom considered that extending his working day was preferable to a long and stressful commute that would have a greater impact on his personal life and wellbeing than working long hours:

> You know, my commute is really busy, and, it's not necessarily a crucial aspect of my life, but it is a factor of what affects it and how I approach work.

All three manifest a degree of agency in the manner in which they manage their work routine to achieve a particular lifestyle and personal time that is as crucial to them as their career (Beck 1992). In making these decisions, they are prepared to risk the opprobrium of others in their workplace who may perceive that they lack professional commitment and motivation towards work (Marston 2007). However, this somewhat negative analysis belies the work ethic that they exhibit. All three work extremely hard and work long hours, including taking work home when necessary and being flexible about meeting the demands of the job, so that when tasks need completing they do whatever is necessary to fulfil their obligations to work. This may include working in the evening at home and over the weekend:

> Probably in a two week period there are about four evenings when I'm working late, and then one of those weekends would be doing something, maybe half a day. Sometimes working the whole weekend. (Kate)

> I might have to continue to send some e-mails in the evening, or possibly do some work…. sometimes you might not finish till eight, nine, ten, or eleven. (Tom)

These accounts suggest a high level of professional attitudes towards work, and all three considered their jobs had professional status. Particular aspects of their working, lives were cited as distinguishing them as a professional. Amongst these were a permanent salaried position, the status of the company and industry they work in, and their role within the company including their title. The opinion of others, particularly significant others, such as parents or close friends, about their jobs was important in supporting their perception of themselves as a professional (Mead 1967; Berger and Luckmann 1974). They were aware that being thought of as a successful professional offered them a certain level of kudos and prestige:

> …it's a decent salary and it's in London and it allows me to travel the world, and a lot of people look at my job from the outside and see that it looks sort of glamorous, and you know, I'm an Associate Director and that job title sounds great, I think there is an external perception that I have this, this career and it's great. (Kate)

> I do think of myself as a professional… because of the industry that I work in. And it's more to do with perhaps other people's thoughts of it… because others think what I do is quite professional you know, one of my best friends, she's a doctor, and she said, 'you're my most successful friend'. (Alice)

However, public perception isn't always supportive in facilitating professional self-perception particularly where there is lack of understanding of the role, as Kate comments, at times it can lead to some humorous notions:

> I work in market research… and people think 'you've got one of those jobs that your grandma wouldn't recognise' and, you know, my Mum for years thought it meant standing on a street with a clipboard!

They also had a realistic view of their professional status. Tom regarded his role akin to those in the semi-professions (Etzioni 1969), '*I guess, more like being a nurse or a teacher*'. Both Kate and Alice compared themselves to the 'traditional' professions such as medicine or law and did not consider that they belonged in the same professional echelon, particularly with respect to the value of the work they do and its impact on society:

> You know, I'm not a surgeon, it's not pressure that has any real urgency in the grand scheme of things. (Kate)

> I don't think I am like …a lawyer… I think that they contribute significantly more than I do. (Alice)

In the past exclusivity and the ability to control entry to a profession created privilege, power and status for the professional classes. Whilst these features of a profession have diminished during the latter part of the twentieth century, certain aspects can still be attributed to the young professionals entering the workforce today. Graduate-level qualification is a prerequisite for entry to many careers. Although what is becoming more readily acknowledged is the importance of the Higher Education Institution where that degree was obtained (Minsk 2015). Tom noted how he felt disadvantaged when discussing his fellow interviewees:

> …they had all been to Oxford, Cambridge….they were all these very, very good universities, and I was feeling a little bit like…whilst I went to a good university, you know, I was definitely, I did feel a little bit on the back foot.

The reputation of the the Higher Education Institution leads to exclusivity of a different kind where entry to a profession as a result of a particular arcane body of knowledge gained over a long period of time is replaced with institutional kudos. This alters the notion of the 'exclusive professions' and creates a new category of professionals in which members of the profession have heterogeneous rather than profession-specific knowledge, and differs from either the full or semi-professionals described by Etzioni (1969). Such changes may alter how individuals reflect on their professional lives and contribute to a more fluid narrative of their professional selves (Bauman 2000).

The widening of professional status and broadening of entry to the professions is often concomitant with lower status and less power within society. Nevertheless certain privileges are afforded to these graduates, for example, a salaried position, comfortable working conditions and other benefits such as private medical insurance. The term professional was not something any of the young graduates necessarily identified with consciously in their daily working lives, and only when prompted by an external event did they think about being a professional as part of their identity, such as applying for a new job or having to complete an official form. However, their understanding of being a professional was more profound than some of the more superficial characteristics; for exmaple, a good salary, the prestige of the company or job title that they mentioned. Kate and Tom suggest that there is an innate trait which guides them to act according to the expected norms whilst also adhering to a personal code of conduct:

> Aaah! So yeah, that's, that's a bit different… being professional, is about your conduct and your behaviour… and what is considered a high quality professionalism, you know, a sort of high level benchmark. (Kate)

> Yeah, for sure [professionalism] has codes and practises… but it's not just that; it's also about behaviours and attitudes. (Tom)

It would seem that these young graduates understand what it means to work professionally and have a deep sense of their own professionalism. They all have a strong work ethic that means that they not only work hard but they are also concerned with doing a proficient and 'good' job. Gaining knowledge and skills and having a sense of achievement gives them satisfaction and this adds to their sense of a professional self:

> I definitely think I work hard … I feel proud of what I'm doing. To feel like I'm learning, and growing and using my skills, that's really important to feel like I'm doing something worthwhile… it's important for me to feel I'm proud of what I do. (Kate)

> So to me a career is something which excites you, motivates you, challenges you... [it] has taught me an awful lot, and I've developed a lot more skills... I enjoy it, I get a lot out of it. (Alice)

The notion of learning and making progress and developing a professional body of knowledge and skills by 'learning on the job' as part of continuous professional development, as well as being successful in their professional life was clearly important to them. From a neoliberal perspective, these young professionals felt that they were responsible for their own professional development and achievements. This was also evident in the auto/biographical accounts of George and Harold as they negotiated their way through the changes to higher education, although there was greater ambivalence in the stories about the teachers in Glenn's chapter where certainly pre-qualification they were at the behest of a competency-based regime that required them to adopt specific performative practices.

The self-regulation the three millennials' practice to make autonomous choices gives them confidence in their own ability to do a proficient job and adds to their sense of professional self:

> I take comfort in the fact that I have experience, and think about how I've changed and learned, and grown, and I feel like I'm deserving of the position I'm in now, due to the experience I've had, I do feel like I know what I'm talking about and when I run training sessions I feel like I do have the authority to know what I'm on about. So that, that makes me feel good in that sense. (Kate)

The sense of personal responsibility for their own professional development was also extended to helping and supporting others in the workplace, particularly junior colleagues or those in difficult circumstances that suggests an ethic of care and altruism:

> I love being able to give advice and coaching and mentoring and all the one on one ... I think I can really help people when they're like in the weeds...help them take a bigger picture and take a step back. (Alice)

Rather than being guided by strict adherence to a precise professional code of ethics determined by a specific profession to define, and monitor professional conduct these millennials' values and attitudes indicate a high sense of moral obligation, sense of civic duty and altruism towards colleagues and their professional behaviour. These characteristics are also evident in the narratives of George and Harold in Chapter 20 when discussing their sense of obligation to their students and the altruism of the pre-service teachers who '*want to make a difference*'. Such a deontological outlook is borne out of a set of personal ethics and values rather than a prescribed code of professional practice and is part of the narrative contributing towards professional identity (MacIntyre 1985). Professional identity does not form in a vacuum but develops as a result of self-formation where values are internalised as part of a process in which social interaction and self-reflection are fundamental (Mead 1967; Berger and Luckman 1974). The development of these millennials professional identity is therefore contingent upon external factors that include social, cultural, historical and political contexts, as well as internally driven factors such as intrinsic and extrinsic motivation, attitudes and values towards work, for example, expecting collaboration, challenge and variety at work that enhances their job satisfaction.

Having personal responsibility for their career development meant that all three regarded themselves as having a certain level of autonomy in their working life to make choices and decisions about their progress and how this can contribute to their success as a professional, and this is evident, for example, in Andrea's and Elizabeth's narratives after qualifying as teachers. Tom considers he is lucky to have the level of autonomy he has and attributes this to the company he works for that has a, '*flat management structure*'. He also takes a socio-historical perspective to compare himself with others whilst noting that he and others like him have the autonomy to move from post to post rather than remaining in the same company for the whole of one's working life:

> Pretty much in control …. Quite a strong level of autonomy… I have more autonomy than many people and I have more autonomy than many people in the past – much more. Many years ago you would have done your family's trade or you would have done an apprenticeship, I feel like there are less people treading such traditional paths these days… people shift …there's less risk around shifting careers than there used to be.

Whilst Tom considers that there is less risk in moving from one post to another, he also notes that the decision to change jobs is a personal negotiation for the individual within their professional life (Beck 1992). He also considers, as a result of policies at work, he can choose to take time to enhance his professional skills and knowledge, and this offers him job satisfaction whilst also being of benefit to the company:

I'm afforded the necessary time to spend reading or going to an exhibition… it's not directly influencing a certain project I'm working on, but it's doing several things: one it's making me feel like a good employee and keeping me a happy worker: two it's giving me information and knowledge which might be useful: three that, it makes us, as a company, interesting and gives us a kind of credential of being a thought provoking place for clients to invest money in.

Alice's sense of autonomy comes from a personal commitment to her work that she can manage in her own way and own time without direct interference from her line manager:

…they leave me to it…it's up to you to kind of push yourself… to kind of churn through it… take accountability for what I'm doing.

However, she recognises herself as having particular attributes of a millennial (Marston 2007) as she values the structured nature of her workplace and appreciates and wants formal appraisals as well as ongoing feedback:

There's a huge amount of research that's gone into like Millennials, and obviously being one of them myself, um, this spirit of on-going feedback we can't bear not to know exactly what people think of us at all times. I think it's important because … I need to know whether I'm providing a good enough service to my clients or not…if they don't respect, or value me, then I need to know how I can perhaps be better.

Kate indicates that she has the freedom to organise her own work and time, as well as having opportunities to develop her own ideas, but counter to this is the knowledge that the company and its clients expect the work to be completed on time and that the onus is on her to deliver what is required. She indicates somewhat ironically that she has the freedom to decide how to manage her work even if it encroaches on her own time:

… if you've got a new idea or a new initiative you're allowed to propose it, and maybe they'll give you some money to go ahead and do it… you don't have somebody breathing down your back…but co-existing with that is the reality that at the end of the day there's a job to be done, and you need to just find a way to get it done [laughs]. You know, that's it, the choice is all on you to figure out how to do it yourself.

The neoliberal attitudes of management within her company means that the onus is on Kate to ensure that tasks are successfully completed but as she indicates operating on one's own is not always beneficial and like many of her generation sees the value in working collegially as a team:

> I do like to work autonomously, but if you're left left alone too much it can start going round in circles and there is real merit in team work; and sometimes it is more effort, especially if you've got to delegate and stuff like that. But overall the results are much better – the team are more creative and more efficient, I do see that.

In a similar vein, Tom enjoys team working and the social side of his workplace. He considers the physical space of his office as a, *'social hub'* where colleagues can congregate and network that is a vital part of his professional life. The collegiality of belonging to a community of practice matters to Tom and enhances his sense of his professional self, as it does for Andrea in Glenn's chapter during her first post after qualifying as a teacher (Wenger 1998). It is also important that the company Tom works for helps to facilitate this *esprit de corp* by offering corporate hospitality to the workforce:

> sharing thinking, new ideas, that kind of stuff... on a Monday we have an internal team catch-up...there's a sense of yes, camaraderie...on a Tuesday we have a staff lunch provided for us, and the idea is that we all take lunch and sit down and talk... they're nice to talk to and spend time with so … at the end of the day that's probably more than you can ask for.

Alice says she gets a buzz out of working in the fast paced, demanding environment, and this is attributed to the collaborative and communicative culture in her workplace:

> …everyone's talking to everyone about everything all the time, so everyone's on the same page... it's really collaborative, and everyone's kind of in it together.

All three enjoy where they work, and perceive that working life is more than the tasks they are expected to do and that personal benefits also accrue to augment their sense of self. Alice feels she has gained personally and grown as a result of the work she does, *'I enjoy it, I get a lot out of it'*, whilst Kate is interested and motivated by the atmosphere and ethos of her workplace, as well as, the extrinsic rewards she has access to, *'it's a young, fun place to work, and there's lots of perks and treats and rewards'*. Tom perceives that although the in-house culture is enjoyable and helps everyone to enjoy their work and be more productive there is perhaps a more insidious ulterior motive that management have surreptitiously imposed so that people tend to work longer hours than they might otherwise do:

> My company feels very modern … well it's a bit like the Google-isation, or FaceBook-isation of work or office practice, isn't it, such as having a slide in the office … the sort of pessimistic view is that making work pleasant and building up a nice environment to be in is that they want you to spend more time there [than at home]…and it's true.

In addition, as Tom notes, mobile technology allows work to be accessed at anytime and anywhere so that it may encroach on personal life. This blending of personal and professional life means that as Kate says, '*the boundaries are getting more blurred*', and this has an impact upon individual agency especially when managerial and client demands mean that professional life intrudes upon personal life to such an extent that there is little or no separation between the two, a point noted particularly about George in Chapter 20. The tensions that this creates causes conflict between personal and professional attitudes and values. However, even though this can cause distress all three indicate that they continue to act professionally even if it causes emotional or personal cost (Hochschild 1983).

At times the long hours and managerial demands placed upon them can interrupt their personal life, so that they become embodied emotionally and physically to such an extent that it causes stress and anxiety and affects health and wellbeing, as Kate describes:

> We have a lot of travel …there's no way to necessarily control how much travel you do. So you're not really in control of your personal life… I don't feel like it's stressful at the time, but you know that you're internalising, it's gonna come out somewhere, like maybe I'll get lots of eczema… and then you get a bit anxious, about all the things that you haven't managed to do while you were away, you know, the upkeep of the household, stupid things like washing… just quite anxious that you're not in control … sad things like if it's somebody's birthday, even someone really close to me, like my sister's birthday, there's been a few years where I haven't sent them a birthday present or a card in time ….and those things make you pause and reflect and really start to think, 'What am I doing?' Things that shouldn't be coming second, but sometimes they do, and it sort of makes you start to reassess your priorities.

Kate's story of how stressful her job can be is caused by lacking sufficient autonomy in how to organise and manage working life. Her reflections indicate that the opposing requirements of the structure of her workplace and her own agency are problematic, and this affects her sense of self. She thinks she should reassess her priorities, and yet she is dictated by deadlines and managerial demands.

The stress for Alice also occurs when she is working extremely long hours at particular points in the year, but this is coupled with difficult tasks she has to deliver on the part of the company, that aren't necessarily her decision:

> I have to be the deliverer of… like, someone else's decision, or someone else's policy, and that can be really tricky. I find that challenging.

This is frequently about the future of certain employees, and this causes her anguish. Alice has little option but to dismiss people which is euphemistically called 'strategic resource allocation', and this makes her feel, *'Pretty crummy'*. Alice experiences complex ethical dilemmas and the moral dimension of Alice's professional self is compromised so that it has a negative emotional impact upon her (Hochschild 1983). In a similar manner in Chapter 21, Karen experienced emotional conflict when her ethic of care for the children having a holiday was opposed by the need to comply with managerial demands for performativity and her decision left her questioning her professional self.

Alice has a sense of responsibility and care towards to the employee, but on the other hand she is at the behest of what the company requires her to do for it to remain efficient and productive. She is compliant and acquiesces to the company's decision and perhaps helps to salve her conscience with the thought that the dismissed individual will soon be able to be employed elsewhere:

> At times like that I feel like that's a little bit ethically grey because, from an employer's perspective it makes sense but really did we exhaust all other opportunities before this individual was let go …but because I work for a firm that's got quite a good reputation, I know how easy it is for people to be employed afterwards, and I suppose that's a nice way to soften it as well.

Tom finds it problematic when clients are unreasonable but is caught up in the grip of their power and authority over of the work he does:

> …if the client sort of like says jump we say how high… some are more demanding than others …nasty, manipulative, demanding, overly demanding … I can't understand their motivation some of the time; they are just nasty,

and …just overly pressurising for, for no benefit, for making things worse in my opinion. Creating bad atmospheres. Of course, they hold all the power because they're the ones spending the money, but just being rude to our partners…that's really my relationship with somebody I work with and I'm having to apologise to theme… and that's just, it's not on in my opinion.

In these stories Alice, Kate and Tom lack any agency to make decisions for themselves and this leaves them feeling powerless and insecure (Sennett 1998). These feelings resonate with Andrea's story in Chapter 21 when she tried to teach in her own style but was overruled by the head teacher. Her professional judgement was queried and left her feeling humiliated, but she had to acquiesce to the demands of organisational professionalism in order to meet the performance criteria to gain qualified teacher status. Similarly, Alice has to come to terms with managerial decisions she finds emotionally difficult and situations not of her making that she then has to enact. Whilst Kate feels a sense of despair about how she can manage the work-life balance that she desires. Tom has to build bridges after powerful clients have been rude and potentially destroyed his working relationship with his colleagues. These aspects of their working lives lead them to question whether they can continue to act professionally.

For Tom, this was exemplified with his frustration about tight deadlines that in his opinion do not provide a good service and lead to a loss of rigorous research and the subsequent reduction in quality of the work he can produce:

> … not doing the best you can do because of saving money and doing a quick job…not as professional as I would like it to be.

In Alice's case, a managerial decision to replace a senior colleague with one of her peers for pragmatic reasons rather than on merit meant that the micro-politics at play made her feel overlooked and yet she was helpless to do anything about it. This has created a dilemma with regard to her professional self, and she is considering whether she wants to stay with the company:

> Promoting this peer above me, that's completely out of my control … and then there's the air of professionalism over it; I'm not going to go to my new boss's boss and say: I'm not gonna work for her any more … but it's extremely de-motivating…and I wouldn't feel guilty if I resigned.

The pressure of impossible deadlines and the quick turnover of work make Kate reflect on her professional identity and future as she questions herself about taking on more responsibility in a higher management role:

> …because of just how much is expected of you; how much sacrifice is needed …the leadership roles don't present an opportunity to have a balanced life.

It is clear that all three participants work very hard and have a strong work ethic. They exhibit values and attitudes that are part of their professional identity. They are concerned with doing a good job to the best of their ability whilst also looking after colleagues in a responsible and caring manner. They take responsibility for their own actions and professional development and may be regarded as operating within a sphere of autonomy and occupational professionalism (Evetts 2009). Yet there are significant factors and incidents such as the pressure of time, tight deadlines, unprofessional behaviour of clients and micro-politics from management and clients that exert unreasonable control that suggests a climate of organisational professionalism that leaves little room for autonomous agency within their professional and personal life (Evetts 2009). This corporate control not only extends to having contractual employment or not, but is exhibited in the control of working practices through increased monitoring, strong line-management, accountability, auditing and performance measures and targets, something the participants in all three chapters in this section experience (e.g. Shore 2008; Darbyshire 2007; Sparkes 2007). This is regarded by many as a threat to professional autonomy that was once regarded as a defining feature of occupational professionalism, but has now been gradually eroded.

These multiple and complex factors situated in the professional context are often diametrically opposed to both personal and professional values and attitudes and can cause emotional conflict that affects these millennials' sense of professionalism and leads all three to question their own professional identity. However (Nygaard 2012) purports that the dichotomy between professionalism with its ideals of collegiality and autonomy, and managerialism represented by control and supervision are not incompatible. Whilst some level of autonomy is important for any job, how that is manifested may be different from previous conceptualisations (Archer 2007). Indeed Alice, Kate and Tom all seem to have a sense of personal agency and moral judgement which enables them to cope with personal and professional pressures that contribute to their professional self as they make sense of their professional life (Erben 1998; Plummer 2001; Polkinghorne 1988; Roberts 2002).

They manage the juggling act required and as they balance the demands of personal and professional life, as Kate reflects, the personal and professional inevitably become entwined, so that professional identity becomes a large component of personal selfhood:

> I'd like to think that my job doesn't really define me, and use that as a mantra to try and remember that it's not all there is in life… but I think it probably does play a bigger role in my identity than I think it does so I'm pretty sure it does make up a big part of who I am.

Conclusion

The auto/biographical narratives of the three young graduates contradict some of the more negative characteristics of millennials such as over-assertiveness and selfishness. Their stories belie these stereotypical notions, particularly of those deciding to work in the private sector rather than the caring or welfare professions where a level of altruism is often assumed. However, their narratives indicate that they do not fully identify with the notion of a traditional profession, for example, they did not have a vocation or calling, or any intrinsic motivation to enter the specific workplace they are in.

Furthermore, Alice, Kate and Tom do not perceive themselves as having the status and kudos or contribution to society such as lawyers or surgeons. Nevertheless they have a deep sense of what it means to work professionally and with professionalism and consider they have a professional identity and role that exhibit many of the qualities, attributes, and criteria that define a 'traditional' professional. It is evident in the stories of their working lives that these three millennials indicate that they are dedicated to their industry, place of work and colleagues. Having interesting work, good working relationships and support as well as a work-life balance are aspects of working life that these young professionals are also looking for. They are hardworking and in spite of high managerial demands and other negative contingencies they strive to meet expectations and targets. This is often in difficult and demanding circumstances that create emotional conflict personally and professionally and this can cause uncertainty about their professional identity. Against this backdrop of constraints to their autonomy, they may be considered to be working in a culture of organisational rather than occupational professionalism. However, despite the managerialism apparent in their workplaces they are able to live in the interstices between personal and professional life, negotiating space so that they can be agentic and enjoy what autonomy their working practice offers. Perhaps these young professionals have accommodated to the reality of their working lives in a similar vein to young public sector professionals, such as doctors, nurses, teachers and social workers, who thought autonomy in their work was not strongly related to job satisfaction but of greater importance was having a job that is interesting with workplace social support (Mastekaasa 2011).

However, these young graduates do not seem to be under such constant scrutiny as their counterparts in the public sector, but this may of course be due to the fact that the controlling factor for them is the market and making a profit rather than auditing, inspection and monitoring so common in the public sector. Nevertheless as expectations of the public sector with its New Public Management and managerialism converge with those in the private sector, these millennials may not have such a different working life or professional identity from young graduates in the caring professions. As these millennials negotiate their way through the work place, they may prefer to construct their professional identity (and autonomy) by employing their agency to engage in creative and professional dialogue and promote mutual respect and collaboration with managers and their peers (Sachs 2001). Whitty's (2000) democratic professionalism with its possibilities for partnership, collaboration and reflective practice may be how these millennials would prefer to manage their professional lives.

Therefore rather than trying to seek similarities with traditional professions, Alice, Kate and Tom are developing their professional identity through new criteria and redefining their professional lives in their own terms. This may change the nature of what it means to have a professional life in the twenty-first century, and as a result, how the discourse of professionalism and professional identity will continue to evolve.

References

Abbott, A. (2015). Sociology of Professions. *International Encyclopaedia of the Social and Behavioural Sciences, 19,* 107–110.

Archer, M. S. (2007). *Making Our Way Through the World: Human Reflexivity and Social Mobility.* Cambridge: Cambridge University Press.

Bauman, Z. (2000). *Liquid Modernity.* Cambridge: Polity Press.

Beck, U. (1992). *Risk Society: Towards a New Modernity.* London: Sage.

Berger, P. L., & Luckman, T. (1974). *The Social Construction of Reality.* Harmondsworth: Penguin.

Carless, S. A., & Wintle, J. (2007). Applicant Attraction: The Role of Recruiter Function, World-Life Balance Policies and Career Salience. *International Journal of Selection and Assessment, 15,* 394–404.

Darbyshire, P. (2007). Never Mind the Quality, Feel the Width: The Nonsense of Quality, Excellence and Audit in Education, Health and Research. *Collegian, 15,* 35–41.

Deal, J. J., Altman, D. G., & Rogelberg, S. G. (2010). Millennials at Work: What We Know and What We Need to Do (If Anything). *Journal of Business and Psychology, 25*(2), 191–199.

Erben, M. (Ed.). (1998). *Biography and Education.* London: Falmer Press.

Etzioni, A. (Ed.). (1969). *The Semi-Professions and Their Organisation: Teachers, Nurses, Social Workers.* London: Collier-Macmillan.

Evetts, J. (2009). New Professionalism and New Public Management: Changes, Continuities and Consequences. *Comparative Sociology, 8*(2), 247–266.

Freidson, E. (1986). *Professional Powers: A Study of the Institutionalization of Formal Knowledge.* Chicago: Chicago University Press.

Mastekaasa, A. (2011). How Important Is Autonomy for Professional Workers? *Professions and Professionalism, 1*(1), 36–51.

Giddens, A. (1991). *Modernity and Self-Identity: Self and Society in the Late Modern Age.* Cambridge: Polity.

Hochschild, A. (1983). *The Managed Heart: Commercialisation of Human Feelings.* Berkeley: University of California Press.

Howe, N., & Strauss, W. (2000). *Millennials Rising.* New York: Vintage Books.

Kumar, K. (1978). *Prophesy and Progress: The Sociology of Industrial and Post-Industrial Society.* Harmondsworth: Penguin Books.

MacIntyre, A. (1985). *After Virtue: A Study in Moral Theory.* London: Gerald Duckworth.

MacLure, M. (1993). Arguing for Your Self: Identity as an Organising Principle in Teachers' Jobs and Lives. *British Educational Research Journal, 19*(4), 311–322.

Marston, C. (2007). *Motivating the "What's in It for Me?" Workforce: Manage Across the Generational Divide and Increase Profits.* Hoboken: Wiley.

Mead, G. H. (1967). *Mind, Self and Society.* Chicago, IL: University of Chicago Press.

Minsk, C. (2015, November 12). The Best UK Universities Chosen by Major Employers. *Times Higher Education Supplement,* p. 1.

Myers, K. K., & Sadaghiana, K. (2010). Millennials in the Workplace: A Communication Perspective on Millennials' Organisational Relationships and Performance. *Journal of Business Psychology, 25,* 225–238.

Ng, E. S. W., Schweitzer, L., & Lyons, S. T. (2010). New Generation, Great Expectations: A Field Study of the Millennial Generation. *Journal of Business and Psychology, 25,* 281–292.

Nygaard, P. (2012). Professional Autonomy Versus Corporate Control. *Professions and Professionalism, 2*(1), 11–26.

Plummer, K. (2001). *Documents of Life 2: An Invitation to Critical Humanism*. London: Sage.

Polkinghorne, D. (1988). *Narrative Knowing and the Human Sciences*. Albany: State University of New York Press.

Roberts, B. (2002). *Biographical Research*. Buckingham: Open University Press. McGraw-Hill.

Roness, D., & Smith, K. (2009). Postgraduate Certificate in Education (PGCE) and Student Motivation. *European Journal of Teacher Education, 32*(2), 111–134.

Sachs, J. (2001). Teacher Professional Identity: Competing Discourses, Competing Outcomes. *Journal of Education Policy, 16*(2), 149–161.

Sennett, R. (1998). *The Corrosion of Character: The Personal Consequences of Work in the New Capitalism*. New York: Norton and Company.

Shore, C. (2008). Audit Culture and Illiberal Governance. *Anthropological Theory, 8*(3), 278–298.

Sparkes, A. C. (2007). Embodiment, Academics, and the Audit Culture: A Story Seeking Consideration. *Qualitative Research, 7*(4), 521–550.

Strauss, W., & Howe, N. (2000). *Millennials Rising: The Next Great Generation*. New York: Vintage.

Twenge, J. M. (2009). Change Over Time in Obedience: The Jury's Still Out, But It Might Be Decreasing. *American Psychologist, 64*, 28–31.

Wenger, E. (1998). *Communities of Practice: Learning, Meaning, and Identity*. Cambridge: Cambridge University Press.

Whitty, G. (2000). Teacher Professionalism in New Times. *Journal of In-Service Education, 26*(2), 281–295.

Part VIII

'Race' and Cultural Difference

Geraldine Brown

Introduction

Hill Collins (1990) argues that she sees her work 'as being part of a larger process, as one voice in a dialogue among people who had been silenced' (xiv). Her words remind us of an important role for Black Feminists in centring the voices of black women who are often rendered silent and/or invisible. This is so we can consider the interconnectedness of our lives to each other and wider systems of power. Key to this approach to scholarship is to seek ways to make explicit our[1] role within knowledge production to make clear how 'the self' is a central instrument in the process itself. The contributors in this part follow in this vein and in employing an auto/biographical approach their work offers a valuable insight into their everyday lives, connections to others and how these things are refracted through multiple systems of power. Paul Grant, Gurnam Singh and Carver Anderson draw attention to the interconnectedness of their lives as self-identified black men living in the UK. Despite growing up in different places, living within different family formations and having variable experiences of schooling and HE, common to their stories is how notions associated with 'race' is implicated in their lives, how it impacts decisions, opportunities and choices they have made along the way. Their stories demonstrate how agency and structure play out in different, yet similar ways. These chapters talk to the minutia of everyday life, but also to a specific world view that privileges notions

---

[1]Our in this context refers to researchers.

of Whiteness and disadvantages black and brown bodies (Said 1978; Malik 1996). This is a world view which sanctions and reproduces specific stereotypes and caricatures of the non-Western 'Other' based on an 'old repertoire', in which biology becomes a marker of superiority and inferiority; used to assign individuals to specific groups in which the process of racialisation is enacted (Brown 2015).

The authors in this part engage auto/biography in order to tell us[2] something about what it means to be perceived different, what it means to inhabit bodies deemed inferior and what it means to engage in a process of resistance in response to a White axis of power that remains and continues to operate today, albeit informed by new ways of thinking about the relationship between populations. This part is a powerful reminder of the material, emotional and lived reality of racism and navigates us as readers to understand racism as something real rather than existing solely as an academic exercise to be studied. Their stories identify racism as something firmly rooted in racist practices within the British State, the British dominant classes and the British working class whose ideas are conditioned, if not determined, by historical developments (Sivanandan 2014, ibid). To this end, whilst 'on the side of' those identified as marginalised, excluded or vulnerable, the contributors in this part are candid in acknowledging how their work also reflects the interests of those who fund research and as researchers ourselves. They speak to how the pursuit of 'objective' science, including social science, is not as easy as our colleagues imagine. This is made vivid by their adoption of auto/biography as it allows for an openness congruent with declaring our interests, biases and the like. Auto/Biography might not be deemed as 'rigorous' as the 'natural' scientists imagine themselves to be, but our interests are all out there. Auto/Biography forces us to be critical of our own positions—the support structures and processes that do not empower or emancipate those we say we speak for.

In this part, the authors in their varying styles and with diverse stories arrive at the same destination. They demonstrate how policy-oriented research inevitably panders to the concerns of the powerful rather than its subjects. They argue that it is not relations between 'races' that need scrutinising but power relations on the ground and they call for research that speaks to the needs of the subjected to overcome oppression and injustice. That in turn means that the research has to translate their authentic experience into action. And that necessitates not taking away

---

[2]Us in this context refers to the reader.

their authority over their own experience through either high theory or ideological orthodoxy, 'for between the experience and the meaning falls the interpreter' (Sivanandan 2014: 2). Auto/Biography provides a way of mediating experience, privileging the interpreter and their methods of interpreting which become the focus rather than the experience and its meanings. Auto/Biography allows us to speak for ourselves, it accepts that we do not require interpreters to tell others what we 'really mean' or 'meant' to say. Hence, as policy-oriented research privileges the concerns of government, so auto/biography privileges the concerns of the auto/biographers. What we learn from this collection is that there has to be an organic relationship between the experience and its meaning for it to lead to action. In other words, there has to be an organic relation between theory and practice—a relationship that takes in the general (state, society, economy, etc.) and the particular (the individual, the community, etc.), both at once, moving between the two levels—seeing the general in the particular and the particular in the general—'the wood and the trees and the trees in the wood' (Sivanandan 2014: 2). This is critical in the fight against racism because it combines the existential and the political, oppression and exploitation, race and class. Paul Grant, Gurnam Singh and Carver Anderson move between theory and practice in their everyday lives. This allows us to see the wood for the trees, but not get lost as we walk through the bushes and undergrowth. They show how our biographies shape our politics, are our politics, and we are still accountable to politics nurtured in communities and experiences, if not families and relationships. They allow the reader to understand how 'our' stories are communal stories, they are not individual stories and that means they show how 'we' write 'communiographies', even when we speak for ourselves. How we remain accountable to our communities, as we are accountable to our disciplines, to our institutions. How this is an important driver in our imperative to do our best, to be soldiers in our people's army rather than legends in our minds and classrooms.

The first chapter is written by Gurnam Singh who reflects on 35 years in Higher Education as a student and faculty member. His work paints a picture seldom seen, that draws on his journey from childhood to adulthood and through the education system as someone from a working-class Sikh family who migrated to a northern town and entered the academy. His story is one of contradictions, this is evident in his description of the academy for Black academics that on the one hand are rendered silent, invisible and erased, yet are simultaneously highly visible. Gurnam offers a valuable insight into navigating and negotiating this contradiction. His description a poignant reminder of what Mirza describes as a black feminist academic as akin to 'being a body out of place' (2012: 153). Gurnam alludes to the emotional labour incurred having to be ever vigilant, how being black in the academy means having to engage in what is deemed to be an acceptable presentation of 'self' whilst simultaneously working to dismantle the racial and racialised system and process that characterise the UK HE system (see Bhopal 2018; Rollock 2019). Auto/Biography provides an effective framework for Gurnam to share daily strategies black academics employ to resist, survive and thrive in the academy and draws attention to broader issues for black working-class students in relation to their access, retention and outcomes in HE. His chapter points to why calls for decolonising the curriculum and the introduction of measures to address the lack of representation of BME staff at all levels of the sector is an imperative we cannot ignore.

Paul Grant's chapter 'Raging against the dying of the light', uses auto/biography to present 'snapshots' of his life. His work points to how our lives cannot not be understood in isolation from social divisions such as 'race', class and gender as they are part and parcel of a reality that is how we experience family life, education, health, migration, housing, community, culture and a factor shaping our politics and activism. Paul's work directs us as readers to think critically about how 'race' operates in the private and public sphere, how this is reproduced over time and how it's by-product, racism is sustained. Paul's story is the sum of multiple stories, it is a story that is personal and aims to develop an approach to theory that bridges the traditional divide between agency and structure. Hence, he shows the interconnectedness of his life to others and to power. Paul's everyday recollection of his family, friends and journey is emotional and hopeful. Whilst accepting that our memories are only every partial (Bell 2010), his recollection of the lives and deaths of close family members and friends replaces the existential, the felt and factual, in discussions around the possibilities for black socialism in the twenty-first century. It offers a corrective to the abstracted wordplay of theoretical discussions that seek simply to change interpretations and language rather than people's everyday realities and their roles in them. His chapter allows us to consider the dynamic nature of auto/biography, to centre our voices, allowing us to interpret our lives in a way that we view to be appropriate and 'right'.

The final chapter in this part is written by Reverend Dr. Carver Anderson. As a Christian, minister, practitioner and researcher, his contribution allows for discernment about what it means to be a black man, a Christian, researching and engaged on a day-to-day basis in work in black inner-city communities. Carver's work with young black men labelled 'problematic' and/or involved in 'gang' associated activities is an explicit how issues of justice and fairness are often born out of our experiences of being 'othered'. Carver's auto/biographical approach shows his multiple connections to the choices he has made in his life (family, education and work). As a young man growing up in 1970s in the UK, he shares his experiences encountering racism and discrimination that eventually directed him to engage in activities in which he could try and make a difference in the life of others. For Carver, supporting young men, their families and working in his community as a minister, academic and community worker is important and about trying to make things better. His chapter shows the power of auto/biography in capturing power relations on the ground.[3] For him, it is difficult to divorce who he is, his beliefs and politics from his identity and experience. This final chapter draws attention to how community can be both a source of solidarity and exclusion, how culture and religious affiliation can lead to internal and external challenges and, raise challenging questions about power.

All the chapters allow for a visibility of the authors which is a testament to acknowledging the value to be found when as researchers we make explicit our connection(s) to what we do (Letherby 2003; Letherby et al. 2013). In these chapters, the authors make no claim to 'objectivity' or as 'value' neutral bystanders. Indeed, they share their anxieties and how they shaped their experiences across multiple spheres such as education, health and employment. Like me, they had encountered racism and been reminded of what it feels like when perceptions of 'my Black body intersect with my material and social reality (Brown 2015: 340)'. Their work helps to show how as black academics we are forced to mask our emotions and stay silent when encountering racism and experience 'race' as it navigates between 'ideological' and the 'real' world (Giddens 1994). How the outcome is experienced as a form of symbolic violence in which power is unleashed and enacted upon those who like me are identified as the 'other' (Du Bois 1903). Also, how hope provides the energy required in the ongoing struggle for change.

References

Bell, L. (2010). *Storytelling for Social Justice: Connecting Narrative and the Arts in Antiracist Teaching*. New York: Routledge.

Bhopal, K. (2018). *White Privilege: The Myth of a Post-Racial Society*. Bristol: Policy Press.

---

[3]On the ground in the context refers to the work conducted in communities.

Brown, G. (2015). *Urban Gun Crime from the Margins: An Auto/Biographical Study of African Caribbean Communities to 'Urban Gun Crime'.* Ph.D. Thesis. Coventry: Coventry University.

Du Bois, W. E. B. (1903). *The Souls of Black Folk: Essays and Sketches.* Chicago: A. C. McClurg and Co.

Giddens, A. (1994). *Beyond Left and Right: The Future of Radical Politics.* Cambridge: Polity Press.

Hill Collins, P. (1990). *Black Feminist Thought: Knowledge, Consciousness and the Politics of Empowerment.* London: Macmillan.

Letherby, G. (2003). Feminist Research. In *Theory and Practice.* Buckingham: Open University Press.

Letherby, G., Scott, J., & Williams, M. (2013). *Objectivity and Subjectivity in Social Research.* London: Sage.

Malik, K. (1996). *The Meaning of Race: Race, History and Culture in Western Society.* London, Palgrave.

Rollock, N. (2019). *Staying Power the Career Experiences and Strategies of UK Black Female Professors.* London: University College Union.

Said, E. (1978). *Orientalism.* London: Penguin

Sivanandan, A., (2014). In A. Gordon, On 'Lived Theory': An Interview with Sivanandan. *Race and Class, 55*(4), 1–7.

23

Now You See Me, Now You Don't! Making Sense of the Black and Minority Ethnic (BME) Experience of UK Higher Education: One Person's Story

Gurnam Singh

Introduction

This chapter seeks to address two linked challenges. The first challenge relates to understanding the ways in which universities in the UK operate to reproduce 'white supremacy' or dominance and how this impacts those who are positioned, both culturally and psychologically, outside of the realms of 'whiteness'. For some, the association of universities with 'white supremacy' may sound harsh and unjustified, particularly given its connotation with right wing extremist hate groups. However, drawing particularly on critical race theory, I invoke the term to both name the prevailing political, economic and institutional arrangements where 'invisible package(es) of unearned assets' (McIntosch 2004: 188) are afforded to people who are accommodated by 'whiteness' and also, to confront the phobia that exists within universities towards the language of racism and anti-racism that allows those in power to abrogate responsibility for racial inequities (Gilborn 2006; hooks 2009).

The second challenge of this chapter is to both ground the challenges faced by BME people navigating the UK education system and also to offer some hope that resistance is possible. This is done through a personal

G. Singh (✉)
Coventry University, Coventry, UK
e-mail: g.singh@coventry.ac.uk

© The Author(s) 2020
J. M. Parsons and A. Chappell (eds.), *The Palgrave Handbook of Auto/Biography*,
https://doi.org/10.1007/978-3-030-31974-8_23

reflection on my journey navigating the British Education system and how being constantly positioned as the 'inferior other' impacted my own sense of being, but also how I have managed to survive and perhaps thrive under these conditions of oppression. Though, until relatively recent times, writing in the first person, i.e. where you are not simply rendered as a neutral observer, commentator or analyst, has been discouraged, there is now greater acceptance of the importance of positionality. In this regard, personally, auto/biography offers two related benefits: first, given that racism and oppression often involves silencing of or misrepresentation of the oppressed, it opens up-space for authenticity of experience to be articulated; second, it enables the writer, and vicariously the reader, to appreciate the development of thought through lived experience. Auto/biographical writing is not without its risks. Writing about personal experience does involve exposing oneself and can be painful, though, as Audre Lorde (2017) in her book '*Your Silence Will Not Protect You*', points out, for the oppressed, silence immobilises and speaking out and telling ones story, sharing ones pain, anger and hopes is powerful.

Institutional Racism and UK Higher Education

The background radiation of empire and colonialism continues to shape much of the curriculum in UK HE, though until relatively recent times, as I have argued previously universities have been mute on the issue of institutional racism (Singh 2011). Back (2004) suggests this could be due a self-concept that 'White' academics align themselves to—as being 'liberal minded rational intellectuals'—coupled with a notion that racism is the product of smallminded, morally degenerate hateful individuals, is the perfect formula for locating the problem somewhere else. He goes on to argue that there is a need for a shift in mindset to an acknowledgement that our capacity to reason is never absolute and 'that racism has damaged reason, damaged academic and civic freedoms and damaged the project of education itself' (Back 2004: 5). Hence, whilst it is not unreasonable to take pride in the broadly free, open and tolerant ethos that HE aspires to, at the same time there needs to be recognition that, like other institutions, universities are not immune from institutional racism.

On 10 March 2014, University College London (UCL) hosted a live panel discussion entitled, 'Why is my Professor not Black?' The response was phenomenal with over 300 people attending. Since then similar events focusing on the issue of race and racism in higher education have been held in universities across the country. These debates have been prompted by ongoing concerns backed up by a growing body of evidence of institutional racism in Higher Education. So, for example, in relation to disparities in degree awarding, students from Black and Minority Ethnic (BME) groups are significantly less likely to achieve a 'good degree' (i.e. 1st or 2:1), and when they do qualify, as a TUC report based on an analysis of the ONS Labour Force Survey highlighted, they are twice as likely to be unemployed as white people (TUC 2017; ECU 2017). As for BME staff they/we tend to be underrepresented at senior levels, over-represented in the lower pay ranks and they report ongoing experiences of discrimination, bullying and exclusion. Recent research by the University and College Union (UCU) noted that 90% of BME staff reported facing barriers to promotion and that out of 159 Higher Education Institutions in the UK, there are just three black Vice Chancellors (https://www.ucu.org.uk/action-against-workplace-racism). And in recognition of a growing body of evidence of subtle and overt racism at UK universities, the Equality and Human Rights Commission, which is a public body that is mandated to enforce equality and non-discrimination laws, launched an inquiry in December 2018 (EHRC, 4 December 2018 https://www.equalityhumanrights.com/en/our-work/news/equality-body-investigate-racial-harassment-universities).

The effects of working in higher educational institutions, where one is routinely subject to significant levels of discrimination and racism, though much of this is in the form of covert and unconscious racism or microaggressions; what I term '*death by a thousand cuts*'! (Singh and Kwhali 2015; Derald Wing 2010). One of the consequences is that BME staff can be rendered mute, invisible and erased on the one hand, yet highly visible on the other. So, for example, we sometimes are positioned as people who possess an abundance of diversity, and therefore a desirable asset for the institution in its claim to be truly international. Positioned thus, as the embodiment of cosmopolitan global culture we can almost become institutional celebrities to be feted and displayed in glossy brochures, websites and YouTube videos.

However, behind the smiling faces and dazzling displays of individual success and achievement is an altogether different experience for minority staff. This is the everyday experience of being rendered, through the discourse of 'non-traditional' and 'widening participation', as 'natural' outsider. This is where our diversity becomes an explanation or worst still a cause for our apparent under attainment. Our diversity is often seen as a weakness, something that narrows our horizons and hence symptomatic of a deficit of cultural capital (Bourdieu 1986). Paradoxically, where we choose to confront the system, we are suddenly perceived as strong, but dangerously so!

The pervasive effects of racism impact all our thinking, wherever one may be positioned in the hierarchy of power. In other words, nobody is totally immune from the poisonous radiation of racism and we have to accept that BME colleagues can be implicated in sustaining white supremacy. Whatever side of the experience of racism one is positioned, be it coloniser of colonised, in his groundbreaking analysis of the psychological effects, Fanon (1967) described the process of colonisation from the colonised person's perspective as 'the epidermalisation of inferiority'. This is where the constructed colonised images of social, cultural and biological inferiority become internalised and rationalised so that the relationship and position of dominance and subjugation becomes accepted as simply natural and normal.

Indeed, one of the central paradoxes of the universities is the dissonance between utopian mission statements and the ongoing subtext of elitism and myth of meritocracy. Though universities, in relation to the student body, are much more diverse than in the past, the higher echelons of most institutions, as is the case in society more generally, remain dominated by materially privileged white middleclass men. In his seminal study on the how those in power rationalise their position, Mills argues that:

> People with advantages are loath to believe that they just happen to be people with advantages. They come readily to define themselves as inherently worthy of what they possess; they come to believe themselves "naturally" elite; and, in fact, to imagine their possessions and their privileges as natural extensions of their own elite selves. (Mills 2000: 14)

There are many effects that such experiences of racism can have, and not all of these are necessarily negative; that is because we also learn how to resist and survive, even if such acts of resistance are not seen as displays of our intellectual prowess but manifestations of an assumed problematic and dysfunctional nature. In her personal reflections on white supremacy and the academy, the African American intellectual bell hooks writes of the suffering and deep sense of isolation that she experienced. But interestingly, she suggests that there are two sources for this pain, one of the obvious and unpleasant effects of racism, but also, a pain that is a result of resistance and struggle. As hooks (1995: 184) suggests, 'The first pain wounds us, the second pain helps us heal our wounds'.

My Story

For us to deal with the pain and oppression we experience and to encourage others to learn from our experiences, though not easy, it is important that we can tell our stories. If our experiences are confined to the realms of 'private troubles', we run the danger of succumbing to, what has been termed internalised oppression which can result in a state of extreme frustration and paralysis (Freire 1970; Fanon 1967). Unless we find avenues to connect our inner troubles with public concerns, where we engage in a realisation that what we perceive as personal, isolated and individual, is at once social and systematic (Mills 2000; Crenshaw 1991), we will be vulnerable to self-blame and what cognitive psychologists' term 'learnt helplessness' (Garber and Seligman 1980).

It is tragic that storytelling, which is a universal phenomenon, is so undervalued within our universities. Indeed, for oppressed people who have historically been deprived the privilege to contribute to 'official' accounts of their lives and aspirations, storytelling and the oral tradition has become an essential requirement for survival. When we think about making sense of the historical and contemporary dynamics of white western racism, or gender and class oppression we instantly recall the remarkable historical fictional work of writers such as the Nobel prize winning author Tony Morrison, who in chronicling various eras of her life through was able to give both voice to black people, but also an intimate insight into mechanisms for oppression and how whiteness can invade black consciousness to devastating effects.

Another person who had a profound impact on my own journey is Audre Lorde, who though a unique ensemble of poetry, philosophy, autobiography and politics, provided me with a deep holistic framework for making sense of my life and the ways that power resided within the conception of a mythical normality. Maya Angelou was another important influence whose detailed accounts the lives of black characters and their struggles to develop a positive sense of identity and self-worth, amidst everyday racism and hostility, has been eye opening. Finally, there was Patricia Hill Collins', whose repudiation of the straight jacket of the 'white academic norms' by refusing to become invisible in her writings enables me to value my own intellectual production. This was especially so in my early years as an academic, where I found my work being rejected by established journals because it was deemed to be overly polemical, descriptive and subjective. Hill Collins talks about the way that oppressed people are only listened to when they adopt the norms and expectations of the dominant group in framing their thoughts. However, in abandoning their own unique standpoint, they can end up changing the meaning of their lived experience and simply elevating the ideas of dominant groups, i.e. reproducing whiteness. As she notes:

> Much of my formal academic training has been designed to show me that I must alienate myself from my communities, my family, and even my own self in order to produce credible intellectual work. Instead of viewing the everyday as a negative influence on my theorizing, I tried to see how the everyday and idea of Black women in my life reflected the theoretical issues I claimed were so important to them. (Collins 2000: viii)

Much of my academic work has stemmed from my lived experience as somebody who has experienced exclusion and a sense of being placed outside of whiteness and white power structure, which is often characterised as 'normative', default position. This can be best illustrated by the ways in which, for example, the problem of segregation is only really perceived in relation to the concentration of non-white students. We are rarely panicked by the existence of white privileged spaces, indeed, such spaces—the lawns of Eton and the spires of Oxford are depicted idyllic educational paradises. The concept of 'whiteness', as Steve Garner (2007) argues in a fluid concept which can function as a lens through which systems of racialised power relationships in both their local and global forms, can be understood.

My black activism has been fought on a number of different fronts, and I would like to explore each one of these through periods/episodes in my own life. Also, having spent most of my life in educational institutions, either as a pupil/student or teacher/academic, inevitably many of the experiences are related to the education, both formal and informal (i.e. the university of life).

Episode 1—1965–70—Infant School Age 5–9

My earliest recollection of anti-racism is from the age of 8 when I learnt about the power of 'direct action'. From the commencement of my schooling in inner city Bradford, I can recall daily incidents of racial abuse and harassment; the words 'Paki', 'Nigger', 'black bastard', 'coon', and so on, became etched into my very being and I would regularly go home bruised and battered following physical attacks. I found one particular taunt of 'go back home!' to be particularly confusing, not least because for me home was Gladstone Street in the City of Bradford, Yorkshire, where I grew-up. Of course, sentiment behind it was that I was in a stranger's land and that my home was some other place. I dealt with this sense of rejection by wishing and dreaming that I was white and developing self-loathing. It was a classic act of the internalisation of racism which the Kenyan writer Ngũgĩ wa Thiong'o, describes as imperialism's cultural bomb which, when unleashed daily, results in the annihilation of:

> a people's belief in their names, in their languages, in their environment, in their heritage of struggle, in their unity, in their capacities and ultimately themselves. It makes them see their past as one wasteland of non-achievement and it makes them want to distance themselves from that wasteland. It makes them want to identify with that which is furthest removed from themselves; for instance, with other peoples' languages rather than their own. (Ngũgĩ wa Thiong'o in Alvares 2012: 140)

This distressing experience went on for three years and I can remember feeling powerless to do anything. I was too young to articulate my experience to teachers, who appeared to be oblivious to the presence of racism in the school, and my parents were understandably preoccupied with providing for our basic material needs. However, I can remember one day in 1967 making a decision to fight back and I ended up beating the particular boy who, to my relief, never bothered me again! The critical lessons I took from these early experiences are:

- Racists and racism will not go away without being confronted; (Malcolm X's Autobiography, Stokley Carmichael, Black Power, Frederic Douglas, A Native Son).
- people in authority, by developing blind spots or through self-preservation, will often collude with racism and oppression (Bauman 1989);
- racism can become internalised and the battle against it begins within oneself (Freire 1970);
- with determination racism can be confronted, although it does have a tendency to reappear in different guises, 'constantly renewed and transformed' (Fanon 1970: 41);
- the importance of balancing up the use of violence against the need for developing non-violent strategies for confronting racist oppression; (Mahatma Gandhi and Martin Luther King).

Episode 2—1972–1976: 13–16—Secondary School, Alienation and Resistance

As my schooling progressed, I found myself struggling to locate myself in the educational process and seeking out alternative and subversive spaces to progress my learning. In this regard, I can recall two linked but quite different experiences that stand out.

Mr. Mitchel: The first experience is related to Mr. Michel, an Oxbridge educated English Teacher who, despite the fact my school had some years previously been converted from a selective Grammar School to a compressive, used to always wear his academic robes. He put on some voluntary classes which were not offered as O levels on the Greek Tragedies, and Greek and Roman Architecture—One might imagine, this was not a very cool thing to do for me, but I used to slip in an out of his classes without being noticed! What he was teaching was truly fascinating and transformative, but I think it was his passion for the subject coupled with the fact that there were just 4 other students and his dialogical approach, that was decisive. I know so because I have forgotten almost everything I learnt during my secondary education besides these classes, which were perhaps on the most obscure of subjects!

Truanting: Truanting from school was one way to escape all kinds of physical and psychological oppression. However, perhaps through serendipity more than design, unlike many of my friends, I truanted to the City Library where at the age of 14 I began to discover a whole history and literature about other parts of the world that was totally denied to me. It was as if I had been allowed to wake-up and make sense of all those negative feelings I had of myself and why I seemed to desire whiteness over my own unique cultural heritage and identity.

Paradoxically, whilst I was struggling at school to engage with the formal curriculum that was being provided, I was flourishing in the library, where I reading quite complex material on such diverse topics as politics, economics, colonialism, architecture, urban planning, science fiction and sport! How do I explain this? Though I had no clue at the time, I later came to understand my experience through the work of Paulo Freire (1970) who argued that education can either act to 'domesticate', or 'liberate' but that is never neutral (See later for a more detailed discussion of this body of work).

Clearly, with the exception of Mr. Mitchel, perhaps, what I was experiencing in school was a form of domestication, that was alienating, and my truanting was an act of resistance and liberation. Though I struggled to gain any descent GCSE's, I did feel like has managed to claim some degree of agency for myself as I progressed further with my education. Jacques Rancière's and in his book, *'The Ignorant Schoolmaster': Five Lessons in Intellectual Emancipation* offers a powerful critique of traditional conceptions of education and also notions of intelligence and ability. For Rancière, equality should be the starting point of education. Educators need to abandon the themes and rhetoric of cultural deficiency on the one hand and salvation on the other—which was/is really how black people were/are configured in terms of education. Rancière (1991) suggests that rather than guide students towards prescribed and alienating ends, educators can channel the equal intelligence in all to facilitate their intellectual growth in virtually unlimited directions.

Episode 3—1976–1981: Involvement in Black Political Organisations

Anti-deportation Protest Outside Armly Prison, Leeds—Aged 16

Like other black youth, living and growing up in inner city Bradford through the 1970s and 1980s one was presented with many challenges related to the question of 'race' and racism. I recall becoming involved in countless anti-racist and anti-fascist activities during this period. Locally, along with other black youth, through forging a political black identity, I recall participating in many successful campaigns against racist attacks, police harassment and deportations.

Numerous black youth organisations and movements mushroomed across the conurbations of the UK during this period and I found myself at the age of 17 immersed in the local and national politics of 'race' and it was a growing realisation that 'the state as it was constituted' was neither capable nor willing to address black people's concerns, and that therefore the only option was a path of self-organisation and political struggle.

My growing politicisation resulted in a more expansive analysis of racism, connecting everyday racism with history and economics. This also led me to develop a conception of anti-racism that was both rooted in our everyday struggles and lived realities but also a utopian bridge towards a post-race settlement.

The slogan 'black and white, unite and fight' encapsulated this important strategic alliance to fight racism and build alternatives. As Sivanandan (1991) points out, our struggle was not simply one against racist attitudes and behaviour, but against the regimes and structures of governance that have and do sustain them:

> If, in the final analysis, racism as I see it is tied up with exploitative systems, our struggle is not only against injustice and inequality and un-freedom, our struggle is against the system of power that allows these things to obtain. (Sivanandan 1991: 45)

My activism during my late teens and early adulthood also enabled me to embark on a personal journey of self-discovery and liberation. A growing sense of self-awareness and critical consciousness led me to ask painful, albeit crucial, questions about my place in this society:

- why did my parents leave their homeland of the Punjab and come to the UK in the first place?
- Despite my activism and insights, why do I, at a psychological level, still display some preference towards whiteness?
- What is it about the nature of racism that can so distort perceptions about self and others?
- In what ways can I heal the damage that racism has caused to me?
- How can I utilise my own growing self-awareness to help others?

And it is these questions that have been central to my ongoing activism and work with black and white communities, professionals and students.

Academic Activist—Late 20s to Present—Decolonising the Curriculum

One of my greatest influences is the Sri Lankan novelist, anti-racist activist and director of the Institute of Race Relations, Ambalavaner Sivanandan, who amongst other things wrote mostly about black activism. The books were particularly influential.

- Race and Resistance: the IRR story, London: Race Today Publications, March 1975
- A Different Hunger: writings on black resistance, London: Pluto Press, 1982

- Communities of Resistance: writings on black struggles for socialism, London: Verso, 1990

One piece in particular, which he published in 1977, entitled, 'The liberation of the black intellectual' (1977), had a profound and transformative impact on me. I was in my early 20s, I was active in anti-racist struggles on the front line of community politics, I was I guess developing my identity as an academic but most of all at the psychological level, I was in search of an identity. If you haven't read this, I would certainly recommend it. In this piece Sivananden does 3 things:

He examines identity, struggle and engagement during what might be termed the post war period of decolonisation and the rise of the Black Power movement in the US which had a significant impact on the development of anti-racism across the globe (Singh and Masocha, 2019). In this text, Sivanandan offers a powerful critique of the choices that black intellectuals are compelled to make within dominant white society and the consequences of making those choices. And third, he offers an alternative conception of knowledge and knowledge production rooted in what one might term a black perspective, where 'black' becomes not a signifier of racial difference, but of collective political identity consciously adopted to unify struggles against white western imperialism.

In his essay, Sivanandan (1977) sought to uncover the tensions and contradictions that black intellectuals are faced with in a racist society. The black intellectual, he suggests has two choices; either s/he adheres to the dominant white norms and culture, thereby effectively becoming a 'servitor of those in power, a buffer between them and his (Sic) people, a shock-absorber of coloured discontent' (Sivanandan 1977), or s/he choses to engage in anti-racist struggles.

To chose to refuse to collude with racism is to take the path of self-liberation, though developing critical consciousness. This existential journey enables one to perceive the reality of one's own oppression, and that of others, thereby shedding the complacency engendered by the system that is infused by racism. For Sivanandan, it is only through the death of the colonised self that the liberated black intellectual can emerge and, by claiming a politicised 'black' identity, s/he is announcing her/his intention to struggle against oppression.

And so as an academic and activist, I have found such critiques of colonialism have had a deep impact on my pedagogical practice. The first thing for me is a realisation that knowledge and knowledge production, particularly within the social sciences and humanities, can never be neutral—it either contributes to oppression or liberation. This means that the act of teaching itself, whether one does this consciously or not, is implicated in a political project—here the work of bell hooks who wrote a book called teaching to transgress (and the work of Paulo Freire is important):

> The academy is not paradise. But learning is a place where paradise can be created. The classroom with all its limitations remains a location of possibility. In that field of possibility, we have the opportunity to labour for freedom, to demand of ourselves and our comrades, an openness of mind and heart that allows us to face reality even as we collectively imagine ways to move beyond boundaries, to transgress. This is education as the practice of freedom. (hooks 1994: 207)

And so one the personal and intellectual project I embarked upon in my post graduate studies was to transgress and to develop a 'black perspective' to both ways of producing knowledge and ways of knowing. Here the work of black feminist writers like bell hooks, Audre Lorde, Patricia Hill-Collins, to name a few, were instrumental.

These are all black intellectuals and activists, but I must stress, in no way am I proposing some form on intellectual apartheid. To the contrary, though not always popular, my struggle against racism has always been orientated towards a universalist vision of humanity as envisaged by the psychiatrist, philosopher and revolutionary, Frantz Fanon. In his book 'The Wretched of the Earth' talks about the need for a new humanity, where the freed black subject does not simply desire what the white coloniser possesses, but to reconstruct desire itself:

> Humanity expects other things from us than this grotesque and generally obscene emulation. If we want to transform Africa into a new Europe, America into a new Europe, then let us entrust the destinies of our countries to the Europeans. They will do a better job than the best of us. But if we want humanity to take one step forward, if we want to take it to another level than the one where Europe has placed it, then we must innovate, we must be pioneers. If we want to respond to the expectations of our peoples, we must look elsewhere besides Europe. Moreover, if we want to respond to the expectations of the Europeans we must not send them back a reflection, however ideal, of their society and their thought that periodically sickens even them. For Europe, for ourselves and for humanity, comrades, we must make a new start, develop a new way of thinking, and endeavor to create a new man. (Fanon 1963)

Moving from the Particular to the Universal

If the task for decolonising the university, or if you like dislodging white-ness as a privileged position, then what does one put in its place? Following the previous quote from Fanon, the challenge as I see it is to reconstruct a de-racialised conception of both humanity and the university so that is can truly claim to reflect the original idea of *universitatem* or universes, referring to 'the whole or entire'.

What then does it mean to be human? For me the conception of human is encapsulated in these two ideas, aesthetics and intellect—interestingly, the latin *homo sapien* means 'thinking animal'—put simply to be human it to be a thinker, to have intellectual ability which far surpasses any other spe-cies. This brain power is coupled with our amazing dexterity that enables us to imagine and make things; art, music, culture, ideas and so on are all the characteristics of being human.

So, from a black or if you like the 'subaltern' perspective, for me the task of decolonisation is essentially project of (re)constructing a universalist con-ception of human-beingness, something that was so damaged by colonial-ism and slavery. I also began to realise that so-called western rationality and knowledge was not the sole solution. It is the realisation of subtle nuances between objectivity and subjectivity, between knowledge and knowing or and truth and wisdom that leads to true understanding. In his essay the lib-eration of the black intellectual, Amblaveer Sivanandan notes that character-istics of the liberated black intellectual:

> Knowledge is not a goal in itself, but a path to wisdom; it bestows not privi-lege so much as duty, not power so much as responsibility. And it brings with it a desire to learn even as one teaches, to teach even as one learns. It is used not to compete with one's fellow beings for some unending standard of life, but to achieve for them, as for oneself, a higher quality of life. (Sivanandan 1977: 89)

Developing a Pedagogy of Liberation

It is this imperative to simultaneously 'learn and teach' that lies at the core of Paulo Freire's conception of a 'pedagogy of liberation'. Central to this approach is the idea of dialogue, an idea that has ancient roots in all world traditions. Within the academy we often hear of the centrality of the Socratic tradition. Besides the fact that Socrates relied entirely on the oral tradition, he claimed he possessed no true wisdom but the gift to engage others in a dialogue process that would be transformative (Gollop 1993).

Dialogue has been referred to as a shared exploration towards greater understanding, connection or possibility, thus, when engaged in true dialogue, the main objective is to move towards greater understanding and the sharing of meaning amongst participants. In dialogue each person meets the other in an attitude of mutuality, reciprocity and co-inquiry. Mutuality occurs in a relationship when each person perceives the self and the other as a person, as a subject rather than as an object, as someone who has the capacity to change, grow and develop rather than as something to be used or as an obstacle to be overcome (Buber 1965: 74–75).

A relationship is reciprocal when each person believes that she is able to both learn from and teach the other, when each give and each receive; this implies both autonomy and interdependence. Each person speaks the truth as he knows it and acknowledges and attempts to understand the truth as the other speaks it. In debate, the goal is to prove one's point and the purpose of the encounter is to win. Dialogue has no such purpose or outcome goal. Ideas and beliefs are not seen as inherently right or wrong in a dialogue process. What is more important in dialogue is the process of moving towards greater understanding and meaning, but as the Russian Philosopher Mikhail Bakhtin argues this is not the same as the traditional Socratic method of dialectics that predominates university academic conventions. In contrast to the linear and oppositional conception associated with Socratic dialogue, simply put Bakhtin offer a view of dialogue as an ensemble of descriptions of the world between speakers. These are formed, he suggests, in a speaker's relation to the Other's words and expressions in a continuum of cultural and political moments (Bakhtin 1986).

Paula Allman (2001), in a book entitled *Critical Education Against Global Capitalism*, argues that much of what passes for discussion in educational practice is nothing more than a 'sharing of monologues' or people taking turns to tell other what they already know of have decided. Dialogue has transformative potential but it needs to be based on a process of trust, care, commitment and collaboration and not competition and individualism. This commitment to co-creation has real potential for the project of decolonising the university, but 'it must be built on a social bond that entails interest in, and a commitment to the other' (Burbules 1993: 19), which is both cognitive and affective, i.e. involves both hearing the words of the other and feeling their presence, pain, suffering, fears, pleasures and successes. And it is in this hearing and feeling for the Other that, not only do we acknowledge the other as a fellow human being, but, we also (re)affirm our own humanity.

Breaking a Culture of Silence

The question remains, how we hear the words of the other, especially when we might be occupying a position of privilege, dominance and power. To overcome the seemingly impossible task of hearing the words, the voices, the silences … and the screams of the Other, one need begin with a unique form of politicised listening, or more profoundly hearing what has not yet been spoken i.e. opening oneself up to receiving the unspoken demand. This process must begin with an understanding that what may seem straightforward to oneself, may be an intensely challenging this for somebody else. So, one needs to ask the question why/how the 'Other' may be silenced, or what are the conditions that may require the other to speak and be heard?

Here is where my own work and thinking has been profoundly influenced by Critical Pedagogy and in particular the work of Brazilian educationalist Paulo Freire (1970) on the ways to counter act the 'cultures of silence' that are rampant in many educational institutions but also how to give voice to marginalised people. For Freire, institutions that embody dominant social relations a 'culture of silence' which that instill a negative, silenced and suppressed self-image into the oppressed. The only solution to overcoming a culture of silence is for the oppressed to embark on a journey from self-delusion (there isn't any problem), self-blame (It must be my fault), dejection (there is nothing I can do about it!), critical consciousness (I cannot continue unless I do something). For those in power, they to engage in their own culture of silence, of if you like condition of alienation. For them the journey is about understanding their own delusion about assumed superiority and being able to truly comprehend the scale of the task of transformation, both personal and institutional.

One of the mechanisms in which one can break out of the state of alienation described here is what Henry Giroux (1993) terms a 'border crosser'. Border in this sense is an inherited enclosed psychic space in which one resides; the default position. Hence becoming a 'border-crosser' requires one to step away from one's inscribed identity/world view, if you like to become a dissident, exile or perhaps even a traitor to one racialised identity. As the metaphor suggests this implies stepping away from one's secure space and entering a new space in which those dominant social relations, ideologies and silencing practices are overcome.

Conclusion—Towards a New World View

The opening up of 'new space' can also be linked to the question of decolonising the curriculum. Whilst we should not underestimate the scale of the task of decolonisation of our minds, the curriculum and our institutions, we must also believe it is not an impossible task. Time doesn't permit me to explore this aspect as any length, but I would like to end by citing Lucius Outlaw (Jnr) (1996) who in a book entitled, *Race and Philosophy,* suggests that the project of decolonising the curriculum, needs to not only enable access for black people to what have traditionally been white privileged spaces, such as universities, but to also challenge the dominant knowledge claims perpetuated through colonial dominance. Likewise, Mekada Graham (2002) suggests that nothing short of a reclamation and restoration of African centred worldviews is need not only to rectify the historical denigration and 'the cultural and spiritual rebirth' of black people it is a necessity for the 'humanity of all people' (p. 67). She goes onto summarise 5 central principles and values that underpin the African-centred worldview;

- Interconnectedness of all things (the I and we are not separable)
- Spiritual nature of being
- Primacy of collective identity
- Oneness of mind, body and spirit
- Primacy of interpersonal relationships. (ibid.: 69)

What is really interesting about these principles is that by and large they represent the antithesis of both neoliberal culture but also increasingly the utilitarian and individualistic nature of higher education. And so, if we are to be serious about new beginning, serious about transformation, both personal and institutional, then we must open our eyes, open our hearts and our minds to sources of learning, knowledge and wisdom that we have thus far erased from our campuses. We talk about progress, but progress is but an empty promise if we leave the vast majority of human beings behind. I leave you will a quote from the Malawian activist, Dunduzu Chisiza (1963):

> 'We excel', declares the African, neither in mysticism nor in science and technology, but in the field of human relations. By loving our parents, our brothers, our sisters, cousins, aunts, uncles, nephews and nieces, and by regarding them as members of our families, we cultivate the habit of loving lavishly, of exuding human warmth, of compassion, and of giving and helping. Once so conditioned, one behaves in this way not only to one's family, but also to the clan, the tribe, the nation, and to humanity as a whole.

References

Allman, P. (2001). *Critical Education Against Global Capitalism: Karl Marx and Revolutionary Critical Education*. Westport, CT: Bergin and Garvey.

Alvares, C. (2012). A Critique of Eurocentric Social Science and the Question of Alternatives. In C. Alvares & S. S. Faruqi (Eds.), *Decolonising The University: The Emerging Quest for Non-Eurocentric Paradigms* (pp. 135–161). Pulau Pinang, Malaysia: Penerbit Universiti Sains Malaysia

Back, L. (2004). Introduction. In I. Law, D. Philips, & L. Turney (Eds.), *Institutional Racism in Higher Education*. Stoke on Trent: Trentham Books.

Bakhtin, M. (1986). Speech Genres and Other Late Essays (Vern W. McGee, Trans.). Austin: University of Texas Press.

Bauman, Z. (1989). *Modernity and the Holocaust*. Cambridge: Polity Press.

Bourdieu, P. (1986). The Forms of Capital. In J. Richardson (Ed.), *Handbook of Theory and Research for the Sociology of Education* (pp. 241–258). Westport, CT: Greenwood.

Buber, M. (1965). Dialogue Between Martin Buber and Carl Rogers. In M. Buber (Ed.), *The knowledge of Man* (pp. 166–184).

Burbules, N. (1993). *Dialogue in Teaching: Theory and Practice*. New York: Teachers College Press.

Chisiza, D. K. (1963, March). The Outlook for Contemporary Africa. *Journal of Modern African Studies, 1*(1), 25–38.

Collins, P. H. (2000). *Black Feminist Thought: Knowledge, Consciousness, and the Politics of Empowerment* (2nd ed.). New York: Routledge.

Crenshaw, K. (1991). Mapping the Margins: Intersectionality, Identity Politics, and Violence Against Women of Color. *Stanford Law Review, 43*(6), 1241–1299.

Derald Wing, S. (2010). *Microaggressions in Everyday Life: Race, Gender and Sexual Orientation*. Hoboken: Wiley.

ECU. (2017). *Equality in Higher Education: Students Statistical Report 2017*. London, Equality Challenge Unit. Available at https://www.ecu.ac.uk/publications/equality-in-higher-education-statistical-report-2017/. Accessed 6 September 2018.

EHRC. (2018). *Equality Body to Investigate Racial Harassment in Universities*. London, Equality and Human Rights Commission. Available at https://www.equalityhumanrights.com/en/our-work/news/equality-body-investigate-racial-harassment-universities. Accessed 21 February 2019.

Fanon, F. (1963). The Wretched of the Earth. 1961. (C. Farrington, Trans.). New York: Grove.

Fanon, F. (1967). *Black Skins, White Masks* (C. Farrington, Trans.). New York: Grove Press.

Fanon, F. (1970). *Toward the African Revolution*. Hamondsworth: Penguin.

Freire, P. (1970). *Pedagogy of the Oppressed* (M. B. Ramos, Trans.). New York: Continuum 2007.

Garber, J., & Seligman, M. E. (Eds.). (1980). *Human Helplessness: Theory and Applications*. New York: Academic Press.

Garner, S. (2007). *Whiteness: An Introduction*. London: Routledge.

Gillborn, D. (2006). Rethinking White Supremacy: Who Counts in 'White World'. *Ethnicities, 6*(3), 318–340.

Giroux, H. (1993). *Border Crossings*. New York: Routledge.

Gollop, D. (1993). *Phaedo, by Plato*. New York: OU Press.

Graham, M. (2002). *Social Work: African-Centred Worldviews*. Birmingham: Ventura Press.

hooks, b. (1994). *Teaching to Transgress: Education as the Practice of freedom*. London: Routledge. 216 + x pages.

hooks, b. (1995). *Killing Rage: Ending Racism*. New York: Henry Holt and Company.

hooks, b. (2009). *Black Looks: Race and Representation*. London: Turnaround Publisher Services.

Lorde, A. (2017). *Your Silence Will Not Protect You*. London: Silver Press.

McIntosh, P. (2004). White Privilege: Unpacking the Invisible Knapsack. In P. S. Rothenberg (Ed.), *Race, Class, and Gender in the United States* (6th ed.), New York: Worth Publishers.

Mills, C. W. (2000). *The Sociological Imagination*. Oxford: Oxford university Press.

Outlaw, L. (1996). *Race and Philosophy*. New York: Routledge.

Rancière, J. (1991). *The Ignorant Schoolmaster: Five Lessons in Intellectual Emancipation*. Stanford: Stanford University Press.

Singh, G. (2011). *Black and Minority Ethnic (BME) Student Participation and Success in Higher Education: Improving Retention and Success—A Synthesis of Research Evidence*. York, Higher Education Academy. Available at https://www.heacademy.ac.uk/system/files/bme_synthesis_final.pdf. Accessed 21 February 2019.

Singh, G., & Kwhali, J. (2015). *How Can We Make Not Break Black and Minority Ethnic Leaders in Higher Education? Stimulus Paper*. London: Leadership Foundation for Higher Education. http://www.academia.edu/13685908/How_can_we_make_not_break_black_and_minority_ethnic_leaders_in_higher.

Sivanandan, A. (1977, April). The Liberation of the Black Intellectual. *Race Class, 18*(4), 329–343.

Sivanandan, A. (1991). *Black Struggles Against Racism, in, Northern Curriculum Development Project, Setting the Context of Change: Anti-racist Social Work Education*. Leeds: CCETSW.

TUC. (2017). *Black, Qualified and Unemployed*. London, Trade Union Congress. Available at https://www.tuc.org.uk/sites/default/files/BlackQualifiedandunemployed.pdf. Accessed 6 September 2018.

24

Raging Against the Dying of the Light

Paul Grant

I am at an age where I get to watch my grandchildren grow and my friends die. I look forward in the children's lives and want their stories to be better and brighter than mine. I look back at my friends' lives and consider the bitterness and brevity of theirs. I wonder how I can give meaning to the life that I have left in the face of their suffering and promise.

I accept that my children and grandchildren will bury me. They will have lives that I will not see or be part of. I have seen my own future in the lives of the families of my dead friends: a character in anecdotes, impressions of a presence or a sense of loss. The question is what I do now, now that I can see the life that I have had and the death that I have to come.

I could continue to encourage others to be their best selves, to live a slightly chaotic black socialism that makes my political commitments into personal responsibilities and gives me some purpose and meaning. I use yoga and play to make children laugh, elders strong and the students soften. However, it is hard to focus on these tasks when it hurts to see resources unused when people are suffering and dying pointlessly. I want to make people see what I see and feel what I feel and to make things better, so it will not hurt so much anymore for anyone.

I understand how people on the left become bitter right-wingers as we get older. The world refused to follow the rules of progress we had imagined

P. Grant (✉)
West Midlands, UK
e-mail: p.grant@wlv.ac.uk

© The Author(s) 2020
J. M. Parsons and A. Chappell (eds.), *The Palgrave Handbook of Auto/Biography*,
https://doi.org/10.1007/978-3-030-31974-8_24

were unbreakable and did not change to make us feel better. We have no great victories to rest on and the young neither recognise our struggles nor want our counsel: it is as though we never lived. And when our revolutionary fervour does not take us any further, it is easy to blame our disappointment on a misled youth and naive dreams. It is easy to limit ourselves to defending our small gains, big mortgages and little lives—our insignificance—the dying of our light in Dylan Thomas' phrase.

The fact that our political dreams might die should not stop us from living them as long as we can. However, I recognise a need to take a step back, to get some perspective on what I do next rather than run from one business to another to distract myself from my littleness. Perhaps, if I tell my own story in my own way, I might regain some sense of myself and remake rather than remember who I can be and what I can do.

Ambalavaner Sivanandan[1] introduced me to Thomas' poem. He introduced me to so much that inspired and directed the socialist light in me. I was so proud to imagine myself his friend, nephew, son, cousin and brother. Sivanandan's death in January 2018 is one of the immediate provocations for my thoughts about life, death and socialism. Another is the death of Howard Reid, my heartical breddrin,[2] in December 2017. As the rastas sing, one bright morning when his work was over, he flew away home, after spending his last energies on one last Christmas at home, one last cuddle with his wife and final man hugs from his boys, when he should have been dead months before. Neither of these deaths was a surprise. Sivanandan was 94 and had been unwell for a long time, but still outlived many of his contemporaries. Howard was 60 and had had various cancers and outlived most of them. My father was born in the same year as Sivanandan and outlived most of his cancers like Howard. He raged against the dying of the light, like them, until it was time to release a body burned out by the fire of its passing. It strikes me that these three men did much to shape me in the same way that iron sharpens iron; they taught me how to live and how to die. A way into my story is to explore their stories and to name and honour some of my other dead.

My father was born in 1923 and arrived in the capital of the British Empire, London, in 1956 from Lucea, the capital of Hanover Parish, Jamaica, with two suitcases. By 1960, he had two 'half-caste' sons, a

---

[1]Ambalavaner Sivanandan was a Sri Lankan novelist and emeritus director of the Institute of Race Relations, a London-based independent educational charity. He is a leading intellectual of the left who changed the way that race relations were viewed in the UK.

[2]A good and close friend.

nineteen-year-old English wife and one room in a house in Stamford Hill, North London. The top of the road had the station, a nunnery, nice family houses and Hassidic Jews, and the bottom of the road had less nice houses full of noisy families. Ours was about halfway down and owned by one of my dad's friends from Jamaica, Mister Stanley. Mister Stanley and Aunt Lee got the deposit money from a pardner hand and savings. They paid the mortgage by working and renting rooms to other black people.

By 1964, we had a sister and my parents had scraped together enough for their own deposit on a house in Walthamstow, a few miles away. They both had to work hard and long to find that money. More than once I was left alone in our room when they were at work with strict instructions not to open the door to anyone ('even if it's Jesus') or to play with the fire. I never opened the door, but I did play with fire. More than once my skin burned when my parents found out. Our new house was a corner house with three bedrooms, an outside toilet and paraffin heaters when we moved in. After a few years, we had an inside toilet, central heating, a telephone and another brother.

There was a swing and grass park just across the road to the new house and the primary school me and my next brother down went to was just beyond that. Its classrooms contained (or, tried to contain) lively children with parents from Jamaica, Pakistan, India, Cyprus, Ireland and England, and we were taught English, French, pounds, shillings and pence and other imperial measurements. We got caned as and when the teachers believed it necessary. My sister and youngest brother went to a 'nicer' Church of England school five minutes further away and across the road to one of my mum's sisters. My mum was the third of four children, with two older sisters and a baby brother. My aunt's three children were the same ages as me and my first brother and sister. My cousins went to the same school as my sister and little brother.

My cousin, Dougal, a few weeks younger than me, joined the army and ended up serving in Northern Ireland when I ended up in sixth form and university. The harshness of life in 1970s East London was no preparation for the brutality of the war in Northern Ireland. He did things there that he knew were wrong—snatch squads in land rovers and severe punishment beatings—and there was nothing to come back to. Violence and alcohol, despair, broke Dougal's mind and killed him young. After a close childhood, we drifted as our school lives parted. I do not remember how I learned of his death, but I do remember him once explaining his cousins' colouring to white schoolmates in terms of holidays in Spain. Better that than we had a black dad and him a black uncle, I guess. He looked after me when I found it difficult to handle the low-level bullying; he had a quicker temper and was a better fighter.

He did this, even though I was the first-born grandchild. Our nan lived about ten minutes' walk away from Dougal's house and mine was a bit nearer. She lived near two of her daughters in a ground floor flat off the Markhouse Road. She drank stera milk in tea and Camp coffee and used to live near King's Cross station. I have been told that I lived there with my mum when I was small but have no memory of that. I do remember being outside there in the bitter cold, wearing a woollen balaclava, mittens joined by wool and cotton shorts. I remember crying with the cold.

Nan gave us special presents on our seventh and fourteenth birthdays. I think that she would have done the same on our twenty-firsts, but she died before any of us got to twenty-one. She had moved from her little ground floor flat to high up a tower block and from there to an old people's home a couple of miles away. I used to get on with her and would visit from a mixture of duty and affection. As she got older and sicker, less my nan, I visited less often. It got harder to accept her decline. I felt guilty, but not enough to keep the relationship alive. The last time I saw her was in hospital and she looked like skin over skeleton in a nylon nightdress. It had been a while. All her flesh and faculties had wasted away and she was dead in all but name. And then she was dead. I never cried. The nan I had grown up with had died years before.

Other relatives from both sides of the family stayed with us from time to time. All adults my parents knew were aunty or uncle or mister or miss. They were all allowed to tell us off, hit us or tell on us to our parents. The big people believed in 'spare the rod and spoil the child' and taught personal responsibility through punishment. We were responsible for our actions, even as children. One time, when I was about five, my mum made Mr. Stanley lock me in the coal cellar at Stamford Hill. I cannot remember what I had done but do remember the terror. The dark and rejection taught me, despite my screaming, begging and door pounding, that I was helpless. My mum could lock me in the dark and not listen.

Our dad's twin brother, Uncle Manscott, was stricter than my dad and once beat all the children playing in his house because no one confessed to breaking something. He and his family lived four miles away from us in Haringey. It always felt much further because it took three buses to get there. It was an occasional Sunday afternoon trip. He had four daughters and there we learned to run without really running and to play without making too much noise. We were told, 'Children should be seen and not heard and preferably not seen'.

Once in junior high school, in a 'dead' lesson after getting back from swimming and starting our next proper class, our big, rugby-playing English teacher caught little Steven Westerman talking after he'd told us to shut up 'for the last time'. He made Steve sail across the classroom with one step and a whack from a massive Dunlop Green Flash plimsoll on his backside. We were shocked silent and were good with him for weeks. A handful of years later, Westy died in a motorcycle accident. He was my first friend to die. We had lost touch, but I took the afternoon off work to pay my respects. It did not make sense. He was bright and cheeky at school and got into a bit of trouble, but he was dead. I could not speak to his parents.

My dad and Uncle Manscott worked in the big factories on the North Circular Road for most of their working lives in this country. The London Rubber Company and then Philips were where the old man spent his life. On Sunday afternoons, when people came around to eat, drink and talk, they often talked of stupid white workers and prejudiced charge hands. There was talk of Enoch Powell forcing people to go home. Most of it went over my head and we could not ask questions, because you 'Don't butt in when big people are talking'. But I understood that the same England that we had loved and supported in 1966 did not like black people. My dad loved Muhammad Ali, and me and my black and brown friends enjoyed floating like butterflies and stinging like bees in playgrounds and classrooms. Henry Cooper, 'Our 'Enry', was always their 'Enry when he got in the ring with Ali. We enjoyed being the greatest and letting everyone know it.

I remember the 1968 Olympics and John Carlos and Tommie Smith holding up black-gloved fists. I was moved by the power of the moment. Black fists. Black Power. Black Panthers. They stood up for black people and I was proud of that (even though I never felt 'fully black', whatever that means) and it drove the stupid white people crazy. It was important that they should be driven crazy by champions who were black and brown. Even as a ten-year-old, I had heard and used all the bad words they used about Jamaican, Pakistani and Indian people. But black people could sprint the fastest, box and sing the best and by the 1970 World Cup had the best and most beautiful football team on the planet. The young, gifted and black were just a fact, even as I was frightened of skinheads, paki-bashers and nig-ger hunters and Enoch Powell.

Dad and uncle said that the union did not really defend the rights of 'the coloureds'. They had to defend themselves and told stories of challenging supervisors, confronting other machine operators and threatening manage-ment with walkouts. The white workers and management learned not to mess with them too much or too often. Violence and intimidation were as much part of the sixties as peace and love and non-violence. I remember the assassination of Martin Luther King. Not the details, but how people cried and got angry and lost. A loss. Someone who had stood up for black people had been shot down. Our parents and teachers beat us, and the stupid white people could complain, kill and maim without anyone stopping them. You dealt with it.

Uncle Manscott and aunt took our four cousins back home to Jamaica for a better education. Two of them are teachers and the other two are nurses. Professionals. Three in Jamaica and one in England. My parents had aspirations for us too. We had to have better lives than theirs. My father did shift work in local factories until he retired and my mother worked at home and in local offices on and off until her mental illness incapacitated her. She was dead at thirty-nine, her mind in pieces, the result of that illness.

I became fully aware of her illness when she had a violent breakdown in the run-up to my GCE exams in 1974. It was the first time that she threatened to kill us. By the time of her death in 1980, it felt like the 'mad mum' had been there forever. I realised that she had been unwell for many years, but the 'nice mum' had overshadowed or normalised the only slightly mad one. That was reversed in the later years. I loved her and she loved us fiercely, but I could not bear her, or, more precisely, how I felt around her. It used to be lovely around her sometimes. She would keep us safe from dad's brought home disappointment and anger and protect us from teachers, bullies or anyone else who troubled us unfairly. Sometimes, she would let us sit on the back of her chair and brush her hair while we watched 'Sunday Night at the London Palladium' after our baths. Of course, she had her own temper, could swear equally well in both East London English and Jamaican patois and was quite handy with sarcasm, slap and slipper.

By the time dad could no longer cope with her increasingly frequent breakdowns, I was no longer living at home. I had a room in Islington. He could not live in the same house as her. He gave up on her and was going to divorce her. He needed to protect himself and my brother and sister (my other brother had joined the army by this time, despite Dougal's experiences in Ireland). I just switched off my mother when she was unwell. Fading her out made it easier not to hear the death threats and abuse and not to see her bright mind and spirit degraded and diminished.

How my father managed so long I do not know. He was neither that kind nor that tolerant. He could get angry quickly and she angered him often by shaming him. But he stayed with her. It wore him down, but, for all her wanderings off, violence, suicide attempts and disappearances, he stayed and got her help. She spent time in the local mental hospital more than once.

They said that there was nothing wrong with her. One time, they phoned to say that she was there and he couldn't face the shame of it all and asked my brother to go for her. She would come home again—sometimes better, sometimes broken—but he could not hold his wife and life together. Sometimes, she would be the old Joan and, then within days, become that cruel parody of herself. He did his best to mind her as she lost hers. It broke him slowly.

I remember seeing the old man cry just the once. It was at his 80th birthday party. He had upset my sister and I took him to one side to find out what was going on. We went into his bedroom and shut the door. I felt uncomfortable. He said he got angry when my sister gave him the money we had collected for his birthday present—he had told us that he did not want us to bother with it. He then got upset and cried. He said that all he wanted was to mind us when we were younger and felt he had failed us. He spoke of our mum and his struggles with her. I have no idea of what I said. My father, who had lost so much and so many with a shrug, wept at his own weaknesses. I do not remember much of what he said. I had to comfort him and then do my best to sort out things with my sister.

The first time that I saw him as a frail old man (before his cancers started to kill him) was when we visited his sister, Aunt Bindy, after she had had a stroke. He sat by her hospital bed in a South London hospital, holding her hand, looking lost and slightly bewildered. I realised that he would need help through this and that it was not really going to get any better for either of them. Aunt's loss of speech and partial paralysis messed up her life, but she did her best to tough it out. She was still as proud as she could be. Her death a while later hit him hard. He was hurt and angry and her powerlessness had terrified him.

I remember when my mum made him leave. I was walking home from school and turned the top of our street to see the old man walking down it with a grip. We had not long moved to a smaller house, closer to dad's work, our schools and Aunt Bindy's house. As I saw him, I knew that he was going to aunt's. Not for a break, but to stay. That was that. No discussion or explanation needed. The cause was obvious, as was my response. I had to sort out the others and make sure that my mum never harmed herself or them. Dad made sure that there was money for shopping and school and that the bills were paid, but he stayed by aunt's. Things needed to be done.

I do not know how long he was away or remember how he came back. I do not think that he was away for that long really, but it felt like it.

We managed. Years later some friends asked why I never said anything to anyone or never asked for help. I got confused. How could they not understand that no one else needed to know and that I did not need any help. I was ashamed that my mum was mad and felt guilty with that shame. I loved her and my dad, but could not make it better for them. I felt rubbish. I had to help him wherever I could and had to turn her off to cope with the grief. There were times when things were better and there was hope. Those came to end early one Sunday morning. My sister and a next cousin came to my flat and told me that my mum was dead.

The person I had faded out over the years had finally disappeared by her own hand. This the coroner later confirmed, despite the police questioning my father about her death. He had worked so hard to keep his 'old-before-her-time' wife alive for so long. The police were there when I arrived and I went to look at her, I think. I felt relief: the wait was over and we could now get on with our lives. It was three years before a tear passed my eyes for her.

By the time that the police and body had left, more of my dad's friends had arrived and the drinking, talking and cooking had begun. Almost thirty years later, as I put the key into the door of my father's house in Southend, I wondered how it would be on the other side. Four hours earlier my sister had called to tell me that our dad had died at home. I was five minutes from my office in Wolverhampton and carried on to work to put some things in place for my students. I was teaching at the university. My father's death was not a surprise. He got close to ninety before the toxic results of smoking and factory life put him on a morphine driver and then killed him. I wondered how it would be on the other side.

I was relieved to see people in the kitchen laughing, joking, drinking and cooking. I said hello to family and friends, as I moved towards his room. The door was open and I saw my brother sitting by my father's bed with the TV on. My dad was laid out and there was no pain on his face. He looked like my dad again. I asked my brother what he was doing. He replied that he and dad had a horse in the race and they were watching it run. That made sense. I kissed the old man and sat with him and my brother for a little while. Racing is not really my thing, but I enjoyed the company and peace, as dad had for many years with William Hill and Joe Coral.

Now that I am older than my father was when he became a widower with four children he knew about (a story for another time), my life is comfortable. Fifty-five years after five of us lived in a single room in Hackney, my house in Birmingham is bought and paid for and I have savings and a pension. Sixty years after my dad left Jamaica and not long after his death, I visited my dad's twin and the wider family. On this visit, my cousin took me to visit our grandparents' graves behind where my father grew up in the hills above Lucea town. As I swept away the leaves, I thought that my grandparents could never have imagined that a nearly white grandson would ever perform this small service when their children left for England. Dad was going to follow his twin to make some money working in England, as he had worked in the United States, swapping agricultural work for factory work. The view from Hilltop is still stunning. I wondered why anyone would leave it.

Dad used to tell stories of the old days all the time. I could not always follow them, as fifty-five years in this country never made much difference to his accent, vocabulary and speed. I miss those stories now. I miss his joy in finding himself in his stories. Now I have questions about the stories he never told me too. Of course, I wonder why he left Hilltop when he did. I would like to know about how the stresses of a 'mixed marriage' with a much older man and teenage pregnancies affected my mother's mental health and her family. I want to understand how those things affected him and his relationship to us, what he felt about it all. I wonder about our grandparents. Why did our white nan move to a tower block and then a care home in her final years and how come none of her children took her in? It seems sad that she should end up like that, when there was talk that she had been in a workhouse when much younger. We never saw or heard of our white grandad. I cannot remember when I realised that I never had one and that you were supposed to have one. We never saw our Jamaican grandparents except in an ancient black and white photo of Papa, who had gone blind, and a colourised one of Mama, who was close to Jamaican white. No one told us about that how that worked either. Of course, some of those are questions for my mum too. I wonder how she managed in the beginning and when the 'struggling through life' times became the 'struggling to live' times. I wonder how it felt to lose your place in a family and then lose yourself. The dream is to sit down and listen to their stories as they understood them and then reason things through as adults, to understand what they saw and felt and thought would happen. To talk with them as I might do with other people I know well.

Uncle Manscott lived a way down the hill from Hilltop, Mama and Papa's house, and he and aunt were happily retired, living off their UK pensions and a little change from selling ice and frozen juice in a house they'd built on land my dad gave them. In Lucea, I'm a nephew of, a cousin of, a son of or simply of the many, many Grants, and we are all defined in relation to the 'breed of Grants' that stretches back well over a hundred years with identifiable traits across generations. One of those traits is the tendency to drive those closest to us slightly mad. Others are bloody-minded stubbornness and being dyam rude.[3]

My uncle's dementia had calmed through a change in his medication. He still sometimes asked my aunt, 'A who dat young lady?', when one of his daughters visited. Her responses often began, 'Manscott, yuh nuh eediyat?' He died last year at the age of 94 and my aunt became a widow after 60 years of marriage. He had been the last man standing—all his brothers and sisters were dead—and died peacefully, outliving his sister by less than a year. The family put up his headstone a year later: gone but not forgotten.

I first visited them in Jamaica was in 1996 when I went to a conference at the University of the West Indies. It was the first time that I had seen them since they had left England, but I could not forget what uncle looked like. He was my dad's identical twin, almost the same person in looks, voice, mannerisms and philosophy. I'd gone to UWI to present a paper on the work of Walter Rodney, the revolutionary Guyanese historian, murdered by the Forbes Burnham government in 1980.

I'd been working at the University of Wolverhampton for a couple of years as an apprentice lecturer. It was a two-year post set up to increase the number of black and minority ethnic lecturers by giving someone a toehold in an institution that they might use to lift themselves into a more permanent position. I was not the first pick candidate, but when offered it, I grabbed it and had the best of two years 'learning my trade', teaching sociology and social policy and working with many different people, both staff and students.

Phil, one of my mentors, taught social policy. He had been a runner but had developed an extremely aggressive rheumatoid and osteoarthritis not long before I met him. He was already walking slowly with two sticks. Within a handful of years, the university had let Phil go on grounds of ill-health. As a socialist social policy lecturer, he understood the workings of educational bureaucracies better than most, but he was disappointed at his treatment at the hands of his employer and some of his colleagues. The facts of his condition were unchangeable, but he felt forgotten and left behind as the disease advanced.

Phil's belief in the principles of the NHS was absolute, despite his experience of many of its actual imperfections and infections. The closest he ever got to private medicine was paying for the cannabis that alone eased

---

[3]Jamaican speech for 'damn rude'.

his pain. His arthritis broke his neck in a coughing fit a while after his hip replacements, but it was pneumonia that killed him when I was in Jamaica in 2002. I had changed my flight to come back for a family matter, only to find out that he had died.

Through his example, Phil taught me about the practice of socialism in a university setting. That included the need for a bloody-minded stubbornness in the face of institutional cockups and setbacks and the everyday practice of fairness and equality. Wherever possible, institutions must be made to follow their own rules rather than the whims of its leaders, professionals or administrators. Integrity for Phil meant doing your best to give all students the best chance to improve themselves, no matter who they were or where they were from. He was always concerned about the impact on the many in need rather than the few in control. He was also concerned about the impact of his individual deterioration on his wife and daughters' quality of life. It was rarely easy, but they did their best to live as well as they could.

I was not sure the university could or would extend my apprentice contract and thought I might be unemployed again. I had been unemployed for a couple of years after I came to Birmingham and had not liked it. I did bits of youth work and volunteered at a Christian anti-racist organisation. Out of that came a chance to see A Sivanandan, the then Director of the Institute of Race Relations, deliver a keynote speech at a teachers' event on racism awareness training in Birmingham in 1985. I had read some of Sivanandan's work in 'Race & Class' and respected it. I didn't understand much of it but knew that he stood up for black and Third World communities against the Thatcher government and the police and popular racism. Respect became love when I watched him shift from engaged and urbane colonially educated black intellectual to an ordinary black man vexed by stupidness.

In the discussion time following his talk, someone got upset by Sivanandan's 'personal' attack on a local racism awareness trainer. Sivanandan's response was simple, clear and effective: 'Fuck off with your bourgeois bullshit'. His outrage at the brutality of Thatcher's war on black people and working-class communities was pure and unrestrained. The room divided into those who gasped into silenced disdain at his bluntness and those who found their voices in it. I loved him in that moment. My wife was driving to London for a business meeting the next day. I cadged a lift and went to the Institute of Race Relations to see him. That connection made me happy when being out of work made me feel useless. Budgeting down to the last pound took some doing, as did budgeting my confidence. It took effort to tell people that yes, I was still out of work and, yes, I was still looking hard. The generosity of the Institute's staff was overwhelming, especially as I had just turned up unannounced (and nervous) and to be taken seriously by them lifted my spirits and ambitions.

Even so, years later, I felt like a fool talking about Rodney at the campus where he became a focus for the Jamaican Black Power struggle in 1968. I'd written about his commitment to improving the everyday lives of people in Guyana and their self-liberation. In his work as a historian and a political activist in Tanzania, Jamaica and Guyana, he focused on the importance of reasoning with the people at the bottom of society, sitting and learning from and with the sufferahs. I saw overlaps between the challenges faced by those like Rodney working to 'liberate' their countries from foreign and neo-colonial domination and those working to 'liberate' their communities from the Tory 'market' and its 'policies of a thousand cuts'. There was much to learn from the Third World about the practice of socialism and community in the First World.

I learned most of my lessons about reasoning with the sufferahs and everyday liberation in Chapeltown, Leeds. Most of my school friends had gone straight from sixth form to redbrick universities. I did not know why I was going to any university and decided to pull out of the UCCA (as UCAS was then) process and take a couple of years out to find out. I found a job as an assistant maintenance man in central London and then got a Community Service Volunteer post at a Black Youth Project, Project Spark, in Chapeltown. That was in 1977. The youth club was a dump of a big five-bedroom corner house on a residential street. The project director loved all the young people, even the 'appalling little shits' (a favourite phrase of his). He was universally known as 'Raggy' and affectionately mocked. He was white and presented himself as committed, eccentric and harmless, a clown with a purpose. He helped everyone who asked and the lads could all feel at home at the club—he did not give the impression of being in charge at all—and there was no need to be too, too careful with the building or the equipment. Of course, money was tight, but being open and accessible was more important. There were enough places working to control and contain the lads and their energies. Project Spark was not going to be another one.

There were the usual pursuits of pool, table tennis and bar football, and there was a sound system based in the downstairs back room. Chapeltown was full of sounds, musical and cultural co-ops. The director nurtured the leadership potential of the lads involved. A couple of them helped in the club and I became good friends with them. They were a year or so younger than me and helped me settle in and taught me so much about life and laughter. I went out with the sister of one of them and had my first experience of Caribbean Pentecostal Christianity at her church. The other, Elton, had two exceptionally large black cats that he named Beelzebub and Lucifer. When his first child was born, I had to feed his cats, his black panthers. This meant standing on his back step, facing another black Pentecostal church when people were there, encouraging Beelzebub and Lucifer to come to me. I was still doing my best to be a committed Christian at the time and I'm sure Elton took joy in my difficulties.

I was thrown into the midst of the 'worst' youth club in Chapeltown and learned what it was to live in the black heart of Leeds. I learned so much about community politics and intrigues, how power plays out in who speaks for who where and when and how it is always better to deal with the few who can say yes rather than the many who like to say no. I also learned about knowing where you live and being known where you live. Once you crossed Scott Hall Road from town, you were broadly safe from casually marauding white people. People would help you if you were attacked. Outside of Chapeltown, you could be at risk and going into the wrong parts of town or the white parts of the city without good cause was simply stupid. One lad was burned with cigarettes for being in the wrong place at the wrong time. One time a white man was shouting at and raising his hands to a black woman in the heart of the area. Some lads badly beat him: he 'needed to know', I was told.

I eventually reapplied for university whilst living in Leeds and got a place at Goldsmiths' College in London. I came home, but I loved the Chapeltown people and community so much, though, that I got a job at the same project when I finished my degree. I went for the manager's job but blew the interview when I realised that I did not know what I was doing and panicked. I got the youth worker post instead at the now rebranded the Palace Youth Project. One of the lads from the sound now managed a team of lads on work experience there and Elton was the project worker. Many years later, one would be convicted of murder and the other would kill himself because he could not face a future of being less than he was.

It was September 1991 and I hadn't spoken to Elton for a while and he'd been due to call me. He had gone back to Leeds after working in Newham for a few years. There was nothing unusual in the delay. I remember walking past his house on the day of his funeral. The long front garden still had bits of his life scattered across the lawn. There were kids' toys, clothes and random other burned debris that the firefighters had pulled out. The worn intimacies of normal life under the watery sun of an autumn day forced me to look away. The church was full to overflowing and big men wept openly. I remember someone reading from Ossie Davis' eulogy for Malcolm X:

Elton was our 'own black shining Prince! – who didn't hesitate to die, because he loved us so'. People raised fists in salute.

At the wake, someone said that if I had been able to talk with Elton that he would still be alive. Although it was probably true, I reeled for a moment. That might well have been the reason he chose not to call. I was told that he had been depressed being back in Leeds and developed a condition that was slowly robbing him of his health, his mind and life, where he had always been effortlessly strong, bright, alive and single-minded. I think that he had made up his mind and did not want to be persuaded otherwise. But what about the lives of his boys and baby mother? The lives of his family and friends all gathered at Harehills Cemetery on that cold, bright and windy day?

Years after there were a couple of times when I saw his gait and style in someone else's walk. I wept with the joy of seeing his spirit again, albeit at a distance and with a stranger's face. Whilst in London, Elton lived at Howard's house in Leyton (about thirty minutes' walk from my dad's in Walthamstow) and through his work in Newham got to know Sivanandan. On a visit to the Institute after the funeral, Sivanandan took me to one side and told me that Elton had been a soldier in the people's army. I was moved. I was moved that the old man had taken the time to comfort me and that he had known my friend. It did not matter that he used the same phrase for others or that he did not know him that well. What mattered was the small act of kindness.

I met Howard not long before I went to Leeds the first time and he came to visit me in there just before I resigned from the youth worker post at the Palace. We were brothers in afros. Him from a solid working-class Christian Jamaican family and me with my shakier Jamaican English working-class family. When we met, he was a banker and I was an assistant maintenance man and we understood each other heartically.[4] There had been a breakdown in communication between me and the Palace manager. It was getting messy with a split between most of the staff and the management in the making. I had reasoned that the future of the project was more important than my position there. My partner at the time had recognised her inability to reach me as I prepared to leave the place where I had found myself. She spoke with Howard, I assume, who arrived as surprise bearing gifts of Gregory Isaacs' 'Night Nurse' and Aswad's 'Not Satisfied'.

He must have spent the best part of eight hours travelling to and from Leeds to spend a few hours with us, with me. Although nothing substantial

---

[4]Heartically in this context means wholehearted and positively.

changed, his presence and presents lifted me and made it all better. It makes me smile that these albums captured both the moment and my character. I still left Leeds with as much integrity as I could and went back to Walthamstow more than a little depressed, without job, money or purpose. I remember the decision to cut my natty hair, the too fine afro I had twisted for months, but had refused to locks up properly. I do not remember the decision to go back to do youth and community work at St Mary's Neighbourhood Centre in Islington, but that is what happened. (I think the youth worker there, who I had worked with before, heard I was back and offered me work.) Howard, however, had come to find me when I was lost and watched out for me on my return.

I remember his return to hospital in November 2017 with stomach troubles. He had not been well for several weeks. I also remember when I realised what terminal meant. The last time I saw him alive turned out to be a couple of weeks before his death. As I left his hospital bedside, I kissed his head top and told him that I loved him and that I would see him soon. The last time that I spoke to him, after leaving 'How you doing?' and 'Just checking in' messages on his phone, was just after Christmas. He told me that he had managed to get the hospital to let him home for a few hours on Christmas Eve and Christmas Day, but that he felt battered. That is when I realised he was dying, properly dying. In that moment, I let him go. I did not want his suffering to continue because I loved him so. So, I was not shocked to see his wife's number come up on my phone a couple of days later. Folk had prayed for his life, a miracle of healing. I had asked for a good clean death. I admired her bravery in making the call herself. A small kindness.

I realised that Sivanandan had died when I was asked if his wife had spoken to me by someone with tears in their eyes. At Sivanandan's funeral, I heard someone ask, 'What do you do when your father dies?' I knew a simple answer and thought that it was self-evident. Before my dad died, there was a moment when I knew it was coming and literally fell to the floor and wept. I then stood up, wiped my face, brushed down my trousers and tucked in my shirt and acted like the person he taught me to be. Things need to be done and others need to be looked after.

That's not to say that dads are always the best examples of sharing and caring. I certainly am not. Too many times my bloody-minded stubbornness, dyam rudeness and quickstep cleverness have blocked my ears to what women have had to say with their words and actions about community, family, resilience and effectiveness. Too often, I have focused on the heroic dead or the grand gesture rather than the everyday responsibilities and ongoing commitments. However, what I want is for my children and grandchildren (and everyone's children and grandchildren) to stand up as tall as they can, leaning on others to offer and receive support as and when necessary.

That is what you do when your father or mother dies, what you do when your friends die and what you do when your politics seem to be dying. You get up and do your best to finish their work and to challenge the system that manufactures everyday misery and ordinary exploitation, the dying of the light.

25

Black Young Men: Problematisation, Humanisation and Effective Engagement

Rev. Carver Anderson

Introduction

This chapter engages with the 'problematisation' of black young men (BYM—with African-Caribbean heritages and backgrounds) in Birmingham, their association with violence, criminality and involvement in 'street life' (culture of life on road). It is concerned with the lack of effective responses to these men and the continued negative labels associated with them and their families (Anderson 2015, 2017). By using an auto/biographical approach, it enables me to offer some thoughts and approaches as I have responded to BYM's needs over the years in my capacity as a pastor, academic and practical theologian working with the Bringing Hope charity in Birmingham (my activism is worked out within this context). These roles have afforded me opportunities to explore some of the wider social and structural factors influencing the men impacted by the above issues.

Central to us understanding the complex 'realities' of BYM, many who I suggest, are misunderstood and misrepresented, it is necessary that they are represented as individuals with 'human needs', to be loved, appreciated, respected, feel secure, and have a sense of hope. This chapter therefore grapples with the structural and statutory labels and negative representations of

Rev. C. Anderson (✉)
Birmingham City University, Birmingham, UK
e-mail: carver.anderson@bringinghope.co.uk

© The Author(s) 2020
J. M. Parsons and A. Chappell (eds.), *The Palgrave Handbook of Auto/Biography*,
https://doi.org/10.1007/978-3-030-31974-8_25

these men and seeks to position their situation, within approaches that are 'needs-led' and solution-focused. In so doing, the narratives of the men become central in how we develop approaches or solutions associated with engaging them. I suggest that, their stories are necessary in helping us to understand causal or influential factors resulting in their involvement in violence and criminality.

The chapter applies a practical theological perspective to understand and respond to the needs and interests of BYM. This has included gaining ethical approval for privileging their voices, some of which are represented later. My aim, my commitment and duty, in continuing to work with BYM, is in Grant's (2006) words, 'saving our sons'. Also, at a time of continued moral panic and serious concerns associated with youth violence (Regan and Hoeksma 2010), this work engages with the notion of a faith-based Christian perspective that seeks to effectively address issues and needs of BYM associated with 'life on road' (Anderson 2017).

The Importance of Creating Space for the Voices of Young Black Men

Hearing some of the pained stories of BYM who have lost friends or family members to violence, acknowledging their expressions about feelings of anger, pain, hopelessness, frustration, revenge and fear, has at times been very emotional leaving me feeling powerless. At the same time, on occasions, I have been involved in supporting families, in planning and officiating funerals for youngsters who have been victims of knife and gun violence. Seeing the inevitable devastation and destructive outcomes of serious violence on families and communities has also been a motivating factor for advocating the need to have 'safe spaces' for BYM to express how they feel.

It is important to acknowledging that a criminal justice or law enforcement response to the issues and challenges associated with BYM does not address the deeper causal factors regarding their criminality or involvement in violence (Glynn 2014). In seeking to capture the thoughts of BYM, as mentioned earlier, I have considered an approach, grounded in my sociological and theological imaginations, that enables me to look at the 'familiar', 'experiential' and my 'common cultural currency', in Walton's words (2014). From this position, I can explore both social and spiritual spheres and capture their lives through several lenses (Thompson et al. 2008). This draws attention to how the use of interdisciplinary tools can offer new insights about this group, deemed 'hard to reach' and/or 'hard to engage'.

Research shows that black young men are over-represented in the criminal justice system and deaths through serious violence (Anderson 2015, 2017). It attests the following:

- As well as historical conflicts, black communities and the police need a process where 'truth and reconciliation' can be explored (Anderson 2017). The media representations of criminality continue to create strong links between images of blackness and criminality (Cushion et al. 2011), and black young men are more likely to be 'stopped and searched' than their white counterparts (Bradford 2017).
- Black young men associated with gangs, guns and violence more likely to receive heavier prison sentences than their white or Asian counterparts (Glynn 2014; Gunter 2010). They are more likely to die from gun and knife-related incidents than their white or Asian counterparts and 60–70% of gun-related murders of black young men are incidents of 'black-on-black' violence (McLagan 2005).
- Black boys are excluded disproportionately from schools (Rendall and Morag 2005) and black families and communities negatively profiled (Brown 2015).

Here, we see a symbiotic relationship between these young men and their families with criminality, bad behaviours, being dangerous and conflict with statutory bodies. According to Newburn, some of these issues serve only to undermine views that:

– [L]evels of offending by African–Caribbeans were little different from those of the white majority and instead gradually created the view that black youths in particular were potent source of danger (2017: 843).

The damage wrought by the disturbing 'realities' of these young men's lives and their reproduction as a dangerous 'other' (Brown 2015) motivates me to engage critically with research and action that seek to develop effective engagement and support for them. My professional and pastoral work and my membership of the wider black community push me to work with black young men to stop death, destruction and violence, whether they are committed randomly or deliberately by them, their peers or through mechanisms unleashed by the state and its institutions.

My first-hand experiences shape my research. As a practical theologian, a 'Progressive Pentecostal' pastor, I have grappled with how to create safe spaces or environments to enable BYM to represent their realities. For several years, as a member and leader within a UK black majority church (BMC) context, I remember challenging leaders regarding their unresponsiveness to issues associated with BYM deemed problematic and who were disconnected from any practical help and support offered by their respective churches. My ongoing concerns about this disconnect have fuelled my activism and directed my research. They have driven me to create space for counter-narratives that humanise, support and empower BYM and their families who have been marginalised, vilified and stereotyped (Brown 2015; Byfield 2008; Rich 2009).

Who I am and what I do reconciles my ambitions to recreate wholeness, shalom, through pastoral and political work with young men, their families and communities. The outcomes of my engagement with BYM and their families make me who I am and are instrumental in re-imagining their personal and community potential and creating a gateway to offer counter-narratives. These stories humanise the 'problems' and reconstruct them as potential role models who make worthwhile contributions to their society, local communities and neighbourhoods. My experiences (historical and current, theological and otherwise), perspectives and understandings continue to shape my practices with BYM and the communities they are from.

Engaging with Black Young Men's 'Realities'

The impetus for my practical work with BYM, alongside my critical research relating to their issues, emanates from several key events and stages in my life. It commences with a vivid recollection of school labelling me, along with other black young men. We were navigating the education and social systems of the 1960s and early 1970s when blatant forms of racism and oppression characterised their interactions with black communities (Byfield 2008; Cork 2005; Scarman 1982).

I can still remember some of the racial abuse I experienced at age twelve from both staff and pupils. It is at this stage, when young men establish tighter friendship groups and often become mutually supportive, that teachers began to 'suspect' our friendship groups. As black young men in a predominantly white school, they stereotyped us as 'troublemakers', 'lively' and 'academically weak'. Whilst not wishing to name the school, I also recall that it 'academically streamed' us into pursuing an 'integrated studies course', with no possibility of being entered for 'O' levels or anything beyond CSEs in Mathematics English and Science regardless of our abilities.

On reflection, there was little structure and less academic support and empowerment in these lessons. For some, this led to truancy, negative behaviours and activities that, I believe, emerged because of the lack of appropriate supervision, care and educational support. Some of my friends were subsequently expelled. Over forty-five years later, the expulsion or exclusion of black children is still a problem for black families and communities. Contemporary evidence highlights disproportionate numbers of black young men excluded from both primary and secondary schools. The impact of these exclusions on the children and their families should be recognised, given the educational achievement gap with excluded pupils (Davidson and Alexis 2012). The causes and outcomes of these practices are clear. Even Lord Scarman, in his report on the 'Brixton Disorders' (10–12 April 1981), stated:

> It was suggested that teachers tend to stereotype black pupils as ill- disciplined or unintelligent and accordingly set too low a performance standard for these pupils; lack of sufficient contact between parents and school; lack of understanding by teachers of the cultural background of black pupils. (Scarman 1982: 64)

More recently, my report for the Commission on Gangs and Violence, 'Uniting to Improve Safety' (Anderson 2017) shows parents sharing their concerns about how schools treated black children, similar to those reported by Scarman some 36 years earlier. Parents expressed concerns with the range of racial disparities in the education system. These include the disproportionate number of black boys excluded without access to alternative full-time educational provision and in danger of being 'educated by the streets' and its negative influences (Anderson 2017).

Whilst it's important to acknowledge that both black and white boys became involved in certain negative behaviours at 'my school', it was the black ones who were labelled 'bad', 'defiant' and 'lively' simply on the basis of skin colour. One may ask where my parents were at this stage. The simple answer would be that they had limited understandings about what the school had done regarding my streaming and I was not about to complain to them about the 'freedom' that I was experiencing with my friends. This reflection still influences me today and I continue to ask critical questions about the treatment of black young men in the education system.

Another influence on me is being a father of two black young men, whose lives I saw negatively impacted by peer pressures and the 'code of the street', where toughness, fearlessness and loyalty are benchmarks for 'street respect' and credibility. This code also governs public and social relations, especially violence between feuding groups (Anderson 1999). My role as a pastor, ministering in areas where gun and gang violence were prevalent, raised more concerns. I felt many of my ministerial and pastoral colleagues in BMCs were not prepared to grapple with some key questions about engaging with black young men and local community concerns. These included:

- How should pastors and church leaders effectively theologically and practically respond to the challenges, interests and social issues facing BYM, their families and communities?
- What responsibilities do Christians have towards marginalised people in general and, more specifically, to support those black youths represented in criminal justice statistics and peer-associated violence?
- How might BYM's narratives influence or inform the statutory, voluntary, community and faith sector leaderships, who may seek to develop interdisciplinary and partnership frameworks to effectively respond to their needs and interests?
- What underlying beliefs, ideologies, practices and theologies inform, shape or inhibit the responses of BMCs to the situation of black young men?
- Are BMCs and the wider faith communities aware of the impact of guns, knives and gang-associated issues within local neighbourhoods, especially on the families of victims and perpetrators?

Although this is not an exhaustive set of questions, it highlights some of the concerns I have had to grapple with regarding the perceived disconnect between the churches I was a part of and the needs and realities of young people categorised as 'problematic' and 'hard to reach' (Anderson 2015, 2017; Glynn 2014). Along with the factors above, through my work with the Bringing Hope charity, I have been into numerous prisons and cells to support these young people, conducted funerals as stated earlier and offered support and advice to agencies and groups impacted by the evils of violence and criminality in local neighbourhoods.

Out of this context, more strategic reflections and interventions emerged. I explored the possibilities of using a practical theological framework to develop more effective engagement with black young men and their issues. Eventually, I came to the pastoral cycle, a tool from practical theology that I used to 'probe' their experiences. It allowed me to gain insights into their worlds and develop an 'effective engagement framework' that can influence how practical theology, sociology and criminology see their needs.

Practical Theological and Interdisciplinary Considerations

I have conducted research over the past 15 years both in prisons and in communities and engaged with individuals and families labelled 'hard to reach'. Most were black men and families from areas associated with gangs, guns, violence and deprivation. For many, the 'code of the street' determined their attitudes, thinking and choices. This is reflected in the following statements from four respondents, active male gang associates who were interviewed for Birmingham's Police and Crime Commissioner Gangs and Violence Report (Anderson 2017: 57):

> 'We will ride and die together, that's how we flex out here. Manz loyal to the end.'
> '....What you saying, we need to stop what manz on, for what blood? You got a job for me? No answer, see, because you dun know that man ain't going to be employed.'
> 'Keeping it real, manz done some things that should have put me six foot under, but you know what? My time ain't come yet.'
> 'You know how this thing goes, blood; when you are on the system of the feds and probation, man still do their thing but keep under the radar.'

Importantly, these men were prepared to talk to someone they believed would listen and understand them. In delineating and responding to these complex and interrelated issues, I want to expose a need for appropriate, culturally competent and interdisciplinary tools to gain insights and understanding regarding the realities of BYM's lives.

In recent years, there has been an increase in interdisciplinary dialogue, enquiry and interventions relating to issues categorised as problematic or of social concern. Many theologians argue that the pastoral situations generated in urban or inner-city communities and neighbourhoods require us to develop insights from a variety of perspectives to translate and apply faith and actions effectively (Cone 1986; Kinast 1999; Osmer 2008; Woodward and Pattison 2000). For Heitink, practical theology is a theological theory of action with a methodology linked to the social sciences and has a global reach (Heitink 1999: 1). Furthermore, Heitink suggests the following about practical theology:

Practical theology should be understood as an empirically descriptive and critically constructive theory of religious practice. The empirical and descriptive dimension, which is pursued in close cooperation with other disciplines in the field of cultural studies, prevents practical theology from wishful speculative thinking and contributes to empirical theory building. (Heitink 1999: xvi)

Conversations about theology and social science have not been without some territorial and contested methodological debates regarding empirical data, sources and recommendations that may or may not lead to effective engagement and changes to given situations. The idea that one discipline and its associated perspectives or approaches are adequate to explore, interpret and address social, community and 'human related problems' or challenges is at best contested and at worst simply wrong.

How then have I used a practical theological framework with interdisciplinary tools to research and contribute to the desistance and rehabilitative process for BYM? In all honesty, I have to acknowledge that my early years as a church leader and minister were void of any approaches or methods that engaged with the realities of unchurched black young men, without some form of judgement about their attitudes, thinking and behaviours that deemed them 'unholy', 'unrighteous', 'bad' and 'ungodly'. My dogmatic and myopic responses echoed those of the denomination to which I was affiliated. They lacked flexibility and the openness to other thoughts and perspectives. It is from this experience that my present work with black church leaders advocates the use of the pastoral cycle to promote critical reflection on their practices and engagement relating to black young men and local communities.

I take very seriously Cornel West's point concerning the need for BMC leaders to consider more critically how they acquire knowledge and understanding regarding sociopolitical issues and concerns. He states:

The black church is going to have to change in order to meet new challenges. Its leadership is going to have to become much more sophisticated, critical and self-critical. This is the only way that democratic sensibilities can become more pronounced and pervasive in the black community. Second, it must become more grounded in intellectual inquiry. We can no longer have leaders who engage simply and primarily in putting forth moral condemnation and ethical rhetoric without any understanding of how power and wealth operate in this society. (cited by Davis 2010: 101–102)

Fig. 25.1 Ballard and Pritchard pastoral cycle

It was by using practical theological tools to critically reflect on my practices that I was able to 're-imagine' alternative ways to engage with the 'realities' of some black families. The pastoral cycle (seen in Fig. 25.1) allowed
me to explore and reflect on West's challenges in my one-to-one and group
training and development sessions with BMC leaders. Practical theology
and its tools for reflection offered me the opportunity to address my fears,
limitations, concerns and inhibitions associated with working with black
young men and local communities. My willingness to learn and use Ballard
and Pritchard's (2006) version of the pastoral cycle supported me to think
more critically, reflect more deeply and analyse more precisely. Ballard and
Pritchard suggest that the pastoral cycle offers the opportunity to use social
scientific enquiry tools to make sense of a given issue or concern and to use
the information gained to redefine methods and approaches. These allow for
more effective engagement with areas of concern or interest. As seen below,
the cycle starts with present experience, which becomes questioned by some
event or crisis. It starts in the concrete reality of where people are (2006: 89).

Importantly, the PC encouraged me to explore the narratives, experiences
and realities of individuals and groups. A multiple methods approach was
used to gain greater insights and understanding from the men who were a
part of both research projects, both in prison and in community. Given that
each project was rooted in a qualitative methodological framework with several sample groups, I used participant observation, interviews, focus groups
and a reflective journal to obtain data. Furthermore, many hours were spent

with relevant literature and navigating hours of social media materials used by young men to tell their 'pained stories' and express disrespect to rival groups on YouTube channels. Some of the content of these videos disturbed me, especially those associated with intended violence and disrespect for women. On the other hand, some expressed real feelings of pain, distrust, anger, trauma and hopelessness, as well as hopes and aspirations. The work of Irwin-Rogers and Pinkney (2017) explores how social media can so easily be a trigger for spontaneous and deliberate violence.

In my research with the Police and Crime Commissioner's Office, I reported that faith groups are active in many of the areas where gang-associated violence and gun and knife crime occur. The challenge was to explore with these faith groups how their capacity, insights and potential could be used to offer faith-based approaches to gang-associated criminality and violence in their localities. The research recommended that:

> The Commission should develop a co-ordinated approach to engage all inter-faith and multi-faith forums/groups in Birmingham. The aims are to discuss the role of faith, values and morals in issues around organised crime, gangs and violence and promote working together, especially in 'priority neighbour-hoods', to increase the peace. (Anderson 2017: 13)

Theological reflection forms a crucial aspect of the process. Importantly, it was my work with the Bringing Hope charity and my doctorial research that encouraged my scriptural reflection in relation to practice. It was from these reflections that revised actions and activities emerged to enable more effective engagement and work with black young men and their families.

Faith, Religion and Spirituality Considerations in Desistance

It is important to point out that my 'faith in action' theology, whilst governed by a Christian ethos, does not seek to recruit, evangelise or proselytise, but to uphold principles of justice, love, integrity and anti-oppressive practice. It enables one to understand the young men's spiritual, moral and ethical concerns, as well as their other needs. In effect, I am advocating for a 'public theology', which seeks to engage and address issues in the public sphere for the public good (Sebastian and Day 2017). Whether an individual or family holds Christian values and beliefs or otherwise, a theology rooted in practical actions is intended to offer help and support to those who may need it. This work takes very seriously an 'advocacy position' regarding the need to see faith-based interventions considered alongside other valid and credible models or perspectives used to support individuals and families. My work through the Bringing Hope charity fully upholds and echoes the 'love principles' represented in 1 Corinthians 13: 1–13 (The Message Bible). Love, faith and action are indeed drivers for my theology of engagement with BYM and their families. Cone argues that:

> Without practical commitment to validate faith's claim, what we say about God, Jesus Christ, and the Holy Spirit becomes nothing but pious talk that makes persons feel good, similar to the excitement derived from musical and sporting events. Theology is the church applying a critical self- evaluation of what it says and does on behalf of the one who defines the church's identity- namely Jesus Christ. (1986: viii)

From Glynn's extensive work with black young men in the UK and USA, he argues for new and more intersectional approaches (considering gender, class, health, race, spirituality, community and education, for example). According to Glynn, these men are more likely to engage with organisations, systems and individuals that support them within 'safe spaces' to talk freely and share their realities, pained or otherwise (Glynn 2014). It is evident from Glynn's assertion that the notion of love highlighted above is not at odds with such intersectionality and can create the 'safe spaces' that offer support without judgement or disrespect.

There is a need to evidence this suggestion that faith-based interventions can effectively engage black young men and support their rehabilitation and resettlement trajectories. My work does this, as does the work of Brown et al. (2016) and Deuchar (2018). Their research explores the use of faith, religion and spirituality in work with offenders and gang associates. As well as interviews and observations with the men themselves, they also interviewed pastors, chaplains and staff involved with the faith groups or organisations working with them. However, whilst Deuchar's research explored a racially diverse group of men from across three continents, Brown et al.'s was more specific. They interviewed 16 black men between the ages of 21 and 36 in prison and community involved in the Bringing Hope charity's 'Second Chance - Damascus Road Community and Prison Programme'. My doctorial work in 2015 highlights the men's responses to questions around faith and spirituality. They represented the following:

CH1—Christian and Rastafarian background—now a professed Christian.
CH2—Christian background—now a professed Christian.
CH3—Rastafarian/Christian background—now a professed Christian.
CH4—Rastafarian/Christian background—now a professed Christian.
CH5—Christian background—now a professed Christian.
P1—Christian background—now a professed Muslim.
P2—Rastafarian background—no active involvement with any faith.
P3—Christian background—no active involvement at present.
P4—Attended Sunday school as a child—now actively exploring the Christian faith in prison.
P5—Had attended church with his grandmother as a child—a professed Muslim.
R1—Christian home and background—attends church, but not a professed Christian.
R2—Christian background—no active involvement but attends church periodically.
R3—From Christian background—not a professed Christian, but an adherent.
R4—Went to Sunday school for a short period—exploring Christian faith at present.

The men felt comfortable enough to disclose these positions. Those who identified as Rastafarians, Christian and Muslim had the potential for deeper explorations of how lifestyle choices are impacted by their understanding of faith, religion and spirituality. Even so, all were happy to discuss ethical and moral actions and their own experiences and struggles to be good men (Anderson 2015).

Given that this chapter aims to highlight and illustrate the potential of faith and spirituality to enable black young men involved or at risk of involvement in offending behaviours to transition into a positive social sphere, the next section does two things. It reiterates some of the key factors associated with their problematisation before using the Bringing Hope approach along with my research to lay out fresh faith-based approaches to supporting desistance and rehabilitative processes in prisons and communities.

Problematisation of BYM

I argue here that the 'constructed images' of black young men are associated with negative pictures emerging from the activities of a minority involved in criminal activities and behaviours. However, the media's sensationalist portrayal of black youth as violent, gangsters and aggressive maximises the moral panic, around them. Madhubuti (1991) argues that there is a 'war on Black men' that seeks to disempower, marginalise and render them 'dysfunctional'. He suggests that where black families are effectively dismantled, this may result in some of their male members entering lifestyles and behaviours that only serve to detract from the creation of 'sane, healthy and energetic youth; provide basic life-giving and life-saving support systems' (Madhubuti 1991: 77). The media portrays black men as violent and uncaring: predators, packs, without sensitivity, morals or responsibility. In 2011, a report from the REACH Media Network highlighted some interesting observations based on their research surrounding, 'Media Representations of Black Young Men and Boys'. By using both quantitative and qualitative methodologies, they utilised content analysis, an approach used for systematically assessing and analysing written, verbal and visual communication, to the representation of black young men. Their very extensive research shows the following:

> [C]lose to 7 in 10 stories of black young men and boys related in some form to crime – a comparatively higher figure than in coverage of young men and boys more generally. Violent crime, murders, and gun and knife crime accounted for the majority of crime coverage featuring black young men and boys in the mainstream news, with little context or explanation for the reasons why crime was committed. (Cushion et al. 2011: 2)

Debates and arguments about causalities regarding these men and boy's over-representation in the criminal justice system are not new; however, there is no denying that media, politicians and policy-makers deliberately or inadvertently, sensationalise or stereotype their involvement in crime. Whilst legitimately challenging this stereotyping, I am not naïve enough to deny the challenges that respondents in my research highlighted regarding the 'code of the street' and the challenges associated with 'street-loyalties' and to live crime-free lives. This code has resulted in unsolved gang-related murders—some respondents said that loyalty means not snitching or selling your friend out, even if they are known to have taken a life. I am aware that Birmingham still has several such unsolved gang-related murders (Heale 2008; McLagan 2005). This code also means that individuals are doing prison sentences 'for a friend', so as not to implicate them, even if there is knowledge that they were present and involved in a serious criminal act.

However, although the code can be related to other groups of young men, Rich (2009), Anderson (2008) and McLagan (2005) consider its consequences for black young men. Anderson (2008), Heale (2008), Pitts (2008) and Gunter (2010) highlight further factors that may contribute to their involvement in activities, lifestyles and behaviours associated with gang association, criminality and violence. These include:

- A need for friendship or brotherhood
- A need for protection and security from other gangs/groups
- A need to make lots of money quickly
- The reduction of youth facilities and competent youth workers
- Easy access to weapons
- Family involvement in gang lifestyles
- The media glorification of the gang lifestyle
- A lack of success in school/education
- Feelings of boredom—nothing to do and
- Feelings of poor self-esteem and being misunderstood.

Gunter (2010) suggests that for some gangs fill a void for belonging and respect and offer a space to enhance their masculinity and feelings of power. Anderson (1999, 2008) and Rich's work (2009) offer insights into black youngsters' lives in some US inner-city areas. Anderson's ethnographic approach explores issues associated with youth violence, crime and social deprivation and their links to moral and ethical lifestyle choices. Rich's (2009) engagement with black young men emerged out of his curiosity as a medical doctor who had to deal with the physical and emotional trauma associated the shooting and maiming of young black men. His concern was not to become desensitised and detached from their pain and realities, but to enter a more critical conversation about how to engage, support and understand them effectively. His reflection is worth quoting at length here, as it supports the practice of humanising these young men:

> Behind the statistics and data, behind the observations of researchers like me and urban ethnographers like Elijah Anderson, are the young men themselves. Sadly, because of their social position and the legacy of violence, racism and poverty into which they have been born, they have become, for many, strange icons of fear. The details of news reports of shootings and stabbings obscure a young man with a story, a young man with real blood running through his veins. Without any access to their voices, we could easily formulate solutions that are out of sync with the realities of their lives and that would be ineffective or outright destructive. Without hearing their stories, we lose sight of the young men who hold real hope for the future, whose visions for community embrace peace and nonviolence. (2009: xv)

Whilst acknowledging the complex web of interactions highlighted by Rich and the challenges associated with young people's lives, it is important to note that most young people in urban and inner-city areas are able to engage with everyday living without involvement with the criminal justice process. In effect, their lifestyle choices and daily activities do not represent any major concerns (Anderson 2017; Regan and Hoeksma 2010). However, as highlighted in Glynn (2014) and Gunter's (2010) work, some of those caught up in the 'criminal justice web' because of their criminality, particularly its association with gangs and violence, have caused damage and devastation to individuals and communities. The moral panics around their activities have resulted in new and revised government legislation and policies regarding gun and knife crime, as highlighted in numerous UK Home Office reports (Anderson 2017). Having said that, the empirical work of Glynn (2014), Anderson (2017) and Brown et al. (2016) highlights that black young men and their families caught up in this context often feel detached and isolated from those in positions of power and influence who could offer them effective help and support to exit their criminal lifestyles.

The next section explores my work with the Bringing Hope charity and how it works to 'humanise' black young men through the 'way of love' outlined in the scripture above.

Bringing Hope's Faith-Based Approach to Humanising Black Young Men

There is no denying it, we can find evidence of good pastoral and ministerial support work offered by faith groups, in particular different church denominations across Birmingham and other UK cities. These range from food banks and lunch clubs to informal education and counselling to leadership training and community advocacy (Adedibu 2012; Anderson 2017). However, there is little evidence of systematic faith-group involvement in working with offenders and those involved in violence. Most of the research and literature on faith-based initiatives or the use of religion and spirituality is American. This began to change with my own research and that of Brown et al. (2016) and Deuchar (2018). Brown et al.'s (2016) evaluation of Bringing Hope charity's work says that faith-based interventions can improve offenders' lives. Whilst other forms of interventions, such as counselling, social work, probation support, coaching and mentoring have been utilised, my concern is focused on the development of a 'Christian response' to the realities of young black men's lives.

My research shows little UK evidence of faith-based initiatives dealing with gang association or serious violence, unlike the USA that has initiatives like, the Ten Point Coalition in Boston and Home Boys Industries in Los Angeles, projects dealing specifically engaging offenders, gang associates and criminally active individuals and families. Having mentioned the work of Bringing Hope, it is now necessary to focus on the approaches and perspectives we have developed over the years. Beyond the media's continued negative representations of black young men and ineffective engagement and support for those individuals and families seeking to exit negative lifestyles, my work with the Bringing Hope continues to penetrate their demonisation and vilification. Bringing Hope enables men in prison and community to explore notions of 'spirituality', 'self-reflection' and 'personal values' as a way of improving their self-concept, attitudes, thinking and behaviours and general well-being.

My research into the narratives of 14 black men aged between 21 and 35 highlights findings that became important for the work with Bringing Hope (Anderson 2015). Some of these men were Bringing Hope service users and their experiences influenced our thinking around how we worked with them and their families. There were ethical issues around interviewing men that I knew professionally. I wondered if my relationship with them would hinder their openness and honesty about their realities. I was conscious of the need to develop and maintain an 'outsider's' perspective, whilst acknowledging my biases. I needed to be rigorous and critical in the information gathering phase, as well as the analysis and evaluation processes. Having worked as a social worker and operated as a pastor in Birmingham, I was indeed familiar with such ethical considerations and regulations. Furthermore, Glynn's work with the project, 'Hard to Access Young People and Drugs Support Services' in Birmingham, shows that:

> Young black people have felt comforted by talking to someone who identifies with who they are, as opposed to their supposed social label. Likewise, disaffected white male and females who are embracing urban culture through music such as hip-hop, garage, drum 'n' bass, dancehall music, etc. have felt more at ease knowing that the researcher had a familiarity with the world they occupy. At all times positive reinforcement without judgment enabled those young people to feel at ease in expressing their views on their terms. (Glynn 2004: 19)

Fetterman's work (2010) also supports the advantage of being a 'known individual' in a community already suspicions of 'outsiders'. This validates the advantages of prior understanding and insights into the community or group being studied. From my position as insider/outsider, the men's responses developed around the following themes:

- Their childhood experiences and early socialisation
- The early/initial involvement in negative, criminal and challenging behaviours
- The impact of being 'On Street' or 'On Road' on self, family and community
- The role of faith, spirituality and religion on lifestyle choices
- The responsibility or blame for 'On Street' lifestyle choices
- Their views on a 'mother's heart'
- Their experiences of fathering and fatherhood
- The relevance or irrelevance of black majority churches to black young men.

I considered these themes as I developed the Life Cycle Perspective (in Fig. 25.2), which represents Bringing Hope's holistic perspective for engaging black young men and their families. Bringing Hope has taken very seriously the need to be family orientated in our work and when we are in contact with someone in need of support, we work with their family and friends wherever necessary.

Bringing Hope has now developed what we call the relationship building imperative, which we share with church leaders and statutory sector providers. This includes the following:

- Deciding how to engage (approaches and modes)
- Commitment and trust to be established
- Heart-to-heart, head-to-head exchanges in safe space
- Knowledge, thoughts and insights to be transferred
- Concerns, challenges and hopes to be expressed
- The unknown context (challenges, doubt and hopes)
- Developing mutual respect through relationship building processes
- Creating space for clarity, instruction and direction
- Planning and action together
- Reflection and review stage.

At the heart of my work with Bringing Hope is our love for the men and their families we work with. We take very seriously each stage of their journeys in the life cycle and remember that crises can emerge at multiple stages. Bringing Hope believes in building open, honest and loving relationships,

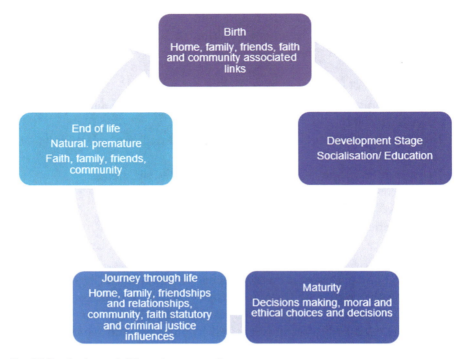

Fig. 25.2 Anderson's life cycle perspective

where trust becomes a valuable currency. This framework for BMCs to engage effectively with black young men applies the pastoral cycle of 'Experience', 'Analysis', 'Biblical Reflection' and 'Revised Action' in a modified form. The adapted version removes the need for biblical or theological reflection and includes moral and ethical reflection instead. The following questions represent this phase in the adapted cycle:

- Does my behaviour cause harm or distress to others?
- How am I influenced to make wrong or right choices?
- How do my actions and attitudes impact others?
- What systems or processes do I apply in seeking to be crime-free?
- What principles guide my actions?
- How important are faith or religion as factors to influence my choices?
- How honest am I about my personal feelings?

Whilst not an exhaustive list, a young man from the 'streets', for example, with no concept of church can use this tool without the fear of having to

Fig. 25.3 An adapted form of the PC for BYM

engage or understand the Bible, which can be a daunting task. He can be encouraged to share how he became involved in gangs or other criminal experiences and then analyses them together with the pastor or church personnel offering support for interpretation and research. His reflections then become ethical and moral one and biblical for the church personnel as the search for ways to develop the engagement. The pastoral cycle encourages both the BMCs and the young black men to reflect on and change their activities and practices (Fig. 25.3).

As Bringing Hope continues to use insights from practical theology alongside other perspectives, it inevitably grapples with the tensions between the BMCs beliefs, traditions and theologies and the lives, beliefs and traditions of black young men. However, Bringing Hope is committed to bringing greater synergy and harmony between both worlds better to meet the needs of these men. These issues remain a priority for its trustees and management team, who work to ensure that these concerns are on the agenda of key internal meetings, as well as planned meetings with church leaders and the black young men.

Conclusion

My research and pastoral experiences over the years of working with black young men have been challenging at times, because of the evidence of misunderstandings and misrepresentations associated with their 'realities'.

I have found that that the programmes and activities within statutory, faith and community sectors regarding them seldom consider their social, political and historical experiences, which for Bringing Hope are crucial in the building relationships of trust and understanding with them. This chapter argues for a re-imagining of our work with BYM. This may mean an active use of the pastoral cycle as highlighted above. It also shows how the interdisciplinary processes between practical theology and social science can be mutually supportive in the work with young black men and the realisation of the love, care and support described in the passage from 1 Corinthians 13. It also echoes Cone's (1986) view that churches that proclaim Christ and support the principles and activities associated with faith as a verbal and active manifestation are obliged to support those identified in the Luke 4:18 or Isaiah1: 17–18 texts. That is, they need to seek justice, support oppressed and fatherless individuals, empower widows and minister to prisoners, whilst bringing comfort and good news to the poor. Cone (1986) concludes that:

> When Faith is understood as a commitment to an ultimate concern, then it is obvious that there can be no separation between faith and obedience, because obedience determines faith. I know your faith not by what you confess but only by what you do. (1986: 40)

Finally, the need for continued reflection and questioning about our effective and relevance to these young men and their families and communities remains vitally important.

References

Adedibu, B. (2012). *Coat of Many Colours: The Origin, Growth, Distinctiveness and Contributions of Black Majority Churches to British Christianity*. Gloucester: Wisdom Summit.

Anderson, C. (2015). *Towards a Practical Theology for Effective Responses to Black Young Men Associated with Crime for Black Majority Churches*. Ph.D. thesis, Birmingham University.

Anderson, C. (2017). *Commission on Gangs and Violence: Uniting to Improve Safety*. Birmingham: Office of West Midlands Police and Crime Commissioner.

Anderson, E. (1999). *Code of the Street: Decency, Violence, and the Moral Life of the Inner City*. New York: W. W. Norton.

Anderson, E. (Ed.). (2008). *Against the Wall: Poor, Young, Black, and Male*. Philadelphia: University of Pennsylvania Press.

Ballard, P., & Pritchard, J. (2006). *Practical Theology in Action: Christian Thinking in the Service of Church and Society* (2nd ed.). London: SPCK.

Bradford, B. (2017). Stop and Search and Police Legitimacy. Abingdon, Oxon: Routledge.

Brown, G. (2015). *Urban Gun Crime from the Margins: An Auto/Biographical Study of African Caribbean Communities to 'Urban Gun Crime'.* Ph.D. thesis, Coventry University.

Brown, G. C., Bos, E., & Brady, G. (2016). *Hear Our Voices: Exploring How Bringing Hope's Damascus Road Second Chance Prison and Community Programme Supports Black Men in Prison and in the Community.* Coventry: Coventry University.

Byfield, C. (2008). *Black Boys Can Make It: How They Overcome the Obstacles to University in the UK and USA.* Stoke on Trent: Trentham Books.

Cone, J. (1986). *Speaking the Truth: Ecumenism, Liberation, and Black Theology.* Grand Rapids, MI: Eerdmans.

Cork, L. (2005). *Supporting Black Pupils and Parents: Understanding and Improving Home-School Relations.* Abingdon, Oxon: Routledge.

Cushion, S., Moore, K., & Jewell, J. (2011). *Media Representations of Black Young Men and Boys: Report of the Reach Media Monitoring Project.* London: DCLG.

Davidson, K., & Alexis, J. (2012). *Education: A Pathway to Success for Black Children.* London: KAD Publishing.

Davis, R. (2010). *The Black Church: Relevant or Irrelevant in the 21st Century?* Macon, GA: Smith and Helwys.

Deuchar, R. (2018). *Gangs and Spirituality: Global Perspectives.* Switzerland: Springer.

Fetterman, D. (2010). *Ethnography: Step-By-Step* (3rd ed.). London: Sage.

Glynn, M. (2004). *Hard to Access Young People and Drugs Support Services in Birmingham: Final Report.* Birmingham: Birmingham Drug Action Team.

Glynn, M. (2014). *Black Men, Invisibility and Crime: Towards a Critical Race Theory of Desistance.* London: Routledge.

Grant, P. (2006). *Saving Our Sons: Strategies and Advice for the Parents of Afrikan Teenage Sons.* Nottingham: Navig8or Press.

Gunter, A. (2010). *Growing Up Bad: Black Youth, Road Culture and Badness in an East London Neighbourhood.* London: Tufnell Press.

Heale, J. (2008). *One Blood: Inside Britain's New Gang Culture.* London: Pocket Books.

Heitink, G. (1999). *Practical Theology: History, Theory, Action Domains: Manual for Practical Theology.* Michigan: Eerdmans.

Irwin-Rogers, K., & Pinkney, C. (2017). Social Media as a Catalyst and Trigger for Youth Violence: Catch 22.

Kinast, R. (1999). *Making Faith-Sense: Theological Reflection in Everyday Life.* Collegeville, MA: Liturgical Press.

Madhubuti, H. (1991). *Black Men: Obsolete, Single, Dangerous? The Afrikan American Family in Transition.* Chicago: Third World Press.

McLagan, G. (2005). *Guns and Gangs: The Inside Story of the War on Our Streets*. London: Allison and Bushy.

Newburn, T. (2017). *Criminology* (3rd ed.). London: Routledge.

Osmer, R. (2008). *Practical Theology: An Introduction*. Michigan: Eerdmans.

Pitts, J. (2008). *Reluctant Gangsters: The Changing Face of Youth Crime*. Devon: Willan.

Regan, P., & Hoeksma, L. (2010). *Fighting Change: Tackling Britain's Gang Culture*. London: Hodder and Stoughton.

Rendall, S., & Morag, S. (2005). *Excluded from School: Systemic Practice for Mental Health and Education*. Hove, East Sussex: Routledge.

Rich, J. (2009). *Wrong Place, Wrong Time: Trauma and Violence in the Lives of Young Black Men*. Maryland: Johns Hopkins University Press.

Scarman, L. (1982). *The Scarman Report: The Brixton Disorders 10–12 April 1981*. Middlesex: Penguin.

Sebastian, K., & Day, K. (2017). *Companion to Public Theology*. Boston: Brill.

Thompson, J., Pattison, S., & Thompson, R. (2008). *SCM Study Guide: Theological Reflection*. London: SCM Press.

Walton, H. (2014). *Writing Methods in Theological Reflection*. London: SCM Press.

Woodward, J., & Pattison, S. (Eds.). (2000). *The Blackwell Reader in Pastoral and Practical Theology*. Oxford: Blackwell.

Part IX

Social Justice and Disability: Voices from the Inside

Chrissie Rogers

Introduction

The following chapters engage with disability and social justice auto/ biographies. They are written from the position of the 'insider' (Cooper and Rogers 2015), an insider as narrating research practices (Rogers), as a mother to a disabled son (Saville) and as an Autistic woman (Simmons). All three chapters weave personal accounts whereby the researchers discuss their positionality and are reflexive in their analysis. The authors highlight through recounting challenges within their specific research contexts, that suffering via auto/biographical storytelling can be a form of resistance that invites social justice (Frank 1995, 2001). Considering this further, Frank (1995: 170) draws on Cassell's three conditions of suffering. In short, the conditions of suffering:

1. involve the whole person.
2. can take place within a state of severe distress.
3. can occur in relation to any aspect of the person.

Frank adds to Cassell's conditions a fourth and fifth which are:

4. resistance
5. its social nature.

Frank's (1995) fourth condition is significant here, as he proposes that telling stories are a form of resistance (and arguably are socially just), which can be considered in the following chapters as the authors auto/biographically discuss carrying out deeply qualitative criminal justice research (Rogers), mothering and dwarfism (Saville), and covering and autism (Simmons). In laying bare their auto/biographies, reflexivity and trust between the story-teller and her narrative(s) are therefore important.

Furthermore, by making the private-public, in this instance the complexity and emotional work of the researcher, mother and Autistic narrator, all three authors can make a claim to 'insider status' but recognise that this is at times messy and uncomfortable. Moreover, while there is increasing literature on, (Bochner and Ellis 2016; Plummer 2009; Potter 1998; Stanley 1992, 1993), and engagement with (Sparkes 2002; Williams 2006) auto/biography, auto/ethnography and creativity within social research, there is still relatively little on the actual practicalities of the problem of managing the self when close to the research material as an 'insider' (Rogers 2018; Rogers and Tuckwell 2016), or how to craft social science. However, in dismissing the auto/biographic, there is a risk of devaluing the stories and voices that impact upon and are impacted by the broader structures of the social world.

The following chapters, as indicated, span sociologically significant areas that include the role of qualitative researcher in the context of those who are, or have been, in the criminal justice system (CJS) and who have learning difficulties (Rogers), broad assumptions about mothering and dwarfism (Saville), and the presentation of the self from the perspective of an Autistic woman (Simmons). Significantly they all highlight aspects of a sociopolitical death of certain research practices or of disabled others. That is for example, where disabled people are not heard or listened to because of partial storytelling, exclusion from mainstream society and stigmatising systems that leave them affectively missing from sociopolitical participation and narratives.

The first chapter highlights how the emotive research journey from the very inception is unpredictable, chaotic and often hidden from the post-project sanitised formal presentation. Rogers' auto/biographical fieldnote reflections evidence how participants, the researcher and their woven stories go 'missing' due to marginalisation and bureaucratic processes, resulting in sociopolitical death. Saville's chapter questions whether experiences of dwarfism could ever be separated from the exploitative historical and cultural portrayals which have plagued and blighted the fight for rights and legitimacy both inside and outside of a community. Saville's auto/biographical reflections as a mother to a son with dwarfism are merged in pursuit of social justice. Simmons' chapter utilises auto/biographical writing, as an autistic woman. She examines disability within the academy and reflects upon her experiences of 'covering' as 'normal'. Critically, she considers the decision-making process behind her reasons to present at an academic conference as a hybrid of an Autistic and non-autistic researcher.

All three chapters highlight the importance, benefits and challenges of doing 'insider' auto/biographical disability research with an emphasis on social justice. What they also implicitly or explicitly emphasise is how critical the sociological imagination is (Mills 1959). That is, how 'personal troubles' of the researcher, mother and Autistic woman are not in a private vacuum and that 'public issues' of research practices, stigma and injustices occur. As it is, for Mills (1959), the private and intimate world is often mistaken for something that can only be understood psychologically or psychoanalytically. However, via auto/biography and a sociological imagination studying the personal lives of individuals, questions and answers about the broader social picture can be addressed. In the case of the following chapters, these relate to research processes, criminal justice, disability, mothering and stigma. Therefore, as outlined in the introduction of this volume, sociological research benefits from considering biography, history and social structure in an authentically creative and a theoretically rigorous manner to highlight sociopolitical death and enable sociopolitical life (Frauley 2016, Rogers this volume; Mills 1959).

Disability and Social Justice

Stories of stigmatisation and embodied injustices are told that include auto/biographic and auto/ethnographic narratives (Harvey 2018; Rogers 2009; Rogers and Tuckwell 2016; Ryan and Runswick-Cole 2008; Thomas 1999). Furthermore, stigmatised identities, social control, injustice and the social/political gaze occur as persistent themes throughout much disability research (Morris 1991; Oliver 1990, 1996; Wilde 2018). Hence, in discussing disability and social justice it would be negligent to attempt to understand any social tradition or norm, for example, the privileging of scientism, intellectual capacity, aesthetic beauty or culturally prescribed presentations of the self without considering its biography, history and social structure.

As suggested, Mills' (1959) proposes history, biography and social structure as crucial within a sociological imagination and asks, what is the structure of the society, where does it stand in human history and what kinds of men and women live in this society? These questions are pertinent in discussing disability and social justice as it could be asked, what is the political, economic and moral context for disabled people? What penalty occurs for a person who breaks the law? What are the laws and who enforces them? How does someone experience normative difference, intellectually, physically or emotionally? How is living with a disabling condition experienced on a day to day basis? What does 'normal' even look like and how is existing outside of this norm experienced? Essentially, what are the social norms of any given society in any given period? Clearly not conforming to the social norms of a society in history differs based on the culture of that time and place (Oliver 1990).

Considering norms therefore, Davis' (2006: 3–6) work on the construction of normalcy reflects upon *Quetelet* the French statistician, Defoe's *Robinson Crusoe* and Marx's work, in positioning 'the normal' and 'the average'. These norms relate, for example, to personhood, civilisation, morality, the body and health. But normality is culturally, historically and auto/biographically specific and more often based on *differences* to a norm. So, one could be described as 'defective', spoilt, stigmatised or 'deformed' (Davis 1995) in any specific time or place. Imagine therefore living with impairments or mental ill health in the seventeenth century where those defined as 'mad' 'bad' and 'sick' were incarcerated in the old leprosaria (Foucault 1967, 1973). Medical science during that period developed and played a role in the production of knowledge and classificatory systems of those who were physically and mentally ill. After the French Revolution, those defined as 'mad', 'bad' and 'sick' were separated further, even if they were institutionalised in the same building, they remained segregated from society (Foucault 1967, 1973).

Notably, during the eighteenth century 'mad', 'bad', 'imbecile', 'lunatic', 'dull', 'cretin', 'idiot' and 'feebleminded' were all legitimate medical terms for those whose behaviour or ability was outside of the norms of society (Goodey 2011). Enlightenment philosophy promoted science, truth, reason and rationality, all of which have been persistently privileged. Scientism moreover dominated knowledge production which included medicine and health and the importance of 'the cure'. Regarding disability, by the latter third of twentieth century in the UK, the social model of disability paved the way for change and was groundbreaking in understanding the differences between disability and impairment, which subsequently affects understanding of social norms around disability and access for example. Prior to the social model, the medical model placed emphasis on impairment and therefore pathologised disabled people. The disability was considered with-in and the person with impairments in need of repair. As such, disability according to Oliver (1996: 22) was considered:

a form of disadvantage which is imposed on top of one's impairment, that is, the disadvantage or restriction of activity caused by a contemporary social organisation that takes little or no account of people with physical impairments.

Therefore, barriers to social and physical inclusion were in place to subjugate those deemed as inferior human beings, leaving them potentially sociopolitically dead.

In terms of auto/biography and the 'insider', disability researchers have faced criticism about their 'involvement' and subjectivity when researching issues close to their hearts. Rogers and Tuckwell (2016: 625) comment that 'often research is maligned if there are too many emotions involved', and Ribbens and Edwards (1998: 13) suggest:

> [t]he central dilemma for us as researchers is that we are seeking to explore such privately based knowledges and personal understandings, but to then reconstitute them within publicly based disciplinary knowledge.

Arguably 'focussing outward on the social and cultural aspects' of personal experience, in exposing the vulnerable self with a view to 'move through, refract, and resist cultural interpretations' (Ellis and Bochner 2003: 209) is critical for creative, authentic intellectual discussion. Furthermore, Sparkes comments, '[m]emories serve particular personal and social functions within the stories we tell ourselves, and others, to explain who we are, what we are, and where we are in life at a particular time and place' (2002: 157). Shakespeare (2006: 195) moreover asserts, 'Just because someone is disabled does not mean they have an automatic insight into the lives of other disabled people'. However, he too recognises having an experience of disability or parenting a disabled person can offer some insight and open debate.

Critically, questions have been raised about authenticity and the self-indulgent nature of the personal leaking into social science research, so what can be said about the 'so what', 'who cares', 'what's the point' questions? Sparkes (2002: 211) responds to those who are disparaging of auto/biographic narrative and asks about social research:

> What substantive contribution to our understanding of social life does it make? What is its aesthetic merit, impact and ability to express complex realities? Does it display reflexivity, authenticity, fidelity and believability? Is it engaging and evocative? Does it promote dialogue and show potential for social action? Does the account work for the reader and is it useful?

Pondering further on authenticity and self-indulgence, arguably in response to a postmodern/structuralist turn, Potter (1998: 173) maintains that those who 'aim to dazzle' with their clever prose are not delivering enlightening research (ibid.: 188). Indeed, in reflecting upon how critique is both understood and produced, perhaps such a lack in story, in narrative, in creativity, hides the fact that the writer has not 'the analytic and articulative capacity to extract and clearly communicate the insights of literature' (ibid.). Stories crafted historically and culturally that involve personal troubles, via auto/biography, autoethnography, life story, fiction, film, photographs and poems, can promote dialogue and show potential for social action and policy changes in rigorously exploring, analysing and critiquing broader social structures (e.g. Potter 1998; Wilde 2018). It is within this disability and social justice context that the subsequent chapters sit.

Chapter Outlines

A feminist and auto/biographic approach along with critiquing social scientific method is highlighted in Rogers' chapter as, while not telling an *auto/biographical* story of offending and criminal justice, she does tell one of her self as the researcher, and how much of the research story is missing, both procedurally and substantively. For example, when she first proposed research with adults who have been through the CJS and their families, she naively assumed her previous links with educators and mothers would be a gatekeeping coup. However, this was not the case. What Rogers found, is that emotive life-story research, from the very inception is unpredictable, chaotic and often hidden from the post-project sanitised formal research processes. Moreover, as data goes 'missing' in several ways (e.g. methodological practices not spoken about, hard to pin down respondents) which can lead to the sociopolitical death of marginalised and oppressed people—the participants and the qualitative researcher.

Saville's chapter reflects on her experiences as an average-statured mother to a child with dwarfism as she explores her evolving relationship with her son through conversational extracts and acknowledges his own autonomy and understanding of his disabled identity. Woven through her narrative Saville considers how the dwarfed body has been the focus of a curious, and often stigmatised gaze in societies throughout history, particularly as the public's fetishism with Othering the dwarfed body gave rise to the 'freak shows' of the nineteenth century. Saville explains how the twenty-first-century entertainment platform has switched, from 'freak show' to reality television. Critically, these cultural portrayals and links to mythology overshadow how our society views *people* with dwarfism. In her chapter, she notes how the dwarfed body is still the objectified commodity of the entertainment industry, and what this may mean for social justice within this community and is overwhelmed by the fear that twenty-first-century society still views dwarf children, and their community, as not quite human. Saville talks of the notion of justice and how it is intrinsically tied into social constructions of humanity, and what it means to be human. She asks, can dwarfism ever be separated from the exploitative historical and cultural portrayals which have plagued and blighted fights for social justice both inside and outside of the community?

Critically, disabled children and adults, particularly those who are intellectually impaired or who have social and emotional difficulties, and/or autism spectrum conditions are still marginalised and stigmatised in the twenty-first century as academic ability and rationality remains revered. Aspects of this are drawn out auto/ biographically by Simmons' chapter, in an exploration of how she presents as a hybrid of her autistic and non-autistic self. Simmons tells of how she disclosed her diagnosis to colleagues at an academic conference, yet, the internalisation of an embodied stigmatised identity resulted in her feeling inferior and positioned in some kind of 'disability closet'. Simmons explores the experience of 'covering' her autism and presenting as 'normal', at the conference. As a result of her exploration of Erving Goffman's (1963) work and her auto/biography, she examines disability within the academy. Significantly she reflects upon her the decision-making process and reasons to present as a hybrid of an autistic and non-autistic researcher.

All three chapters reflect upon history, biography and social structure in relation to disability and social justice. Past narratives form discourses on social justice/injustice, stigma/tolerance and have been woven into legislation and cultural perceptions of what 'normal'/'abnormal' is. For example, what are 'normal' or acceptable research practices? How is living in an ableist society experienced? What differences, if any, are tolerated? Critically, a person, a custom, a method or behaviour might be tolerated, as in, the person, custom, way of being/doing are put up with and not necessarily accepted in any one society. Indeed, tolerance ideologically is the dark side of diversity as neoliberalism utters empty rhetoric around social justice while different practices and ways of being are 'celebrated' (see also Davis 2013). This diversity rhetoric is something we need to caution as Rogers, Saville and Simmons explore sociopolitical death and interrogate the disabled and unjust world around them.

References

Bochner, A. P., & Ellis, C. (Eds.). (2016). *Evocative Autoethnography: Writing Lives and Telling Stories.* New York: Routledge.

Bochner, A. P., & Ellis, C. (2003). An Introduction to the Arts and Narrative Research: Art as Inquiry. *Qualitative Inquiry, 9*(4), 506–514. https://doi.org/10.1177/1077800403254394.

Cooper, L., & Rogers, C. (2015). Mothering and 'insider' dilemmas: Feminist sociologists in the research process. *Sociological Research Online, 20*(2), 5.

Davis, L. J. (1995). *Enforcing normalcy: Disability, Deafness, and the Body.* London: Verso.

Davis, L. J. (2006). Constructing normalcy: The bell curve, the novel, and the invention of the disabled body in the nineteenth century. In L. J. Davis (Ed.), *The Disability Studies Reader* (2nd ed.). Oxon: Routledge.

Davis, L. J. (2013). *The End of Normal: Identity in a Bicultural Era.* Ann Arbor: The University of Michigan Press.

Foucault, M. (1967). *Madness and Civilisation.* Cambridge: Tavistock Publications.

Foucault, M. (1973). *The birth of the Clinic.* Kent: Tavistock Publications.

Frauley, J. (Ed.). (2016). *C. Wright Mills and the Criminological Imagination: Prospects for Creative Inquiry.* London: Routledge.

Frank, A. W. (1995). *The Wounded Storyteller: Body, Illness and Ethics.* Chicago: The University of Chicago Press.

Frank, A. W. (2001). Can we Research Suffering? *Qualitative Health Research, 11*(3), 353–362. https://doi.org/10.1177/104973201129119154.

Goodey, C. F. (2011). *A History of Intelligence and "Intellectual Disability".* Surrey: Ashgate.

Harvey, J. (2018). *A Sociological Approach to Acquired Brain Injury and Identity.* Abingdon: Routledge.

Morris, J. (1991). *Pride Against Prejudice: Transforming Attitudes to Disability.* London: The Women's Press ltd.

Oliver, M. (1990). *The Politics of Disablement.* Basingstoke: Palgrave Macmillan.

Oliver, M. (1996). *Understanding Disability: From Theory to Practice.* Basingstoke: Palgrave Macmillan.

Mills, C. W. (1959). *The Sociological Imagination.* New York: Oxford University Press.

Plummer, K. (2009). Autoethnography of sexualities: Introduction. *Sexualities, 12*(3), 267–269.

Potter, G. (1998). Truth in fiction, science and criticism. *Journal of Literary Semantics, 27*(3), 173–189.

Ribbens, J., & Edwards, R. (Eds.). (1998). *Feminist Dilemmas in Qualitative Research: Public Knowledge and Private Lives.* London: Sage.

Rogers, C. (2009). (S)excerpts from a life told: Sex, gender and learning disability. *Sexualities, 12*(3), 270–288.

Rogers, C. (2018). Life stories, criminal justice and caring research. In G. Noblit. (Ed.), *Oxford Research Encyclopedia of Education.* New York: Oxford University Press.

Rogers, C., with Tuckwell, S. (2016). Co-constructed research and intellectual disability: An exploration of friendship, intimacy and being human. *Sexualities, 19*(5–6), 623–640.

Ryan, S., & Runswick-Cole, K. (2008). Repositioning mothers: Mothers, disabled children and disability studies. *Disability and Society, 23*(3), 199–210.

Shakespeare, T. (2006). *Disability Rights and Wrongs.* Oxon: Routledge.

Sparkes, A. C. (2002). Autoethnography: Self-indulgence or something more? In A. Bochner & C. Ellis (Eds.), *Ethnographically Speaking: Autoethnography, Literature, and Aesthetics.* New York: Altamira Press.

Stanley, L. (1992). *The Auto/Biographical I.* Manchester: Manchester University Press.

Stanley, L. (1993). On auto/biography in sociology. *Sociology, 27*(1), 41–52.

Thomas, C. (1999). *Female Forms: Experiencing and Understanding Disability.* Buckingham: Open University Press.

Wilde, A. (2018). *Film, Comedy, and Disability Understanding Humour and Genre in Cinematic Constructions of Impairment and Disability.* Oxon: Routledge.

Williams, D. J. (2006). Autoethnography in offender rehabilitation research and practice: addressing the "Us vs. Them" Problem. *Contemporary Justice Review 9*(1), 23–38.

26

Missing Data and Socio-Political Death: The Sociological Imagination Beyond the Crime

Chrissie Rogers

Introduction

This chapter is about missing data and its core socio-political death, as outlined in the section introduction. For example, socio-political death is where disabled people are not heard or listened to because of partial storytelling, exclusion from mainstream society and stigmatising systems that leave them affectively missing from socio-political participation and narratives. Missing data are partial stories that equate to the socio-political death of marginalised and oppressed people (e.g. prisoners and their families, intellectually and physically disabled people, those on the autism spectrum and people with mental health conditions). Marginalised and oppressed people are silenced due to researchers having limited access to them, a disabling condition, participant scepticism about 'powerful' others, personal trauma and governing and punitive institutional practices.[1] This chapter is also about my auto/biographical research narrative. Auto/biographies from the position of the researcher and/or research participants are too often missing

---

[1]For example, restrictive ethical procedures, the research excellence framework (REF) in the UK and a disdain for creative methods.

C. Rogers (✉)
University of Kent, Canterbury, UK
e-mail: c.a.rogers@kent.ac.uk

© The Author(s) 2020
J. M. Parsons and A. Chappell (eds.), *The Palgrave Handbook of Auto/Biography*,
https://doi.org/10.1007/978-3-030-31974-8_26

in the post-project sanitised data analysis. Subsequently, this leads to the socio-political death of certain communities, people and research practices.

Linking missing data and socio-political death to auto/biographical narrative, I reflect upon a story I have told about nothingness and trauma—a twin miscarriage (Rogers 2017a). In that story, I paint a pen picture of something that is missing, but also silenced within the context of women's leaky bodies. Scott (2018: 15) has more recently discussed nothingness and suggests two categories that are:

> social nothingness: doing/being a non-something (through acts of commission) and not-doing/not-being something (through acts of omission). In the first case, nothing is demonstrably performed through non-participation, eschewal and repudiation, leading to the constitution of symbolic objects such as non- and never-identities, conspicuous absence and rejected options. In the second case, nothing is more passively arrived at by default, through failures to act, inertia and unrealised potential.

Both these aspects of nothingness can result in missing data that lead to socio-political death. Yet telling and hearing the personal stories of marginalised and oppressed others and then embedding them within a broader sociological landscape will undoubtedly aid resistance and socio-political living (see also Frank 1995, 2001; Plummer 2013).

Below I introduce a sociological imagination and discuss fieldnotes, the blurring of boundaries and the importance of situating the self within sociological research. I go on to map from scholars and my own study, how social science research practices can lead to socio-political death and injustice. I then outline the research project this chapter is grounded upon. The following sections chart my auto/biographical narratives and fieldnotes with a view to identify the challenges faced when carrying out deeply qualitative research with marginalised others. I conclude by returning to Mills' (1959) sociological imagination and suffering as auto/biographical storytelling can play a part in resistance to injustice and socio-political death.

A Sociological Imagination—Looking Back, Moving Forward

Sociology and criminological sociology have long since had a tradition where fieldnotes, interviews and auto/biography play an integral part in the research process and the documentation of life. They have also sought to uncover and bring to the social and political table the lives of people who are marginalised, stigmatised, excluded, oppressed and poor. Furthermore, the blurring of boundaries between a fieldworker's personal and researcher life is evident (Goffman 2014; Worley et al. 2016). For example, from early twentieth century Anderson and Park ([1923]), Becker ([1963] 1991) and Whyte ([1943] 1993) carried out deeply qualitative research in areas of homelessness, deviance and criminality. They drew upon interview data, fieldnotes and auto/biography to construct narratives that were culturally, politically and historically challenging.

More recently, Goffman (2014) in her ethnography *On the Run* has received significant critique from both inside and outside the academy as to how she wrote about her findings as highlighted by Lewis-Kraus (2016: n.p.). Talking about Goffman, he said:

> another young professor told me, with the air of reverent exasperation that people use to talk about her, "Alice used a writing style that today you can't really use in the social sciences." He sighed and began to trail off. "In the past," he said with some astonishment, "they really did write that way." The book smacked, some sociologists argued, of a kind of swaggering adventurism that the discipline had long gotten over.

Putting aside any ethical discussion that one might have, this comment alone regarding the style of writing that is expected within social research is deeply problematic as it assumes there is a *right way of writing*—perhaps objective—and that any deviation from such a style lacks rigour and academic credibility.

Arguably sociological research still has much to learn from deeply qualitative and auto/biographical narratives as Reisman and Becker ([1984] 2017) commenting on the work of Hughes' (a key figure in Chicago School sociology) reveal he (Hughes) would get students to reflect upon their personal history. He said small events help to highlight larger matters and proffered that looking from the inside out aided a sociological understanding (ibid.: viii–ix). And while perhaps not considered the best teacher of his time, his views on the discipline were convincing, particularly as he was 'dismayed by the boundaries between the humanities and social sciences, between history and sociology' (Reisman and Becker [1984] 2017: xii). It is therefore significant that Hughes regarded the interview as an important tool in sociological research because it was 'able to surmount barriers of class, occupation, status, gender, race, even nation' (ibid.: xii). Also, during this period, Robert E. Park played a defining role in the Chicago

School, where sociology students were encouraged to go and get the seats of their pants dirty while carrying out qualitative research (Worley et al. 2016). Both Park and Hughes had influence on the nature of 'doing' sociological research, recording the micro-politics of everyday life and the blurring of boundaries between the auto/biographical self and other during the twentieth century.

Although there was much notable qualitative inquiry throughout the twentieth century, by the late 1950s, Mills (1959) had written 'The Sociological Imagination' as he was frustrated with the direction of sociological research. Namely, that there was a glut of atheoretical empirical studies where statistics or narrative had little or no theoretical base and abstract theory, where philosophical and theoretical writing was not grounded in the micro-politics of everyday life.[2] Mills (1959) proposed that sociological research include history, biography and social structure to interrogate the 'personal troubles' and 'public issues' of society. That is, private experiences can open a window into the auto/biographical micro-politics of society, but that these experiences are embedded within much broader political, structural and historical contexts. For example, experiencing continual stigmatisation and exclusion as a child in school and then breaking the law as an adult are a personal trouble (Gillies 2016). Experiencing violent attacks from a son and then caring about him while he is incarcerated are a personal trouble (Condry and Miles 2014, 2016; Holt 2013). Yet crime and violence are public issues, as the law is rooted in legal and moral mores of the social structure at any given time. So how the criminal justice system (CJS) processes a criminal act, what punishment is recommended for that crime and how others perceive and treat the lawbreaker is publicly *and* sociologically significant. So significant, the following sub-section draws on lengthy narratives from auto/biographic/ethnographic research and fieldnotes (Williams 2006; Johns 2018; Fish 2018) and my auto/biographical research fieldnotes as a way into storying missing data, auto/biography and social justice methodologically.

---

[2]I could discuss Wootton's (1959) work, as a woman scholar who, for all intents and purposes, discredited 'value-free' social science and was a contemporary of Mills (1959) as she has been largely airbrushed out of sociological storytelling and has therefore gone 'missing', but this would take us in a slightly different direction.

Resisting Socio-Political Death

I'm not worthy of being loved, am I? I devastated my family. I am too skeptical. Sometimes I drink alcohol. I left Church. I divorced. I've made too many wrong decisions. I hurt everyone; except one little person, the person who matters most to me. I can't hurt her. Tears roll down my cheeks and my crying won't stop. My eyes burn and there is a pounding inside my head. I notice that my fist hurts now and my knuckles are bleeding. Most of all, my heart hurts. I need help – professional help. (Williams 2006: 33)

Most days, he carries a box cutter and an ice pick on him, just in case, just like you do in jail, except jail you make them yourself. His preferred weapon inside was a modified toothbrush: you shave off all the bristles with a razor, then melt razor blades into the head, in different directions, so it doesn't matter which way you cut someone, it'll cut them. […] During the hour and a half I spend with Scott, we become 'sort of friends', as he puts it: 'I might be a thief but mate because I know you, you could leave your purse there with five grand in it and I wouldn't touch a cent because I know you. And we're sort of friends now, you know?' […] Driving home, I am aware of the clinging sense of wretchedness. I feel heavy with the weight of Scott's story and with what it means to be his 'friend'. (Johns 2018: 2–3)

Building friendships was difficult to avoid. There were a few instances where one of the clients 'took me under her wing' and I spent more time with some of the women rather than others. […] Spending time on the wards was enjoyable, but also distressing, intense and sometimes daunting. I had some fun with the clients and staff, but seeing people feeling angry, spending time with weeping women who had just self-harmed and listening to some stories from people's pasts was extremely distressing. (Fish 2018: 10–11)

I started the interview with Mum and her son wandered into the lounge and said, 'where's the axe?!' Apparently, he wanted to chop some wood in the garden. Who knew? Then after being in the garden, and having cut his finger, he walked past with a knife; not a kitchen knife, but one in a sheath. I mean he's 22, been in 'special' schools, got mental health problems, not been out of prison that long, and he now wanted to be interviewed. I had said 'okay', but I hadn't planned for it at this time. I also didn't know if the axe and knife business were for effect, to provoke a reaction. Perhaps if a social worker or probation officer, someone else, perhaps they might have said something? But I didn't. I didn't bat an eyelid, I mean what am I going to say? 'What are you going to do with that knife?' To be perfectly honest, I didn't feel in any danger. (personal fieldnotes, Autumn 2016)

One of the things so far about all of this is the enormity of the relational ground work that you have to do, or that is appropriate to do in order to access and importantly maintain connections with participants. And then get, let's say, some kind of interview. Because ultimately the people I'm talking to have chaotic lives, mental health problems, learning difficulties/disabilities, medical problems, incarcerated or offending sons. One mother I interviewed hasn't, as yet, agreed to a second interview. She said she wanted one. We've had some communications, and since all the prison riots stuff - that has been an issue. I have also had contact with another mother, and it was touch and go if she was going to have another interview, and then weeks and weeks of no communication and then I'll get a contact. Then there's this negotiation of whether we are going to meet. She lives a long way from me, and she said in an email that she and her son were suicidal. I'd interviewed both her and her son, previously. But was I going to get to see here again? Another participant ex-prisoner told me about her stage 4 throat cancer and during the interview had to take her morphine and was awaiting treatment. Then she corresponded telling me she'd had her voice box removed! But then no contact, and sometimes you just wonder what has happened and even if people are still alive! (personal fieldnotes, February 2017)

The first excerpt here from Williams (2006) is drawn from his autoethnographic research around prisoner rehabilitation. It is not clear whether the voice narrated is that of his own or of a research participant. It *could* be either, but it is his. The second two excerpts are from Johns' (2018) and Fish's (2018) ethnographies. Johns and Fish are evidently talking about their research participants and how their own voice and indeed their own feelings are affected by the research process. The final excerpts are fieldnotes from my current research (outlined below) that highlight both the 'risky' and emotive elements and the auto/biographical features that ground this chapter.

What these narratives underline quite explicitly is that carrying out qualitative research, whether the researcher is auto/biographically part of the substantive subject or auto/biographically integrated into the research process, is challenging, practically and emotionally. Such sociological research can leak into everyday life for the researcher, as he/she makes connections between his or her participants and his or her own biography. For example, Fassin (2017) remarks on subjectivity and objectivity within his prison ethnography, while reflecting upon the comments of an elderly inmate who said, 'to understand something you have to live it' (ibid.: 296). Fassin (ibid.) continued:

Speaking within benevolent certainty, he [the elderly inmate] sought to alert me to the pointlessness of my enterprise: "you can't do an objective study of a prison. You're going to write on the basis of what we say. But to be able to analyse something, you have to experience it." A striking paradox, in which he seemed to be asserting that subjectivity as the necessary condition for objectivity.

In many ways, this paradox is critical within auto/biographic sociology and when considering the sociological (or criminological) imagination (Frauley 2016; Mills 1959; Young 2011). I am not suggesting that sociological research ought to be objective, but like Mills (1959), and scholars since (e.g. Frauley 2016; Stanley 1992, 2013), the micro-world of personal storytelling, whether auto/biographically or via others' life stories, the macro-world of culture and politics, and historical context is significant within sociological and criminological research. Yet notably, as Carrabine commenting on Mills states, 'the more radical implications of his [Mills] argument over how the sociological imagination can offer liberation from oppressive conditions are largely forgotten' (2015: 73).

Perhaps this could be interpreted as missing data and socio-political death, as research processes and outputs are sanitised: cleaned up omitting the dirty and messy parts of social life, including that of the researcher's own embodied auto/biography, as highlighted above, for example, by Lewis-Kraus (2016) on Alice Goffman. But missing data and therefore socio-political death are two-fold, for as we 'clean up' the research, perhaps via overly bureaucratic ethics procedures, or research excellence governance, we survey: (1) *Whose* story is important and (2) *How* we hear these stories. Moreover, are we unable to hear these stories because they are simply too emotionally traumatic to tell, especially if we sanitise the process? Conceivably, if due to restrictive ethics procedures we are unable to access what might be considered high-risk research, we will never hear the stories of those people, groups and communities who are most oppressed. If we fear reprisal for overcommitment or connection to our research participants (Goffman 2014; Worley et al. 2016), we could ask, how will the sociological imagination even continue to exist? We therefore need to revisit how biography, history and social structure merge.

As I consider auto/biography, I reflect upon feminist philosophy, as matters that emerge in connection with closeness to a subject matter or story are evident. For example, Carlson (2010: 3) suggests issues connected to learning disability:

not only are worthy of scholarly interest but speak to the deepest problems of exclusion, oppression, and dehumanisation; [...] one's proximity to persons with intellectual disabilities should be neither assumed as a basis for participation in this conversation nor grounds for disqualification when speaking philosophically about this topic.

What Carlson (2010) notably alludes to is that there are people who are actually silenced, whether that is because of a relationship to those judged as marked or those who are indeed considered inferior to more powerful others (see also Goffman 1963).

There are many who 'experience' socio-political death, for example, prisoners and their families, disabled people, those with mental health problems (e.g. Codd 2008; Condry 2007; Gormley 2017) and all those who are considered different from the cultural and historical norm of that time. Furthermore, as Ahmed (2010: xvi) suggests, silencing is a tool of oppression, as 'when you are silenced, whether by explicit force or by persuasion, it is not simply that you do not speak but that you are barred from participation in a conversation which nevertheless involves you'. Yet, if we cannot trust 'powerful others' to perform and embody ethical and moral research practices, can we ever really *hear* the stories of those most at risk of oppression? Being silenced whether through restrictive research practices or through socio-political death (exclusion from policy and process) is unacceptable.

The Project—Care-Less Spaces: Prisoners with Learning Difficulties and Their Families

Funded by The Leverhulme Trust, in 2016–2017, I carried out in-depth life-story interviews with 13 men and 2 women who had been through the CJS and who self-identified as having learning difficulties (LD) and/or mental health problems, 5 mothers to sons with LD and/or mental health problems and 10 professionals who have worked in the LD/mental health forensic or education settings. In total, 43 interviews were completed as I revisited several participants over 18 months (Rogers 2018). The purpose of the research was to:

- Explore the life-story experiences of people with LD and/or mental health problems who have been through the CJS.
- Explore the life-story experiences of mothers who have a family member as above.

- Examine how those who break the law make sense of, and cope with prison culture, routines, rules, and practices, and how this pathway impacts upon all their lives on release.

As part of the life-story method, for those who wanted to contribute further, I asked participants to take photographs between the first and second interview. I chose photographs because for some, articulating feelings was not easy, and the process of doing, seeing and imagining is often how we make a connection to something, someone or our feelings (Booth and Booth 2003). Therefore, I gave participants who wanted to be involved, a disposable camera and encouraged them to use it to record 'feelings photographs' (Rogers 2019). Ten of those who had offended and 4 mothers participated in taking photographs with 8 having at least one follow-up interview. The photographs were an aid to our subsequent interviews and gave an additional account of 'feelings', as well as facilitated discussion in a more in-depth way (Aldridge 2007; Rogers 2019). All interviews were recorded.

Ethical Considerations

In the UK, social science research requires ethical approval when involving human participants (BSA 2017). I cannot make 'truth' claims about my participants and their lives, as they are not a homogenous group. Yet, it is important to understand from the very beginning of an investigation into such areas of injustice, inequalities and social life that doing, or at least attempting to do ethical and meaningful research, is vital. As I have asked with Geeta Ludhra (Rogers and Ludhra 2012: 43) before (although adapted for this research):

- Whose voice is narrated throughout the research?
- Who consents to the research?

  – The gatekeeper or person with learning difficulties or mental health problems?

- How included in the whole research process (from design to analysis) is the participant?
- What role do you as the researcher play in the life of the participant, and how does a relationship develop?

  – Are you a friend, a counsellor or an 'objective' observer?

There is never one easy answer to these questions, as negotiation is often key. In my current research, therefore, I needed to be flexible, empathetic, caring and responsive as I gained access and listened to people's life stories. As it is many, 'disabled' others are excluded from being heard or are represented in different and sometimes negative ways, and in my research, these offenders and families are amongst those most marginalised others. I did gain university ethical approval to carry out the research and all participants had the capacity to consent, but it is a negotiated process. No real names are used in any work I present. Below I weave my auto/biography with the criminal justice research journey thus far.

Auto/Biographical Beginnings

Sociologically Speaking

My sociological imagination was roused as an undergraduate in the 1990s, but it was in 2004 I submitted my Ph.D. for examination. The research 'A sociology of parenting children identified with "special educational needs": The private and public spaces parents inhabit' (Rogers 2005) were driven by my desire to make a difference and a personal connection to the subject matter, just like many of the feminist scholars I had been reading. I certainly recognised women writers played a significant role in bringing the private sphere into the public arena. Over two centuries ago, Wollstonecraft (1792) discussed the socialisation of girls, as women were 'hidden' from the public sphere. But it was not until the twentieth century that feminist sociology really took shape for me, as influences of women such as Harding (1986, 1991, 1993) and Oakley (1981) questioned social research processes, for example, who to access, how to interpret and analyse data and then how to theorise.

Standpoint feminists, Smith (1988) and Hartsock (1998), and those commenting, such as Smart (1990), argued feminist sociology is not simply the *experience of women*, but that their experience comes from struggle with oppression. Hertz (1997), moreover, discusses in some depth the need for reflexivity to shift our understanding of data collection and therefore suggests it is 'important to admit that we study things that trouble us or intrigue us, beginning from our own standpoints' (xvi), and asks, '[h]ow do we find the parallels in our experiences to make sociological sense of our own routines, or chaos for that matter?' (ibid.). This is a significant point, as some feminist sociology, and indeed sociologically informed personal storytelling (e.g. auto/biography, autoethnography) has been critiqued for mere navel-gazing (Sparkes 2002; Plummer 2009). Such works and critique inspired me to make public the experiences of parenting a disabled child, largely because I was a mother to a disabled daughter and because Plummer (2013: 209) asserts:

> we humans tell our stories, listen to the stories of others and the story of our own lives, our tales come to haunt, shape and transform our social worlds. […] These stories have significance and we need always be mindful of the tales we tell and the tales we hear: stories have their consequences, for stories and their documents are our futures. We should ask just how stories work their ways in human social life.

My Ph.D. was a story of parenting and difficult differences. It was not auto/biographical although it did include auto/biography (Rogers 2005). However, the mothers and fathers I interviewed shared deeply emotive tales about their experiences of childrearing, education, surveillance and exclusion.

At that time as a mother to a disabled daughter, a sociology graduate and a learning disability support worker, I was catapulted into reflecting upon the broader sociological landscape. Policy processes around inclusion and 'special educational needs' and 'good enough' mothering discourses led me back to those auto/biographical challenges faced by many parents to disabled children. It might therefore come as no surprise the opening quotation to my Ph.D. thesis was one from Mills (1959: 8) where he suggests:

> Perhaps the most fruitful distinction with which the sociological imagination works is between 'the personal troubles of milieu' and 'the public issues of social structure'. This distinction is an essential tool of the sociological imagination and a feature of all classic work in social science.

Significantly for my auto/biography, the influences that brought attention to the personal as political, for example, the feminists highlighted above and Mills' (1959) sociological imagination, whereby history, biography and social structure, have a part to play and have shaped much of my work. For the purposes here, missing data and socio-political death have been implicit themes in my research process. For example, as I worked on my first monograph, I was asked to omit the methods chapter. I explained that methods were a significant part of my research (Rogers 2007), but to no avail—it was excluded from the final manuscript. Furthermore, in my research, some participants, past and current, have felt unable to revisit their stories in a follow-up interview as reflecting upon trauma was emotionally too draining, resulting in untold or partial stories. Below, my auto/biography merges more explicitly with my current criminal justice research.

Auto/Biographically Speaking

My husband jumped in and we screeched off like something from a movie. 'I don't think I can drive, I feel sick,' I screamed, my heart pounding. Still I didn't want to stop. This lad was not someone you would want to upset, as rationale in this sort of a mood was not part of his personality once provoked. [...] 'It's all such a mess.' I broke down and cried. Sarah, my daughter, then 20 years old was taken to her Nan and Granddad's in an inconsolable state and wanting to leave home, this was before we went to the police station. She is moderately learning disabled. [...] 'I'm coming to your house and I'm going to kill you. I will be with Sarah till we die,' he had hollered as we speedily left the rough road. I was scared. We fled, and for that summer if she was not palmed off on accommodating family members, she remained a prisoner in her own home. Not least of all because of the danger this violent young man posed, who himself was learning disabled and had other emotional and behavioural difficulties. (Rogers 2009: 270–271).

My daughter, a 27-year-old intellectually disabled adult was yesterday morning apprehended at her learning disability club by two police officers. She was arrested, taken in a police car to the station, searched, and relieved of all her belongings and jewellery, finger printed, put in a cell, interviewed, charged and bailed. Luckily, her step father was at home, went to the station, and stayed in the cell with her and attended the interview. They said she was caught on CCTV shoplifting (the two times I can corroborate she was actually with me or in bed). This footage was not shown to either my daughter or hubby. TWO big officers! They then called for another (a female). So policing the town and ridding the centre of – who? People like my daughter? She is traumatised, and scared. What concerns me? Yes, my daughter's physical and mental health. But also, is this how it is? What if she were guilty of robbing £18 of stuff over two days? But is this how the CJS deals with vulnerable adults? It is such easy pickings for arrest figures, but had she not been in the family she is – what then? Maybe in care, or with parents who have difficulties themselves, this would likely be processed, and she would end up with a criminal record? (Personal reflections 2014)

These two quotations identify a personal relationship with learning disability, violence and the CJS. In response to the narratives, the first one, my daughter returned to residential college in the autumn and she never saw this young man again, despite the experience having a frightening and disruptive impact upon all our lives. The second narrative was a reflection on the beginning of a 6-month process in dealing with the aftermath of one significant event—the arrest of my daughter. Because of this experience, my daughter wanted to be accompanied to and from her day services due to fear of being arrested for some time. It took months for her criminal record to be quashed, via the then independent police complaints commission (IPCC), even though there was no evidence of her involvement in any crime committed.

These deeply personal experiences cannot give a broad insight into the criminal justice terrain, violence and mothering alone, but they can provoke our sociological imagination (Mills 1959) and open our sociological eyes (Hughes [1984] 2009). For example, based on the excerpts above, if, as in the case of the first, a young woman was not collected after her date by a carer or parent, then perhaps no one would know of the violent and abusive relationship. Concerning the second, if a young woman had no one to take the wrongful arrest to the IPCC, she would have a criminal record: impactful for future life chances. Founded on my sociological beginnings and personal troubles identified above, my sociological imagination was provoked to explore the wider cultural and political structures of criminal justice for disabled people and their families (see also, Rogers 2018; Gormley 2017; Peay 2016; Talbot et al. 2015). Arguably because aspects of social life are *missing* from the formal research produced based on the sanitisation of social science and the 'silencing' of stories different or too harrowing to tell, many groups, people and communities experience socio-political death.

Auto/Biography and Research Reflections—Gaining and Maintaining Access in the Field

In the Leverhulme project outlined above, I did not anticipate the enormity of time it would take to gain access, nurture relationships and then maintain access. Perhaps I was naïve? It was certainly not so simple as setting a date, meeting participants and gathering stories. Arguably it ought not to be simple, clean or easy. After all, I was going to speak to people about their criminal pathways, including their childhood and post-prison experiences. People I had contact with did not necessarily want to use email and so I had to use my phone and social media, as a form of enabling access. Blurred boundaries for me as a researcher, between my private and professional life (Rogers 2003), became evident, and although I was carrying out life-story research, it had elements of ethnographic methods (Goffman 2014; Worley et al. 2016), largely because I spent a year or so managing people, fielding phone calls and living with the research process continuously.

In addition to blurred boundaries, I made assumptions about how people might respond to my calls for participants. I realised, quite quickly that even if I made contact, it did not mean an interview was imminent or even happening at all. In that moment, the respondent to the call wanted to talk about their life, but in a different moment, they would not have responded, and then some potential participants simply changed their mind. I rapidly began to learn, if someone contacted me, I was not to leave them. I had to be in response mode. This level of engagement was only possible because I was carrying out this research full time. Universities or research funders who limit full 'buy out' of academic time due to lack of full economic costing, over teaching/administrative responsibilities or who lack, reduce or over-regulate sabbatical time, effectively restrict such qualitative inquiry and therefore silence those who are oppressed, leading to missing data and socio-political death (see also Rogers 2017b).

It was a challenge to gain access to and then maintain access with participants (McClimens 2007). For example, 4 mothers contacted me because of my posts on social media, and 1 was accessed via snowballing (from an ex-offender participant). The (ex)offenders were obtained via a range of charity/supporting gatekeepers who enabled access and vouched for my credibility (see also Girling 2017). It was not a straightforward process, as cancelled appointments, communication difficulties and the time spent nurturing relationships were factors that added to the reality of maintaining contact. Therefore, assumptions about access for the purposes of research with groups considered 'hard to reach' are imprudent. For example, I thought perhaps my personal links with educators who knew young men and their families who went on to offend was a gate-keeping coup. I also assumed that my previous research would enable access to specific families (Rogers 2007, 2016). These potential access pathways did not prove fruitful (Rogers 2018). As an auto/biographical note in my research diary said, '*I will get people, but perhaps not the actual brief I originally focused on, that of learning disability. Getting hold of families seems to be quite tricky too*' (fieldnotes, September 2016). Clearly, I was frustrated, but what could I do? My notes indicate this further:

> In the early stages I made lots of phone calls, trying to source participants and make relevant links to the charities and individuals and so on. This was a hard start in terms of finding gatekeepers. So I began to look for professionals who worked in the forensic setting, or in education that deals with challenging young people. I was struggling to get any ex-offenders and was worried I would fall, at the first hurdle. So, for example, those I wanted, those with learning difficulties were incredibly difficult to find, due to all sorts of reasons, not least, how do I find them? (fieldnotes September 2016)

What these excerpts express is that the struggles of gaining access to one group, and therefore people's stories, meant shifting the focus at that time. But accessing professionals who work with the group I wanted to talk to then compounded the silencing. Albeit relevant, their stories were second hand, so to speak. Yet talking to professionals showed me further, how difficult accessing 'disabled' offenders would be, as evidenced in this fieldnote below:

> One professional said, I have asked some of our clients about this type of research, and being involved (those ex-offenders now in the community) and they said about their criminal past, 'that was then, why the fuck would I want to talk to anyone now, dredging it all up? Anyway, who wants to know?' He tried to explain to this guy that it was for the 'greater good, and that we could all learn from it'. That didn't work. I am beginning to realise that getting hold of these participants is going to be tricky. I'm worried! (fieldnotes, September 2016)

This passage not only highlights the challenges in gaining access to participants, but that potential participants, as this professional indicated, would not want to talk to me. This supports a two-tier element to missing data at an institutional level and at an auto/biographic level.

Furthermore, optimistic expectations around *maintaining* access with participants once contact was established were rash. Largely because a small number of offenders and/or their families who heard about my call for participants via prison charity adverts, social media and word of mouth made contact to say they wanted to be a part of the research, but then withdrew before the interview could be carried out. This was despite numerous convincing and upbeat email exchanges and phone calls about their desire to participate. For example, the passages from my fieldnotes below clearly show how I was thinking and feeling about this process:

> I was going to see an ex-offender, a woman, and we had email communication, several. We set a date, she seemed genuinely interested and enthusiastic. We had emailed the day before said date, and then on the date nothing. I had a date, but she had not responded with a where to meet. I emailed several times on the day, but nothing. The next day I emailed saying I hoped she was okay, and not to worry. We can re-schedule, or if you've changed your mind don't worry. Still nothing. I emailed once more and thought I better leave her alone. She never got back to me. […] I had another cancellation! We had already re-scheduled once. I drove all the way from Glasgow to Yorkshire and sat outside her house. I had spoken to her the night before and she was still okay with me coming. I rang her while sitting outside. Nothing. I waited for a bit, but it seemed quite a deprived area, and didn't want to hang around for too long as I might look out of place sitting there in my car and knocking on the door. (fieldnotes, September 2016)

I discovered from the beginning the unpredictability and chaotic nature of my research participants' lives. This was mirrored in my chaotic and unpredictable research process (Rogers 2018). Therefore, reflections upon how we connect with our participants, especially those who are marginalised and oppressed and have challenges that impact upon their comprehension, concentration or interaction with others, can fracture and complicate access to their stories and consequently their lives. Sometimes it can block access altogether and result in a dearth of stories that are crucial for our understanding of injustice—socio-political death—but how can we then bring them back to life or resurrect the stories, the lives?[3] How can we resist social injustice and suffering? Perhaps the answer is via storytelling (see also Frank 1995, 2001; Plummer 2013).

Reflecting further upon access and how making connections with participants is critical especially for people who might face challenges that impede their storytelling. For example, during an interview with Kip (a professional who works in the community with offenders who have learning difficulties and/or autism),[4] he told me how police officers wanted to speak to one of his service-users about historical sexual abuse. His storying underlines the fact that a researcher, an unknown other, cannot simply

---

[3]Socio-political death in these examples can also illustrate 'social nothingness' (Scott 2018: 15), as identified in the opening of this chapter.

[4]I note here, learning difficulties *and/or* autism, and while I accept there are significant differences between those who have autism and those who have intellectual impairments, in the case of this instance here, and generally in my research, it was that some had learning difficulties, while some had autism too. Not that participants had autism only.

walk into someone's life and expect a person to open up and 'spill their guts', to meet a research agenda because asked. Kip made this point in our interview as he revealed, 'that is quite often how research is experienced' (due to lack of time and, critically, understanding). He recalled:

> So, they arrived together [the police officers], and he said [the service user], 'I didn't know I was going to talk to lesbians', and they said, 'we're not lesbians', 'but you said you travelled together'? And I said [to the officers] 'you need to be careful of your choice of language when you're dealing with someone with autism. This is going to be really difficult for him'. And in the end, they wanted to get this story out of him, and they couldn't do it. And I tried to say, 'it's your first day, and you won't do it'. I told them 'you need to have a cup of coffee with him, then you need to come and have a sarnie with him, then you need to come and spend just a little bit of time with him. How can you expect this guy to tell you, unless you are prepared to invest?' So, in the end, he [the service user] told me what had happened, and he named a person, after the officers had left. They said, 'if this name comes up again, we can do something but if it doesn't we can't'. So, people open up people, and then leave them vulnerable, even now, and people don't seem to get it. They just don't seem to get that you have to invest just a little bit more sometimes.

This example about walking into the life of a person who is autistic and then potentially opening them up emotionally is clear in how *not* to make a connection: investment is key. This understanding of autism is critical (see also Simmons, this volume). It also explicitly demonstrates how life-story data can go missing altogether if the person carrying out the research does not understand the research context, for example everyday living conditions/impairment, or does not have the time to invest due to institutional restrictions or limited funding.

Therefore, carrying out sociological or criminological research warrants personal skills too. Qualitative research, moreover, needs the recognition that 'the interview' is not quantifiable or predictable. For example, I spent a minimum of 11 hours with one of my mother participants (Elaine) spanning three interviews. This is because, when I carried out the two follow-up interviews, Elaine's son had been recalled to prison and it seemed unethical to leave immediately, given the emotional content of our discussion. Furthermore, she was alone. Consequently, on both follow-up occasions, we went out to lunch after the interview. The last time I visited, on my return I received a positive email, saying:

'Lovely to spend time with you today - even though it can be painful it seems also to be cathartic - which is good. It really helps talking stuff over with someone who can understand the situation and does not judge. […] Thank you'. (Elaine, email excerpt, December 2017)

Elaine went on to say that the time after the interview 'helps me to "normalise"', which is an important aspect of carrying out such emotive data collection (Rogers 2018). Critically, some of my participants have said telling their life story brings painful memories of suffering and feelings to the fore which brings us back to reflecting upon the fine line between hearing their story and them not telling it. It is socio-political life and death in the balance.

Nevertheless, some time spent with participants is perhaps more mundane, yet necessary. Nothing however can prepare you, so blocking out two hours out of a busy schedule is not helpful or appropriate. You as the researcher might become a taxi service or a temporary 'carer'. For example, below one man I interviewed said he did not want to stay in his house. His partner was in her dressing gown, and so he said, 'can we go to the café'. And from my fieldnotes, I was reflecting upon these issues as it is clear such research requires more than skills in interviewing. It requires sensitivity, time and flexibility as evidenced in this excerpt.

A guy, an ex-offender with learning difficulties, after the interview in his lounge wanted to be dropped off in his town. It's the little additional things that go on, that are perhaps unanticipated, or outside of any formal research design process. We certainly don't often write them into our research. It's the unknowable things that you can't plan. So when asking about ethics, it's not easy, you can't pre-empt it. When discussing ethics. Important but unknowable. I mean one interviewee turned up for an interview in a coffee shop, having done a night shift, he has learning difficulties/autism and he's in a massive panic. He's lost his wallet. And because I know about autism, I know that we need to sort this out. He's certainly not going to be in any fit state to do an interview, so we went through his bag, where he's been, and he said he'd been to Wetherspoon's for breakfast, so I got on my phone, and googled the pub, and he said, 'have you got the number? Will you ring them?' I said 'yeah, okay', so I rung Wetherspoon's and spoke to the lady there, and he knew what table he'd been sitting at, and the lady said, 'yes, we've got his wallet'. So I said to him, 'she's waiting for you, with your wallet', and so off he went, while I sat there with our coffees, and then he came back with his wallet and everything was fine. But that was a major thing as it had his travel card and a bank card. So that threw the timings, and so you cannot bank on the timings. (fieldnotes, February 2017)

All this groundwork is crucial for enabling socio-political life, resisting injustice and resurrecting the socio-politically dead—sociologically and auto/biographically.

Conclusion

> I have dreamed about participants and one was about Harry's (offender/prisoner) older self, but he's only 22! These stories seep into our essence, and our identity as a sociologist. Elaine (Harry's Mum and a mother participant), really wanted to go out so we had 'done some normality'. I think that lunch out, after the formal interview, was good for me too. I need to stop now and smell the coffee! Anyway, I am going to stop now, and possibly take a couple of days out. (fieldnotes, February 2017)

'No social study that does not come back to the problems of biography, of history and of their intersections within a society has completed its intellectual journey' (Mills 1959: 6) and is, arguably, nothing (Scott 2018). Part of the sociological imagination is the ability to shift between thinking politically and reflecting upon the personal biography (that of the people or communities being researched and the researcher's auto/biographical self).

Notably, considering Mills' work, Frauley (20162016: 33) says, within criminology and criminal justice studies, we 'must reject scientism and its bureaucratic ethos and embrace intellectual craftsmanship'. He continues that no one story is in a silo, without the weight of history or culture behind it. Like Mills' imagination, craftwork is required as a 'creative, imaginative and speculative criminology is one that we must build' (Frauley 2016: 25). The point is to reveal that the problems suffered by the individuals are hardly ever only individual in nature or solvable at that level (Frauley 2016: 30). Reflecting upon problems suffered, Wilkinson (2005: 3) says that sociological research often ignores what the actual '*experience* of suffering *does* to people' [emphasis in original] and what is more, the lived experience is rarely the direct focus.

In addition to Wilkinson's (2005) work, Frank (2001: 355) explains that loss and suffering (whether present or anticipated) is an 'instance of no thing, an absence of what was missed and now is no longer recoverable and the absence of what we fear will never be'. I wonder too, if this form of suffering and resistance (to socio-political death) can be linked back to Scott's (2018) social nothingness? Currently, bureaucratic processes, in for example the criminal justice system, legal procedures, prisons, universities and schools, cannot manage this suffering, therefore enabling socio-political death. Without revealing the broader picture, people go missing, 'communities' and groups die a slow socio-political death and institutions such as legal structures and procedures, schools and universities stay alive, albeit like machines all producing 'cheerful' robots (Mills 1959; Frauley 2016). If however, we ask imaginative questions, enable 'speaking' auto/biographically (e.g. Bochner and Ellis 2016; Williams 2006), draw out creativity and visual methods (e.g. Rogers 2019) and utilise literature, the Arts and comedy (e.g. Piamonte 2016; Potter 1998; Stanley 2013; Wilde 2018), then perhaps we might rouse resistance and socio-political living for oppressed and marginalised people, and sociologists and criminologists committed to social justice.

References

Ahmed, S. (2010). Secrets and Silence in Feminist Research. In R. Ryan-Flood & R. Gill (Eds.), *Secrecy and Silence in the Research Process: Feminist Reflections*. Routledge: Oxon.

Aldridge, J. (2007). Picture This: The Use of Participatory Photographic Research Methods with People with Learning Disabilities. *Disability and Society, 22*(1), 1–17.

Anderson, M., & Park, R. E. (1923). *The Hobo: The Sociology of the Homeless Man*. Chicago: The University of Chicago Press.

Becker, H. S. ([1963] 1991). *Outsiders: Studies in the Sociology of Deviance*. New York, NY: The Free Press.

Bochner, A. P., & Ellis, C. (2016). *Evocative Autoethnography: Writing Lives and Telling Stories*. Abingdon: Routledge.

Booth, T., & Booth, W. (2003). In the Frame: Photovoice and Mothers with Learning Difficulties. *Disability & Society, 18*(4), 431–442.

BSA. (2017). *Statement of Ethical Practice for the British Sociological Association*. British Sociological Association.

Carrabine, E. (2015). Contemporary Criminology and the Sociological Imagination. In J. Frauley (Ed.), *C. Wright Mills and the Criminological Imagination: Prospects for Creative Inquiry* (pp. 73–98). London: Routledge.

Carlson, L. (2010). *The Faces of Intellectual Disability: Philosophical Reflections*. Bloomington: Indiana University Press.

Codd, H. (2008 [2011]). *In the Shadow of Prison: Families, Imprisonment and Criminal Justice*. London: Routledge.

Condry, R. (2007). *Families Shamed: The Consequences of Crime for Relatives of Serious Offenders*. Cullompton: Willan Publishing.

Condry, R., & Miles, C. (2014). Adolescent to Parent Violence: Framing and Mapping a Hidden Problem. *Criminology and Criminal Justice, 14*(3), 257–275.

Condry, R., & Miles, C. (2016). Adolescent to Parent Violence and the Challenge for Youth Justice. In M. Bosworth, C. Hoyle, & L. Zedner (Eds.), *Changing Contours of Criminal Justice*. Oxford: Oxford University Press.

Fassin, D. (2017). *Prison Worlds: An Ethnography of the Carceral Condition*. Cambridge: Polity Press.

Fish, R. (2018). *A Feminist Ethnography of Secure Wards for Women with Learning Disabilities: Locked Away*. London: Routledge.

Frank, A. W. (1995). *The Wounded Storyteller: Body, Illness and Ethics*. London: University of Chicago Press.

Frank, A. W. (2001). Can We Research Suffering? *Qualitative Health Research, 11*(3), 353–362.

Frauley, J. (2016). For a Refractive Criminology: Against Science Machines and Cheerful Robots. In J. Frauley (Ed.), *C Wright Mills and the Criminological Imagination: Prospects for Creative Inquiry* (pp. 21–57). London: Routledge.

Gillies, V. (2016). *Pushed to the Edge: Inclusion and Behaviour Support in Schools*. Bristol: Policy Press.

Girling, E. (2017). Ethical Challenges: Doing Research with Children. In M. Cowburn, L. Gelshthorpe, & A. Wahidin (Eds.), *Research Ethics in Criminology: Dilemmas, Issues and Solutions*. Abingdon: Routledge.

Goffman, A. (2014). *On the Run: Fugitive Life in an American City*. London: University of Chicago Press.

Goffman, E. (1990 [1963]). *Stigma: Notes on the Management of Spoiled Identity*. London: Penguin.

Gormley, C. (2017). An Extended Social Relational Approach to Learning Disability Incarcerated. In D. Moran & A. K. Schliehe (Eds.), *Carceral Spatiality* (pp. 43–74). Houndmills: Palgrave Macmillan.

Harding, S. (1986). *The Science Question in Feminism*. New York: Cornell University Press.

Harding, S. (1991). *Whose Science? Whose Knowledge? Thinking from Women's Lives*. New York: Cornell University Press.

Harding, S. (1993). Rethinking Standpoint Epistemology: What Is "Strong Objectivity"? In L. Alcoff & E. Potter (Eds.), *Feminist Epistemologies* (pp. 49–82). London: Routledge.

Hartsock, N. C. M. (1998). *The Feminist Standpoint Revisited*. Oxford: Westview Press.

Hertz, R. (Ed.). (1997). *Reflexivity and VOICE*. London: Sage.

Holt, A. (2013). *Adolescent-to-Parent Abuse: Current Understandings in Research, Policy and Practice*. Bristol: Policy Press.

Hughes, E. ([1984] 2017). *The Sociological Eye: Selected Papers*. Abingdon: Routledge.

Johns, D. F. (2018). *Being and Becoming an Ex-prisoner*. Abingdon: Routledge.

Lewis-Kraus, G. (2016). The Trials of Alice Goffman. *New York Times Magazine.* https://www.nytimes.com/2016/01/17/magazine/the-trials-of-alice-goffman. html.

McClimens, A. (2007). This Is My Truth, Tell Me Yours: Exploring the Internal Tensions Within Collaborative Learning Disability Research. *British Journal of Learning Disabilities, 36,* 271–276.

Mills, C. W. (1959). *The Sociological Imagination.* New York: Oxford University Press.

Oakley, A. (1981). Interviewing Women. In H. Roberts (Ed.), *Doing Feminist Research* (pp. 30–61). London: Routledge and Kegan Paul.

Peay, J. (2016). An Awkward Fit: Offenders with Mental Disabilities in a System of Criminal Justice. In M. Bosworth, C. Hoyle, & L. Zedner (Eds.), *Changing Contours of Criminal Justice.* Oxford: Oxford University Press.

Piamonte, S. (2016). The Criminological Imagination and the Promise of Fiction. In J. Frauley (Ed.), *C Wright Mills and the Criminological Imagination: Prospects for Creative Inquiry* (pp. 241–254). London: Routledge.

Plummer, K. (2009). Introduction: Autoethnography of Sexualities. *Sexualities, 12*(3), 267–269.

Plummer, K. (2013). A Manifesto for Social Stories. In L. Stanley (Ed.), *Documents of Life Revisited: Narrative and Biographical Methodology for a 21st Century Critical Humanism* (pp. 209–220). Abingdon: Routledge.

Potter, G. (1998). Truth in Fiction, Science and Criticism. *Journal of Literary Semantics, 27*(3), 173–189.

Reisman, D., & Becker, H. S. ([1984] 2017). Introduction to the Transaction Edition. In E. Hughes (Ed.), *The Sociological Eye: Selected Papers.* Abingdon: Routledge.

Rogers, C. (2003). The Mother/Researcher in Blurred Boundaries of a Reflexive Research Process. *Auto/Biography, XI*(1&2): 47–54.

Rogers, C. (2005). *A Sociology of Parenting Children Identified with Special Educational Needs: The Private and Public Spaces Parents Inhabit* (Unpublished PhD thesis). University of Essex.

Rogers, C. (2007). *Parenting and Inclusive Education: Discovering Difference, Experiencing Difficulty.* Houndmills: Palgrave Macmillan.

Rogers, C. (2009). (S)excerpts from a Life Told: Sex, Gender and Learning Disability. *Sexualities, 12*(3), 270–288.

Rogers, C. (2016). *Intellectual Disability and Being Human: A Care Ethics Model.* London: Routledge.

Rogers, C. (2017a). Hope as a Mechanism in Emotional Survival: Documenting Miscarriage. *Journal of Gynecol, 2*(3). ISSN: 2474–9230.

Rogers, C. (2017b). 'I'm Complicit and I'm Ambivalent and That's Crazy': Care-Less Spaces for Women in the Academy. *Women's Studies International Forum, 61,* 115–122.

Rogers, C. (2018). Life Stories, Criminal Justice and Caring Research. In G. Noblit (Ed.), *Oxford Research Encyclopedia of Education*. New York: Oxford University Press.

Rogers, C. (2019). Necessary Connections: "Feelings Photographs" in Criminal Justice Research and Doing Visual Methods. Special Issue: Collaborations in Research, *Methodological Innovations*.

Rogers, C., & Ludhra, G. (2012). Research Ethics: Participation, Social Difference and Informed Consent. In S. Bradford & F. Cullen (Eds.), *Research and Research Methods for Youth Practitioners*. London: Routledge.

Scott, S. (2018). A Sociology of Nothing: Understanding the Unmarked. *Sociology, 52*(1), 3–19.

Smart, C. (1990). Feminist Approaches to Criminology or Postmodern Woman Meets Atavistic Man. In A. Morris & L. Gelsthorpe (Eds.), *Feminist Perspectives in Criminology*. Milton Keynes: Open University Press.

Smith, D. (1988). *The Everyday World as Problematic: A Feminist Sociology*. Milton Keynes: Open University Press.

Sparkes, A. C. (2002). Autoethnography: Self-Indulgence or Something More? In A. Bochner & C. Ellis (Eds.), *Ethnographically Speaking: Autoethnography, Literature, and* Aesthetics. New York: Altamira Press.

Stanley, L. (1992). *The Auto/Biographical I*. Manchester: Manchester University Press.

Stanley, L. (2013). *Documents of Life Revisited: Narrative and Biographical Methodology for a 21st Century Critical Humanism*. Abingdon: Routledge.

Talbot, J. with Cheung, R., & O'Sullivan, S. (2015). *Relative Justice: The Experiences and Views of Family Members of People with Particular Needs in Contact with Criminal Justice and Liaison and Diversion Services*. London: Prison Reform Trust and Partner of Prisoners and Families Support Group (POPS).

Whyte, W. F. ([1943] 1993). *Street Corner Society: The Social Structure of an Italian Slum*. Chicago, IL: University of Chicago Press.

Wilkinson, I. (2005). *Suffering: A Sociological Introduction*. Cambridge: Polity Press.

Wilde, A. (2018). *Film, Comedy, and Disability: Understanding Humour and Genre in Cinematic Constructions of Impairment and Disability*. Abingdon: Routledge.

Williams, D. J. (2006). Autoethnography in Offender Rehabilitation Research and Practice: Addressing the "Us vs. Them" Problem. *Contemporary Justice Review, 9*(1), 23–38.

Wootton, B. (1959). *Social Science and Social Pathology*. London, UK: Allen and Unwin.

Worley, R. M., Worley, V. B., & Wood, B. A. (2016). 'There Were Ethical Dilemmas All Day Long!': Harrowing Tales of Ethnographic Researchers in Criminology and Criminal Justice. *Criminal Justice Studies, 29*(4), 289–308.

Young, J. (2011). *The Criminological Imagination*. Cambridge: Polity Press.

27

Co-constructed Auto/Biographies in Dwarfism Mothering Research: Imagining Opportunities for Social Justice

Kelly-Mae Saville

Introduction

This chapter is about learning. It is about me as a nondisabled mother, learning my place in my son's disabled community. It is also about finding my own self in his story, 'our' story. As 'relational others', our auto/biographies are entwined, yet we come to understand the world around us differently (Toyosaki and Pensoneau-Conway 2013). This chapter is about listening: listening to the 'voices' around and within the dwarfism community. Listening to my son as he starts to define his own self: a disabled child, but more importantly to him, as a Dwarf. That capitalisation is unreservedly explicit in its meaning. My son recognises his disability as an inherent part of his identity; it is socio-political in nature. The twenty-first century has been historic for Dwarfs as Adelson (2005: 212) says, 'as a result of the social changes of the past several decades, this "people who were not a people" have now joined other minorities, identity groups, and disability groups in demanding "a seat at the table"'. Like other disabled communities, my son now embraces dwarfism as part of a distinct subculture, with values and 'logics' at times opposed to those in medical fields (Radić-Šestić et al. 2015). This chapter is about the body. It is about Dwarf

K.-M. Saville (✉)
Aston University, Birmingham, UK
e-mail: savillkm@aston.ac.uk

bodies resisting the stigma and 'spoiled' identity that has been levied at them throughout the ages (Goffman 1963). Finally, this chapter is about imagining an opportunity for social justice. I say 'imagining' because I do not think we are there yet. People with dwarfism occupy a contested space; they sit at society's margins; even as a disability, dwarfism is given 'liminal status' (Shakespeare et al. 2010).

Co-constructed Auto/Biographies in Contested Spaces: The Ethics of Ownership

I occupy a contested space within the dwarfism community. My height is average, I am 5 feet 7, I do not have dwarfism, yet, by association, I am part of this community. When telling stories which involve, or I should say, which are co-constructed within a landscape blighted by social injustices, as an average statured member of this community my experiences are narrow and, some may argue quite rightly, incomplete. Certainly, 'one trouble with telling stories about disclosure is getting started. It is difficult to know where to start, especially when the story being told is not yours alone to tell. Stories implicate others' (Aubrecht and La Monica 2017: 2). In the confines of private reflection, I often doubt my own position as 'storyteller' for this community. Indeed, who am I to front this cause when there are many good writers within the dwarfism community who can tell you the stories from their own experiences? As Rogers (2009: 275) argues, '[t]here are contentious ethical issues related to the ownership of particular knowledge and experience'. My own accounts of knowledge and experience within the dwarfism community have, and are still, manifested through observation and interaction, rather than an embodied experience of having dwarfism. At times, I have struggled to make sense of this situation, being a nondisabled member of a disabled community. Indeed, the issue of 'ownership' to the stories of social injustices is an extension to this ethical dilemma (Rogers and Tuckwell 2016). People with dwarfism can tell you in vivid detail the scale of discrimination against them because of the size of their bodies; they can describe the intense and fiery visceral reactions within their bodies when the threat of harm comes close (Ellis 2018; Shakespeare et al. 2010). Those stories are not mine to tell. Instead, I occupy a peculiar space: not quite insider, not quite outsider. My knowledge and understanding of the community are shaped from my own experiences in being a mother to a child with achondroplasia. So, when considering space and place, who best to go on this writing journey with than my own son?

Like Aubrecht and La Monica (2017) in their deliberations over the 'start' of their stories, I have come to acknowledge the depth of implication and intrusion, both directly and indirectly, and my work has on the life of my son. And so, our story has to start somewhere. Berger and Quinney (2005: 10) say about storytelling:

> the writing is part of the research process. It is not merely a 'report' of one's observations, but an integral part of the process of creating meaning […] It is through the writing that we discover our 'voice', as we emerge from silence, in our search to discover or rediscover ourselves.

I have recently started having open and frank discussions with him about how he understands his disability and about my position as his mother. This seemingly simple adjustment is no mean feat; at this moment in time, he is eight years old. The political and social implications around disabled identities, and which language frame to use (Dunn and Andrews 2015), are not an easy conversation to have in the lecture hall, let alone in the private space of the car—where most of our important conversations seem to happen (thank you hospital appointments in far-away places!).

Mothering at the Margins of Care-Less Space: The Research

The goal of this project was to challenge and build upon the academic debates around both the stigmatisation of dwarfism (Ablon 1984; Adelson 2005; Ellis 2018; Goffman 1963) and the auto/biographies of women who mother children with dwarfism. I was particularly interested in mothers' views of stigmatisation and how this was reproduced in the choices available to them and the decisions they make, on behalf of both themselves and their children. This research was underpinned by three main research goals:

1. To document and explore the auto/biographies of mothers with children with dwarfism,
2. To discover what 'care' means and entails for mothers of children with dwarfism, and
3. To explore how is 'care' experienced in their lives (in relation to them and their children).

Reflective Methods

Throughout my writing and researching process, I have been influenced and inspired by Ribbens' (1998) and Rogers' (2003, 2007, 2009) work which, by adopting the use of feminist frameworks, opens up a channel to discuss mothering auto/biographically. Rogers (2003), for example noting the potential loss of her own 'voice' within the research process, decided to engage with and document her 'established' and 'developing selves' during her fieldwork. I endeavour to understand my sense of self as it emerges and evolves throughout my mothering journey, and my writing acts as a mirror to these experiences. During my time within this research process, I have been careful not to conflate my own understandings and experiences with those of the wider population. Although some of our experiences and stories may overlap, my stature is in contrast with the embodied realities experienced by people with dwarfism; therefore, my own 'voice' is shaped through and moulded by, the experiences I have whilst mothering my achondroplastic son. Retelling our stories through auto/biography is an organic part of the process and interpretation.

As auto/biography has no strict method, its practices are guided through the belief that meanings that affect our understandings of the social world are derived from our stories (Ellis 2009; Tillmann 2009). During this research process, I have challenged myself to find my own 'voice' in the story. As a mother to a disabled child, researching other mothers' experiences within the community we share, I have often questioned my place in this research. Like Rogers (2009: 275):

> I have thought about pseudonyms, or writing it as a case study as if I were not the mother. But this then assumes that autoethnography is not a legitimate method in revealing social meaning and processes. I also came back to thinking that I have a particular interpretation. That is different and necessary. I am privileged to be able to write about this and bring it to the public table, not as something dirty, but as an important part of the fabric and dilemmas in social life.

The public and private spheres become blurred when you undertake research so 'close to home' (Ribbens 1998; Rogers 2003). Ellis (2007) warns that those adopting auto/biographical methods should consider the consequences and 'relational ethics' of such approaches. Indeed, the telling of my own personal story and experiences implicate, not only myself, but the person I cherish most—my son. I am all too aware that, one day, my son may decide to read my work—and what then, *what would he make of it?*

Ethical Considerations

Ethical approval for this research project was gained through my university's Ethics Committee. The BSA (2017) sets out what it considers to be ethical research. Responsibility in obtaining informed consent is levied at the sociologist. I adopted Liamputtong's (2007) position—that ethical practice in research is a process and undertook Miller and Bell's (2002) approach of 'negotiated consent'. This approach sees participation as a completely voluntary act which can be adapted and changed throughout the course of the research.

Steinberg (2017), in what she terms 'sharenting', argues that children's rights to privacy are also betrayed when parents reveal private aspects of their children's lives with others. With regard to my own research, this issue is of particular importance, crucially the subject of 'ownership' over shared experiences and stories—and who has the right to tell. In order to overcome some of these issues, Steinberg (2017) recommends that older children be consulted about what can and cannot be told, giving them 'vetoing' powers. Moreover, Steinberg (2017) recommends that parents be reflective to their own hierarchal position and contemplate how their children would feel if they came across the stories online or in publications. However, Steinberg (2017) argues that parents 'right to share' as well as the overall benefit of creating knowledge should not be risked by removing these types of narratives from online forums and research. Instead, by following the suggested steps, children's rights to privacy can be maintained by a constant reflective cycle.

Relational Ethics in 'Insider' Research: Negotiating Consent

In the car, alone with my thoughts, I cannot shake the need to explain to my son—to justify and seek permission—about the stories I want to share about our lives, his life. Cautiously, I approach the subject of auto/biography:

> "My boy, I want to ask you some things and I need you to tell me how you feel about them, okay?"

> In his distinctive Midlands accent, he replied, "Okay Mom".

I carried on looking forward to the road not knowing how to proceed with this conversation. A wave of dread washed over me, and I was not sure how to go into the details and implications of the choices I wanted to offer him (MacDonald 2013). After all, he is only a young child. How was he supposed to understand the complexities surrounding consent in auto/biographical research if I did not tell him myself? Even then, would he understand the implications of consent, the part where if I write it, someone might read it—read about his life? Or was I making a bigger deal out of this than necessary? Minutes passed in silence. I decided to start with the basics, and I told him I was writing about what it was like to be a mother to a child with achondroplasia. Like Rogers (2009) in the above quote, it felt unnecessary, pointless even, to start writing about our lives using pseudonyms. However, I wanted—I needed—to ascertain my writing's parameters with my son: What bits of our lives, his life, could I share with others? When considering the implications of 'relational ethics' (Ellis 2007) alongside the advocating of social justice for the dwarfism community, these layers had to be peeled back to the core, and for me, that core starts with my son.

> 'So, when I write about mothering and dwarfism, what I'm really writing about is us, is you, and what it's like to be your mum. But I need to know what to call you, some writers don't use their real names and the people in the stories have pretend names. What would you want to be called?'
>
> 'Luqman', he replied without hesitation.
>
> 'Luqman? That's your real name, so you want to be called your real name?'
>
> 'Yes', he shot back.

When considering the subject and ethics of disabled voices being 'heard', especially in the context of nondisabled academics writing, and auto/biographies about the lives of disabled people, there have understandably, been issues raised about 'not hearing' or 'talking over' disabled voices. This is a complex topic, not least when it is often not just about the social justice perspective of listening to disabled people—interdependency—the notion that as a society, we need people, and are needed by people, is another important aspect when thinking about voices and who gets to be heard (Kittay and Feder 2002). With regard to my own son, of course I champion his voice. However, as a disabled child he still relies upon his trusted adults to facilitate a platform in order for him to be heard (Carpenter and McConkey 2012; Ryan and Runswick-Cole 2009).

'Okay, now I need to know how I should refer to your size. So, I can say "Luqman has dwarfism, it's called achondroplasia" or I can say "Luqman is a Dwarf"'.

'Say "Luqman is a Dwarf, he has achondroplasia"'.

'No wait, are you sure? Before you decide, let me just add some details about both terms. If I say "somebody with dwarfism" that is called person-first language. Some people in the dwarfism community think it's completely different from saying "you're a Dwarf". Referring to yourself as a "Dwarf" is called identity-first language, for some people their dwarfism is an important part of their identity. Both ways of describing dwarfism are used in the community, but some people prefer saying "with dwarfism" and in all my writing as somebody without dwarfism I've followed that lead, but when I write about you it's your choice, you get to decide but you have to understand that the terms mean slightly different things'.

'I prefer "Luqman is a Dwarf"' he repeated to me, quite frustrated that I had not taken his word for it.

I had attempted to play it down and not go into identity politics with an eight-year-old. This was the first time we had ever talked about language in the community, and I stopped short of going into the politics of disabled identities, not wanting to overwhelm him or to change the direction of the conversation (Dunn and Andrews 2015). Fundamentally, the purpose of this interaction was for me to seek his permission and point of view regarding his own stories, so I came to the realisation that this was a moment for me to listen. Listen to the voice of Luqman, aged eight, knowing full well that as he gets older, his position and language may change or indeed become more entrenched,

'Okay Luqman, now another question: you know I'm writing about parts of your life, and mine, our life together. Well, I need to know what stories I can write about and which ones I can't. You get to decide, and if you don't want me to tell a story, you just have to say. But I want to tell people what it's like to have dwarfism from your perspective, and mine too, as your mum. So, can I tell people about the time you played tennis and that boy called you that word?'

'No' he swiftly rebutted.

'Can I ask why? It's an important part of your story don't you think?'

'Because it made me sad'.

I took a deep gulp. That event, though a common occurrence for people in the dwarfism community, was unexpected—it had happened in a place which we often frequented, surrounded by people we were mildly acquainted with. If anything, it stung more—them not being strangers—for me at least. As Rogers (this volume) observes, 'reflecting upon trauma was emotionally too draining, resulting in untold or partial stories'. Missing data, or the 'silencing' of stories too traumatic to relive, disabled communities may experience socio-political death. In not-narrating Luqman's story, his experiences, which are often shared by his community, are left for now, untold. However, the story was solely owned by Luqman. Like Rebecca Cokley (2018, Rewire News) in her article, her son held vetoing powers for the retelling of stories which included him:

> He was right. It's not my story to tell. And being a good mom, especially in this digital age, means teaching my kids that they have the right to consent, or not consent, to how their images, their words, their bodies, and their experiences are used […] So I'm not going to tell you about what happened to my son. I'm not going to tell you the reaction my husband and I had to a grave injustice. Because that's his reality, and even at 7—especially at 7—I want him to know that he has the right to own his experience without his parents putting it out there into the universe as a teaching moment. Because a mother's trust is important, and I want my son to know that what he brings to me, he brings to me, and not the rest of the world. I want him to know that I won't share it unless he wants me to.

'Can I tell them about this conversation, the one happening right now?'

'Yes'.

'Okay, so what about the hospital appointments, can I tell stories about those ones?'

'Yes', he replied in his usual cheerful tone.

Finding Our Feet

With the parameters set, the storytelling can now go forward—but to go forward, I had to look back—to a story, a time, and a place I had almost forgotten. My first memory, a story that I retold through auto/biographical reflection within my Masters dissertation, was to be pivotal in shaping how I came to understand Luqman and his body and also, importantly, how I reacted to 'threats' from 'normative gazes'. At the time of writing, he was six years old. I queried how important the encounter would be; my subsequent stance and attitude retold in my second memory lead me to believe that those first reflective encounters in the surgeon's office crucially influenced and informed me in a way that at the time, I could not comprehend (Freeman 2015; Giorgio 2013).

***

Luqman is six years old. However, I have often imagined him as an adult reading my work and scrutinising the choices I made for him on his behalf. In years to come, this work will be but a memory of a time and place in my life—his life—its significance on his future, I do not yet know (Freeman 2015). As Sparkes (2002: 157) relays, '[m]emories serve particular personal and social functions within the stories we tell ourselves and others, to explain who we are, what we are, and where we are in life at a particular time and place'. The telling of my story (actually, 'our story'), at this time in his life, leaves me and my choices open to future criticism from one of the people I love most in the world—Luqman. Normative discourses around motherhood reduce the experience to one of joy and unconditional love, where maternal sacrifice is the order of the day and the emotional state of the mother who does the care-work is not given a second thought (Kittay 1999; Landsman 2003, 2009; Lynch 2007; Rogers 2007, 2013, 2016).

Worlds Apart

The poem, 'Worlds Apart', by Green (2002: 27) emotively depicts how a nondisabled mother imagines switching places with her disabled child:

In dream time, I am my child - or she is me.

I feel the rock hard muscles in my arms and legs.

I sit held fast by metal bars and nylon straps.

As an average statured mother to a son with dwarfism, as Green (2002: 27) does here, I have often tried to place myself in his position:

I'm braced against the spasms that will stiffen limbs.

I also know the sadness that my presence sometimes brings,

and feel the need to squelch the hidden source from which it springs.

I remember being advised by social workers in Luqman's early years, to walk around on my hands and knees to get a 'feel' for what it is like to be short. The experience was supposed to equip me with the information I needed to keep him safe, away from obstacles and dangers, and to see life through his eyes. Yet, like Green (2002: 27):

I wonder,

In her dreams can she be me?

Does she then know the freedom of unbounded moves through space

and can she see the look of need upon another's face?

Among my deepest hopes is that this may be so.

Yesterday, I cried. A silent cry. A cry so pained that my eyes were blinded by a watery haze as what felt like fire engulfed my throat and I held my breath begging myself to stop. A cry of despair. A cry in solitude:

For in the daylight hours,

each other's worlds we cannot know.

(Green 2002: 27)

Yesterday was a hard day. Trauma: it is hard to predict when it will strike and, like all things that come unexpected, you try to hold on for the ride—or at least survive the fall (Tummala-Narra 2009). Yesterday started out like any other appointment day. I drove the eighty-odd miles to the hospital for Luqman's review and we got there early, so we could avoid the morning rush hour traffic. A common complication of having achondroplasia, one which Luqman had, was bowing in the legs. For Luqman, the bowing was so severe it was damaging the ligaments in his legs, causing him pain and constant discomfort to the extent that it was impacting upon his everyday activities. He had spent the year prior to surgery, dependent upon a wheelchair—dependent, like other children with dwarfism in wheelchairs, requiring an adult to push him around school.

 Back to the hospital; it was all going so well. We were there on the premise that we would be discussing removing the plates from his knees that had helped with the bowing. X-rays had been taken and then came the physical examination. Luqman lay on the table, with no less than four surgeons poking and prodding his little, cute, chubby folds of muscle on his legs.

'It's gone really well', one of them muttered.

I could sense the tone: personal pride and accomplishment.

'Yes, but look lower, below the ankle', one replied.

Another surgeon placed his seemingly oversized arm across Luqman's ankles, hiding his feet beneath.

'But … if we do this (still hiding Luqman's feet) it's all been *corrected*. So the *deformity* is just in the lower limbs now'.

There, they had said it, '*deformity*'. I am sensitive to subtle shifts in language; having spent three years studying half of my degree in English language, I know of its importance in creating, influencing, and controlling societal discourse (Fairclough 2010; Van Dijk 1995, 1996). In that brightly lit room, a group of people had assembled, for the sole purpose of discussing how best to *care* for my son's health and future well-being. Pushing the 'deformity' remark out of my mind, I decided to brave the question:

'So, ankle wise, what are you thinking?'

Finally, the lead surgeon spoke up – 'Oh, we'll cage them'.

Such a detached and off the cuff remark. '*Cage them*'. It is as grotesque and cruel as it sounds. Completely and wholly, like Green (2002) in her poem, I imagined being my child. I looked over to him, and there he was, smiling. He had been a good boy for the surgeons and X-ray technicians, done everything that was asked of him; he knew I would be pleased. But at that moment, my heart, that mother's heart, the one which must fight and protect against threat, I could feel it crack. 'When we are together, my body does the work for two wills' (Green 2002: 23); I suppressed the instinct to grab Luqman and run us for cover. Instead, I told my boy that we would talk in the car. I thanked the surgeons and left. Luqman and I, we never had that conversation.

In thinking through my own experiences theoretically using Rogers' (2016) care ethics model of disability as a framework, it becomes clear that the caring spheres work and interact in complex—and at times, emotionally detrimental ways. Rogers (2016: 90) observes how:

> Carefullness, resilience, survival and skills development are evident in mothers with disabled children […] Caring and care-full-ness ought to be privileged and positioned as not simply about the practical day-to-day aspects of caring (although these are important) but about how practical caring work and emotional work co-exist. Moreover, in addition to this, the mother who is caring for, about and with her 'child' faces potential prejudice, in addition to self-doubt about her own mothering abilities.

In the car, (almost) alone with my thoughts for eighty-odd miles as we ventured home, the sadness and despair rose from deep within. Caging, also commonly referred to as framing, is a metal apparatus which is drilled into the bone and wrapped around the limb on the outside of the body—controlled by external fixators. Controversially, it is most commonly used on the dwarfism community to lengthen limbs—an invasive surgical procedure in which bones are broken then supported through guided growth to increase height. Current research on the surgical outcomes of limb lengthening on achondroplastic children in the UK put complication rates at 70% (Donaldson et al. 2015). Whilst I acknowledge that Luqman's risks may be lower as we do not intend to lengthen his limbs, invasive surgery such as this still poses extreme challenges and restrictions to his social, emotional, and physical well-being.

Clutching onto the steering wheel, I imagined the surgical steel: the plates, the rods, the screws, and the pins. Luqman's perfect, cute, little feet. I imagined the process: first cutting, then piercing through the muscle, and drilling into the bone multiple times to ensure all the rods were in. I imagined Luqman, the boy who trusts me, trusts me to care. I imagined having to hold him down as he struggled against the anaesthetic mask (as he always does) begging me not to let them put him to sleep. I imagined him waking up and looking down at his legs, then looking back up at me. I imagined watching his heartbreak as he realised that he could no longer trust me, because I had done this to him—I had caused him this pain. How could I ever explain to my six-year-old, beautiful, cheerful, happy little boy that drilling rods and pins into and out of his legs would be good for him? I imagined the years of pain he would endure as he learned to walk with steel frames screwed around his legs and into his body. *When we are together I am him, and he is me—my body, my mind, will forever do 'the work of two wills'* (Green 2002: 23, italics added).

Letting Him Choose? Hearing Luqman

For mothers in the dwarfism community, a significant part of their role— and time—is focused on resisting the societal and cultural representations of dwarfism that get tied onto their children's bodies—and, in the case where mothers also have dwarfism, their own. Schwalbe (1998) argues that it is important to examine how cultural depictions have been represented historically, especially in relation to embodiment; with regard to dwarfism, substantial literature and empirical research have noted the religious, cultural, societal, and 'spectator' development of the condition (Ablon 1984; Adelson 2005; Backstrom 2012; Bogdan 1988; Dasen 2013; Koren and Negev 2004; Shakespeare 2013; Shakespeare et al. 2010). Dwarfism, for example under Goffman's (1963: 4) classification of stigma, was denoted as 'abominations of the body'. Ablon (1984: 81) has observed that 'all dwarfs must live with the constant stares, curiosity, and often gross or rude comments and questions of the average-sized populations around them as the explicit reminders of their difference'. During fieldwork, many mothers within the dwarfism community used words such as 'exhibit' and 'spectacle' to describe how they felt in public spaces. One mother, who along with her children also has dwarfism, recounted her experiences with occupational therapists. During her child's occupational assessment for preschool, the two therapists' initial reactions to seeing an adult with dwarfism were to crawl up to her on their knees and speak to her as if she were a child:

Then they came towards me on their knees in front of everybody and went, 'Hello, you must be Mum'. I went, 'What are you doing? You're being patronising and rather alarming and I don't know who you are!' So I asked, 'Why are you on your knees?' And she said 'Oh, I've got a bad back' and I was like 'Well does being on your knees help?' They were woefully ill-prepared, and they treated the preschool like a zoo; they could pop in and see the 'exhibit'.

Most poignantly, these feelings of being watched and ridiculed are exacerbated by the negative reactions of others. Shakespeare et al. (2010: 26) argue that as dwarfism is a visible difference with links to folklore and comedy, the condition's novelty value means that it is impossible 'to escape the curiosity, and occasionally the hostility' acted out towards people with dwarfism. A quantitative analysis of their research found that within the dwarfism community:

- 96% have experienced staring or pointing.
- 77% have been on the receiving end of verbal abuse.
- 75% feel they often attract unwanted attention.
- 63% of respondents have often felt unsafe when out.
- 33% have been physically touched by people in public.
- 12% have experienced physical violence.

At the time of that interview, Luqman was six years old; the notion that adults with dwarfism were still being infantilised and ridiculed because of their stature was a distant possibility. However, I could detach myself from the realities that Luqman would face in the future because it had not happened to him yet. Of course, we had had issues with people mistaking his age, but at six years old, he was a child, and so being treated a few years younger did not seem a massive problem by comparison. Yet, as Luqman gets older, I often reflect back to that interview; the years are going by, and one day this will be him. What then? How can I prepare him? *Why should I have to?*

Recently, I undertook an interview with a mother who had a young child with achondroplasia. She was relatively new to the community, having only made contact with the larger group of online mothers a few months prior to our interview. As such, she often paused and asked for clarification of 'correct' terminology when referring to both the community as a whole and individuals with dwarfism conditions. During our meeting, she spoke about her desire to enrol her toddler onto the BioMarin trials of vosoritide. In a recent press release, the drug was described as 'an innovative therapy to treat the underlying cause of achondroplasia. At the molecular level, vosoritide corrects the signaling process that determines skeletal growth and proportionality of bones, while the body is still growing' (Fuchs 2018, Cision PR Newswire). As a clinician herself, she felt excited that a potential therapy had been created which could possibly address both stature and the potentially fatal complications of having achondroplasia. Even if the trials proved ineffective, she remained positive that the condition itself was still at the forefront of medical advancements. She had made formative steps by contacting the doctors in charge of recruiting for the trial but had been informed that as her child had previously undergone surgery within the last twelve months, she would be excluded from the current round of intakes. At this stage, she had not made her mind up definitively; all she wanted was the choice to remain open even if she decided at a later stage that the drug trial was not the best option for her child. We both acknowledged the struggle and the heavyweight of responsibility that we felt in making decisions on behalf of our young children. As she walked away from the table to tend to her child, she asked about Luqman and what 'our' position was concerning the drug trials. Suddenly, I realised, I had never raised the issue of vosoritide with my son; 'we' did not have a position on the topic, because *he did not know about the trials.*

> Oh that's a really interesting question. Well actually, thinking about it, Luqman doesn't know about the drug trials because I've never told him. So he can't really make a choice about vosoritide. I've never realised until you've just asked, but we've never talked about it. He's a little older now, and the trials are quite new, so we never had that as an option like you do, when he was younger. Thinking about it, we've dodged a massive bullet. I wouldn't like to have had to make that decision for him as a baby.

> Looking at me from across the room she calmly responded, 'Well don't you think he's old enough now to get a choice? Maybe you have an ethical obligation to inform him and let him choose for himself. He's still below the age cap, so there's still time to enrol if that's what he wanted'.

> Attempting to explain myself, I positioned, 'It's really difficult to introduce this idea to him now. He's settled in himself. He's been part of the larger community since he was a few months old. This is all he knows. Having dwarfism and being around others like him is normal for him. Dwarfism is a huge part of his identity and how he understands himself and the world around him. The disability sports he participates in through the Dwarf Sports Association is a massive part of his life. If he was to enrol on the trials and get taller, how would that decision impact his participation in those sporting events? Would he even qualify to partake in the sports? Would he be ostracised by the community for wanting to be taller? Would he end up being in a metaphorical no man's land: not 'Dwarf' enough for the community, not 'average' enough for society?'

The mothers within my research are diverse: some have dwarfism, and some are average stature like myself. Some recognise dwarfism as an identity sub-culture, some see the condition in terms of health and disability, and some acknowledge all of these as factors which come together and inform their sense of self. In talking through these, at times, contested positions with my participant, I came to realise that she was right. Even if I was following Luqman's lead in the decisions he was making, how truthful was this 'freedom of choice' if I was hiding or glossing over the facts and options available to him. At that moment, I had to be honest with myself: I had been providing him with fragments of information. I had told him about the operations available to straighten his legs, but I did not tell him about drug trials that potentially would make him taller and less prone to medical complications.

***

Here, we were again, en route home after another lengthy hospital journey. Another prime opportunity to casually ask him important questions without the prospect of interruption from the television or his two brothers. I had been dreading this moment (most children love the idea of growing!). I steadied myself, gripping the steering wheel tight. We had just come out of a pre-operative assessment for the procedure that would insert pins into his fibulas in order to restrict their growth whilst his tibias caught up in length. Hopefully, this would address the rolling ankles and pain in his legs. With the prospect of more surgery on the horizon, I decided to broach the subject of vosoritide with Luqman for the first time:

> 'Hypothetically if there was an injection that would make you taller – you'd still be a Dwarf that doesn't change – but taller, would you want to be average height like me and your brothers or smaller just like you are now?'

> 'Smaller like me', he shot back.

I was not sure if he grasped my meaning. I decided to probe further. After all, this was not a hypothetical situation. I was hedging my bets with the use of the abstract. I wanted to see what he thought about his body, without flashing some magic beans in front of his eyes.

> 'Okay, if you had a choice, no medicine or operations involved. If you got to choose, would you ever want to be average height?'

> 'No, I'd always choose to be a Dwarf'.

'Why? What do you like about being a Dwarf?'

'I have fun. I get to do Dwarf sports with my friends.'

'Anything else?'

'I don't know anything else. I can't explain, it's just fun'.

And there it was: he did not know anything else. *Why would he?* His friends and community were just like him, why would he want to be different from them? There was I, trying to ask a child to imagine being something he was not—more than that—asking what he liked about being in his body. Of course, he could not explain it! I was asking him to separate his sense of self—his physical body and his identity. He could not do it. It was unimaginable. Turning my attention back to the journey ahead, a wave of relief washed over me. In all honesty, I had not thought where the conversation would go if Luqman had decided that he would like to take a drug which would make him grow. It was a risk going forward with such an important conversation without having at least done some groundwork. I knew which centres offered the trial, so I reckoned that if pushed, I could get him referred. However, if I was being entirely honest with myself, I knew that if he wanted vosoritide, I would have tried to talk him out of it. I see Luqman's dwarfism as part of his identity—part of my identity. The activities he participates in are mainly based within the community. This, of course, is my doing. I had wholly embraced this new environment; I had hit the ground running. As a nondisabled mother, having a disabled child, I wanted to submerge him—well, us—into a community where he would be treated normally and where his size was ordinary. I knew he would have experiences and questions I could not help with. I had reached out to other parents and adults in the community to help us navigate these situations. This new drug route had made our once seemingly easy decisions that much harder. But why?

Acceptance. Actually, more than that. For me as Luqman's mother, it came down to how I *needed* Luqman to perceive himself. I wanted him to not just accept the path that fate had handed to him; I wanted him to love it: to love himself just the way he is and to validate my own mothering choices. *Would offering him a 'way out' make him think I was not happy with the way he was born? Would it put doubt in his mind that his body was not good enough the way it was?* Parents who have to make these types of life-changing decisions do not do so easily. Just having to weigh up all the potential angles and possibilities is a feat in itself. The weight of responsibility is nothing short of colossal. *To choose or not to choose? That is the question*. On one side, there is the issue of his health. Why would I knowingly choose for him not to have a drug which could eradicate the potentially fatal complications of achondroplasia, without him having to go through surgery? Swallowing that pill is hard. At the moment, the drug trial is just that: a trial. Provisional results concentrate on height gain, with anecdotal mentions concerning the wider health implications of growth. Parents who have decided to trial vosoritide have done so in the hope that their children's lives will be easier, less painful. Emotionally, the consequences of living in a society and culture which dehumanises people with dwarfism are distressing to all involved, not least to the person who is targeted in the abuse (Ellis 2018; Grant 2016, 2018). Then comes the other charge against me: Why would I 'let' him go through the experiences of bullying and ridicule that stem from our societal and cultural views of dwarfism? I have never and will never know or experience what it is like to be the focus of mockery and abuse that people with dwarfism endure (Ellis 2018). Historically and culturally, people with dwarfism have been subjected to various degrees of public curiosity. People with dwarfism have been stigmatised or considered not quite part of humanity (Adelson 2005; Goffman 1963). As a nondisabled mother to a child with dwarfism, I am spared this experience. Luqman is not. People considered 'abnormal' were employed as spectacles for public entertainment. In contemporary society, we still have this curiosity, although the platform has shifted: from 'freak show' to reality television (Backstrom 2012). These fictional portrayals have generated distance and skewed our understandings of the genuine lived reality and experiences of dwarfism, from the point of view of both the people with the condition and their families.

Imagining Opportunities for Social Justice?

The importance of using auto/biography as a way to explore how justice could be achieved in the lives of disabled individuals is key, as is the 'critique of unjust systems' which create barriers to justice and liberation (Toyosaki and Pensoneau-Conway 2013: 566). In that respect, it is paramount to *hear from the inside* the multiple voices within the community which make up the collective. Another way to position this notion is to think about the opportunities for social justice within our everyday interactions, by disrupting in the moment the layers of social injustice. 'Maybe seeking social justice is not only about seeking social justice, but about critiquing and interrupting the minute moments of social injustice that permeate our everyday identity performances, and hoping for a better tomorrow with others in our lives' (Toyosaki and Pensoneau-Conway 2013: 561).

When discussing the concept of social justice with dwarfism activist and writer, Eugene Grant, he challenged the defeatist nature of our conversation:

> Isn't there something about reality versus hope or a vision for a better world? Just because we should expect or be prepared for things (abuse against Dwarf bodies) doesn't mean we must stop longing for their end. There's the world as it is and the world that we want and they're not mutually exclusive. People seem to act as if the world that we want is the world we live in now, that everything's all good, that we shouldn't talk about such problems, and that doing so is having some sort of detrimental effect or scaring children and I just don't believe that's true. People with dwarfism have told me that they've stayed away from certain gatherings because they didn't feel there was a place for their – darker – experiences or stories. But these experiences and stories are (a) critical to many people's lived experiences and shouldn't be silenced or muffled, and (b) don't have to stop our pursuit of justice. After all, dishonest justice isn't really justice at all. There's the world we live in (see Shakespeare, Thompson and Wright 2010) and the world we want.

When space is not given for stories to be told by disabled communities and other marginalised groups, missing data—the details of their lives—are silenced and stolen, eventually resulting in socio-political death: a form of systematic symbolic violence against a whole community. To resist this outcome, and enable socio-political living, we must aid the hearing and (re)telling of the 'personal stories of marginalised and oppressed others and then embedding them within a broader sociological landscape' (Rogers, this volume). Through our conversations and my observations of his life, social justice for Luqman is making sure that I make his environments safe from abusive outsiders. This includes him not being around conversations which position his body as problematic. Social justice is intended to marry together individual rights and freedoms, with active participation within the wider society. People in the dwarfism community belong in our society; participation is a right, yet barriers remain. As Mladenov (2016) argues, the subject of disability is socio-political. How is justice to be achieved, if in order to participate, you have to assimilate to an environment that is hostile towards people they perceive as nonconforming? *Why should Luqman have to change himself just to be accepted? Why should I have to prepare him for abuse? Why is that a part of my mothering role?*

Conclusion

As a mother researching within my own disabled community, I have become aware of the relationality I have to others. Through auto/biographical reflections, we negotiate our positions as we critique and challenge the unjust structures around disability and, more specifically, dwarfism. Our co-constructed stories cement our relationships as we become more socio-politically astute. Reflecting upon our stories, our auto/biographies, returns us to the emotional sphere in caring *for* and *about* our disabled children (Rogers 2016). In returning to the emotional, I acknowledge that my researcher self and mothering self were never distinct identities. The boundaries were too often blurred that I question if there was even a divide present at all (Adler and Adler 1997; Cooper and Rogers 2015).

Using memory as a basis for this chapter has opened up the possibility to 'listen' to my son as he developed awareness of his own embodied self. Indeed, '[w]e live our lives in the present and yet all forms of research […] are backwards looking' (Freeman 2015: 10). The use of past field notes has enabled me to document not only my son's life as he grows up within the dwarfism community, but the interactions which inform how we make decisions about his life. It is this critique of society's conforming culture which fuels the desire to embrace a community which removes Dwarf bodies from the margins of humanity by redefining what the community consider 'normal'.

When thinking about the opportunities for social justice, I am often caught between hope and despair. Social justice cannot be truly implemented within the context of the dwarfism community, if in order to participate within the wider society, people with dwarfism were made to expect abusive interactions by members of the public, as is the current status-quo. But we live in hope. Hope for a better tomorrow, a better future for our generation and the next. Hope that by telling outsiders our stories, they can see and feel our humanity (Rogers 2016). Auto/Biography can inform social justice by permitting social actors to engage in a cycle of reflexivity and resistance work. Critiquing structures which hold up discrimination and working towards their dismantlement.

References

Ablon, J. (1984). *Little People in America: The Social Dimensions of Dwarfism*. New York: Praeger.

Adelson, B. (2005). *The Lives of Dwarfs: Their Journey from Public Curiosity Toward Social Liberation*. New Brunswick, NJ: Rutgers University Press.

Adler, P., & Adler, P. (1997). Parent-as-Researcher: The Politics of Researching in the Personal Life. In R. Hertz (Ed.), *Reflexivity and Voice* (pp. 21–44). London: Sage.

Aubrecht, K., & La Monica, N. (2017). (Dis)Embodied Disclosure in Higher Education: A Co-constructed Narrative. *Canadian Journal of Higher Education, 47*(3), 1–15.

Backstrom, L. (2012). From the Freak Show to the Living Room: Cultural Representations of Dwarfism and Obesity. *Sociological Forum, 27*(3), 682–706.

Berger, R., & Quinney, R. (2005). *Storytelling Sociology: Narrative as Social Inquiry*. London: Lynne Rienne.

Bogdan, R. (1988). *Freak Show: Presenting Human Oddities for Amusement and Profit*. Chicago: University of Chicago Press.

British Sociological Association. (2017). *Statement of Ethical Practice for the British Sociological Association* [online]. Available from https://www.britsoc.co.uk/media/24310/bsa_statement_of_ethical_practice.pdf. Last Accessed on 14 August 2018.

Carpenter, J., & McConkey, R. (2012). Disabled Children's Voices: The Nature and Role of Future Empirical Enquiry. *Children and Society, 26*(3), 251–261.

Cokley, R. (2018). *On Parenting and Consent: When Sharing Isn't Caring*. Rewire News. Available here https://rewire.news/article/2018/05/09/parenting-consent-sharing-isnt-caring/. Last Accessed on 30 July 2018.

Cooper, L., & Rogers, C. (2015). Mothering and 'Insider' Dilemmas: Feminist Sociologists in the Research Process. *Sociological Research Online, 20*(2), 5.

Dasen, V. (2013). *Dwarfs in Ancient Egypt and Greece*. Oxford: Oxford University Press.

Donaldson, J., Aftab, S., & Bradish, C. (2015). Achondroplasia and Limb Lengthening: Results in a UK Cohort and Review of the Literature. *Journal of Orthopaedics, 12*(1), 31–34.

Dunn, D. S., & Andrews, E. E. (2015). Person-First and Identity-First Language: Developing Psychologists' Cultural Competence Using Disability Language. *The American Psychologist, 70*(3), 255–264.

Ellis, C. (2007). Telling Secrets, Revealing Lives: Relational Ethics in Research with Intimate Others. *Qualitative Inquiry, 13*(1), 3–29.

Ellis, C. (2009). *Revision: Autoethnographic Reflections on Life and Work*. Walnut Creek, CA: Left Coast Press.

Ellis, L. (2018). Through a Filtered Lens: Unauthorized Picture-Taking of People with Dwarfism in Public Spaces. *Disability and Society, 33*(2), 218–237.

Fairclough, N. (2010). *Discourse and Social Change*. Cambridge: Polity Press.

Freeman, J. (2015). *Remaking Memory: Autoethnography, Memoir and the Ethics of Self*. Faringdon, Oxfordshire: Libri Publishing.

Fuchs, H. (2018). *BioMarin Doses First Participant in Phase 2 Study of Vosoritide for Treatment of Infants and Young Children with Achondroplasia*. Cision PR Newswire. Available here https://www.prnewswire.com/news-releases/biomarin-doses-first-participant-in-phase-2-study-of-vosoritide-for-treatment-of-infants-and-young-children-with-achondroplasia-300666321.html. Last Accessed 30 July 2018.

Giorgio, G. A. (2013). Reflections on Writing Through Memory in Autoethnography. In S. Holman Jones, T. E. Adams, & C. Ellis (Eds.), *Handbook of Autoethnography* (pp. 406–424). Walnut Creek, CA: Left Coast Press.

Goffman, E. (1963). *Stigma: Notes on the Management of Spoiled Identity*. Harmondsworth: Penguin.

Grant, E. (2016). Laughing at Dwarfism Is the Last Acceptable Prejudice—But Don't Seek My Approval for Your Intolerance. *The Independent*. Available here https://www.independent.co.uk/voices/laughing-at-dwarfism-is-the-last-acceptable-prejudice-but-dont-seek-my-approval-for-your-intolerance-a6879106.html. Last Accessed on 30 July 2018.

Grant, E. (2018). Verne Troyer's Tragic Death Underlines the Harm Mini-Me Caused People with Dwarfism. *The Guardian*. Available here https://www.theguardian.com/film/2018/apr/23/verne-troyer-mini-me-dwarfism-abuse-austin-powers. Last Accessed on 30 July 2018.

Green, S. E. (2002). Mothering Amanda: Musings on the Experience of Raising a Child with Cerebral Palsy. *Journal of Loss and Trauma, 7*(1), 21–34.

Kittay, E. F. (1999). *Love's Labor: Essays on Women, Equality and Dependency*. New York: Routledge.

Kittay, E., & Feder, E. (2002). *The Subject of Care: Feminist Perspectives on Dependency*. Oxford: Rowman and Littlefield.

Koren, Y., & Negev, E. (2004). *In Our Hearts We Were Giants: The Remarkable Story of the Lilliput Troupe—A Dwarf Family's Survival of the Holocaust*. New York: Carroll and Graf Publishers.

Landsman, G. (2003). Emplotting Children's Lives: Developmental Delay vs. Disability. *Social Science and Medicine, 56*(9), 1947–1960.

Landsman, G. (2009). *Reconstructing Motherhood and Disability in the Age of 'Perfect' Babies*. New York: Routledge.

Liamputtong, P. (2007). *Researching the Vulnerable*. London: Sage.

Lynch, K. (2007). Love labour as a Distinct and Non-Commodifiable Form of Care Labour. *Sociological Review, 55*(3), 550–570.

MacDonald, A. (2013). Researching with Young Children: Considering Issues of Ethics and Engagement. *Contemporary Issues in Early Childhood, 14*(3), 255–269.

Miller, T., & Bell, L. (2002). Consenting to What? Issues of Access, Gate-Keeping and 'Informed' Consent. In M. Mauthner, M. Birch, J. Jessop, & T. Miller (Eds.), *Ethics in Qualitative Research* (pp. 53–69). London: Sage.

Mladenov, T. (2016). Disability and Social Justice. *Disability and Society, 31*(9), 1226–1241.

Radić-Šestić, M., Ostojić, S., & Đoković, S. (2015). Attitude of Deaf Culture Toward Cochlear Implantation. *Specijalna Edukacija I Rehabilitacija, 14*(1), 101–124.

Ribbens, J. (1998). Hearing My Feeling Voice? An Autobiographical Discussion of Motherhood. In J. Ribbens & R. Edwards (Eds.), *Feminist Dilemmas in Qualitative Research: Public Knowledge and Private Lives* (pp. 24–38). London: Sage.

Rogers, C. (2003). The Mother/Researcher in Blurred Boundaries of a Reflexive Research Process. *Auto/Biography, XI*(1 and 2), 47–54.

Rogers, C. (2007). *Parenting and Inclusive Education: Discovering Difference, Experiencing Difficulty*. Houndmills: Palgrave Macmillan.

Rogers, C. (2009). (S)excerpts from a Life Told: Sex, Gender and Learning Disability. *Sexualities, 12*(3), 271–289.

Rogers, C. (2013). Intellectual Disability and Mothering: An Engagement with Ethics of Care and Emotional Work. In C. Rogers & S. Weller (Eds.), *Critical Approaches to Care: Understanding Caring Relations, Identities and Cultures* (pp. 132–143). London: Routledge.

Rogers, C. (2016). *Intellectual Disability and Being Human: A Care Ethics Model*. London: Routledge.

Rogers, C. (this volume). Missing Data: The Sociological Imagination Beyond the Crime. In J. Parsons & A. Chappell (Eds.), *The Palgrave Macmillan Handbook of Auto/Biography*. Houndmills: Palgrave.

Rogers, C., & Tuckwell, S. (2016). Co-constructed Research and Intellectual Disability: An Exploration of Friendship, Intimacy and Being Human. *Sexualities, 19*(5–6), 623–640.

Ryan, S., & Runswick-Cole, K. (2009). From Advocate to Activist? Mapping the Experiences of Mothers of Children on the Autism Spectrum. *Journal of Applied Research in Intellectual Disabilities, 22*(1), 43–53.

Schwalbe, M. (1998). Goffman Against Postmodernism: Emotion and the Reality of the Self. *Symbolic Interaction, 16*(4), 333–350.

Shakespeare, T. (2013). *Disability Rights and Wrongs Revisited*. Abingdon: Routledge.

Shakespeare, T., Thompson, S., & Wright, M. (2010). No Laughing Matter: Medical and Social Experiences of Restricted Growth. *Scandinavian Journal of Disability Research, 12*(1), 19–31.

Sparkes, A. C. (2002). Autoethnography: Self-Indulgence or Something More? In A. Bochner & C. Ellis (Eds.), *Ethnographically Speaking: Autoethnography, Literature, and Aesthetics*. Walnut Creek, CA: AltaMira Press.

Steinberg, S. B. (2017). Sharenting: Children's Privacy in the Age of Social Media. *Emory Law Journal, 66*(4), 839–884.

Tillmann, L. M. (2009). Body and Bulimia Revisited: Reflections of "A Secret Life". *Journal of Inquiry, 15*(2), 545–560.

Toyosaki, S., & Pensoneau-Conway, S. L. (2013). Autoethnography as a Praxis of Social Justice: Three Ontological Contexts. In S. Holman Jones, T. Adams, & C. Ellis (Eds.), *Handbook of Autoethnography* (pp. 557–575). Walnut Creek, CA: Left Coast Press.

Tummala-Narra, P. (2009). Contemporary Impingements on Mothering: Identity in the Contemporary World. *American Journal of Psychoanalysis, 69*(1), 4–21.

Van Dijk, T. (1995). Aims of Critical Discourse Analysis. *Japanese Discourse, 1*(1), 17–25.

Van Dijk, T. (1996). *Discourse, Power and Access in Texts and Practice: Readings in Critical Discourse Analysis* (C. R. Caldas-Coulthard & M. Coulthard, Eds., pp. 84–104). London: Routledge.

28

An Auto/Biographical Account of Managing Autism and a Hybrid Identity: 'Covering' for Eight Days Straight

Amy Simmons

Introduction

This chapter is concerned with the value of 'Autistic'[1] as a sociopolitical identity and the consequences for an Autistic person's emotional well-being and self-concept. This chapter is about conforming to social and cultural rules when circumstances dictate certain behaviours, for example, an academic conference. This chapter is about me. I self-identify as Autistic, receiving my diagnosis of Asperger's syndrome (on the autistic spectrum) in 1998, at the age of thirteen (I am now thirty-four, and I was thirty-one at the time of the conference). Before I go any further, I introduce one of the 'lead characters' in my auto/biography, my support worker, Steve. Steve's role is to monitor my progress and 'manage' my behaviour, communicate with others on my behalf and facilitate my smooth trajectory through further and higher education (FHE).

---

[1]'Autistic' separates Autism as a foundation of personal, social and political identity from autism as a diagnosis. Although Autism and autism do not exist in isolation from each other, they are quite separate.

A. Simmons (✉)
University of Bradford, Bradford, UK
e-mail: a.l.simmons@bradford.ac.uk

J. M. Parsons and A. Chappell (eds.), *The Palgrave Handbook of Auto/Biography*,
https://doi.org/10.1007/978-3-030-31974-8_28

Below, I introduce the personal auto/biographical context, some key concepts and discussion around autism, as well as a brief synopsis of method used. I then go on to reflect upon some of my experiences of attending three academic conferences, over an eight-day period, connecting it to the theoretical assumptions about stigma, shame and normalisation (Goffman 1963; Foucault 1975). Finally, I draw some conclusions.

Auto/Biographical and Autism Context

From 1 April 2016 to 8 April 2016, as a Ph.D. student, I was a delegate at three consecutive sociology conferences, hosted by my university at that time. From April 1 to 4, I was also a student representative, welcoming and orientating international delegates, and acting as a source of local knowledge. During this period, I 'covered' my autism—those traits that seem to leak out, that might be deemed inappropriate, socially unacceptable or simply plain strange (Goffman 1963; Thomas 2007). I positioned myself as autistic in conversation, but decided to downplay my differentness, and mask my meltdowns, which I experience as a rush of adrenaline, followed by a brief period of intense anger or distress, and self-stimulatory behaviour ('stimming' or 'to stim'), e.g. absent-mindedly plaiting strands of my hair.

Covering is 'admitting to the stigmatised feature or attribute, but working hard to minimise its significance' (Thomas 2007: 23), and 'persons who are ready to admit possession of a stigma [...] may nonetheless make a great effort to keep the stigma from looming large' (Goffman 1963: 103). Covering usually describes the situation of a person whose stigma is known about, one who cannot 'choose' to pass, but who nonetheless minimises the extent to which their condition obtrudes into their everyday interactions. But it can also describe the position of any person, myself included, during that eight-day period, who makes 'an effort to restrict the display of those failings most centrally identified with the stigma' (Goffman 1963: 104). Stigma is 'the situation of the individual who is disqualified from full social acceptance' (Goffman 1963: 9). Stigma, therefore, can be said to have occurred when an individual is found to:

> [possess] an attribute that makes him different from others in the category of persons available for him to be, and of a less desirable kind – in the extreme, a person who is quite thoroughly bad, or dangerous, or weak. He is thus reduced in our minds from a whole and usual person to a tainted, discounted one. (Goffman 1963: 11)

Autism fits this description quite comfortably and the discourse surrounding any stigmatised identity, including autism, can perpetuate or challenge these negative stereotypes. The language of autism is highly contested. To consciously self-identify as a 'person with autism' is to favour person-first language. For the person with autism, autism is not an integral part of their self-identity. To consciously describe oneself as an 'autistic person' is to favour identity-first language. Commonly, Autistic people see autism as an integral part of their identity (Kapp et al. 2012; Brown 2011). I wonder, is it preferable to use person-first language or identity-first language?

Language choices are personal to the autistic individual, but I will use identity-first language here. Brown (2011) described how:

> In the autism community, many self-advocates and their allies prefer terminology such as "Autistic," "Autistic person," or "Autistic individual" because we understand autism as an inherent part of an individual's identity – the same way one refers to "Muslims," "African-Americans," "Lesbian/Gay/Bisexual/Transgender/Queer," "Chinese," "gifted," "athletic," or "Jewish." (Brown 2011: n.p.)

The terminology used to describe individuals not on the autistic spectrum has also received attention in recent years. 'Non-autistic' is sometimes used interchangeably with narrower concepts, for example, 'neurotypical', 'neurologically typical' or the derogatory colloquialism 'allistic', but this is a misnomer. A person might be non-autistic, but neurologically atypical, for example, a schizophrenic person.

Autistic individuals are pigeon-holed into superficial 'high-functioning' or 'low-functioning' categories, but recent thinking on autism does not support this binary system (Tate 2014; Des Roches Rosa 2018). I have been identified as 'high-functioning' and I hold several qualifications, and I am after all, currently in the latter stages of my Ph.D. research. But I meltdown and stim, my social circle is limited. I do not live or travel independently, and I have been in paid work for two months and one week in total. Some identified as 'low-functioning' (and I am describing people I know or have known) have a wide circle of friends, some are in paid employment and travel independently, and if any of these 'low-functioning' people 'meltdown', none have ever done so in my company. Functionality is also context-dependent. On the same day, the same autistic individual could exhibit 'high' and 'low' functioning behaviours. A fire drill, a withering look from a passer-by, a gotcha joke (a joke which works by convincing the 'victim' that false information is true) or a 'scary face' video on social media, any of these and more besides are likely to result in a meltdown in me ('low-functioning' behaviour). I, however, redirect my attention to my research shortly afterwards, continuing work on my Ph.D. thesis as before ('high-functioning' behaviour). Covering (Goffman 1963) required me to mask these 'low-functioning' behaviours, to give a positive impression, but I acknowledge the ambiguity of concepts such as 'low-functioning' and 'high-functioning', and the privileges my status as a 'high-functioning' autistic individual affords me.

In the spring of 2016, I was quite unfamiliar with the term covering (Goffman 1963); besides, I am not comfortable with the ideas around covering, or indeed, pretence. In childhood, even in adolescence, when peer pressure to 'fit in' is at its highest (Humphrey and Lewis 2008), I would never downplay my differentness—never 'act normal' to win friends. And a Ph.D. is a solitary affair, with few opportunities for social interaction. I work in a largely deserted office, or I work from home, and I have not attended any taught courses for several months. Goffman's (1963) use of the concept covering, and how I interpret it, contravened my principles and my self-integrity, and it demanded a performance I had not rehearsed, but with Steve's support, I duly covered, self-presenting as an autistic-NT hybrid (Ahmed 1999; Sion 2013). Sion (2013) presents hybridity as a paradox. The hybrid's stigmatised identity is known. In some contexts, this might be in the best interests of the stigmatised person.

There are many careers where 'insider' knowledge of the stigmatised group is an advantage. But the person acting out their hybridity downplays and minimises their differentness to be viewed more favourably by the majority in any given social situation. Given my position as an Autistic individual, I therefore felt it made sense to introduce auto/biographic and auto/ethnographic sociology as a tool to understand covering and hybrid identity further. Auto/biographical sociology positions 'the autobiographical as a basis for sociological analysis and understanding in its own right' (Coffey 2004: 141). Auto/ethnography 'is an approach to research and writing that seeks to describe and systematically analyse (*graphy*) personal experience (*auto*) in order to understand cultural experience (*ethno*)' (Ellis et al. 2011: para. 1, emphasis in original). Auto/Biography is more than navel-gazing (Rogers, this volume). The telling of one story can illuminate issues effecting a wider group of people. An auto/biography is one of the most personal forms of academic writing. This auto/biography is about my Self-sacrifice, the decline in my self-concept and my emotional well-being. But other autistic people are advised to cover, to circumvent negative attention and stigma. Other autistic people Self-sacrifice, for the arbitrary label 'high functioning' and the privileges which accompany a higher position in the hierarchy of impairment (Rogers 2016). The deeply personal experiences I describe here are mine alone. The experiences of covering and Self-sacrifice, and the subsequently lowered self-esteem are not.

Utilising auto/biographical sociology (Stanley 1995; Coffey 2004) and auto/ethnography (Ellis 2004), I reflect on my experiences of covering for eight days at three consecutive conferences and with sociological analysis. Used to its best effect, auto/ethnography, and auto/biographical sociology, is a methodologically sound analytical tool, which can make a significant contribution to sociological research (Allen-Collinson and Hockey 2008). Far from being self-indulgent, it is usually necessary when writing an auto/biography to revisit some difficult, often painful memories (Ellis 2004). Rogers' (this volume) concept of sociopolitical death is a macabre but a useful metaphor for the filtering out of stories too harrowing to be told, and stories 'not worth hearing' from voices 'not worth listening to'. Autistic voices, the voices of people with learning difficulties or mental health conditions, are often silenced. This auto/biography is my sociopolitical survival. All names except Steve are pseudonyms. Steve was happy to be named as an integral part of my academic journey.

The fieldnotes included here were taken as part of my Ph.D. research on autism and transition in FHE, which also involved interviewing thirty-seven autistic students. Application for ethical approval for my research was a relatively prolonged process. Including 'vulnerable' adults in the project meant I had to be especially rigorous when outlining possible ethical complications and detailing how I intended to address them. The concept of 'vulnerability' is contentious. Vulnerability is universal. We are all susceptible to death, injury, illness and disability, but certain groups are more vulnerable than others, 'Vulnerable persons are those with reduced capacity, power or control to protect their interests relative to other agents […] inequalities of power, dependency, capacity or need render some agents vulnerable to harm or exploitation by others' (Mackenzie et al. 2014: 6). The notion of 'vulnerability' conjures images of 'victimhood, deprivation, dependency or pathology' (Fineman 2008: 8). I acted in the participants' best interests, and I took care to equalise the balance of power between us as far as possible, but I was always attentive to their needs. The ethics committee in my department approved my application.

Eight Days: A Hybrid Identity

1 April 2016 was the first day of the first conference. It also marked the beginning of autism awareness/acceptance month. It was an irony not lost on me. Autism awareness/acceptance month is a month I associate

with celebrations of Autism (and autism), proud displays of autism and challenging some of the misconceptions around the condition. I do not associate autism awareness/acceptance month with covering (Goffman 1963), the purpose of which is surely unawareness. April 1 is also April Fools' Day (a Western tradition, which began in 1582), the tradition of tomfoolery, practical jokes and 'gotcha' jokes. It is not that I cannot appreciate humour, but I have never responded well to 'gotcha' jokes. I experience a meltdown as a rush of adrenaline, and a subsequent, indeterminate period of intense distress. My frustrations would escalate into a meltdown, something which is heavily stigmatised (Ryan 2010).

The following account details my fretful attempts to pre-empt the potential April foolery, given the first day of the conference was indeed April Fools' Day, and avert a 'meltdown'. I therefore presumed anything anyone said was a joke because everyone knew it was April Fools' Day, did they not? In this reflection from that time, I was sitting in a room at the beginning of the postgraduate conference:

> 'Sorry I'm late, the car wouldn't start!' A dishevelled young woman flings open the door to the seminar room, apologising unreservedly to Andrew, the facilitator, momentarily interrupting his housekeeping. Andrew is not disturbed. He welcomes the latecomer and indicates an unoccupied seat. I begin to smile, in amusement, smelling a rat. I await the 'April fools!' with bated breath, but none is forthcoming. (personal fieldnotes, April 2016)

Amina had not been joking, but I had panicked, knowing how alienating a meltdown could be. I must have seemed quite insensitive, seeming to laugh at this latecomer's misfortune. It was quite the conclusion to leap to. It would have been inappropriate for Amina to arrive late and interrupt the facilitator's opening remarks, for a relatively elaborate April Fools' joke, and triumphantly exclaim 'April fools!' in a bid to fool a group of sociologists, and twenty international students, not all of whom would observe the tradition. I was in a state of high vigilance, fearful of the consequences of being 'caught out', of the consequences of a meltdown, of humiliating and disappointing Steve. The reprimand and eventual exclusion from the labour market were surely to arrive if I failed to recognise and be a part of social traditions. Besides, I am acutely aware, only 32% of autistic individuals are in full- or part-time paid employment (National Autistic Society 2016a), and I was determined to make a favourable impression at this event.

April Fools' Day was only one worry of mine that morning, as there were many others. Sometimes I knew conference or course facilitators organised 'ice-breaker' games, and I have never been able to distance myself from the 'failure' of losing. Games have always made me feel anxious, in anticipation of a meltdown, but covering was an added pressure, knowing I would have to 'play pretend', if necessary, as the following shows:

> Is that a knot or a butterfly in my stomach? Other delegates seem composed, mature. I explore the possibility of 'nipping out to the toilet' if Andrew has organised a game. I have Googled 'ice-breaker games', 'Ha!' sounds uncomfortable, embarrassing. We will be like sardines in a tin, lying side by side on the floor. And when it is my turn, someone will touch my stomach, with a 'ha!' and if I giggle (although I could not feel less like laughing), I will be eliminated. I have seen enough episodes of The Chase and Strictly Come Dancing to know what a good loser is supposed to look like, but will that translate into my own behaviour? I will probably have a meltdown! I do not want to be a sardine! Or any food. What if we are asked one of those 'if you were a food, what would you be?' questions? How do you answer those sorts of questions without cringing? (personal fieldnotes, April 2016)

Andrew, however, as he concluded his introductions, did not ask too much of us. He only asked for our names, where we came from and our research interests. I may have been spared the indignity of answering any comparative journey or research questions, but as the other delegates introduced themselves, and I put faces to the names on the conference papers, I made comparisons of quite a different kind. In my imagined scenarios, the delegates had travelled confidently and independently from far afield. In my imagination, the delegates were comfortable spending several nights in a city centre hotel, and the conversation had flowed easily between them. I imagined, by the close of the conference, these delegates would have become good friends. Whether some, all or none of this was the reality for any of the delegates, these were some of the conclusions I came to.

Unlike these delegates, I had never travelled independently, or spent time in a city centre hotel room with a stranger. Steve and I commuted daily to and from the conference, as we lived relatively locally. He would come, first thing, to collect me from my home, where I lived with my parents. Some suggest society places too much emphasis on disabled individuals' independence and shames or stigmatises those who are seemingly 'dependent' (French 1991). Rogers (2016: 14), notably described about shame, it 'can be a feeling based on a sense of failure to attain particular goals grounded in cultural expectations'. Goffman (1963), moreover, described how 'we' (non-stigmatised persons or 'normals') make a set of assumptions when we meet a stranger, expecting them to be like 'us'.

I also made a groundless set of assumptions about this group of strangers, somehow expecting them to have attained these particular goals, with no evidence to suggest this, or otherwise. As the day progressed, I continued to compare myself unfavourably to the other delegates, as I describe below:

> I smile and nod encouragingly, and stare intently at the bridge of the presenter's nose, to seem attentive. My concentration is waning, but I cannot let the presenter know that. I begin to compare my presentation to theirs. Mine is colourful, I have written in a few jokes, I have included photographs of autistic celebrities, singer Björk, and television personality Anne Hegerty, (who is also autistic). Their presentations are sophisticated, professional, not much attempt at humour. And I realise, too, I am the only presenter who did not submit a conference paper to a panel of judges. I submitted a conference paper, but as a student representative, I was given a 'free pass', my paper had been accepted automatically. Would I be sitting here today if my paper had been held to the same rigorous standards? The other delegates are listening intently, contributing sensible questions to group discussions. I clock-watch, I cannot follow the conversation. It is the first of eight days of feigning interest, and competence. I begin to feel 'less than'. (personal fieldnotes, April 2016)

Over the next few days, I withdrew further into myself as reflected upon here:

> Today is the fourth day of the first conference. It is half an hour until 'show time' (although it has been 'show time' since Friday morning). It is difficult not to reflect on my previous experiences of presenting, a panic attack, instigated by an audience of seven, two other presenters, Steve, the chair, and three vaguely interested parties. I had not slept, and I had struggled to breathe, stimming and sipping water unnecessarily to moisten my bone-dry mouth. But this morning, almost noon, I am relatively confident. I am the first presenter after lunch. The perfect scheduling for a nervous presenter. I can compose myself, listen to some music, and deliver my presentation before I can overthink things, before the fear can consume me.
> Andrew is making an announcement, there is an exhibition in a local university which might be of interest to some of the delegates. 'Is it far?' Rachel, a confident young woman who contributes regularly to group discussions, asks. 'No,' I flinch, startled by the sound of my own voice. But the ice has been broken, and determined, emboldened, I continue, 'it's not far. Just down the road.' I pass this university on my daily commute, I walk past it most days, and I have interviewed someone there. I become conscious of how little I have spoken in the past few days. Aside from evening meals, when we were on an even footing, I was reluctant to engage other delegates in conversation.

The less I speak, the less possibility there is of unwittingly displaying my autism. The less possibility of humiliating and disappointing Steve, who has worked with me for thirteen years, who has encouraged me to present myself in the best possible light. But I feel qualified to speak now. What hope for me as a speaker, if I cannot bring myself to speak in a low-stakes, non-academic group discussion? (personal fieldnotes, April 2016)

These auto/biographies indicate quite pointedly, how much emotion work is used in any attempt to cover, largely due to conversations with the self. On reflection, self-isolation (Audet et al. 2013; Cairns 2013) and self-discrimination (Corrigan and Rao 2012), whether by avoiding social situations which might expose a stigmatised identity (Goffman 1963) or by maintaining a self-imposed silence, as I did, is a response to stigma.

When I spoke so infrequently during those first four days of the conference, to the extent that I was startled by the sound of my own voice, I was self-isolating. When I contemplated 'nipping out to the toilet' if Andrew introduced a game, I was self-isolating. When, during housekeeping, before a plenary, on day six of the conference, the speaker warned us of a scheduled fire alarm test, and I made a note to myself to come prepared with earphones. What actually happened was Steve knowing me well decided not to subject me to this fire alarm, and we arrived late on Friday morning. I was constantly self-isolating. I was unconvinced I would be able to avert or manage a meltdown, so I avoided, or planned to avoid, potential triggers that are in common with 50% of autistic people and their families (National Autistic Society 2016b).

On April 6, the first day of the third conference, and the sixth day in all, the university had organised a drinks reception, to launch a new publication and to celebrate the beginning of the conference proper. There were research posters on display and I circulated the room alone, conscious of my below-average reading speed, seeming to skim-read the information, without absorbing a word. Some of the international delegates cheerily greeted me as they passed by together. It was a disappointment. We were on good terms, but I was a 'hello friend' (a friend you would say 'hello' to, but not pass the time of day with). We had, I guessed, spent only three and a half days in each other's company, and I had not contributed much to any conversations. Were my expectations too high? I stimmed. I would twirl my hair between my fingers, or push my glasses up my nose, or my right hand would protectively clutch my left. Fellow delegates milled about, socialising with apparent ease, seemingly enjoying the opportunity to unwind and mingle with peers. I spotted my supervisor who was casually sipping a glass of wine and sharing a joke with one of her colleagues. I recognised other senior members of staff too, one seemed to be preparing to deliver a speech.

A young woman unknowingly attracted my attention. The woman was dressed from head to toe in a vibrant purple outfit and she used a wheelchair. I had noticed her at registration, and again in a paper session. She seemed pleasant and softly spoken, I promised myself I would begin a conversation with her before close of play on Friday. I envied her. Natalie could socialise without fear of being 'caught out'. The wheelchair was a visible signifier of her stigmatised identity, she could not pass for non-disabled. Part of her being was discredited, whereas part of my being was discreditable (Goffman 1963). I suspected there would have been some overlap in our experiences (Oliver 1990), such as infantilisation and the 'supercrip-vegetable' dichotomy, where the disabled individual is upheld on a pedestal as an 'inspiration' or conceptualised as a helpless 'vegetable' (Morris 1991), but camouflaging (or covering) is more common (and possible) in invisible disabilities. With the possibility of covering comes the expectation to do so. Conferences are inherently social occasions. Delegates are expected to socialise with other delegates, make conversation and contribute to group discussions (Kelsky 2011). Delegates are expected to conduct themselves in a mature fashion (Hargittai 2009). A social, emotional, behavioural condition seemed more likely to preclude this than a physical disability.

A day later, at lunch, I struggled with the few remaining grains of rice and slices of mushroom on my plate. I resented the caterers' policy to withhold knives from us, supposedly in the interests of health and safety (perhaps on the off-chance that one of those in attendance was violent?). I briefly entertained the possibility that the caterers had been warned that one of the delegates would be autistic. My emotional well-being was beginning to decline. After seven days of covering (Goffman 1963), seven days of normalising, I was beginning to self-stigmatise and experience quite irrational thoughts. Plate cleared of mushroom stroganoff, I retrieved my already well-thumbed conference book from my 'free' tote bag and browsed the post-lunch paper sessions. Frontiers was primarily a disability studies strand, and one of the two Frontiers sessions scheduled for after lunch featured a presentation on mental well-being that piqued my interest. I made my intentions known to Steve, and we left the dining area for the now familiar conference suite:

I sit several rows back, clock-watching. Steve and I are the sole occupants of the room. I watch as the advertised start time approaches, then passes. 'Steve, can you pass my conference bingo card, please?' Steve hands me the joke bingo card and a pen, but before I can check the 'A paper session is cancelled' box, we have company. The chair, and three presenters, bustle into the conference suite. An image of a computer desktop flickers onto the projector screen, updating in real-time as the presenters upload their PowerPoint presentations. I frown, not recognising any of the titles. 'We're in the wrong room!' Steve too, has realised there must have been a miscommunication. 'Oh well!' I affect nonchalant airs, with as much conviction as I can muster. 'This is a round table,' the chair warns me, which does not communicate much to me, and I continue 'That's alright, we'll stay anyway!' 'We'll go,' Steve makes an executive decision to leave, and, 'tail between my legs', I stand to leave. The dining area is deserted now. I double-check the room number and tearfully 'turn the air blue', overwhelmed by panic, anger, shock and shame. 'Remember where you are' Steve warns me. 'I suggest we go back to the office for a bit, then come back down for the next one,' he advises me. There is no alternative now, short of interrupting a presentation. I stand to leave without a word of complaint. Masking a meltdown is especially difficult. A meltdown is a frightening experience, the loss of control, the absence of emotional and behavioural self-regulation. Masking is a reminder that autistic ways of being are not okay. (personal fieldnotes, April 2016)

Cold air filled my lungs! Freedom! I could sing, quite literally! I expressed myself through song. Releasing some of my frustrations, that are the pressures and confines of the Autistic 'closet', the expectation on me to be 'good', the performance ongoing since Friday and the consequences of 'breaking character', of being a good research student, I began to sing a song from the Disney film musical Frozen. 'Don't let them in, don't let them see, be the good girl you always have to be, conceal, don't feel, put on a show, make one wrong move and everyone will know' (Anderson-Lopez and Lopez 2013).

'Remember where you are!' Steve interjects in low tones, my second warning in two minutes. 'But I didn't think it mattered now, I mean, I'm not in the conference centre, I thought it was okay' I gabble, little more than a child in trouble, caught doing 'something naughty'. 'Someone's bound to say something, you know what they're like!' Steve remarks. 'True!' I capitulate and make my way to the office in silence. I round the corner, the office comes into my line of vision and storm-like, I stride towards the sanctuary and solitude it promises. I am angry, I am embarrassed, I am tired of the pretence. And it seems I am not alone. The promise of sanctuary and solitude has been broken. The ordinarily unoccupied office has one other occupant. Under any other circumstances, I would have delighted in the company. I get on well with Priyanka, but I need breathing space. 'Hi, how are you?' Tired of acting. Confused. Desperate for release, embarrassed, 'not bad thanks, you?' (personal fieldnotes, April 2016)

These reflections on the early stages of a 'meltdown', my difficult behaviours, and how Steve manages these difficult behaviours, underline the emotion work involved in covering, and managing my self-presentation. In the latter stages of the 'meltdown', when I was asked a phatic question (Malinowski 1923), 'how are you?' the emotion work continued. A phatic question is not asked for information, but to convey sociability. I have had to learn this. So even at that point, when I am not okay, not one bit, and I am then asked, 'how are you'? I am supposed to say 'fine thanks'! Despite not being fine at all. It seems to be one of the unwritten rules governing the question, how are you? It must always be answered with a positive statement. 'Not too bad' is the bare minimum. The conversation progressed for a brief period, before we continued with our respective projects in silence. I used the unanticipated spare time productively, applying for a (day-long, department-wide) conference but I was suffering, my need for release going unmet.

Normalisation: What Is This Thing?

Given what has been discussed, it is possible to reconcile an Autistic self-identity with an appreciation of the difficulties of autism. As Kapp et al. (2012: 10) suggest, 'Neurodiversity advocates, while often emphasising social barriers, [and] have acknowledged this interrelationship between internal and social challenges' (Kapp et al. 2012: 10). But placing such a high value on normalisation (e.g. Wolfensberger 1972) did not sit comfortably with my Autistic identity. Normalisation makes 'available to all people with disabilities patterns of life and conditions of everyday living which are as close as possible to the regular circumstances and ways of life or society' (Nirje 1982: n.p.). It is difficult to oppose this principle.

In covering (Goffman 1963), in normalising, what was I hoping to achieve if not a 'regular' way of life, a career, an income, a standard of living? But the process of normalising can negatively affect the disabled person's self-concept as according to Milton and Moon (2012: 2) 'attempts to normalise people through behaviourist means or any other, would send them into disequilibrium and a state of personal anomie and possibly rather than leading someone away from a state of mental ill-health, be actually leading someone toward it'. Furthermore, applied behavioural analysis (ABA) is one of the most popular, but controversial therapies used to normalise autistic children (Devita-Raeburn 2016). ABA practitioners build a profile of the autistic child to develop a personalised programme. When an autistic child exhibits the desired behaviour (e.g. making eye contact), the therapist rewards them (e.g. they might be given access to a favourite toy). If an autistic child does not exhibit the desired behaviour, or exhibits 'inappropriate' (autistic) behaviour, the therapist temporarily withholds a privilege. But some of the underlying principles and some of the unintended consequences of ABA are troubling to many autistic commentators, and parents of autistic children. Citing Pellicano, Lambert (2013) described how:

> Although therapists wouldn't say that they're trying to normalise children with autism, that is the underlying ideology of ABA – to make them indistinguishable from their peers […] Being told there's something wrong with you is going to potentially make you more anxious and more depressed, which is already highly prevalent in people with autism. (Lambert 2013: online)

I have never experienced therapy, but this is consistent with my (thankfully brief) experiences of normalisation and the (thankfully temporary) consequences for my emotional well-being.

Normalisation reinforces to the autistic person that they are flawed, damaged, broken, the idea that to be who they are is to fail, the idea that they are not good enough, that there is something inherently wrong with autistic ways of being. Pellicano's (2013) and Lambert's (2013) critique of ABA also shows how this is not the fault of the therapists, just as Steve was not accountable for how I responded to normalisation. The problem does not lie in the aims and values of therapists or support workers. The problem lies in a society which undervalues differentness and stigmatises those perceived as different.

Normalisation is a worthy end goal, revolutionary in its time, but the process of normalisation (the downplaying of difference, mimicking NT behaviours to be seen to be 'doing well') amounts to Self-sacrifice. For the possibility of a 'regular' standard of living, for the opportunity to build a career as a sociologist, I temporarily sacrificed my Self. And normalisation (or in my case covering) seems to resign profoundly autistic individuals to the bottom of a hierarchy of impairment (Rogers 2016), the 'less autistic' the autistic person is, the more human they are. Normalisation as a process is not only potentially harmful to an autistic individual's emotional well-being, it is a gross injustice to individuals towards the other, more heavily stigmatised end of the autistic spectrum.

This intersects with the controversy of the 'straight-acting' gay man (Myers 2013; Stehler 2018). For example, some gay men camouflage their femininity or specify 'straight-acting only' on dating apps or denounce feminine gay men as an embarrassment. Myers (2013) summarised the position of feminine gay men:

> Whether we're carefully arranging ourselves into 'tribes' or behaving in a more traditionally masculine way to avoid 'standing out', we just want to belong, even if it means we have to alienate or deny the existence of everyone else along the way. (Myers 2013)

It is not possible to draw direct comparisons here, but there are some similarities between an autistic individual who masks their autism and a gay man who masks his femininity (if indeed he is feminine), confining the profoundly autistic person, or the feminine gay man respectively, to the lower reaches of an unnecessary hierarchy.

Autistic ways of being also languish at the bottom of (what I will call) a 'hierarchy of weirdness'. It is not unusual for NT persons to want to deviate from socially prescribed norms, to be quirky, but only within the confines of social acceptability, and only ever temporarily (Waldschmidt 2005). Disabled identities are forever outside the boundaries of socially accepted difference. Davis (1997: 9) noted the '"problem" is not the person with disabilities; the problem is the way that normalcy is constructed to create the "problem" of the disabled person'. The 'problem' is created concurrently with 'normalcy', and the 'problem' of autism is, to some extent, created when any society privileges NT ways of being above autistic ways of being. What is autistic has been defined in relation to NT norms, and usually unfavourably.

The Consequences of Covering

It is not unusual for any academic to become conscious of their self-presentation during academic conferences. This is something Ford (2013) became aware of when she tried to balance her career as a sociologist, with her role as a mother to a young girl at a conference. She discretely bade her daughter goodnight, over the phone, in a quiet corner of the room, as though her status as a parent would preclude her from being taken seriously as an academic. Similarly, Goffman (1956) described the ways in which most people manage their self-presentation in daily life. It is not unusual to (consciously or unconsciously) manage how others perceive you. But the stigma of autism added another dimension to everyday perception management, and common conference behaviour. Non-stigmatised persons are not compelled to pass, camouflage, cover, mask or compensate. Livingstone and Happé (2017) defined compensation as 'the processes contributing to improved behavioural presentation of a neurodevelopmental disorder, despite persisting core deficit(s) at cognitive and/or neurobiological levels' (Livingstone and Happé 2017: 731). When I prepared for the possibility of playing an elimination game at the beginning of the conference, the idea was to compensate. Despite ongoing issues with kakorrhaphiophobia (the irrational and intense fear of losing or failure), the aim was to be seen to behave in an age-appropriate way. Likewise, when I prepared for the possibility of a gotcha joke to mark April Fools' Day, the aim was to compensate. But, as I began to realise, the effects of compensation were more serious, and longer lasting than I had anticipated, as considered below:

> Charlie and I say goodbye, with a hug, as he leaves my house for his own. Charlie is my brother, three years my junior, and we have always been close. Our parents are at a wedding. The bride, Danielle, is the same age as me. I had a ready-made group of friends, growing up. Our parents would organise and supervise us. We would go camping, canoeing, our parents would pack a picnic and we would play rounders on a field somewhere (mostly I would be a spectator, sport was not for me), we would see in the new year together. But the friendships were not enduring, most of the younger generation lost touch, and in the silence, with only a dog for company, I contemplate the loss of childhood, the loss of friendship. Weddings are costly affairs. The price per head might be close to £100. Would I be willing to spend £100 on Danielle? Truthfully, no. But I am emotionally and physically exhausted from eight days of suppressing the very essence of me. I am 'less than'. My parents know Danielle no better than I do, but I am 'not the kind of person you'd want at your wedding'. I am too broken. I am too damaged. I am too autistic. I curl up in an armchair and insert my Frozen DVD into my ageing laptop. Emotion overwhelms me as the film begins, I picture the delegates on their homeward journeys, or parting company. Set to music, these mental images are more powerful somehow, and I realise I have been left behind. Left behind while my parents attend Danielle's wedding. Left behind while the other delegates travelled home. I need a release. I need to cry. I need to be Amy, before I forget what it means to be Amy, before I lose my Self. (personal fieldnotes, April 2016)

This clearly identifies my autistic self is considered, even by those around me, that I might perhaps not 'cover' enough? I might shame or embarrass those around me (Rogers 2016).

Covering (Goffman 1963) had affected my mental well-being, and I entertained several quite disturbing ideas, '"Amy Simmons" is not okay at a conference", '"be yourself" does not apply to you', 'my greatest victory is not being myself!' and 'if autism is not a bad thing, why do I have to hide it all the time?' Over an eight-day period, I had begun to lose my Self, and sense of pride in my Autistic identity. A fortnight earlier, I had been a bubbly, confident Autistic self-advocate, but this was no longer so. Hull et al. (2017) summarised the consequences of the use of camouflaging in autistic persons, 'In the short term, camouflaging results in extreme exhaustion and anxiety; although the aims of camouflaging are often achieved, in the long term there are also severe negative consequences affecting individuals' mental health, self-perception' (Hull et al. 2017: 2532).

I began a meltdown cycle in the weeks which followed the eight days of covering. To the uninitiated (and the initiated alike), I seemed to regress. The regression was quite startling. Steve was concerned I might be exhibiting signs of a breakdown. He warned me to manage these outbursts and warned me I had not shown such challenging behaviours since I was a college student. He and my parents were worried. But I was reconnecting with my Autistic Self. My meltdowns were disturbing, even petrifying, but they were also liberating. During the conference, I had covered, I had masked, I had averted my meltdowns or managed them, unwilling to risk exclusion from the labour market, with no safe space, and very few 'safe people'. With only 'safe people' (my parents or Steve) for company, there would be no repercussions. I could vent some of my frustrations, and I could give expression to my autism. Attwood (2015) describes this pattern of behaviour (more commonly observed in autistic children) as the Jekyll and Hyde effect, something my own research on autism and transition in FHE supports. At school, the autistic child is not 'safe'. There will be unwanted consequences for their behaviour (not 'bad' behaviour, but autistic ways of being). The autistic child's frustrations are not self-limiting and worsen throughout the day. Once the child is at home, safe and loved, they allow themselves to express any distress which has accumulated throughout the day (Myers 2015; Rogers 2007). This is often mistaken for 'naughty' behaviour or ineffective parenting, but it is neither of these (Attwood 2015). And there was not a day, but a week of frustration and feelings of inadequacy for me to release.

The deterioration in my emotional well-being, and my self-concept, raises questions of cause and effect. Is it shame which causes people to cover, or does covering (Goffman 1963) instil a sense of shame in the individual? These are not mutually exclusive possibilities, but in my experience, it was the latter. I chose to cover to enhance my job prospects, conscious of how few job opportunities are usually available to autistic people. I chose to cover because I was under Steve's surveillance, regulated because I cannot self-regulate (Foucault 1975), in common with many other autistic individuals (Whitman 2004). I did not choose to cover because I am ashamed of my Autistic identity, although 'Stigma […] is intimately bound up with shame. In moments of stigma, Goffman famously noted, "shame becomes a central possibility"' (Lyons and Dolezal 2017: 208). Stigmatised individuals cover for reasons other than internalised stigma, usually to circumnavigate the consequences of social stigma (Kanuha 1999; Olney and Brockelman 2010). My mental well-being began to decline as the conference progressed, not aided by continuous covering, for a prolonged period of time.

There is no deliverance in confession when covering (Goffman 1963). Foucault (1978) described how the confession is an apparatus of power, sometimes freely given, reconceptualised as a source of personal liberation. The confessor is encouraged to confess to uncomfortable feelings or vices in intimate detail, to 'get it off their chest', but this produces truth, knowledge and power concurrently. When I 'confessed', when I positioned myself in conversation as an autistic researcher, I had hoped for freedom, the discourse of confession as liberation is a convincing one, deeply embedded in today's thinking, and the promise of 'a weight off my shoulders' was difficult to resist. But not only did this continue the knowledge-power cycle, the 'show' had to go on, with me in another role, switching from 'the NT individual' to 'the asymptomatic autistic individual' (there was no leeway, but now my status as an autistic individual was known). This is the nature of covering (Goffman 1963).

The person who covers is never free. The downplaying of differentness requires almost as much energy, and as much concentration, as passing (Goffman 1963). Covering is a tightrope walk. The autistic person is expected to perform before an audience, cautiously treading a 'high wire', on which there is little to no room for error or manoeuvre. Covering gives the autistic individual a safety net to fall back on, 'sorry, it's just my autism', giving the autistic person a legitimate 'excuse' for their atypical behaviours, but they have 'fallen', they have 'failed', and there is no freedom even in 'failure', only humiliation, and self-loathing. If I 'fail' while covering, it is not *carte blanche* to be my Autistic Self. The show must go on.

Covering, however, would not be quite so necessary if there was no stigma attached to what Rogers (2016) described as 'difficult differences'. The most recent statistics and analysis in several key areas, including the number of homeless people with autistic indicators, autistic adults' under-employment, the likelihood of an autistic person experiencing hate crime and public responses to filicides (a parent, or set of parents, murders their child) involving the death of an autistic child make for difficult reading. 73% of people with learning delays and autistic people have reported hate crime and the rate of incidence is likely to be much higher as not all instances of hate crime go reported (Dimensions 2018). The National Autistic Society (2016a) reports that only 16% of autistic adults are in *full-time*, paid employment, a figure which has remained static for a decade. A disproportionate number of autistic individuals are homeless (Churchard et al. 2018), relative to the number of autistic individuals as a percentage of the population as a whole. And Willingham (2013) described, and challenged, the public outpouring of sympathy for the perpetrator(s) in response to most cases of filicide involving an autistic child. This undermines the value of autistic life. The life of the autistic child and their parents is a life not worth living (Morris 1991), and filicide is seen as reasonable under these circumstances.

What these seemingly disparate statistics indicate is autism is still a heavily stigmatised, badly misunderstood condition. It would be a disservice to the other delegates if I was to imply that I had encountered any stigma during the conference. Most of my interactions with the other delegates were very positive, and I had no reason to assume that, where they were not, autism had played a part. But vicariously experienced stigma, and mediated stigma (Essed 1991), stigma experienced through others, or through mass, and now social media left me very conscious of the stigma of autism, led me to self-present in ways which did not feel authentic, and ways which did not sit comfortably with my Self.

Gray (2002: 735) summarised the social situation of autistic individuals, when he described how autistic people 'are people with a disability who must deal with the social world as if they were not disabled. The implications of this for problematic social interaction are considerable. One of the problems they experience through social interaction is stigma'. Some people will make allowances for an autistic person. It would be an unfair generalisation to suggest otherwise. Some people have insider knowledge of the condition. Familiarity and a close relationship with a stigmatised person often reduce the possibility that a non-stigmatised person will stigmatise others with that identity (Goffman 1963). A brief conversation with Rachel on the eighth day of the conference illustrates this:

> The university have arranged another drinks reception, to mark the close of the conference. Broken, emotionally exhausted, I seek out Rachel, and hesitantly apologise for myself, although I have not wrongfooted her, 'just so you know, not all autistic people are like me, so, you know, if I haven't done very well, don't think all autistic people are like me!' 'My little cousin is autistic, so, you haven't done badly, but even if you had, I wouldn't think that you were all the same!' Rachel exclaims. (personal fieldnotes, April 2016)

Rachel had some familial experiences of autism, and so she made allowances for me. But others will not make allowances for autistic individuals, and it is not always possible for the autistic person to know who will, and who will not. Autistic people come under pressure to conduct themselves in public as if they were not disabled, at all times, never knowing if the next person they come into contact with will, or will not, make allowances. Although there is no direct comparison here, there are some similarities with Foucault's (1975) work on the panoptic. Bentham's panopticon prisons were designed to allow a single guard, stationed in a central watchtower, to observe inmates without being seen. The guard could only see one inmate at a time, but as none of the inmates knew which of them was being watched when, they would behave as if they were under surveillance all the time, and I felt as if I was expected to behave as though I was NT for similar reasons, 'you never know who is watching'.

Conclusion

This chapter is concerned with Autistic identity, and the consequences of camouflaging for an Autistic individual's emotional well-being. Perhaps to 'be yourself' is a privilege afforded to the NT. The autistic individual cannot, quite literally, afford to be themselves. To achieve a certain quality of life, for the possibility of an income, of meaningful employment, the autistic person must cover, an emotionally and physically exhausting task, which can damage their self-esteem and mental health. I described how feelings of shame were a consequence, not a cause of covering (Goffman 1963). The feelings I describe here were temporary, I no longer feel 'less than', to be who I am no longer feels like failure. But what of the autistic person covering (Goffman 1963) and camouflaging on a regular, maybe daily basis, over a prolonged period, perhaps a lifetime? What of the autistic person for whom there is no freedom, no release, from passing and masking, whether in public or at home? More ought to be done to challenge the injustice of the 'less is more' narratives surrounding autism, reinforced to the autistic person with supposed compliments, like 'I never would have guessed you were autistic, you hide it well' (May 2018; 'Anonymously Autistic' 2016). It should never be necessary to hide it well. It should never be necessary to sacrifice the Self to gain access to the opportunities most people take for granted.

References

Ahmed, S. (1999). 'She'll Wake Up One of These Days and Find She's Turned into a Nigger': Passing Through Hybridity. *Theory, Culture and Society, 16*(2), 87–106.

Allen-Collinson, J., & Hockey, J. (2008). Autoethnography as 'Valid' Methodology? A Study of Disrupted Identity Narratives. *International Journal of Interdisciplinary Social Sciences, 3*(6), 209–218.

Anderson-Lopez, K., & Lopez, R. (2013). For the First Time in Forever. In *Frozen.* Burbank, CA: Walt Disney Records.

'Anonymously Autistic'. (2016). *Autistic People Should Not Have to Pretend Not to Be Autistic.* Available at https://themighty.com/2016/10/passing-the-problem-with-autistic-people-being-forced-to-act-normal/. Accessed 13 October 2018.

Attwood, T. (2015). *The Complete Guide to Asperger's Syndrome* (2nd ed.). London: Jessica Kingsley.

Audet, C. M., McGowan, C. C., Wallston, K. A., & Kipp, A. M. (2013). Relationship Between HIV Stigma and Self-Isolation Among People Living with HIV in Tennessee. *PLoS One, 8*(8), 1–8.

Brown, L. X. Z. (2011). *The Significance of Semantics: Person-First Language: Why It Matters.* Available at https://www.autistichoya.com/2011/08/significance-of-semantics-person-first.html. Accessed 11 October 2018.

Cairns, G. (2013). *The Diminished Self—HIV and Self-Stigma.* Available at http://www.aidsmap.com/The-diminished-self-HIV-and-self-stigma/page/2657859/. Accessed 10 July 2018.

Churchard, A., Ryder, M., Greenhill, A., & Mandy, W. (2018). The Prevalence of Autistic Traits in a Homeless Population. *Autism.* Available to download at http://journals.sagepub.com/doi/10.1177/1362361318768484. Accessed 6 October 2018.

Coffey, A. (2004). *Reconceptualising Social Policy: Sociological Perspectives on Contemporary Social Policy.* Maidenhead: Open University Press.

Corrigan, P. W., & Rao, D. (2012). On the Self-Stigma of Mental Illness: Stages, Disclosure, and Strategies for Change. *Canadian Journal of Psychiatry, 57*(8), 464–469.

Davis, L. J. (1997). *Enforcing Normalcy: Disability, Deafness, and the Body*. London: Verso.

De Roches Rosa, S. (2018). *The Problems with Functioning Labels*. Available at http://www.thinkingautismguide.com/2018/03/the-problems-with-functioning-labels.html. Accessed 6 October 2018.

Devita-Raeburn, E. (2016). *The Controversy Over Autism's Most Common Therapy*. Available from https://www.spectrumnews.org/features/deep-dive/controversy-autisms-common-therapy/. Accessed 12 October 2018.

Dimensions. (2018). *Say NO More Autism and Learning Disability Hate Crime*. #ImWithSam. Available at https://www.dimensions-uk.org/get-involved/campaigns/say-no-autism-learning-disability-hate-crime-imwithsam/. Accessed 6 October 2018.

Ellis, C. (2004). *The Ethnographic I: A Methodological Novel About Autoethnography*. Pasadena, CA: Almira Press.

Ellis, C., Adams, T. E., & Bochner, A. P. (2011). Autoethnography: An Overview. *Forum: Qualitative Social Research, 12*(1), Art. 10.

Essed, P. (1991). *Understanding Everyday Racism: An Interdisciplinary Theory*. Thousand Oaks, CA: Sage.

Fineman, M. A. (2008). The Vulnerable Subject: Anchoring Equality in the Human Condition. *Yale Journal of Law and Feminism, 20*(1), 1–23.

Ford, S. (2013). *Impression Management at an Academic Conference*. Available at http://sociologyinfocus.com/2013/11/impression-management-at-an-academic-conference/. Accessed 10 July 2018.

Foucault, M. (1975). *Discipline and Punish: The Birth of the Prison* (2nd ed.). New York: Vintage Books.

Foucault, M. (1978). *The History of Sexuality, Volume 1: An Introduction*. New York: Vintage Books.

French, S. (1991). What's So Great About Independence? *The New Beacon, 75*(886), 153–156.

Goffman, E. (1956). *The Presentation of Self in Everyday Life*. Edinburgh: University of Edinburgh.

Goffman, E. (1963). *Notes on the Management of Spoiled Identity* (1st ed.). London: Penguin.

Gray, D. E. (2002). 'Everybody Just Freezes. Everybody Is Just Embarrassed': Felt and Enacted Stigma Among Parents of Children with High Functioning Autism. *Sociology of Health and Illness, 24*(6), 734–749.

Hargittai, E. (2009). *Conference Do's and Dont's*. Available from https://www.insidehighered.com/advice/2009/10/19/conference-dos-and-donts. Accessed 11 October 2018.

Hull, L., Petrides, K. V., Allison, C., Smith, P., Baron-Cohen, S., Lai, M., et al. (2017). Putting on My Best Normal. *Journal of Autism and Developmental Disorders, 47*(8), 2519–2534.

Humphrey, N., & Lewis, S. (2008). 'Make Me Normal': The Views and Experiences of Pupils on the Autistic Spectrum in Mainstream Secondary Schools. *Autism, 12*(1), 23–46.

Kapp, S. K., Gillespie-Lynch, K., Sherman, L., & Hutman, T. (2012). Deficit, Difference or Both? Autism and Neurodiversity. *Developmental Psychology*. Available to download at https://www.researchgate.net/publication/224869514_Deficit_Difference_or_Both_Autism_and_Neurodiversity. Accessed 6 October 2018.

Kanuha, V. K. (1999). The Social Process of "Passing" to Manage Stigma: Acts of Internalized Oppression or Acts of Resistance? *The Journal of Sociology and Social Welfare, 26*(4), Art. 3.

Kelsky, K. (2011). *How to Work the Conference (Part Two of Three)*. Available from http://theprofessorisin.com/2011/08/26/how-to-work-the-conference-part-two-of-three/. Accessed 11 October 2018.

Lambert, C. (2013). *Is It Right to Try to 'Normalise' Autism?* Available at https://www.theguardian.com/education/2013/oct/29/specialeducationneeds-autism. Accessed 10 July 2018.

Livingstone, L. A., & Happé, F. (2017). Conceptualising Compensation in Neurodevelopmental Disorders: Reflections from Autism Spectrum Disorder. *Neuroscience and Biobehavioural Reviews, 80*(September), 729–742.

Lyons, B., & Dolezal, L. (2017). Shame, Stigma and Medicine. *Medical Humanities, 43*(4), 208–210.

Mackenzie, C., Rogers, W., & Dodds, S. (2014). Introduction: What Is Vulnerability and Why Does It Matter for Moral Theory? In C. Mackenzie, W. Rogers, & S. Dodds (Eds.), *Vulnerability: New Essays in Ethics and Feminist Philosophy* (pp. 33–59). New York: Oxford University Press.

Malinowski, B. (1923). The Problem of Meaning in Primitive Languages. In C. K. Ogden & I. A. Richards (Eds.), *The Meaning of Meaning* (pp. 296–336). London: Kegan Paul, Trench and Trubner.

May, K. (2018). *The Problem with "I'd Never Have Guessed"*. Available from https://www.headtalks.com/electricity-every-living-thing/. Accessed 12 October 2018.

Milton, D., & Moon, L. (2012). The Normalisation Agenda and the Psycho-Emotional Disablement of Autistic People. *Autonomy, the Critical Journal of Interdisciplinary Autism Studies, 1*(1), 1–12.

Morris, J. (1991). *Pride Against Prejudice: Transforming Attitudes to Disability*. London: The Women's Press.

Myers, J. (2013). *Sorry, 'Straight-Acting' Boys, but Gay Stereotypes Exist Despite You… Get Over It*. Available at http://theguyliner.com/opinion/straight-acting-boys-gay-stereotypes-exist-despite-you/. Accessed 10 July 2018.

Myers, M. (2015, September 28). Autism and the Delayed Effect. *Kathy Brodie*. Available from http://www.kathybrodie.com/guest-post/autism-and-the-delayed-effect/. Accessed 14 August 2018.

National Autistic Society. (2016a). *Government Must Tackle the Autism Employment Gap (27 October 2016)*. Available at http://www.autism.org.uk/get-involved/media-centre/news/2016-10-27-employment-gap.aspx. Accessed 10 July 2018.

National Autistic Society. (2016b). *Too Much Information*. London: National Autistic Society.

Nirje, B. (1982). The Basis and Logic of the Normalisation Principle. *Sixth International Congress of IASSMD*, Toronto.

Oliver, M. (1990). *The Politics of Disablement*. London: Macmillan.

Olney, M. F., & Brockelman, K. F. (2010). Out of the Disability Closet: Strategic Use of Perception Management by Select University Students with Disabilities. *Disability and Society, 18*(1), 35–50.

Pellicano, E. (2013). Sensory Symptoms in Autism: A Blooming, Buzzing Confusion? *Child Development Perspectives, 7*(3), 143–148.

Rogers, C. (2007). *Parenting and Inclusive Education: Discovering Difference, Experiencing Difficulty*. London: Palgrave Macmillan.

Rogers, C. (2016). *Intellectual Disability and Being Human: A Care Ethics Model*. London: Routledge.

Rogers, C. (this volume). Missing Data: The Sociological Imagination Beyond the Crime. In J. Parsons & A. Chappell (Eds.), *The Palgrave Macmillan Handbook of Auto/Biography*. Houndmills: Palgrave.

Ryan, S. (2010). 'Meltdowns', Surveillance and Managing Emotions: Going Out with Children with Autism. *Health Place, 16*(5), 868–875.

Sion, L. (2013). Passing as Hybrid: Arab-Palestinian Teachers in Jewish Schools. *Ethnic and Racial Studies, 37*(14), 2636–2652.

Stanley, L. (1995). *The Auto/Biographical I: Theory and Practice of Feminist Auto/Biography, Volume 1 (Cultural Politics)*. Manchester: Manchester University Press.

Stehler, D. (2018). *The Internalized Homophobia of "Straight-Acting" Gay Men: IDAHOTB Starts with Looking at Ourselves*. Available at https://medium.com/th-ink/the-internalized-homophobia-of-straight-acting-gay-men-82012d5ddc87. Accessed 30 July 2018.

Tate, R. (2014). *What's the Difference Between High Functioning and Low Functioning Autism?* Available at https://awnnetwork.org/whats-the-difference-between-high-functioning-and-low-functioning-autism/. Accessed 6 October 2018.

Thomas, C. (2007). *Sociologies of Disability and Illness: Contested Ideas in Disability Studies and Medical Sociology*. Basingstoke: Palgrave Macmillan.

Waldschmidt, A. (2005). Who Is Normal? Who Is Deviant? "Normality" and "Risk" in Genetic Diagnostics and Counseling. In S. Tremain (Ed.), *Foucault and the Government of Disability* (pp. 191–207). Michigan: University of Michigan Press.

Whitman, T. L. (2004). *The Development of Autism: A Self-Regulatory Perspective.* New York: Jessica Kingsley.

Willingham, E. (2013). *If a Parent Murders an Autistic Child, Who Is to Blame?* Available at https://www.forbes.com/sites/emilywillingham/2013/09/05/if-a-parent-murders-an-autistic-child-who-is-to-blame/#19ad415f7ae3. Accessed 6 October 2018.

Wolfensberger, W. P. J. (1972). *The Principle of Normalization in Human Services.* Toronto: National Institute on Mental Retardation.

Index

Printed in the United States
By Bookmasters